Spell Compendium™

Matthew Sernett

Jeff Grubb Mike McArtor

CREDITS

DESIGNERS
Matthew Sernett, Jeff Grubb, Mike McArtor

DEVELOPMENT TEAM
Jesse Decker, Mike Donais, Stephen Schubert, Rob Watkins

EDITORS
Michele Carter, Jennifer Clarke Wilkes, Kim Mohan, Chris Youngs

MANAGING EDITOR
Kim Mohan

SENIOR PRODUCER
Christopher Perkins

D&D R&D GROUP MANAGER
Mike Mearls

SENIOR CREATIVE DIRECTOR
Jon Schindehette

ART DIRECTORS
Kate Irwin, Stacy Longstreet

COVER ARTIST
Mat "czarofhappiness" Smith

COVER PHOTOGRAPHER
Katie L. Wright

INTERIOR ARTISTS
Steven Belledin, Mitch Cotie, Chris Dien, Wayne England, Jason Engle, Carl Frank, Brian Hagan, Fred Hooper, Ralph Horsley, Jeremy Jarvis, David Martin, Jim Nelson, William O'Connor, Lucio Parrillo, Michael Phillippi, Eric Polak, Wayne Reynolds, Ron Spears, Joel Thomas, Franz Vohwinkel

GRAPHIC DESIGNER
Dee Barnett

PUBLISHING PRODUCTION MANAGER
Angelika Lokotz

PREPRESS MANAGER
Jefferson Dunlap

IMAGING TECHNICIAN
Carmen Cheung

PRODUCTION MANAGER
Cynda Callaway

Much of the material in this book was taken from or derived from other sources. For a list of all these sources, see page 285.

Based on the original Dungeons & Dragons® rules created by E. Gary Gygax and Dave Arneson, and the new Dungeons & Dragons game designed by Jonathan Tweet, Monte Cook, Skip Williams, Richard Baker, and Peter Adkison.

This product uses updated material from the v.3.5 revision.

U.S., CANADA, ASIA, PACIFIC, & LATIN AMERICA
Wizards of the Coast LLC
P.O. Box 707
Renton WA 98057-0707, USA
Tel: +1-800-324-6496

EUROPE, U.K., EIRE & SOUTH AFRICA
Wizards of the Coast LLC c/o Hasbro UK Ltd.
P.O. Box 43
Newport, NP19 4YD, UK
Tel: +800 22 427276
email wizards@hasbro.co UK

620A3577000001 EN
9 8 7 6 5 4 3 2 1
ISBN: 978-0-7869-6448-2 Original Publication December 2005 This Edition First Printing April 2013

Visit our website at www.DungeonsandDragons.com

Contents

Introduction

Pockets full of bat guano, incomprehensible speech, and twisted hands making bizarre gestures—it sounds crazy, but in the DUNGEONS & DRAGONS game, these are the earmarks of power, for they are the signs of spellcasting. Spells and spellcasters form a cornerstone of fantasy, and *Spell Compendium* builds on that cornerstone by presenting over a thousand spells in one place.

This introduction describes the features of this book and how to use them. After reading it, open this book to any page; you'll find something magical on every one.

USING THIS BOOK

This book puts over a thousand spells at your fingertips. That fact might be a little intimidating, but *Spell Compendium* is easy to use. It works just like Chapter 11: Spells in the *Player's Handbook*. When selecting spells for your character, simply open and place *Spell Compendium* next to your *Player's Handbook* and use both books' spell lists for your character's class to make your spell selections. Use the same spellcasting rules presented in the *Player's Handbook* when casting spells from *Spell Compendium*, and look to Chapter 10 of the *Player's Handbook* for explanations of elements of the spell's descriptions.

Spell Compendium presents spells slightly differently from the *Player's Handbook* format.

Descriptive Passages: The first thing you're likely to note is a descriptive passage in italics. This serves much the same purpose as the italicized descriptions of monsters in the *Monster Manual*: It lets you know what the spell looks like, sounds like, or feels like to cast. The text in this section presents the spell from the spellcaster's view and describes what it's typically like to cast the spell. The descriptive passages shouldn't be considered to be binding rules. A grand gesture indicated by a spell's descriptive passage is unnecessary if you use the Still Spell feat to cast it, and even though a descriptive passage describes you casting a spell on another creature, it might be possible to cast the spell on yourself, depending on the spell's target entry and the rules for spellcasting in the *Player's Handbook*.

References to Other Books: When *Spell Compendium* mentions a spell, monster, or some other rule element from one of the three core rulebooks, that mention is frequently accompanied by an abbreviation (PH, DMG, MM) and a page number in parentheses, so you can find the necessary information quickly. On occasion, a spell in this book mentions or makes use of material from a D&D supplement, such as *Complete Arcane* or *Planar Handbook*. Those mentions are accompanied by parenthetical cross-references as well.

Deities for Domains: The domains presented in this book do not include lists of deities that provide these domains to their clerics. You can assign the domains to deities as you see fit, or leave the domains as options for generalist clerics who don't devote themselves to a particular deity.

INTRODUCING SPELLS

The simplest way to introduce the spells in this book to your character or your campaign is to have a character choose them and cast them in play. You can assume that spellcasters always possessed the ability to cast the spells but they simply hadn't been cast in the presence of the PCs before. Alternatively, spells might be discovered in lost books of lore or newly created by a PC or NPC. Wands, scrolls, and other magic items also present great ways to introduce the spells you want your character to cast or you want to see cast by your players' PCs. Whichever way you choose to introduce *Spell Compendium* spells, don't hesitate or wait for the perfect moment; the best way to get the most from this or any rules supplement is to put it into play right away.

OTHER SPELLCASTING CLASSES

Spell Compendium deals exclusively with spells used by the classes and prestige classes introduced in the *Player's Handbook* and *Dungeon Master's Guide*, but even if you're playing a different spellcasting class, you can still use this book. The advice below should help you decide how to adopt spells for your character. If the spellcasting class or prestige class you're playing isn't mentioned here, find a similar class and follow its advice. Also, many new classes and prestige classes reference the spell lists of existing classes. If your spellcaster uses the spell list of a character class mentioned in Chapter 2, your character gains access to all the spells presented for that class.

When deciding if other classes should have spells added to their spell lists, consider the advice below.

Demonologist (*Book of Vile Darkness*): The demonologist's spell list is intentionally narrow. Carefully consider the consequences of expanding the list. If you chose to expand the spell list, the spells you select should emphasize the demonologist's focus on demons and demonic abilities.

Disciple of Thrym (*Frostburn*): The disciple of Thrym's spell list is intentionally narrow. Carefully consider the consequences of expanding the list. If you choose to add spells to the disciple of Thrym's spell list, add cold spells.

Fatemaker (*Planar Handbook*): The fatemaker's spell list is intentionally narrow. Carefully consider the consequences of expanding the list. If you choose to expand the spell list, the spells you add should focus on personal empowerment as opposed to defense or smiting foes from afar.

Healer (*Miniatures Handbook*): Add spells concerned with healing, removing affliction, providing protections, and providing for needs. In particular, add higher-level versions of spells the healer can already cast, such as *mass restoration*.

Maho-Tsukai (*Oriental Adventures*): The maho-tsukai's spell list is intentionally narrow. Carefully consider the consequences of expanding the list. When adding spells to the maho-tsukai's spell list, add mainly spells with the evil descriptor.

Mortal Hunter (*Book of Vile Darkness*): The mortal hunters's spell list is intentionally narrow. Carefully consider the consequences of expanding the list. Examine the assassin, blackguard, and ranger spells in this book for likely additions to the mortal hunter's spell list.

Prime Underdark Guide (*Underdark*): The prime Underdark guide's spell list is intentionally narrow. Carefully consider the consequences of expanding the list. When adding to the spell list, look for spells that emphasize survival and exploration.

Spellthief (*Complete Adventurer*): The spellthief can learn sorcerer/wizard spells from several specific schools. Thus, spells in this book from those schools are available to a spellthief to learn.

Shaman (*Oriental Adventures*): Shamans have a spell list that is a blend of druid and cleric, but they should not get all the spells clerics and druids do. Examine the spell lists of both those classes for good choices. Also, consider using the cleric domains presented in this book as shaman domains.

Shugenja (*Complete Divine*): Add spells with strong elemental or weather themes. The druid spell list is a good place to look.

Sohei (*Oriental Adventures*): The sohei spell list is intentionally narrow. Carefully consider the consequences of expanding the list. If you choose to do so, add spells that deal with personal protection and martial ability.

Warmage (*Miniatures Handbook*): Expanding the warmage spell list isn't recommended. The warmage has a limited list of spells to balance its power and adding spells might tip that balance. If you'd like to add to the list anyway, try replacing access to spells rather than simply giving the warmage a wider range of spells to choose from. Of course, when a warmage gains the advanced learning class feature, the evocation spells in this book offer many options.

Wu Jen (*Complete Arcane*): Add spells with element (except air), wood, and metal themes.

WHAT YOU NEED TO PLAY

Spell Compendium makes use of the information in the three D&D core books—*Player's Handbook*, *Dungeon Master's Guide*, and *Monster Manual*. Other books might increase your enjoyment of this product, most notably *Complete Arcane* and *Complete Divine*, but they are not strictly necessary.

SWIFT AND IMMEDIATE ACTIONS

Some spells in this book have a casting time of "1 swift action" or "1 immediate action." These action types, not described in the core rulebooks, are defined and explained below.

Swift Action: A swift action consumes a very small amount of time, but represents a larger expenditure of effort and energy than a free action. You can perform one swift action per turn without affecting your ability to perform other actions. In that regard, a swift action is like a free action. However, you can perform only a single swift action per turn, regardless of what other actions you take. You can take a swift action any time you would normally be allowed to take a free action.

Casting a quickened spell is a swift action (instead of a free action, as stated in the Quicken Spell feat description in the *Player's Handbook*).

Casting a spell with a casting time of 1 swift action does not provoke attacks of opportunity.

Immediate Action: Much like a swift action, an immediate action consumes a very small amount of time, but represents a larger expenditure of effort and energy than a free action. However, unlike a swift action, an immediate action can be performed at any time—even if it's not your turn. Casting *feather fall* is an immediate action (instead of a free action, as stated in the spell description in the *Player's Handbook*), since the spell can be cast at any time.

Using an immediate action on your turn is the same as using a swift action, and counts as your swift action for that turn. You cannot use another immediate action or a swift action until after your next turn if you have used an immediate action when it is not currently your turn. You also cannot use an immediate action if you are currently flat-footed.

Magic Items: Activating a spell completion item, activating a spell trigger item, or drinking a potion is a standard action even if the spell from which the scroll, potion, or item is made can be cast as a swift action. In other words, it takes a standard action to drink a *potion of quick march*(page 164), even though casting the spell itself requires only a swift action.

SOURCES

This book includes spells from many sources, including *Dragon* magazine, web articles previously published on the Wizards of the Coast website, and supplements such as *Complete Arcane* and *Manual of the Planes*. Most of the spells are presented with little change, but some material has been revised to v.3.5 based on feedback from thousands of D&D players comparing and debating the strengths and weaknesses of spells at gaming conventions, on message boards, on email lists, and over the counters of their friendly local gaming stores. We hope you like the changes we made to some of these spells.

If you have been playing with a spell we've picked up and revised for this book, you should strongly consider updating your character or campaign to the new version. The simplest way to do this is simply offer a "mulligan" to any character who needs tweaking. It's pretty easy to note that a spell has a different duration or that another class can now cast the spell.

Most of the changes we made to previously published material we made to create an improved version of that material—to help out spells that were formerly suboptimal choices, to adjust spells that were simply too good, or take whatever steps the D&D 3.5 revision made necessary. Of course, if you're playing with older material and it's working fine in your game, you shouldn't feel compelled to change. It's your game, after all.

Chapter One
Spell Descriptions

Illus. by D. Martin

The spells herein are presented in alphabetical order (with the exception of those whose names begin with "greater," "lesser," "mass," "superior," "swift," or "final"; see Order of Presentation, PH 181). For explanation of spell terminology, see Chapter 10 of the *Player's Handbook*.

RENAMED SPELLS

The following spells were renamed before their inclusion in this book. If you look for a particular spell in this chapter and don't find it, check this list to see if the spell has a new name.

Previous Name	Present Name
Aganazzar's scorcher	*scorch*
air bubble	*deep breath*
Alamanther's return	*replicate casting*
analyze opponent	*know opponent*
assay resistance	*assay spell resistance*
Auril's flowers	*ice flowers*
Azuth's exalted triad	*triadspell*
Azuth's spell shield	*mass spell resistance*
Balagarn's iron horn	*ironthunder horn*
bane bow	*foebane*
Barlen's crabwalk	*crabwalk*
Bigby's slapping hand	*slapping hand*
bridge of sound	*dark way*
Caligarde's claw	*force claw*
chamber	*ethereal chamber*
chameleon	*camouflage*
claws of the beast	*claws of the bear*
climb	*climb walls*
curse of petty failing	*curse of ill fortune*
curse of petty failing, legion's	*mass curse of ill fortune*
Darsson's potion	*quick potion*
deafening breath	incorporated into *breath weapon*
	admixture
Dhulark's glassstrike	*glass strike*
Eilistraee's grace	*grace*
Elminster's effulgent epuration	*effulgent epuration*
Elminster's evasion	*instant refuge*
favor of Ilmater	*favor of the martyr*
force ram	*battering ram*
force whip	*sonic whip*
frost fingers	*frost breath*
fugue of Tvash-Prull	*fugue*
gate seal	*seal portal*
Ghorus Toth's metal melt	*metal melt*
great shout	incorporated into *greater shout*
green oath	*plant body*
Grimwald's greymantle	*graymantle*
guided arrow	*guided shot*
hand of Torm	*hand of the faithful*
harmony	*inspirational boost*

Horizikaul's boom	*sonic blast*
Horizikaul's cough	*sonic snap*
Horizikaul's versatile vibration	*sonic rumble*
Igedrazaar's miasma	*malevolent miasma*
improved alarm	*greater alarm*
ironguard, greater	*ironguard*
Kaupaer's skittish nerves	*nerveskitter*
Kelemvor's grace	*life's grace*
Khelben's suspended silence	*suspended silence*
Laeral's cutting hand	*cutting hand*
Laogzed's breath	*nauseating breath*
Leomund's hidden lodge	*hidden lodge*
manifest, mass	*mass make manifest*
Mestil's acid breath	*acid breath*
Mestil's acid sheath	*acid sheath*
minor reflection	*ray deflection*
minor servitor	*awaken construct*
monstrous regeneration	*greater vigor*
Mordenkainen's buzzing bee	*buzzing bee*
Mordenkainen's force missiles	*force missiles*
Mystra's miasma	*magic miasma*
Nchaser's glowing orb	*glowing orb*
Nybor's gentle reminder	*rebuke*
Nybor's mild admonishment	*greater rebuke*
Nybor's stern reproof	*rebuke, final*
Nybor's wrathful castigation	*wrathful castigation*
Otiluke's dispelling screen	*dispelling screen*
Otiluke's greater dispelling screen	*greater dispelling screen*
Presper's moonbow	*moonbow*
Rary's interplanar telepathic bond	*interplanar telepathic bond*
recall spirit	*revenance*
remedy moderate wounds	*vigor*
righteous fury	The version of this spell from the *Minatures Handbook* has been renamed *rhino's rush*
rogue wave	*tidal surge*
Shelgarn's persistent blade	*persistent blade*
Simbul's skeletal deliquescence	*corporeal instability*
Simbul's spell sequencer	*spell matrix*
Simbul's spell trigger	*greater spell matrix*
Simbul's spell matrix	*lesser spell matrix*
Simbul's synostodweomer	*synostodweomer*
Snilloc's snowball swarm	*snowball swarm*
teleport, mass	incorporated into *teleport*
Tenser's floating disk, greater	*greater floating disk*
Tirumel's energy spheres	*energy spheres*
Tvash-Prull's bonefiddle	*bonefiddle*
undeniable gravity	*earthbind*
Vaeraun's nightshield	*nightshield*
Zajimarn's avalanche	*obedient avalanche*
Zajimarn's ice claw prison	*ice claw*

SPELL DESCRIPTIONS

ABSORB WEAPON

Transmutation
Level: Assassin 2
Components: V, S
Casting Time: 1 standard action
Range: Touch
Effect: One touched weapon not in another creature's possession
Duration: 1 hour/level (D)
Saving Throw: Will negates (object); see text
Spell Resistance: Yes (object)

The weapon you hold in your hand begins to fade from existence as you complete the spell. With the last words of the spell it disappears completely. At the same moment, a weapon-shaped red blotch appears on your arm.

You can harmlessly absorb a weapon you are touching (even a poisoned one) into your arm, as long as it is not in another creature's possession. The weapon must be a light weapon for you at the time you cast the spell. The absorbed weapon cannot be felt under the skin and doesn't restrict your range of motion in any way. An absorbed weapon cannot be detected with even a careful search, although *detect magic* reveals the presence of a magical aura. The only evidence of its presence is a faint blotch on your skin shaped vaguely like the weapon.

When you touch the spot (an action equivalent to drawing a weapon), or when the spell duration expires, the weapon appears in your hand and the spell ends. If you attack with the weapon in the same round that you retrieve it from its hiding place, you can attempt a Bluff check to feint in combat as a free action, and you gain a +4 bonus on the Bluff check. An intelligent magic weapon gets a saving throw against this spell, but other weapons do not.

ABSORPTION

Abjuration
Level: Sorcerer/wizard 9
Components: V, S
Casting Time: 1 standard action
Range: Personal
Target: You
Duration: Until expended or 10 minutes/level

As you complete the spell's intricate gestures, you detect a slight buzz at the edge of your hearing. Your body feels warmer, and a feeling of security fills you.

Spells and spell-like effects that target you are absorbed, their energy stored to power spells of your own. *Absorption* absorbs only ranged spells that have you as a target. Touch spells, effect spells, and area spells that affect you cannot be absorbed.

Once the spell is cast, you can absorb 1d4+6 spell levels (rolled secretly by the DM). The level of each spell you absorb is subtracted from the total. If a spell is only partially absorbed (because its level exceeds the number of levels remaining to be absorbed), divide the number of spell levels left unabsorbed by the original spell level. For spells that deal damage, use the result to determine what fraction of the damage you take. For spells that create effects, use the result as a percentage chance to be affected.

For example, you have three spell levels of *absorption* remaining and are struck by *dominate person* cast as a

5th-level spell. *Absorption* absorbs three levels of the spell, resulting in a 40% chance (2/5) that you will be affected normally. If affected, any saving throw the spell allows you still applies. Likewise, if you're struck by *disintegrate* cast as a 6th-level spell with four levels of *absorption* remaining, two levels of the spell remain, and you take only 33% (1/3) of the damage you would normally take from the spell.

You can use captured spell energy to cast any spell you know or have prepared, but spells so cast don't disappear from your list of prepared spells or count against the number of spells you can normally cast per day (so you so must keep a running total of spell levels absorbed and used). The levels of spell energy you have stored must be equal to or greater than the level of the spell you want to cast, and you must have at hand (and expend) any material components required for the spell.

ABYSSAL ARMY

Conjuration (Summoning) [Chaotic, Evil]
Level: Cleric 9, sorcerer/wizard 9
Components: V, S
Casting Time: 10 minutes
Range: Medium (100 ft. + 10 ft./level)
Effect: Two or more summoned creatures, no two of which are more than 30 ft. apart
Duration: 10 minutes/level (D)
Saving Throw: None
Spell Resistance: No

You complete the spell and a hot fog rises from the ground, coiling round you. Stepping out of the billowing steam comes a handful of squat, blubbery demons. Other, greater silhouettes loom behind them, answering your call.

This spell summons a pack of demons from the Infinite Layers of the Abyss to serve you.

When the spell is complete, 2d4 dretches (MM 42) appear. Ten minutes later, 1d4 babau demons (MM 40) appear. Ten minutes after that, one vrock demon (MM 48) appears. Each creature has maximum hit points per Hit Die. Once these creatures appear, they serve you for the duration of the spell.

The demons obey you explicitly and never attack you, even if someone else manages to gain control over them. You do not need to concentrate to maintain control over the demons. You can dismiss them singly or in groups at any time.

ACCELERATED MOVEMENT

Transmutation
Level: Bard 1, ranger 1, sorcerer/wizard 1
Components: S, M
Casting Time: 1 swift action
Range: Personal
Target: You
Duration: 1 round/level (D)

An azure glow surrounds you as you complete the motions that unleash the spell. You immediately feel lighter of foot.

While this spell is in effect, you can move at your normal speed when using Balance, Climb, Hide, Move Silently, and Tumble without taking any penalty on your check. This spell does not affect the penalty for using these skills while running or charging.

Material Component: A dead cockroach.

ACID BREATH

Conjuration (Creation) [Acid]
Level: Sorcerer/wizard 3
Components: V, S, M
Casting Time: 1 standard action
Range: 15 ft.
Area: Cone-shaped burst
Duration: Instantaneous
Saving Throw: Reflex half
Spell Resistance: Yes

You pop the fire ants into your mouth and exhale quickly. The ants distill into drops of pure acid in midair, spattering against your foes and leaving smoking holes.

You breathe forth a cone of acidic droplets. The cone deals 1d6 points of acid damage per caster level (maximum 10d6).

Material Component: A handful of fire ants (alive or dead).

ACID SHEATH

Conjuration (Creation) [Acid]
Level: Sorcerer/wizard 5
Components: V, S, M, F
Casting Time: 1 standard action
Range: Personal
Target: You
Duration: 1 round/level (D)

You crush the fire ants between your fingers and rub the smashed mixture over your exposed flesh. The smashed ants liquefy, and the liquid covers your body in a thick, translucent sheath.

You enclose yourself in a fluid sheath of acid that does not harm you. You can breathe normally and cast spells while the acid sheath is present. Any creature striking you deals normal damage, but at the same time the attacker takes 2 points of acid damage per caster level (maximum 30 points). Reach weapons, such as longspears, do not endanger their users in this way. The acid sheath does not protect you against other attack forms, such as fire.

If you are in a grapple, other creatures in the grapple take acid damage once per round at the beginning of their turns.

Any spell you cast with the acid descriptor while the sheath surrounds you deals an extra 1 point of damage per die.

Material Component: A handful of fire ants (alive or dead).

Focus: A glass sculpture of a humanoid (worth 50 gp).

ACID STORM

Conjuration (Creation) [Acid]
Level: Sorcerer/wizard 6
Components: V, S, M
Casting Time: 1 standard action
Range: Medium (100 ft. + 10 ft./level)
Area: Cylinder (20-ft. radius, 20 ft. high)
Duration: Instantaneous
Saving Throw: Reflex half
Spell Resistance: No

A dark green cloud whirls into being before unleashing a shower of foul-smelling, yellow-green rain.

Acid rain deals 1d6 points of acid damage per caster level (maximum 15d6) to each creature in the area.

Material Component: A flask of acid (10 gp).

AID, MASS

Enchantment (Compulsion) [Mind-Affecting]
Level: Cleric 3
Range: Close (25 ft. + 5 ft./2 levels)
Targets: One or more creatures, no two of which are more than 30 ft. apart

You hold your holy symbol aloft and cast the spell. A silvery radiance dances from your hands, leaping over all the nearby party members and strengthening them.

This spell functions like *aid* (PH 196), except that it affects multiple subjects at a distance and each subject gains temporary hit points equal to 1d8 + caster level (to a maximum of 1d8+15).

AIMING AT THE TARGET

Abjuration
Level: Sorcerer/wizard 2
Components: S
Casting Time: 1 immediate action
Range: Personal
Target: You
Duration: Concentration, up to 20 minutes; see text

As you intone the words of power to release this spell, you feel far more focused on the spell on which you have been concentrating.

When you cast this spell, you increase your ability to concentrate on a spell you have already cast. You can cast this spell while maintaining concentration on another spell. *Aiming at the target* gives you a +10 circumstance bonus on Concentration checks you make to maintain concentration on the other spell, and its effect lasts as long as you concentrate on the other spell (to a maximum of 20 minutes).

AIR BREATHING

Transmutation
Level: Cleric 3, druid 3, sorcerer/wizard 3
Components: S, M/DF
Casting Time: 1 standard action
Range: Touch
Target: Living creatures touched
Duration: 2 hours/level; see text
Saving Throw: Will negates (harmless)
Spell Resistance: Yes (harmless)

Tiny bubbles form on your hands as you complete the spell. As you touch each subject, its chest heaves and shudders, then begins to rhythmically expand and contract.

The transmuted creatures can breathe air freely. Divide the duration evenly among all the creatures you touch. This spell does not make creatures unable to breathe the water.

Arcane Material Component: A short reed or piece of straw.

ALARM, GREATER

Abjuration
Level: Bard 2, sorcerer/wizard 2
Components: V, S, F
Duration: 4 hours/level (D)

Uttering a low chant, you ring a crystal bell with the drumming of your fingernails, bringing into being an invisible warded area.

This spell functions like *alarm* (PH 197), and in addition the spell works on creatures traveling through the area on coterminous or coexistent planes (DMG 150), such the Ethereal Plane and the Plane of Shadow.

Focus: A bell made of carved crystal, worth at least 100 gp.

Illus. by W. Reynolds

Nebin surprises the trolls with acid breath

ALIGN FANG

Transmutation [see text]
Level: Druid 2, ranger 2
Components: V, S, DF
Casting Time: 1 standard action
Range: Touch
Target: Living creature touched
Duration: 1 minute/level
Saving Throw: Will negates (harmless)
Spell Resistance: Yes (harmless)

You kneel beside your animal companion and press a sprig of mistletoe against its forehead, calling upon the power of nature.

Align fang makes a creature's natural weapons good-, evil-, lawful-, or chaotic-aligned, as you choose. A natural weapon that is aligned can overcome the damage reduction of certain creatures, usually outsiders of the opposite alignment. This spell has no effect on a natural weapon that is already treated as being aligned, such as the claw or bite attack of most demons.

You can't cast this spell on a manufactured weapon, such as a sword.

When you cast this spell to make a natural weapon good-, evil-, lawful-, or chaotic-aligned, *align fang* is a good, evil, lawful, or chaotic spell, respectively.

ALIGN FANG, MASS

Transmutation [see text]
Level: Druid 3, ranger 3
Range: Close (25 ft. + 5 ft./2 levels)
Targets: One creature/level, no two of which are more than 30 ft. apart

You hold a sprig of mistletoe aloft and invoke the powers of nature. Your animal allies glow pale blue at their muzzles and paws.

This spell functions like *align fang*, except that it affects multiple allies at a distance.

ALIGN WEAPON, MASS

Transmutation [see text]
Level: Cleric 3
Range: Close (25 ft. + 5 ft./2 levels)
Targets: One weapon/level, no two of which are more than 30 ft. apart

You hold your holy symbol high and speak old words of power. Your party's weapons take on a pale blue radiance.

This spell functions like *align weapon* (PH 197), except that it affects multiple weapons or projectiles at a distance.

ALLEGRO

Transmutation
Level: Bard 3
Components: V, S, M
Casting Time: 1 swift action
Range: 20 ft.
Area: 20-ft.-radius burst centered on you
Duration: 1 minute/level (D)
Saving Throw: Fortitude negates (harmless)
Spell Resistance: Yes (harmless)

With a quick wiggle of your fingers and a few arcane words, you release the feather in your hand to complete the spell. Suddenly, translucent blue motes burst outward from you and collect on yourself and your nearby allies before fading away.

Each creature within the spell's area gains a 30-foot enhancement bonus to its land speed, up to a maximum of double the creature's land speed. Affected creatures retain these effects for the duration of the spell, even if they leave the original area.

Material Component: A tail feather from a bird of prey.

AMANUENSIS

Transmutation
Level: Cleric 0, sorcerer/wizard 0
Components: V, S
Casting Time: 1 standard action
Range: Close (25 ft. + 5 ft./2 levels)
Target: Object or objects with writing
Duration: 10 minutes/level
Saving Throw: Will negates (object)
Spell Resistance: Yes (object)

You point at the writing and then move your hand as though holding a stylus or quill. As you intone the spell, the script appears on a sheet of paper close at hand.

You cause writing from one source (such as a book) to be copied into a book, paper, or parchment. This spell copies 250 words per minute and creates a perfect duplicate of the original. The spell copies only nonmagical text, not illustrations or magical writings (such as the text of a spellbook, a spell scroll, or a *sepia snake sigil*). If the target contains normal and magical writing (such as a letter with *explosive runes*), only the normal text is copied, leaving blank space in the copied text where the magical writing would be expected. Likewise, if the target contains text and illustration, only the text is copied.

The spell triggers (but does not copy) writing-based magic traps in the material being copied.

Blank paper, parchment, or a book must be provided for the spell to write upon. If the target has multiple pages, the spell automatically turns to the next blank page whenever necessary. If more pages in the target exist than blank pages are available, the spell copies the original until it runs out of blank pages. At any time during the spell's duration you can redirect the magic to copy from another target, copy onto a different blank source, or resume a duplication that was interrupted by a shortfall of blank pages.

The spell does not translate the copied writing. If you do not understand the original, you have no additional ability to understand the copy.

AMORPHOUS FORM

Transmutation
Level: Assassin 3, sorcerer/wizard 3
Components: S, M
Casting Time: 1 standard action
Range: Touch
Target: Willing corporeal creature touched
Duration: 1 minute/level (D)
Saving Throw: Will negates (harmless)
Spell Resistance: Yes (harmless)

You dust your ally with gelatin and silently evoke the spell. Immediately her bones begin to soften and she and her belongings slump, becoming malleable ooze.

The subject and all its gear become amorphous and oozelike. This new form is boneless and fluid, enabling the subject to pass through holes or narrow openings as small as 2 inches in diameter. While amorphous, the subject is immune to poison, polymorphing, and stunning, it cannot be flanked, and it is not subject to extra damage from critical hits. It gains a swim speed (if it does not have one already) equal to its land speed. The subject can remain submerged as long as desired without breathing.

The subject's armor (including natural armor) becomes worthless, though its modifiers for size, Dexterity, and deflection still apply to Armor Class, as do armor bonuses from force effects (for example, from the *mage armor* spell). While amorphous, the subject can't attack or cast spells that require verbal, somatic, material, or focus components. (This limitation does not rule out the casting of any spells that the subject might have prepared using the metamagic feats Eschew Materials, Silent Spell, and Still Spell.) The subject loses all supernatural abilities while in amorphous form, and its magic items, aside from those bonuses noted above, cease functioning as long as it remains amorphous.

Material Component: A pinch of gelatin.

Illus. by C. Frank

AMPLIFY

Transmutation [Sonic]
Level: Bard 1
Components: S
Casting Time: 1 standard action
Range: Long (400 ft. + 40 ft./level)
Area: 20-ft.-radius emanation centered on a creature, object, or point in space
Duration: 1 minute/level (D)
Saving Throw: Will negates; see text
Spell Resistance: Yes; see text

You need to hear what's going on. A hand motion or two, and the voices become louder to your ears.

You cause an amplification of all sounds within the spell's area. This decreases the DC to hear those sounds by 20. Those creatures within the spell's area do not notice the increased amplification. Thus, anyone whose voice is amplified remains unaware of the increase in volume.

The spell can be centered on a creature, and the effect then radiates from the creature and moves as it moves. An unwilling creature can attempt a Will save to negate the spell and can apply spell resistance, if any. Items in a creature's possession receive the benefits of saves and spell resistance, but unattended objects and points in space do not. *Amplify* counters and dispels *silence*, and is also countered and dispelled by *silence*.

Gaining the benefits of the amorphous form spell can be disconcerting

ANALYZE PORTAL

Divination
Level: Bard 3, Portal 2, sorcerer/wizard 3
Components: V, S, M
Casting Time: 1 minute
Range: 60 ft.
Area: Cone-shaped emanation from you to the extreme of the range
Duration: Concentration, up to 1 round/level (D)
Saving Throw: See text
Spell Resistance: No

Seeing with a magic eye, you sense the portal. Studying it, knowledge about the portal comes into your mind as though it was a memory you could not recall until now.

You can tell whether an area contains a magical portal or the effect of a *gate* spell. If you study an area for 1 round, you know the sizes and locations of any such portals in the area. Once you find a portal, you can study it. (If you find more than one portal, you can study only one at a time.)

Each round you study a portal, you can discover one property of the portal, in this order.

- Any key or command word needed to activate the portal.
- Any special circumstances governing the portal's use (such as specific times when it can be activated).
- Whether the portal is one-way or two-way.
- A glimpse of the area where the portal leads. You can look at the area where the portal leads for 1 round; the range of your vision is the spell's range. *Analyze portal* does not allow other divination spells or spell-like abilities to extend through the portal. For example, you cannot also use *detect magic* or *detect evil* to study the area where the portal leads while viewing the area with *analyze portal*.

For each property, you make a caster level check (1d20 + caster level) against DC 17. If fail, you can try again in the next round.

Analyze portal has only a limited ability to reveal unusual properties, as follows.

- Random Portals: The spell reveals only that the portal is random and whether it can be activated now. It does not reveal when the portal starts or stops functioning.
- Variable Portals: The spell reveals only that the portal is variable. If you study the portal's destination, the spell reveals only the destination to which the portal is currently set.
- Creature-Only Portals: The spell reveals this property. If you study the portal's destination, the spell reveals where the portal sends creatures. If it is the kind of portal that sends creatures to one place and their equipment to another place, the spell does not reveal where the equipment goes.

- Malfunctioning Portals: The spell reveals only that the portal is malfunctioning, not what sort of malfunction the portal produces.

Material Components: A crystal lens and a small mirror.

ANARCHIC STORM

Conjuration (Creation) [Chaotic, Water]
Level: Cleric 3
Components: V, S, M, DF
Casting Time: 1 standard action
Range: 20 ft.
Area: Cylinder (20-ft. radius, 20 ft. high)
Duration: 1 round/level (D)
Saving Throw: None
Spell Resistance: No

You call upon the powers of chaos, and a heavy rain begins to fall around you, its drops a rainbow of soft radiances. Above you, a multicolored lightning bolt flashes.

The downpour created by this spell falls in a fixed area once created. The storm reduces hearing and visibility, resulting in a –4 penalty on Listen, Spot, and Search checks. It also applies a –4 penalty on ranged attacks made into, out of, or through the storm. Finally, it automatically extinguishes any unprotected flames and has a 50% chance to extinguish protected flames (such as those of lanterns).

The rain damages lawful creatures, dealing 2d6 points of damage per round (lawful outsiders take double damage). In addition, each round, a bolt of lightning strikes a randomly selected lawful outsider within the spell's area, dealing 5d6 points of electricity damage. After the spell's duration expires, the water disappears.

Material Component: A flask of anarchic water (see the *anarchic water* spell, below).

ANARCHIC WATER

Transmutation [Chaotic]
Level: Cleric 1
Components: V, S, M
Casting Time: 1 minute
Range: Touch
Target: Flask of water touched
Duration: Instantaneous
Saving Throw: Will negates (object)
Spell Resistance: Yes (object)

You speak the ancient, slippery words as you pour the iron and silver into the flask. Despite the fact that there is more powder than room in the bottle, all of it dissolves, leaving a flask of water swirling with motes of gold.

This transmutation imbues a flask (1 pint) of water with the energy of chaos, turning it into anarchic water. Anarchic water damages lawful outsiders the way holy water damages undead and evil outsiders. A flask of anarchic water can be thrown as a splash weapon. Treat this attack as a ranged touch attack with a range increment of 10 feet. A flask breaks if thrown against the body of a corporeal creature, but to use it against an incorporeal creature, the bearer must open the flask and pour the anarchic water out onto the target. Thus, a character can douse an incorporeal creature with anarchic water only if he is adjacent to it. Doing so is a ranged touch attack that does not provoke attacks of opportunity.

A direct hit by a flask of anarchic water deals 2d4 points of damage to a lawful outsider. Each such creature within 5 feet of the point where the flask hits takes 1 point of damage from the splash.

Material Component: 5 pounds of powdered iron and silver (worth 25 gp).

ANGELSKIN

Abjuration [Good]
Level: Paladin 2
Components: V, S, DF
Casting Time: 1 standard action
Range: Touch
Target: Lawful good creature touched
Duration: 1 round/level
Saving Throw: Will negates (harmless)
Spell Resistance: Yes (harmless)

You touch your ally with the holy symbol and invoke the blessed words. An opalescent glow spreads across her skin, imbuing it with a pearl-like sheen.

The subject gains damage reduction 5/evil.

ANGER OF THE NOONDAY SUN

Evocation [Light]
Level: Druid 6
Components: V, S
Casting Time: 1 standard action
Range: 20 ft.
Area: All sighted creatures within a 20-ft.-radius burst centered on you
Duration: Instantaneous
Saving Throw: Reflex negates; see text
Spell Resistance: Yes

Your body explodes with radiance that bathes the area around you in sunlight.

Any creature within the area of the spell that can see you must make a saving throw or be temporarily blinded. The blindness lasts for 1 minute per caster level.

An undead creature caught within the spell's area takes 1d6 points of damage per two caster levels (maximum 10d6), or half damage if a Reflex save is successful. In addition, the beam results in the destruction of any undead creature specifically harmed by bright light (such as a vampire) if it fails its save.

The ultraviolet light generated by the spell deals damage to fungi, mold, oozes, and slimes as if they were undead creatures.

ANIMATE BREATH

Transmutation
Level: Sorcerer/wizard 7
Components: S
Casting Time: 1 standard action
Range: Personal
Target: Your breath weapon
Duration: 1 round/level

You exhale a flaming tongue of fire, but instead of lashing out against your foes, it produces a creature made of flames that answers to your bidding.

For this spell to function, you must have a breath weapon, either as a supernatural ability or as the result of casting a spell such as *dragon breath* (page 73). When you successfully cast this spell, you imbue the energy of your breath weapon with coherence, mobility, and a semblance of life. The

Illus. by F. Hooper

Animate breath gives a lone dragon a powerful ally

animated breath then attacks whomever or whatever you designate. The spell works only on breath weapons that deal energy (acid, cold, electricity, fire, or sonic) damage. The animated breath uses the statistics of a Huge fire elemental (MM 99), with the following exceptions.

- The creature's subtype changes to match the energy damage dealt by the breath weapon.
- The creature deals 2d8 points of damage of the same type as the breath weapon with each successful slam attack, instead of 2d8 points of fire.
- The creature has immunity to its own energy type, but no vulnerability to another energy type.
- The creature does not have the burn ability.

ANIMATE FIRE

Transmutation [Fire]
Level: Druid 1
Components: V, S, M
Casting Time: 1 round
Range: Close (25 ft. + 5 ft./2 levels)
Target: One Small fire
Duration: Concentration, up to 1 round/level (D)
Saving Throw: None
Spell Resistance: No

By casting the mixture in your hand at the fire, you complete the spell. Immediately thereafter, a part of the flame coalesces into a vaguely humanoid shape more solid looking than the rest.

You animate a fire, which must be approximately the size of a campfire. The animated fire has the statistics of a Small fire elemental (MM 98), and attacks as you direct. It cannot move beyond the range of its source fire (25 ft. + 5 ft./2 levels).

Material Component: A handful of charcoal, sulfur, and soda ash.

ANIMATE SNOW

Transmutation [Cold]
Level: Druid 6
Components: V, S
Casting Time: 1 standard action
Range: Medium (100 ft. + 10 ft./level)
Target: Cube of snow up to 20 ft. on a side
Duration: 1 round/level
Saving Throw: None
Spell Resistance: No

Nearby snow rapidly draws together with an audible crunch, coalescing into a vaguely human-shaped form.

You cause snow in the area to become 1d3+2 Large animated objects, 1d3 Huge animated objects, or one Gargantuan animated object (MM 14). The animated snow attacks as directed by your vocal commands.

Animated snow does not have a hardness score. It possesses improved speed as if it had legs, granting it a speed of 30 feet, as well as the blind special ability (MM 13). In addition, each animated snow object has the cold subtype and deals an extra 1d6 points of cold damage on a successful hit.

Animated snow objects take 1d6 points of damage per round in a place where the temperature is above freezing.

ANIMATE WATER

Transmutation [Water]
Level: Druid 1
Range: Close (25 ft. + 5 ft./2 levels)
Target: Cube of water up to 5 ft. on a side

You indicate a patch of water with a hand shaking from pent-up divine spell power, and the liquid rises into a vaguely humanoid shape.

This spell functions like *animate fire*, but you can instead animate a quantity of water of at least 4 cubic feet into a Small water elemental (MM 100).

Material Component: A vial of pure spring water mixed with cinnabar oil.

ANIMATE WOOD

Transmutation
Level: Druid 1
Components: V, S, M
Casting Time: 1 round
Range: Touch
Target: One Small or smaller wooden object
Duration: Concentration, up to 1 round/level (D)
Saving Throw: None
Spell Resistance: No

By touching a piece of wood you release the energy of the spell into it. The wood begins to writhe and twist before your eyes and then rises to move in the direction you indicate.

This spell imbues a Small or smaller wooden object with mobility and a semblance of life, then causes it to immediately attack whomever or whatever you initially designate. Statistics for the animated wood are as for a Small animated object (MM 13). Wooden objects animated by this spell have hardness 5. The spell cannot animate objects carried or worn by a creature.

Material Component: A mixture of powdered cinnabar and ground peach pit.

ANTICIPATE TELEPORTATION

Abjuration
Level: Sorcerer/wizard 3
Components: V, S, F
Casting Time: 10 minutes
Range: One willing creature touched
Area: 5-ft./level radius emanation from touched creature
Duration: 24 hours
Saving Throw: None
Spell Resistance: No

The arcane words that activate this spell linger in the air for a moment. As they fade from your hearing, you become more aware of both your surroundings and the possibility of intrusion.

The subject of the spell is surrounded with an invisible aura that anticipates and delays the teleportation of any creature into the spell's area. Any teleportation spell or effect (including all spells with the teleportation descriptor) can be anticipated, making the spell's recipient instantly aware of the exact location where the teleporting creature will arrive (subject to the restrictions below), the creature's size, and how many other creatures (and their sizes) are arriving with the teleporting creature. The spell also delays the arrival of the teleporting creature by 1 round (so that it arrives on its initiative count immediately before its next turn), generally giving the recipient of the spell and anyone else made aware of the information 1 round to act or ready actions. The teleporting creature does not perceive this delay.

Since a teleporting creature doesn't necessarily arrive at the precise location it intends, the spell also functions against a creature that arrives in range even though its intended destination was elsewhere. For a creature that intends to teleport into range but inadvertently arrives outside the spell's area, the spell gives the recipient awareness that a creature has attempted to teleport into range and delays the creature as normal, but doesn't give any awareness as to the actual location of its imminent arrival.

The spell has no effect on creatures attempting to teleport away from the spell's area, although if their destination is within the area, the spell will affect their reentry as normal.

Focus: A tiny hourglass of platinum and crystal costing at least 500 gp, which must be carried or worn by the spell's recipient while the spell is in effect.

ANTICIPATE TELEPORTATION, GREATER

Abjuration
Level: Sorcerer/wizard 6

This spell functions like *anticipate teleportation*, except that *greater anticipate teleportation* identifies the type of the arriving creature (and any companions accompanying it) and creates a delay of 3 rounds, providing the recipient with even more warning and preparation time.

Focus: A tiny hourglass of platinum and crystal filled with diamond dust, costing at least 1,000 gp. The hourglass must be carried or worn by the spell's recipient while the spell is in effect.

ANTICOLD SPHERE

Abjuration [Cold]
Level: Druid 5, sorcerer/wizard 5
Components: V, S
Casting Time: 1 standard action
Range: 10 ft.
Area: 10-ft.-radius emanation centered on you
Duration: 10 minutes/level (D)
Saving Throw: None
Spell Resistance: Yes

As a rosy color flickers into being in the surrounding air, you feel a sense of warmth and well-being.

All creatures within the area of the spell gain immunity to cold damage. In addition, the emanation prevents the entrance of any creature with the cold subtype. The effect hedges out such creatures in the area when it is cast.

Note: Forcing an abjuration barrier against creatures that the spell keeps at bay collapses the barrier (PH 172).

ANTIDRAGON AURA

Abjuration
Level: Cleric 3, sorcerer/wizard 3
Components: V, S, M, DF
Casting Time: 1 standard action
Range: Close (25 ft. + 5 ft./2 levels)
Targets: One creature/2 levels, no two of which are more than 30 ft. apart
Duration: 1 minute/level
Saving Throw: Will negates (harmless)
Spell Resistance: Yes (harmless)

You unleash the power of this spell and the nugget of platinum vanishes from your palm. Your companions are bathed in a white aura with a silver scale pattern overlaid upon it.

All subjects gain a +2 luck bonus to Armor Class and on saving throws against the attacks, spells, and special attacks (extraordinary, supernatural, and spell-like) of dragons. This bonus increases by 1 for every four caster levels above 5th (to +3 at 9th, +4 at 13th, and a maximum of +5 at 17th).

Material Component: A chunk of platinum worth at least 25 gp (slightly less than 1 ounce).

ANTIMAGIC RAY

Abjuration
Level: Sorcerer/wizard 7
Components: V, S, M
Casting Time: 1 standard action
Range: Close (25 ft. + 5 ft./2 levels)
Effect: Ray
Duration: 1 round/level
Saving Throw: Will negates (object)
Spell Resistance: Yes

The gestures for casting arc of lightning...

Illus. by F. Vohwinkel

As you cast this spell, an invisible ray projects from your fingers. Where it strikes your foe, it ripples across his body, like water spreading across a calm pond.

You must succeed on a ranged touch attack with the ray to strike a target. The target, if struck, functions as if it were inside an *antimagic field* (PH 200) if it fails its Will save.

If this spell is used against a creature, the subject can't cast spells or use supernatural or spell-like abilities, nor do such abilities have any effect on the creature. However, the creature can still use spell completion items (such as scrolls) or spell trigger items (such as wands), even though it can't cast the spells required.

If this spell is used against an object, that object's magical powers are suppressed—including any spells previously cast and currently in effect on the item, as well as any spells or magical effects targeted on the object during the *antimagic ray's* duration.

The spell doesn't affect any objects other than the subject itself, even if those objects are worn, carried by, or in contact with the subject. For instance, if a creature is the target, the equipment it carries remains unaffected.

Material Component: A pinch of iron filings mixed with ruby dust worth 100 gp.

ANYSPELL

Transmutation
Level: Spell 3
Components: V, S, DF (and possibly M, F, and XP)
Casting Time: 15 minutes
Range: Personal
Target: You
Duration: Instantaneous

Although there is no visible effect from this spellcasting, you channel divine power through your mind, shaping and transforming this energy into the potential to cast one arcane spell.

Anyspell allows you to read and prepare any arcane spell of up to 2nd level. You must have an arcane magical writing (a scroll or spellbook) on hand to cast *anyspell*. During the spell's 15-minute casting time, you can scan the spells available and choose one to read and prepare.

Once you choose and prepare an arcane spell, you retain it in your mind. The prepared spell occupies your 3rd-level domain spell slot. If you read the spell from a spellbook, the book is unharmed, but reading a spell from a scroll erases the spell from the scroll.

When you cast the arcane spell, it works just as though cast by a wizard of your cleric level except that your Wisdom score sets the save DC (if applicable). You must have a Wisdom of at least 10 + the arcane spell's level to prepare and cast it. Your holy symbol substitutes for any noncostly material component. If the spell has a costly material component (one to which a gold piece value is assigned), you must provide it. If the spell has another focus, you must provide the focus. If the spell has an XP component, you must pay the experience point cost.

ANYSPELL, GREATER

Transmutation
Level: Spell 6

This spell functions like *anyspell*, except you can read and prepare any arcane spell of up to 5th level, and the prepared spell occupies your 6th-level domain spell slot.

APPRAISING TOUCH

Divination
Level: Bard 1, sorcerer/wizard 1
Components: V, S
Casting Time: 1 standard action
Range: Personal
Target: You
Duration: 1 hour/level

Encircling your eye with thumb and forefinger as if holding a jeweler's lens, you speak the arcane words that complete the spell. Objects near you suddenly seem clearer, more in focus. You note blemishes and imperfections you had missed before.

You gain an intuitive insight into the value of objects you come into contact with. You gain a +10 insight bonus on Appraise checks to determine the value of items you touch while this spell is in effect. Using the Appraise skill in this fashion requires 2 minutes instead of the normal 1 minute.

Even if you fail an Appraise check while this spell is in effect, you never mistakenly estimate the worth of an item by more than 50%.

ARC OF LIGHTNING

Conjuration (Creation) [Electricity]
Level: Druid 4, sorcerer/wizard 5, Windstorm 5
Components: V, S, M/DF
Casting Time: 1 standard action
Range: Close (25 ft. + 5 ft./2 levels)
Area: A line between two creatures
Duration: Instantaneous
Saving Throw: Reflex half
Spell Resistance: No

Static fills the air as you complete the spell. With a gesture you create magical conductivity between two creatures, and a bolt of electricity arcs between them with a shockingly loud crackle.

This bolt deals 1d6 points of electricity damage per caster level (maximum 15d6) to both creatures and to anything in the line between them.

Both creatures must be in range, and you must be able to target them both (as if this spell had them as its targets). Draw the line from any corner in one creature's space to any corner in the other's space. The bolt affects all squares in this line.

Arcane Material Component: Two small iron rods.

ARMOR OF DARKNESS

Abjuration [Darkness]
Level: Darkness 4
Components: V, S, DF
Casting Time: 1 standard action
Range: Touch
Target: Creature touched
Duration: 10 minutes/level
Saving Throw: Will negates (harmless)
Spell Resistance: Yes (harmless)

The spell envelops the creature in a shroud of flickering shadows.

The shroud grants the subject a +4 deflection bonus to Armor Class plus an additional +1 for every three caster levels above 7th (for a total of +5 at 10th level, +6 at 13th, +7 at 16th, to a maximum of +8 at 19th level). The subject can see through the armor as if it did not exist and is also afforded darkvision out to 60 feet. The subject gains a +2 saving throw bonus against any holy, good, or light spells or effects.

Undead creatures that are subjects of *armor of darkness* also gain +4 turn resistance.

ARROW MIND

Divination
Level: Ranger 1, sorcerer/wizard 1
Components: V, S, M
Casting Time: 1 immediate action
Range: Personal
Target: You
Duration: 1 minute/level (D)

. . . leave no doubt as to the source of the spell

The bow in your hand feels more like an extension of your body as you complete the spell—as if it's become a part of your arm. Creatures nearby seem sharper to your eyes, more in focus.

While this spell is in effect and you are wielding a projectile weapon that fires arrows, such as a longbow or shortbow, you threaten all squares within your normal melee reach (5 feet if Small or Medium, 10 feet if Large) with your bow, allowing you to make attacks of opportunity with arrows shot from the bow. In addition, you do not provoke attacks of opportunity when you shoot a bow while you are in another creature's threatened square.

Material Component: A flint arrowhead.

ARROW OF BONE

Necromancy [Death]
Level: Sorcerer/wizard 7
Components: V, S, M
Casting Time: 10 minutes
Range: Touch
Target: One projectile or thrown weapon touched
Duration: 1 hour/level or until discharged
Saving Throw: Fortitude partial
Spell Resistance: Yes

You complete the long ritual needed to cast the spell, scribing arcane runes into the item. It changes before your eyes into an identical item made of bone. The runes glow with dark magic and the weapon feels cold to the touch.

When thrown or fired at a creature as a normal ranged attack, the weapon gains a +4 enhancement bonus on attack rolls and damage rolls. In addition, any living creature struck by an *arrow of bone* must succeed on a Fortitude save or be instantly slain. A creature that makes its save instead takes 3d6 points of damage +1 point per caster level (maximum +20). Regardless of whether the attack hits, the magic of the *arrow of bone* is discharged by the attack, and the missile is destroyed.

Material Component: A tiny sliver of bone and an *oil of magic weapon* (50 gp).

ARROW STORM

Transmutation
Level: Ranger 3
Components: V
Casting Time: 1 swift action
Range: Personal
Target: You
Duration: 1 round

Your bow glows blue for an instant and now feels as light as a feather in your hand. In your mind's eye you see the arrows in your quiver, and your hand feels drawn to them.

You can cast this spell only at the beginning of your turn, before you take any other actions. After casting *arrow storm*, you can use a full-round action to make one ranged attack with a bow with which you are proficient against every foe within a distance equal to the weapon's range increment. You can attack a maximum number of individual targets equal to your character level. If you choose not to spend a full-round action in this fashion after casting the spell, the spell has no effect.

ASPECT OF THE EARTH HUNTER

Transmutation
Level: Druid 6, ranger 4
Components: V, S, M, DF
Casting Time: 1 standard action
Range: Personal
Target: You
Duration: 10 minutes/level (D)

By completing the spell you call upon the world's primal energies. You feel disoriented for a moment as your face elongates into a snout, your limbs thicken, and your skin turns into silvery chitin.

When you cast this spell, you assume the physical appearance and many of the qualities and abilities of a bulette (MM 30). While under the effect of the spell, your creature type changes to magical beast, and your size changes to Huge. You have the space and reach of a bulette (15 feet/10 feet). You gain the Strength, Dexterity, and Constitution of an average bulette (Str 27, Dex 15, Con 20), but you retain your own mental ability scores. Your base land speed becomes 40 feet, and you gain a burrow speed of 10 feet. You gain darkvision out to 60 feet. You also gain low-light vision, scent, and tremorsense out to 60 feet.

Your class and level, hit points, alignment, base attack bonus, and base saving throw bonuses all remain the same. You lose any extraordinary special abilities of your own form, as well as spell-like and supernatural abilities. You keep all extraordinary special attacks derived from class levels (such as a barbarian's rage or a rogue's sneak attack), but you lose any from your normal form that are not derived from class levels. You cannot speak or cast spells while in bulette form. However, if you have the Natural Spell feat, you can cast spells normally. Your natural armor bonus becomes +12, regardless of any natural armor bonus from your normal form. You can make two claw attacks, which are natural weapons that deal 2d8+8 points of damage. While in bulette form, you gain the bulette's leap extraordinary attack form, allowing you to make four claw attacks instead of two. Your equipment melds into your new form and becomes nonfunctional.

Material Component: A small piece of a bulette's armored shell.

ASPECT OF THE WOLF

Transmutation
Level: Druid 1, ranger 1
Components: V, S, M/DF
Casting Time: 1 standard action
Range: Personal
Target: You
Duration: 10 minutes/level (D)

With a howl you complete the spell. Instantly, your body sprouts short, thick fur. Your spine and neck bend, causing you to drop to your hands and knees—which quickly shorten into canine limbs.

When you cast this spell, you assume the physical appearance and many of the qualities and abilities of a wolf (MM 283). While under the effect of the spell, your creature type changes to animal, and your size changes to Medium. You have the space and reach of a wolf (5 ft./5 ft.). You gain the Strength, Dexterity, and Constitution of an average wolf (Str 13, Dex 15, Con 15), but you retain your own mental ability scores. Your base land speed becomes 50 feet. You gain low-light vision and scent. You gain a bite attack, which is a primary natural attack that deals 1d6+1 points of damage with each successful hit.

Your class and level, hit points, alignment, base attack bonus, and base saving throw bonuses all remain the same. You lose any extraordinary special abilities of your own form, as well as spell-like and supernatural abilities. You keep all extraordinary special attacks derived from class levels (such as a barbarian's rage or a rogue's sneak attack), but you lose any from your normal form that are not derived from class levels. You cannot speak or cast spells while in wolf form. However, if you have the Natural Spell feat, you can cast spells normally. Your natural armor bonus becomes +2, regardless of any natural armor bonus from your normal form. While in wolf form, you gain the wolf's trip extraordinary attack form, allowing you to make a free trip attempt against any opponent that you hit with your bite attack. Your equipment melds into your new form and becomes nonfunctional.

Arcane Material Component: A whisker from a wolf.

ASSAY SPELL RESISTANCE

Divination
Level: Cleric 4, sorcerer/wizard 4
Components: V, S
Casting Time: 1 swift action
Range: Personal
Target: You
Duration: 1 round/level

Finishing the spell, your eyes glow with a pale blue radiance, and you understand how to overcome your foe's resistance to your magic.

This spell gives you a +10 bonus on caster level checks to overcome the spell resistance of a specific creature. *Assay resistance* is effective against only one specific creature per casting, and you must be able to see the creature when you cast the spell.

ASTRAL HOSPICE

Conjuration (Teleportation)
Level: Cleric 4
Components: V, S, M
Casting Time: 1 standard action
Range: Close (25 ft. + 5 ft./2 levels)
Effect: See text
Duration: 24 hours/level
Saving Throw: None
Spell Resistance: No

You fish out the gem and, floating in the Astral Plane, cast the spell. A small pinprick of light appears next to you, widening to form a circular portal of a bronze hue. You step through the portal and begin the process of healing.

This spell can be cast only upon the Astral Plane (DMG 154). It opens up a small planar portal to a demiplane where natural healing can occur (unlike on the Astral Plane itself). The firm surface of the demiplane is roughly 50 feet square, and the demiplane extends 50 feet above the surface. The demiplane's traits (including time, gravity, and magic) match those of the Material Plane, and the demiplane is self-contained; walking to one end returns a character to the point from which he began. The demiplane has no unusual planar traits.

The only way in or out of the demiplane is through the entrance created by you, and only those named or described by you upon the casting of the spell can enter. The portal continues to exist and remains visible on the Astral Plane only while the hospice demiplane exists. When you leave the demiplane, the portal seals shut and vanishes. Anyone still in the hospice demiplane at that time appears on the Astral Plane at the location of the hospice's entrance.

Material Component: A single flawless gemstone of at least 250 gp value.

Augment familiar makes a familiar more threatening than it appears

Illus. by J. Nelson

ATTUNE FORM

Transmutation
Level: Cleric 3, druid 3, sorcerer/wizard 4
Components: V, S, M/DF
Casting Time: 1 standard action
Range: Touch
Target: One creature/3 levels
Duration: 24 hours
Saving Throw: None
Spell Resistance: No

You touch the pebble against your allies' flesh and bring them into attunement with the plane.

This spell allows you to attune the affected creatures to the plane you are currently on, negating the harmful effects of that plane. Affected creatures gain the protections described in the *avoid planar effects* spell (page 19).

Arcane Material Component: A bit of stone or earth from your home plane.

AUGMENT FAMILIAR

Transmutation
Level: Sorcerer/wizard 2
Components: V, S
Casting Time: 1 standard action
Range: Close (25 ft. + 5 ft./2 levels)
Target: Your familiar
Duration: Concentration + 1 round/level
Saving Throw: Fortitude negates (harmless)
Spell Resistance: Yes (harmless)

Reaching out with magic, you empower your familiar, making it quicker and stronger.

This spell grants your familiar a +4 enhancement bonus to Strength, Dexterity, and Constitution, damage reduction 5/magic, and a +2 resistance bonus on saving throws.

AURA AGAINST FLAME

Abjuration
Level: Cleric 2, druid 1
Components: V, S
Casting Time: 1 standard action
Range: Personal
Target: You
Duration: 1 round/level

With the casting of this spell you are surrounded with a cool, blue mist that clings to your body, dampening the heat of the nearby flames.

You create an aura of blue mist that protects you against fire, absorbing the first 10 points of fire damage as a *resist energy (fire)* spell (PH 272). In addition to the *resist energy (fire)* effect, the spell can be used to snuff out fires.

Any nonmagical flame that the aura contacts is immediately extinguished if the flame's maximum damage is 10 or fewer points per round. This means that torches, small fires, and hurled alchemist's fire are snuffed out and cause no damage if used against you or if you touch them.

You can use a standard action to touch an existing magical fire (such as a *flaming sphere* or a *wall of fire*) and attempt to dispel it as if using a *dispel magic* spell against it (use the caster level of *aura against flame* for the caster level check). If you succeed, you take no damage from the touch and the magical fire and aura both vanish. If you fail, you take damage from the magical fire source normally (reduced by your *aura against flame*), and both spells remain.

With a readied action, you can use the aura as a *dispel magic* effect to counterspell a magical fire attack against you. If successful, the spell is counterspelled and the aura disappears. If you fail the dispel check, or if the attack is not a fire attack, the aura remains.

AURA OF EVASION

Abjuration
Level: Cleric 5, sorcerer/wizard 6
Components: V, S, M, DF
Casting Time: 1 standard action
Range: 10 ft.
Area: 10-ft.-radius emanation centered on you
Duration: 1 minute/level
Saving Throw: No
Spell Resistance: No

"Stay together," you shout, and intone the words of this spell, casting the crushed gemstone in the air at its conclusion. You are all bathed in a silver-green nimbus of light.

You and all creatures within 10 feet of you gain evasion, but only against breath weapons. (If a breath weapon would normally allow a Reflex saving throw for half damage, a creature within an aura of evasion that successfully saves takes no damage instead.) Creatures within the spell's area that already have evasion or improved evasion get a +4 bonus on Reflex saving throws against breath weapons.

Material Component: Powdered emerald worth 500 gp.

AURA OF GLORY

Transmutation
Level: Paladin 2
Components: V, DF
Casting Time: 1 swift action
Area: 10-ft.-radius spread
Duration: Instantaneous
Saving Throw: None
Spell Resistance: No

You invoke the holy words and a soft golden light radiates from you. You feel surer of yourself, bolstered by the power of your beliefs.

You channel divine power into yourself, spreading glory to your comrades. This spell removes any fear effect from all allies within your aura of courage.

AURA OF TERROR

Necromancy [Fear, Mind-Affecting]
Level: Sorcerer/wizard 6
Components: V
Casting Time: 1 standard action
Range: 30-ft.-radius emanation centered on you
Duration: 1 minute/level
Saving Throw: Will negates; see text
Spell Resistance: Yes

You speak a few curt words and your face is briefly overlaid with the image of a violet-shaded skull. The skull fades, but the nimbus of violet light remains around you.

You become surrounded by an aura of fear, granting you a frightful presence not unlike that of a dragon. Whenever you charge or attack, you inspire fear in all creatures within 30 feet that have fewer Hit Dice than your caster level. Each potentially affected opponent must succeed on a Will save or become shaken—a condition that lasts until the opponent is out of range. A successful save leaves that opponent immune to your frightful presence for 24 hours.

If you cast this spell when you already have the frightful presence ability or a fear aura, the existing ability becomes more effective in the following ways:

- The radius of the area affected by the ability increases by 10 feet.
- The DC of your frightful presence ability increases by 2.
- Creatures that would normally be shaken by your fear aura are frightened instead, and creatures that would normally be frightened are panicked.

AURA OF VITALITY

Transmutation
Level: Druid 7
Components: V, S
Casting Time: 1 standard action
Range: Close (25 ft. + 5 ft./2 levels)
Targets: One creature/3 levels, no two of which are more than 30 ft. apart
Duration: 1 round/level
Saving Throw: Will negates (harmless)
Spell Resistance: Yes (harmless)

One after another, your companions begin to radiate a soft, golden glow. They breathe deeply, suffused with additional mystic power.

All subjects receive a +4 morale bonus to Strength, Dexterity, and Constitution.

AVASCULAR MASS

Necromancy [Death, Evil]
Level: Deathbound 8, sorcerer/wizard 8
Components: V, S
Casting Time: 1 standard action
Range: Close (25 ft. + 5 ft./2 levels)
Effect: Ray
Duration: See text
Saving Throw: Fortitude partial and Reflex negates; see text
Spell Resistance: Yes

You shoot a black ray of necromantic energy from your outstretched hand, causing your foe to violently purge blood vessels through its skin. The purged blood vessels spread outward, creating a many-layered mass of bloody, adhesive tissue that traps nearby creatures in a gory horror.

You must succeed on a ranged touch attack with the ray to strike a target. If the attack is successful, the subject loses half its hit points (rounded down) and is stunned for 1 round. On a successful Fortitude saving throw, the subject is not stunned. Oozes and plants are not affected by this spell.

The *avascular mass* instantaneously erupts from the subject and must be anchored to at least two opposed points—such as floor and ceiling or opposite walls—or else the mass collapses and has no effect. Creatures caught within a 20-foot-radius *avascular mass* become entangled. The original target of the spell is automatically entangled. Because the *avascular mass* is magically animate and gradually tightens on those it holds, an entangled character who attempts to cast a spell must make a DC 25 Concentration check or lose the spell.

Anyone within 20 feet of the primary target when the spell is cast must make a Reflex save. If this save succeeds, the creature is not stuck in the avascular mass and is free to act, though moving might be a problem (see below). If the save fails, the creature is stuck. A stuck creature can break loose by spending 1 round and succeeding on a DC 20 Strength check or a DC 25 Escape Artist check. Once loose (either from making the initial Reflex save or a later Strength check or Escape Artist check), a creature can progress through the writhing blood vessels very slowly. Each round devoted to moving allows the creature to make a new Strength check or Escape Artist check. The creature moves 5 feet for each full 5 points by which the check result exceeds 10.

If you have at least 5 feet of avascular mass between you and an opponent, it provides cover. If you have at least 20 feet of avascular mass between you, it provides total cover.

The avascular mass of entangling tissue persists for 1 round per caster level. When the duration elapses, the blood vessel mass becomes so much limp, decaying tissue.

AVASCULATE

Necromancy [Death, Evil]
Level: Deathbound 7, sorcerer/wizard 7
Components: V, S
Casting Time: 1 standard action
Range: Close (25 ft. + 5 ft./2 levels)
Effect: Ray
Duration: Instantaneous
Saving Throw: Fortitude partial
Spell Resistance: Yes

You shoot a black ray of necromantic energy from your outstretched hand, causing your foe to violently purge blood or other vital fluids through his skin.

You must succeed on a ranged touch attack with the ray to strike a target. If the attack succeeds, the subject is reduced to half of its current hit points (rounded down) and stunned for 1 round. On a successful Fortitude saving throw, the subject is not stunned.

AVOID PLANAR EFFECTS

Abjuration
Level: Cleric 2, druid 2, sorcerer/wizard 3
Components: V
Casting Time: 1 immediate action
Range: 20 ft.
Targets: One creature/level in a 20-ft.-radius burst centered on you
Duration: 1 minute/level
Saving Throw: None
Spell Resistance: Yes (harmless)

The danger of the plane surprises you, and you have barely time to bark out a few elder words of power. In a moment you're safe, and you gain a brief respite—time enough to cast more permanent protective spells.

You gain a temporary respite from the natural effects of a specific plane. These effects include extremes in temperature, lack of air, poisonous fumes, emanations of positive or negative energy, or other attributes of the plane itself (DMG 150).

Avoid planar effects provides protection from the 3d10 points of fire damage that characters normally take when on a plane with the fire-dominant trait. *Avoid planar effects* allows a character to breathe water on a water-dominant plane and ignore the threat of suffocation on an earth-dominant plane. A character protected by *avoid planar effects* can't be blinded by the energy of a major positive-dominant plane and automatically stops gaining temporary hit points when they equal the character's full normal hit point total. Negative-dominant planes don't deal damage or bestow negative levels to characters protected by *avoid planar effects*.

In addition, some effects specific to a plane are negated by *avoid planar effects*. In the D&D cosmology, *avoid planar effects* negates the deafening effect of Pandemonium and the cold damage on the Cania layer of the Nine Hells. The DM can add additional protections for a cosmology he creates. If the campaign has an Elemental Plane of Cold, for example, *avoid planar effects* protects against the base cold damage dealt to everyone on the plane.

The effects of gravity traits, alignment traits, and magic traits aren't negated by *avoid planar effects*, nor is the special entrapping trait of certain planes (such as Elysium and Hades).

The spell does not provide protection against creatures, native or otherwise, nor does it protect against spells, special abilities, or extreme and nonnatural formations within the plane. This spell allows you to survive on the Elemental Plane of Earth, for instance, but it won't protect you if you walk into a pool of magma on that same plane.

Mass awaken creates powerful allies for a druid

AWAKEN, MASS

Transmutation
Level: Druid 8
Components: V, S, DF, XP
Casting Time: 24 hours
Range: Medium (100 ft. + 10 ft./level)
Target: One animal or tree/3 levels, no two of which are more than 30 ft. apart
Duration: Instantaneous
Saving Throw: See text
Spell Resistance: Yes

After a full day of constant spellcasting, you finally succeed in bringing sentience to the subjects.

You awaken one or more trees or animals to humanlike sentience. All awakened creatures must be of the same kind. To succeed, you must make a Will save (DC 10 + the HD of the highest-HD target, or the HD the highest-HD target has once awakened, whichever is greater). Failure indicates that the spell fails for all targets.

The awakened animal or tree is friendly toward you. You have no special empathy or connection with it, but it serves you in specific tasks or endeavors if you communicate your desires to it.

An awakened tree has characteristics as if it were an animated object (MM 13), except that its Intelligence, Wisdom, and Charisma scores are all 3d6. Awakened plants gain the ability to move their limbs, roots, vines, creepers, and so forth, and they have senses similar to a human's. An awakened animal has 3d6 Intelligence, a +1d3 bonus to Charisma, and +2 HD.

An awakened tree or animal can speak one language that you know, plus one additional language that you know per point of its Intelligence bonus, if it has one. (See MM 290 for information on skills and feats the creature gains.)

XP Cost: 250 XP per creature awakened.

AWAKEN CONSTRUCT

Transmutation
Level: Cleric 9, sorcerer/wizard 9
Components: V, S, M, XP
Casting Time: 8 hours
Range: Touch
Target: One construct
Duration: Instantaneous
Saving Throw: Will negates (harmless)
Spell Resistance: Yes (harmless)

Tendrils of writhing light cover your hand and the brain it holds. The light disperses into the construct you touch, enveloping it in a soft white corona for several seconds before the creature's body absorbs the radiance.

This spell awakens a humanoid-shaped construct to humanlike sentience. An awakened construct's Intelligence, Wisdom, and Charisma scores are all 3d6. The spell does not work on constructs that are constructs only temporarily (such as objects affected by an *animate objects* spell). The awakened creature is independent of both you and the being who originally made it, though it is initially friendly toward both you and its maker. (See MM 290 for information on skills and feats the creature gains.)

Material Component: The brain of a humanoid that has been dead less than 8 hours.

XP Cost: 5,000 XP.

AWAKEN SIN

Enchantment (Compulsion) [Fear, Good, Mind-Affecting]
Level: Cleric 3, paladin 2
Components: V, S, DF
Casting Time: 1 standard action
Range: Touch
Target: One evil creature with Intelligence 3+
Duration: Instantaneous
Saving Throw: Will negates
Spell Resistance: Yes

A command for repentance issues from your mouth, carrying with it the power of the spell. The crushing feeling of guilt that grew within you while you cast the spell lifts as you project the feeling at your target.

The subject immediately takes 1d6 points of nonlethal damage per caster level (maximum 10d6) and is stunned for 1 round. If this knocks the subject unconscious, it also takes 1d6 points of Wisdom damage.

AWAKEN UNDEAD

Necromancy [Evil]
Level: Deathbound 6, sorcerer/wizard 7
Components: V, S, M, XP
Casting Time: 1 standard action
Range: Close (25 ft. + 5 ft./2 levels)
Targets: All mindless undead within a circle with a radius of 25 ft. + 5 ft./2 levels
Duration: Instantaneous
Saving Throw: None (harmless)
Spell Resistance: Yes (harmless)

Whispering secret words to the undead before you, you call forth a glimmer of intelligence in its dead eyes.

This spell grants intelligence to mindless undead such as skeletons and zombies. Undead creatures with Intelligence scores are unaffected. A mindless undead gains an Intelligence score of 1d6+4, subject to the limitation that an undead cannot be more intelligent than is typical of a living creature of the same kind. A dog skeleton simply has Intelligence 2 (no roll needed), while an orc skeleton makes the die roll but can't have more than Intelligence 8. (See MM 290 for information on skills and feats the creature gains.)

Undead regain the armor and weapon proficiencies they had in life (assume the undead were formerly warriors unless the DM specifies otherwise) and will don armor and take up weapons while obeying your commands. A zombie fighter can wear any armor and wield any simple or martial weapon, and a warhorse zombie can wear any armor.

Undead also regain any extraordinary racial abilities they had in life, such as poison or scent.

Awakened undead gain a +2 profane bonus on their Will saving throws to resist *control undead*. Awakened undead also gain +2 turn resistance (or retain their own turn resistance, if any, and if it is better than +2).

Material Component: A humanoid finger bone.

XP Cost: 250 XP.

Illus. by J. Jarvis

AXIOMATIC STORM

Conjuration (Creation) [Lawful, Water]
Level: Cleric 3, paladin 3
Components: V, S, M, DF
Casting Time: 1 standard action
Range: 20 ft.
Area: Cylinder (20-ft. radius, 20 ft. high)
Duration: 1 round/level (D)
Saving Throw: None
Spell Resistance: No

You call upon the forces of law and a heavy rain begins to fall around you, its raindrops harsh and metallic. Above you, a jet of caustic acid lances down from the heavens.

A driving rain falls around you. It falls in a fixed area once created. The storm reduces hearing and visibility, resulting in a –4 penalty on Listen, Spot, and Search checks. It also applies a –4 penalty on ranged attacks made into, out of, or through the storm. Finally, it automatically extinguishes any unprotected flames and has a 50% chance to extinguish protected flames (such as those of lanterns).

The rain damages chaotic creatures, dealing 2d6 points of damage per round (chaotic outsiders take double damage). In addition, each round, a gout of acid strikes a randomly selected chaotic outsider within the spell's area, dealing 5d6 points of acid damage. After the spell's duration expires, the water disappears.

Material Component: A flask of axiomatic water (see the *axiomatic water* spell, below).

AXIOMATIC WATER

Transmutation [Lawful]
Level: Cleric 1, paladin 1
Components: V, S, M
Casting Time: 1 minute
Range: Touch
Target: Flask of water touched
Duration: Instantaneous
Saving Throw: Will negates (object)
Spell Resistance: Yes (object)

You speak the ancient, slippery words as you pour the iron and silver into the flask. Despite the fact that there is more powder than will fit in the container, all of it dissolves, leaving a flask of water dotted with motes of gunmetal gray.

This transmutation imbues a flask (1 pint) of water with the order of law, turning it into axiomatic water. Axiomatic water damages chaotic outsiders the way holy water damages undead and evil outsiders. A flask of axiomatic water can be thrown as a splash weapon. Treat this attack as a ranged touch attack with a range increment of 10 feet. A flask breaks if thrown against the body of a corporeal creature, but to use it against an incorporeal creature, the bearer must open the flask and pout the axiomatic water out onto the target. Thus, a character can douse an incorporeal creature with axiomatic water only if he is adjacent to it. Doing so is a ranged touch attack that does not provoke attacks of opportunity.

A direct hit by a flask of axiomatic water deals 2d4 points of damage to a chaotic outsider. Each such creature within 5 feet of the point where the flask hits takes 1 point of damage from the splash.

Material Component: 5 pounds of powdered iron and silver (worth 25 gp).

BABAU SLIME

Transmutation
Level: Abyss 3, druid 1, sorcerer/wizard 1
Components: V, S, M/DF
Casting Time: 1 standard action
Range: Touch
Target: Creature touched
Duration: 1 minute/level
Saving Throw: Fortitude negates (harmless)
Spell Resistance: Yes (harmless)

You press the viscous ball of demon sweat between your fingers and speak the eldritch words. Your flesh and equipment begin to weep hot red tears that quickly form a coating over your body.

This demon-inspired transmutation causes the subject to secrete a slimy red layer of jelly that coats its skin, armor, and equipment. A creature that strikes a slime-protected subject with an unarmed strike, a touch attack (including a touch spell), or a natural weapon takes 1d8 points of acid damage. Any creature in a grapple with the target of *babau slime* takes 1d8 points of acid damage at the beginning of its turn.

Arcane Material Component: A drop of babau slime.

Backbiter turns a weapon against its wielder

Illus. by C. Frank

BACKBITER

Necromancy
Level: Sorcerer/wizard 1
Components: V, S, F
Casting Time: 1 standard action
Range: Close (25 ft. + 5 ft./2 levels)
Target: One weapon
Duration: 1 round/level or until discharged
Saving Throw: Will negates; see text
Spell Resistance: Yes (object)

The weapon you indicate during the spell's casting briefly shimmers with a black aura that disappears in an eyeblink.

You cast this spell on any melee weapon. The next time that weapon is used to make a melee attack, its shaft twists around so that the weapon strikes the wielder instead. The weapon hits automatically, and no attack roll is made.

The wielder gets no warning or knowledge of the spell's effect on his weapon, and although he makes the attack, the self-dealt damage can't be consciously reduced (though damage reduction applies) or changed to nonlethal damage. Once the weapon attacks its wielder (whether successfully or not), the spell is discharged.

Magic weapons targeted by this spell receive a Will save. An item in a creature's possession uses its own Will save bonus or its wielder's bonus, whichever is higher.

Focus: A dagger.

BACKLASH

Transmutation
Level: Sorcerer/wizard 4
Components: V, S
Casting Time: 1 standard action
Range: Touch
Target: Creature touched
Duration: 10 minutes/level or until discharged
Saving Throw: Will negates
Spell Resistance: Yes

You touch your opponent and a red aura entwines him, then fades without further effect. You back away as your opponent laughs and begins to cast a spell.

The first time the target creature attempts to cast a spell or use a spell-like ability, the magic of that spell backfires. The spell is expended, and the creature takes 1d6 points of damage per level of the spell being cast. This discharge ends the spell.

BALANCING LORECALL

Divination
Level: Druid 2, ranger 2, sorcerer/wizard 2
Components: V, S, M/DF
Casting Time: 1 standard action
Range: Personal
Target: You
Duration: 1 minute/level (D)

As you perform the final gestures of the spell you feel magic surround you, pushing on you from all sides as if trying to help keep you standing tall.

You gain a +4 insight bonus on Balance checks. If you have sufficient ranks in the Balance skill, you can even balance on an otherwise-impossible surface with a DC 20 Balance check.

If you have 5 or more ranks in Balance, you can balance on vertical surfaces; the normal modifier for a sloped or angled surface no longer applies to you, though other DC modifiers (such as for a slippery surface) do apply. If you balance on a vertical surface, you can move up or down as if you were climbing. However, you are not actually climbing, so you can make attacks normally, retain your Dexterity bonus to Armor Class, and generally follow the rules of the Balance skill rather than the Climb skill.

If you have 10 or more ranks in Balance, you can balance on liquids, semisolid surfaces such as mud or snow, or similar surfaces that normally couldn't support your weight. For each consecutive round that you begin balanced on a particular surface of this sort, the DC of your Balance check increases by 5. As with all uses of the Balance skill, you move at half speed unless you decide to use the accelerated movement option (thereby increasing the DC of the Balance check by 5).

Arcane Material Component: A thin, 3-inch-long wooden dowel.

BALEFUL TRANSPOSITION

Conjuration (Teleportation)
Level: Sorcerer/wizard 2
Components: V
Casting Time: 1 standard action
Range: Medium (100 ft. + 10 ft./level)
Targets: Two creatures of up to Large size
Duration: Instantaneous
Saving Throw: Will negates
Spell Resistance: Yes

Seeing your friend imperiled, you cast about for a likely target and settle upon a nearby foe. With a word, your ally stands free while your foe faces death.

Two target creatures, of which you can be one, instantly swap positions. A solid object such as the ground, a bridge, or a rope must connect the creatures. Both subjects must be within range. Objects carried by the creatures (up to the creatures' maximum loads) go with them, but other creatures do not, even if they are carried. The movement is instantaneous and does not provoke attacks of opportunity.

If either creature succeeds on its Will save, the spell is negated.

BALL LIGHTNING

Evocation [Electricity]
Level: Sorcerer/wizard 5
Components: V, S, M
Casting Time: 1 standard action
Range: Medium (100 ft. + 10 ft./level)
Effect: One lightning ball
Duration: 1 round/level
Saving Throw: Reflex negates
Spell Resistance: Yes

With a circuitous pass of your hand through the air, a crackling ball of lightning appears before you, accompanied by the smell of ozone.

You create a 5-foot-diameter ball of concentrated electricity that rolls in whichever direction you point, dealing electricity damage to creatures it strikes. It moves 30 feet per round. As part of this movement, it can ascend or jump up to 30 feet to strike a subject. If it enters a space with a creature, it stops moving for the round and deals 1d6 points of electricity damage per caster level (maximum 15d6), though a successful Reflex save negates that damage.

The ball moves as long as you actively direct it (a move action for you); otherwise it merely stays at rest, damaging any creature in its space. It cannot push aside unwilling creatures or batter down large obstacles. The lightning winks out if it exceeds the spell's range.

Material Component: A handful of copper and iron pellets.

BALOR NIMBUS

Transmutation
Level: Abyss 4, Cleric 2, sorcerer/wizard 2
Components: V, S, M/DF
Casting Time: 1 standard action
Range: Personal
Target: You
Duration: 1 round/level

You smash the soot against your flesh and intone the ancient, dark words. Like the legendary balor, your body bursts into lurid flames.

The flames created by this spell do not harm you or any equipment you carry or wear. Each round, the flames deal 6d6 points of fire damage to any creature grappling you (or any creature you grapple) on your turn.

Arcane Material Component: A pinch of soot.

BANDS OF STEEL

Conjuration (Creation)
Level: Sorcerer/wizard 3
Components: V, S, M
Casting Time: 1 standard action
Range: Medium (100 ft. + 10 ft./level)
Target: One Medium or smaller creature
Duration: 1 round/level
Saving Throw: Reflex partial
Spell Resistance: No

The interlocking hoops become briefly hot then disappear even as similar, larger bands streak from your outstretched hand toward the creature you indicate. With a satisfying metallic clank, the bands wrap around the indicated creature.

The victim must succeed on a Reflex save or be immobilized and thus unable to move. If the saving throw succeeds, the victim is only partially trapped by the bands, and is entangled.

A creature immobilized by the bands can attempt to escape as a full-round action, either by bursting free (Strength DC 18) or wriggling out (Escape Artist DC 18).

An entangled creature can use a full-round action to break free (Strength DC 13) or disentangle itself (Escape Artist DC 13).

Material Component: Three small silver hoops, interlocked.

Illus. by M. Phillippi

Ball lightning's versatility makes it an effective spell in many situations

BARGHEST'S FEAST

Necromancy [Evil]
Level: Cleric 6, sorcerer/wizard 7
Components: V, S, M
Casting Time: 1 round
Range: Touch
Target: Corpse touched
Duration: Instantaneous
Saving Throw: Will negates (object)
Spell Resistance: Yes (object)

The diamond in your hand turns to coal, and then to dust, which sprinkles down upon the corpse. Where it strikes, ebon flames spring up, and when the flames pass nothing remains, not even grave dust. "Return from that one," you mutter.

Black flames flicker over a corpse, utterly consuming it. You destroy the remains of a dead person or creature,

preventing any form of raising or resurrection that requires part of the corpse. There is a 50% chance that a *wish*, *miracle*, or *true resurrection* spell cannot restore to life a victim consumed by a *barghest's feast* spell. Check once for each destroyed creature. If the d% roll fails, the creature cannot be brought back to life by mortal magic.

Material Component: A diamond worth 5,000 gp.

BATTERING RAM

Evocation [Force]
Level: Sorcerer/wizard 2
Components: V, S, F
Casting Time: 1 standard action

Range: Close (25 ft. + 5 ft./2 levels)
Target: One object or creature
Duration: Instantaneous
Saving Throw: None
Spell Resistance: Yes

You point the shard of ram's horn at your foe and snap off the last words of the spell. An invisible wedge of force slams into the creature, doubling it over and driving it back.

You create a ramlike force that can strike with considerable power. The force can target a creature or an object. The force deals 1d6 points of damage to the subject. If the subject is a creature, this attack initiates a bull rush (as a Medium creature with Strength 30, for a +10 bonus on the bull rush attempt). If the subject is a movable object, such as a door, you can make a Strength check (with a +10 bonus) to attempt to force open the door.

Focus: A piece of carved ram's horn.

BATTLE HYMN

Enchantment (Charm) [Mind-Affecting]
Level: Bard 2, sorcerer/wizard 4
Components: V, S
Casting Time: 1 standard action
Range: 30 ft.
Targets: All allies within 30 ft.
Duration: 1 round/level
Saving Throw: Will negates (harmless)
Spell Resistance: Yes (harmless)

You wave your hand as if a conductor and hum an uplifting tune under your breath. As the energy of the spell releases, you hear the air around you fill with the song you are humming, as if performed by a small troupe.

This spell brings forth a stirring martial tune that inspires all creatures within the area who are friendly to you. These creatures can reroll one Will save that they have just made each round for the duration of the spell. The reroll must be made before the DM declares whether the roll results in success or failure, and the result of the second roll must be used, even if it is a lower result.

BEAST CLAWS

Transmutation
Level: Druid 1
Components: V, S, M
Casting Time: 1 standard action
Range: Personal
Target: You
Duration: 1 hour/level

With a crackle of popping joints and tendons, your hands and fingers become long curving claws with heavy knuckles.

You gain two claw attacks that act as slashing melee weapons, dealing 1d4 points of damage with a threat range of 19–20. Attacks with your transformed hands do not provoke attacks of opportunity.

Your claws work just like the natural weapons of many monsters. You can make an attack with one claw or a full attack with two claws at your normal attack bonus, replacing your normal attack routine. You take no penalties for two-weapon fighting, and neither attack is a secondary attack. If your base attack bonus is +6 or higher, you do not gain any additional attacks—you simply have two claw attacks at your normal attack bonus.

If you attack with a manufactured weapon or another natural attack, you can't make any claw attacks in that round. The claws do not hinder your manual dexterity or spellcasting.

Material Component: The claw of a bird of prey, such as an eagle or falcon.

BEASTLAND FEROCITY

Enchantment (Compulsion) [Mind-Affecting]
Level: Bard 1, druid 1
Components: V, S, DF
Casting Time: 1 standard action
Range: Touch
Target: Creature touched
Duration: 1 minute/level
Saving Throw: Fortitude negates (harmless)
Spell Resistance: Yes (harmless)

You cast the spell and lay your hand upon your ally, and beneath your glowing fingers, give him a mixed gift—the ability to fight on, but at the cost of not knowing when to stop.

The subject becomes such a tenacious combatant that it continues to fight without penalty even while disabled or dying. While between –1 and –9 hit points, the creature gains a +4 enhancement bonus to Strength. If the creature is reduced to –10 hit points, it dies normally.

BEGET BOGUN

Conjuration (Creation)
Level: Druid 1
Components: V, S, M, XP
Casting Time: 1 standard action
Range: Touch
Effect: Tiny construct
Duration: Instantaneous
Saving Throw: None
Spell Resistance: No

With the bogun made, you take the final step and imbue it with sentience, breathing life into your new servant and companion.

Beget bogun allows you to infuse living magic into a small mannequin that you have created from vegetable matter. This is the final spell in the process of creating a bogun. See the bogun's description for further details.

Material Component: The mannequin from which the bogun is created.

XP Cost: 25 XP.

BELKER CLAWS

Transmutation [Air]
Level: Sorcerer/wizard 2
Components: V, S, M
Casting Time: 1 standard action
Range: Touch
Target: Living creature
Duration: Instantaneous
Saving Throw: None
Spell Resistance: Yes

You uncork the vial and speak the old words. The smoke issues from the bottle and

---

BOGUN — CR 1

N, CN, LN, NE, or NG Tiny construct
Init +3; **Senses** darkvision 60 ft., low-light vision; Listen +1, Spot +1
Languages telepathic link with master

AC 15, touch 15, flat-footed 12
hp 11 (2 HD)
Fort +0, **Ref** +3, **Will** +1

Speed 20 ft. (4 squares), fly 50 ft. (good)
Melee nettles +1 (1d4–2 plus poison)
Space 2-1/2 ft.; **Reach** 0 ft.
Base Atk +1; **Grp** –5
Atk Options poison (nettles, DC 11, 1d6 Dex/1d6 Dex)

Abilities Str 7, Dex 16, Con —, Int 8, Wis 13, Cha 10
SQ construct traits (*MM* 307)
Feats Stealthy
Skills Hide +10, Move Silently +9

A bogun is a small nature servant created by a druid. Like a homunculus, it is an extension of its creator, sharing the same alignment and link to nature. A bogun does not fight particularly well, but it can perform any simple action, such as attacking, carrying a message, or opening a door or window. For the most part, a bogun simply carries out its creator's instructions. Because it is self-aware and somewhat willful, however, its behavior is not entirely predictable. On rare occasions (5% of the time), a bogun might refuse to perform a particular task. In that case, the creator must make a DC 11 Diplomacy check to convince the creature to cooperate. Success means the bogun performs the task as requested; failure indicates that it either does exactly the opposite or refuses to do anything at all for 24 hours (DM's option as to which).

A bogun cannot speak, but the process of creating one links it telepathically with its creator. It knows what its creator knows and can convey to him or her everything it sees and hears, up to a range of 500 yards. A bogun never travels beyond this range willingly, though it can be removed forcibly. In that case, it does everything in its power to regain contact with its creator. An attack that destroys a bogun also deals its creator 2d10 points of damage. If its creator is slain, a bogun also dies, and its body collapses into a heap of rotting vegetation.

A bogun looks like a vaguely humanoid mound of compost. The creator determines its precise features, but a typical bogun stands about 18 inches tall and has a wingspan of about 2 feet. Its skin is covered with nettles and branches.

Combat: A bogun attacks by brushing against opponents with harsh nettles that deliver an irritating poison.

Construction: Unlike a homunculus, a bogun is created from natural materials available in any forest. Thus, there is no gold piece cost for its creation. All materials used become permanent parts of the bogun.

The creator must be at least 7th level and possess the Craft Wondrous Item feat to make a bogun. Before casting any spells, the creator must weave a physical form out of living (or once-living) vegetable matter to hold the magical energy. A bit of the creator's own body, such as a few strands of hair or a drop of blood, must also be incorporated into this crude mannequin. The creator can assemble the body personally or hire someone else to do it. Creating this mannequin requires a DC 12 Craft (basketweaving or weaving) check.

Once the body is finished, the creator must animate it through an extended magical ritual that requires a week to complete. The creator must labor for at least 8 hours each day in complete solitude in a forest grove; any interruption from another sentient creature undoes the magic. If the creator is personally weaving the creature's body, that process and the ritual can be performed together.

When not actively working on the ritual, the creator must rest and can perform no other activities except eating, sleeping, or talking. Missing even one day causes the process to fail. At that point, the ritual must be started anew, though the previously crafted body and the grove can be reused.

On the final day of the ritual, the creator must personally cast *control plants, wood shape,* and *beget bogun.* These spells can come from outside sources, such as scrolls, rather than being prepared, if the creator prefers.

wraps itself around your hand, turning it into smoke as well.

With a successful touch attack, you deal 2d12 points of damage. For every three caster levels, the smoke lasts for another round (to a maximum of 4 additional rounds at 12th level), dealing another 2d12 points of damage per round.

Material Component: A small vial of smoke.

The belker claws spell makes a spellcaster's touch a potent weapon

Illus. by E. Polak

BENIGN TRANSPOSITION

Conjuration (Teleportation)
Level: Sorcerer/wizard 1
Components: V
Casting Time: 1 standard action
Range: Medium (100 ft. + 10 ft./level)
Targets: Two willing creatures of up to Large size
Duration: Instantaneous
Saving Throw: None
Spell Resistance: No

Calling out the arcane words, you suddenly stand where your companion was, and he has taken your place, outside the reach of his foes.

Two target creatures, of which you can be one, instantly swap positions. Both subjects must be within range. Objects carried by the creatures (up to the creatures' maximum loads) go with them, but other creatures do not, even if they are carried. The movement is instantaneous and does not provoke attacks of opportunity.

BESTOW CURSE, GREATER

Necromancy
Level: Cleric 7, sorcerer/wizard 8
Components: V, S
Casting Time: 1 standard action
Range: Touch
Target: Creature touched
Duration: Permanent
Saving Throw: Will negates
Spell Resistance: Yes

Channeling your hatred into binding words of power, you thrust your hand at your foe and proclaim a terrible curse.

The spellcaster places a curse on the creature touched, choosing one of the three following effects.

- One ability score is reduced to 1, or two ability scores take –6 penalties (to a minimum score of 1).
- –8 penalty on attack rolls, saving throws, ability checks, and skill checks.
- Each turn, the subject has a 25% chance to act normally; otherwise, it takes no action.

You can also invent your own curse, but it should be no more powerful than those described above, and the Dungeon Master has the final say on the curse's effect.

A *greater curse* cannot be dispelled, nor can it can be removed with *break enchantment* or *limited wish.* A *miracle* or *wish* spell removes a *greater curse,* as does *remove curse* cast by a spellcaster of at least 17th level.

BINDING WINDS

Evocation [Air]
Level: Druid 2, Windstorm 2
Components: V, S
Casting Time: 1 standard action
Range: Medium (100 ft. + 10 ft./level)
Target: One creature
Duration: Concentration
Saving Throw: Reflex negates
Spell Resistance: Yes

Calling upon the power of elemental air, you encircle the target in whipping winds.

The subject can act normally, but it cannot move from its current location. The winds carry its voice away, so it can speak but cannot be heard, and it cannot hear anything but the roar of the winds. This spell distracts spellcasters, and so a Concentration check is required to successfully cast any spell (DC equal to this spell's DC + the level of the spell being cast).

Furthermore, no sonic or language-dependent spells or effects can be cast into or out of the winds (though spells cast by you upon yourself function normally). Ranged attacks made into or out of the winds take a –2 penalty. *Binding winds* holds flying creatures in midair.

BITE OF THE KING

Necromancy
Level: Gluttony 8, Hunger 8
Components: V
Casting Time: 1 standard action
Range: Touch
Target: One living creature of a size that does not exceed caster's
Duration: 1 round/level
Saving Throw: Fortitude negates
Spell Resistance: Yes

Your mouth opens impossibly wide and engulfs your foe. You swallow loudly and your mouth returns to normal size, leaving no trace of your foe behind.

When you cast this spell, you can send a creature to a pocket "stomach" dimension with a successful melee touch attack. The target you touch must make a successful Fortitude save. If it fails its saving throw, the creature is sent to the stomach dimension. The victim takes 2d8+12 points of bludgeoning damage and 12 points of acid damage per round while in the stomach dimension. The victim can cut its way out by using a light slashing or piercing weapon to deal 35 points of damage to the stomach dimension (AC 21). A creature that successfully exits appears to cut its way free from thin air, appearing in a space adjacent to you.

Each time you cast this spell, you create a separate temporary stomach dimension.

BITE OF THE WEREBEAR

Transmutation
Level: Druid 6, sorcerer/wizard 7
Components: V, S, M
Casting Time: 1 standard action
Range: Personal
Target: You
Duration: 1 round/level

With an inhuman roar, your face extends and expands, and your hands enlarge into clawed paws. Powerful muscle builds under your skin, and you become a half-bear creature.

You gain a +16 enhancement bonus to Strength, a +2 enhancement bonus to Dexterity, a +8 enhancement bonus to Constitution, and a +7 enhancement bonus to natural armor. Your hands become claws, granting you two claw attacks, and your mouth becomes that of a bear, giving you a bite attack. You can attack with both claws at your full attack bonus, but your bite attack takes a –2 penalty (as if you had the Multiattack feat). Each claw deals 1d8 points of damage (1d6 if you are Small) + your Str modifier, and your bite deals 2d8 points of damage (2d6 if you are Small) + 1/2 your Str modifier. You gain the benefits of the Blind-Fight and Power Attack feats, as well. If your base attack bonus is +6 or higher, you do not gain any additional attacks.

Material Component: A tuft of bear fur.

BITE OF THE WEREBOAR

Transmutation
Level: Druid 4, sorcerer/wizard 5
Components: V, S, M
Casting Time: 1 standard action
Range: Personal
Target: You
Duration: 1 round/level

You shake your head, and your face reshapes itself into the visage of a boar. As this happens, your body becomes bulkier, and your shoulders and back bristle with hair.

You gain a +4 enhancement bonus to Strength, a +6 enhancement bonus to Constitution, and a +8 enhancement bonus to natural armor. Your face becomes that of a boar, and you gain a bite attack that deals 1d8 points of damage (or 1d6 points if you are Small) + 1-1/2 times your Str modifier. You also gain the benefit of the Blind-Fight feat. If your base attack bonus is +6 or higher, you do not gain any additional attacks.

Material Component: Four boar bristles.

BITE OF THE WERERAT

Transmutation
Level: Druid 2, sorcerer/wizard 3
Components: V, S, M
Casting Time: 1 standard action
Range: Personal
Target: You
Duration: 1 round/level

With a sneeze, you grow a whiskered snout and ratlike tail as fine gray fur covers your thickening skin.

You gain a +6 enhancement bonus to Dexterity, a +2 enhancement bonus to Constitution, and a +3 enhancement bonus to natural armor. Your face lengthens into a ratlike snout, and you gain a bite attack that deals 1d4 points of damage (or 1d3 points if you are Small) + 1-1/2 times your Str modifier. You also gain the benefit of the Weapon Finesse feat. If your base attack bonus is +6 or higher, you do not gain any additional attacks.

Material Component: A rat's tail.

BITE OF THE WERETIGER

Transmutation
Level: Druid 5, sorcerer/wizard 6
Components: V, S, M
Casting Time: 1 standard action
Range: Personal
Target: You
Duration: 1 round/level

You snarl, and your features shift into those of a tiger. Your hands grow sharp claws, and the thick skin and striped fur of a tiger covers your body.

You gain a +12 enhancement bonus to Strength, a +4 enhancement bonus to Dexterity, a +6 enhancement bonus to Constitution, and a +5 enhancement bonus to natural armor. Your hands become claws, granting you two claw attacks, and your mouth becomes that of a tiger, giving you a bite attack. You can attack with both claws at your full base attack bonus, but your bite attack takes a –2 penalty (as if you had the Multiattack feat). Each claw deals 1d8 points of damage (1d6 if you are Small) + your Str modifier, and your bite deals 2d6 points of damage (2d4 if you are Small) + 1/2 your Str modifier. You gain the benefits of the Blind-Fight and Power Attack feats, as well. If your base attack bonus is +6 or higher, you do not gain any additional attacks.

Material Component: A tiger's claw.

BITE OF THE WEREWOLF

Transmutation
Level: Druid 3, sorcerer/wizard 4
Components: V, S, M
Casting Time: 1 standard action
Range: Personal
Target: You
Duration: 1 round/level

A howl erupts from your lips as your face contorts and expands into a wolflike form.

You gain a +2 enhancement bonus to Strength, a +4 enhancement bonus to Dexterity, a +4 enhancement bonus to Constitution, and a +4 enhancement bonus to natural armor. You gain a bite attack that deals 1d6 points of damage (or 1d4 points if you are Small) + 1-1/2 times your Str modifier. You also gain the benefit of the Blind-Fight feat. If your base attack bonus is +6 or higher, you do not gain any additional attacks.

Material Component: A wolf's tooth.

BLACK BLADE OF DISASTER

Conjuration (Creation)
Level: Sorcerer/wizard 9
Components: V, S
Casting Time: 1 standard action
Range: Close (25 ft. + 5 ft./2 levels)
Effect: Sword-shaped planar rift
Duration: Concentration, up to 1 round/level
Saving Throw: None
Spell Resistance: Yes

As you cast the spell, a large black tear in the universe appears in the form of a crackling ebony sword made of the material of the planes. The blade flies off at your mental command to destroy your foes.

You create a black blade-shaped planar rift about 3 feet long. The blade strikes at any creature within its range, as you desire, starting the round you cast the spell. The blade makes a melee touch attack against its designated target once each round. Its attack bonus is equal to your base attack bonus + your Intelligence bonus or your Charisma bonus (for wizards and sorcerers, respectively).

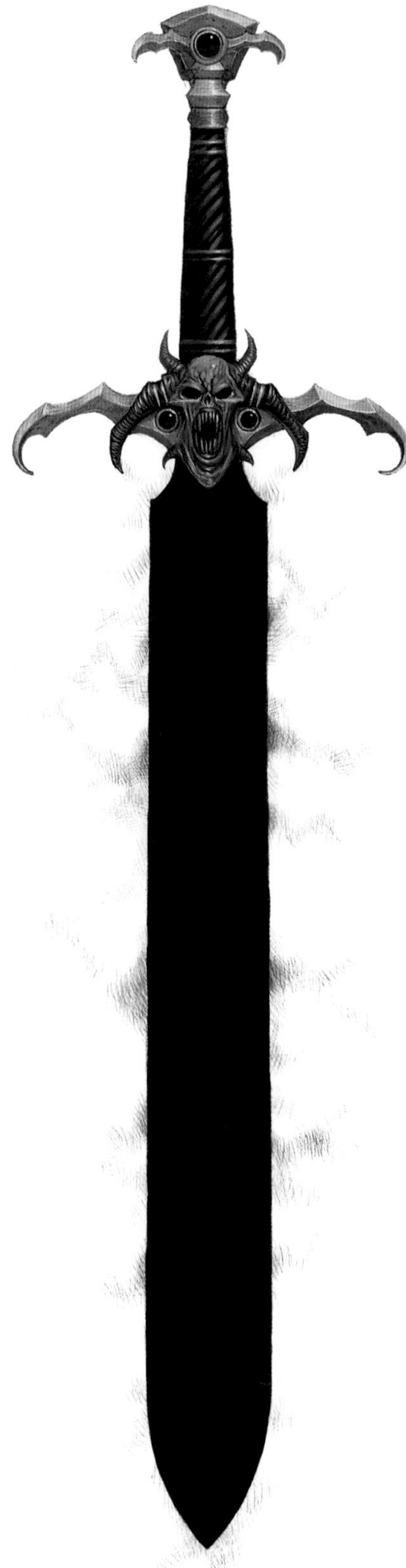

A black blade of disaster can bring death to any creature it touches

Anything hit by the blade is disintegrated if it fails a Fortitude save, taking 2d6 points of damage per caster level (maximum 40d6), or 5d6 points of damage if the saving throw is successful. The blade can pass through any magical barrier equal to or less than its spell level, but cannot penetrate dead magic areas or an *antimagic field*. It can harm ethereal and incorporeal creatures as if it were a force effect.

The blade always strikes from your direction. It does not get a flanking bonus or help a combatant get one. If the blade exceeds its range or goes out of your line of sight, the spell ends. You can direct the blade to attack another target as a standard action.

A *gate* spell can be used to counterspell a *black blade of disaster*. A *dimensional anchor* spell cast at the blade dispels it automatically. The blade cannot be harmed by physical attacks, but *dispel magic*, a *sphere of annihilation*, or a *rod of cancellation* can affect it. Its touch attack AC is 13.

BLACKFIRE

Necromancy [Evil]
Level: Sorcerer/wizard 8
Components: V, S, M
Casting Time: 1 standard action
Range: Medium (100 ft. + 10 ft./level)
Effect: Ray
Duration: 1 round/level
Saving Throw: Fortitude partial and Reflex negates; see text
Spell Resistance: Yes

With the dark words still on your tongue, a ray of black energy springs from your hand to wrap the indicated target in black flames that absorb heat rather than create it. The black fire crackles and hisses, emanating the smells of hot metal and sulfur.

You must succeed on a ranged touch attack with the ray to strike a target. On a successful attack, a living target is engulfed in chill black flames that feed on the fuel of their victim's life force. A creature engulfed in blackfire must make a successful Fortitude save each round that the spell is in effect or take 1d4 points of Constitution damage and become nauseated. A creature that makes its Fortitude save takes no

Illus. by W. England

damage for that round and is sickened instead. In addition to its effects on the subject, blackfire can spread rapidly. Each round on its turn, any living creature adjacent to a creature engulfed in blackfire must succeed on a Reflex save or become engulfed itself.

Any creature that has its Constitution reduced to 0 or lower by the spell is turned into a pile of black ash and can be returned to life only by *true resurrection* or *wish*, the caster of which must succeed on a DC 30 caster level check to restore the victim to life. If a creature succeeds on its Fortitude save in 3 consecutive rounds, the *blackfire* affecting it gutters out. The black flames cannot otherwise be extinguished by normal means (such as immersion in water or smothering), but *antimagic field*, a successful *dispel magic*, *remove curse*, or *break enchantment* snuffs it out. As well, a creature protected by *death ward* has immunity to *blackfire's* effects.

Material Component: A pinch of dust from a vampire destroyed by sunlight.

BLACKLIGHT

Evocation [Darkness]
Level: Darkness 3, sorcerer/wizard 3
Components: V, S, M
Casting Time: 1 standard action
Range: Close (25 ft. + 5 ft./2 levels)
Area: A 20-ft.-radius emanation centered on a creature, object, or point in space
Duration: 1 round/level (D)
Saving Throw: Will negates or none (object)
Spell Resistance: Yes or no (object)

With a few short words of power, you draw the light from the surrounding area. Within just a few seconds, the light dims to utter darkness.

You create an area of total darkness. The darkness is impenetrable to normal vision and darkvision, but you can see normally within the blacklit area. Creatures outside the spell's area, even you, cannot see through it.

You can cast the spell on a point in space, but the effect is stationary unless you cast it cast on a mobile object. You can cast the spell on a creature, and the effect then radiates from the creature and moves as it moves. Unattended objects and points in space do not get saving throws or benefit from spell resistance.

Wands provide spellcasters with a way to keep spells on hand even when their daily spells are exhausted

Illus. by C. Frank

Blacklight counters or dispels any light spell of equal or lower level, such as *daylight*.

Material Component: A piece of coal and the dried eyeball of any creature.

BLADE OF PAIN AND FEAR

Evocation
Level: Assassin 2, blackguard 2, cleric 3, Deathbound 2, sorcerer/wizard 3
Components: V, S, DF
Casting Time: 1 standard action
Range: 0 ft.
Effect: Swordlike column of gnashing teeth
Duration: 1 round/level (D)
Saving Throw: Will partial
Spell Resistance: Yes

A three-foot-long column of disembodied gnashing teeth springs forth from your hand.

For the duration of the spell, you can make melee touch attacks that deal 1d6 points of damage +1 point per two caster levels (maximum +10). Your Strength modifier does not apply to the damage. A creature that you successfully deal damage to must also make a Will saving throw or become frightened for 1d4 rounds.

BLADE STORM

Transmutation
Level: Ranger 3
Components: V
Casting Time: 1 swift action
Range: Personal
Target: You
Duration: 1 round

With a thought and a word you complete the spell. Your weapons shift color, becoming blue for a moment, and feel lighter in your hands. An unseen force guides them, pulling them toward your enemies.

You can cast this spell only at the beginning of your turn, before you take any other actions. After casting *blade storm*, you can take a full-round action to make one attack with each melee weapon you are currently wielding against every foe within reach. If you wield more than one weapon, or a double weapon, you can attack each foe once with each weapon or end, using the normal rules for two-weapon fighting (PH 160). So, a ranger wielding a longsword and a short sword could attack each opponent he can reach with both weapons. If you choose not to spend a full-round action in this fashion after casting the spell, the spell has no effect.

BLADE THIRST

Transmutation
Level: Ranger 3
Components: V
Casting Time: 1 swift action
Range: Touch
Target: One slashing weapon
Duration: 1 round/level
Saving Throw: None (object)
Spell Resistance: Yes (object)

You touch a blade, and it catches fire. Unearthly blue flames crackle along its length while the weapon beneath remains cold and unharmed.

You grant a slashing weapon a +3 enhancement bonus. The weapon sheds illumination as if it were a torch.

BLADES OF FIRE

Conjuration (Creation) [Fire]
Level: Ranger 1, sorcerer/wizard 1
Components: V
Casting Time: 1 swift action
Range: Touch
Targets: Up to two melee weapons you are wielding
Duration: 1 round
Saving Throw: None
Spell Resistance: No

With a word your weapons burst into flame. You feel no heat and the flames merely tickle your skin.

Your melee weapons each deal an extra 1d8 points of fire damage. This damage stacks with any energy damage your weapons already deal.

BLADEWEAVE

Illusion [Pattern]
Level: Bard 2, sorcerer/wizard 2
Components: V
Casting Time: 1 swift action
Range: Personal
Target: You
Duration: 1 round/level (D)
Saving Throw: See text
Spell Resistance: See text

With a shout you unleash the power of the spell, causing every movement you make with your weapon to seem beautiful and full of flourish.

Once per round, choose one target that you successfully attacked with a melee weapon. That creature must succeed on a Will save or be dazed for 1 round. Spell resistance applies to this effect.

BLAST OF FLAME

Conjuration (Creation) [Fire]
Level: Sorcerer/wizard 4
Components: V, S, M
Casting Time: 1 standard action
Range: 60 ft.
Area: Cone-shaped burst
Duration: Instantaneous
Saving Throw: Reflex half
Spell Resistance: No

As you cast the spell, your hand becomes sheathed in barely perceptible yellow flames. With a roar, the flames burst from your hand in the shape of a cone, leaving your hand trailing wisps of smoke.

Flames fill the area, dealing 1d6 points of fire damage per caster level (maximum 10d6) to any creature in the area that fails its saving throw.

Material Component: A bit of wick soaked in oil.

BLAST OF FORCE

Evocation [Force]
Level: Force 3, sorcerer/wizard 2
Components: V, S
Casting Time: 1 standard action
Range: Medium (100 ft. + 10 ft./level)
Effect: Ray
Duration: Instantaneous
Saving Throw: Fortitude partial
Spell Resistance: Yes

Drawing upon magic in its purest form, you send invisible energy whistling through the air to batter your foe.

You must succeed on a ranged touch attack with the ray to strike a target. A *blast of force* deals 1d6 points of damage per two caster levels (maximum 5d6). In addition, a successful hit forces the subject to make a Fortitude save or be knocked prone (size and stability modifiers apply to the saving throw as if the spell were a bull rush).

BLESS WEAPON, SWIFT

Transmutation
Level: Paladin 1
Components: V
Casting Time: 1 swift action
Duration: 1 round

You invoke the holy words quickly, and your weapon flashes a momentary blue-white radiance.

This spell functions like *bless weapon* (PH 205), except as noted above.

BLESSED AIM

Divination
Level: Blackguard 1, cleric 1, paladin 1
Components: V, S
Casting Time: 1 standard action
Range: 50 ft.
Effect: 50-ft.-radius spread centered on you
Duration: 1 minute/level
Saving Throw: Will negates (harmless)
Spell Resistance: No

With the blessing of your deity, you bolster your allies' aim with an exhortation.

This spell grants your allies within the spread a +2 morale bonus on ranged attack rolls.

BLESSING OF BAHAMUT

Abjuration [Good]
Level: Paladin 3
Components: V, S, M
Casting Time: 1 standard action
Range: Personal
Target: You
Duration: 1 round/level

You hear a distant dragon's roar that no one else detects, and your skin takes on a platinum sheen.

You gain damage reduction 10/magic for the spell's duration.

Material Component: A canary feather, which is flung into the air.

BLINDING BREATH

Transmutation [Light]
Level: Sorcerer/wizard 4

You expel your breath weapon, which crackles with eye-splitting intensity.

Illus. by W. England

The blessed aim spell grants all of a blackguard's nearby allies a better chance to hit with ranged attacks

This spell functions like *breath flare* (page 38), except that targets that fail their saving throws against your breath weapon are permanently blinded, rather than dazzled.

BLINDING SPITTLE

Transmutation
Level: Druid 2
Components: V, S
Casting Time: 1 standard action
Range: Close (25 ft. + 5 ft./2 levels)
Effect: One missile of spit
Duration: Instantaneous
Saving Throw: None
Spell Resistance: Yes

Whipping your head forward with the last word of the spell, you spit a globule of dark liquid at your foe.

You spit caustic saliva into your target's eyes with a successful ranged touch attack. A –4 penalty applies to the attack roll. The subject is blinded until it can wash its eyes with water or some other rinsing fluid, which requires a standard action.

This spell has no effect on creatures without eyes or creatures that don't depend on eyes for vision.

BLINDSIGHT

Transmutation
Level: Cleric 3, druid 3
Components: V, S
Casting Time: 1 standard action
Range: Touch
Target: Creature touched
Duration: 1 minute/level
Saving Throw: Will negates (harmless)
Spell Resistance: Yes (harmless)

You touch your intended subject, which then turns its head rapidly about as if looking for the source of some sound.

This spell grants the subject the blindsight ability (MM 306) effective out to 30 feet.

BLINDSIGHT, GREATER

Transmutation
Level: Cleric 4, druid 4

This spell functions like *blindsight*, except as noted above and that the blindsight granted by the spell is effective out to 60 feet.

BLINK, GREATER

Transmutation
Level: Bard 5, Celerity 8, sorcerer/wizard 5

An immaterial fog descends over your eyes as you complete the spell. You perceive the closeness of a parallel, ethereal reality, and you know that you can pass freely between that world and the one upon which you stand.

This spell functions like *blink* (PH 206), except that you have control over the timing of your "blinking" back and forth between the Ethereal Plane and the Material Plane. You can also ready an action to blink away from any physical or magical attack. The attack misses automatically unless it also affects ethereal targets (as a force effect does). While blinking, you have no chance of interfering with your own attacks or your own spells. When moving through solid objects, you do not risk materializing inside one unless you actually end your movement there, in which case you materialize and are shunted off to the nearest open space, taking 1d6 points of damage per 5 feet traveled in this manner.

BLISTERING RADIANCE

Evocation [Fire, Light]
Level: Cleric 5, sorcerer/wizard 4
Components: V, S, M
Casting Time: 1 standard action
Range: Long (400 ft. + 40 ft./level)
Area: 50-ft.-radius spread
Duration: 1 round/level
Saving Throw: None and Fortitude partial; see text
Spell Resistance: Yes

As you conclude the ritual to release the energy of the spell, you hurl a blazing ball of light toward the point you designate, and it erupts into a brilliant hovering sphere.

All sighted creatures in the area are dazzled (no save), and the heat from the blistering radiance deals 2d6 points of fire damage to all creatures and objects in the area each round on your turn (Fortitude half). Like a *fireball* spell, *blistering radiance* erupts if it strikes any material body or solid barrier before attaining the prescribed range, and you must make a successful ranged touch attack to send the sphere through a narrow opening or passage.

Blistering radiance counters or dispels any darkness spell of equal or lower level.

Material Component: A bit of tinder and a small lens.

BLOOD FRENZY

Transmutation
Level: Druid 2
Components: V, S
Casting Time: 1 standard action
Range: Touch
Target: Any creature with the rage ability
Duration: Special; see text
Saving Throw: Will negates
Spell Resistance: Yes

A hot rush of anger flows through your target's veins.

The target creature enters a rage, as its rage special ability, but this rage does not count toward the creature's number of rage attempts per day.

BLOOD SIROCCO

Evocation
Level: Druid 6
Components: V, S
Casting Time: 1 standard action
Range: 60 ft.
Effect: Cone-shaped emanation centered on you or on a point in space
Duration: 1 round/level
Saving Throw: Fortitude negates; see text
Spell Resistance: Yes

With a hot exhalation and a circular wave of your outstretched arm, a stifling wind tears across the landscape, kicking up clouds of dust and sand and spreading out to blow over your foes.

A *blood sirocco* blows out from your location with the force of a windstorm (DMG 95). Creatures in the affected area of Small or smaller size are knocked prone and rolled 1d4×10 feet, taking 1d4 points of nonlethal damage per 10 feet. Medium creatures are knocked prone, and creatures of Large or Huge size are unable to move toward the origin point of the cone. A successful Fortitude save allows the creature to move normally in that round.

In addition, the stifling winds dehydrate those within the cone. In each round when an affected living creature fails its saving throw, it takes 2 points of damage.

The wind of a *blood sirocco* automatically extinguishes candles, torches, and similar unprotected flames. It causes protected flames, such as those of lanterns, to dance wildly and has a 50% chance to extinguish these lights. The wind of a *blood sirocco* continues to blow from the origin point to the wide end of the cone for the duration of the spell. Any creature within this area is entitled a saving throw each round to ignore the effects of the *blood sirocco*.

BLOOD TO WATER

Necromancy [Water]
Level: Cleric 7
Components: V, S
Casting Time: 1 standard action
Range: Close (25 ft. + 5 ft./2 levels)
Effect: Up to five living creatures, no two of which are more than 30 ft. apart
Duration: Instantaneous
Saving Throw: Fortitude half
Spell Resistance: Yes

You forcefully spit, ending your spellcasting. From where you spat arises a sea-green orb of energy for each creature you intend as a subject of the spell. The orbs fly to their designated targets and turn blood red as they impact.

You transmute the subjects' blood into pure water, dealing 2d6 points of Constitution damage. A successful Fortitude save halves the Constitution damage.

This spell has no effect on living creatures with the fire or water subtype.

BLOOD WIND

Evocation
Level: Cleric 1, sorcerer/wizard 1
Components: V, S
Casting Time: 1 swift action
Range: Close (25 ft. + 5 ft./2 levels)
Target: A single creature with Intelligence 4 or higher
Duration: 1 round
Saving Throw: Will negates (harmless)
Spell Resistance: Yes (harmless)

After you complete the spell, the subject's limbs ripple with power and grow slightly in length.

The subject can take a full attack action to use all of its natural weapons or unarmed strikes as if they were thrown weapons with a 20-foot range increment. The subject gestures as if making a melee attack, but the result of the attack affects a target within range. This spell does not actually grant reach, and so does not help provide a flanking bonus or allow the subject to make attacks of opportunity at any range greater than normal. The subject uses its normal melee attack bonuses and deals damage normally if it hits, though the target of the attacks can benefit from cover or concealment.

BLOODHOUND

Divination
Level: Ranger 1
Components: V, S
Casting Time: 1 standard action
Range: Personal
Target: You
Duration: 24 hours (D)

A white film slips over your vision. Strangely, your eyes seem more focused and you note barely perceptible traces of passage that you had missed before.

If you fail a Survival check to track a creature while this spell functions, you can immediately attempt another roll against the same DC to reestablish the trail. If the reroll fails, you must search for the trail for 30 minutes (if outdoors) or 5 minutes (if indoors) before trying again.

BLOODSTAR

Conjuration (Creation)
Level: Sorcerer/wizard 4
Components: V, S, F
Casting Time: 1 standard action
Range: Medium (100 ft. + 10 ft./level)
Effect: A bloodstar
Duration: 1 round/level
Saving Throw: Fortitude negates
Spell Resistance: Yes

In a ruby flash a blood-colored, glowing crystal appears near your foes to suck the blood from their wounds.

You create a magic construct called a bloodstar that shoots from your hand and hovers in the air anywhere within the limit of the range (each round, you can move the bloodstar anywhere within range with a standard action spent concentrating on the new position). The bloodstar pulses with ruby light (providing illumination in a 20-foot radius). Any creature you initially designate within 10 feet of the bloodstar that takes damage from any source must make a saving throw. On a failed save, the victim takes 1 point of Constitution damage. Each time victims are damaged, they can attempt new saves.

The bloodstar cannot be attacked or harmed by physical attacks.

Focus: A ruby worth at least 30 gp.

BODAK'S GLARE

Necromancy [Death, Evil]
Level: Abyss 8, Cleric 8
Components: V, S, F
Casting Time: 1 standard action
Range: 30 ft.
Target: One living creature
Duration: Instantaneous
Saving Throw: Fortitude negates
Spell Resistance: Yes

You invoke the powers of deep darkness and your eyes vanish, looking like holes in the universe itself.

Upon completion of the spell, you target a creature within range that can see you. That creature dies instantly unless it succeeds on a Fortitude save. The target need not meet your gaze.

If you slay a humanoid creature with this attack, 24 hours later it transforms into a bodak (*MM* 28) unless it has been resurrected in the meantime. The bodak is not under your command, but can be controlled as normal with a rebuke undead check.

Focus: A black onyx gem worth at least 500 gp.

A blood sirocco leeches away life by drawing blood into its howling winds

Illus. by C. Frank

BODY BLADES

Transmutation
Level: Cleric 2
Components: V, S
Casting Time: 1 standard action
Range: Personal
Target: You
Duration: 1 minute/level

You finish the spell's casting and shudder as slender, sharp-tipped spikes erupt from your body, limbs, and clothing.

You sprout daggerlike blades from all the surfaces of your body and clothing. The blades appear metallic but are not actually metal, and never harm you or interfere with your movement or actions. You are proficient with your blades, and they allow you to deal piercing damage equal to 1d6 + your caster level (maximum 1d6+5) with a successful grapple attack. You can also make a regular melee attack (or off-hand attack) with the spikes, and they count as a light weapon in this case. If a creature initiates a grapple with you, it takes the same damage, and you gain a bonus on grapple checks to resist the grapple equal to the damage dealt. You get a +4 bonus on Escape Artist checks to escape from a net, rope, grappler, or spell that entangles.

BODY HARMONIC

Transmutation
Level: Bard 5
Components: V, S, F
Casting Time: 1 standard action
Range: Medium (100 ft. + 10 ft./level)
Target: One living creature
Duration: Concentration, up to 1 round/level
Saving Throw: Will negates
Spell Resistance: Yes

You rub the rim of a water-filled glass, causing it to emit a piercing tone. As you chant a simple poem you feel the glass in your hand crackle with energy, causing the hand holding it to become slightly numb.

As you rub the glass, the targeted creature's body begins to vibrate loudly and painfully in harmony with the tone. Each round you continue to concentrate on this spell, the victim takes 1d10 points of damage to one ability score. You must select a different ability score each round, and cannot damage any one ability score more than once every 5 rounds. The creature can attempt a Will saving throw each round to negate that round's effect.

While the subject is under the effect of *body harmonic*, its body whines and hums discordantly. The victim takes a –20 penalty on Move Silently checks.

Focus: A crystal water-filled goblet worth at least 500 gp.

BODY OF THE SUN

Transmutation [Fire]
Level: Druid 2, sorcerer/wizard 2
Components: V, S, DF
Casting Time: 1 standard action
Range: 5 ft.
Area: 5-ft.-radius emanation centered on you
Duration: 1 round/level
Saving Throw: Reflex half
Spell Resistance: Yes

By drawing on the power of the sun, you cause your body to emanate fire.

Fire extends 5 feet in all directions from your body, illuminating the area and dealing 1d4 points of fire damage per two caster levels (maximum 5d4). Adjacent creatures take fire damage each round on your turn.

BODY OF WAR

Transmutation
Level: Sorcerer/wizard 7
Components: V, S, M
Casting Time: 1 standard action
Range: Personal
Target: You
Duration: 1 round/level (D)

Throwing back your arms as you complete the spell, you feel your body grow heavy and unresponsive. A moment of panic grips you as your chest ceases to expand and you realize you are no longer breathing. Cold sweeps over your body as you glance down at your now-metallic flesh.

When you cast this spell, you assume the physical appearance and many of the qualities and abilities of a warforged titan (EBERRON *Campaign Setting* 302). While under the effect of the spell, your creature type changes to construct, and your size changes to Huge. You have the space and reach of a warforged titan (15 feet/15 feet). Your mindset changes so that you relish combat and cannot cast spells, even from magic items. You gain the Strength and Dexterity of an average warforged titan (Str 28, Dex 8), but you retain your own mental ability scores. You have no Constitution score while affected by this spell. Your base land speed becomes 50 feet. You gain darkvision out to 60 feet. You also gain low-light vision.

Your class and level, hit points, alignment, base attack bonus, and base saving throw bonuses all remain the same. You lose any extraordinary special abilities of your own form, as well as spell-like and supernatural abilities. You keep all extraordinary special attacks derived from class levels (such as a barbarian's rage or a rogue's sneak attack), but you lose any from your normal form that are not derived from class levels. You cannot speak or cast spells while in warforged titan form. Your natural armor bonus becomes +18, regardless of any natural armor bonus from your normal form, and you gain damage reduction 10/adamantine.

As a construct, you have the following qualities: immunity to all mind-affecting spells and abilities, poison, sleep effects, paralysis, stunning, disease, death effects, necromancy effects, critical hits, nonlethal damage, ability drain, fatigue, exhaustion, energy drain, and to any effect that requires a Fortitude save (unless the effect also works on objects or is harmless). You also gain the warforged titan's two attack forms (axe and maul), along with the trample special ability (damage 1d8+13; Reflex DC 25 half). The warforged titan's axe deals 2d8 points of slashing damage and has a ×3 critical modifier; its maul (essentially a huge warhammer) deals 2d8 points of bludgeoning damage and also has a ×3 critical modifier. Your equipment melds into your new form and becomes nonfunctional.

Material Component: A miniature bronze hammer.

BOLT OF GLORY

Evocation [Good]
Level: Cleric 6, Glory 6
Components: V, S, DF
Casting Time: 1 standard action
Range: Close (25 ft. + 5 ft./2 levels)
Effect: Ray
Duration: Instantaneous
Saving Throw: None
Spell Resistance: Yes

The body of war spell turns any sorcerer or wizard into a potent combatant

Calling upon the Positive Energy Plane and the power of your faith, you project a white bolt of hissing positive energy at your foe.

You must succeed on a ranged touch attack with the ray to strike a target. A creature struck takes varying damage, depending on its nature or its home plane of existence and your level.

Creatures native to the Negative Energy Plane, evil-aligned outsiders, and all undead creatures take 1d12 points of damage per caster level (maximum 15d12).

Creatures native to the Material Plane or an Elemental Plane, or any other neutral-aligned outsiders, take 1d12 points of damage per two caster levels (maximum 7d12).

Creatures native to the Positive Energy Plane and all good-aligned outsiders are not affected by this spell.

BOLTS OF BEDEVILMENT

Enchantment [Mind-Affecting]
Level: Bard 5, Madness 5
Components: V, S
Casting Time: 1 standard action
Range: Medium (100 ft. + 10 ft./level)
Effect: Ray
Duration: 1 round/level
Saving Throw: Will negates
Spell Resistance: Yes

With a strangled peal of laughter to complete the spell, you point your hand at your enemy and fire a black beam from your finger.

This spell grants you the ability to make one ray attack per round. You must succeed on a ranged touch attack with the ray to strike a target. A living creature struck by the ray is dazed for 1d3 rounds if it fails its save.

BOMBARDMENT

Conjuration (Creation)
Level: Druid 8
Components: V, S, F
Casting Time: 1 standard action
Range: Long (400 ft. + 40 ft./level)
Area: Cylinder (15-ft. radius, 40 ft. high)
Duration: Instantaneous
Saving Throw: Reflex half; see text
Spell Resistance: No

As you point to the empty air, boulders tumble into being and cascade down, burying your opponents.

You designate the spot on which the cylinder is centered. Each creature in the area that fails a Reflex saving throw takes 1d8 points of damage per caster level (maximum 20d8) and is buried under 5 feet of rubble. A successful save halves the damage and avoids burial. A buried creature can free itself with a DC 20 Strength check (a full-round action), or it can be dug free by others (a single creature working alone requires 1 minute to free a trapped creature). A buried creature is unable to move, and cannot cast spells with somatic components, and any material components must be in hand.

After this spell is cast, its area is covered in 5 feet of dense rubble (DMG 90).

Focus: A quartz crystal embedded in rock.

BONEFIDDLE

Necromancy
Level: Bard 2, sorcerer/wizard 2
Components: V, S, F
Casting Time: 1 standard action
Range: Close (25 ft. + 5 ft./2 levels)
Target: One creature with a skeleton or exoskeleton
Duration: Concentration, up to 1 round/level
Saving Throw: Fortitude negates
Spell Resistance: Yes

You rub your middle finger across your thumb like a bow against a fiddle while simultaneously humming a discordant tune under your breath. Nearby, you see a translucent bone-white fiddle bow appear and sink into the flesh of your target. It begins sawing, as if playing your target like a fiddle.

You call up a ghostly fiddle bow in the air above the targeted creature. This bow immediately descends into the target body and begins to saw back and forth against its skeleton. Although the music produced is eerily beautiful, it causes intense pain and anguish in the victim. Each round on its turn, the victim must make a Fortitude save or take 3d6 points of sonic damage and a –20 penalty on Move Silently checks. A successful save negates the damage and ends the spell. The spell's effects continue even if the subject moves so that you no longer have line of sight or line of effect to it.

Focus: A miniature silver fiddle worth at least 30 gp.

BOTTLE OF SMOKE

Conjuration (Creation)
Level: Druid 3, ranger 3
Components: V, S, F
Casting Time: 10 minutes
Range: Touch
Effect: One smoky, horselike creature
Duration: 1 hour/level
Saving Throw: None
Spell Resistance: No

You wave an ornate bottle about and smoke twists into it, filling it with a white cloud.

You create a plume of smoke that you capture in a special bottle you're holding. If the bottle is thereafter opened before the spell duration expires, the smoke emerges to form a vaguely horselike creature made of wisps of smoke. It makes no sound, and anything that touches it simply passes through it.

To mount this smoke horse, the would-be rider must make a DC 10 Ride check while holding the bottle in one hand. Anyone attempting to mount without the bottle simply passes through the horse's form. Letting go of the bottle after mounting causes the rider to fall through the horse's smoky form; he or she cannot thereafter remount without the intact bottle in hand. If the bottle is broken, the spell ends immediately and the rider (if mounted) falls to the ground.

The smoke horse has a speed of 20 feet per caster level, to a maximum of 240 feet. It can send smoke billowing out behind it at the rider's behest, leaving behind a bank of smoke 5 feet wide and 20 feet high as it moves. A severe wind, or magical wind of any kind, disperses the horse (and any smoke it has produced) instantly. Otherwise, the bank of smoke lasts 10 minutes, starting on the turn it was laid down. Starting or stopping the smoke trail is a free action. The mount and the smoke trail it produces give concealment to anyone behind them.

The mount is immune to all damage and other attacks because material

Illus. by W. Reynolds

objects and spells simply pass through it. It cannot attack.

The rider can return the smoke horse to the bottle, and thus pause the spell, at any time by simply uncorking it (a move action) and stoppering it again (another move action) in the next round after the horse is inside. If the bottle is reopened later, the spell reactivates with its remaining duration intact. Regardless of how much duration remains unused, the spell ceases functioning 24 hours after it is cast. If dispelled at any time while the bottle is corked, the spell ends.

Focus: An ornate, corked bottle worth at least 50 gp.

Branch to branch allows a druid or ranger to swing through the trees like a monkey

Illus. by J. Nelson

BRAIN SPIDER

Divination [Mind-Affecting]
Level: Cleric 7, Mind 7
Components: V, S, M, DF
Casting Time: 1 round
Range: Long (400 ft. + 40 ft./level)
Targets: Up to eight living creatures
Duration: 1 minute/level
Saving Throw: Will negates
Spell Resistance: Yes

You touch a spider's body and think of the targets. As each target succumbs to the spell, a leg of the spider vanishes into nothingness.

For the duration of the spell, as a standard action, you can eavesdrop on the thoughts of up to eight other creatures at once, hearing as desired:

- A creature's surface thoughts.
- Individual trains of thought in whatever order you desire.
- One nugget of information per caster level from all the minds regarding one particular topic, thing, or being.
- The thoughts and memories of one creature of the group in detail.

Once per round, if you do not perform a detailed study of one creature's mind, you can attempt (as a standard action) to implant a *suggestion* (PH 285) in the mind of any one of the affected creatures. The creature can make another Will saving throw to resist the *suggestion*, using the original save DC. (Creatures with special resistance to enchantment spells can use this resistance to keep from being affected by the *suggestion*.) Success on this saving throw does not negate the other effects of the brain spider for that creature.

Material Component: A dead spider of any size or type. It must still have all eight legs.

BRAMBLES

Transmutation
Level: Cleric 2, druid 2
Components: V, S, M
Casting Time: 1 standard action
Range: Touch
Target: Wooden weapon touched
Duration: 1 round/level
Saving Throw: None
Spell Resistance: No

With the sound of twisting wood, the weapon you touch grows sharp spikes like rose thorns.

For the duration of the spell, the weapon deals both piercing and bludgeoning damage. It gains a +1 enhancement bonus on its attacks and also gains a +1 enhancement bonus per caster level on melee damage rolls (maximum +10). This spell works only on melee weapons with wooden striking surfaces. For instance, it does not work on a bow, an arrow, or a metal mace.

Material Component: A small thorn.

BRANCH TO BRANCH

Transmutation
Level: Druid 1, ranger 1
Components: V, S
Casting Time: 1 standard action
Range: Personal
Target: You
Duration: 1 hour/level (D)

With the last guttural utterance, your fingers thicken and your arms lengthen slightly. You have the impression that you would feel more at ease in a canopy of trees.

You gain a +10 competence bonus on Climb checks made in trees. As long as you remain at least 10 feet above the ground, you can brachiate (swing by branches and vines) in medium or dense forest, but not in sparse forest. When you brachiate, you gain a 10-foot enhancement bonus to your land speed and ignore the hampered movement penalties for undergrowth and other terrain features. You can charge while brachiating, but you can't run. Naturally, some local conditions, such as areas of sparse forest, clearings, wide rivers, or other breaks in the forest canopy, might force you to return to the ground.

BREATH FLARE

Transmutation [Light]
Level: Sorcerer/wizard 1

Components: S
Casting Time: 1 swift action
Range: Personal
Target: Your breath weapon
Duration: 1 round

You exhale your breath weapon, and it flashes brilliantly, surprising your foes.

For this spell to function, you must have a breath weapon that uses fire or electricity, either as a supernatural ability or as the result of casting a spell such as *dragon breath* (page 73). When you successfully cast this spell, your breath weapon is suffused with bright light. In addition to taking the normal fire or electricity damage, creatures that fail their saving throws against the breath weapon are dazzled for 1 minute per caster level. Sightless creatures are not affected by *breath flare*.

BREATH OF THE JUNGLE

Transmutation
Level: Druid 1
Components: V, S, DF
Casting Time: 1 standard action
Range: Medium (100 ft. + 10 ft./level)
Effect: Mist spreads in a 40-ft. radius, 20 ft. high
Duration: 1 minute/level
Saving Throw: None
Spell Resistance: No

With a word of power and flick of your wrist, a foul-smelling, fine mist appears.

The DC of any saving throw made within the mist against poison or disease increases by 2.

The mist does not provide concealment.

BREATH WEAPON ADMIXTURE

Transmutation [see text]
Level: Sorcerer/wizard 9
Components: S
Casting Time: 1 swift action
Range: Personal
Target: Your breath weapon
Duration: 1 round

You spit out two forms of energy as your breath weapon streaks toward your opponents.

For this spell to function, you must have a breath weapon, either as a supernatural ability or as the result of casting a spell such as *dragon breath* (page 73). When you successfully cast this spell, you choose one type of energy other than that normally associated with your breath weapon: acid, cold, electricity, fire, or sonic. You can modify your breath weapon to add an equal amount of the energy you choose. For example, a great wyrm red dragon whose breath weapon normally deals 24d10 points of fire damage could use this spell to produce a cone dealing 24d10 points of fire damage and 24d10 points of acid damage. Even opposed types of energy, such as fire and cold, can be combined using this spell. If you choose sonic energy, the save DC of your breath weapon is reduced by 2.

When you use this spell to produce acid, cold, electricity, or fire energy, it is a spell of that type. For example, *breath weapon admixture* is an acid spell when you cast it to add acid damage to your breath weapon.

BREATH WEAPON SUBSTITUTION

Transmutation [see text]
Level: Sorcerer/wizard 5
Components: S
Casting Time: 1 swift action
Range: Personal
Target: Your breath weapon
Duration: 1 round

Your foes, prepared for your terrible fiery breath weapon, are caught off guard as you exhale a cone of caustic acid in their surprised faces.

For this spell to function, you must have a breath weapon, either as a supernatural ability or as the result of casting a spell such as *dragon breath* (page 73). When you successfully cast this spell, you choose one type of energy other than that normally associated with your breath weapon: acid, cold, electricity, or fire. You can modify your breath weapon to use the selected energy type instead of its normal energy type. For example, an old red dragon whose breath weapon normally deals 16d10 points of fire damage could use this spell to produce a cone dealing 16d10 points of acid damage instead.

When you use this spell to produce acid, cold, electricity, or fire energy, it is a spell of that type. For example, *breath weapon substitution* is an acid spell when you cast it to change your breath weapon to deal acid damage.

BRIAR WEB

Transmutation
Level: Druid 2, ranger 2
Components: V, S, DF
Casting Time: 1 standard action
Range: Medium (100 ft. + 10 ft./level)
Area: 40-ft.-radius spread
Duration: 1 minute/level
Saving Throw: None
Spell Resistance: No

With a sound like a thousand knives being unsheathed, the plants in the area grow sharp thorns and warp into a thick briar patch.

This spell causes grasses, weeds, bushes, and even trees to grow thorns and wrap and twist around creatures in or entering the area. The spell's area becomes difficult terrain, and creatures move at half speed within the affected area. Any creature moving through the area also takes 1 point of nonmagical piercing damage for each 5 feet moved.

A creature with *freedom of movement* or the woodland stride ability is unaffected by this spell.

BRILLIANT AURA

Transmutation
Level: Cleric 8, druid 8, sorcerer/wizard 7
Targets: Weapons carried by one creature/2 levels, no two of which are more than 30 ft. apart
Duration: 1 round/level
Saving Throw: Will negates (harmless)
Spell Resistance: Yes (harmless)

Taking fresh insight from contemplation of light, you cast the spell and set your allies aglow with white brilliance.

This spell functions like *brilliant blade* (see below), except as noted here, and that all weapons of the subject creatures gain the brilliant energy special ability.

BRILLIANT BLADE

Transmutation
Level: Cleric 7, druid 7, sorcerer/wizard 6
Components: V, S
Casting Time: 1 standard action
Range: Close (25 ft. + 5 ft./2 levels)
Target: One melee or thrown weapon, or fifty projectiles (all of which must be in contact with each other at the time of casting)
Duration: 1 minute/level
Saving Throw: Will negates (harmless, object)
Spell Resistance: Yes (harmless, object)

With a word, the indicated weapon glows with a soft blue-white halo that emits a low, slowly pulsating hum. The faint smell of ozone permeates the air.

You transform a single melee weapon, natural weapon, thrown weapon, or group of projectiles into a weapon with the brilliant energy special ability (DMG 224). If this spell is cast on arrows or crossbow bolts, the effect on a particular projectile ends after one use, whether or not the missile strikes its intended target. Treat shuriken as arrows, rather than as thrown weapons, for the purpose of this spell.

BRISTLE

Transmutation
Level: Sorcerer/wizard 2
Components: V, S
Casting Time: 1 standard action
Range: Touch
Target: Suit of armor touched
Duration: 1 minute/level (D)
Saving Throw: None
Spell Resistance: No

With a word and the sudden opening of your hand you complete the spell. Touching a suit of armor instantly causes the armor to sprout long, deadly-looking spines.

The *bristle* spell temporarily enhances one suit of armor, causing it to grow long hard spikes that stick out in all directions. This spell does not work on clothing other than armor, but it does function with armor that already has spikes built in. The spikes are flexible enough not to hamper the creature wearing the armor. Each round, the first time the armor wearer attacks a target in melee, the spikes strike out as well, growing in length and hardness. The spikes have an attack bonus equal to your caster level and deal 2d6 points of damage. Your Strength modifier does not apply to this damage.

Briar web wraps creatures in the thorny grip of nearby plants

Illus. by W. England

BUOYANT LIFTING

Evocation
Level: Druid 1
Components: S, DF
Casting Time: 1 immediate action
Range: Close (25 ft. + 5 ft./2 levels)
Target: One willing creature/level, no two of which are more than 20 ft. apart
Duration: 1 minute/level (D); see text
Saving Throw: None
Spell Resistance: No

With a sharp jab of your finger, the water around your indicated subjects begins to push them toward the surface.

The subjects of this spell are borne toward the surface at 60 feet per round until they are floating on it. The subject then rests at the top of the liquid (rescuing it from drowning if it was a sinking air-breather) and can swim away under its own power or be moved by others (such as with a rope). If the subject is removed from the liquid, the spell ends.

BURNING BLOOD

Necromancy
Level: Sorcerer/wizard 4
Components: V, S, M
Casting Time: 1 standard action
Range: Medium (100 ft. + 10 ft./level)
Target: One living creature; see text
Duration: 1 round/level (D)
Saving Throw: Fortitude partial; see text
Spell Resistance: Yes

The taste of copper fills your mouth and bloody spatters punctuate the last few words that unlock the spell. You gag slightly as the blood in your mouth congeals, but disappears even as you release the spell.

You taint a living creature's blood with a hot, corrosive infusion, dealing 1d8 points of acid damage and 1d8 points of fire damage per round. The subject can attempt a Fortitude save each round to negate the damage, but a successful save does not prevent damage in future rounds. Searing pain limits the subject to a single move action in any round when it fails its Fortitude save.

Burning blood does not affect creatures of the construct, elemental, ooze, plant, or undead types.

Material Component: A drop of blood and a pinch of saltpeter.

BURNING SWORD

Evocation [Fire]
Level: Sorcerer/wizard 2
Components: V, S
Casting Time: 1 standard action
Range: Touch
Target: Weapon touched
Duration: 1 minute/level (D)
Saving Throw: None
Spell Resistance: No

By chopping your hand like an axe and uttering the last few phrases of the spell, you cause the weapon you've touched to become wreathed in flickering blue flames.

The flames from this spell shed azure light out to 30 feet. These flames do not harm the weapon or its wielder, but for the duration of the spell, it delivers fire damage in addition to its normal damage.

The enchanted weapon deals an extra 1d6 points of fire damage on a successful hit. Also, on a critical hit, the weapon deals additional fire damage based on the weapon's critical multiplier:

Critical Multiplier	Additional Fire Damage
×2	+1d10
×3	+2d10
×4	+3d10

BURROW

Transmutation
Level: Druid 2, ranger 2
Components: V, S, F/DF
Casting Time: 1 standard action
Range: Touch
Target: Creature touched
Duration: 1 minute/level (D)
Saving Throw: Will negates (harmless)
Spell Resistance: Yes (harmless)

You invoke the spell and your hands glow with a yellow aura, the aura lengthening and forming into translucent mole hands. The smell of freshly turned earth fills the air.

The subject can burrow through earth and loose rock (but not solid stone) with a speed of 30 feet (or 20 feet if it wears medium or heavy armor, or if it carries a medium or heavy load).

Arcane Focus: A claw from a burrowing creature.

BURROW, MASS

Transmutation
Level: Druid 4, ranger 3
Targets: One creature/level, no two of which are more than 30 ft. apart

You call upon the power of the spell and, in turn, each of your allies' hands gain a yellow nimbus, forming into the hands of large moles.

This spell functions like *burrow*, except that it affects multiple creatures.

BUZZING BEE

Conjuration (Creation)
Level: Sorcerer/wizard 1
Components: V, S, M
Casting Time: 1 standard action
Range: Medium (100 ft. + 10 ft./level)
Target: One creature
Duration: 1 minute/level (D)
Saving Throw: None
Spell Resistance: No

A small but extremely loud bee appears, buzzing around the head of the designated target.

This spell creates an unnerving noise that disrupts the subject's concentration. The subject is distracted and takes a –10 penalty on Move Silently checks. Creatures that can't hear are not distracted. The DC of Concentration checks to cast spells or maintain concentration while distracted is equal to this spell's DC + the level of the spell being cast.

The bee has a fly speed of 180 feet (perfect). It remains near the subject in spite of darkness, invisibility, polymorph, cover, concealment, or any other attempt at disguising or hiding. The bee remains until the spell's duration expires or the subject moves out of range.

The bee can't be attacked, but it can be dispelled.

Material Component: A dab of honey.

CACOPHONIC BURST

Evocation [Sonic]
Level: Bard 5, sorcerer/wizard 5
Components: V, S
Casting Time: 1 standard action
Range: Long (400 ft. + 40 ft./level)
Area: 20-ft.-radius burst
Duration: Instantaneous
Saving Throw: Reflex half
Spell Resistance: Yes

You complete the spell with a scream, and echoes of your cry travel outward and burst into ear-shattering sounds.

You cause a burst of low, discordant noise to erupt at the chosen location. It deals 1d6 points of sonic damage per caster level (maximum 15d6) to all creatures within the area.

Cacophonic burst cannot penetrate the area of a *silence* spell.

CACOPHONIC SHIELD

Evocation [Sonic]
Level: Bard 4, sorcerer/wizard 5
Components: V, S
Casting Time: 1 standard action
Range: 10 ft.
Area: 10-ft.-radius emanation centered on you
Duration: 1 minute/level (D)
Saving Throw: Fortitude partial
Spell Resistance: Yes

Your words speed into a jumble of sounds that mix together until only a constant, faint buzzing sound remains.

You create a barrier of sonic energy at a distance of 10 feet from yourself. Creatures on either side of the barrier hear it as a loud but harmless buzzing. Nonmagical sound (including sound produced by a thunderstone) does not cross the barrier. Supernatural or spell-based sounds or sonic effects penetrate the barrier only if the caster or originator of the effect succeeds on a caster level check (DC 11 + your caster level).

A creature that crosses the barrier takes 1d6 points of sonic damage +1 point per caster level (maximum +20) and must make a Fortitude save or be deafened for 1 minute. The sonic vibrations create a 20% miss chance for any missiles (including siege weapon attacks) crossing the barrier in either direction. The barrier moves with you, but you cannot force another creature to pass through it (for example, by moving adjacent to an enemy). If you force a creature to pass through, the barrier has no effect on that creature.

CALL KOLYARUT

Conjuration (Calling) [Lawful]
Level: Cleric 7, sorcerer/wizard 7
Components: V, S, DF, XP
Casting Time: 10 minutes
Range: Close (25 ft. + 5 ft./2 levels)
Effect: One called kolyarut
Duration: Instantaneous
Saving Throw: None
Spell Resistance: No

As you complete the spell, the powers of Mechanus respond. The kolyarut does not manifest before you as much as assembles itself in your presence, a single whirling cog unfolding until the construct stands complete. "Who is to be punished?" it asks in the flat voice of a clock mechanism.

By casting this spell, you receive the aid of a kolyarut inevitable (MM 159). If you know an individual kolyarut's name, you can request that individual by speaking the name during the spell (though you might get a different creature, anyway).

You can ask the kolyarut to perform one duty for you. The task must take no more than 1 hour to complete. The inevitable does not ask for any payment for the task.

XP Cost: 250 XP.

CALL MARUT

Conjuration (Calling) [Lawful]
Level: Cleric 9, Mechanus 9, sorcerer/wizard 9
Components: V, S, DF, XP
Casting Time: 10 minutes
Range: Close (25 ft. + 5 ft./2 levels)
Effect: One called marut
Duration: Instantaneous
Saving Throw: None
Spell Resistance: No

You call across the boundaries of the multiverse, and the powers of Mechanus respond. The marut warps into place in an eyeblink with a whirling throb of thunder. "Who denies death?" it asks with the voice of an avalanche.

Illus. by J. Nelson

A zelekhut only answers the call of a spellcaster who seeks justice

By casting this spell, you receive the aid of a marut inevitable (MM 159). If you know an individual marut's name, you can request that individual by speaking the name during the spell (though you might get a different creature, anyway).

You can ask the marut to perform one duty for you. The task must take no more than 1 hour to complete. The inevitable does not ask for any payment for the task.

XP Cost: 500 XP.

CALL ZELEKHUT

Conjuration (Calling) [Lawful]
Level: Cleric 5, sorcerer/wizard 5
Components: V, S, DF, XP
Casting Time: 10 minutes
Range: Close (25 ft. + 5 ft./2 levels)
Effect: One called zelekhut
Duration: Instantaneous
Saving Throw: None
Spell Resistance: No

You make the necessary conjurations and the powers of Mechanus respond. The zelekhut fades into view, its centaur form accompanied by the sound of rattling silver chains. "Who seeks to escape justice?" it asks with the solemn tones of a judge's gavel.

By casting this spell, you receive the aid of a zelekhut inevitable (MM 160). If you know an individual zelekhut's name, you can request that individual by speaking the name during the spell (though you might get a different creature, anyway).

You can ask the zelekhut to perform one duty for you. The task must take no more than 1 hour to complete. The inevitable does not ask for any payment for the task.

XP Cost: 100 XP.

CALTROPS

Conjuration (Creation)
Level: Sorcerer/wizard 0
Components: V, S
Casting Time: 1 standard action
Range: Close (25 ft. + 5 ft./2 levels)
Area: See text
Duration: 1 round/level
Saving Throw: None
Spell Resistance: No

You speak the words and spread your palm open, as if you were throwing jacks. Coppery sparks spring from your palm, filling the corridor with small four-pronged spikes.

A *caltrops* spell covers one 5-foot-by-5-foot square with caltrops. Every time a creature moves into an area covered by caltrops or spends a round fighting while standing in such an area, it might step on one. The caltrops make one attack roll (+0 melee) against the creature. For this attack, the target's shield and deflection bonuses do not count, nor does its armor bonus for armor worn. A target wearing shoes or other footwear gains a +2 armor bonus to Armor Class (which does count). If the caltrops succeed on the attack, the creature has stepped on one.

A successful attack by a caltrop deals 1 point of damage. If the target is Small, Medium, or Large, its land speed is reduced by one-half because of the injury. This movement penalty lasts for 24 hours, until the creature is successfully treated with a DC 15 Heal check, or until it receives at least 1 point of magical healing. A charging or running creature must immediately stop if it steps on a caltrop. Any creature moving at half speed or slower can pick its way through a bed of caltrops with no trouble.

The DM judges the effectiveness of caltrops against unusual opponents or opponents outside the size range given above. A giant centipede, for example, can scramble among the caltrops with no chance of hurting itself, and a fire giant wearing thick, massive boots might be immune to their attacks.

For every two caster levels beyond 1st, you can affect an additional 5-foot-by-5-foot square, and the caltrops' attack bonus increases by 1. Thus, you affect two squares at 3rd level (+1 melee), three at 5th level (+2 melee), four at 7th level (+3 melee), and a maximum of five at 9th level or higher (+4 melee maximum).

Multiple *caltrops* spells (or mundane caltrops) occupying the same space have no additional effect.

CAMOUFLAGE

Transmutation
Level: Druid 1, ranger 1
Components: V, S
Casting Time: 1 standard action
Range: Personal
Target: You
Duration: 10 minutes/level

Upon finishing the spell, your skin and clothing change color, warping tint and hue to match your surroundings.

Throughout the duration of the spell, your coloration changes instantly to match the background of any new environment you enter, with no effort on your part. This effect grants you a +10 circumstance bonus on Hide checks.

CAMOUFLAGE, MASS

Transmutation
Level: Druid 2, ranger 2
Range: Medium (100 ft. + 10 ft./level)
Target: Any number of creatures, no two of which are more than 60 ft. apart
Saving Throw: Will negates (harmless)
Spell Resistance: Yes (harmless)

Reaching out to your environment, you wrap your allies in the patterns and shifting colors of their surroundings, concealing them from prying eyes.

This spell functions like *camouflage*, except the effect is mobile with the group. The spell is broken for any individual who moves more than 60 feet from the nearest member of the group. (If only two individuals are affected, the one moving away from the other one loses its camouflage. If both are moving away from each other, they both become visible when the distance between them exceeds 60 feet.)

CAPRICIOUS ZEPHYR

Evocation [Air]
Level: Druid 3, sorcerer/wizard 3
Components: V, S
Casting Time: 1 standard action
Range: Medium (100 ft. + 10 ft./level)
Effect: 5-ft.-diameter sphere
Duration: 1 round/level
Saving Throw: None or Reflex partial; see text
Spell Resistance: Yes

Blowing on your twirling hand, you complete the spell, creating a roiling ball of dust and gale-force winds.

A ball of swirling wind and dust moves as you direct it, pushing your foes across the battlefield. From its starting point, a *capricious zephyr* moves 30 feet per round in the direction you point, regardless of the presence or absence of terrain.

If the sphere enters a space with a creature, it stops moving for that round and tries to bowl over the creature with its wind force. That creature must resist a bull rush attack from the *capricious zephyr,* which has a +6 bonus on the check. If the spell wins the bull rush, it pushes the creature as far as it can in a random direction (roll 1d8; 1 indicates a push into the square closest to you, and 2 through 8 indicate the other squares, moving clockwise around the creature). Any creature pushed by the sphere must succeed on a Reflex save or fall prone.

A *capricious zephyr* moves as long as you actively direct it (a move action for you). Otherwise, it merely stays at rest and attempts to bowl over anyone in its square. The spell ends if the distance between the sphere and you ever exceeds the spell's range.

CAST IN STONE

Transmutation
Level: Druid 9
Components: V, S
Casting Time: 1 standard action
Range: Personal
Target: You
Duration: 1 round/level (D)
Saving Throw: None and Fortitude negates; see text
Spell Resistance: No

Your eyes become like gray stone orbs traced with golden veins. The change catches the foes fighting you by surprise, and they turn to stone.

Any creature within 30 feet that meets your gaze is permanently turned into a mindless, inert statue (as *flesh to stone*), unless it succeeds on a Fortitude save. You can free the victim of your own *cast in stone* at any time by speaking a command word you establish during the casting.

Each creature within range of the gaze must attempt a saving throw against the gaze effect each round at the beginning of its turn. A creature can avert its eyes, which grants a 50% chance to avoid the gaze but in turn grants you concealment relative to it. A creature can close its eyes or turn away entirely; doing so prevents the gaze from affecting it but grants you total concealment from that creature.

In addition, you can actively attempt to use the gaze as a standard action each round. To do so, you choose a target within range, and that target must attempt a saving throw. A target that is averting or shutting its eyes gains the above benefits.

Illus. by R. Spears

Chain missile puts magic missile to shame

CASTIGATE

Evocation [Sonic]
Level: Cleric 4, paladin 4, Purification 4
Components: V
Casting Time: 1 standard action
Range: 10 ft.
Area: 10-ft.-radius burst centered on you
Duration: Instantaneous
Saving Throw: Fortitude half
Spell Resistance: Yes

Shouting your deity's teachings, you rebuke your foes with the magic of your sacred words.

This spell has no effect on creatures that cannot hear. All creatures whose alignment differs from yours on both the law–chaos and the good–evil axes take 1d4 points of damage per caster level (maximum 10d4). All creatures whose alignment differs from yours on one component take half damage, and this spell does not deal damage to those who share your alignment. For example, a lawful good cleric who casts this spell deals full damage to any creature that is not lawful and not good, half damage to any creature that is lawful or good (but not both), and no damage to lawful good creatures.

A Fortitude saving throw reduces damage by half.

CELEBRATION

Enchantment (Compulsion) [Mind-Affecting, Sonic]
Level: Bard 4
Components: V, S
Casting Time: 1 standard action
Range: Close (25 ft. + 5 ft./2 levels)
Targets: All creatures in a 15-ft.-radius burst
Duration: 1 round/level
Saving Throw: Will negates; see text
Spell Resistance: Yes

With a few slurred words and fumbling motions, you complete the spell and prepare to perform.

You cause any creatures in the area to feel increasingly more intoxicated the longer you perform a drinking song. In the round this spell is cast, all creatures that fail their saving throws take a –2 penalty to Dexterity, Intelligence, and Wisdom.

If you use a standard action to continue performing in a second consecutive round, each affected creature must succeed on a second Will saving throw or become nauseated. Succeeding on this saving throw prevents the nausea, and the creature is immune to further effects of this spell.

If you use a standard action to continue performing in a third consecutive round, any affected creatures must succeed on a Will save or pass out, becoming unconscious and helpless.

CHAIN MISSILE

Evocation [Force]
Level: Sorcerer/wizard 3
Components: V, S
Casting Time: 1 standard action
Range: Long (400 ft. + 40 ft./level)

Target: One creature, plus one more creature/2 levels (each of which must be within 30 ft. of the primary target)
Duration: Instantaneous
Saving Throw: None
Spell Resistance: Yes

Bolts of pale blue energy spring forth from your finger and slam into the desired target. An instant later, the bolts bounce away toward other creatures, slamming into each one.

Missiles of magical energy dart from your fingertip to unerringly strike a creature. The missiles strike one creature initially, then spring to other targets. Each missile deals 1d4+1 points of force damage. One missile strikes the primary target per two caster levels, to a maximum of ten missiles (dealing 10d4+10 points of damage). After the missiles strike, they ricochet to a number of targets up to the number of missiles created by the spell. Each secondary target takes 1d4+1 points of damage, as if struck by a single *magic missile*. You choose secondary targets as you like, but they must all be within 30 feet of the primary target, and no secondary target can be struck more than once. You can choose to affect fewer secondary targets than the maximum (to avoid allies in the area, for example). Missiles without a secondary target do not ricochet off the primary target.

Spells, magic items, and abilities that protect against *magic missile* (such as the *shield* spell or a *brooch of shielding*) also protect against this spell. If the primary target has that sort of protection, the spell has no effect against it but still springs to all secondary targets. (A *brooch of shielding* loses a number of charges equal to the number of missiles hitting the creature—up to ten missiles.) If spell resistance causes the spell to fail to harm the primary target, the spell fails and missiles do not ricochet to additional targets.

The missiles strike unerringly, even if the targets are in melee or have anything less then total cover or concealment. You cannot single out specific parts of a creature to strike. This spell cannot target or damage inanimate objects.

CHAIN OF EYES

Divination
Level: Cleric 3, druid 4, sorcerer/wizard 2
Components: V, S
Casting Time: 1 standard action
Range: Touch
Target: Living creature touched
Duration: 1 hour/level
Saving Throw: Will negates
Spell Resistance: Yes

With the creature's will to resist brushed aside, you gaze out from its eyes to see your own satisfied smile.

You can use another creature's vision instead of your own. While this spell gives you no control over the subject, each time it comes into physical contact with another living being, you can choose to transfer your sensor to the new creature. During your turn in a round, you can use a free action to switch from seeing through the current creature's eyes to seeing normally or back again.

Each transfer attempt allows the new target a saving throw and spell resistance. If a target resists, the spell ends.

CHARGE OF THE TRICERATOPS

Transmutation
Level: Druid 3, ranger 3
Components: V, S, DF
Casting Time: 1 standard action
Range: Touch
Target: Living creature touched
Duration: 1 round/level (D)
Saving Throw: Will negates (harmless)
Spell Resistance: Yes

Holding your hand to your head—index and middle fingers extended in a V—you call upon the ancient power of the triceratops. You touch your intended target,

A druid can cast charge of the triceratops on herself, an ally, or an animal companion

Illus. by J. Nelson

which then grows large horns, a bony skull plate, and a thickened hide.

The horns created by this spell grant a natural gore attack that deals 1d8 points of damage (1d6 points of damage if the subject creature is Small, 2d6 if Large). If the gore attack is used as part of a charge, it deals double damage.

If the gore attack is used as a primary weapon, the subject adds 1-1/2 times its Strength bonus to the damage of the attack. If it is used as a secondary weapon, the subject adds only 1/2 its Strength bonus to the damage roll, and takes a –5 penalty on the attack roll.

The recipient also gains a +4 enhancement bonus to its natural armor.

CHEAT

Transmutation
Level: Bard 1, Greed 1, sorcerer/wizard 1
Components: V, S, F
Casting Time: 1 standard action
Range: Personal
Target: You
Duration: 1 minute/level or until discharged
Saving Throw: Will negates; see text
Spell Resistance: No

You rattle the dice in your hand and mutter the words of the spell, then check your facedown cards again. The two low cards have somehow become trumps.

At one point during the duration of this spell, you can attempt to alter the outcome of a game of chance. This spell can affect only nonmagical games, such as those using cards or dice. It cannot affect a game involving magic, nor a magic item involved in a game of chance (such as a *deck of many things*). Whenever a dice roll is made to determine the outcome of the game, a character under the effect of this spell can demand a reroll and take the better of the two rolls.

Anyone observing the game of chance is allowed a Will saving throw to realize something fishy is going on, and might suspect that the outcome of the game has been magically altered.

For example, Darkon is playing a game that he has a 1 in 4 chance of winning. The DM secretly rolls 1d4 and tells the player that Darkon lost. Because Darkon is under the effect of a *cheat* spell, the player can have the DM reroll. The spell alters probability, so there is no subterfuge that another character could notice (except for the casting of the spell itself).

Focus: A pair of dice made from human bones.

CHECKMATE'S LIGHT

Evocation [Lawful]
Level: Cleric 3, paladin 2
Components: V, S, DF
Casting Time: 1 standard action
Range: Touch
Target: Melee weapon touched
Duration: 1 round/level (D)
Saving Throw: None
Spell Resistance: No

You intone your deity's name and the weapon you touch hums a harmonic response before it lights up with a soothing red glow.

You imbue the touched weapon with a +1 enhancement bonus per three caster levels (maximum +5 at 15th level), and it is treated as lawful-aligned for the purpose of overcoming damage reduction. In addition, you can cause it to cast a red glow as bright as a torch. Any creature within the radius of its clear illumination (20 feet) gets a +1 morale bonus on saving throws against fear effects.

If the weapon leaves your grasp, the spell effect is suppressed until you or another worshiper of your deity picks it up. Time that passes while the spell's effects are suppressed counts against the spell's duration.

CHILL OF THE GRAVE

Necromancy
Level: Deathbound 1
Components: V, S
Casting Time: 1 standard action
Range: Close (25 ft. + 5 ft./2 levels)
Effect: Ray
Duration: Instantaneous
Saving Throw: None
Spell Resistance: Yes

A pale ray erupts from your pointing finger, and a moaning sound fills the air as it streaks toward your target.

You must succeed on a ranged touch attack with the ray to strike a target. The subject takes 1d10 points of cold damage. This damage increases to 2d10 at caster level 4th, 3d10 at caster level 7th, and 4d10 at caster level 10th.

CIRCLE DANCE

Divination
Level: Bard 2, cleric 3, druid 3, sorcerer/wizard 3
Components: V, S
Casting Time: 1 minute
Range: Personal
Target: You
Duration: Instantaneous

You dance to each point of the compass rose, then finish the spell in a wide, circular sweep. At the end, you know that the creature you seek lies in the direction you face.

You divine the relative direction and condition of another creature. You must have firsthand knowledge of the creature for the spell to function.

If the creature is alive and on the same plane as you, the spell leaves you facing in its direction. You also get an impression of its physical and emotional condition (unharmed, wounded, unconscious, dying, and so on). If the creature you seek is on a different plane or dead, you feel nothing.

CLARITY OF MIND

Abjuration
Level: Balance 3
Components: V, S, DF
Casting Time: 1 standard action
Range: Touch
Target: Living creature touched
Duration: 1 hour/level
Saving Throw: Will negates (harmless)
Spell Resistance: Yes (harmless)

A nimbus of silver rays surrounds the warrior's head as you touch him and invoke the spell's holy power. His thoughts grow clearer, and he is better able to see through the mind-warping effects of spells.

You grant the subject a +4 insight bonus on saving throws against all mind-affecting spells and effects. If the subject of *clarity of mind* attacks a creature that has concealment and fails the miss chance roll, he can reroll the miss chance once to see if his attack actually hit the target.

CLAWS OF THE BEAR

Transmutation
Level: Druid 1, ranger 1
Components: V, S
Casting Time: 1 standard action
Range: Personal
Target: You
Duration: 1 round/level

Howling a curse at your enemies, pain explodes in your hands as they suddenly sport long claws. Almost instantly the pain fades. Too bad your foes won't be able to say the same.

When you cast this spell, your hands become natural weapons that deal 1d8 points of damage each or your normal unarmed damage, whichever is greater. You are considered armed while this spell is in effect. If you are Small, your claws deal 1d6 points of damage, and if you are Large, they deal 2d6 points of damage. You add your Strength modifier to your claw damage rolls.

Your claws work just like the natural weapons of many monsters. You can make an attack with one claw or a full attack with two claws at your normal attack bonus, replacing your normal attack routine. You take no penalties for two-weapon fighting, and neither attack is a secondary attack. If your base attack bonus is +6 or higher, you do not gain any additional attacks—you simply have two claw attacks at your normal attack bonus.

CLAWS OF DARKNESS

Illusion (Shadow)
Level: Sorcerer/wizard 2
Components: V, S
Casting Time: 1 standard action
Range: Personal
Target: You
Duration: 1 round/level (D)
Saving Throw: Fortitude partial
Spell Resistance: Yes; see text

You draw material from the Plane of Shadow to cause your hands and forearms to elongate and change shape into featureless claws of inky blackness.

The climb walls spell helps make treacherous ascents simple work

When you cast this spell, your hands become shadowy claws. Starting on your next action, you can use the claws to make unarmed attacks as if they were natural weapons. (You attack with one claw and can use the other claw for an off-hand attack. If you have multiple attacks, you use them normally when attacking with the claws.) Attacks with the claws are melee touch attacks. Each claw deals 1d8 points of cold damage. If you grapple an opponent, you deal claw damage with each successful grapple check, and the grappled target is under the effect of a *slow* spell for as long as you maintain the grapple. An opponent that makes a successful Fortitude save is not *slowed*, and it cannot be *slowed* by this casting of *claws of darkness*.

You can extend the claws up to 6 feet, which gives you a natural reach of 10 feet, or retract them as a free action.

When the spell is in effect, you cannot cast spells with components other than verbal ones, nor can you carry items with your hands. Any magic items worn on your hands are temporarily absorbed and cease functioning while the spell is active.

CLEAR MIND

Abjuration
Level: Paladin 1
Components: V, S, DF
Casting Time: 1 standard action
Range: Personal
Target: You
Duration: 10 minutes/level

A silver glow sheathes your body as you complete the spell. As the glow fades, you feel a touch of the divine at the back of your mind. This divine touch spreads until you feel your concerns and anxieties fade away.

You gain a +4 sacred bonus on saving throws made against mind-affecting spells and effects.

CLIMB WALLS

Transmutation
Level: Druid 1, ranger 1
Components: V, S, M
Casting Time: 1 standard action
Range: Touch
Target: Creature touched
Duration: 1 minute/level (D)
Saving Throw: Will negates (harmless)
Spell Resistance: Yes (harmless)

You brush the target with your finger, and she now perceives handholds and toeholds where others see smooth stone.

The subject gains a +10 enhancement bonus on Climb checks. The bonus increases to +20 at caster level 5th, and to +30 (the maximum) at caster level 9th. Unlike with *spider climb*, this spell does not allow the subject to climb on ceilings, and it does not give the creature a climb speed.

Material Component: A drop of tree sap or equally sticky material.

CLOAK OF BRAVERY

Abjuration [Mind-Affecting]
Level: Cleric 3, Courage 3, paladin 2
Components: V, S
Casting Time: 1 standard action
Range: 60 ft.
Area: 60-ft.-radius emanation centered on you
Duration: 10 minutes/level
Saving Throw: Will negates (harmless)
Spell Resistance: Yes (harmless)

Summoning up your courage, you throw out your arm and sweep it over the area, cloaking all your allies in a glittering mantle of magic that bolsters their bravery.

Illus. by M. Cotie

All allies within the emanation (including you) gain a morale bonus on saves against fear effects equal to your caster level (to a maximum of +10 at caster level 10th).

CLOAK OF BRAVERY, GREATER

Abjuration [Mind-Affecting]
Level: Courage 9
Range: 1 mile; see text
Area: 1-mile-radius emanation centered on you
Duration: 1 hour/level

This spell functions like *cloak of bravery*, except all allies within the emanation (including you) are immune to fear effects and gain a +2 morale bonus on attack rolls. Allies who don't have line of sight to you are unaffected.

CLOAK OF DARK POWER

Abjuration
Level: Drow 1
Components: V, S
Casting Time: 1 standard action
Range: Touch
Target: Creature touched
Duration: 1 minute/level
Saving Throw: Will negates (harmless)
Spell Resistance: Yes (harmless)

A dim gray haze appears around the creature. Light bends around this haze, leaving the creature in a patch of strange and shifting darkness.

Cloak of dark power creates a dusky haze around the subject. The haze does not interfere with vision, but the subject and anything it wears or carries is protected from the effects of full sunlight, even under the open, daytime sky of the surface world. A drow subject suffers no blindness or bright illumination combat penalties while under the effect of *cloak of dark power*.

The subject also gains a +4 resistance bonus on saves against *light* or *darkness* spells or effects.

CLOAK OF THE SEA

Transmutation
Level: Druid 5, sorcerer/wizard 6
Components: V, S, DF
Casting Time: 1 standard action
Range: Touch
Target: Creature touched
Duration: 1 hour/level (D)
Saving Throw: Will negates (harmless)
Spell Resistance: Yes (harmless)

A blue-green glow surrounds your hand as you complete the spell. With a touch you release it into your intended target, which then turns the same shade of blue-green.

While underwater, the subject functions as if affected by *blur* (PH 206), *freedom of movement* (PH 233), and *water breathing* (PH 300), and doesn't take nonlethal damage for the duration of the spell. When out of the water (or even partially out), the subject gains none of these advantages except *water breathing*. The subject can leave and reenter water without ending the spell.

CLOAK POOL

Illusion (Glamer)
Level: Bard 2, sorcerer/wizard 2
Components: V, S
Casting Time: 1 standard action
Range: Close (25 ft. + 5 ft./2 levels)
Target: One color pool
Duration: 1 hour/level (D)
Saving Throw: Will negates (harmless, object)
Spell Resistance: No

A few words and motions, and the swirling color pool becomes as silver-gray as the rest of the Astral Plane.

This spell causes a color pool on the Astral Plane (DMG 154)—an irregular patch of color containing a portal to another plane—to seemingly cease to exist. In truth, the color pool is only hidden from view. The use of this spell does not hide the area around the pool; it masks only the fact that a pool is present. *See invisibility* or *true seeing* reveals the presence of the pool, as does *analyze portal*.

CLOSE WOUNDS

Conjuration (Healing)
Level: Cleric 2
Components: V
Casting Time: 1 immediate action
Range: Close (25 ft. + 5 ft./2 levels)
Target: One creature
Duration: Instantaneous
Saving Throw: Will half (harmless); see text
Spell Resistance: Yes (harmless)

Your ally falls from a crushing blow, but you don't have time to reach him. You quickly speak words of power, and the worst of his injuries glow golden and begin to heal.

This spell cures 1d4 points of damage +1 point per caster level (maximum +5).

If you cast this spell immediately after the subject takes damage, it effectively prevents the damage. It would keep alive someone who had just dropped to –10 hit points, for example, leaving the character at negative hit points but stable.

Used against an undead creature, *close wounds* deals damage instead of curing the creature (which takes half damage if it makes a Will saving throw).

CLOUD OF BEWILDERMENT

Conjuration
Level: Bard 2, sorcerer/wizard 2
Components: V, S, M
Casting Time: 1 standard action
Range: Close (25 ft. + 5 ft./2 levels)
Area: 10-ft. cube
Duration: 1 round/level
Saving Throw: Fortitude negates; see text
Spell Resistance: No

As you exhale the last syllables of the incantation, your breath forms an invisible spray of noxious air.

This spell creates a small cloud of nauseating vapors. Any living creature in the area becomes nauseated. This condition lasts as long as the creature is in the cloud and for 1d4+1 rounds after it leaves. Any creature that succeeds on its save but remains in the cloud must continue to save each round on your turn.

The cloud obscures sight, including darkvision, providing concealment to creatures within the area or against attacks made through the cloud.

Material Component: A rotten egg.

CLOUD WINGS

Transmutation
Level: Druid 2
Components: V, S
Casting Time: 1 standard action
Range: Touch
Target: Creature touched
Duration: 1 hour/level
Saving Throw: Fortitude negates (harmless)
Spell Resistance: Yes (harmless)

As you touch the subject, mist forms crude wings that cling to his back.

This spell increases the subject's fly speed by 30 feet. It has no effect on other modes of movement, nor does it allow the subject to fly if it cannot already do so.

CLOUDBURST

Evocation [Water]
Level: Druid 1
Components: V, S
Casting Time: 1 round
Range: Long (400 ft. + 40 ft./level)
Area: 100-ft.-radius emanation
Duration: 10 minutes/level (D)
Saving Throw: None
Spell Resistance: No

Clouds whirl into existence and, with a peal of thunder, let loose a drenching downpour.

You cause clouds to gather and a heavy rain to fall. The rain reduces visibility ranges by half, resulting in a –4 penalty on Spot and Search checks. It automatically extinguishes unprotected flames and has a 50% chance of extinguishing protected flames. Ranged weapon attacks and Listen checks take a –4 penalty. Fire damage in this spell's area is reduced by 1 point per die of damage.

This spell does not function indoors, underground, underwater, or in desert climates. After the spell ends, the water created evaporates over the next 10 minutes. The water created with this spell does not slake thirst or provide any nourishment to plants.

The cloud wings spell gives great speed to a flying creature

CLOUD-WALKERS

Transmutation
Level: Druid 7, Windstorm 6
Components: V, S, DF
Casting Time: 1 standard action
Range: Touch
Targets: One creature/level
Duration: 10 minutes/level (D)
Saving Throw: Reflex negates (harmless)
Spell Resistance: Yes (harmless)

With a kiss blown to each subject, you create gaseous pads of cloudstuff on their feet, allowing them to walk on the clouds.

Each subject of the spell can move with a fly speed of 60 feet (perfect maneuverability), but only outdoors. To touch the earth again, a subject must use a standard action to shake off the cloudstuff, which ends the spell for that creature. You can dismiss the spell, but only for all subjects at once—an act that can have significant consequences for subjects already in the air.

CLUTCH OF ORCUS

Necromancy [Evil]
Level: Cleric 3
Components: V, S
Casting Time: 1 standard action
Range: Medium (100 ft. + 10 ft./level)
Target: One humanoid
Duration: Concentration, up to 1 round/level
Saving Throw: Fortitude negates
Spell Resistance: Yes

Reaching out a hand twisted by tension into a grasping claw, you squeeze your foe's heart from afar, anticipating the moment its remains will rest in your palm.

Magical force grips the subject's heart (or similar vital organ) and begins crushing it. The victim is paralyzed and takes 1d12 points of damage per round. Concentration is required to maintain the spell each round. A conscious victim can attempt a new Fortitude saving throw each round to end the spell. If the victim dies as a result of this spell, its smoking heart appears in your hand.

COCOON

Conjuration (Creation)
Level: Druid 8
Components: V, S, M, XP
Casting Time: 1 round
Range: Close (25 ft. + 5 ft./2 levels)
Target: One corpse
Duration: Instantaneous
Saving Throw: Fortitude negates
Spell Resistance: Yes

The silkworm cocoon disappears from your palm, and silk threads coalesce from thin air around your target, quickly wrapping about the body until it is fully encased.

When cast upon a deceased creature (whose death can be no less recent than 1 round per caster level), this spell preserves the body and begins a slow process of rebirth. If the corpse is *raised*, *resurrected*, or *reincarnated* at any point

Illus. by R. Spears

during the next week, the creature takes no level loss or Constitution loss normally associated with such spells.

At the conclusion of the week, if the subject has not been returned to life, the creature is automatically *reincarnated*, as the spell, with no loss of level or Constitution.

Material Component: A silkworm cocoon.

XP Cost: 250 XP

COLD FIRE

Transmutation [Cold]
Level: Cleric 1, druid 1
Components: V, S, DF
Casting Time: 1 standard action
Range: Close (25 ft. + 5 ft./2 levels)
Target: One fire source (up to a 20-ft. cube) or one creature; see text
Duration: 1 minute/level (D) (fire source) or Instantaneous (creature)
Saving Throw: No (fire source) or Fortitude half (creature)
Spell Resistance: No (fire source) or Yes (creature)

As you complete the spell you widen your eyes slightly at the fire you wish to affect. Its flames instantly turn a blue-white. The air between you and the fire feels much colder.

You are able to change the normal flames of a fire (any blaze that lasts for more than 1 round) into cold flames. Affected flames deal cold damage to creatures that come into contact with them. The spell can also affect magical fires such as those generated by a *wall of fire*, provided the affected fire is small enough. *Cold fire* flames burn blue and white for the duration of the spell.

If the target is a creature with the fire subtype or vulnerability to cold, the spell deals 1d6 points of cold damage per two caster levels (maximum 5d6) to the creature, but has no further effect.

COLD SNAP

Transmutation [Cold]
Level: Cleric 6, druid 5
Components: V, S
Casting Time: 1 minute
Range: 1 mile
Area: 1-mile-radius circle centered on you
Duration: 2d4 hours
Saving Throw: None
Spell Resistance: No

As you call upon divine power to fuel your spell, you feel the air around you become chilled. The drop in temperature creates a thin fog that exacerbates the cold in the air without hindering your vision or movement whatsoever.

This spell causes a powerful cold front to form, lowering the temperature in the affected area by 5 degrees Fahrenheit per caster level (maximum change of 50 degrees Fahrenheit), to a maximum low of –20 degrees Fahrenheit (see Cold Dangers, DMG 302). Spells with the cold descriptor deal an extra 1 point of damage per die when cast in the area.

COMBUST

Evocation [Fire]
Level: Sorcerer/wizard 2
Components: V, S, M
Casting Time: 1 standard action
Range: Touch
Target: Touched creature or combustible object that weighs no more than 25 lb./level
Duration: Instantaneous; see text
Saving Throw: Reflex partial
Spell Resistance: Yes

You rub the oil against the flint and murmur the ancient words, touching your target. It immediately smolders and then bursts into bright flames.

This spell makes a combustible object or a creature's combustible equipment burst into flame, even if damp.

If the target is a creature, the initial eruption of flame causes 1d8 points of fire damage per caster level (maximum 10d8) with no saving throw. Further, the creature must make a DC 15 Reflex save or catch fire (DMG 303).

If the target is a combustible, unattended object, the initial eruption of flame deals fire damage to the object as noted above. The object catches fire and takes 1d6 points of fire damage each round until consumed or someone puts out the fire.

Material Component: A drop of oil and a piece of flint.

COMETFALL

Conjuration (Creation)
Level: Cleric 6, druid 6
Components: V, S, DF
Casting Time: 1 standard action
Range: Medium (100 ft. + 10 ft./level)
Effect: 400-pound ball of rock and ice
Area: 5-ft.-radius burst
Duration: Instantaneous
Saving Throw: Reflex half
Spell Resistance: No

You conjure a bright, glowing comet, which appears in midair above your enemies, then strikes the ground with tremendous force and a thunderous boom.

You conjure a comet that immediately falls to the ground, dealing 1d6 points of damage per caster level (maximum 15d6) to everything in the area. The force of the comet can also knock creatures over. Creatures who fail their Reflex save are knocked prone. A creature that succeeds on its saving throw takes half damage from the comet and is not knocked down.

The comet breaks apart on impact, filling the 10-foot-square area with dense rubble (DMG 90).

You must cast this spell in an area with at least 40 feet of vertical space above the point of impact. If you do not have 40 feet of space, the spell fails.

CONE OF DIMNESS

Illusion (Phantasm) [Mind-Affecting]
Level: Sorcerer/wizard 3
Components: V, S
Casting Time: 1 standard action
Range: 60 ft.
Area: Cone-shaped burst
Duration: 1 round/level
Saving Throw: Will negates; see text
Spell Resistance: Yes

Splaying your fingers, you call upon the energies that dwell within the shadowy places of the world. Your arm shakes with barely contained power, causing a translucent gray cone to burst forth from your outstretched hand.

Creatures in the cone must succeed on a Will save or believe darkness has engulfed them, rendering them blinded. A creature that makes its initial Will save suffers no ill effects.

A creature that fails its initial save can attempt a new saving throw each round until it succeeds or the spell expires. Failing the subsequent saving throws results in continued blindness. Success on a later save means the creature feels its vision beginning to clear, although its vision remains dim and hazy for the remainder of the spell. This results in a 20% miss chance for any attack the creature makes.

CONSUMPTIVE FIELD

Necromancy [Death, Evil]
Level: Cleric 4
Components: V, S
Casting Time: 1 standard action
Range: 30 ft.
Area: 30-ft.-radius emanation centered on you
Duration: 1 round/level
Saving Throw: Will negates
Spell Resistance: Yes

Sweeping your arm about and clutching it to your chest, you draw the last breaths of fallen foes from their choking mouths and inhale them to fuel your own power.

All creatures in the area with fewer than 0 hit points that fail their saving throws die, and you gain 1d8 temporary hit points and a +2 bonus to Strength for each death caused by this spell and until the spell's duration expires.

Additionally, your effective caster level increases by one per death caused by this spell, to a maximum increase of half your original caster level, improving spell effects that are dependent on caster level. (This increase in effective caster level does not grant you access to more spells, and it does not increase the duration of this spell.)

Creatures that fall to –1 hit points or lower in the area after the spell is cast are likewise subject to its effect.

No creature can be affected by this spell more than once per casting, regardless of the number of times that the area of the spell passes over them.

CONSUMPTIVE FIELD, GREATER

Necromancy [Death, Evil]
Level: Cleric 7

This spell functions like *consumptive field*, except that the field affects all creatures in the area with 9 hit points or fewer. Such creatures that fail their saving throws die, and creatures that fall to 9 hit points or lower in the area after the spell is cast are likewise subject to its effect.

CONTAGION, MASS

Necromancy [Evil]
Level: Cleric 5, druid 5, sorcerer/wizard 6
Range: Medium (100 ft. + 10 ft./level)
Area: 20-ft.-radius spread

Forcing a hacking cough, you complete the spell. In the area you've designated, you see swirling red and black mist rise up, accompanied by the distant sound of your echoing cough.

This spell functions like *contagion* (PH 213), but all creatures within the area are infected.

Illus. by R. Horsley

Greater consumptive field snuffs out the lives of the weak and grants tremendous power to evil clerics

CONTAGIOUS FOG

Conjuration (Creation)
Level: Sorcerer/wizard 3
Components: V, S, M
Casting Time: 1 standard action
Range: Medium (100 ft. + 10 ft./level)
Duration: 1 round/level
Saving Throw: See text

Spitting the last phrase of the spell, you throw out your arm, and a brown mist whirls into being around your foes.

This spell functions like *fog cloud* (PH 232), except as noted here. Each round that a creature is within the fog, it must make a Fortitude save or contract a disease equivalent to the shakes (DMG 292), which strikes immediately (no incubation period). A creature afflicted with this disease takes 1d8 points of Dexterity damage immediately, and each day that the disease persists, it must make a DC 13 Fortitude save or take another 1d8 points of Dexterity damage.

The fog moves away from you at 10 feet per round, rolling along the surface of the ground or water. (Figure out the cloud's new spread each round based on its new center, which is 10 feet farther away from the point of origin where you cast the spell.) Because the vapors are heavier than air, they sink to the lowest level of the surface over which they move, pouring down sinkhole openings, and even down through minute cracks. *Contagious fog* cannot penetrate liquids, nor can it be cast underwater.

Material Component: A used handkerchief.

CONTAGIOUS TOUCH

Necromancy
Level: Druid 4
Components: V, S
Casting Time: 1 standard action
Range: Touch
Target: Creature touched
Duration: 1 round/level
Saving Throw: Fortitude negates
Spell Resistance: Yes

Holding out your hand like it's dead, you croak out magic words and imbue your limb with a terrible disease.

Upon casting this spell, you choose one disease from this list: blinding sickness, cackle fever, filth fever, mindfire, red ache, the shakes, or slimy doom (DMG 292). Any living creature you hit with a melee touch attack during the spell's duration is affected as though by the *contagion* spell, immediately contracting the disease you have selected unless it makes a successful Fortitude save. You cannot infect more than one creature per round.

CONTINGENT ENERGY RESISTANCE

Abjuration
Level: Cleric 4, druid 4, sorcerer/wizard 5
Components: V, S, M
Casting Time: 1 minute
Duration: 1 hour/level (D)

As you finish chanting the words, a pearlescent film covers your body before fading into your skin, a pale rainbow of colors offering their protection against potential damage to come.

This spell functions similarly to *contingency* (PH 213), but with a more limited scope. While *contingent energy resistance* is in effect, if you are dealt damage associated with one of the five types of energy (acid, cold, electricity, fire, or sonic), the spell automatically grants you resistance 10 against that type of energy for up to 10 minutes per caster level, or until the remainder of the spell's duration, just as if you were under the effect of a *resist energy* spell of the appropriate type.

Once the energy type protected against by a particular casting of this spell is determined, it can't be changed. You can't have more than one *contingent energy resistance* in effect on yourself at the same time—if you cast the spell a second time while an earlier casting is still in effect, the earlier spell automatically expires.

The energy resistance granted by this spell does not stack with similar benefits against the same energy type (such as from the *resist energy* spell). However, it is possible to be simultaneously under the effect of *resist energy (fire)* and *contingent energy resistance (electricity)*, or any other two such spells that protect against different types of energy.

Material Component: An oyster shell.

CONVICTION

Abjuration
Level: Cleric 1
Components: V, S, M
Casting Time: 1 standard action
Range: Touch
Target: Creature touched
Duration: 10 minutes/level
Saving Throw: Will negates (harmless)
Spell Resistance: Yes (harmless)

You hold the holy passage in your hand and touch your ally, intoning the spell. A sea-blue nimbus of light blossoms about his head and shoulders, strengthening his resolve.

This spell bolsters the mental, physical, and spiritual strength of the creature touched. The spell grants the subject a +2 morale bonus on saving throws, with an additional +1 to the bonus for every six caster levels you have (maximum +5 morale bonus at 18th level).

Material Component: A small parchment with a bit of holy text written upon it.

CONVICTION, MASS

Abjuration
Level: Cleric 3
Range: Medium (100 ft. + 10 ft./level)
Targets: Allies in a 20-ft.-radius burst

You hold the holy passage aloft and invoke the power of its words. Around you, your friends are bathed in a sea-blue nimbus of light.

This spell functions like *conviction*, except that it affects multiple allies at a distance.

CORONA OF COLD

Evocation [Cold]
Level: Cleric 3, druid 3
Components: V, S, DF
Casting Time: 1 standard action
Range: 10 ft.
Area: 10-ft.-radius emanation centered on you
Duration: 1 round/level (D)
Saving Throw: Fortitude negates
Spell Resistance: Yes

As you complete the spell you feel your extremities turn ice cold, numb, and sluggish. The feeling subsides as the cold drains away from your body into the air around you, causing your breath to emerge as white puffs in the now-chill air.

You are surrounded by a protective aura of cold that also causes damage to others within its radius. You gain resistance to fire 10.

Starting in the round you cast the spell, *corona of cold* also deals 1d12 points of cold damage each round at the beginning of your turn to all other creatures within the area. A successful save prevents the damage caused by the spell in that round, but does not prevent damage in future rounds. Creatures damaged by the spell shiver uncontrollably, taking a –2 penalty to their Strength and Dexterity and moving at half speed for as long as they remain within the area; these penalties do not stack with consecutive rounds of damage or additional *corona of cold* spells.

CORPOREAL INSTABILITY

Transmutation
Level: Sorcerer/wizard 4
Components: V, S
Casting Time: 1 standard action
Range: Touch
Target: Living creature touched
Duration: 1 round/level (D)
Saving Throw: Fortitude negates
Spell Resistance: Yes

You brush your fingers against the enemy, and immediately his bones begin to soften until he flows down into a flesh-colored puddle.

Your touch transforms a living creature into a spongy, amorphous mass, its shape melting and writhing uncontrollably. An affected creature is unable to hold or use any item. Soft or misshapen feet and legs reduce speed to 10 feet, or one-quarter normal, whichever is less (minimum 5 feet). The victim becomes blinded and cannot cast spells or use magic items, and searing pain renders it incapable of attacking. While in this form, the creature has immunity to extra damage from critical hits and sneak attacks due to its amorphous nature. A conscious victim can regain its own shape by taking a standard action to attempt a new save in any later round. Success ends the spell effect.

Each round the victim spends in an amorphous state, it takes 1 point of Wisdom drain from mental shock. If the victim's Wisdom is reduced to 0, it falls unconscious.

CORPSE CANDLE

Conjuration (Creation)
Level: Sorcerer/wizard 3
Components: S, M
Casting Time: 1 standard action
Range: Close (25 ft. + 5 ft./2 levels)
Effect: Ghostly hand and candle
Duration: 1 minute/level (D); see text
Saving Throw: None
Spell Resistance: No

You hold out a piece of flesh before you, and as you concentrate on your desired spell effect, the flesh dissolves into nothingness. Nearby, in the place of your choosing, a severed hand appears bearing a lit candle.

The ghostly hand carries a lit candle that sheds light in a 5-foot radius. You can move the hand at the beginning of your turn as you desire—forward or back, up or down, straight or around corners—up to 50 feet per round. Directing the candle is a free action. The hand and candle are incorporeal and can pass through objects. A corpse candle illuminates hidden, ethereal, and invisible beings and items, all of which become faintly visible as wispy outlines. Ethereal creatures remain unreachable from the Material Plane (except with force effects), but illuminated incorporeal and invisible creatures do not benefit from concealment, and so attacks against them suffer no miss chance.

The hand cannot be attacked or damaged, though *dispel magic* and similar spells can dispel it. The hand winks out if the distance between you and it exceeds the spell's range.

Material Component: A piece of a corpse untreated by any kind of preservative.

CORROSIVE GRASP

Conjuration (Creation) [Acid]
Level: Sorcerer/wizard 1
Components: V, S
Casting Time: 1 standard action
Range: Touch
Targets: Creatures touched
Duration: Instantaneous
Saving Throw: None
Spell Resistance: Yes

Your hand glistens and smokes from a viscous coating of acid. It does not harm you, but your opponents are less fortunate.

A touch attack with this hand causes 1d8 points of acid damage. You can use this melee touch attack up to one time per level. You can also deal this damage as extra damage with an unarmed strike or an attack with a natural weapon. If you grapple an opponent, you can deal this damage in addition to other damage you deal with a successful grapple check.

COUNTERMOON

Abjuration
Level: Druid 2
Components: V, S, M
Casting Time: 1 standard action
Range: Close (25 ft. + 5 ft./2 levels)
Target: One lycanthrope
Duration: 12 hours
Saving Throw: Will negates (D)
Spell Resistance: Yes

Translucent red chains fly from your outstretched hand to wrap around the target before fading away.

This spell forces a lycanthrope back to its natural form and keeps it from changing form, preventing both voluntary shapechanging through the alternate form ability and involuntary shapechanging because of lycanthropy.

Material Component: A hair, scale, or other cast-off item from the type of creature.

CRABWALK

Transmutation
Level: Bard 1, druid 1, ranger 1
Components: V, S, M
Casting Time: 1 standard action
Range: Touch
Target: Creature touched
Duration: 1 minute/level
Saving Throw: None
Spell Resistance: No

Corpse candle sometimes reveals things you wish you hadn't seen

The creature you touch now moves much faster, scuttling about with disconcerting ease.

When the subject of this spell charges, it gains a +4 bonus on its attack roll and takes no penalty to Armor Class. This benefit replaces the normal +2 bonus on attack rolls and –2 penalty to AC that a charge attack normally confers. If the creature is capable of multiple attacks after a charge, such as a lion with the pounce ability, the bonus applies only to the first attack.

Material Component: A crab's leg.

CRAWLING DARKNESS

Conjuration (Creation)
Level: Cleric 5
Components: V, S, DF
Casting Time: 1 round
Range: Personal
Target: You
Duration: 1 minute/level (D)

A shroud of dark, writhing tentacles forms around your body as you speak the spell's final syllables.

This spell creates a number of tentacles that surround you but do not interfere with your movement or spellcasting. They provide concealment and completely hide your features. You gain a +4 competence bonus on grapple checks, Climb checks, and Escape Artist checks.

When you are attacked, the tentacles strike back at your attacker. They have an attack bonus equal to your base attack bonus + your Wis modifier, and a successful attack deals 1d12 points of damage.

CREAKING CACOPHONY

Illusion (Figment) [Sonic]
Level: Bard 3, druid 3
Components: V, S
Casting Time: 1 standard action
Range: Medium (100 ft. + 10 ft./level)
Area: 40-ft.-radius spread
Duration: 1 round/level
Saving Throw: None
Spell Resistance: Yes

Noise swells into a cacophonous din, as if hundreds of intertwined trees and branches were rubbing together in a chaotic medley of groans and creaks.

The sound from this spell is as loud as a pitched battle and is audible far beyond the spell's area. Outside the spell's area, the sound is merely loud. Inside the spell's area, the sound is overwhelming. All creatures within the spell's area take a –4 penalty on Listen checks. Spellcasters are distracted and must make a Concentration check to cast any spell (DC equals this spell's DC + the level of the spell being cast).

A *creaking cacophony* spell enhances and focuses sonic energy. Creatures in the area that do not have immunity to sonic damage gain vulnerability to sonic damage.

CREATE MAGIC TATTOO

Conjuration (Creation)
Level: Sorcerer/wizard 2
Components: V, S, M, F
Casting Time: 10 minutes
Range: Touch
Target: Creature touched
Duration: 24 hours
Saving Throw: None
Spell Resistance: Yes (harmless)

You finish the last detail and lean back to look at your work. The tattoo looks good. It should prove useful.

This spell creates a single magic tattoo. You determine the exact type of tattoo, though the selection is limited by your caster level, as indicated below. You must possess a modicum of artistic talent to sketch the desired tattoo—at least 1 rank of Craft (drawing), Craft (painting), Craft (calligraphy), or a similar Craft skill. Inscribing a magic tattoo requires a successful Craft check. The DC varies with the kind of tattoo, as noted below.

If you are a 3rd- to 6th-level caster, you can inscribe a tattoo that generates any one of the following effects (Craft DC 10).

- +2 resistance bonus on one type of saving throw (Fortitude, Reflex, or Will).
- +1 luck bonus on attack rolls.
- +1 deflection bonus to AC.

At 7th to 12th caster level, you can add the following tattoos to the list that you can inscribe (Craft DC 15).

- +2 resistance bonus on saving throws.
- +2 competence bonus on attack rolls.

When your caster level reaches 13th, you can add the following to the list of tattoos you can inscribe (Craft DC 20).

- Spell resistance equal to 10 + 1 per three caster levels.
- +2 enhancement bonus to any one ability score.
- +1 spellcaster level. This effect increases the subject's effective level, but not the total number of spells. For example, an 11th-level caster who receives this tattoo functions as a 12th-level caster for the purpose of determining level-based spell variables (such as range, area, effect, and so on), but he does not receive any extra spells.

A single creature can have only three magic tattoos at a time. Any attempt to apply more than that automatically fails.

A successful *erase* spell removes a single magic tattoo. A successful *dispel magic* spell can remove multiple magic tattoos if targeted on the creature bearing them.

Material Components: Tattoo inks in appropriate colors costing at least 100 gp.

Focus: Tattoo needles.

CREEPING COLD

Transmutation [Cold]
Level: Druid 2
Components: V, S, F
Casting Time: 1 standard action
Range: Close (25 ft. + 5 ft./2 levels)
Target: One creature
Duration: 3 rounds
Saving Throw: Fortitude half
Spell Resistance: Yes

Reaching out your hand and making a crushing motion, you turn the subject's sweat to ice, creating blisters as the ice forms on and inside the skin.

Illus. by C. Dien

The subject takes 1d6 cumulative points of cold damage per round (that is, 1d6 on the 1st round, 2d6 on the second, and 3d6 on the third). Only one save is allowed against the spell; if successful, it halves the damage each round.

Focus: A small glass or pottery vessel worth at least 25 gp filled with ice, snow, or water.

CREEPING COLD, GREATER

Transmutation [Cold]
Level: Druid 4
Duration: See text

This spell is the same as *creeping cold*, but the duration increases by 1 round, during which the subject takes 4d6 points of cold damage. If you are at least 15th level, the spell lasts for 5 rounds and deals 5d6 points of cold damage. If you are at least 20th level, the spell lasts for 6 rounds and deals 6d6 points of cold damage.

CRITICAL STRIKE

Divination
Level: Assassin 1, bard 1, sorcerer/wizard 1
Components: V
Casting Time: 1 swift action
Range: Personal
Target: You
Duration: 1 round

Upon uttering the ancient phrase that completes the spell, you feel the weapon in your hand drawn toward a creature standing nearby.

Whenever you make a melee attack against a flanked foe or against a foe denied its Dexterity bonus, you deal an extra 1d6 points of damage, your weapon's threat range is doubled (as if under the effect of *keen edge*), and you gain a +4 insight bonus on rolls made to confirm critical threats. The increased threat range granted by this spell doesn't stack with any other effect that increases your weapon's threat range. Creatures immune to extra damage from sneak attacks are immune to the extra damage dealt by your attacks.

CROWN OF GLORY

Enchantment (Compulsion) [Mind-Affecting]
Level: Glory 8
Components: V, S, DF
Casting Time: 1 round
Range: 20 ft.
Targets: You and one creature/level in a 20-ft.-radius burst centered on you
Duration: 1 minute/level
Saving Throw: Will negates (harmless)
Spell Resistance: Yes (harmless)

When you cast this spell, you crown yourself with your deity's favor and draw all eyes toward you.

You are imbued with an aura of celestial authority, inspiring awe in all lesser creatures that behold your terrible perfection and righteousness. You gain a +4 enhancement bonus to Charisma for the duration of the spell.

In addition, the subject creatures gain a +4 morale bonus on attack rolls, saves, and skill checks, immunity to fear effects, and temporary hit points equal to your caster level (maximum 20).

CRUMBLE

Transmutation
Level: Druid 3
Components: V, S
Casting Time: 1 standard action
Range: Medium (100 ft. + 10 ft./level)
Target: One structure or construct
Duration: Instantaneous
Saving Throw: Fortitude half (object)
Spell Resistance: Yes (object)

With a final word and gesture, time takes control of the object, eroding it away before your eyes, aging it several centuries in a few seconds.

You bring the forces of erosion to bear on a fabricated structure such as a stone bridge, a wooden building, an iron wall, a construct, or any other object not formed by nature itself.

The erosion deals 1d8 points of damage per caster level to the object (hardness does not apply) to a maximum of 10d8. The maximum size of the object affected depends on your level. If you cast this spell on an object of greater size than you can affect, the spell fails.

Level	Size of Object Affected
Up to 9th	Large
10th–15th	Huge
16th–18th	Gargantuan
19th–20th	Colossal

CURSE OF ILL FORTUNE

Transmutation
Level: Blackguard 2, cleric 2
Components: V, S, DF
Casting Time: 1 standard action
Range: Medium (100 ft. + 10 ft./level)
Target: One living creature
Duration: 1 minute/level
Saving Throw: Will negates
Spell Resistance: Yes

Letting loose a stream of foul incantations, you curse the subject.

You place a temporary curse upon the subject, giving it a –3 penalty on attack rolls, saving throws, ability checks, and skill checks. *Curse of ill fortune* is negated by any spell that removes a *bestow curse* spell.

CURSE OF ILL FORTUNE, MASS

Necromancy
Level: Cleric 5
Targets: Enemies in a 20-ft.-radius burst

This spell functions like *curse of ill fortune*, except that it affects multiple enemies.

CURSE OF IMPENDING BLADES

Necromancy
Level: Bard 2, ranger 2, sorcerer/wizard 2
Components: V, S, M/DF
Casting Time: 1 standard action
Range: Medium (100 ft. + 10 ft./level)
Target: One creature
Duration: 1 minute/level
Saving Throw: None
Spell Resistance: Yes

You grip the nail-pierced hunk of leather and cast the spell. A small black dagger jets from the tip of the nail and strikes your opponent squarely in the chest.

The target of the spell has a hard time avoiding attacks, sometimes even seeming to stumble into harm's way. The subject takes a –2 penalty to AC.

The curse cannot be dispelled, but it can be removed with a *break enchantment, limited wish, miracle, remove curse,* or *wish* spell.

Arcane Material Component: A nail through a piece of leather.

CURSE OF IMPENDING BLADES, MASS

Necromancy
Level: Bard 3, ranger 3, sorcerer/wizard 3
Targets: Enemies in a 20-ft.-radius burst

This spell functions like *curse of impending blades,* except that it affects multiple enemies.

CURSE OF LYCANTHROPY

Necromancy
Level: Pestilence 6
Components: V, S, M, DF
Casting Time: 1 standard action
Range: Touch
Target: Humanoid touched
Duration: Instantaneous
Saving Throw: Fortitude negates
Spell Resistance: Yes

Dipping your hand in blood and then gripping the target fiercely, you call on the curse of lycanthropy to destroy your foe.

If the target fails its saving throw, it dies, and 1d6 wererats (in wererat form; MM 173) claw their way out of its body. The wererats do not attack you or your allies, but might attack nearby living creatures. If no target is available, the wererats scurry away to spread their lycanthropy.

Material Component: A pint of animal blood.

CURSED BLADE

Necromancy
Level: Assassin 4
Components: V
Casting Time: 1 swift action
Range: Touch
Target: One melee weapon
Duration: 1 minute/level
Saving Throw: None
Spell Resistance: No

Drawing upon dark powers, you whisper a vehement curse and draw your finger down the weapon.

A weapon affected by this spell deals wounds that can't be healed in the usual fashion. Any damage dealt by the weapon (not including damage from special weapon properties such as flaming, holy, wounding, and so on) cannot be cured by any means until the damaged individual has received a *remove curse* spell (or some other effect that neutralizes a curse).

If a creature is slain by a weapon that is under the effect of this spell, it can't be raised from the dead unless a *remove curse* spell (or similar effect) is cast on the body or a *true resurrection* spell is used.

CUTTING HAND

Transmutation
Level: Sorcerer/wizard 1
Components: V, S
Casting Time: 1 standard action
Range: Personal
Target: Your hand
Duration: 1 round/level (D)

Your hand tingles as a smooth, metallic edge extrudes from the outside of your palm and curls up along your fingertips, forming a flexible, razor-sharp blade.

You alter the structure of your hand so that it becomes as hard and sharp as a blade. Your hand deals 1d6 points of damage (1d4 if you are Small, and 1d8 if you are Large) and gains a +2 enhancement bonus on attack rolls and damage rolls. You are considered armed with this hand. Your hand's enhancement bonus does not apply to melee touch attacks.

CYCLONIC BLAST

Evocation [Air]
Level: Sorcerer/wizard 5
Components: V, S, F
Casting Time: 1 standard action
Range: 120 ft.
Area: 120-ft. line
Duration: Instantaneous
Saving Throw: Reflex half
Spell Resistance: Yes

Cupping a child's top, you forcefully thrust your hand forward, simultaneously speaking the final words of the spell's proscribed formula. Immediately thereafter, a blast of whirling wind issues forth from your outstretched fingers, sweeping up within it all who stand in its way.

You send a twisting torrent of wind, not unlike a tornado turned on its side, toward your enemies. A *cyclonic blast* deals 1d6 points of damage per caster level (maximum 15d6 points of damage) to all creatures and objects in the area. Objects bigger than Large take half damage. The *cyclonic blast* begins at your fingertips.

Creatures who fail their Reflex saving throws against a *cyclonic blast* are additionally in danger of being knocked back by the force of the wind. Treat this as a bull rush attack made with a +12 bonus on the Strength check. The *cyclonic blast* always moves with the opponent to push that target back the full distance allowed, and (unlike a normal bull rush) you can exceed your normal movement limit with a sufficiently high check result. Airborne creatures are treated as if they were one size category smaller for the purpose of resisting the bull rush.

If the damage caused to an interposing barrier by the blast shatters or breaks through it, the *cyclonic blast* can continue beyond the barrier if the spell's range permits; otherwise, it stops at the barrier just as any other spell effect does.

Focus: A child's spinning top.

DAGGERSPELL STANCE

Abjuration
Level: Druid 2, sorcerer/wizard 2
Components: V, F
Casting Time: 1 swift action
Range: Personal
Target: You
Duration: 1 round/level (D)

The daggers in your hands glow silver as you complete the spell. They feel as if they have become a part of your body.

While this spell is in effect, if you make a full attack while holding a dagger in each hand, you gain a +2 insight bonus on attack rolls and damage rolls made with daggers in that round.

The magical energy that permeates your daggers while this spell is active allows you to deflect the magical energy of spells. When wielding two daggers and fighting defensively, you gain spell resistance equal to 5 + your caster level.

The spell focuses your concentration so that when you devote all of your attention to defense, you can turn the force of most blows away from your body with your daggers. When wielding two daggers and using the total defense action, you gain both the spell resistance benefit described above and damage reduction 5/magic.

Focus: A pair of daggers.

Illus. by R. Horsley

Daggerspell stance turns its caster into a deadly dervish

DANCE OF THE UNICORN

Abjuration
Level: Druid 5, Purification 5
Components: V, S
Casting Time: 1 standard action
Range: 5 ft./level
Area: 5 ft./level-radius emanation centered on you
Duration: 1 minute/level (D)
Saving Throw: None
Spell Resistance: No

Whirling your pointed finger through a complex gesture, you create a cool and fresh mist that cleanses the air of pollutants.

You surround yourself with a purifying, swirling mist that washes the air clean of smoke, dust, and poisons. Nonmagical contaminants, including inhaled poisons, are automatically negated within the cloud. *Dance of the unicorn* also grants everyone within the mist a +4 bonus on saving throws against magical or supernatural gas effects, such as *acid fog, cloudkill,* and green dragon breath.

The cloud of mist leaves everything within its area damp.

DARK WAY

Illusion (Shadow)
Level: Bard 2, cleric 2, sorcerer/wizard 2
Components: V, S, DF
Casting Time: 1 standard action
Range: Close (25 ft. + 5 ft./2 levels)
Effect: One bridge of force 5 ft. wide, 1 in. thick, and up to 20 ft./level long
Duration: 1 round/level
Saving Throw: None
Spell Resistance: Yes

You stand at the edge of the canyon and invoke the power. At your feet appears a thin black bridge that arches over the canyon.

You create a ribbonlike, weightless, unbreakable bridge. A *dark way* must be anchored at both ends to solid objects, but otherwise can be at any angle. Like a *wall of force* (PH 298), it must be continuous and unbroken when formed. It is typically used to cross a chasm or a hazardous space. Creatures can move on a *dark way* without penalty, since it is no more slippery than a typical dungeon floor.

A *dark way* can support a maximum of 200 pounds per caster level. Creatures that cause the total weight on a *dark way* to exceed this limit fall through it as if it weren't there. You never fall through a *dark way* unless your own weight exceeds the spell's maximum capacity.

DARKBOLT

Evocation [Darkness]
Level: Darkness 5
Components: V, S
Casting Time: 1 standard action
Range: Medium (100 ft. + 10 ft./level)
Effect: One ray/2 levels (maximum seven rays)
Duration: Instantaneous; see text
Saving Throw: Will partial
Spell Resistance: Yes

With a quick invocation to your deity, you call forth a nimbus of jet-black night. This terrible radiance, laced with the will of your deity, allows you to shoot black bolts of power.

You unleash beams of darkness from your open palm. You must succeed on a ranged touch attack to strike your target. You can hurl one bolt for every two caster levels you have (maximum seven bolts). You can hurl all the bolts at once, or you can hurl one bolt per round as a free action, starting in the round when you cast the spell. You do not have to hurl a bolt in every round, but if you don't hurl the bolt you were entitled to in a round, it is lost. If you hurl all the bolts at once, all your targets must be within 60 feet of each other.

A *darkbolt* deals 2d8 points of damage to a living creature, and the creature is dazed for 1 round unless it makes a Will save (a creature struck by multiple bolts during the same round is dazed for a maximum of 1 round, no matter how many times it fails its save). An undead creature takes no damage, but is dazed if it fails its save.

DARKFIRE

Evocation [Fire]
Level: Cleric 3
Components: V, S
Casting Time: 1 standard action
Range: 0 ft.
Effect: Flame in your palm
Duration: 1 round/level (D)
Saving Throw: None
Spell Resistance: Yes

Your hand feels warm cupping the eldritch flames. You cannot see the fire in the shadows, but you know it is there, as will those who will soon feel the hungry flames.

Dark flames appear in your hand. You can hurl them or use them to touch enemies. The flames appear in your open hand and harm neither you nor your equipment. They emit no light but produce the same amount of heat as an actual fire.

Beginning the following round, you can strike opponents with a melee touch attack, dealing 1d6 points of fire damage per two caster levels (maximum 5d6). Alternatively, you can hurl the flames up to 120 feet as a thrown weapon. When doing so, you make a ranged touch attack (with no range penalty) and deal the same damage as with the melee attack. No sooner do you hurl the flames than a new set appears in your hand.

The *darkfire* is invisible to normal vision but can be seen with darkvision as easily as a normal flame can be seen in darkness (this means that *darkfire* can be used as a signal or beacon for creatures with darkvision).

The spell does not function underwater.

DARKVISION, MASS

Transmutation
Level: Sorcerer/wizard 4
Range: 10 ft.
Targets: Allies in a 10-ft.-radius burst centered on you

As you conclude the spell's casting, you are aware of being able to see without light. A glance at your allies show that they too perceive more than before.

This spell functions like *darkvision* (PH 216), except that all target creatures receive the spell's benefits. Unlike with *darkvision*, recipients of this spell cannot have the ability made permanent with a *permanency* spell.

Material Component: A dried carrot or three small agates.

DAWN

Abjuration
Level: Druid 0, ranger 1
Components: V
Casting Time: 1 swift action
Range: 15 ft.
Target: All creatures in a 15-ft.-radius burst centered on you
Duration: Instantaneous
Saving Throw: Fortitude negates (harmless)
Spell Resistance: Yes (harmless)

With a cry similar to a rooster's you cast the spell. For a moment you feel as if you had just awakened from a comfortable nap, but as the feeling fades, those around you begin to stir.

All sleeping creatures in the affected area awaken. Those who are unconscious because of nonlethal damage wake up and are staggered. This spell does not affect dying creatures.

DEAD END

Illusion (Shadow)
Level: Assassin 1, bard 1, sorcerer/wizard 1
Components: V, S, M
Casting Time: 1 standard action
Range: Touch
Targets: One creature/level touched
Duration: 10 minutes/level (D)
Saving Throw: Will negates (harmless) or Will disbelief (if interacted with); see text
Spell Resistance: Yes

Sprinkling spice on the ground, you complete the final step of the spell. Upon touching your intended targets, you note with satisfaction that the area around all of you seems a little cleaner and less trod upon.

This spell flawlessly disguises the spoor left by the subjects, concealing their tracks, scent, and other signs of their passage with an illusion that defeats even the senses of taste and touch. Any creature making a Search check, using the scent ability, or using the Survival skill to track a creature affected by this spell interacts with the illusion and can make a Will save to disbelieve. Creatures that succeed on the save can detect the subjects normally. Creatures merely passing through an area the subjects passed through do not count as interacting with the illusion.

Targets of this spell can make a Will save to negate it, and spell resistance applies.

Material Component: A pinch of some odoriferous spice.

DEADFALL

Conjuration (Creation)
Level: Druid 8
Components: V, S
Casting Time: 1 standard action
Range: Long (400 ft. + 40 ft./level)
Effect: Mass of dead wood forming in a cylinder (20-ft. radius, 40 ft. high); see text
Duration: Instantaneous; see text
Saving Throw: Reflex partial; see text
Spell Resistance: No

With the final word of the spell you call into being a huge tower of logs and branches. It collapses to the ground with a roar, crushing creatures beneath its weight.

Pick a point on the ground as the center of the radius and bottom of the cylinder. *Deadfall* creates a tangled mass of huge branches, logs, and fallen trees on the ground. The deadfall immediately collapses in on itself with terrific force and noise. Creatures and objects in the area take 1d6 points of damage per caster level (maximum 20d6). In addition, creatures in the area must succeed on a Reflex save or be knocked prone.

Once you cast the spell, a considerable volume of dead wood remains behind. This pile of brush is 5 feet high, with a 20-foot radius, and it counts as dense rubble (DMG 90).

DEAFENING CLANG

Transmutation [Sonic]
Level: Paladin 1
Components: V, S, DF
Casting Time: 1 swift action
Range: Touch
Target: Your weapon
Duration: 1 round
Saving Throw: Fortitude partial; see text
Spell Resistance: No

At your touch, the weapon rings like a struck tuning fork. The sound diminishes until it's imperceptible, but when you touch the weapon you can feel the vibration.

You empower the touched weapon with magic that causes it to emit a loud clang when it is struck against a hard surface, such as a floor, wall, or creature. The weapon deals 1d6 points of sonic damage with each successful hit, and any creature struck by the weapon must succeed on a Fortitude saving throw or be deafened for 1 minute.

DEATH ARMOR

Necromancy
Level: Sorcerer/wizard 2
Components: V, S, M, F
Casting Time: 1 standard action
Range: Personal
Target: You
Duration: 1 round/level

You smear yourself with white paste, drawing a skull on your bare flesh. Immediately, a wreath of black flames crackles to life around you.

The black flames created by this spell injure creatures that contact them. Any creature striking you with its body or handheld weapons takes 1d4 points of damage +1 point per two caster levels (maximum +10). If the creature has spell resistance, it applies to the damage. Weapons with reach, such as longspears, do not endanger their users in this way.

Material Component: Paste made from ground bones.

Focus: An onyx worth 50 gp.

DEATH DRAGON

Necromancy [Evil, Fear, Mind-Affecting]
Level: Cleric 7
Components: V, S, DF
Casting Time: 1 round
Range: Personal
Effect: Dragon-shaped armor of energy and bones
Duration: 1 round/level (D)

You summon unholy power to gird yourself in a dragon-shaped cocoon of bones and negative energy.

The cocoon created by this spell gives you a +4 enhancement bonus to natural armor and a +4 deflection bonus to Armor Class. You are treated as armed when you make unarmed attacks, and you deal damage as if your limbs were short swords of an appropriate size. You can use your off hand to attack, incurring the standard two-weapon fighting penalties (PH 160). The cocoon prevents you from casting spells with somatic, material, or focus (but not divine focus) components, but does not otherwise hinder your actions or movement.

As a standard action, you can project a cone of *fear* or make a melee touch attack to use *inflict critical wounds* on the creature touched (the caster level of these effects equals your own). These effects are otherwise identical to the spells of the same names, but have saving throw DCs equal to what this spell's save DC would be if the spell allowed a save.

DEATH PACT

Necromancy
Level: Cleric 8, Pact 8
Components: V, S, M, DF
Casting Time: 10 minutes
Range: Touch
Target: Willing living creature touched
Duration: Permanent until triggered
Saving Throw: None
Spell Resistance: No

With the last words of power, you make the convert's oath binding and ensure your deity's aid when the worst befalls his new servant.

This spell allows the target to enter into a binding agreement with your deity that brings the target back to life if it is slain.

When this spell is cast, the subject's Constitution is permanently lowered by 2 points. In exchange for this, if the subject should die, a *true resurrection* spell (PH 296) is immediately cast upon the subject. However, the resurrected creature does not regain the 2 Constitution points when returned to life.

If the spell is dispelled before the subject dies, it does not regain its 2 lost Constitution points. A *wish* or *miracle* spell can return the lost Constitution, but only after the *death pact* has been activated or dispelled.

Material Component: A diamond worth at least 1,000 gp.

DEATH THROES

Necromancy [Force]
Level: Cleric 5, sorcerer/wizard 5
Components: V, S

The deadfall spell crushes the life from its victims

Illus. by J. Jarvis

Casting Time: 1 standard action
Range: Personal
Target: You
Duration: 1 hour/level or until you are killed
Saving Throw: None
Spell Resistance: No

As the killing blow falls, you smile with grim satisfaction even as the light of life fades, knowing that your enemy will soon be joining you in the afterlife.

If you are killed, your body is instantaneously destroyed in an explosion that deals 1d8 points of damage per caster level to everyone in a 30-foot-radius burst.

This explosion destroys your body, preventing any form of raising or resurrection that requires part of the corpse. A *wish*, *miracle*, or *true resurrection* spell can restore life.

DEATH WARD, MASS

Necromancy
Level: Cleric 8, druid 9
Range: Close (25 ft. + 5 ft./2 levels)
Targets: One creature/level, no two of which are more than 30 ft. apart

Sensing the spark of life in your allies through your magic, you bolster that spark and protect it from harm.

This spell functions like *death ward* (PH 217), except as noted above.

DECOMPOSITION

Necromancy
Level: Druid 2
Components: V, S, DF
Casting Time: 1 standard action
Range: 50 ft.
Area: Living enemies within a 50-ft.-radius emanation centered on you
Duration: 1 round/level
Saving Throw: None
Spell Resistance: Yes

Using your link to the natural world, you create an air of decay that makes death come quicker to the wounded.

Whenever an enemy within the area takes normal (not nonlethal) damage, that wound festers for an additional 3 points of damage at the beginning of its turn each round thereafter for the duration of the spell. A DC 15 Heal check or the application of any *cure* spell or other healing magic stops the festering. Only one wound festers at a time; additional wounds taken while the first is still festering are not subject to this effect. Once festering has been stopped, however, any new wound taken while the subject is within the area (before the spell expires) begins the process anew.

The deep breath spell gives Mialee some confidence she'll survive being dragged beneath the water by the sahuagin

For example, a subject who takes 6 points of damage from an attack while within the area of a *decomposition* spell takes 3 points of damage from the festering wound in the next round, and another 3 points in the round after that. In the following round, that subject receives 4 points of healing from a *cure light wounds* spell, so the festering stops and the subject takes no festering damage that round. In the next round, the subject remains within the emanation and takes another 3 points of damage in battle. The festering begins again, dealing 3 points of festering damage in the following round.

DECOY IMAGE

Illusion (Figment)
Level: Ranger 3
Components: V, S
Casting Time: 1 round
Range: Long (400 ft. + 40 ft./level)
Effect: Figment that mimics you and all allies within 50 ft. of you
Duration: 8 hours (D)
Saving Throw: Will disbelief; see text
Spell Resistance: No

You finish the spell, and mystic duplicates of you and your allies appear ahead of you. As you move forward, they set out as well.

In order to flush ambushes, you project a duplicate image of yourself and your companions.

This spell creates an illusion complete with visual images, sounds (including speech), smells, textures, and temperature. It mimics exactly what you and any of your allies within 50 feet of you do. If the terrain differs significantly between that of the illusion and that of the characters, or if any character takes an action the illusion can't duplicate (for instance, climbing a tree if none are present for the illusory duplicate to mimic) onlookers automatically receive a saving throw. In addition, anyone who moves out of the spell's area disappears from the illusion.

DEEP BREATH

Conjuration (Creation) [Air]
Level: Druid 1, ranger 1, sorcerer/wizard 1
Components: V
Casting Time: 1 immediate action
Range: Personal
Target: You
Duration: 1 round/level

You let out a quick cry and instantly feel your chest swell with air, as if you had taken a deep breath. Strangely, you feel no need to exhale.

Your lungs instantly fill with air, and continue to refill with air for the duration of the spell. When the spell's duration expires, you can continue

Illus. by R. Spears

to hold your breath as if you had just gulped down a lungful of air.

You can cast this spell with an instant utterance, quickly enough to save yourself from drowning after being suddenly plunged into water.

DEEPER DARKVISION

Transmutation
Level: Ranger 4, sorcerer/wizard 3
Components: V, S, M
Casting Time: 1 standard action
Range: Touch
Target: Creature touched
Duration: 1 hour/level
Saving Throw: Will negates (harmless)
Spell Resistance: Yes (harmless)

You toss the powdered dried carrot into the air as you cast this spell, and it vanishes. You choose yourself as the spell's recipient and your eyes begin to glow with an alien purple luster.

The subject gains the ability to see 90 feet in total darkness and ignores the 20% miss chance normally present in shadowy illumination (such as might be created by a *darkness* spell). *Deeper darkvision* is black and white only but otherwise similar to normal sight.

Material Component: A pinch of dried carrot or an agate.

DEFENESTRATING SPHERE

Evocation [Air]
Level: Sorcerer/wizard 4
Components: V, S, F
Casting Time: 1 standard action
Range: Medium (100 ft. + 10 ft./level)
Effect: 2-ft.-radius sphere
Duration: 1 round/level (D)
Saving Throw: Fortitude partial; see text
Spell Resistance: Yes

From the pearl you hold between your thumb and ring finger erupts a cloudy gray sphere of whirling air and howling wind that flies to attack your enemies.

When you cast this spell, you create a violently swirling sphere of air. As a move action, you can make the sphere travel up to 30 feet per round and strike a creature or object you indicate as a ranged touch attack. Any creature struck by the sphere takes 3d6 points of damage from the force of its winds. In addition, Medium or smaller creatures must succeed on a Fortitude save or be knocked prone. Creatures that fall prone must then succeed on a second Fortitude save or be swept up by the sphere and driven 1d8×10 feet into the air, dropping 1d6 squares from their original position in a random direction and taking falling damage as normal. If a window is within range, the subject is automatically thrown in that direction.

If some obstacle prevents the subject creature from reaching its expelled height, it takes 1d6 points of damage for every 10 feet of movement it was unable to complete, so that a creature hurled 50 feet up in a room with a 20-foot ceiling would take 3d6 points of damage from the impact, then take 2d6 points of damage when it falls back to the ground.

The sphere can affect a maximum of one creature or object per round, and winks out if it exceeds the spell's range.

Focus: A gray pearl worth at least 100 gp.

Scrolls provide spellcasters with a cheap way to have access to spells they don't normally prepare

DEHYDRATE

Necromancy
Level: Druid 3
Components: V, S, DF
Casting Time: 1 standard action
Range: Medium (100 ft. + 10 ft./level)
Target: One living creature
Duration: Instantaneous
Saving Throw: Fortitude negates
Spell Resistance: Yes

With a squeezing gesture, you indicate your target and see sweat pour off it.

You afflict the target with a horrible, desiccating curse that deals 1d6 points of Constitution damage, plus 1 additional point of Constitution damage per three caster levels, to a maximum of 1d6+5 at 15th level. Oozes, plants, and creatures with the aquatic subtype are more susceptible to this spell than other targets. Such creatures take 1d8 points of Constitution damage, plus 1 additional point of Constitution damage per three caster levels, to a maximum of 1d8+5.

DEIFIC VENGEANCE

Conjuration (Summoning)
Level: Cleric 2, Purification 2
Components: V, S, DF
Casting Time: 1 standard action
Range: Close (25 ft. + 5 ft./2 levels)
Target: One creature
Duration: Instantaneous
Saving Throw: Will half
Spell Resistance: Yes

You call out to your deity, declaring your foe's crimes and asking your deity to punish him.

This spell deals 1d6 points of damage per two caster levels (maximum 5d6), or 1d6 points per caster level (maximum 10d6) if the target is undead.

Illus. by W. England

DELAY DEATH

Necromancy
Level: Cleric 4
Components: V, S, DF
Casting Time: 1 immediate action
Range: Close (25 ft. + 5 ft./2 levels)
Target: One creature
Duration: 1 round/level
Saving Throw: Will negates (harmless)
Spell Resistance: Yes (harmless)

You gesture toward your ally and call upon the power of your beliefs. A soft, golden glow appears on your companion's chest, around his heart.

The subject of this powerful spell is unable to die from hit point damage. While under the protection of this spell, the normal limit of –9 hit points before a character dies is extended without limit. A condition or spell that destroys enough of the subject's body so as to not allow *raise dead* to work, such as a *disintegrate* effect, still kills the creature, as does death brought about by ability score damage, level drain, or a death effect.

The spell does not prevent the subject from entering the dying state by dropping to –1 hit points. It merely prevents death as a result of hit point loss.

If the subject has fewer than –9 hit points when the spell's duration expires, it dies instantly.

DELAY DISEASE

Conjuration (Healing)
Level: Cleric 1, druid 1
Components: V, S, DF
Casting Time: 1 standard action
Range: Touch
Target: Creature touched
Duration: 24 hours
Saving Throw: Will negates (harmless)
Spell Resistance: Yes (harmless)

You press your focus to the creature and implore the contagion that ravages it to lie dormant. As the spell takes effect, a dim yellow glow passes over the creature's body.

The progress of any nonmagical disease that already afflicts the target is halted for the duration of the spell. *Delay disease* allows the subject to skip the required saving throw against the disease for the day that the spell is in effect. During this period, the subject accrues no further ability damage from the disease. A skipped saving throw counts as neither a success nor a failure for the purpose of recovery from the disease. Furthermore, the incubation period of any disease to which the subject is exposed during the spell's duration does not begin until the spell expires. *Delay disease* does not cure any damage that a disease might already have dealt, and it has no effect on magical or supernatural diseases.

DELUSIONS OF GRANDEUR

Illusion (Phantasm) [Mind-Affecting]
Level: Bard 2, sorcerer/wizard 2
Components: V
Casting Time: 1 standard action
Range: Medium (100 ft. + 10 ft./level)
Target: One creature
Duration: 10 minutes/level
Saving Throw: Will negates
Spell Resistance: Yes

By shouting flattering comments at your intended subject, you release the energy of the spell. The target of your spell glows momentarily with a white nimbus of crackling energy that fades to a sickly gray before disappearing completely.

This powerful phantasm fools the subject into believing itself more competent and safe than it really is. The spell makes any action the subject considers attempting seem easily accomplished, requiring only a token effort. Deadly wounds seem like mere scratches, stalwart foes appear weak and intimidated, and the subject's own attacks seem stronger and more effective. As a result of its skewed perceptions, the subject takes a –2 penalty on attack rolls, saves, ability checks, and skill checks, as well as to Wisdom. This penalty cannot reduce the subject's Wisdom below 1. Finally, the subject becomes so completely enamored with its own (false) abilities that it cannot fight defensively or take the total defense action.

DEMON DIRGE

Transmutation
Level: Cleric 3, sorcerer/wizard 3
Components: V, S, DF
Casting Time: 1 standard action
Range: Close (25 ft. + 5 ft./2 levels)
Target: Living creature
Duration: 1d6 rounds; see text
Saving Throw: None or Fortitude partial; see text
Spell Resistance: Yes

You cry out the ancient words and make the prescribed motions, and your foe lets out a howl of pain as his blood boils in his veins.

Demon dirge deals 2d6 points of damage each round for the duration of the spell to any creature that has both the chaotic and evil subtypes (such as a howler or a demon). No saving throw is allowed against this damage.

If the target creature also possesses the tanar'ri subtype (MM 316), the spell has a much more powerful effect. In addition to the damage, a tanar'ri is stunned for the duration of the spell unless it succeeds on a Fortitude save.

DEMONHIDE

Abjuration [Evil]
Level: Blackguard 2
Components: V, S, DF
Casting Time: 1 standard action
Range: Touch
Target: Evil creature touched
Duration: 1 round/level
Saving Throw: Will negates (harmless)
Spell Resistance: Yes (harmless)

You touch your minion with your holy symbol and invoke the horrid words of the lower planes. A fiery glow spreads across your servant's skin, leaving it with a deep red luster.

The subject gains damage reduction 5/cold iron or good.

DESICCATING BUBBLE

Necromancy
Level: Sorcerer/wizard 2
Components: S, M/DF
Casting Time: 1 standard action
Range: Medium (100 ft. + 10 ft./level)
Effect: 3-ft.-radius sphere of air
Duration: 1 round/level
Saving Throw: Reflex negates
Spell Resistance: Yes

From your outstretched hand bursts a small sphere similar in appearance to a soap bubble. It quickly expands and speeds in the direction you indicate.

A globe of supernaturally dry air rolls in whichever direction you point and engulfs those it strikes. It moves 30 feet per round and can leap up to 30 feet to strike a target. If it enters a space with a creature, it stops moving for the round and deals 2d4 points of damage as it evaporates moisture from the subject. (The subject can negate this damage with a successful Reflex save.) Oozes, creatures composed of water (such as water elementals), and creatures with the aquatic subtype take 2d6 points of damage.

The bubble moves as long as you actively direct it (a move action for you); otherwise, it merely stays at rest. The surface of the bubble has a spongy, yielding consistency (similar to that of a soap bubble, but not fragile and allowing objects to pass through it without affecting the spell) and so does not cause damage except by absorbing moisture. It cannot batter down large obstacles. The bubble winks out if it exceeds the spell's range.

Arcane Material Component: A tiny bag or bladder filled with air, and a sprinkle of dust.

DETECT FAVORED ENEMY

Divination
Level: Ranger 1
Components: V, S, DF
Casting Time: 1 standard action
Range: 60 ft.
Area: Quarter circle emanating from you to the extreme of the range
Duration: Concentration, up to 10 minutes/level (D)
Saving Throw: None
Spell Resistance: No

Using your passion for fighting your foe, you reach out with your magic and your mind to sense the presence of your enemies.

You can sense the presence of a favored enemy. The amount of information revealed depends on how long you study a particular area.

1st Round: Presence or absence of a favored enemy in the area.

2nd Round: Types of favored enemies in the area and the number of each type.

3rd Round: The location and HD of each individual present.

Note: Each round you can turn to detect things in a new area. The spell can penetrate barriers, but 1 foot of stone, 1 inch of common metal, a thin sheet of lead, or 3 feet of wood or dirt blocks detection.

DEVIL BLIGHT

Transmutation
Level: Cleric 3, sorcerer/wizard 3
Components: V, S, DF
Casting Time: 1 standard action
Range: Close (25 ft. + 5 ft./2 levels)
Target: Living creature
Duration: 1d6 rounds
Saving Throw: None or Fortitude partial; see text
Spell Resistance: Yes

You cry out the ancient words and make the prescribed motions, and your foe lets out a shriek of agony as it stumbles under the force of the spell.

This spell deals 2d6 points of damage per round for the duration of the spell to creatures that have both the lawful and evil subtypes (such as a barghest or a devil). No saving throw is allowed against this damage.

If the target creature also possesses the baatezu subtype (MM 306), it must succeed on a Fortitude save or be stunned for the duration of the spell.

DIAMONDSTEEL

Transmutation
Level: Paladin 3, sorcerer/wizard 3
Components: V, S, M
Casting Time: 1 standard action
Range: Touch
Target: Suit of metal armor touched
Duration: 1 round/level
Saving Throw: Will negates (object)
Spell Resistance: Yes (object)

You pass your hand over the suit of armor several times before finally touching it. As you do so, you feel a warmth grow in the palm of your hand. The warmth passes into the armor and manifests as a sparkling shine.

Diamondsteel enhances the strength of one suit of metal armor. The armor provides damage reduction equal to half the AC bonus of the armor. This damage reduction can be overcome only by adamantine weapons. For example, a suit of full plate would provide damage reduction 4/adamantine, and a *+1 breastplate* (+6 AC) would provide damage reduction 3/adamantine.

Material Component: Diamond dust worth at least 50 gp.

DIMENSION DOOR, GREATER

Conjuration [Teleportation]
Level: Sorcerer/wizard 5
Range: Touch
Target: You and touched objects or other touched willing creatures
Duration: 1 round/2 levels

Your flesh gives an involuntary shudder as you will yourself elsewhere. You vanish, reappearing some distance away.

This spell functions like *dimension door* (PH 221), except as noted above and that you can transfer the targets once per round, up to a distance of 25 feet + 5 feet per two levels, as a move action that does not provoke attacks of opportunity.

DINOSAUR STAMPEDE

Evocation [Force]
Level: Druid 6
Components: V, S, M
Casting Time: 1 standard action
Range: Medium (100 ft. + 10 ft./level)
Area: 20-ft.-radius spread
Duration: 1 round/level (D)
Saving Throw: Reflex half
Spell Resistance: Yes

Throwing down and shattering a fossil to complete the spell, you call upon potent natural forces and energies, and manifest them in the form of a swath of intangible, spectral, stampeding dinosaurs.

Creatures in the spell's area take 1d12 points of damage +1 point per caster level (up to +20). Creatures more than 10 feet above the ground are not affected by *dinosaur stampede*.

With a simple gesture (a free action), you can make the spectral forms move along the ground up to 40 feet per round (moving its effective point of origin). Creatures cannot be damaged more than once per round by *dinosaur stampede.*

Material Component: A fossil.

DIRE HUNGER

Transmutation
Level: Druid 5
Components: V, S
Casting Time: 1 standard action
Range: Close (25 ft. + 5 ft./2 levels)
Target: One living creature
Duration: 1 round/level
Saving Throw: Fortitude negates
Spell Resistance: Yes

You feel pangs of hunger well up within your abdomen as you complete the spell. A blood-red glow of energy radiates from your intended target and the hunger you felt subsides. The target creature's face elongates into a toothy, dinosaurlike snout filled with serrated teeth, and its belly distends as if the creature were undernourished.

The spell's subject becomes maddened by terrible pangs of hunger, viewing all creatures as food sources.

The subject creature gains a new bite attack that does damage according to the creature's size:

Fine	1
Diminutive	1d2
Tiny	1d3
Small	1d4
Medium	1d6
Large	1d8
Huge	2d6
Gargantuan	2d8
Colossal	4d6

The subject creature adds 1-1/2 times its Strength bonus to this damage. If the creature already has a bite attack that deals more damage, use that damage value instead.

The subject creature eschews all other attacks or actions except for its new bite attack, but it defends itself normally. It moves to attack the nearest living creature it can get to and attacks this creature until it is dead or until another living creature is closer. The subject creature attacks whatever living creature is nearest, regardless of former allegiance or personal connection. If moving toward the nearest living creature would move the creature into a dangerous area (precarious footing, a huge fire, or a deadly trap is in the way) the subject creature moves around the hazard if it can or moves to attack another creature if moving around the hazard isn't possible. If such movement brings the subject creature closer to another living creature, it attacks that creature instead. If the subject of the spell cannot detect or get to a living creature nearby, it goes looking for one to attack.

DIRGE

Evocation [Sonic]
Level: Bard 6
Components: V, S
Casting Time: 1 round
Range: 50 ft.
Area: All enemies within a 50-ft.-radius burst centered on you
Duration: 1 round/level
Saving Throw: Fortitude negates
Spell Resistance: Yes

As you sing, translucent spectral skulls float down from the sky like falling snow.

Your song draws the energies of death and destruction down on your enemies. Each round, any enemy in the area takes 2 points of Strength and Dexterity damage. Subjects can attempt a Fortitude save each round to negate the damage, but a successful save does not prevent damage in future rounds.

A dinosaur stampede mows down anything in its path

Illus. by J. Jarvis

DIRGE OF DISCORD

Enchantment (Compulsion) [Evil, Mind-Affecting]
Level: Bard 3
Components: V, S, M
Casting Time: 1 standard action
Range: Close (25 ft. + 5 ft./2 levels)
Area: 20-ft.-radius spread
Duration: Concentration + 1 round/level
Saving Throw: Will negates
Spell Resistance: Yes

You create an unholy, cacophonous dirge that fills the targets' minds with the screams of the dying, the wailing of the damned, and the howling of the mad.

Creatures affected by this spell take a –4 penalty on attack rolls and Dexterity, a 50% reduction in their speed (to a minimum of 5 feet), and must make a Concentration check to cast any spell (DC equal to this spell's DC + the level of the spell being cast).

Material Component: A pinch of ashes from a destrachan.

Illus. by W. England

DISCERN SHAPECHANGER

Divination
Level: Sorcerer/wizard 2
Components: V, S, M
Casting Time: 1 round
Range: Personal
Target: You
Duration: 1 round/level

The smell of wet animal dander assaults your nose even as the perfume of the material component fades. You feel suddenly more suspicious of beings around you, as if some of them might not be what they seem.

By taking a standard action to concentrate, you can see the true form of creatures within 60 feet. Each round, you can examine one creature you can see to determine whether it is polymorphed, disguised, or transmuted, and what its true form is. If you look at a shapechanger in its true form, you immediately sense its shapechanging ability, but you can't determine what other forms it might be capable of assuming.

For the purpose of this spell, a shapechanger is any creature with the shapechanger type or a supernatural or extraordinary ability that allows it to assume an alternate form. A wizard who knows *alter self* is not a shapechanger (since a spell is not a supernatural or extraordinary ability), but a barghest is (since it has the supernatural ability to assume alternate forms, even though its type is outsider).

Material Component: A balm of honey and lotus flower costing 25 gp, smeared on your eyelids.

Many wizards jealously guard their spellbooks, placing magical and mundane wards upon them

DISCOLOR POOL

Illusion (Glamer)
Level: Bard 2, sorcerer/wizard 2
Components: V, S, M
Casting Time: 1 standard action
Range: Close (25 ft. + 5 ft./2 levels)
Target: One color pool
Duration: 1 hour/level (D)
Saving Throw: Will disbelief (if interacted with)
Spell Resistance: No

The color pool glows with the rust-shade of Hades, but a few words and a spattering of ink, and it glows with the amber of the Blessed Fields of Elysium. Those who pass through it will not know their error until it is too late.

This spell causes a color pool on the Astral Plane—an irregular patch of color containing a portal to another plane—to appear to be a different color, and thus, to lead to another plane. *True seeing* or *analyze portal* reveals the true nature of the pool.

Material Component: Four drops of colored ink.

DISGUISE UNDEAD

Illusion (Glamer)
Level: Sorcerer/wizard 2
Components: V, S, F
Casting Time: 1 standard action
Range: Touch
Target: 1 corporeal undead
Duration: 24 hours
Saving Throw: None
Spell Resistance: Yes (harmless)

One cannot just march a ghoul into the Duke's Court. But as the fumes issuing from the cocoon surround the creature, the form of the ghoul is replaced with that of a stately courtier armed with a rapier. Of course, it will have to keep its mouth shut.

You make one undead—including its clothing, armor, weapons, and equipment—look different. You can make it seem 1 foot shorter or taller, thin, fat, or in between. You cannot change the creature's body type. For example, a wight could look human, humanoid, or like any other generally human-shaped bipedal creature. Otherwise, the extent of the apparent change is up to you. You could add or obscure a minor feature, such as a mole or a beard, or make it look like an entirely different creature.

The spell does not provide the abilities or mannerisms of the chosen form. It does not alter the perceived tactile (touch) or audible (sound) properties of the undead or its equipment. For example, a battleaxe made to look like a dagger still functions as a battleaxe.

This spell also foils magical means of detecting undead. The subject of *disguise undead* detects as a creature of the type simulated.

Creatures get Will saves to recognize the glamer as an illusion if they interact with the subject (such as by touching the undead and having that not match what they see, in the case of this spell).

Focus: A cocoon of a death's head moth.

DISPEL WARD

Abjuration
Level: Cleric 1, sorcerer/wizard 1
Components: V, S
Casting Time: 1 standard action
Range: Medium (100 ft. + 10 ft./level)
Target: One warded object or area
Duration: Instantaneous
Saving Throw: None
Spell Resistance: No

Your head throbs with energy as you recite the final few phrases of the spell. A moment later, the energy releases and the area you designated as the spell's target glows silver for several seconds. You hear a sound like a mechanical object winding down.

This spell functions like *dispel magic* (PH 223), except that it can be used only in the targeted or area version, and it affects only abjuration magic placed upon objects or areas (such as *arcane lock, explosive runes, fire trap, glyph of warding,* and *guards and wards.*) The maximum bonus on the level check is +10.

DISPELLING BREATH

Abjuration
Level: Sorcerer/wizard 5
Components: S
Casting Time: 1 swift action
Range: Personal
Target: Your breath weapon
Duration: 1 round

You exhale a cloud of poisonous gas mixed with starlight motes that gravitate toward the spellcasters and summoned monsters within the cloud.

For this spell to function, you must have a breath weapon, either as a supernatural ability or as the result of casting a spell such as *dragon breath* (page 73). When you successfully cast this spell, your breath weapon acts as a targeted *dispel magic* (PH 223).

For each creature or object that fails its saving throw against your breath weapon and that is the subject of one or more spells, you make a dispel check against the highest level spell currently in effect on the object or creature. A dispel check is 1d20 + 1 per caster level (maximum +15) against a DC of 11 + the spell's caster level. If that check fails, you make dispel checks against progressively weaker spells until you dispel one spell or until you fail all your checks. A creature's magic items are not affected, and creatures and objects that rolled successful saving throws against your breath weapon are likewise not affected.

If a creature that is the effect of an ongoing spell (such as a monster summoned by *monster summoning*), is in the area and fails its saving throw against your breath weapon, you can also make a dispel check to end the spell that conjured the creature (returning it whence it came).

For each ongoing area or effect spell centered within the area of your breath weapon, you make a dispel check to dispel the spell.

Spells are dispelled prior to the effect of your breath weapon being resolved.

You can choose to automatically succeed on dispel checks against any spell in the area that you have cast.

DISPELLING SCREEN

Abjuration
Level: Sorcerer/wizard 4
Components: V, S, M
Casting Time: 1 standard action
Range: Close (25 ft. + 5 ft./2 levels)
Effect: Energy wall whose area is up to one 10-ft. square/level, or a sphere or hemisphere with a radius of up to 1 ft./level
Duration: 1 minute/level (D)
Saving Throw: None
Spell Resistance: No

By tossing down the sheet of crystal in your hand and completing the mysterious words of power needed to release the energy of the spell, you create an immobile, shimmering screen of violet energy.

Any spell effect operating on a creature or unattended object that passes through the screen is affected as by a targeted *dispel magic* (PH 223) at your caster level. Attended items that pass through are not affected by the screen, which is the only way the screen differs from a normal targeted casting of *dispel magic*—attended items are essentially not targeted by the screen. Make a caster level check (1d20 + 1 per caster level, maximum +10) to dispel spell effects (DC 11 + caster level) or suppress an unattended object's magical properties for 1d4 rounds (DC equal to the item's caster level). Spell effects not operating on objects or creatures cannot pass through the screen. A *disintegrate* or successful *dispel magic* removes *dispelling screen,* while an *antimagic field* suppresses it.

Material Component: A sheet of fine lead crystal.

DISPELLING SCREEN, GREATER

Abjuration
Level: Drow 6, sorcerer/wizard 7

This spell functions like *dispelling screen,* except that the maximum caster level bonus on the dispel check is +20.

DISPLACER FORM

Transmutation
Level: Sorcerer/wizard 4
Components: V, S, M
Casting Time: 1 standard action
Range: Personal
Target: You
Duration: 1 round/level (D)

You drop to your hands and knees a moment before your extremities morph into the limbs of a great black panther.

When you cast this spell, you assume the physical appearance and many of the qualities and abilities of a displacer beast (MM 66). While under the effect of the spell, your creature type changes to magical beast, and your size changes to Large. You have the space and reach of a displacer beast (15 feet/5 feet [10 feet with tentacles]). You gain two tentacle attacks, which each deal 1d6 points of damage + your Str modifier. You gain the Strength, Dexterity, and Constitution of an average displacer

Displacer form gives a spellcaster some obvious advantages

Illus. by J. Engle

beast (Str 18, Dex 15, Con 16), but you retain your own mental ability scores. Your base land speed becomes 40 feet. You gain darkvision out to 60 feet. You also gain low-light vision.

Your class and level, hit points, alignment, base attack bonus, and base saving throw bonuses all remain the same. You lose any spell-like abilities of your own form, and you lose any extraordinary special abilities from your own form. You retain any supernatural abilities of your own form. You keep all extraordinary special attacks derived from class levels (such as a barbarian's rage or a rogue's sneak attack), but you lose any from your normal form that are not derived from class levels. You can speak and cast spells while in displacer beast form, but you must physically touch any necessary material components. Your natural armor bonus becomes +5, regardless of any natural armor bonus from your normal form. While in displacer beast form, you gain the displacer beast's displacement and resistance to ranged attacks abilities. Your equipment melds into your new form and becomes nonfunctional.

Material Component: A single claw from a displacer beast.

DISQUIETUDE

Enchantment (Compulsion) [Mind-Affecting, Sonic]
Level: Bard 2
Components: V, S
Casting Time: 1 standard action
Range: Close (25 ft. + 5 ft./2 levels)
Target: One living creature
Duration: 1 round/level
Saving Throw: Will negates
Spell Resistance: Yes

Your spell warns of unseen dangers and untrustworthy allies. As you sing, your target eases away from her compatriots, doubt written on her face.

The affected subject restricts its movement to avoid any physical contact, even with allies. Any ally that wishes to touch the subject must make a successful melee touch attack to do so. The subject must stay 15 feet away from all other creatures. If, at the beginning of its turn, the creature is within 15 feet of any creature, it must first move away (beyond 15 feet from any creature) before taking any action. If the subject cannot safely move that distance, it instead must take the total defense action and remain in its space.

DISRUPT UNDEAD, GREATER

Necromancy
Level: Sorcerer/wizard 3
Components: V, S
Casting Time: 1 standard action
Range: Close (25 ft. + 5 ft./2 levels)
Effect: Ray
Duration: Instantaneous
Saving Throw: None
Spell Resistance: Yes

A black ray fires from your outstretched hand, piercing and passing through nearby undead.

You must succeed on a ranged touch attack with the ray to strike a target. This spell functions like *disrupt undead* (PH 223), except that this ray deals 1d8 points of damage per caster level to any undead, to a maximum of 10d8. If the damage is sufficient to destroy the first target, then you can redirect the ray to another undead target within 15 feet of the first target. If you make a successful ranged touch attack on the second target, that target takes half of the damage rolled for the first target.

DISSONANT CHANT

Abjuration [Sonic]
Level: Bard 2, sorcerer/wizard 2
Components: V, S
Casting Time: 1 standard action
Range: Close (25 ft. + 5 ft./2 levels)
Area: 100-ft.-radius emanation
Duration: 1 round/level (D)
Saving Throw: None; see text
Spell Resistance: Yes

Your intricate hand motions slow and then stop even as you begin chanting the arcane words that unlock the spell's power. As you conclude, your disembodied words continue on, growing both in tempo and volume.

You create a distracting and discordant chant. Affected creatures that attempt spellcasting or other activities that require concentration must make Concentration checks (DC equal to this spell's DC + the level of the spell being cast).

The DCs of activities that already require Concentration checks, such as casting defensively, increase by 4.

Creatures within the area gain a +4 bonus on saving throws against language-dependent effects.

DISSONANT CHORD

Evocation [Sonic]
Level: Bard 3
Components: V, S
Casting Time: 1 standard action
Range: 10 ft.
Area: 10-ft.-radius burst centered on you
Duration: Instantaneous
Saving Throw: Fortitude half
Spell Resistance: Yes

You emit a terrible, piercing note. The note pulses in the air, radiating like a shockwave. It slams into nearby creatures and rattles loose objects.

Creatures (other than you) in the affected area take 1d8 points of sonic damage per two caster levels (maximum 5d8).

DISTORT SPEECH

Transmutation [Sonic]
Level: Bard 1
Components: V, S
Casting Time: 1 standard action
Range: Close (25 ft. + 5 ft./2 levels)
Target: One creature
Duration: 1 round/level
Saving Throw: Fortitude negates
Spell Resistance: Yes

By pointing and making a number of loud, nonsensical sounds you release the power of the spell. The target attempts to speak, but spews forth only gibberish instead.

For the duration of this spell, the subject has a 50% chance to miscast spells that have verbal components, and any time the subject speaks (including the use of magic items activated by command words), there is a 50% chance that the utterance is completely incomprehensible and therefore ineffective.

DISTRACT

Enchantment (Compulsion) [Mind-Affecting]
Level: Bard 1, sorcerer/wizard 1
Components: S
Casting Time: 1 standard action
Range: Medium (100 ft. + 10 ft./level)
Targets: One creature/level, no two of which are more than 30 ft. apart
Duration: 1 round/level
Saving Throw: Will negates
Spell Resistance: Yes

This spell arouses a zest and appreciation for life in the targets. The targets are distracted as they study the shapes of the clouds, the texture of tree bark, the patterns carved into a stone wall, the temperature and scent of a breeze—anything and everything gets their attention, if just for a moment.

The targets of this spell must succeed on a Will save or lose themselves to the urge to experience nearly everything. Failure indicates the creatures take a –4 penalty on all Concentration, Listen, Search, and Spot checks, and can take only a single standard or move action each round, but not both. Creatures with more than 6 HD are unaffected.

DISTRACT ASSAILANT

Enchantment (Compulsion) [Mind-Affecting]
Level: Assassin 1, sorcerer/wizard 1
Components: V, S, M
Casting Time: 1 swift action
Range: Close (25 ft. + 5 ft./2 levels)
Target: One creature
Duration: 1 round
Saving Throw: Will negates
Spell Resistance: Yes

Buzzing under your breath like a fly, you swat at the sky and toss the fly's wing in your hand into the air. The target of your spell becomes distracted, starting at shadows and looking about for unseen assailants.

A creature affected by this spell is flat-footed until the beginning of its next turn.

Material Component: The dried wing of a fly.

DISTRACTING RAY

Abjuration
Level: Bard 2, sorcerer/wizard 2
Components: V, S
Casting Time: 1 standard action
Range: Close (25 ft. + 5 ft./2 levels)
Effect: Ray
Duration: Instantaneous
Saving Throw: None
Spell Resistance: No

You blast a nearby creature with a multicolored ray. The ray explodes on contact to form a dizzying array of bizarre swirling and flashing lights around the targeted creature.

You must succeed on a ranged touch attack with the ray to strike a target. This ray attempts to undo magic as it is being cast. Used in the same manner as a counterspell (as a readied action), the ray interferes with the manipulation of divine or arcane magic by dazzling the target. If the ray successfully strikes a spellcaster, and that spellcaster is in the process of casting a spell, then the target spellcaster must make a Concentration check to avoid losing the spell. The DC of the Concentration check is equal to 17 + the level of the spell the target is casting.

DIVINE AGILITY

Transmutation
Level: Cleric 5
Components: V, S
Casting Time: 1 standard action
Range: Touch
Target: Living creature touched
Duration: 1 round/level
Saving Throw: Will negates (harmless)
Spell Resistance: No

Calling aloud on the divine power of your deity, you imbue a living creature with agility and skill in combat.

You grant the subject a +10 enhancement bonus to Dexterity.

DIVINE INSIGHT

Divination
Level: Cleric 2, paladin 2
Components: V, S, DF
Casting Time: 1 standard action
Range: Personal
Target: You
Duration: 1 hour/level or until discharged (D)

Clutching the focus of your spells to your chest, you let your eyes flutter shut. As you complete the short prayer you feel your deity's presence fill you with confidence.

Once during the spell's duration, you can choose to use its effect. This spell grants you an insight bonus equal to 5 + your caster level (maximum bonus of +15) on any single skill check. Activating the effect requires an immediate action. You must choose to use the insight bonus before you make the check you want to modify. Once used, the spell ends.

You can't have more than one *divine insight* effect active on you at the same time.

DIVINE INTERDICTION

Abjuration
Level: Cleric 2
Components: V
Casting Time: 1 standard action
Range: Close (25 ft. +5 ft./2 levels)
Area: 10-ft.-radius emanation centered on a creature, object, or point in space
Duration: 1 round/level
Saving Throw: Will negates or None (object); see text
Spell Resistance: Yes or No (object); see text

You shout out a plea, calling upon your deity to quell the power of another deity's follower.

This spell can be cast at a point in space, but the effect is stationary unless cast on a mobile object. The spell can be cast on a creature, and the effect then radiates from the creature and moves as it moves. A creature can attempt a Will save to negate the spell, and spell resistance, if any, applies if the spell is cast on a creature.

Divine interdiction interferes with a cleric's connection to her divine source of power, resulting in a temporary loss of the ability to turn or rebuke creatures and loss of granted domain powers. Paladins, blackguards, and other classes capable of rebuking and turning also suffer a temporary loss of this ability. This affects the subject's ability to channel energy through the use of a turn or rebuke attempt, and so also interferes with the use of many divine feats.

DIVINE PROTECTION

Enchantment (Compulsion) [Mind-Affecting]
Level: Cleric 2, paladin 2
Components: V, S, DF
Casting Time: 1 standard action
Range: Medium (100 ft. + 10 ft./level)
Targets: Allies in a 20-ft.-radius burst
Duration: 1 minute/level
Saving Throw: Will negates (harmless)
Spell Resistance: Yes (harmless)

You call upon your holy powers to aid your companions and a golden light appears from above, bathing them with sparkling radiance.

Allies gain a +1 morale bonus to their Armor Class and on saving throws.

DIVINE SACRIFICE

Evocation
Level: Blackguard 1, paladin 1
Components: V, S
Casting Time: 1 standard action
Range: Personal
Target: You
Duration: 1 round/level

Giving up some of your life force to win the battle, you empower your next blow against your foe.

Your first attack each round for the duration of the spell deals an extra 5d6 points of damage if it hits, and you take 10 points of damage each time you make such an attack, whether or not the attack is successful.

DOLOROUS BLOW

Transmutation
Level: Bard 3, sorcerer/wizard 3
Components: V, S
Casting Time: 1 standard action
Range: Touch
Target: Weapon touched
Duration: 1 minute/level
Saving Throw: None
Spell Resistance: No

A longing for battle fills you as you complete this spell. Upon touching the intended weapon, the feeling fades even as a dull red aura encompasses the weapon.

For the duration of the spell, the weapon's threat range is doubled, and its critical threats automatically confirm, so every threat is a critical hit. The latter effect does not apply to any weapon that already has a magical effect related to critical hits.

Multiple effects that increase a weapon's threat range (such as this spell and the Improved Critical feat) don't stack. You can't cast this spell on a natural weapon, such as a claw.

DOOMTIDE

Illusion (Pattern)
Level: Cleric 5
Components: V, S, DF
Casting Time: 1 standard action
Range: 80 ft.
Effect: Eight 10-ft. cubes extending straight from you
Duration: 1 round/level
Saving Throw: Will negates
Spell Resistance: Yes

You fill an area with illusory black, creeping mist that vaguely resembles thousands of slender grasping tentacles.

Creatures within the area must make Will saves or be dazed for 1 round. Any creature moving into the mist, or a creature that begins its turn in the mist, must succeed on a Will save or also be dazed for 1 round.

The mist filling the area obscures all sight, including darkvision, beyond 5 feet. A creature within 5 feet has concealment. Creatures farther away have total concealment.

When you cast the spell, you decide if the effect remains stationary or

Illus. by W. O'Connor

Denied the power to turn undead by her foe's divine interdiction, a cleric falls before a horde of undead

if its point of origin moves straight away from you at a rate of 10 feet per round.

A moderate wind disperses the effect in 4 rounds; a strong wind disperses the mist in 1 round.

DOWNDRAFT

Evocation [Air]
Level: Cleric 3, druid 3
Components: V, S, M
Casting Time: 1 standard action
Range: Long (400 ft. + 40 ft./level)
Area: Cylinder (20-ft. radius, 100 ft. high)
Duration: Instantaneous
Saving Throw: Reflex partial; see text
Spell Resistance: Yes

Dropping the small carving in your hand to the ground, you crush it with your foot as you recite the last few words of the spell. In the distance you see a column of air turn a hazy gray. The air column then blasts toward the ground, and you hear a distant whoosh.

Downdraft sends a column of turbulent air rushing toward the earth. Airborne creatures caught in the area of a downdraft must succeed on a Reflex save or immediately plummet up to 100 feet straight downward, taking falling damage (1d6 points of damage per 10 feet fallen) if the downdraft makes them hit the ground or collide with an object. Those who succeed on the Reflex save plummet only 50 feet.

Creatures already on the ground must succeed on a Reflex save or be knocked prone by the spell.

Material Component: A balsa-wood bird carving, which is crushed underfoot.

DRACONIC MIGHT

Transmutation
Level: Paladin 4, sorcerer/wizard 5
Components: V, S
Casting Time: 1 standard action
Range: Touch
Target: Living creature touched
Duration: 1 minute/level (D)
Saving Throw: Fortitude negates (harmless)
Spell Resistance: Yes (harmless)

Dragon ally summons a dragon to do your bidding, but only at a great price

Upon casting this spell, your ally's face is covered briefly with a fine pattern of yellow scales. The scales fade, but the golden radiance remains.

The subject of the spell gains a +4 enhancement bonus to Strength, Constitution, and Charisma. It also gains a +4 enhancement bonus to natural armor. Finally, it has immunity to magic sleep and paralysis effects.

Special: Sorcerers cast this spell at +1 caster level.

DRAGON ALLY

Conjuration (Calling)
Level: Dragon 7, sorcerer/wizard 7
Effect: One called dragon of 18 HD or less

This spell functions like *lesser dragon ally*, except you can call a single dragon of up to 18 HD.

XP Cost: 250 XP.

DRAGON ALLY, GREATER

Conjuration (Calling)
Level: Sorcerer/wizard 9
Effect: One called dragon of 22 HD or less

This spell functions like *lesser dragon ally*, except you can call a single dragon of up to 22 HD.

XP Cost: 500 XP.

DRAGON ALLY, LESSER

Conjuration (Calling)
Level: Sorcerer/wizard 5
Components: V, XP
Casting Time: 10 minutes
Range: Close (25 ft. + 5 ft./2 levels)
Effect: One called dragon of 15 HD or less
Duration: Instantaneous
Saving Throw: None
Spell Resistance: No

You feel some of your lifeforce being pulled from you in the casting of the spell. A large dragon lands nearby. "You wish to discuss something?" it asks, eying your belongings.

This spell calls a dragon. You can ask the dragon to perform one task in exchange for a payment from you. Tasks might range from the simple (fly us across the chasm, help us fight a battle) to the complex (spy on our enemies, protect us on our foray into the dungeon). You must be able to communicate with the dragon to bargain for its services.

Illus. by F. Vohwinkel

The summoned dragon requires payment for its services, which takes the form of coins, gems, or other precious objects the dragon can add to its hoard. This payment must be made before the dragon agrees to perform any services. The bargaining takes at least 1 round, so any actions by the creature begin in the round after it arrives.

Tasks requiring up to 1 minute per caster level require a payment of 50 gp per HD of the called dragon. For a task requiring up to 1 hour per caster level, the creature requires a payment of 250 gp per HD. Long-term tasks (those requiring up to 1 day per caster level) require a payment of 500 gp per HD.

Especially hazardous tasks require a greater gift, up to twice the given amount. A dragon never accepts less than the indicated amount, even for a nonhazardous task.

At the end of its task, or when the duration bargained for elapses, the creature returns to the place it was called from (after reporting back to you, if appropriate and possible).

XP Cost: 100 XP.

Special: Sorcerers cast this spell at +1 caster level.

DRAGON BREATH

Evocation [Good or Evil]
Level: Cleric 5, sorcerer/wizard 4
Components: V, S, M/DF
Casting Time: 1 standard action
Range: Personal
Target: You
Duration: 1 round/level

Using magic to mimic a dragon's breath, you spew forth a gout of energy.

You gain the ability to breathe a gout of energy as a standard action that mimics a dragon's breath. Once you've used the breath attack, you must wait 1d4 rounds before doing so again.

When you cast *dragon breath*, you choose one true dragon whose breath you're emulating. If you choose a chromatic dragon, then the spell gains the evil descriptor. If you choose a metallic dragon, then it gains the good descriptor. Particulars for the breath weapons of each of the true dragons are provided below.

Chromatic Dragons

Black: 30-ft. line of acid, 1d8/2 caster levels (maximum 10d8); Reflex half.

Blue: 30-ft. line of electricity, 1d8/2 caster levels (maximum 10d8); Reflex half.

Green: 15-ft. cone of acid, 1d8/2 caster levels (maximum 10d8); Reflex half.

Red: 15-ft. cone of fire, 1d8/2 caster levels (maximum 10d8); Reflex half.

White: 15-ft. cone of cold, 1d8/2 caster levels (maximum 10d8); Reflex half.

Metallic Dragons

Brass: 15-ft. cone of *sleep*, lasts 1d6 rounds; Will negates.

Bronze: 30-ft. line of electricity, 1d8/2 caster levels (maximum 10d8); Reflex half.

Copper: 15-ft. cone of *slow*, lasts 1d6 rounds; Will negates.

Gold: 15-ft. cone of fire, 1d8/2 caster levels (maximum 10d8); Reflex half.

Silver: 15-ft. cone of paralysis, lasts 1d6 rounds; Fort negates.

Arcane Material Component: A dragonscale of the appropriate color.

DRAGONSIGHT

Transmutation
Level: Bard 5, sorcerer/wizard 5
Components: V, S, F
Casting Time: 1 standard action
Range: Personal
Target: You
Duration: 1 hour/level (D)

You cast this spell and your eyes enlarge and turn yellow and catlike, like those of a dragon.

You gain the visual acuity of a dragon, including low-light vision, darkvision, and blindsense.

You can see four times as well as a normal human in low-light conditions and twice as well in normal light. Your darkvision is effective out to 10 feet per caster level. You take half the normal penalties for distance on Spot checks.

Your blindsense has a range of 5 feet per caster level.

None of these effects stack with any low-light vision, darkvision, or blindsense you might already have.

Focus: A dragon's eye.

DRAGONSKIN

Transmutation
Level: Sorcerer/wizard 3
Components: S, M
Casting Time: 1 standard action
Range: Personal
Target: You
Duration: 10 minutes/level

You say nothing, but make the motions in the prescribed pattern and hold the dragon's scale aloft. Your flesh erupts with hard, colorful scales.

Your skin toughens and becomes scaly like that of a chromatic dragon, of a color that you select. You gain an enhancement bonus to natural armor equal to +1 per two levels (to a maximum of +5 at 10th level), as well as energy resistance 10 against the type of energy appropriate to the color you select: acid (black or green), cold (white), electricity (blue), or fire (red). Your energy resistance increases to 20 at 10th level.

Material Component: A dragon's scale.

Special: Sorcerers cast this spell at +1 caster level.

DREAM CASTING

Illusion (Phantasm) [Mind-Affecting]; see text
Level: Sorcerer/wizard 6
Casting Time: 1 hour
Target: You and one dreamer
Duration: 24 hours/level; see text
Saving Throw: Will negates; see text

You complete the spell with a few last gestures and arcane words. You feel a pressure in your mind as you begin to relay the intent of your dreaming contact.

This spell functions like *dream* (PH 225), except as noted above and that you can alter the sleeping person's dreams to produce a specific desired effect. The dreamer gets a Will saving throw to resist the additional effects of this spell; if the save succeeds, the *dream casting* spell can send only a message, in the manner of the *dream* spell. If the saving throw fails, you decide what additional effect the message carries.

Fear: Your image in the dream is surrounded by intimidating imagery and an aura of power. For the duration of the spell, any time the dreamer can see you or knows you are present, he is shaken. This is a compulsion and fear effect.

Charm: Your image in the dream appears particularly helpful and kind. For the duration of the spell, the dreamer is under the effect of a *charm monster* spell. This is a charm effect.

Rage: Your image in the dream taunts and harasses the dreamer. For the duration of the spell, any time the dreamer can see you or knows you are present, he preferentially attacks you if in a combat situation. The dreamer gains a +2 morale bonus on saving throws, attack rolls, ability checks, skill checks, and weapon damage rolls when attacking you while under this effect. This is a compulsion effect.

Dream sight gives a sleeping character the ability to pass through the world like a ghost

Illus. by B. Hagan

Harrow: Your image in the dream behaves in a bizarre and irrational manner. For the duration of the spell, the dreamer behaves in an unusual manner, gaining two random traits from Table 4–24: One Hundred Traits (DMG 128), rerolling any results not pertinent to behavior. If the dreamer can see you or knows you are present, he is *confused* for 1 round/level.

DREAM SIGHT

Divination
Level: Dream 6
Components: S, DF
Casting Time: 1 round
Range: See text
Target: You
Duration: 1 minute/level (D)

In sleep your spirit rises to travel about and observe the world.

You fall into a deep sleep while your spirit leaves your body invisibly in incorporeal form and travels to distant locations. Your spirit can move 100 feet per round, and can see and hear anything you could if you were in the same location. The spirit can be blocked by any spell that wards incorporeal creatures, and it can be detected and attacked in the same way as incorporeal creatures can. Your spirit can do nothing but move and observe—it cannot speak, attack, cast spells, or perform any other action.

At the end of the spell, your spirit instantaneously returns to your body and you wake up. If your body is disturbed or attacked while your spirit is wandering, the spell ends immediately.

DROWN

Conjuration (Creation) [Water]
Level: Druid 6
Components: V, S
Casting Time: 1 standard action
Range: Close (25 ft. + 5 ft./2 levels)
Target: One living creature
Duration: Instantaneous
Saving Throw: Fortitude negates
Spell Resistance: Yes

You speak the words and make the sign of the wave. Your foe sputters, water gushing from his mouth, then collapses.

You create water in the lungs of the subject, causing it to begin drowning (DMG 304) as if it had failed to continue holding its breath. The subject's hit points immediately drop to 0, and it falls unconscious. In the next round, it loses another hit point (bringing its hit points to –1) and is dying. In the following round, it dies.

Coughing and other attempts by the subject to physically expel the water from its lungs are useless. However, another creature can stabilize the subject by making a DC 15 Heal check on the creature before it dies.

Undead, constructs, creatures that do not need to breathe, and creatures that can breathe water are unaffected by this spell.

DROWN, MASS

Conjuration (Creation) [Water]
Level: Druid 9
Targets: One or more creatures, no two of which are more than 30 ft. apart.

You speak the words and make the sign of the wave, indicating each of your foes in turn. They sputter and pitch forward, water gushing from their mouths and nostrils.

This spell functions like *drown*, except that it affects multiple creatures.

DUELWARD

Abjuration
Level: Sorcerer/wizard 5
Components: V, S, M
Casting Time: 1 standard action

Range: Personal
Target: You
Duration: 1 round/level or until discharged (D)

The air around you crackles with magical energy as you finish uttering the last syllables of the spell's formula. You immediately feel as if your link to the arcane somehow has increased, filling you with confidence and a sense of security.

While a *duelward* spell is in effect, counterspelling is an immediate action for you, allowing you to counterspell even when it is not your turn without having previously readied an action. You also gain a +4 competence bonus on Spellcraft checks made to identify spells being cast.

The first time you successfully counterspell while the spell is in effect (whether you counterspell as an immediate action or not), *duelward* is discharged.

Material Component: A miniature silk glove.

EARTH LOCK

Abjuration [Earth]
Level: Sorcerer/wizard 2
Components: V, S, M
Casting Time: 1 standard action
Range: Close (25 ft. + 5 ft./2 levels)
Target: One 1-foot length of tunnel with a diameter of up to 10 feet
Duration: Permanent
Saving Throw: None
Spell Resistance: No

You scribe a spiral in the air with the diamond-tipped bit of charcoal, chanting the words of the spell. Immediately the sides of the cavern begin to contract, sealing the passage behind you.

You cause a 1-foot length of subterranean tunnel to constrict, "locking" it against others who might wish to traverse its length. This spell affects only naturally occurring tunnels or worked tunnels that are surrounded on all sides by unworked, natural, subterranean earth. You can affect any tunnel whose diameter does not exceed 10 feet. A square-sided or rough tunnel can also be affected, as long as its diameter at the point where the spell is cast does not exceed 10 feet.

An earth lock spell causes a tunnel to constrict seconds before charging minotaurs reach the gap

The constriction takes 1 round to complete. Any Large or smaller object or creature that partially blocks the constriction point is pushed, unharmed, to one side or the other. (A creature can decide which way to move; an object moves randomly.) A Huge or larger object or creature that blocks the constriction point prevents the spell from working until moved.

You can freely pass through tunnels that you have secured with this spell. (The constriction opens and closes on your command, taking 1 round for either process). A tunnel secured with *earth lock* can be bypassed by others in several ways. A DC 20 Escape Artist check allows the creature making the check to squeeze through the constriction but leaves it intact. A DC 25 Strength check breaks the constriction and ends the spell. A successful *dispel magic* or *knock* spell opens the constriction—the former by ending the spell and the latter by suppressing it for 10 minutes. If a creature burrows through the *earth lock*, the spell ends. The constricted tunnel can also be dug out normally.

Identifying a tunnel secured with *earth lock* (as opposed to a tunnel that just ends) requires a DC 20 Search check.

Material Component: A diamond chip worth at least 50 gp, embedded in a piece of charcoal.

Illus. by R. Spears

EARTH REAVER

Transmutation [Fire]
Level: Cleric 5, sorcerer/wizard 5
Components: V, S
Casting Time: 1 standard action
Range: Medium (100 ft. + 10 ft./level)
Area: 20-ft.-radius spread
Duration: Instantaneous
Saving Throw: Reflex partial
Spell Resistance: Yes

With a stern, commanding word, you point at a spot on the ground. An instant later, the earth at the indicated spot erupts in a shower of rock, dirt, and fire.

Creatures and objects within the area take 4d6 points of damage from the impact of the rock shards, as well as 3d6 points of fire damage; no saving throw applies to the damage. Creatures in the area must also succeed on a Reflex saving throw or be knocked prone.

EARTHBIND

Transmutation
Level: Druid 2, sorcerer/wizard 2
Components: V, S
Casting Time: 1 standard action
Range: Medium (100 ft. + 10 ft./level)
Target: One creature
Duration: 1 minute/level (D)
Saving Throw: Fortitude negates
Spell Resistance: Yes

Your foe will reach you in seconds. You cast this spell, and yellow strips of magical energy loop about its wings, hampering its flight and dragging it to ground.

You hinder the subject creature's ability to fly (whether through natural or magical means) for the duration of the spell. If the target fails its saving throw, its fly speed (if any) becomes 0 feet. An airborne creature subjected to this spell falls to the ground as if under the effect of a *feather fall* spell. Even if a new effect would grant the creature the ability to fly, that effect is suppressed for the duration of the *earthbind* spell.

Earthbind has no effect on other forms of movement, or even on effects that might grant airborne movement without granting a fly speed (such as jumping or *levitate* or *air walk* spells).

EARTHEN GRACE

Abjuration [Earth]
Level: Druid 2, sorcerer/wizard 3
Components: V, S, M
Casting Time: 1 standard action
Range: Touch
Target: Living creature touched
Duration: 1 minute/level
Saving Throw: Will negates (harmless)
Spell Resistance: Yes (harmless)

You sprinkle the spell's component on your target, causing its skin to momentarily take on the speckled gray look of granite. The smell of dust hangs heavily in the air.

You grant the subject an affinity for earth and stone. Any damage the subject takes from a stone or earthen source counts as nonlethal damage for the duration of the spell. Natural attacks by creatures made of earth or stone (such as stone golems), natural attacks by creatures of the earth subtype, and attacks by stone weapons (such as a stone hammer or a sling stone) instead deal nonlethal damage, as does falling damage when the subject lands on rock or earth. When the nonlethal damage the subject has taken (from any source) equals the subject's current hit points, the spell ends, and any further damage from a stone or earthen source causes damage normally.

Material Component: A chunk of granite.

EARTHEN GRASP

Transmutation [Earth]
Level: Sorcerer/wizard 2
Components: V, S, M
Casting Time: 1 standard action
Range: Close (25 ft. + 5 ft./2 levels)
Effect: Animated earthen arm
Duration: 2 rounds/level
Saving Throw: None
Spell Resistance: Yes

You raise your arm above your hand, your fingers flexed like talons. Nearby, an arm made of earth but as large as a person erupts from the ground, its hand grasping at the air.

You bring forth from the ground an arm made of dense, compacted earth or soil that can grapple your foes. You can cause the arm to rise only out of earth, mud, grass, or sand, and the spell fails if you attempt to cast it in an area with the wrong materials (including stone).

Treat the arm as a Medium creature, with a base attack bonus equal to your caster level and a Strength of 14 +2 per three caster levels (16 at 3rd level, 18 at 6th level, and so on). The arm doesn't move from the square it appears in, but can make one grapple attempt per round against any creature in its square or any adjacent square. Doing so does not provoke attacks of opportunity. If the arm can target multiple creatures, you choose one. If you are unable to choose a target, the arm attacks a random creature within reach (possibly including your allies). Each round when it successfully pins a target, the hand deals lethal damage equal to 1d6 points + its Str modifier.

The earthen arm has AC 15, hardness 4, and 3 hit points per caster level. If reduced to 0 or fewer hit points, it crumbles to dust.

Material Component: A miniature hand sculpted from clay.

EARTHFAST

Transmutation
Level: Druid 2
Components: V, S
Casting Time: 1 standard action
Range: Close (25 ft. + 5 ft./2 levels)
Area: One stone structure or rock formation, up to 25 cubic ft./level
Duration: Instantaneous
Saving Throw: None
Spell Resistance: Yes (object)

Gray bands extend from your fingertips, wrapping themselves around the wall like a brace, strengthening it for the coming assault.

You reinforce a rock formation or stone structure. The *earthfast* spell doubles the structure's hit points and increases its hardness to 10. This spell does not function on constructs.

EASY CLIMB

Transmutation
Level: Ranger 2
Components: V, S
Casting Time: 1 standard action
Range: Medium (100 ft. + 10 ft./level)
Area: Vertical path 10 ft. wide and 20 ft. tall/level
Duration: 10 minutes/level (D)
Saving Throw: None (object)
Spell Resistance: Yes (object)

By pushing upward with your hand and speaking in a commanding voice, you cause sturdy rungs to form on the surface you designate.

You create a path of handholds and footholds up the surface of a cliff face, tree trunk, wall, or other vertical obstacle. This effect changes the surface to the equivalent of a very rough wall (Climb DC 10).

EASY TRAIL

Abjuration
Level: Druid 2, ranger 1
Components: V, S
Casting Time: 1 standard action
Range: 40 ft.
Area: 40-ft.-radius emanation centered on you
Duration: 1 hour/level (D)
Saving Throw: None
Spell Resistance: Yes

The easy climb spell can create a path of escape where none existed before

You sweep your arm as if to push aside a branch and simultaneously call out for the plants around you to move aside. Obediently, the plants surrounding you oblige.

Anyone in the area of the spell (including you) finds the undergrowth held aside while they pass. This effect essentially provides a trail through any kind of undergrowth, and you treat any trackless terrain as having a trail (PH 164). Once the effect of the spell passes, the plants return to their normal shape. The DC to track anyone who traveled within the area of this spell increases by 5 (the equivalent of hiding the trail).

This spell has no effect on plant creatures (that is, they aren't pushed or held aside by its effect).

EBON EYES

Transmutation
Level: Assassin 1, cleric 1, sorcerer/wizard 1
Components: V, S, M
Casting Time: 1 standard action
Range: Touch
Target: Creature touched
Duration: 10 minutes/level
Saving Throw: None
Spell Resistance: Yes (harmless)

You feel, more than see, a black haze form at the corner of your eyes. Upon touching your intended subject the haze disappears and the creature's eyes become shrouded in blackness.

The subject of this spell gains the ability to see normally in natural and magical darkness, although it does not otherwise improve the subject's ability to see in natural dark or shadowy conditions. The subject ignores the miss chance due to lack of illumination other than total darkness. While the spell is in effect, a jet-black film covers the subject's eyes, a visual effect that gives the spell its name.

Material Component: A pinch of powdered black gemstone of any type.

ECHO SKULL

Divination
Level: Druid 5
Components: V, S, F
Casting Time: 1 standard action
Range: Touch
Target: Animal skull touched
Duration: 1 hour/level (D)
Saving Throw: None
Spell Resistance: Yes (object)

You cast the spell and the animal skull in your hand glows green, the radiance fading quickly. You cast your perception into the skull and see your own form holding it. You switch your viewpoint back and set the skull aside, able to eavesdrop and surprise any trespassers.

You can see, hear, and speak through a tiny dried animal skull at any distance. As long as you and the skull remain on the same plane, you can see and hear as if you were standing where it is, and during your turn you can switch your perception from its location to your own or back again as a free action.

Focus: A tiny dried animal skull.

ECTOPLASMIC ARMOR

Abjuration
Level: Sorcerer/wizard 1
Components: V
Casting Time: 1 standard action
Range: Touch
Target: Creature touched
Duration: 1 hour/level (D)
Saving Throw: Will negates (harmless)
Spell Resistance: No

With a final word, shimmering translucent slime appears around the target and fits to its form like a suit of plate.

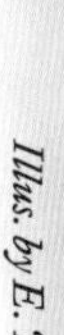

Illus. by E. Polak

The subject of the spell gains a +5 armor bonus to AC, with an additional +1 to the bonus for every four caster levels you have (maximum +9 bonus at 16th level). This armor bonus applies only against incorporeal touch attacks. All other attacks ignore the armor bonus from *ectoplasmic armor.*

ECTOPLASMIC FEEDBACK

Abjuration
Level: Sorcerer/wizard 2
Components: V, S
Casting Time: 1 standard action
Range: Personal
Target: You
Duration: 1 minute/level (D)
Saving Throw: None
Spell Resistance: See text

A shimmering sheath of energy surrounds you, promising harm to incorporeal creatures that touch you.

Any creature that hits you with an incorporeal touch attack takes 1d6 points of force damage +1 point per caster level (maximum +10). If the attacker has spell resistance, it applies to this effect.

EFFULGENT EPURATION

Abjuration
Level: Sorcerer/wizard 9
Components: V, S
Casting Time: 1 standard action
Range: Close (25 ft. + 5 ft./2 levels)
Effect: One magic-absorbing sphere per caster level
Duration: 1 round/level
Saving Throw: Will negates (harmless)
Spell Resistance: Yes (harmless)

Completing the powerful spell, you bring into being floating spheres of silver, like bubbles of mercury.

When you cast this spell, you bring forth one floating, silvery sphere per caster level, each about the size of your head. These spheres hover around you to provide protection from magical effects. As a standard action, you can shift the spell's effect (and thus all the spheres) to any other creature within range. You can shift the effect once per round.

Each of these spheres can absorb and completely negate any spell or spell-like ability, regardless of level, that directly targets the subject. The spheres do not automatically absorb all spells; the subject can choose whether or not to let them absorb any given spell cast upon it. (This option allows the creature to benefit from helpful spells.) Area spells and spells that do not actually have a target cannot be absorbed. Once a sphere has absorbed a spell or spell-like ability, it simply fades away. Only spells and spell-like abilities of deific power can overcome the protection provided by *effulgent epuration.*

ELECTRIC JOLT

Evocation [Electricity]
Level: Sorcerer/wizard 0
Components: V, S
Casting Time: 1 standard action
Range: Close (25 ft. + 5 ft./2 levels)
Effect: Ray
Duration: Instantaneous
Saving Throw: None
Spell Resistance: Yes

A white-hot electric spark dances on your fingertip and then bolts toward your target.

You release a small stroke of electrical energy. You must succeed on a ranged touch attack with the ray to strike a target. The spell deals 1d3 points of electricity damage.

ELECTRIC LOOP

Evocation [Electricity]
Level: Sorcerer/wizard 2
Components: V, S, M
Casting Time: 1 standard action
Range: Close (25 ft. + 5 ft./2 levels)
Targets: One creature/3 levels, each of which is adjacent to another target
Duration: Instantaneous
Saving Throw: Reflex half; see text
Spell Resistance: Yes

Spitting a harsh-sounding arcane word, you snap your fingers, and lightning leaps among your foes.

You create one small stroke of lightning that targets one creature per three caster levels you possess (maximum four creatures). Each target must be in a square adjacent to another target. The spell deals 1d6 points of electricity damage per two caster levels (maximum 5d6) to each target. A creature that fails its Reflex save must make a successful Will save or be stunned for 1 round.

Material Component: A loop of copper wire and a magnet.

ELEMENTAL BODY

Transmutation [see text]
Level: Sorcerer/wizard 7
Components: V, S, M
Casting Time: 1 standard action
Range: Personal
Target: You
Duration: 1 hour/level

Drawing upon the power of the elemental planes, your transform your body in a flash of light.

You can transform your body into a particular type of elemental substance. You and your possessions appear to be made of that element, though in the same general shape and size as your normal appearance.

You gain the following abilities when you cast *elemental body:*

- You have the benefits of the *attune form* spell (page 17) with respect to the appropriate element. If you choose a water body, for example, you can breathe normally on water-dominant planes.
- You are immune to poison, sleep, paralysis, and stunning, and are not subject to extra damage from critical hits or flanking. You gain darkvision out to 60 feet.
- Your creature type remains unchanged, so you are unaffected by spells that target elementals, but you gain the air, earth, fire, or water subtype depending on the elemental substance you chose.

In addition, you gain the following exceptional abilities according to the element chosen:

Air: Fly at your normal speed (perfect maneuverability), air mastery (airborne creatures take a –1 penalty on attack rolls and damage rolls against you).

Earth: Earth mastery (you gain a +1 bonus on attack rolls and damage rolls if both you and your foe touch the ground), push (you can start a bull rush maneuver without provoking attacks of opportunity), +3 natural armor bonus to AC.

Fire: Fire immunity, burn (those you hit in melee and those who attack you with natural weapons must make a Reflex save or catch fire, with a save DC equal to that of a fire elemental of the same size).

Water: Swim at your normal speed, water mastery (you gain a +1 bonus on attack rolls and damage rolls if both you and your opponent touch water), drench (you can use your elemental form to put out nonmagical open flames and dispel magical fire you touch as if casting *dispel magic* at your caster level).

The *elemental body* spell has the descriptor of the element you choose. So, if you choose a body of fire, *elemental body* is a fire spell.

Material Component: A bit of the element in question from a plane other than the one where the spell is being cast.

EMBRACE THE WILD

Transmutation
Level: Druid 2, ranger 1
Components: V
Casting Time: 1 standard action
Range: Personal
Target: You
Duration: 10 minutes/level (D)

While picturing a certain kind of animal in your mind, you cry out in imitation of its most common call. Immediately thereafter, you perceive your surroundings as the animal you imagined would.

Upon casting the spell, you gain the senses of animal creatures. You gain low-light vision and either blindsense out to 30 feet or scent (your choice). You also gain a +2 bonus on Listen and Spot checks.

EMERALD FLAME FIST

Evocation [Fire]
Level: Sorcerer/wizard 7
Components: V, S
Casting Time: 1 standard action
Range: Touch
Target: Creature or object touched
Duration: 1 round/level; see text
Saving Throw: See text
Spell Resistance: Yes

Crackling emerald flames wreathe your hand as you finish the spell, lighting the area around you in a green glow.

Emerald flame fist sends a strong message to your foes

One of your hands bursts into an aura of brilliant emerald flame, shedding light equal to that of a torch. With a standard action, you can make a melee touch attack that deals 3d6 points of fire damage +1 point per caster level (maximum +20). The creature you touch is engulfed by the fiercely hot aura of flame. Each round at the beginning of its turn, the creature is allowed a Fortitude save to prevent further damage, but on a failed save the creature is still engulfed in the flaming aura and again takes 3d6 points of fire damage +1 point per caster level (maximum +20).

An engulfed creature that fails its Fortitude save can use a full-round action to attempt a DC 15 Reflex save, which extinguishes the flames and ends the spell.

You can use this spell to attack an object. Nonmagical, unattended objects are automatically engulfed in green flame and take 3d6 points of fire damage +1 point per caster level each round.

ENERGIZED SHIELD

Abjuration [see text for *lesser energized shield*]
Level: Cleric 3, paladin 2

This spell functions like *lesser energized shield*, except that the energy resistance is 10 and damage dealt is 2d6.

ENERGIZED SHIELD, LESSER

Abjuration [see text]
Level: Cleric 2, paladin 1
Components: V, S, DF
Casting Time: 1 standard action
Range: Touch
Target: Shield touched
Duration: 1 round/level
Saving Throw: None
Spell Resistance: No

A silver aura surrounds the touched shield for a moment before it appears to transform into the chosen type of energy. The shield hums with power.

When this spell is cast, the shield touched appears to be made entirely out of one type of energy (fire, cold, electricity, acid, or sonic). Whoever bears the shield gains resistance 5 against the chosen energy type. Additionally, if the wielder successfully hits someone with the shield with a shield bash attack, the victim takes 1d6 points of the appropriate energy damage in addition to the normal shield bash damage. The energy type must be chosen when the spell is cast and cannot be changed during the duration of the spell. The energy resistance overlaps (and does not stack) with *resist elements*. A given shield cannot be the subject of more than one *lesser energized shield* or *energized shield* spell at the same time.

Illus. by C. Frank

The descriptor of this spell is the same as the energy type you choose when you cast it.

ENERGY EBB

Necromancy [Evil]
Level: Cleric 7, sorcerer/wizard 7
Components: V, S
Casting Time: 1 standard action
Range: Close (25 ft. + 5 ft./2 levels)
Effect: Ray
Duration: 1 round/level
Saving Throw: Fortitude partial; see text
Spell Resistance: Yes

You point your finger and utter the incantation, releasing a black needle of crackling negative energy that suppresses the life force of any living creature it strikes.

This spell functions like *enervation* (PH 226), except the creature struck gains negative levels over an extended period.

You must succeed on a ranged touch attack with the ray to strike a target. If the attack succeeds, the subject initially gains one negative level, then continues to gain another negative level each round thereafter as its life force slowly bleeds away. The drain can be stopped only by a successful DC 23 Heal check or the application of a *heal*, *restoration*, or *greater restoration* spell.

Each round after the first, on your turn, the affected creature can attempt a Fortitude saving throw to end the effect.

If you strike an undead creature, that creature gains 4d4×5 temporary hit points that last for up to 1 hour.

ENERGY IMMUNITY

Abjuration
Level: Cleric 6, druid 6, sorcerer/wizard 7
Components: V, S
Casting Time: 1 standard action
Range: Touch
Target: Creature touched
Duration: 24 hours
Saving Throw: None
Spell Resistance: Yes (harmless)

A sense of security fills you as you complete the spell. As you touch the intended target of the spell, the feeling lingers for a moment before fading.

This abjuration grants a creature and its equipment complete immunity to damage from one of the five energy types—acid, cold, electricity, fire, or sonic. *Energy immunity* absorbs only hit point damage, so the recipient could still suffer side effects such as drowning in acid, being deafened by a sonic attack, or becoming immobilized in ice (and thus helpless).

Energy immunity overlaps *protection from energy* and *resist energy*. As long as *energy immunity* is in effect, the other spells absorb no damage.

ENERGY SPHERES

Evocation [Acid, Cold, Electricity, Fire, Sonic]
Level: Sorcerer/wizard 4
Components: V, S, M
Casting Time: 1 standard action
Range: Close (25 ft. + 5 ft./2 levels)
Effect: Five floating spheres
Duration: 1 round/level or until discharged
Saving Throw: Reflex half; see text
Spell Resistance: Yes; see text

You toss each of the marbles into the air, making the incantation as you do so. Each marble turns a different color—pale green, white, blue, red, and violet—and settles into orbit around your head.

You create a circle of five colored spheres that orbit your head at a distance of 1 foot. These spheres provide as much light as a torch and can be used offensively or defensively. Each sphere corresponds to one of the five types of energy (acid, cold, electricity, fire, sonic).

If used to attack, on your turn as a standard action you can direct one or more spheres to strike a creature or creatures in range, no two of which are more than 30 feet apart. Each sphere deals 5 points of energy damage per five caster levels (maximum 20 points of damage) to a single creature, so an 11th-level caster's sphere deals 10 points of energy damage. The subject can make a Reflex save for half damage against each sphere.

If you are attacked with an effect that causes energy damage, and the sphere of that type of energy is still present, you can have that sphere absorb some of that energy damage. Each sphere grants you energy resistance 5 per five caster levels. If a sphere is used to absorb damage, that sphere is destroyed.

When used to attack a creature with spell resistance, make one spell resistance roll for all spheres that attack the target in a round. Success or failure applies to all spheres striking the creature that round.

Material Component: Five glass marbles.

ENERGY TRANSFORMATION FIELD

Transmutation
Level: Sorcerer/wizard 7
Components: V, S, M, XP
Casting Time: 4 rounds
Range: Close (25 ft. + 5 ft./2 levels)
Area: 40-ft.-radius spread
Duration: Permanent
Saving Throw: None
Spell Resistance: Yes

You hold the eye in your palm, sprinkle it with blood and diamonds, and speak the words. Slowly it rises from your hand, emitting a soft beam that illuminates the chosen area. Then it disappears, and you place the spell within the magic trap.

You create a lingering zone of transformative magic that absorbs magic energy from magic items or spellcasting and uses it to power another spell tied to that location. For example, you could have an *energy transformation field* tied to a *summon monster* V spell that would summon a monster when the field had absorbed enough magic.

The field absorbs the magic of spells cast, spell-like or supernatural abilities that are activated, and magic items used within its dimensions. Each source of magic provides spell levels of energy to the field equal to the spell level of the effect used. Supernatural abilities that emulate spells provide energy equal to the spell level of the effect. Supernatural abilities that do not emulate spells provide energy equal to the HD of the creature using the ability. For example, a cast *fireball* spell or a charge from a *wand of fireball* would add three spell levels to the field's store, a potion of cure *light wounds* would add one, and a *wish* from a *ring of three wishes* would add nine. Items that don't have a clearly defined spell level (such as the effects of most rods) use the prerequisite caster level needed to create that item (so an *immovable rod* would provide two spell levels every time it was activated because of its *levitate* prerequisite). Effects that are absorbed give no indication of where the magic went; they simply vanish.

The field absorbs only magic that is actually used within its area. Ongoing magical effects that enter the area, including spells cast from outside the area into the field or continually functioning items such as a *+1 mace*, are often visibly reduced, but do not have their actual effects hindered. For example, a *continual flame* would dim slightly, but its overall magic would not be affected.

An *energy transformation field* has a single spell linked to it. When the field has absorbed spell levels equal to the spell level of its linked spell, it automatically casts that spell at a point within the field designated by you at the time of the casting of the field. This expends those absorbed spell levels (although unused levels remain until they are used or expire). The cast spell functions as if cast by you in terms of duration and all level-based spell effects. Absorbed spell levels fade at a rate of one per day if not used. The field automatically triggers its linked spell if it has enough stored spell levels and the duration of its previous casting has expired. If a linked spell requires concentration to maintain, the field expends one spell level for every hour of concentration (the field's concentration is interrupted only by its complete destruction). Spells that require a target will target the living creature nearest to the field.

Typical spells linked to an energy transformation field are *blindness/deafness*, *fireball*, *suggestion*, *summon monster*, or *wall of force*. Spells that have a costly material component or an XP cost cannot be linked to a field, but those with a costly focus can if the focus object is present within the field (typically sealed into a wall or in a secret compartment).

Only *Mordenkainen's disjunction*, *limited wish*, *wish*, or similar spells can destroy the *energy transformation field*. Spells of lower level, such as *dispel magic* and *greater dispel magic*, are absorbed by it, and an *antimagic field* prevents it from absorbing magical energy within the field but does not otherwise hamper this spell. If two or more field spells share an overlapping area, each field has an equal chance of absorbing a spell effect in that area.

Material Component: Three drops of your blood, an eye from any humanoid, and 5,000 gp worth of powdered diamond.

XP *Cost*: 250 XP.

ENERGY VORTEX

Evocation [see text]
Level: Cleric 3, druid 3
Components: V, S
Casting Time: 1 standard action
Range: 20 ft.
Targets: All creatures within a 20-ft.-radius burst centered on you
Duration: Instantaneous
Saving Throw: Reflex half
Spell Resistance: Yes

Energy wells up inside you and explodes outward in a furious burst.

When you cast *energy vortex*, you choose one of four energy types: acid, cold, electricity, or fire. A blast of that energy type bursts in all directions from you, dealing 1d8 points of damage +1 point per caster level (maximum +20) to nearby creatures other than you. If you are willing to take the damage yourself, you deal twice as

This gnome druid chose to cast a cold version of energy vortex

Illus. by R. Horsley

much damage. You don't get a Reflex save, but spell resistance applies, as do any resistances and immunities you have to the energy type.

The descriptor of this spell is the same as the energy type you choose when you cast it.

ENERVATING BREATH

Necromancy
Level: Sorcerer/wizard 9
Components: S
Casting Time: 1 swift action
Range: Personal
Target: Your breath weapon
Duration: 1 round

Your breath weapon explodes from your mouth, brilliant but mixed with sharp spikes of living darkness.

For this spell to function, you must have a breath weapon, either as a supernatural ability or as the result of casting a spell such as *dragon breath* (page 73). When you successfully cast this spell, you can modify your breath weapon so that it is laced with negative energy. In addition to the normal energy damage your breath weapon deals, creatures that fail their saving throws against the breath weapon gain 2d4 negative levels.

If the subject gains at least as many negative levels as it has Hit Dice, it dies. Each negative level gives a creature the following penalties: –1 penalty on attack rolls, saving throws, skill checks, ability checks, and effective level (for determining the power, duration, DC, and other details of spells or special abilities). Additionally, a spellcaster loses one spell or spell slot from her highest available level.

Assuming the subjects survive, they regain lost levels after a number of hours equal to your caster level. Ordinarily, negative levels have a chance of permanently draining the subject's level, but the negative levels from *enervating breath* don't last long enough to do so.

If an undead creature is caught within the breath weapon, it gains 2d4×5 temporary hit points before taking damage from the breath weapon. These temporary hit points last for up to 1 hour.

ENHANCE FAMILIAR

Universal
Level: Sorcerer/wizard 3
Components: V, S
Casting Time: 1 standard action
Range: Touch
Target: Familiar touched
Duration: 1 hour/level
Saving Throw: None
Spell Resistance: Yes (harmless)

After you touch the target familiar, the creature perks up and appears more alert.

You infuse your familiar with vigor, granting it a +2 competence bonus on saves, attack rolls, and melee damage rolls, as well as a +2 dodge bonus to Armor Class.

ENHANCE WILD SHAPE

Transmutation
Level: Druid 4
Components: V, S
Casting Time: 1 minute
Range: Personal
Target: You
Duration: 1 hour/level

You call upon the primordial energies of nature to fill you with the raw power of nature. A feral feeling grows within you, seeking release.

This spell infuses your wild shape ability with magical energy, magnifying and enhancing its power. The type of enhancement must be chosen at the time the spell is cast and cannot be changed once the spell is in effect. The next time you activate your wild shape ability (during the duration of *enhance wild shape*), this spell enhances your new form in the way you selected. The enhancement to your wild shape remains as long as you stay in that form (or until the spell's duration expires) but does not apply to your next wild shape form. If you do not activate your wild shape ability during the duration of *enhance wild shape*, the spell has no effect.

You select one of the following enhancements when you cast this spell.

- Assume the form of a plant with your next wild shape.
- Gain the extraordinary abilities of the new form.
- The new form assumed is stronger than normal and gains a +2 bonus to Strength.
- The new form assumed is more agile than normal and gains a +2 bonus to Dexterity.
- The new form assumed is healthier than normal and gains a +2 bonus to Constitution.

A druid can be affected by more than one *enhance wild shape* spell at a time, but a different wild shape enhancement must be chosen each time.

ENLARGE PERSON, GREATER

Transmutation
Level: Sorcerer/wizard 5
Range: Touch
Duration: 1 hour/level (D)

Your intended subject begins to grow rapidly as you complete the spell.

This spell functions like *enlarge person* (PH 226), except as noted above.

ENRAGE ANIMAL

Enchantment (Compulsion) [Mind-Affecting]
Level: Druid 1, ranger 1
Components: V, S
Casting Time: 1 standard action
Range: Medium (100 ft. + 10 ft./level)
Target: One animal
Duration: Concentration +1 round/level
Saving Throw: None
Spell Resistance: Yes

You feel inexplicably angry as you near the conclusion of the spell's casting. The feeling subsides slightly as you release the spell into your target.

Enrage animal affects only creatures of the animal type and bestows a +4 morale bonus to Strength and Constitution, a +2 morale bonus on Will saves, and a –2 penalty to Armor Class. This effect is otherwise identical to a barbarian's rage (PH 25), except that the animal is not fatigued at the end of the rage.

ENTANGLING STAFF

Transmutation

Level: Druid 3, sorcerer/wizard 4

Components: V, S, F

Casting Time: 1 swift action

Range: Touch

Target: Quarterstaff touched

Duration: 1 round/level (D)

Saving Throw: Fortitude negates (harmless, object)

Spell Resistance: Yes (harmless)

Rapping your staff with a knuckle, you cause it to sprout wriggling vines that grab and lash at the air.

Each time you successfully strike a foe with the staff (a normal melee attack), you deal normal damage and can attempt to start a grapple as a free action without provoking attacks of opportunity. This grapple attempt does not require a separate touch attack. You gain a +8 bonus on grapple checks you cause by striking a foe with the entangling staff. You can attempt to grapple creatures up to one size category larger than you.

If your grapple check succeeds, your quarterstaff's vines constrict your foe, dealing 2d6 points of damage (you can choose to deal nonlethal damage instead of normal damage if you wish). You then have two choices:

Release: You release your opponent from the grapple. Some vines remain clinging to your foe, leaving it entangled for the duration of the spell. You can attack different enemies in later rounds with the staff, potentially grappling and constricting or entangling them.

Maintain: You maintain your hold. In subsequent rounds, you deal constriction damage with a successful grapple check. You can then choose to release or maintain the hold again.

Focus: A quarterstaff.

ENTICE GIFT

Enchantment [Mind-Affecting]

Level: Bard 2, Greed 2, sorcerer/wizard 2

Components: V, S

Casting Time: 1 standard action

Range: Close (25 ft. + 5 ft./2 levels)

Target: One creature

Duration: 1 round

Saving Throw: Will negates

Spell Resistance: Yes

You cast the spell and a purple glow appears in your mark's eyes. You hold out your hand and demand the object it holds in a compelling voice.

Entangling staff makes a simple piece of wood into a surprisingly versatile weapon

You enchant a creature so that it feels suddenly compelled to give you what it is holding when you cast this spell. On the creature's next action, it moves as close to you as it can get in a single round and offers you the object as a standard action. This spell allows you to act out of turn and accept the "gift" if the creature reaches you to hand you the object (assuming you have a free hand and can accept it). The subject defends itself normally and acts as it wishes on subsequent rounds, including attempting to get the object back if desired. If the subject is prevented from doing as the spell compels, the spell has no effect. For example, if the subject is paralyzed and cannot move or drop the item, nothing happens.

ENVELOPING COCOON

Evocation [Force]

Level: Druid 6

Components: V, S, M

Casting Time: 1 standard action

Range: Medium (100 ft. + 10 ft./level)

Effect: Cocoon of force around one Large or smaller creature

Duration: 1 round/level (D)

Saving Throw: Reflex negates

Spell Resistance: Yes

Crushing a caterpillar between your fingers, you create a tight cocoon of shimmering blue-green energy around your foe.

A cocoon of force encloses a creature of size Large or smaller, containing it for the spell's duration or until the cocoon is destroyed. The cocoon has hardness 10 and 10 hit points per caster level. The enveloping cocoon prevents the creature trapped inside from moving or casting spells with somatic components. The cocoon is too confining to permit effective attacks with anything larger than a natural or light weapon (and the creature inside can attack only the cocoon in any event).

You can attach a second spell to the cocoon by casting it at the cocoon. When the *enveloping cocoon* spell ends or is dismissed, the attached spell automatically affects the creature inside, with no save allowed (although spell resistance, if any, still applies). If the cocoon is destroyed before it is dismissed or the spell duration ends, the attached spell is wasted.

Any of the following spells from this book can be attached to an enveloping cocoon: *infestation of maggots, languor, miasma,* and *phantasmal disorientation.* In addition, a cocoon can be used in conjunction with these spells from the *Player's Handbook*: *baleful polymorph, blight, contagion, dominate animal, flame strike,* and *poison* (the subject fails the initial save but can attempt the second save).

Material Component: A live caterpillar.

Illus. by M. Phillippi

ERADICATE EARTH

Abjuration [Earth]
Level: Sorcerer/wizard 3
Components: V, S, M
Casting Time: 1 standard action
Range: 40 ft.
Area: 40-ft.-radius burst centered on you
Duration: Instantaneous
Saving Throw: Fortitude half
Spell Resistance: Yes

You grasp the stone firmly and point your fist outward. You feel the stone vanish, and a huge, silent explosion ripples through the air.

A shock wave radiates from you, seismically damaging all nearby creatures that have the earth subtype. Any such creature that is within the area of the spell takes 1d8 points of damage per caster level (maximum 10d8).

Material Component: A small stone.

ESSENCE OF THE RAPTOR

Transmutation
Level: Druid 4
Components: V, S
Casting Time: 1 standard action
Range: Personal
Target: You
Duration: 10 minutes/level (D)

You infuse yourself with the essence of a prehistoric raptor. New sensations assault you as you notice sounds, smells, and other elements of your surroundings that you could not perceive before.

Your physical appearance does not change. Your speed increases to 60 feet (if it is already 60 feet or faster, it does not change), and you gain a +8 bonus on Hide, Jump, Listen, Spot, and Survival checks.

You also gain the scent ability (MM 314).

ETHEREAL BREATH

Transmutation
Level: Sorcerer/wizard 5
Components: S
Casting Time: 1 swift action
Range: Personal
Target: Your breath weapon
Duration: 1 round

After the casting of ethereal breath, a dragon's breath weapon affects incorporeal creatures

Illus. by R. Spears

You exhale a blast of fire down the corridor, but none of the furnishings take any damage. On another plane of existence, a horde of ethereal marauders is now nothing more than smoldering meat.

For this spell to function, you must have a breath weapon, either as a supernatural ability or as the result of casting a spell such as *dragon breath* (page 73). When you successfully cast this spell, you can modify your breath weapon to manifest on the Ethereal Plane instead of on the Material Plane. (You must be on the Material Plane, or on another plane with a coexistent Ethereal Plane, for this spell to function.) Your breath weapon affects ethereal creatures as if they were material, and does not affect material creatures in its area.

ETHEREAL CHAMBER

Evocation [Force]
Level: Sorcerer/wizard 2
Components: V, S, M
Casting Time: 1 standard action
Range: Close (25 ft. + 5 ft./2 levels)
Target: One ethereal creature
Duration: 1 minute/level
Saving Throw: Reflex negates
Spell Resistance: Yes

You pinch a piece of glass between your fingers and as it crumbles to nothingness, a glassy prison springs into being.

You create a translucent prison of pure crystalline force around a target on the Ethereal Plane. You must be able to see or otherwise target the creature you wish to affect.

The subject affected by the chamber cannot move on either the Ethereal Plane or its coterminous planes for the duration of the spell but is otherwise unaffected. The subject cannot move onto another plane while inside the chamber, including the Material Plane.

The subject within the crystalline prison cannot make physical attacks or be attacked and is unaffected by most spells and supernatural abilities. Gaze attacks and sonic spells function through the walls of the crystalline prison, but a creature within the chamber gains a +2 bonus on saving throws.

The target of *ethereal chamber* can break the crystalline prison by making a Strength check (DC 10 + caster level). A *disintegrate* spell destroys an *ethereal chamber.*

Material Component: A piece of translucent glass.

ETHEREAL MOUNT

Conjuration (Creation)
Level: Bard 4, sorcerer/wizard 4
Effect: One quasi-real mount, plus one additional mount/2 levels

Your spell draws ether into form, creating a misty mount for you to ride.

This spell functions like *phantom steed* (PH 260), except as noted here. You call into being one or more quasi-real mounts. These mounts accept only you and those that you designate as riders. The mounts appear as horses or any other commonly ridden mounts, but they have a foggy, almost translucent nature, and their colors shift across the spectrum over time.

These mounts have AC 18 (–1 size, +4 natural armor, +5 Dex), and hit points equal to 10 + your caster level. They do not fight and have no attacks. If reduced to 0 hit points, an *ethereal mount* melts into the ethereal fog from which it came.

An ethereal mount has a speed of 240 feet on the Ethereal Plane and can carry its rider's weight plus 10 pounds per level. (If the Deep Ethereal is used in your cosmology, then the amount of time to reach destinations is halved while on an ethereal mount.)

EVIL GLARE

Necromancy [Evil, Fear, Mind-Affecting]
Level: Cleric 7, sorcerer/wizard 7
Components: V, S, DF
Casting Time: 1 standard action
Range: 30 feet
Target: Living creatures
Duration: 1 round/level; see text
Saving Throw: Will negates
Spell Resistance: Yes

You cast this spell and your eyes begin to tingle, brimming with dark energy. You shoot a glance at your rival, and she freezes in her tracks from your malignant glare.

Immediately upon completion of the casting of this spell, you target a living creature within range with your glare; that creature becomes paralyzed with fear for 1d8 rounds. You must be able to see the creature, and it must be able to see you (though it need not meet your gaze).

Once per round after that for the duration of the spell, you can target another creature with your glare as a standard action. You can't target the same creature twice with a single casting of the spell, regardless of the outcome of its saves.

EXACTING SHOT

Transmutation
Level: Ranger 2
Components: V, S
Casting Time: 1 swift action
Range: Touch
Target: Ranged weapon touched
Duration: 1 minute/level
Saving Throw: Will negates (harmless, object)
Spell Resistance: Yes (harmless, object)

As you complete the complicated ritual of the spell you see in your mind's eye the vital areas of your favored enemy's anatomy.

All rolls made to confirm critical threats by the target weapon against your favored enemies automatically succeed, so every threat is a critical hit. The affected weapon also ignores any miss chance due to concealment whenever you fire at a favored enemy (unless the target has total concealment, in which case the normal miss chance applies). If the ranged weapon or the projectile fired has any magical effect or property related to critical hits, this spell has no effect on it.

EXCAVATE

Transmutation
Level: Sorcerer/wizard 8
Components: V, S, M
Casting Time: 1 standard action
Range: Close (25 ft. + 5 ft./2 levels)
Effect: One 5-ft.-by-5-ft. opening, 1 ft./level deep
Duration: Instantaneous
Saving Throw: None
Spell Resistance: No

You toss the bit of earth against the wall and it glitters and burns as it strikes the stone. The rock vaporizes where it hits and a passage opens before you, burrowing into the wall.

As with *passwall* (PH 259), this spell allows you to create a passage through wooden, plaster, or stone walls, but not through metal or harder materials. If a wall's thickness is more than 1 foot per caster level, then a single *excavate* spell simply makes a niche or short tunnel with the stated dimensions. Several *excavate* spells can be used in succession to breach very thick walls by forming a continuing passage. Unlike *passwall*, *excavate* is an instantaneous effect that does not end and cannot be dispelled; any passage it creates is permanent.

Material Component: A pinch of excavated earth.

EXPEDITIOUS RETREAT, SWIFT

Transmutation
Level: Bard 1, sorcerer/wizard 1
Components: V
Casting Time: 1 swift action
Duration: 1 round

In a breathless voice you call out, as if you were already running a race.

This spell functions like *expeditious retreat* (PH 228), except as noted above.

EXPLOSIVE CASCADE

Evocation [Fire]
Level: Sorcerer/wizard 4
Components: V, S, M
Casting Time: 1 standard action
Range: Close (25 ft. + 5 ft./2 levels)
Area: One 5-ft. square/level, all of which must be connected in one continuous path (S)
Duration: Instantaneous
Saving Throw: Reflex half
Spell Resistance: Yes

You hold the metal tube out from your body and cast the spell. A bright ball of flame manifests and skips across the battlefield, immolating targets in its path.

You create a path of flame when you cast this spell. Anything along this path takes 1d6 points of fire damage per caster level (maximum 10d6) to all creatures and objects it touches. The flame lights up the area as if it were a torch, and small sparks and decaying flames remain in the area for 1 round, shedding light as candles but dealing no damage. A creature or object can be affected only once by each casting of this spell.

If the damage from the flame destroys an interposing barrier, the flame can move beyond the barrier if it has area remaining.

Material Component: Bat guano, sulfur, and copper packed into a metal tube with one closed end.

EXTEND TENTACLES

Transmutation
Level: Cleric 2, sorcerer/wizard 2
Components: V
Casting Time: 1 standard action
Range: Personal
Target: You
Duration: 1 round/level

You wriggle your tentacles in a complicated choreography of movement, and your tentacles lengthen.

This spell lengthens your tentacles, increasing the reach of your tentacle attacks by 5 feet. The tentacles attack as normal. If you do not already have tentacles, the spell has no effect on you.

EXTRACT WATER ELEMENTAL

Transmutation [Water]
Level: Druid 6, sorcerer/wizard 6
Components: V, S
Casting Time: 1 standard action
Range: Close (25 ft. + 5 ft./2 levels)
Target: One living creature
Duration: Instantaneous
Saving Throw: Fortitude half
Spell Resistance: Yes

Calling upon the essence of elemental water, you surround your target creature with a swirling blue and red aura. The aura seeps into the creature a moment before water spurts forth from its pores. It cries out in pain.

This brutal spell causes the targeted creature to dehydrate horribly as the moisture in its body is forcibly extracted through its eyes, nostrils, mouth, and pores. This deals 1d6 points of damage per caster level (maximum 20d6), or half damage on a successful Fortitude save. If the targeted creature is slain by this spell, the extracted moisture is transformed into a water elemental of a size equal to the slain creature (up to Huge). The water elemental is under your control, as if you summoned it, and disappears after 1 minute.

This spell has no effect on living creatures with the fire subtype.

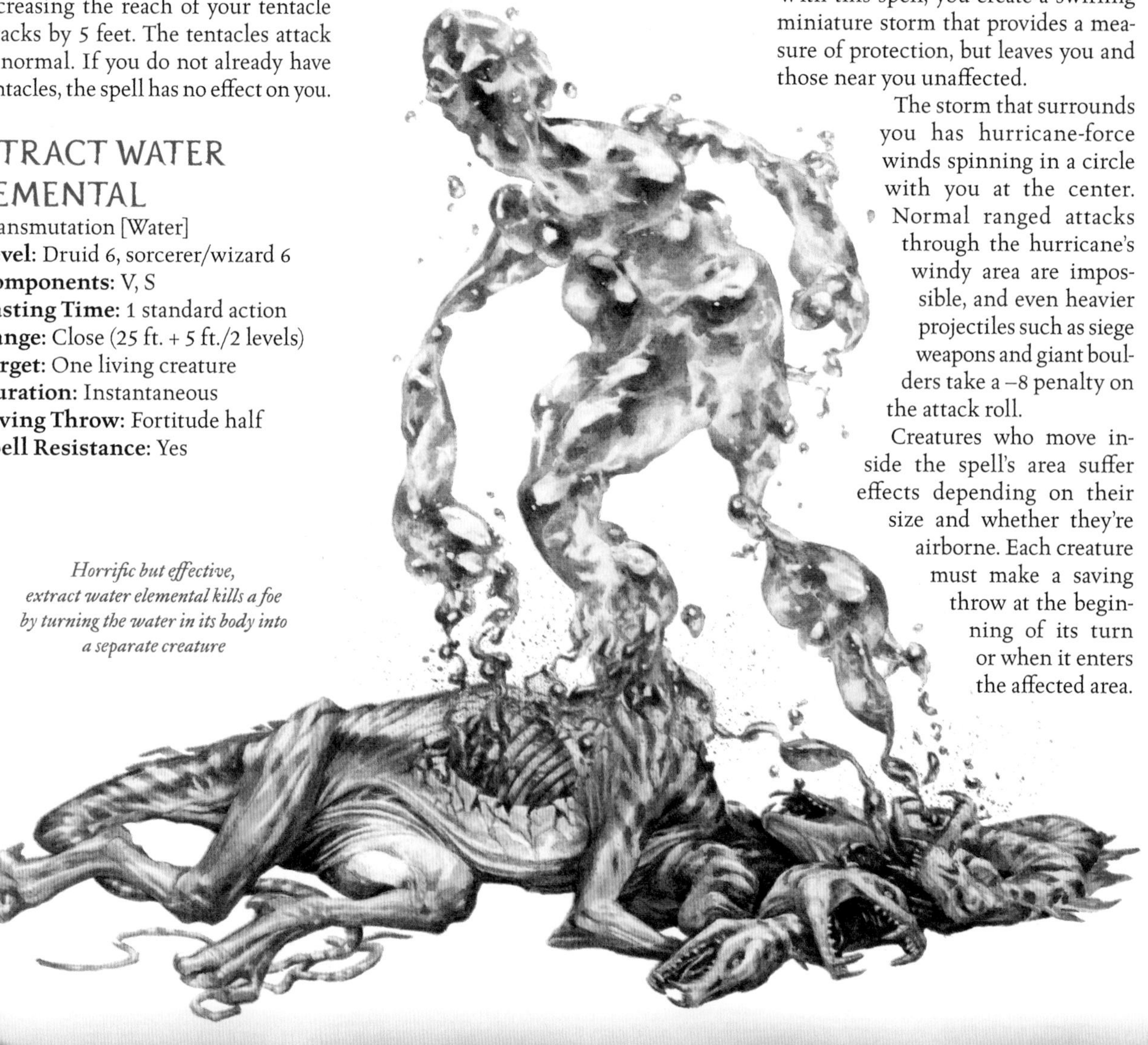

Horrific but effective, extract water elemental kills a foe by turning the water in its body into a separate creature

Illus. by J. Jarvis

EYE OF THE HURRICANE

Abjuration [Air]
Level: Druid 4
Components: V, S
Casting Time: 1 standard action
Range: 40 ft.
Area: 40-ft.-radius emanation centered on you, with 10-ft.-radius quiet area centered on you
Duration: 1 round/level
Saving Throw: Fortitude negates; see text
Spell Resistance: Yes

Your voice trails off into whispers as you near the end of the spell's complex ritual. The whispers begin to build upon one another, echoing in the air around you, swirling and twisting until they become a steady cacophony. The wind gathers speed, creating a spherical vortex around you.

With this spell, you create a swirling miniature storm that provides a measure of protection, but leaves you and those near you unaffected.

The storm that surrounds you has hurricane-force winds spinning in a circle with you at the center. Normal ranged attacks through the hurricane's windy area are impossible, and even heavier projectiles such as siege weapons and giant boulders take a –8 penalty on the attack roll.

Creatures who move inside the spell's area suffer effects depending on their size and whether they're airborne. Each creature must make a saving throw at the beginning of its turn or when it enters the affected area.

Medium or smaller creatures must succeed on a Fortitude save or be knocked 1d4×10 feet away from the eye of the hurricane's center and take 1d4 points of nonlethal damage per 10 feet traveled in this manner. Creatures blown away are knocked prone as well. Flying creatures are blown back 2d6×10 feet and take 2d6 points of nonlethal damage.

Large creatures must succeed on a Fortitude save or be knocked prone by the force of the wind. Flying creatures are instead blown back 1d6×10 feet.

Huge creatures must succeed on a Fortitude save or be checked. Flying creatures are instead blown back 1d6×5 feet.

Gargantuan and Colossal creatures can move through the spell's area without adverse consequences.

Even creatures that succeed on their saving throws must attempt them again whenever they start a turn inside the spell's area or whenever they move back into it.

The spell's area is effectively a sphere. Although the area is centered on you, you're not within the wind. If you move, the eye of the hurricane moves as well to keep you in the center. If you cast *eye of the hurricane* so that creatures are inside the eye when the spell begins, they must make Fortitude saves when your movement brings the area of wind upon them. Thereafter, if you move the spell area into a square occupied by another creature, that creature makes a Fortitude save at the beginning of its next turn (assuming the windy area of the spell is still on it).

EYE OF POWER

Divination (Scrying)
Level: Sorcerer/wizard 9
Components: V, S, M
Casting Time: 10 minutes
Range: Unlimited
Effect: Magical sensor
Duration: 1 minute/level (D)
Saving Throw: None
Spell Resistance: No

Your invocation creates a miniature floating eye of faintly glowing blue energy. Spying your enemy from the safety of your magical sensor, you unleash your spell.

This spell functions like *arcane eye* (PH 200), except as noted here. You can cast any spell of 3rd level or lower that has a range other than personal through the eye. Any spell so cast functions as though it had been cast from the eye's location rather than yours. Casting any spell of higher than 3rd level through the eye not only produces no effect (though the spell is still expended), but it destroys the *eye of power* and ends the spell.

Unlike an *arcane eye*, an *eye of power* is visible and corporeal, so it can be destroyed. The eye is a Fine object with AC 18 and 77 hit points. It uses your save bonuses for saving throws.

Material Component: A bit of bat fur.

EYES OF THE KING

Conjuration (Summoning) [Evil]
Level: Hunger 6
Components: V, S, M
Casting Time: 1 minute
Range: Unlimited
Effect: Magical sensor
Duration: Concentration + 5 rounds, up to 1 minute/level (D)
Saving Throw: None
Spell Resistance: No

Letting a bit of bat fur loose to float on the air, you summon huge, glowing green bats to serve as your eyes.

You summon four fiendish dire bats (MM 62) that blaze with a faint ghoul-green light (they glow as bright as a candle). These fiendish dire bats have damage reduction 5/magic; resistance to acid 5 and fire 5; spell resistance 9; and a smite good attack that provides a +4 bonus on one damage roll.

The bats allow you to see through their eyes, from their perspective, using your own visual senses. If you have darkvision, low-light vision, or spells cast that enhance your visual senses, such as *true seeing* or *see invisibility*, you continue to gain the benefit of those abilities or spells through the eyes of your bat minions. The bats also give you the benefit of their blindsense ability for the purpose of viewing their surroundings for the duration of the spell.

You can summon the bats at any point you can see, but they can then travel outside your line of sight without hindrance. Even while outside your line of sight, they follow your mental directions on where to explore. The dire bats travel together, never separating by more than 40 feet. They fly with a speed of 40 feet if viewing an area ahead as a human would (primarily looking at the floor) or at half speed (speed 20 feet) if examining the ceiling and walls as well as the floor ahead. The bats can travel in any direction as long as the spell lasts.

You must concentrate to control the dire bats. If you do not concentrate, the bats move to attack the closest active creature. Once concentration lapses, the spell ends 5 rounds later.

Material Component: A bit of bat fur.

FAITH HEALING

Conjuration (Healing)
Level: Blackguard 1, cleric 1, paladin 1
Components: V, S
Casting Time: 1 standard action
Range: Touch
Target: Living creature touched
Duration: Instantaneous
Saving Throw: Will half (harmless)
Spell Resistance: Yes (harmless)

You place your hands on your loyal acolyte and blue-silver radiance discharges from your hands. The horrendous wounds across his chest heal, leaving no scar.

When laying your hand upon a living creature, you channel positive energy that cures 8 points of damage +1 point per caster level (up to +5). The spell works only on a creature that worships the same deity as you. A target with no deity or a different deity from yours is unaffected by the spell, even if the target would normally be harmed by positive energy.

FALSE GRAVITY

Transmutation
Level: Sorcerer/wizard 3
Components: V, S, M
Casting Time: 1 standard action
Range: Touch
Target: Creature touched
Duration: 1 minute/level
Saving Throw: Will negates (harmless)
Spell Resistance: Yes (harmless)

You clatter the magnets in your hand and set your foot on the wall. Your second step carries you onto the wall, and you can walk up it with ease.

The subject of this spell can travel on any solid surface as though that surface possessed its own gravity. For example, the subject could walk or even run up a wall as though the wall were a perfectly level floor. The subject can switch "down" as often as it likes during the spell's duration, though only once per round, as a free action. Unattended objects fall, as normal.

The subject of *false gravity* can fly by choosing a solid surface and letting itself fall through the air toward it. A character "flying" in this fashion moves at 30 feet per round and can make one turn, in any direction, once per round, by redefining its personal gravity. A creature falling in this fashion loses all "downward" momentum when it changes its gravity.

Material Component: A pair of magnets.

FAMILIAR POCKET

Universal
Level: Sorcerer/wizard 1
Components: V, S, M
Casting Time: 1 standard action
Range: Touch
Target: One container or garment with a pocket touched
Duration: 1 hour/level (D)
Saving Throw: None
Spell Resistance: No

You move your hand along the mouth of the pocket intended for your familiar, and a line of glowing white energy follows in its wake. The glow fades, and the space seems strangely larger inside than a normal pocket.

When you cast this spell, a garment or container becomes a safe haven for a Tiny or smaller familiar. The spell turns the target pocket into a comfortable extradimensional space (about 1 cubic foot). The familiar can fit inside the space without creating any noticeable bulge in the item. Whenever the familiar is touching you, you can whisk it inside the space as a free action by speaking a command word chosen by you when the spell is cast. If the familiar can speak, it can command itself inside. As a free action, you can call the familiar forth or it can leave the space on its own.

Once inside, the familiar has total cover and total concealment, and as a free action, you or the familiar can further seal the space to make it airtight and waterproof. The air supply inside the sealed space lasts for 1 hour, but with the pocket unsealed, the familiar can remain inside indefinitely. The familiar cannot attack or cast spells from within the space, but can use supernatural or spell-like abilities as normal (provided they don't require line of sight, which the pocket blocks). You continue to gain the special ability granted by your familiar. While inside the pocket, the familiar continues to benefit from the share spells ability as if it were adjacent to you.

The spell ends if the *familiar pocket* is placed within or taken into another extradimensional space (such as a *portable hole*). If your familiar is within the pocket when the spell duration expires or if the spell ends abnormally (as above), the familiar appears in your space unharmed.

Material Component: A tiny golden needle and a strip of fine cloth given a half twist and fastened at the ends.

Fangs of the vampire king turns a spellcaster into a bloodsucking horror

Illus. by C. Frank

FANGS OF THE VAMPIRE KING

Transmutation [Evil]
Level: Assassin 3, blackguard 3, Deathbound 3
Components: V, S
Casting Time: 1 standard action
Range: Personal
Target: You
Duration: 1 minute/level

Hissing an evil laugh, you sprout sharp fangs to drain the blood of your foes.

You grow vampirelike fangs that allow you to make bite attacks as a natural attack. Your bite attack deals 1d6 points of damage + your Str modifier, and 1 point of Constitution damage. If you make a full attack with other weapons, you can make a bite attack as a natural secondary attack (–5 penalty on the attack roll).

FANTASTIC MACHINE

Conjuration [Creation]
Level: Craft 6, Gnome 6
Components: V, S, DF
Casting Time: 1 standard action
Range: Medium (100 ft. + 10 ft./level)
Effect: A 10-ft. machine
Duration: 1 minute/level (D)
Saving Throw: None
Spell Resistance: No

Your spell generates an illusory, many-armed, noisy, massive mechanical construct of impressive appearance.

This spell creates a bizarre, but useful, machine that you can command to perform any simple, physical task that can be described in twenty-five words or less. You can order the machine to perform the same task over and over, but you can't change the task. You must specify the task when you cast the spell. The machine always acts on your turn in the initiative order. (It can act during the turn you cast the spell.)

The machine functions as a Large animated object (MM 13). It trundles over the ground at a speed of 40 feet. It can swim or fly at a speed of 10 feet (clumsy). It has 22 hit points, AC 14 (–1 size, +5 natural), and hardness 10. Its saving throw modifiers are Fortitude +1, Reflex +1, Will –4.

The machine has a Strength of 16. A light load for the machine is up to 172 pounds; a medium load is 173–346 pounds; and a heavy load is 347–520 pounds. The machine can fly or swim only when lightly loaded.

The machine can lift a weight of up to 1,040 pounds to a height of 15 feet. It can push or drag 2,600 pounds. It can excavate 7,000 pounds of loose rock each minute (which is sufficient to clear a 5-by-5-by-5-foot space in 3 rounds). It can excavate sand or loose soil at twice that rate.

The machine has an attack bonus of +5 and can make one slam attack each round that deals 1d8+4 points of damage. It deals triple slam damage (3d8+12) against stone or metal. The machine can hurl Small rocks (if any are at hand) with an attack bonus of +3. Its range increment is 150 feet, and it can throw a rock up to 10 range increments. A thrown rock deals 2d6+4 points of damage.

FANTASTIC MACHINE, GREATER

Conjuration [Creation]
Level: Craft 9

This spell functions like *fantastic machine*, but you can concentrate on controlling the machine's every action or specify a simple program, such as to collect all the logs in an area and stack them in a neat pile, plow a field, drive piles, or the like. The machine can perform only fairly simple physical tasks. Directing the machine's actions or changing its programmed movement is a standard action for you. The machine always acts on your turn in the initiative order. (It can act during the turn you cast the spell.)

Except where noted below, the machine functions as a Large animated object (MM 13) constructed from adamantine. It trundles over the ground at a speed of 60 feet. It can swim or fly at a speed of 20 feet (poor). It has 16 HD, 88 hit points, AC 20 (–1 size, +11 natural), and hardness 20. Its saving throw modifiers are Fortitude +5, Reflex +5, and Will +0.

The machine has a Strength of 22. A light load for the machine is up to 346 pounds, a medium load is 347–692 pounds, and a heavy load is 693–1,040 pounds. The machine can fly or swim only when lightly loaded.

The machine can lift a weight of up to 2,080 pounds to a height of 15 feet. It can push or drag 5,200 pounds. It can excavate 20,000 pounds of loose rock each minute (which is sufficient to clear a 5-by-5-by-5-foot space in 1 round). It can excavate sand or loose soil at twice that rate.

The machine makes slam attacks with an attack bonus of +17/+12 for 1d8+9 points of damage. It deals triple slam damage (3d8+27) against stone or metal. The machine can hurl Small rocks (if any are at hand) with an attack bonus of +12/+7. Its range increment is 150 feet, and it can throw a rock up to 10 range increments. A thrown rock deals 2d6+9 points of damage.

FAVOR OF THE MARTYR

Necromancy
Level: Paladin 4
Components: V, S
Casting Time: 1 standard action
Range: Medium (100 ft. + 10 ft./level)
Target: One willing creature
Duration: 1 minute/level
Saving Throw: None
Spell Resistance: Yes (harmless)

Calling upon the saints of your order, you imbue the person in need with the power to resist the dire forces arrayed against you.

The subject gains immunity to nonlethal damage, charm and compulsion effects, and attacks that function specifically by causing pain, such as the *wrack* spell (see page 243). It is further immune to effects that would cause it to be dazed, exhausted, fatigued, nauseated, sickened, staggered, or stunned. The subject remains conscious at –1 to –9 hit points and can take a single action each round while in that state, and does not lose hit points for acting. If any of the above conditions were in effect on the subject at the time of casting, they are suspended for the spell's duration. (Thus, an unconscious subject becomes conscious and functional.) When the spell ends, any effects suspended by the spell that have not expired in the interim (such as the fatigued condition, which normally requires 8 hours of rest to recover from) return. Effects that expired during the duration of this spell do not resume when it ends.

In addition to these effects, the subject gains the benefit of the Endurance feat for the duration of the spell.

FAVORABLE SACRIFICE

Abjuration
Level: Cleric 3
Components: V, S, M
Casting Time: 1 standard action
Range: Touch
Target: Creature touched
Duration: 1 hour/level
Saving Throw: Will negates (harmless)
Spell Resistance: Yes (harmless)

The gems vaporize in your hand as you intone the spell. The rising vapors surround your ally, granting him the blessing of your beliefs.

The subject receives the protection of a divine power commensurate with the value of the expended material component. Only one of the benefits described below applies per casting of this spell; they do not stack.

By expending 250 gp, you grant the subject damage reduction 5/magic; resistance to acid, cold, electricity, fire, and sonic 10; and spell resistance equal to your caster level.

By expending 1,000 gp, you grant the subject damage reduction 10/magic; resistance to acid, cold, electricity, fire, and sonic 15; and spell resistance equal to your caster level +5.

By expending 10,000 gp, you grant the subject damage reduction 20/magic; resistance to acid, cold, electricity, fire, and sonic 20; and spell resistance equal to your caster level +10.

Material Component: Gems worth a total of 250 gp, 1,000 gp, or 10,000 gp.

FEARSOME GRAPPLE

Transmutation
Level: Sorcerer/wizard 2
Components: V
Casting Time: 1 immediate action
Range: Personal
Target: You
Duration: 1 round/level

Two short, otyughlike tentacles sprout from under your arms to hang limply at your sides. When you think of grappling, the tentacles twitch to life and wave about as if seeking a foe.

You grow two tentacles that grant you a +4 circumstance bonus on grapple checks. These tentacles cannot attack, hold objects, manipulate items, or perform any action other than grappling. If your caster level is at least 9th, you grow four tentacles instead, and the circumstance bonus increases to +8.

FELL THE GREATEST FOE

Transmutation
Level: Assassin 2, cleric 3, paladin 2, ranger 2
Components: V, S, M
Casting Time: 1 standard action
Range: Touch
Target: Creature touched
Duration: 1 round/level
Saving Throw: Fortitude negates (harmless)
Spell Resistance: Yes (harmless)

You touch the creature, and its muscles ripple with yellow energy.

The subject gains the ability to deal greater damage against larger creatures. For every size category of an opponent bigger than the subject of the spell, the subject deals an extra 1d6 points of damage on any successful melee attack. For example, a Medium creature would deal an extra 1d6 points of damage against a Large creature, 2d6 against Huge, 3d6 against Gargantuan, or 4d6 against a Colossal creature.

Material Component: A dragon's claw or a giant's fingernail.

FIELD OF GHOULS

Necromancy [Death, Evil]
Level: Hunger 7
Components: V, S
Casting Time: 1 standard action
Range: 30 ft.
Area: 30-ft.-radius emanation centered on you
Duration: 1 round/level
Saving Throw: Will negates
Spell Resistance: Yes

Wrenching life from their bodies with your magic, your foes' remains stir and rise as ghouls under your control.

Humanoid creatures in the area with –1 to –9 hit points that fail their saving throws die and immediately rise as ghouls (MM 118) under your control. You choose whether the ghouls follow you, or whether they can remain where formed and attack any creature (or just a specific kind of creature) the ghouls notice. The ghouls remain until they are destroyed.

The ghouls that you create remain under your control indefinitely. No matter how many ghouls you generate with this spell, however, you can control only 4 HD worth of undead creatures per caster level (this includes undead from all sources under your control). If you exceed this number, all the newly created creatures fall under your control, and any excess undead from previous castings become uncontrolled (you choose which creatures are released). If you are a cleric, any undead you might command by virtue of your power to command or rebuke undead do not count toward the limit.

Creatures that fall to –1 hit points or fewer in the area after the spell is cast are likewise subject to its effect and rise as ghouls on your next turn.

No creature can be affected by this spell more than once per round, regardless of the number of times that the area of the spell passes over it. This spell does not affect creatures that are already dead, or creatures that are killed by reducing their hit points to –10.

FIELD OF ICY RAZORS

Evocation [Cold]
Level: Sorcerer/wizard 8
Components: V, S, F
Casting Time: 1 standard action
Range: Medium (100 ft. + 10 ft./level)
Targets: One creature/level, no two of which are more than 60 ft. apart
Duration: Instantaneous plus 1 round/level; see text
Saving Throw: Reflex partial
Spell Resistance: Yes

Your breath becomes cold and frosty as you intone this spell, and blue-white crystals erupt from the soil, chill air swirling around their needle-sharp tips.

Razor-sharp ice crystals surround the targets. Each target takes 1d6 points of damage per caster level (maximum 20d6); half of this damage is cold damage, and half is slashing. In addition, each target's speed is reduced by 20 feet for 1 round per caster level. Creatures that succeed on Reflex saving throws take half damage and their movement is unaffected.

Focus: A silver shuriken worth 50 gp that looks like a snowflake.

FIENDFORM

Transmutation [Evil]
Level: Sorcerer/wizard 5
Components: V, S, M
Casting Time: 1 standard action
Range: Personal
Target: You
Duration: 1 minute/level

The bone in your hand cracks and then crumbles to dust as you complete the spell. You see within your subconscious a bestiary of terrible fiends even as dark whispers in your mind attempt to convince you which form to take.

This spell functions like *alter self* (PH 197), except that you can take the form of any fiendish creature, demon, or devil that can be summoned by a *summon monster* I, II, III, or IV spell (MM 287), regardless of size. You can assume only one form with each use of the spell, but you gain all that form's extraordinary, spell-like, and supernatural abilities, and your type changes to outsider. Spells and effects that harm or ward evil outsiders affect you, and any effect that would normally banish an outsider to its home plane instead ends the spell and leaves you dazed for 1 round per caster level.

Material Component: A bone from any fiendish creature, half-fiend, demon, or devil.

A field of icy razors stops a centaur's charge

Illus. by B. Hagan

FIERCE PRIDE OF THE BEASTLANDS

Conjuration (Summoning) [Chaotic, Good]
Level: Cleric 8, sorcerer/wizard 8
Components: V, S
Casting Time: 10 minutes
Range: Medium (100 ft. + 10 ft./ level) **Effect:** Two or more summoned creatures, no two of which are more than 30 ft. apart
Duration: 10 minutes/level (D)
Saving Throw: None
Spell Resistance: No

Green-white fog rises from the ground as you intone this spell, and great feline shadows take shape within the misty cloud. The first of a pride of golden-pelted lions with silver eyes emerges from the fog.

When the spell is complete, 2d4 celestial lions (MM 274) appear. Ten minutes later, 1d4 celestial dire lions (MM 63) appear. Each creature has maximum hit points per Hit Die. Once these creatures appear, they serve you for the duration of the spell.

A celestial lion called by this spell has damage reduction 5/magic; resistance to acid 5, cold 5, and electricity 5; spell resistance 9; and a smite evil attack that provides a +5 bonus on one damage roll.

A celestial dire lion called by this spell has damage reduction 5/magic; resistance to acid 10, cold 10, and electricity 10; spell resistance 13; and a smite evil attack that provides a +8 bonus on one damage roll.

The creatures obey you explicitly and never attack you, even if someone else manages to gain control over them. You do not need to concentrate to maintain control over the creatures. You can dismiss them singly or in groups at any time.

FIND THE GAP

Divination
Level: Assassin 3, paladin 3, ranger 3
Components: V
Casting Time: 1 standard action
Range: Personal
Target: You
Duration: 1 round/level

You speak the words of this spell, and a blue mark that only you can see appears on your opponent, highlighting a weak spot in her defense.

You gain the ability to perceive weak points in your opponent's armor. Your first melee or ranged attack each round is resolved as a touch attack, disregarding the subject's armor, shield, and natural armor bonuses (including any enhancement bonuses) to Armor Class. Other AC bonuses, such as dodge bonuses, deflection bonuses, and luck bonuses, still apply.

FIND TEMPLE

Divination
Level: Paladin 1
Components: V, S, DF
Casting Time: 1 standard action
Range: 10 miles + 1 mile/level
Area: Circle centered on you, with a radius of 10 miles + 1 mile/level
Duration: 1 hour/level
Saving Throw: None
Spell Resistance: No

At ease and filled with a reassuring calm, you close your eyes for a moment to allow your deity to guide you to a holy place.

With this spell, you can easily find a place to worship and possible aid or shelter from the priests within. When the spell is cast, you sense the direction of the nearest temple to your god. If there is none within the spell's area, the spell instead shows you the direction of the nearest temple dedicated to a god of the same alignment as yours. You can also specify a particular temple to search for, but you must have visited the temple personally at some point in the past (seeing the temple through a divination does not count).

FINS TO FEET

Transmutation
Level: Druid 2, sorcerer/wizard 2
Components: V, S
Casting Time: 1 standard action
Range: Touch
Target: Willing creature touched
Duration: 1 hour/level
Saving Throw: Fortitude negates (harmless)
Spell Resistance: Yes (harmless)

The naga's lower extremities thrash about and slowly transform into humanoid limbs.

This spell transforms tails, tentacles, or finned extremities into humanoid legs and feet. Creatures so affected lose any natural swim speed they possess, but gain a land speed instead. Transmuted Medium creatures have a base land speed of 30 feet, Small and smaller creatures have a base land speed of 20 feet, and Large or larger creatures have a base land speed of 40 feet.

The subject loses any natural attacks based on its tail or tentacles.

FIRE SHIELD, MASS

Evocation [Fire or Cold]
Level: Sorcerer/wizard 5
Components: V, S, M
Casting Time: 1 round
Range: Close (25 ft. + 5 ft./2 levels)
Targets: One or more allied creatures, no two of which are more than 30 ft. apart
Duration: 1 round/level (D)
Saving Throw: Will negates (harmless)
Spell Resistance: Yes (harmless)

With a few frenzied motions you complete the spell, bathing your allies in halos of magical flame.

This spell functions like *fire shield* (PH 230), except as noted above.

FIRE SHURIKEN

Evocation [Fire]
Level: Assassin 2
Components: V, S, M
Casting Time: 1 standard action
Range: 0 ft.
Effect: One magic shuriken/3 levels
Duration: Instantaneous
Saving Throw: None
Spell Resistance: Yes

With dark intent you complete the quick motions of the spell and find in your hand several shuriken composed of flame.

This spell creates shuriken formed of magical fire that you can throw as a normal ranged attack. You are automatically considered proficient with the fire shuriken, which have a range increment of 10 feet, threaten a critical hit on a roll of 19–20, and deal 3d6 points of fire damage each on a successful hit (although you and your possessions take no damage as the shuriken are thrown). Any additional damage dealt by the fire shuriken (including your Strength bonus and sneak attack damage) is also fire damage. The shuriken disappear when they hit, so they cannot set fire to combustibles or damage objects.

You can create one fire shuriken per three caster levels, up to a maximum of six at 18th level.

Material Component: A shuriken coated with pine sap and sulfur.

FIRE SPIDERS

Conjuration (Summoning) [Fire]
Level: Sorcerer/wizard 6
Components: V, S, M
Casting Time: 1 standard action
Range: Close (25 ft. + 5 ft./2 levels)
Effect: Fiery spiders that cover a 10-ft.-radius spread
Duration: 1 round/level
Saving Throw: Reflex half
Spell Resistance: Yes

Tiny lights appear in the darkness—one, ten, over a hundred. As they appear, the sound of insectile chittering increases, until a swarming army of flaming, otherworldly arachnids is gathered together at your command.

You call forth a teeming mass of fire elementals the size of common spiders. A creature that starts its turn in the affected area takes 4d6 points of fire damage. Each round, you can use a move action to direct the spiders to move up to 30 feet. If the spiders are left undirected, they move at a speed of 15 feet toward the nearest living

Illus. by D. Martin

Fire spiders are nearly impossible to defeat by attacking individual ones

creature, if one isn't already in the affected area.

As fire elementals, the fire spiders have immunity to fire and are thwarted by barriers that block neutral outsiders. Any cold spell of 3rd level or higher can disperse the fire spiders, ending the spell.

Material Component: A pinch of sulfur.

FIRE STRIDE

Transmutation [Teleportation]
Level: Sorcerer/wizard 4
Components: V, S
Casting Time: 1 standard action
Range: Personal
Target: You
Duration: 10 minutes/level or until expended; see text

You draw arcane power into your body, wrapping your feet and legs with wisps of flame.

You gain the ability to step into fires and move from one fire to another. The fires you enter and move between must be at least as big around as you are. Fire elementals and other fire creatures are not considered "fires" for the purpose of this spell, nor are sources of great heat, such as pools of lava.

Once in a fire, you instantly know the locations of all suitable fires within long range (400 ft. + 40 ft./level) and can transport yourself to one of them. Each transport counts as a full-round action. With each casting of the spell, you can transport yourself once per caster level. If a fire's location doesn't offer enough space for you (for example, a fire contained inside a furnace too small to hold you or a fire already occupied by a big cauldron), it is not a viable destination and you don't sense its location. If a fire rests on a surface that can't support you, it is still a viable destination and you suffer the appropriate consequences if you transport yourself to it. For example, if you transport yourself into a fire burning in a pit full of oil, you fall into the oil when you arrive there.

Fire stride provides no protection against fire, so it is advisable to obtain such protection before using the spell.

FIRE WINGS

Transmutation [Fire]
Level: Druid 3
Components: V, S, M, F
Casting Time: 1 round
Range: Personal
Target: You
Duration: 1 minute/level

In a flash of light and a roar of fire, your arms become wings of flame.

This spell transforms your arms into wings of brilliant fire. The flame does not damage you or any items you carry. Because your arms are transformed, you cannot hold items in your hands or cast spells that require somatic components, but rings, bracers, and other items worn on your arms when you cast the spell still function normally. The wings allow you to fly at a speed of 60 feet (or 40 feet if you wear medium or heavy armor), with good maneuverability. You can charge but not run while flying, and you cannot carry more than a light load aloft. Using a *fire wings* spell requires only as much concentration as walking, so you can take other actions normally.

If the spell duration expires while you are aloft, you descend at a rate of 60 feet per round for 1d6 rounds, then fall the rest of the distance if you haven't already landed. Because dispelling a spell effectively ends it, the subject also descends in this way if the *fire wings* spell is dispelled, but not if it is negated by an *antimagic field*.

If you are not flying, you can make up to two attacks each round with the fire wings as if they were natural weapons. A successful attack deals 2d6 points of fire damage.

The wings can be extinguished (and the spell canceled) by a *quench* spell, immersion in water, or a wind of hurricane or greater force.

Material Component: The feather of a bird, which you must burn when you cast the spell.

Focus: A golden amulet shaped like a phoenix (worth 150 gp).

FIREBRAND

Evocation [Fire]
Level: Sorcerer/wizard 5
Components: V, S, M
Casting Time: 1 standard action
Range: Medium (100 ft. + 10 ft./level)
Area: One 5-ft.-radius burst/level (S)
Duration: Instantaneous
Saving Throw: Reflex half
Spell Resistance: Yes

The flask of alchemist's fire vanishes from your hand and the ground erupts beneath your foes, shooting multiple fountains of fiery liquid upward.

You create up to one burst of flame per level and cause those bursts to explode upon the battlefield. Each burst of flame deals 1d6 points of fire damage per caster level (maximum 15d6) to all creatures within the area.

The bursts do not need to be contiguous, and may be distributed within range as you see fit. Burst effects that overlap do not deal additional damage (a creature can be affected by only one burst).

Material Component: A flask of alchemist's fire (worth 20 gp).

FIREBURST

Evocation [Fire]
Level: Sorcerer/wizard 2
Components: V, S, M
Casting Time: 1 standard action
Range: 10 ft.
Effect: Burst of fire extending 10 ft. from you
Duration: Instantaneous
Saving Throw: Reflex half
Spell Resistance: Yes

With a grand circular gesture the air around you fills with flame. An instant later the fire explodes outward, engulfing everything close to you.

Fireburst causes a powerful explosion of flame to burst from you, damaging anyone within 10 feet of you. All creatures and objects within that area, except for you and any creatures or objects that share your space, take 1d8 points of fire damage per caster level (maximum 5d8).

Material Component: A bit of sulfur.

FIREBURST, GREATER

Evocation [Fire]
Level: Sorcerer/wizard 5
Effect: Burst of fire extending 15 ft. from you

This spell functions like *fireburst,* except that it affects creatures within 15 feet of you and deals 1d10 points of fire damage per caster level (maximum 15d10).

FIRES OF PURITY

Evocation [Fire]
Level: Druid 6, Purification 6, sorcerer/wizard 6
Components: V, S, DF
Casting Time: 1 standard action
Range: Touch
Target: Creature touched
Duration: 1 round/level
Saving Throw: See text
Spell Resistance: Yes (harmless); see text

You touch the target, and it bursts into flames that do not harm it, although the heat you feel from the fire seems quite real to you.

The creature you touch bursts into magical flames that do not harm the subject, but are capable of harming anyone else who comes into contact with the creature.

With a successful melee attack, the subject deals an extra 1 point of fire damage per caster level (maximum +15). If the defender has spell resistance, it applies to this effect. Creatures that make successful melee attacks against the subject are susceptible to the same damage unless they attack with weapons that have reach, such as longspears.

The subject of *fires of purity* takes only half damage from fire-based attacks. If such an attack allows a Reflex save for half damage, the subject takes no damage on a successful save.

FIREWARD

Transmutation
Level: Druid 5
Components: V, S, DF
Casting Time: 1 standard action
Range: Medium (100 ft. + 10 ft./level)
Area: One 20-ft. cube/level (S)
Duration: 1 hour/level
Saving Throw: None
Spell Resistance: No

You stomp on the ground, and fire snuffs out all around you, rippling away to nothingness faster than you can blink.

This spell functions like *quench* (PH 267), except as noted above. In addition, it has the following effects.

A sorcerer keeps a flame dagger at the ready while she casts another spell

While *fireward* remains in effect, no magical fire effect can function inside its area. This effect is similar to that of an *antimagic field*, but only magical fire is suppressed. Any nonmagical fire created inside or brought into the spell's area is immediately extinguished as well.

FIST OF STONE

Transmutation [Earth]
Level: Sorcerer/wizard 1
Components: V, S, M
Casting Time: 1 standard action
Range: Personal
Target: You
Duration: 1 minute

The complicated gestures of the spell end with a punch of your fist, which now has the texture and look of stone.

You transform one of your hands into a mighty fist of living stone, gaining a +6 enhancement bonus to Strength for the purposes of attack rolls, grapple checks, or breaking and crushing items. In addition, you gain the ability to make one natural slam attack, dealing 1d6 points of damage + your new Strength bonus (or 1-1/2 times your Strength bonus if you make no other attacks in that round). You can make the slam attack as a natural secondary attack with the normal –5 penalty, or a –2 penalty if you have the Multiattack feat (MM 304), as part of a full attack action. However, you cannot gain more than one slam attack per round with this spell due to a high base attack bonus (+6 or higher).

Your fist undergoes no change in size or form, remaining as flexible and responsive as it would normally be while under the spell's effect.

Material Component: A pebble inscribed with a stylized fist design.

FLAME DAGGER

Evocation [Fire]
Level: Sorcerer/wizard 2
Components: V, S, M
Casting Time: 1 standard action
Range: 0 ft.
Effect: A daggerlike beam
Duration: 1 minute/level (D)
Saving Throw: None
Spell Resistance: Yes

You evoke the spell and a blazing beam of red-hot fire springs forth from your hand, ready to be used as a weapon.

You create a bladelike beam that you can wield as if it were a dagger. Attacks with a *flame dagger* are melee touch attacks, and the blade deals 1d4 points of fire damage +1 point per caster level (to a maximum of +10). Because the blade is immaterial, your Strength

Illus. by C. Frank

modifier does not apply to the damage. A *flame dagger* can ignite combustible materials such as parchment, straw, dry sticks, cloth, and so on.

This spell does not function underwater.

Material Component: A candle.

FLAME OF FAITH

Evocation
Level: Cleric 3, paladin 2
Components: V, S, M
Casting Time: 1 standard action
Range: Touch
Target: Nonmagical weapon touched
Duration: 1 round/level
Saving Throw: None
Spell Resistance: No

Using your faith as a guide for your magic, you touch the weapon and it bursts into flame.

You can temporarily turn any single normal or masterwork melee weapon into a magic, flaming one. For the duration of the spell, the weapon acts as a *+1 flaming burst weapon.*

Material Component: A lump of phosphorus, touched to the target weapon.

FLAME WHIPS

Transmutation
Level: Sorcerer/wizard 4
Components: V, S
Casting Time: 1 standard action
Range: Personal
Effect: Flaming whips
Duration: 1 round/level (D)

At the conclusion of this spell, your arms stretch into whiplike appendages and burst into flames.

Your forelimbs transform into flaming whips. You gain two melee touch attacks with a 15-foot reach that each deal 6d6 points of fire damage. Attacks with these flaming whips replace any natural attacks you had with those limbs.

While this spell is in effect, you cannot cast spells with material components, nor can you carry items with your forelimbs. Any items worn on your forelimbs cease functioning while the spell is active.

FLASHBURST

Evocation [Fire]
Level: Sorcerer/wizard 3
Components: V, S, M/DF
Casting Time: 1 standard action
Range: Long (400 ft. + 40 ft./level)
Area: 20-ft.-radius burst
Duration: Instantaneous; see text
Saving Throw: Will partial; see text
Spell Resistance: Yes

A blinding flash of light follows the casting of this spell.

Flashburst creates a blinding, dazzling flash of light. Sighted creatures within the area are blinded for 2d8 rounds. A successful Will save negates the blindness. Creatures in the area are dazzled for 1 round even if their save was successful. Creatures outside the area, but within 120 feet of the burst, can be blinded for 2d8 rounds if they have line of sight to the burst (Will negates). Creatures outside the burst area are not dazzled.

Arcane Material Component: A pinch of sulfur or phosphorus.

FLENSING

Transmutation [Evil]
Level: Sorcerer/wizard 8
Components: V, S, M
Casting Time: 1 standard action
Range: Close (25 ft. + 5 ft./2 levels)
Target: One corporeal creature
Duration: 4 rounds
Saving Throw: Fortitude partial; see text
Spell Resistance: Yes

With a cruel utterance, you complete the spell and unleash its terrible energy. A sickeningly wet ripping sound accompanies the sight of strips of flesh being torn away, as if some invisible hand was attempting to peel your target like an onion.

When you cast this spell, you literally strip the flesh from a corporeal creature's body, inflicting incredible pain and psychological trauma. Each round, the subject takes 2d6 points of damage, 1d6 points of Charisma damage, and 1d6 points of Constitution damage. A successful Fortitude save negates the ability damage and reduces the hit point damage by half for that round, but does not end the spell.

Flensing has no effect on creatures in gaseous form.

Material Component: An onion.

FLESHSHIVER

Necromancy
Level: Sorcerer/wizard 6
Components: V, S, M
Casting Time: 1 standard action
Range: Close (25 ft. + 5 ft./2 levels)
Target: One living creature
Duration: Instantaneous
Saving Throw: Fortitude partial; see text
Spell Resistance: Yes

Breaking the bone in the grip of your fist, you hear the sickening but satisfying crunch of your foe's bones breaking beneath his squeezing flesh.

A creature with Hit Dice less than or equal to your caster level is automatically stunned for 1 round (no saving throw). A creature with Hit Dice greater than your caster level is allowed a saving throw to negate the stunning effect.

In the following round, the target must make a Fortitude save or take 1d6 points of damage per caster level (maximum 15d6) and be nauseated by the pain for 1d4+2 rounds.

Material Component: A bone, which is snapped during the casting of the spell.

FLIGHT OF THE DRAGON

Transmutation
Level: Sorcerer/wizard 4
Components: V, M
Casting Time: 1 standard action
Range: Personal
Target: You
Duration: 10 minutes/level (D)

The wing-claw vaporizes in a puff of acrid smoke, and you feel the muscles of your shoulders warm from the eldritch energies coursing within. Great draconian wings unfurl from your shoulders and reach toward the sky.

A powerful pair of wings sprout from your shoulders, granting you a fly speed of 100 feet (average). You can't carry aloft more than a light load.

When flying long distances, you can fly at 15 miles per hour (or 24 miles per hour at a hustle).

Material Component: A dragon's wing claw.

Special: Sorcerers cast this spell at +1 caster level.

FLOATING DISK, GREATER

Evocation [Force]
Level: Sorcerer/wizard 4
Components: V, S, M
Casting Time: 1 standard action
Range: Close (25 ft. + 5 ft./2 levels)
Effect: 3-ft.-diameter disk of force
Duration: 1 hour/level
Saving Throw: None
Spell Resistance: No

Letting the mercury drip to the ground you create a slightly concave disk of energy. It hovers several feet above the ground.

This spell functions like *Tenser's floating disk* (PH 294), except that the created disk does not need to stay within 3 feet of the surface beneath it. However, the disk must remain within 15 feet of you at all times. You can concentrate (as a standard action) on the disk to make it move with a fly speed of 20 feet (perfect). This allows you to sit on the disk and command it to carry you about.

Material Component: A drop of mercury.

FLY, MASS

Transmutation
Level: Sorcerer/wizard 5
Components: V, S
Range: Close (25 ft. + 5 ft./2 levels)
Targets: One creature/level, no two of which are more than 30 ft. apart

As your gestures point out which creatures receive the benefits of your spell, they seem lighter on their feet.

Illus. by R. Horsley

Mass fly allows a whole squad of drow to gain control of the battlefield

This spell functions like *fly* (PH 232), except as noted here. This spell confers the power of flight upon all targeted creatures. Each recipient of the spell must remain within 30 feet of at least one other recipient, or the spell ends for the creature that is separated from the others. If only two individuals are affected, the spell ends for both if the distance between them exceeds 30 feet.

FLY, SWIFT

Transmutation
Level: Bard 2, druid 3, sorcerer/wizard 2
Components: V
Casting Time: 1 swift action
Range: Personal
Target: You
Duration: 1 round

You squawk twice like an eagle and suddenly long for the freedom of the skies.

This spell functions like *fly* (PH 232), except as noted above.

FOCUSING CHANT

Enchantment (Compulsion) [Mind-Affecting]
Level: Bard 1
Components: V
Casting Time: 1 swift action
Range: Personal
Target: You
Duration: 1 minute (D)

You chant softly under your breath and concentrate on the sound of your voice. Distractions fade from your consciousness, allowing you to focus on the task at hand.

You gain a +1 circumstance bonus on attack rolls, skill checks, and ability checks for the duration of the spell.

FOEBANE

Evocation
Level: Ranger 4
Components: V, S
Casting Time: 1 standard action
Range: Touch
Target: Weapon touched
Duration: 1 round/level (D)
Saving Throw: Will negates (harmless, object)
Spell Resistance: Yes (harmless, object)

Holding aloft the weapon, you name the kind of creature you wish to slay. With a flash, the weapon takes on a blue glow that quickly fades to a barely perceptible aura surrounding it.

When you cast this spell, choose one of your favored enemies. Against creatures of the selected enemy kind, the weapon acts as a +5 magic weapon and deals an extra 2d6 points of damage. Furthermore, while you wield the weapon, you gain a +4 resistance bonus on saving throws against effects created by creatures of that kind.

The spell is automatically canceled 1 round after the weapon leaves your hand for any reason. You cannot have more than one foebane weapon active at a time.

If this spell is cast on a magic weapon, the powers of the spell supersede any that the weapon normally has, rendering the normal enhancement bonus and powers of the weapon inoperative for the duration of the spell. This spell is not cumulative with any other spell that might modify the weapon in any way. This spell does not work on artifacts.

FORCE CHEST

Evocation [Force]
Level: Sorcerer/wizard 4
Components: V, S, M
Casting Time: 1 standard action
Range: 0 ft.
Effect: Box of force 2 ft. on a side
Duration: 24 hours/level (D)
Saving Throw: None
Spell Resistance: No

Holding your hands as if to grip a box, you feel the pressure of one appear as you complete the spell. The password you choose to unlock the box echoes through your mind.

This spell brings into being a lidded box of force. The box appears in your hands, and you can choose to make it either invisible or merely translucent. The chest has no weight worth noting.

Solid walls of force form the chest's five sides and lid. You and other creatures cannot open the lid except by first speaking the password (determined by you at the time of casting). Both objects and Tiny and smaller creatures can fit in the box; it holds enough air to supply one Tiny, two Diminutive, or four Fine creatures for 1 hour.

Like a *wall of force* spell, a *force chest* is immune to damage of all kinds and resists *dispel magic*, but it is susceptible to *disintegrate* and *Mordenkainen's disjunction*, and it can be destroyed by a *sphere of annihilation* or a *rod of cancellation*. The box is a spell effect, and Open Lock and Use Magic Device cannot open it.

A force chest spell gives a lich a sense of security when confronted by troublesome adventurers

Material Component: A 2-inch-square glass cube.

FORCE CLAW

Evocation [Force]
Level: Sorcerer/wizard 4
Components: V, S, M
Casting Time: 1 standard action
Range: Medium (100 ft. + 10 ft./level)
Effect: Invisible claw of force
Duration: 1 round/level (D)
Saving Throw: None
Spell Resistance: Yes

Curling your hand into a claw, you finish the final gesture. Your foes see no result from your spell, but you know they're in for a surprise.

Force claw creates a Medium claw of invisible force at any spot you designate within the spell's range. The claw guards the area of a 20-foot cube that you specify. You can move the claw's location up to 60 feet to another point within range each round on your turn as a move action.

The claw is able to make attacks of opportunity against any enemy that provokes such attacks within the guarded area. It has a +10 bonus on the attack roll and deals 1d8+6 points of damage with a successful hit. It can make an unlimited number of attacks of opportunity each round, though it can make only one such attack per opportunity.

Material Component: A small, dried claw from an animal.

FORCE LADDER

Evocation [Force]
Level: Sorcerer/wizard 2
Components: V, S, F
Casting Time: 1 standard action
Range: Close (25 ft. + 5 ft./2 levels)
Effect: One ladder of force up to 60 ft. long
Duration: 1 minute/level
Saving Throw: None
Spell Resistance: No

You concentrate on the small silver model of the ladder in your outstretched hand. A transparent ladder, visible only by its edges, appears.

You create an immobile transparent ladder made of force. The ladder is 2 feet wide and anywhere from 10 to 60 feet long, with rungs spaced 1 foot apart. The ladder functions as a normal ladder and can support any weight. It can be destroyed by anything that destroys a *wall of force*.

Focus: A miniature silver ladder (50 gp).

Illus. by R. Spears

FORCE MISSILES

Evocation [Force]
Level: Sorcerer/wizard 4
Components: V, S
Casting Time: 1 standard action
Range: Medium (100 ft. + 10 ft./level)
Targets: Up to four creatures, no two of which are more than 30 ft. apart
Duration: Instantaneous
Saving Throw: None
Spell Resistance: Yes

Sparking bolts of blue magic, like giant magic missiles, streak from your outstretched hand to strike your foes and explode in sparkling bursts.

You create powerful missiles of magical force, each of which darts from your fingertips and unerringly strikes its target, dealing 2d6 points of damage. The missile then explodes in a burst of force that deals half this amount of damage to any creatures adjacent to the primary target.

The missile strikes unerringly, even if the target is in melee or has anything less than total cover or concealment. A caster cannot single out specific parts of a creature. The spell can target and damage unattended objects.

You gain one missile for every four caster levels. You can make more than one missile strike a single target, if desired. However, you must designate targets before rolling for spell resistance or damage.

FORCEWARD

Abjuration [Force]
Level: Sorcerer/wizard 4
Components: V, S
Casting Time: 1 round
Range: 15 ft.
Effect: 15-ft.-radius sphere centered on you
Duration: 1 minute/level
Saving Throw: Will negates; see text
Spell Resistance: Yes

Waving your arm about your head to trace the curve of a dome, you call up a hemisphere of force as clear as glass.

You create an unmoving, transparent sphere of force centered on you. The sphere negates force effects and provides an impassable barrier against incorporeal creatures. Spells with the force descriptor do not affect anything within the sphere, and any force spell that overlaps the area, such as *wall of force*, is automatically countered. Incorporeal creatures, or creatures with the force descriptor must make a Will save to enter the area of the sphere.

Forceward does not push a creature out of the way if you move toward an incorporeal creature or force effect, and such creatures are treated as if they automatically succeeded on their saving throws against this spell.

FORCEWAVE

Evocation [Force]
Level: Sorcerer/wizard 4
Components: V, S, F
Casting Time: 1 swift action
Range: 10 ft.
Effect: 10-ft. burst of force centered on you
Duration: Instantaneous
Saving Throw: None
Spell Resistance: Yes

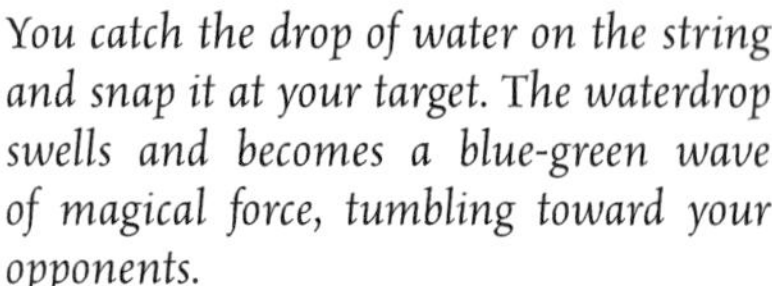

You catch the drop of water on the string and snap it at your target. The waterdrop swells and becomes a blue-green wave of magical force, tumbling toward your opponents.

This spell initiates a bull rush against all creatures within 10 feet. The *forcewave* has a +10 bonus on the bull rush attempt. All creatures are pushed to the extent of the bull rush result, and the result of the bull rush can push creatures beyond the spell's normal range.

Focus: A small piece of string and a drop of water.

FORESTFOLD

Transmutation
Level: Druid 3, ranger 3
Components: V, S
Casting Time: 1 standard action
Range: Personal
Target: You
Duration: 1 hour/level (D)

Warmth fills your feet, and as you glance down, you see that your feet have changed shape slightly, enabling you to better traverse a particular type of terrain. You also notice a shift in the color of your skin and clothing to match the colors most commonly found in your environment.

You change your coloring and attune your footfalls to one specific kind of terrain (aquatic, desert, plains, forest, hills, mountains, marsh, or underground). While you are in terrain of that kind, you gain a +10 competence bonus on Hide and Move Silently checks. You retain these bonuses even if you leave the designated terrain and return within the duration of the spell.

FORTIFY FAMILIAR

Universal
Level: Sorcerer/wizard 3
Components: V, S
Casting Time: 1 standard action
Range: Touch
Target: Familiar touched
Duration: 1 hour/level
Saving Throw: None
Spell Resistance: Yes (harmless)

You touch your familiar, and you see that the creature seems more robust.

Illus. by S. Belledin

A druid uses the freeze spell to encase a despoiler of nature in ice

This spell makes your familiar tougher, granting it 2d8 temporary hit points and a +2 enhancement bonus to its natural armor. It also has a 25% chance to avoid extra damage from sneak attacks or critical hits (although such attacks still deal normal damage if successful). Temporary hit points gained in this fashion last for up to 1 hour.

FORTUNATE FATE

Conjuration (Healing)
Level: Cleric 7
Components: V, S
Casting Time: 1 minute
Range: Touch
Target: Living creature touched
Duration: 10 minutes/level or until discharged
Saving Throw: None (harmless)
Spell Resistance: Yes (harmless)

A golden aura spreads out from your fingertips, suffusing your ally with a golden glow that brightens, then fades into her skin.

You surround the subject with an aura that immediately heals the creature if it is subjected to an effect that would kill it (reduce its hit points to –10 or below). When this event occurs, the *fortunate fate* spell intervenes by immediately triggering a *heal* spell upon the target. If the effect is one that causes harm in a way that a *heal* spell can repair (disease, hit point damage, ability damage, or poison), the target does not actually die, saved by the *heal.* If the effect is one that *heal* cannot countermand (such as ability drain, old age, negative levels, disintegration, ability drain, or death effects), the *fortunate fate* spell cannot prevent the creature's death.

FOUNDATION OF STONE

Transmutation [Earth]
Level: Cleric 1, druid 1
Components: V, S, DF
Casting Time: 1 standard action
Range: Close (25 ft. + 5 ft./2 levels)
Target: One creature/level, no two of which are more than 30 ft. apart
Duration: 1 round/level
Saving Throw: None
Spell Resistance: No

Calling upon the strength of the earth, you lend some of the stability of stone to your allies.

As long as they do not move and remain standing on solid ground, the subject creatures gain a +2 bonus to Armor Class and a +4 bonus on Strength checks made to resist being bull rushed or tripped.

If this spell is cast in mountainous terrain, the bonus on Strength checks granted by this spell increases to +6.

FREEZE

Conjuration (Creation) [Cold]
Level: Druid 6
Components: V, S, DF
Casting Time: 1 standard action
Range: Medium (100 ft. + 10 ft./level)
Effect: Ray
Duration: 1 round/2 levels
Saving Throw: Reflex partial; see text
Spell Resistance: Yes

Calling upon divine power, your hand turns cold and numb as you complete the spell. A moment later, a thin blue ray swirled with white streaks from your outstretched hand, leaving a light fog in the air where it passed.

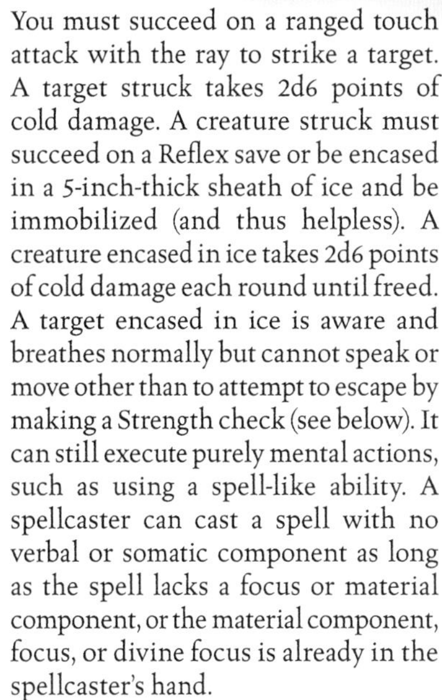

You must succeed on a ranged touch attack with the ray to strike a target. A target struck takes 2d6 points of cold damage. A creature struck must succeed on a Reflex save or be encased in a 5-inch-thick sheath of ice and be immobilized (and thus helpless). A creature encased in ice takes 2d6 points of cold damage each round until freed. A target encased in ice is aware and breathes normally but cannot speak or move other than to attempt to escape by making a Strength check (see below). It can still execute purely mental actions, such as using a spell-like ability. A spellcaster can cast a spell with no verbal or somatic component as long as the spell lacks a focus or material component, or the material component, focus, or divine focus is already in the spellcaster's hand.

The ice blocks line of effect. A winged creature cannot flap its wings and falls. A swimmer can't swim but, because ice floats, the encased swimmer will rise to the surface and bob about.

A DC 22 Strength check breaks the ice, freeing the encased creature. Creatures other than the target can also attack the ice. The ice has hardness 0 and 15 hit points. When the duration of the spell expires, the ice melts and the encased creature is freed. Damage that would harm the creature must first deal enough damage to destroy the ice before the creature takes damage, and damage dealt to the ice is subtracted from damage that would be dealt to the creature.

FREEZING FOG

Conjuration (Creation) [Cold]
Level: Sorcerer/wizard 6
Components: V, S
Casting Time: 1 standard action
Range: Medium (100 ft. + 10 ft./level)
Effect: Fog spreads in a 20-ft. radius, 20 ft. high
Duration: 1 minute/level
Saving Throw: Reflex partial; see text
Spell Resistance: No

A cool mist rises from the area you indicate. The thick mist blocks your ability to see within it, but the ground at its edge has turned white with frost.

A bank of freezing mist billows out from the point you designate, obscuring all sight (including darkvision) beyond 5 feet. A creature within 5 feet has concealment, while creatures farther away have total concealment.

Each round on your turn, the frigid mist deals 1d6 points of cold damage to each creature and object within it. The fog is so thick that any creature attempting to move through it progresses at a maximum speed of 5 feet (regardless of its normal speed) and takes a –2 penalty on melee attack rolls and damage rolls and a –6 penalty on ranged weapon attack rolls (but not ranged spell attack rolls). A creature or object that falls into the fog from above is slowed, so that each 10 feet of mist it passes through effectively reduces overall falling damage by 1d6.

Freezing fog also coats all solid surfaces in its area with a slick, icy rime, and on your turn each round, each creature in the area of the fog must make a successful Reflex save or fall prone. A creature that manages to stand must make a DC 10 Balance check in order to move, falling prone if it fails its save by 5 or more. Creatures in the fog can't take a 5-foot step.

A severe wind disperses the cloud in 1 round. The spell does not function underwater.

FROST BREATH

Evocation [Cold]
Level: Cleric 2, druid 2, sorcerer/wizard 2
Components: V, S, M
Casting Time: 1 standard action
Range: 30 ft.
Area: Cone-shaped burst
Duration: Instantaneous
Saving Throw: Reflex half
Spell Resistance: Yes

Giving a forceful exhale across your cupped hand, your breath shoots forth tinged with frost and crystals of ice.

You breathe a cone of intense cold at your foes. The spell deals 1d4 points of cold damage per two caster levels (maximum 5d4). In addition, all creatures damaged by the frost breath that fail their Reflex save are dazed for 1 round by the sudden shock of cold.

Material Component: Three drops of water or fragments of ice (which are held in a cupped palm and blown toward the target).

FUGUE

Evocation [Sonic]
Level: Bard 4
Components: V, S, F
Casting Time: 1 standard action
Range: Medium (100 ft. + 10 ft./level)
Area: 30-ft.-radius spread
Duration: Concentration, up to 1 round/level
Saving Throw: Will negates
Spell Resistance: Yes

Upon completing the spell, a discordant cacophony of haunting and alien music rises up in the area you designate. Although the strange music reaches your ears, you feel no effect from it.

Creatures that fail their save become affected by the haunting fugue in semirandom ways. On each affected creature's turn (as long as it remains in the affected area), you make a Perform check. The check result determines how the victim's mind and body are affected by the spell. You can select any of the effects for which your Perform check equals or exceeds the required DC.

DC	Result
15	Victim takes 3d6 points of nonlethal damage
20	Victim takes 3d6 points of sonic damage
25	Victim is knocked prone
30	Victim is nauseated for 1 round
35	Victim is stunned for 1 round
40	Victim attacks nearest target

All creatures that succeed on their saves against the spell are disoriented and take a –2 penalty on attack rolls and skill checks as long as they remain in the affected area.

Focus: A miniature violin bow made of platinum worth 250 gp.

FUSE ARMS

Transmutation
Level: Cleric 2, sorcerer/wizard 2
Components: V, S
Casting Time: 1 standard action
Range: Touch
Target: Creature with at least two arms or tentacles touched
Duration: 10 minutes/level
Saving Throw: Fortitude negates (harmless)
Spell Resistance: Yes (harmless)

Convulsing, the touched subject's limbs begin to ooze together with a sickening noise like a pot of melted wax splattering on the floor. With a lurch they form into one pair of massive limbs.

You cause a creature's multiple arms or tentacles to fuse together into a single pair of stronger limbs. Only limbs that the creature can use as arms or grasping limbs are affected by the spell (so basilisks and monstrous centipedes, neither of which use their limbs to attack or manipulate objects, are unaffected).

For every set of limbs fused into the primary set of limbs, the creature gains +4 to Strength when using those fused limbs (affecting activities that would use those limbs, but not activities relying on its bite, legs, and so on). For example, a girallon under the effect of this spell would have one pair of arms and Strength 26 for the purpose of using those arms. A behir, which has three pairs of limbs that it can use as arms, would end up with one pair of arm-limbs with a +8 bonus to Strength for those arms (its six legs would be unaffected).

The loss of limbs might reduce the number of attacks available to the subject.

If the subject has only two arms or tentacles, they are fused into a single limb, and the creature gains a +4 bonus to Strength on attack rolls made with that limb.

G'ELSEWHERE CHANT

Conjuration [Sonic, Teleportation]
Level: Bard 3
Components: V, S
Casting Time: 1 standard action
Range: Touch
Target: One creature or object touched
Duration: Instantaneous
Saving Throw: Will negates
Spell Resistance: Yes

A marilith makes good use of the fuse arms spell

You touch the target and it vanishes in a shower of golden sparks. Almost instantly, it appears a short distance away.

You teleport a target to a random, safe location up to 100 feet distant and visible to you.

To randomly determine the subject's destination, roll 1d8 to determine the direction, then roll 1d10×10 to determine the distance from the subject's previous location. Roll direction and distance again if this new destination is outside your line of sight, within a solid object, or more than 5 feet above the ground.

If your target is being held (whether an object held by a character or a character being grappled by a creature), the holding or grappling creature also receives a Will saving throw to resist.

GEMBOMB

Evocation [Force]
Level: Gnome 2, Trade 2
Components: V, S, M
Casting Time: 1 round
Range: Touch
Target: Gem touched
Duration: 10 minutes/level or until used
Saving Throw: Reflex half
Spell Resistance: Yes

You place a small spark of energy in the heart of a valuable gem.

You turn a gem into a bomb that you (and only you) can lob at enemies. You must hold the gem in your hand when casting the spell.

You can toss the bomb with perfect accuracy anywhere within 60 feet. The gembomb explodes in a 5-foot-radius burst dealing 1d8 points of force damage per two caster levels (maximum 5d8). Tossing a gembomb is a standard action.

Material Component: A gem worth at least 1 gp.

GEMJUMP

Conjuration [Teleportation]
Level: Sorcerer/wizard 6
Components: V, S, F
Casting Time: 1 round
Range: Unlimited; see text
Target: You and willing creatures totaling up to one/3 levels; see text
Duration: Until triggered
Saving Throw: None; see text
Spell Resistance: No; see text

You mutter over the iridescent, faceted gem. It twinkles in response, and you feel a strong link between you and the stone. When you speak the word, the two of you will be reunited.

Illus. by E. Polak

The general of undeath spell makes an evil cleric into a true leader of those beyond fear and death

Illus. by R. Horsley

This spell teleports you to the location of a specially prepared gem.

You initially cast *gemjump* upon the focus, which you must touch. As a standard action any time after you prepare the stone, you can utter a command word and instantly teleport to the location of the gem, provided you and the stone are on the same plane.

The teleport is always on target (as though you are using a *greater teleport* spell). If the area containing the gem is too small for you, you appear in the nearest sufficiently large space.

You can transport, in addition to yourself, one Medium or smaller creature per three caster levels, and can bring along objects as long as their weight does not exceed your maximum load.

An unwilling creature can't be teleported by *gemjump*. Likewise, a creature's Will save (or spell resistance) prevents items in its possession from being teleported. Unattended, nonmagical objects receive no saving throw.

Focus: A gem worth 500 gp.

GENERAL OF UNDEATH

Necromancy [Evil]
Level: Cleric 8
Components: V, S, DF
Casting Time: 1 standard action
Range: Personal
Target: You
Duration: 24 hours

You focus on the darkness within your soul, willing it to grow and grant you the power to control a greater number of undead minions.

This spell increases the number of Hit Dice of undead that you can control by an amount equal to your caster level. When the duration expires, you lose control of the extra undead as if you had voluntarily relinquished control of them.

GHOST TOUCH ARMOR

Transmutation
Level: Cleric 2, sorcerer/wizard 2
Components: V, S, M
Casting Time: 1 standard action
Range: Touch
Target: Armor of creature touched
Duration: 1 minute/level
Saving Throw: Will negates (harmless)
Spell Resistance: Yes (harmless)

Confronted with incorporeal enemies, you give the armor you touch the power to defend against such foes.

The subject's armor gains the ghost touch special ability (DMG 219).

Material Component: A tiny shield made of resin.

GHOST TOUCH WEAPON

Transmutation
Level: Cleric 3
Components: V, S
Casting Time: 1 standard action
Range: Close (25 ft. + 5 ft./2 levels)
Target: One weapon or fifty projectiles (all of which must be in contact with each other at the time of casting)
Duration: 1 minute/level

Saving Throw: Will negates (harmless, object)
Spell Resistance: Yes (harmless, object)

With a few words and a gesture, you empower a weapon to strike true against incorporeal foes.

Ghost touch weapon makes a weapon magically capable of dealing damage normally to incorporeal creatures, regardless of its enhancement bonus. (An incorporeal creature's 50% chance to avoid damage does not apply to attacks made with weapons under the effect of this spell.) A ranged weapon affected by this spell does not bestow the ability on its ammunition.

The weapon can be picked up and moved by an incorporeal creature at any time. A manifesting ghost can wield the weapon against corporeal foes. Essentially, a weapon under the effect of this spell counts as either corporeal or incorporeal at any given time, whichever is more beneficial to the wielder.

GHOST TRAP

Abjuration
Level: Cleric 6, sorcerer/wizard 7
Components: V, S
Casting Time: 1 standard action
Range: 5 ft./level
Area: 5 ft./level-radius emanation centered on you
Duration: 1 minute/level (D)
Saving Throw: None
Spell Resistance: No

Energy ripples outward from you, rendering solid the insubstantial.

You are surrounded by a field of energy that negates incorporeality. The radius of the field is 5 feet per caster level. All incorporeal creatures in this field become corporeal. Creatures cannot turn ethereal while in this area, and ethereal creatures cannot enter or affect the plane this spell was cast on while in this field.

GHOSTFORM

Transmutation
Level: Sorcerer/wizard 8
Components: V, S
Casting Time: 1 standard action
Range: Personal
Target: You
Duration: 1 round/level (D)

Laughing at death, you assume a ghostly form in which you can pass through walls.

You assume a visible, incorporeal form like that of a manifesting ghost. You gain the incorporeal subtype for the duration of the spell, providing you with the following abilities and characteristics.

You have no physical body while in this state. You can be harmed only by other incorporeal creatures, magic weapons or creatures that strike as magic weapons, and spells, spell-like abilities, or supernatural abilities. You are immune to all nonmagical attack forms. Even when hit by spells, including touch spells, or magic weapons, you have a 50% chance to ignore any damage from a corporeal source (except for positive energy, negative energy, force effects, or attacks made with ghost touch weapons). Nondamaging spell effects affect you normally unless they require corporeal targets to function (such as *implosion*) or they create a corporeal effect that incorporeal creatures would normally be unaffected by (such as a *web* or *wall of stone* spell).

Your attacks while in *ghostform* pass through (ignore) natural armor, armor, and shields, although deflection bonuses and force effects (such as *mage armor*) work normally against you. Nonmagical attacks you make with a melee weapon have no effect on corporeal targets, and any melee attack you make with a magic weapon against a corporeal target has a 50% miss chance, except for attacks you make with a ghost touch weapon, which are made normally (no miss chance). Spells you cast while in *ghostform* affect corporeal targets normally, including spells that require you to make an attack roll (such as rays or melee touch spells).

Any equipment you are wearing or carrying is also incorporeal as long as it remains in your possession. An object that you relinquish loses its incorporeal quality (and you lose the ability to manipulate the object). If you use a thrown weapon or a ranged weapon, the projectile becomes corporeal as soon as it is fired and can affect a corporeal target normally (no miss chance). Magic items you possess work normally with respect to their effects on you or on another target.

As an incorporeal creature, you have no natural armor bonus but have a deflection bonus equal to your Charisma bonus (always at least +1, even if your Charisma score does not normally provide a bonus).

You can enter or pass through solid objects while in *ghostform*, but you must remain adjacent to the object's exterior, and so you cannot pass entirely through an object whose space is larger than your own. You can sense the presence of creatures or objects within a square adjacent to your current location, but enemies have total concealment from you while you are inside an object. In order to see farther from the object you are in and attack normally, you must emerge. While inside an object, you have total cover, but when you attack a creature outside the object you have cover only, so a creature outside with a readied action could strike at you as you attack. You cannot pass through a force effect.

You can pass through and operate in water as easily as you do in air. You cannot fall or take falling damage. You cannot make trip or grapple attacks, nor can you be tripped or grappled. In fact, you cannot take any physical action that would move or manipulate an opponent or its equipment, nor are you subject to such actions. You have no weight while in *ghostform* and do not set off traps that are triggered by weight.

You move silently and cannot be heard with Listen checks if you don't wish to be while in *ghostform*. You have no Strength score while incorporeal, so your Dexterity modifier applies to both your melee attacks and ranged attacks. Nonvisual senses, such as scent and blindsight, are either ineffective or only partly effective with regard to you. You have an innate sense of direction and can move at full speed even when you cannot see.

Illus. by C. Dien

Already shaken by the appearance of the ghostly bard, the azers flee upon hearing the spirit's haunting tune

GHOSTHARP

Divination
Level: Bard 0
Components: V, S
Casting Time: 1 minute
Range: Touch
Target: Object touched
Duration: 5 minutes/level (D)
Saving Throw: None
Spell Resistance: No

You place the coin on the table, touch it, and whisper the words of the spell. Softly the coin begins to replay the music of the previous night's performance.

You prepare an object that records and replays a song previously played or sung in its vicinity. When cast, the spell searches a radius of 50 feet for the lingering notes of a tune played there within the last day. It records these notes and reverberations. At your verbal command, "Play," the ghostharp replays the music. The tune repeats until you command it to stop, or until its duration comes to an end. The ghostharp does not record conversations. Its imperfect replay can't reproduce bardic music or other magical effects, nor can it cast spells.

GHOUL GAUNTLET

Necromancy [Death, Evil]
Level: Hunger 5, sorcerer/wizard 6
Components: V, S
Casting Time: 1 standard action
Range: Touch
Target: One living humanoid creature
Duration: Instantaneous
Saving Throw: Fortitude negates
Spell Resistance: Yes

Your touch gradually transforms a living victim into a ravening, flesh-eating ghoul.

The subject takes 3d6 points of damage per round while its body slowly dies and its flesh is transformed into the cold, undying flesh of the undead. When the victim reaches 0 hit points, it becomes a ghoul (MM 118).

If the target fails its initial saving throw, *remove disease, dispel magic, heal, limited wish, miracle, Mordenkainen's disjunction, remove curse, wish,* or *greater restoration* negates the gradual change. Healing spells can temporarily prolong the process by increasing the victim's hit points, but the transformation continues unabated.

The ghoul that you create remains under your control indefinitely. No matter how many ghouls you generate with this spell, however, you can control only 4 HD worth of undead creatures per caster level (this includes undead from all sources under your control). If you exceed this number, all the newly created creatures fall under your control, and any excess undead from previous castings become uncontrolled (you choose which creatures are released). If you are a cleric, any undead you might command by virtue of your power to command or rebuke undead do not count toward the limit.

GHOUL GESTURE

Necromancy
Level: Hunger 3
Components: V, S, M
Casting Time: 1 standard action
Range: Medium (100 ft. + 10 ft./level)
Effect: Ray
Duration: 1 round/level

Saving Throw: Fortitude partial
Spell Resistance: Yes

A green ray stabs from your pointing finger to strike the belly of your enemy.

You must succeed on a ranged touch attack with the ray to strike a target. A subject that is successfully targeted must make a Fortitude save or be paralyzed for the duration of the spell.

A subject of the ray that succeeds on its Fortitude save is instead sickened for the duration of the spell. *Neutralize poison* removes the sickened condition.

Material Component: A small scrap of cloth taken from clothing worn by a ghoul, or a pinch of earth from a ghoul's lair.

GHOUL GLYPH

Necromancy
Level: Hunger 2, sorcerer/wizard 2
Components: V, S, M
Casting Time: 1 minute
Range: Touch
Target: Object touched
Duration: Permanent until discharged
Saving Throw: Fortitude partial
Spell Resistance: Yes

The faint, green glow of the glyph flares to life. A sickly green light fills the room, illuminating the paralyzed forms of its victims, and bringing with it the stench of death.

You inscribe a glyph, approximately 1 foot across, that paralyzes any living creature of Large or smaller size that comes within 5 feet of the glyph. You can scribe the glyph to be visible as faintly glowing lines, or invisible. You can inscribe a *ghoul glyph* on a portable object, but if the object is moved more than 5 feet, the glyph fades.

Conditions for triggering a *ghoul glyph* are stringent. It takes effect on any creature except yourself that moves within 5 feet. It affects invisible creatures normally but is not triggered by those that travel past it ethereally. Only a single *ghoul glyph* can be inscribed in a 5-foot square.

Ghoul glyphs cannot be affected or bypassed by such means as physical or magical probing, though they can be dispelled. *Mislead* and *nondetection* can fool a *ghoul glyph*.

Read magic allows identification of a *ghoul glyph* with a successful DC 13 Spellcraft check, if the glyph is noticed before it is activated. A rogue can use the Search skill to find a *ghoul glyph* and Disable Device to thwart it. The DC in each case is 27.

Girallon's blessing gives Krusk a hand in dealing with foes

Illus. by W. England

When a glyph is activated, the target is paralyzed for 1d6+2 rounds. Additionally, if the target fails a Fortitude save, the paralyzed subject exudes a carrion stench that causes distress in all creatures within a 10-foot radius. Those in the radius, including the target, must make a Fortitude save or take a –2 penalty on attack rolls, weapon damage rolls, saving throws, skill checks, and ability checks until the paralysis effect wears off.

Material Component: You trace the glyph with earth from a ghoul's lair.

GHOUL LIGHT

Necromancy
Level: Hunger 1
Components: V, S, M
Casting Time: 1 standard action
Range: Touch
Effect: Magical, heatless flame
Duration: 10 minutes/level
Saving Throw: None
Spell Resistance: No

A sickly green flame springs forth from an object that you touch.

The effect looks like a regular flame, equivalent in brightness to a torch, except for its green hue, but it creates no heat and doesn't use oxygen. Ghoul light can be covered and hidden, but not smothered or quenched.

All undead within 30 feet of a source of ghoul light gain +1 turn resistance. Multiple ghoul light sources do not stack.

Darkness spells of 2nd level or higher can counter *ghoul light*.

Material Component: A bit of rendered fat.

GIANT'S WRATH

Transmutation [Earth]
Level: Druid 3, sorcerer/wizard 3
Components: V, S, M
Casting Time: 1 swift action
Range: Personal
Targets: One pebble/3 levels
Duration: 1 round/level
Saving Throw: None
Spell Resistance: None

With your best giant's shout you rattle some pebbles in your closed hand, completing the spell that will allow them to become boulders.

You infuse a handful of stone pebbles with powerful transmutation magic. For the duration of the spell, you can hurl one pebble as an attack action that provokes attacks of opportunity. The instant the pebble leaves contact with your hand, its size and the force of your throw increase dramatically, as the pebble transforms into a boulder. The boulder has a range increment of 120 feet, and you must succeed on a ranged attack to strike a target with the boulder. If you hit the target, the boulder deals 2d6 points of bludgeoning damage + your Str modifier. You gain an insight bonus equal to your caster level on attack rolls and damage rolls (maximum +10) with these boulders.

If you drop a pebble or give it to another creature, the pebbles' magic dissipates harmlessly.

Material Component: The pebbles to be transmuted.

GIRALLON'S BLESSING

Transmutation
Level: Cleric 3, druid 3, sorcerer/wizard 3
Components: V, S, M
Casting Time: 1 standard action
Range: Touch
Target: Creature touched
Duration: 10 minutes/level
Saving Throw: Fortitude negates (harmless)
Spell Resistance: Yes (harmless)

The touched subject appears to be in discomfort for an instant before arms erupt from its torso with a damp squelch.

You give the subject an additional pair of arms. Each of its arms—new and old—ends in a clawed hand with fingers and an opposable thumb. The creature's original arms (if any) are its primary arms, and new limbs are secondary limbs (if the subject had no arms, the arms created by the spell are its primary arms).

The creature gains four claw attacks, each using its base attack bonus + its Str modifier for attack rolls. Each claw deals 1d4 points of damage + the subject's Str modifier, and if an opponent is struck by two or more claws in 1 round, the subject can rend it for an additional 2d4 points of damage + 1-1/2 times its Str modifier.

A creature cannot use normal weapons and the claw attacks in the same round, and the subject does not gain additional claw attacks from a high base attack bonus.

Material Component: A few strands of girallon hair.

GLASS STRIKE

Transmutation
Level: Sorcerer/wizard 7
Components: V, S, F
Casting Time: 1 standard action
Range: Close (25 ft. + 5 ft./2 levels)
Target: One creature or 4 cubic ft. of material
Duration: 1 hour/level
Saving Throw: Fortitude negates
Spell Resistance: Yes

The spell erupts from the surface of the mirror you hold, striking your foe square in the chest and transforming it to glass.

You transform the target into glass. You can cast either of these two versions:

Glass Creature: As *flesh to stone* (PH 232), but the subject becomes glass.

Glass Object: An object of up to 4 cubic feet in volume is affected. Part of a larger object (such as a floor or wall) can be transformed by this spell. Glass has hardness 1, and 1 hit point per inch of thickness.

Neither version of the spell affects magic items (magic items carried by a transformed creature remain intact). When the duration ends, the subject returns to its original materials. If the subject was broken or damaged while in glass form, its normal form has similar damage.

Focus: A piece of glass from a mirror.

GLOWING ORB

Evocation [Light]
Level: Cleric 4, sorcerer/wizard 3
Components: V, S, F
Casting Time: 1 standard action
Range: Touch
Effect: Magical, controllable light source
Duration: Permanent
Saving Throw: None
Spell Resistance: No

Calling on the limitless light of the Positive Energy Plane, you coax a tiny portion of its power into a fragile glass sphere.

This spell places a magical light source inside a glass sphere roughly the size of a human fist. You can control the light level generated by a glowing orb by mental command (a standard action), provided that the orb is within 30 feet of you. The light level ranges from no light at all to illumination within a 60-foot radius. There is no limit to the number of glowing orbs you can possess, and you can control their light levels independently or in concert.

If a glowing orb is smashed, the magic is lost. If you die, however, an orb retains its magic. Any character with an Intelligence or Wisdom of at least 13 can gain control of an orb simply by touching it.

Focus: A glass sphere (50 gp) into which the light is placed. An orb usable for this purpose has hardness 0 and 2 hit points.

GOLDEN BARDING

Conjuration (Creation)
Level: Blackguard 1, paladin 1
Components: V, DF
Casting Time: 1 standard action
Range: Touch
Target: Special mount touched
Duration: 1 hour/level
Saving Throw: None
Spell Resistance: No

With a flash, a glowing, golden suit of barding for your special mount appears.

You create a suit of barding for your mount to wear. The armor appears on your mount, fitting perfectly. The golden barding you create has no armor check penalty and has no effect on your mount's speed. The exact nature of the barding depends on your caster level.

2nd–3rd: Scale mail barding (+4 armor bonus).

4th–5th: Chainmail barding (+5).

6th–7th: Splint mail barding (+6).

8th–9th: Half-plate barding (+7).

10th+: Full plate barding (+8).

You can cast *magic vestment* or other spells that target a suit of armor on the *golden barding*.

GOLEM STRIKE

Divination
Level: Sorcerer/wizard 1
Components: V
Casting Time: 1 swift action
Range: Personal
Target: You
Duration: 1 round

A dim glow fills your eyes, allowing you to see—briefly—weak points in the magic infused within a nearby construct.

For 1 round, you can deliver sneak attacks against constructs as if they were not immune to extra damage from sneak attacks. To attack a construct in this manner, you must still meet the other requirements for making a sneak attack.

This spell applies only to sneak attack damage. It gives you no ability to affect constructs with critical hits, nor does it confer any special ability to overcome the damage reduction or other defenses of constructs.

GRACE

Transmutation [Good]
Level: Bard 2, cleric 3
Components: V
Casting Time: 1 swift action
Range: Personal
Target: You
Duration: 1 round/level

With a single word, you call upon the might and grace of your deity, bathing your body with divine energy. Your body glows with silvery light and you feel quick and light on your feet.

You create a silvery glow around your body that provides illumination to a radius of 60 feet. You gain a –20 circumstance penalty on Hide checks made while under the effect of this spell.

For the duration of the spell, you gain a +2 sacred bonus to Dexterity, and your base land speed increases by 10 feet.

Your touch attacks and any melee weapons you wield become infused with this power as well. They are treated as good-aligned weapons for the purpose of overcoming damage reduction.

GRAVE STRIKE

Divination [Good]
Level: Cleric 1, paladin 1
Components: V, DF
Casting Time: 1 swift action
Range: Personal
Target: You
Duration: 1 round

Golden motes of light dance before your eyes. They converge on undead you look at, hovering about them and forming wedges of positive energy.

For 1 round, you can deliver sneak attacks against undead as if they were not immune to extra damage from sneak attacks. To attack an undead creature in this manner, you must still meet the other requirements for making a sneak attack.

A rogue and a cleric of Olidammara, this halfling delivers a fatal blow to a vampire with the grave strike spell

This spell applies only to sneak attack damage. It gives you no ability to affect undead with critical hits, nor does it confer any special ability to overcome the damage reduction or other defenses of undead creatures.

GRAYMANTLE

Necromancy
Level: Sorcerer/wizard 5
Components: V, S, M
Casting Time: 1 standard action
Range: Medium (100 ft. + 10 ft./level)
Target: One living creature
Duration: 1 round/level
Saving Throw: Fortitude negates
Spell Resistance: Yes

You create a cloud of sickly gray energy that streaks toward a living creature, wrapping it in the foul essence of unlife.

A skull-shaped cloud of gray energy strikes your target. The gray radiance is transferred to the creature, covering it entirely. For the duration of the spell, a living subject cannot regain hit points or ability score points by any means (undead creatures can still gain hit points), nor can the creature remove negative levels. Regeneration or fast healing abilities the subject has from any source are suppressed for the duration of the spell. Spells that heal damage do not work on that individual. The subject can improve its current hit points by boosting its Constitution score and can receive temporary hit points (from an *aid* spell, for example).

When the spell ends, automatic healing abilities, such as a troll's regeneration, and items that restore hit points, such as a *ring of regeneration*, begin to function again.

Material Component: A skull.

GREAT THUNDERCLAP

Evocation [Sonic]
Level: Sorcerer/wizard 3
Components: V, S, F
Casting Time: 1 standard action
Range: Medium (100 ft. + 10 ft./level)
Area: 20-ft.-radius spread
Duration: Instantaneous
Saving Throw: See text
Spell Resistance: No

You grip the bell in your fist and raise it over your head, intoning the spell and calling down a thunderous blast in the midst of those who oppose you.

You create a loud noise equivalent to a peal of thunder. The spell has three effects. First, all creatures in the area must make Will saves to avoid being stunned for 1 round. Second, the creatures must make Fortitude saves or be deafened for 1 minute. Third, they must make Reflex saves or fall prone.

Illus. by M. Phillippi

Creatures that cannot hear are not stunned, but might still fall prone.

Focus: An iron bell.

GREATER (SPELL NAME)

Any spell whose name begins with *greater* is alphabetized in this chapter according to the second word of the spell name. Thus, the description of a *greater* spell appears near the description of the spell on which it is based, unless that spell appears in the *Player's Handbook*.

GUIDED SHOT

Divination

Level: Ranger 1, sorcerer/wizard 1
Components: V
Casting Time: 1 swift action
Range: Personal
Target: You
Duration: 1 round

With a guttural utterance made with unmoving lips, you magically focus your attention on a distant foe. Upon aiming your weapon, you note how clearly defined your intended target is.

While this spell is in effect, your ranged attacks do not take a penalty due to distance. In addition, your ranged attacks ignore the AC bonus granted to targets by anything less than total cover, and also ignore the miss chance granted to targets by anything less than total concealment.

This spell does not provide any ability to exceed the maximum range of the weapon with which you are attacking, nor does it confer any ability to attack targets protected by total cover.

GUIDING LIGHT

Evocation [Light]

Level: Bard 1, cleric 1, sorcerer/wizard 1
Components: V, S
Casting Time: 1 standard action
Range: Long (400 ft. + 40 ft./level)
Targets: Creatures in a 5-ft.-radius burst
Duration: 1 minute/level (D)
Saving Throw: None
Spell Resistance: Yes

Across the murky plain, a beam of radiance shoots down, highlighting your foes.

A hail of stone spell pummels its target

Illus. by D. Martin

Bright lights shine at the targets. The lights grant a +2 circumstance bonus on ranged attack rolls against any highlighted target. If a creature gains total cover or total concealment relative to you, or if it leaves the area, the spell ends for that target.

GUTSNAKE

Transmutation

Level: Sorcerer/wizard 5
Components: V, S, F
Casting Time: 1 standard action
Range: Personal
Target: You
Duration: 1 round/level (D)

You concentrate on the tooth, speak the words, and a 15-foot-long tentacle sprouts from your stomach. The tentacle has no eyes, but it ends in a set of snapping reptilian jaws.

The tentacle created by the *gutsnake* spell is equivalent to a giant constrictor snake (MM 280) except that it is completely obedient to you and moves as you command. The snake has hit points equal to your own full normal total. Attacks against the snake cause you no discomfort and do not disrupt your spellcasting. If it is "killed," the tentacle disappears without causing harm to you. The tentacle does not interfere with spellcasting in any way.

Once each round as a free action, you can have the tentacle attack a creature up to 10 feet away with its bite attack, and if it successfully hits, the tentacle can use the snake's improved grab ability to deal damage through constriction.

In each round when the *gutsnake* is constricting a target, you cannot move more than 5 feet away from that target, unless the *gutsnake* makes a successful grapple check to carry the opponent with you when you move (see PH 155 for grappling rules). This is the only way in which the tentacle restricts movement. While the snake is present, you can use its Balance and Climb skill modifiers instead of your own, and you gain a climb speed of 20 feet.

Focus: A fang from any reptile.

HAIL OF STONE

Conjuration (Creation) [Earth]

Level: Sorcerer/wizard 1
Components: V, S, M
Casting Time: 1 round
Range: Medium (100 ft. + 10 ft./level)
Area: Cylinder (5-ft. radius, 40 ft. high)
Duration: Instantaneous
Saving Throw: None
Spell Resistance: No

You hold the jade chip before you and blow on it as you end the spell. The chip flares with a green flame and vanishes as rocks begin to fall on your pursuers.

You create a rain of stones that deals 1d4 points of damage per caster level (maximum 5d4) to creatures and objects within the area.

Material Component: A piece of jade worth at least 5 gp.

HAILSTONES

Evocation [Cold]
Level: Sorcerer/wizard 3
Components: V, S, M
Casting Time: 1 standard action
Range: Medium (100 ft. + 10 ft./level)
Effect: One frigid globe/5 levels
Duration: Instantaneous
Saving Throw: None
Spell Resistance: Yes

The crystal globes in your hand vibrate intensely before turning ice-cold. As you hurl them, they resemble balls of ice, an observation borne true when they strike and shatter into a shower of ice crystals.

You create frigid hailstones that strike your enemies. You must succeed on a ranged touch attack to hit with a globe. Each hailstone deals 5d6 points of cold damage. For every five caster levels, you gain an additional hailstone (maximum of four stones at 20th level), and all globes must be aimed at enemies that are all within 30 feet of each other.

Material Component: A handful of crystal globes.

HAMATULA BARBS

Transmutation
Level: Cleric 3, sorcerer/wizard 3
Components: V, S, M
Casting Time: 1 standard action
Range: Touch
Target: Creature touched
Duration: 10 minutes/level
Saving Throw: Fortitude negates (harmless)
Spell Resistance: Yes (harmless)

You invoke the dark nature of the spell and slender, sharp-edged barbs sprout from your body and clothing, glowing with hellish energy.

Any creature hitting the subject of this spell with a handheld weapon or a natural weapon takes 1d8 points of slashing and piercing damage from the subject's barbs. This damage does not apply to attackers using reach weapons, such as longspears. The subject itself is not harmed by its own barbs.

Arcane Material Component: A barb from a hamatula.

HAND OF DIVINITY

Evocation [see text]
Level: Blackguard 2, cleric 2, paladin 2
Components: V, S, DF
Casting Time: 1 minute
Range: Touch
Target: Creature touched
Duration: 1 minute/level
Saving Throw: None
Spell Resistance: No

You call upon your beliefs and a great pair of hands appears around your target, cradling it in its power. The effect fades, but your target briefly glows with a healthy orange nimbus.

If your deity is non-evil, this spell grants a +2 sacred bonus on saving throws, and the spell is a good spell. If your deity is evil, this spell grants a +2 profane bonus on saving throws, and the spell is an evil spell.

This spell works only on a creature with the same deity as you or the same alignment as your deity. If cast on a target that does not meet this criteria, the spell has no effect.

HAND OF THE FAITHFUL

Abjuration [see text]
Level: Cleric 4, paladin 3
Components: V, S, DF
Casting Time: 1 minute
Range: 10 ft.
Area: 10-ft.-radius emanation centered on a point in space
Duration: 1 hour/level
Saving Throw: Fortitude negates
Spell Resistance: Yes

You summon the protective field, and the shimmering border limns out along the floor, carrying with it the ephemeral image of blocking hands.

You create an immobile zone of warding that is permeable to those of your religion but repels all others. Creatures that have the same deity as you, or are wearing the holy symbol of your deity, can enter and move within the warded area unhindered. Other creatures that try to enter or move within the area must make a Fortitude save each round or be stunned for 1 round. If the creature's only action is to try to move completely out of the area, the ward does not hinder it. Once a creature succeeds on its saving throw, it is no longer affected by that casting of *hand of the faithful.*

This spell has the alignment components of your deity, so if your deity is good and lawful, this is a lawful and good spell.

HARDENING

Transmutation
Level: Sorcerer/wizard 6
Components: V, S, M
Casting Time: 1 standard action
Range: Touch
Target: One item of a volume no greater than 10 cu. ft./level; see text
Duration: Permanent
Saving Throw: None
Spell Resistance: Yes (object)

You rub your hands along the length of the object, intoning the spell. A warm red glow emits from your hands, strengthening the object.

This spell increases the hardness of materials. Paper becomes harder to tear, glass becomes harder to break, wood becomes more resilient, and so on. For every two caster levels, add 1 point of hardness to the material targeted by the spell. This hardness increase improves only the material's resistance to damage. Nothing else is modified by the improvement. For example, a longsword (treat steel as iron, base hardness 10) affected by a *hardening* spell cast by a 12th-level caster would have hardness 16 for the purpose of ignoring damage caused by someone making a sunder attack. The sword's hit points, attack and damage modifiers, and other factors are not affected. A *hardening* spell does not in any way affect a substance's resistance to other forms of transformation. Ice still melts, paper and wood still burn, rock still becomes transmutable to mud with the proper spell, and so on.

This spell affects up to 10 cubic feet of material per level of the caster. If cast upon a metal or mineral, the spell affects only 1 cubic foot per level.

Material Component: An ointment made with 50 gp of diamond dust per 10 cubic feet of material.

HARMONIC CHORUS

Enchantment (Compulsion) [Mind-Affecting]
Level: Bard 2
Components: V, S, F
Casting Time: 1 standard action
Range: Close (25 ft. + 5 ft./2 levels)
Target: One living creature
Duration: Concentration, up to 1 round/level (D)
Saving Throw: Will negates (harmless)
Spell Resistance: Yes

Sweeping your arm as if presenting a gift to someone, you call out to the intended subject of your spell. A mantle of sweet tones settles about your subject, whose face is now twisted in concentration.

Harmonic chorus lets you improve the spellcasting ability of another spellcaster. For the duration of the spell, the subject gains a +2 morale bonus to caster level and a +2 morale bonus on save DCs for all spells it casts.

Focus: A tuning fork.

HASTE, SWIFT

Transmutation
Level: Ranger 2
Components: V
Casting Time: 1 swift action
Range: Personal
Target: You
Duration: 1d4 rounds

Two quick syllables release the power of the spell, and the world moves a bit slower about you.

This spell functions like *haste* (PH 239), except as noted above. This spell counters and dispels any *slow* effect on you.

HAUNTING TUNE

Enchantment (Compulsion) [Fear, Mind-Affecting, Sonic]
Level: Bard 3
Components: V, S
Casting Time: 1 round
Range: Medium (100 ft. + 10 ft./level)
Targets: One creature/level, no two of which are more than 30 ft. apart
Duration: 10 minutes/level
Saving Throw: Will negates
Spell Resistance: Yes

The spell wrapped within your music makes even the most hard-hearted quail.

Targets that fail their saves become shaken.

HAWKEYE

Transmutation
Level: Druid 1, ranger 1
Components: V
Casting Time: 1 standard action
Range: Personal
Target: You
Duration: 10 minutes/level (D)

By crying out like a hawk, you improve your eyesight. Distant objects and creatures seem closer and more distinct.

Your range increment for ranged weapons increases by 50%, and you gain a +5 competence bonus on Spot checks.

HEAL ANIMAL COMPANION

Conjuration (Healing)
Level: Druid 5, ranger 3
Components: V, S
Casting Time: 1 standard action
Range: Touch
Target: Your animal companion touched
Duration: Instantaneous
Saving Throw: Will negates (harmless)
Spell Resistance: Yes (harmless)

You lay your hand on your animal companion, and as you do, its eyes become clear and focused, and it breathes easier.

This spell functions like *heal* (PH 239), except that it affects only your animal companion.

HEALING LORECALL

Divination
Level: Cleric 2, druid 2, ranger 1
Components: V, S, M
Casting Time: 1 standard action
Range: Personal
Target: You
Duration: 10 minutes/level

With a mint leaf under your tongue, you whisper quiet words of soothing comfort. You feel a divine touch guiding your healing hand.

A caster with 5 or more ranks in Heal can, when casting a conjuration (healing) spell, choose to remove any one of the following conditions affecting the subject of the spell, in addition to the spell's normal effects: dazed, dazzled, or fatigued. A caster with 10 or more ranks in Heal can choose from the following conditions in addition to those above: exhausted, nauseated, or sickened.

Also, when determining the amount of damage healed by your conjuration (healing) spells, you can substitute your total ranks in Heal for your caster level. The normal caster level limit for individual spells still applies; thus, a 3rd-level cleric with 6 ranks in Heal when under the effect of *healing lorecall* cures 1d8+5 points of damage with a *cure light wounds* spell.

Material Component: A mint leaf.

HEALING STING

Necromancy
Level: Druid 2
Components: V, S, M
Casting Time: 1 standard action
Range: Touch
Targets: You and one living creature
Duration: Instantaneous
Saving Throw: None
Spell Resistance: Yes

Your palms tingle as you smash the dead wasps between your hands. The tingling intensifies as you strike the opposing warrior, pulling his vitality into yourself.

Focusing the power of negative energy, you deal 1d12 points of damage +1 per caster level (maximum 1d12+10) to a living creature and gain an equal amount of hit points if you make a successful melee touch attack. A *healing sting* cannot give you more hit points than your full normal total. Excess hit points are lost.

Material Component: Five dried wasp bodies.

HEALING TOUCH

Necromancy (Healing)
Level: Sorcerer/wizard 3
Components: V, S
Casting Time: 1 standard action
Range: Touch
Target: Creature touched
Duration: Instantaneous
Saving Throw: Will negates (harmless)
Spell Resistance: Yes (harmless)

The skin of your hands turns translucent, showing the muscle and bone beneath. You touch your badly injured ally and feel your own vitality leave your body and enter his damaged form.

You transfer some of your life essence to the subject of the spell, healing it. You can heal up to 1d6 points of damage per two caster levels (maximum 10d6), and you decide how many dice to roll when you cast the spell. You take damage equal to half the amount your subject was healed. This spell cannot heal a subject of more damage than your current hit points +10, which is enough to kill you.

HEALTHFUL REST

Conjuration (Healing)
Level: Bard 1, cleric 1, druid 1
Components: V, S
Casting Time: 10 minutes
Range: Close (25 ft. + 5 ft./2 levels)
Targets: One creature/level, no two of which are more than 30 ft. apart
Duration: 24 hours
Saving Throw: Will negates (harmless)
Spell Resistance: Yes (harmless)

A diffuse glow of golden light spreads from you, wrapping those you have chosen in a soft nimbus. The subjects of your spell look relaxed and rested, the stresses of the day forgotten.

Healthful rest doubles the subjects' natural healing rate. Each affected creature regains twice the hit points and ability damage it otherwise would have regained during that day, depending on its activity level (PH 76).

Collecting material components can be a laborious process, so alchemists often offer them for sale

HEART OF STONE

Necromancy
Level: Sorcerer/wizard 8
Components: V, S, F, XP
Casting Time: 1 hour
Range: Personal
Target: You
Duration: 1 year

You feel a hard shove from within your chest as you finally complete the complicated phrases and intricate motions of this taxing spell. Sweat beads on your forehead and your breath comes shallow and fast. The rhythmic rush of sound in your ears that usually accompanies such heavy physical exertion is disquietingly absent.

You exchange your own living heart for a finely crafted heart of perfect, unblemished stone, altering the nature of your body. Your living heart can be stored or hidden anywhere you like, where it continues to beat for the duration of the spell. While under the effect of *heart of stone,* you gain damage reduction 5/— and resistance to cold 5, fire 5, and electricity 5, but are subject to the following disadvantages. Your rate of natural healing slows to only 1 hit point per day (regardless of character level or whether you rest). In addition, your own living heart is susceptible to attack; if it is damaged or destroyed, you are instantly slain.

Heart of stone can be dispelled, in which case your living heart instantly returns to its proper place while the stone heart is transported to the place where you left your heart. Your heart and the stone heart likewise switch places if you enter an *antimagic field* (temporarily negating the spell's effects), but the spell resumes when you leave it. *Stone to flesh* can also end the spell, though you get a Fortitude saving throw to resist.

Focus: A carved stone heart of exceptional quality (jade, obsidian, or gold-veined marble) worth 5,000 gp.

XP Cost: 500 XP.

HEART RIPPER

Necromancy [Death]
Level: Assassin 4
Components: V, S
Casting Time: 1 standard action
Range: Close (25 ft. + 5 ft./2 levels)
Target: One living creature
Duration: Instantaneous
Saving Throw: Fortitude negates
Spell Resistance: Yes

Illus. by W. England

Illus. by B. Hagan

The assassin didn't even bother to speak to the guards before he killed them with a heart ripper spell

With a sweep of your hand, invisible magic slams into your target. With a bloody pop and squelch, the heart of your target bursts out its back, dropping the creature like a discarded rag doll.

Invisible bolts of force instantly slay the target you designate by driving its heart from its body unless it succeeds on a Fortitude save. If the target has HD higher than your caster level, it does not die on a failed saving throw, but instead is stunned for 1d4 rounds. Creatures that don't depend on their hearts for survival, creatures with no anatomy, and creatures immune to extra damage from critical hits are unaffected by the spell.

HEARTFIRE

Evocation [Light, Fire]
Level: Bard 2, druid 2
Components: V, S, DF
Casting Time: 1 standard action
Range: Close (25 ft. + 5 ft./2 levels)
Area: Living creatures within a 5-ft.-radius burst
Duration: 1 round/level
Saving Throw: Fortitude partial
Spell Resistance: Yes

A flickering red fire bursts in the area you intended. Creatures in the area are outlined in the flame, some more intensely than others.

Outlined subjects shed light as torches. Outlined creatures do not benefit from the concealment normally provided by darkness (although a 3rd-level or higher magical darkness effect functions normally), *blur, displacement, invisibility,* or similar effects. In addition, if they fail a Fortitude save, affected creatures take 1d4 points of fire damage each round as their passions manifest as physically damaging fire. Creatures that make a successful Fortitude save take only half damage each round for the duration of the spell (minimum 1 point per round). Spellcasters affected by this spell who try to cast spells must make Concentration checks (DC 10 + half the continuous damage last dealt) each round as they take continuous damage from the spell. The fire created by this spell can be extinguished by normal means; doing so ends the outlining effect.

HEAT DRAIN

Necromancy [Cold]
Level: Cleric 8
Components: V, S, DF
Casting Time: 1 standard action
Range: 20 ft.
Area: 20-ft.-radius burst centered on you
Duration: Instantaneous
Saving Throw: Fortitude negates
Spell Resistance: Yes

The heat in the room seems to rush toward you, leaving everyone around you in bone-chilling pain while you feel amazingly refreshed and alive.

You drain the heat from all living creatures within the affected area except you. This influx of warmth heals and empowers you. All affected living creatures take 1d6 points of cold damage per caster level (maximum 20d6). For every living creature that takes damage from this spell, you gain 2 temporary hit points. The temporary hit points last for up to 1 minute per level.

HEATSTROKE

Transmutation
Level: Druid 3
Components: V, S
Casting Time: 1 standard action
Range: Medium (100 ft. + 10 ft./level)
Target: One creature
Duration: Instantaneous
Saving Throw: Fortitude partial
Spell Resistance: Yes

With a wave of your hand and a few hissed words, you cause the target creature to suffer as if it had been toiling for hours on end under the merciless hammer of the desert sun.

If the target creature fails to resist the spell, it immediately becomes fatigued. If it is already fatigued, it instead becomes exhausted. The subject takes 2d6 points of nonlethal damage from the oppressive heat as well, even if it makes the Fortitude saving throw to avoid fatigue or exhaustion.

A creature wearing heavy armor takes a –4 penalty on its save. Creatures with immunity or resistance to fire are not affected by this spell.

HEAVENLY HOST

Conjuration (Summoning) [Good, Lawful]
Level: Cleric 9, sorcerer/wizard 9
Components: V, S
Casting Time: 10 minutes
Range: Medium (100 ft. + 10 ft./level)
Effect: Two or more summoned creatures, no two of which are more than 30 ft. apart
Duration: 10 minutes/level (D)
Saving Throw: None
Spell Resistance: No

You invoke this spell and heavenly rays lance down from above. Out of these sparkling rays manifest great glowing balls of power. The shadows of greater warriors coalesce within this light.

When the spell is complete, 2d4 lantern archons (MM 16) appear. Ten minutes later, 1d4 hound archons (MM 17) appear. Each creature has maximum hit points per Hit Die. Once these creatures appear, they serve you for the duration of the spell.

The creatures obey you explicitly and never attack you, even if someone else manages to gain control over them. You do not need to concentrate to maintain control over the creatures. You can dismiss them singly or in groups at any time.

HELLISH HORDE

Conjuration (Summoning) [Evil, Lawful]
Level: Cleric 9, sorcerer/wizard 9
Components: V, S
Casting Time: 10 minutes
Range: Medium (100 ft. + 10 ft./level)
Effect: Two or more summoned creatures, no two of which are more than 30 ft. apart
Duration: 10 minutes/level (D)
Saving Throw: None
Spell Resistance: No

A wave of spectral fire bursts forth, and out of the curling smoke steps the hunched form of a barbazu, followed by a second, and other shadowy forms loom behind them.

When the spell is complete, 2d4 bearded devils (MM 52) appear. Ten minutes later, 1d4 chain devils (MM 53) appear. Ten minutes after that, one bone devil (MM 52) appears. Each creature has maximum hit points per Hit Die. Once these creatures appear, they serve you for the duration of the spell.

The devils obey you explicitly and never attack you, even if someone else manages to gain control over them. You do not need to concentrate to maintain control over the devils. You can dismiss them singly or in groups at any time.

HERALD'S CALL

Enchantment (Compulsion) [Mind-Affecting, Sonic]
Level: Bard 1
Components: V, S
Casting Time: 1 swift action
Range: 20 ft.
Area: 20-ft.-radius burst centered on you
Duration: 1 round
Saving Throw: Will negates
Spell Resistance: Yes

By placing your hand to your mouth and calling out, you gain the attention of creatures around you. For a moment, all eyes snap to you. Some creatures seem reluctant or unable to pull their eyes away.

Any creature with 5 Hit Dice or less is slowed (PH 280) for 1 round. Creatures beyond the radius of the burst might hear the shout, but they are not slowed. An affected creature under the effect of a *haste* spell has the *haste* spell suppressed (not dispelled) for 1 round.

HEROICS

Transmutation
Level: Sorcerer/wizard 2
Components: V, S, M
Casting Time: 1 standard action
Range: Touch
Target: Creature touched
Duration: 10 minutes/level
Saving Throw: None
Spell Resistance: Yes

Your heart swells with martial vigor and you feel like marching off to war. Upon touching your intended subject the desire to do battle wanes, but you see a hint of the lust for glory in the recipient's eyes.

The *heroics* spell temporarily grants the subject a feat from the fighter's bonus feat list. For the duration of the *heroics* spell, the subject can use the feat as if it were one of those the creature had selected. All prerequisites for the feat must be met by the target of this spell.

Material Component: A bit of a weapon or armor that has been used in combat by a fighter of at least 15th level.

HIDDEN LODGE

Conjuration (Creation)
Level: Bard 5, sorcerer/wizard 5
Components: V, S, F; see text
Duration: 24 hours

You picture in your mind the desired appearance of a camouflaged lodge even as you complete the motions and words of the spell. When you finish, you open your eyes and note a new feature in the landscape roughly the size of a house.

This spell functions like *Leomund's secure shelter* (PH 247), except as noted here. The house created by *hidden lodge* is perfectly camouflaged to blend in with whatever terrain or surroundings are appropriate. It might appear as a house-sized boulder in a rocky or mountainous area, as a sand dune in the desert, as a densely tangled thicket, a grassy knoll, or even a mighty tree. The lodge also obscures all telltale signs of habitation, including any smoke, light, or sound coming from within.

At any distance of more than 30 feet, the lodge is indistinguishable from natural terrain. Any creature approaching within 30 feet is entitled to a DC 30 Survival check to spot the hidden lodge as an artificial dwelling and not a natural part of the landscape.

Focus: The focus of an *alarm* spell (silver wire and a tiny bell), if this benefit is to be included in the *hidden lodge* (see *Leomund's secure shelter* for more information).

HIDE FROM DRAGONS

Abjuration
Level: Assassin 4, bard 5, sorcerer/wizard 7
Components: S, M
Casting Time: 1 standard action
Range: Touch
Targets: One creature touched/2 levels
Duration: 10 minutes/level (D)
Saving Throw: Will negates (harmless)
Spell Resistance: Yes (harmless)

Silently you make the motions and the dragon's scale smolders in your hand. The rising smoke wraps around you and sinks into your skin.

Dragons cannot see, hear, or smell the warded creatures, even with blindsense. They act as though the warded creatures are not there. Warded creatures could stand before the hungriest of red dragons and not be molested or even noticed. If a warded character touches or attacks a dragon or the dragon's hoard, even with a spell, the spell ends for all recipients.

Material Component: A dragon scale.

HIDE THE PATH

Abjuration
Level: Cleric 6, druid 6
Components: V, S, F
Casting Time: 10 minutes
Range: Anywhere in the area to be warded
Area: Up to 200 sq. ft./level (S)
Duration: 24 hours (D)
Saving Throw: None
Spell Resistance: No

After what feels like an hour, you finish the chant and rest your hands on the onyx sphere, envisioning the places you wish to protect from those seeking your secrets.

Hide the path wards a large, continuous area against divination magic. The ward protects 200 square feet per caster level and can be shaped as you desire. The warded area can be as much as 20 feet high.

Find the path won't function in an area warded by *hide the path*. In addition, any spellcaster attempting to cast a 1st- through 6th-level divination spell in the warded area must make a caster level check (DC 11 + your caster level) or the spell fails. Higher-level divinations function normally. *Hide the path* has no effect on divination spells cast outside the warded area.

Focus: A 6-inch onyx sphere mounted upon an obsidian stand; the entire focus must be worth no less than 1,000 gp. Any creature in physical contact with the focus can cast divination spells without restriction from the *hide the path* effect. If the focus is destroyed or brought beyond the boundaries of the *hide the path* spell, the spell is immediately dismissed.

HINDSIGHT

Divination
Level: Bard 6, sorcerer/wizard 9
Components: V, S, M
Casting Time: 1 hour
Range: 60 ft.
Area: 60-ft.-radius emanation centered on you
Duration: Instantaneous
Saving Throw: None
Spell Resistance: No

The rigorous ritual of the spell finally draws to a close. You breathe a sigh of relief even as phantom images appear before your eyes, moving in reverse. Suddenly they cease their movements and seem more real. You watch as the phantom images play out their parts in quick succession, showing you the knowledge of the past you seek.

You can see and hear into the past, getting a look at events that happened previously at your current location. The level of detail you see and hear by means of this spell depends on the span of time you wish to observe; concentrating on a span of days renders a more detailed perspective than a span of centuries, for example. You can view only one span of time per casting, chosen from the following options.

Days: You sense the events of the past, stretching back one day per caster level. You gain detailed knowledge of the people, conversations, and events that transpired.

Weeks: You gain a summary of the events of the past, stretching back one week per caster level. Exact wording and details are lost, but you know all the participants and the highlights of the conversations and events that took place.

Years: You gain a general idea of the events of the past, stretching back one year per caster level. You notice only noteworthy events such as deaths, battles, scenes of great emotion, important discoveries, and significant happenings.

Centuries: You gain a general idea of the events of the past, stretching back one century plus an additional century for every four caster levels beyond 1st. For instance, a 16th-level caster would gain insight into the events of four centuries in the past, and a 17th-level caster would see back across five centuries. You notice only the most remarkable of events: coronations, deaths of important personages, major battles, and other truly historic happenings.

Material Component: An hourglass-shaped diamond worth at least 1,000 gp.

HISS OF SLEEP

Enchantment (Compulsion) [Mind-Affecting]
Level: Sorcerer/wizard 7
Components: V
Casting Time: 1 round
Range: Close (25 ft. + 5 ft./2 levels)
Targets: One creature/level
Duration: 1 round/level
Saving Throw: Will negates
Spell Resistance: No

From your hiding place, you whisper the spell softly, your words taking on a sono-

The holy mount spell bolsters a paladin's special mount with many useful resistances

rous drone. One by one, your foes drop to ground, asleep.

The targets of this spell fall into a comatose slumber. Sleeping creatures are helpless. Slapping or wounding the subjects awakens them, but normal noise does not. Awakening a creature is a standard action.

HOLY MOUNT

Transmutation
Level: Paladin 2
Components: V, S
Casting Time: 1 standard action
Range: Touch
Target: Your special mount
Duration: 1 round/level
Saving Throw: None
Spell Resistance: Yes (harmless)

Touching your special mount, you feel the divine power seep into your trusted friend and watch as a golden nimbus surrounds it.

Your special mount gains the celestial template (MM 31) for the duration of the spell.

HOLY SPURS

Transmutation
Level: Paladin 1
Components: V
Casting Time: 1 swift action
Range: Close (25 ft. + 5 ft./2 levels)
Target: Your special mount
Duration: 1 round
Saving Throw: Will negates (harmless)
Spell Resistance: Yes (harmless)

You invoke the holy powers and your mount's legs glow with a brilliant yellow radiance.

This spell increases your special mount's base land speed by 40 feet. This adjustment is treated as an enhancement bonus.

HOLY STAR

Abjuration
Level: Cleric 7
Components: V, S
Casting Time: 1 standard action
Range: 0 ft.
Effect: Protective star of energy
Duration: 3 rounds (D)

By calling upon the power of your deity, you bring into existence a glowing mote of energy near your shoulder. While no brighter than a candle, the mote of light fills your body with an inner warmth and feeling of reassuring protection.

You create a glowing mote of energy that stays near your shoulder, providing light equal to that of a candle. This star has the following three functions, and you can designate which function to activate as a free action on your turn.

Spell Turning: A *holy star* can turn a total of four to seven (1d4+3) spell levels, as the *spell turning* spell (PH 282). Any turning potential depleted through this use remains so for the duration of the spell; the *holy star* does not return to full capacity every time you choose this function. If its entire spell turning capacity is expended, this function no longer works, but the others do.

Protection: A *holy star* gives you a +6 circumstance bonus to AC.

Fire Bolt: A *holy star* lashes out with a beam of energy as a ranged touch attack against a creature (you choose the target) up to 90 feet away (no range increment). This attack uses your attack bonus and deals fire damage equal to 1d6 points per two caster levels (maximum 10d6).

HOLY STORM

Conjuration (Creation) [Good, Water]
Level: Cleric 3, paladin 3
Components: V, S, M, DF
Casting Time: 1 standard action
Range: 20 ft.
Area: Cylinder (20-ft. radius, 20 ft. high)
Duration: 1 round/level (D)
Saving Throw: None
Spell Resistance: No

You call upon the forces of good, and a heavy rain begins to fall around you, its raindrops soft and warm.

A driving rain falls around you. It falls in a fixed area once created. The storm reduces hearing and visibility, resulting in a –4 penalty on Listen, Spot, and Search checks. It also applies a –4 penalty on ranged attacks made into, out of, or through the storm. Finally, it automatically extinguishes any unprotected flames and has a 50% chance to extinguish protected flames (such as those of lanterns).

The rain damages evil creatures, dealing 2d6 points of damage per round (evil outsiders take double damage) at the beginning of your turn.

Material Component: A flask of holy water (25 gp).

Illus. by J. Thomas

HOLY TRANSFORMATION

Transmutation [Good]
Level: Cleric 7

This spell functions like *lesser holy transformation,* but when you cast this spell, you assume the physical appearance and many of the qualities and abilities of a hound archon (MM 16). While under the effect of the spell, your creature type changes to outsider (archon, good, lawful), and your size changes to Medium. You have the space and reach of a hound archon (5 feet/5 feet). You gain a +4 sacred bonus to Strength and Constitution. You gain darkvision out to 60 feet. You gain a +4 sacred bonus on saving throws. You gain damage reduction 5/evil. Evil creatures within 10 feet of you take a –2 penalty on attack rolls and saving throws. You gain the ability to speak and understand Celestial.

Illus., by M. Cotie

HOLY TRANSFORMATION, LESSER

Transmutation [Good]
Level: Cleric 4
Components: V, S, DF
Casting Time: 1 standard action
Range: Personal
Target: You
Duration: 1 round/level (D)

A charge of holy energy courses through you, causing a barely visible golden aura to surround you. You feel a closeness to your deity as well as a noticeable increase in physical girth and power.

When you cast this spell, you assume the physical appearance and many of the qualities and abilities of a protectar (*Miniatures Handbook* 66). While under the effect of the spell, your creature type changes to outsider (good), and your size changes to Medium. You have the space and reach of a protectar (5 feet/5 feet). You gain a +2 sacred bonus to Strength and Constitution. You gain a fly speed of 60 feet (good). You gain darkvision out to 60 feet. You gain a +2 sacred bonus on saving throws. You gain the ability to speak and understand Celestial.

Howling chain is tremendously useful against enemy spellcasters

HORRIBLE TASTE

Transmutation
Level: Druid 1, ranger 1, sorcerer/wizard 1
Components: V, S, M
Casting Time: 1 standard action
Range: Touch
Target: Creature or object touched
Duration: 10 minutes/level
Saving Throw: Fortitude negates; see text
Spell Resistance: No

After a few mystic words, you touch a piece of rotten meat to the subject and it sinks inside the creature's body.

Any creature that bites the spell's subject must succeed on a Fortitude saving throw or be nauseated until the end of its next turn.

If a creature of animal Intelligence (2 or lower) fails its saving throw, it will not willingly bite the subject a second time; someone trying to direct the creature to bite the subject again must make a Handle Animal check as if he was trying to "push" the creature. This check must be made every time he tries to make the creature bite.

Creatures that are immune to poison or that lack the ability to taste are unaffected by this spell.

Material Component: A pinch of rotten meat.

HOWLING CHAIN

Evocation [Force]
Level: Sorcerer/wizard 6
Components: V, S, F
Casting Time: 1 standard action
Range: Medium (100 ft. + 10 ft./level)
Effect: One chain of force
Duration: 1 round/level
Saving Throw: See text
Spell Resistance: Yes

A blood-red chain of pure force appears, howling instead of rattling as it shakes and twines.

You create a chain of force, which lashes out and attacks your enemies. The chain has a reach of 15 feet, but cannot move from the space you designate. The chain attacks by attempting to trip your foes (+12 melee touch attack, +15 on the opposed Strength check). It does not provoke attacks of opportunity for tripping, nor can it be tripped in response on a failed attempt. If it succeeds in tripping an enemy, it immediately follows up with a melee attack on the prone defender (+12 melee attack, 2d6+10 points of damage). Any creature struck by the chain must make a Will saving throw or become shaken.

A *howling chain* can make one attack of opportunity each round for every four caster levels you have, using the same tactic as above.

A *howling chain* has as many hit points as you do when you're undamaged, and its AC is AC 20 (–1 size, +11 natural). It takes damage as a normal creature, but most magical effects that don't deal damage do not affect it. It makes saving throws as its caster. *Disintegrate* or a successful *dispel magic* destroys it.

Focus: A small length of platinum chain worth at least 500 gp.

HUNGRY GIZZARD

Conjuration (Creation)
Level: Druid 6
Components: V, S, M
Casting Time: 1 standard action
Range: Medium (100 ft. + 10 ft./level)
Target: One Medium or smaller creature
Duration: 1 round/level (D)
Saving Throw: Reflex negates
Spell Resistance: Yes

What appears to be a massive gizzard from a bird attempts to consume a creature you indicate. The gizzard pulses with glowing red blood and supernatural energy.

A Large bulbous, fleshy mass seethes into being around a single Medium or smaller target within range. The target can make a Reflex save to avoid becoming engulfed by the hungry gizzard, otherwise it is entombed within the disembodied digestive organ. If the target successfully saves, the gizzard immediately vanishes without further effect.

Each round a creature remains trapped inside a hungry gizzard (starting in the round the spell is cast), the target creature is considered grappled and takes 2d8+8 points of crushing damage per round and 1d8 points of acid damage.

While engulfed, the target creature can cast a spell only if the spell has no somatic component, the material components are in hand, and it makes a Concentration check (DC 20 + spell level). An engulfed creature can cut its way out by using claws or a light slashing weapon to deal 25 points of damage to the gizzard (AC 12). Once the creature exits, the gizzard immediately melts into a pool of blood and meaty chunks.

There is no immediate physical exit; the only way for those trapped inside to escape is to cut their way free, to dispel the spell, or to have allies outside destroy the gizzard. The gizzard is fairly easy to strike in combat from a vantage point outside of its interior, due to its size (AC 4). A newly formed hungry gizzard has 5 hit points per caster level. The gizzard is treated like an unattended object for the purpose of saving throws. A hungry gizzard reduced to 0 hit points is immediately destroyed.

Material Component: A dried gizzard.

HUNTERS OF HADES

Conjuration (Summoning) [Evil]
Level: Cleric 9
Components: V, S, M
Casting Time: 1 minute
Range: Medium (100 ft. + 10 ft./level)
Effect: Two summoned pack fiends, which can be no more than 30 ft. apart, or one retriever
Duration: 10 minutes/level (D)
Saving Throw: None
Spell Resistance: No

You evoke the dark powers and the ground splits near you. Up from the smoking depths comes a pair of creatures, each resembling a mating of wolf and cockroach.

This spell summons either a single retriever (MM 46) or a pair of pack fiends (*Planar Handbook* 128) from the Gray Waste of Hades to serve you. The creatures magically understand your spoken commands (regardless of your language). They are treated as trained hunting beasts, so you can command them to track if you so choose.

The creatures obey you explicitly and never attack you, even if someone else manages to gain control over them. You do not need to concentrate to maintain control over the creatures. You can dismiss them singly or in groups at any time.

Material Component: A pinch of ash. If a retriever is summoned, a 500 gp bloodstone must also be used.

HUNTER'S MERCY

Transmutation
Level: Ranger 1
Components: S
Casting Time: 1 standard action
Range: Personal
Target: You
Duration: 1 round

Your eyes glow red, but you see the world as normal except when you look at your target. A small glowing dot reveals the creature's weakest point.

This transmutation makes a bow strike true. Your first hit with a bow (not including crossbows) in the next round is automatically a critical hit. If you don't hit in the round following the casting of this spell, the effect is wasted.

HURL

Transmutation
Level: Sorcerer/wizard 2
Components: V, S
Casting Time: 1 standard action
Range: Touch
Target: Weapon touched
Duration: 1 minute/level
Saving Throw: None
Spell Resistance: No

You picture with your mind's eye the target weapon returning to its owner. Upon completion of the spell, the weapon glows with a dull yellow radiance.

The *hurl* spell enhances one melee weapon so that it returns to the thrower after being thrown. For the duration of the spell, when thrown, the weapon returns to its wielder at the beginning of the wielder's next action. The weapon returns whether it hit or missed its target. On its return, the thrown weapon hovers for 1 round next to the wielder and can then be seized and thrown again. After 1 round, the weapon falls to the ground. The weapon returns to its wielder only if thrown; it doesn't automatically fly back if dropped or seized by another creature. (An improvised weapon or a weapon not designed for throwing has a range increment of 10 feet.) Throwing a two-handed weapon is a full-round action.

HYMN OF PRAISE

Evocation [Good, Sonic]
Level: Bard 3
Components: V, S
Casting Time: 1 standard action
Range: 50 ft.
Area: 50-ft.-radius emanation centered on you
Duration: 1 round/level (D)
Saving Throw: Will negates
Spell Resistance: Yes

Your heart light and joyful, you feel a sense of optimism as you launch into an inspiring melody.

You can strike up a rousing, inspirational song that temporarily boosts by 2 the effective caster level of each good-aligned divine spellcaster within range. This increase does not grant access to additional spells, but it does improve all spell effects that are dependent on caster level. Within the spell's area, each good-aligned divine spellcaster gains a +4 sacred bonus on Charisma checks to turn undead, and each evil-aligned divine spellcaster takes a –4 sacred penalty on Charisma checks to rebuke undead.

HYPOTHERMIA

Evocation [Cold]
Level: Cleric 4, druid 3
Components: V, S
Casting Time: 1 standard action
Range: Close (25 ft. + 5 ft./2 levels)
Target: One creature
Duration: Instantaneous
Saving Throw: Fortitude partial
Spell Resistance: Yes

The fighter drops to her knees, her face pale and a bluish cast to her lips and fingers. A cloud of frosted breath escapes her lips as she whispers, "So . . . c-c-cold . . ."

The subject takes 1d6 points of cold damage per caster level (maximum 10d6) and becomes fatigued. A successful Fortitude save halves the damage and negates the fatigue.

ICE AXE

Evocation [Cold]
Level: Cleric 3
Components: V, S, M
Casting Time: 1 standard action
Range: 0 ft.
Effect: Battleaxe-shaped weapon of swirling ice
Duration: 1 round/level (D)
Saving Throw: None
Spell Resistance: Yes

A thin layer of frost forms around your hand as shards of ice descend from the sky and coalesce into the form of a battleaxe.

This spell creates a battleaxe-shaped formation of jagged, fast-swirling ice shards in your hand. You are automatically considered proficient with the *ice axe*. Attacks with the ice axe are melee touch attacks. The axe deals 2d12 points of cold damage +1 point per two caster levels (maximum +10) with a successful hit. You cannot be disarmed of the ice axe nor can it be sundered. Since the axe is virtually weightless, your Strength modifier does not apply on damage rolls. If your base attack bonus is high enough to allow for multiple attacks in a round, you can make them with the *ice axe*.

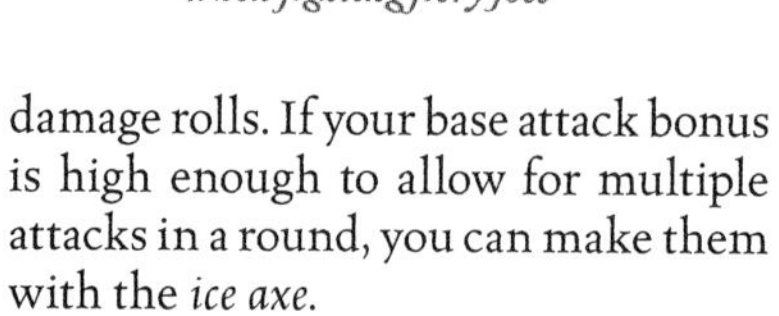
Dwarf clerics employ the ice axe spell when fighting fiery foes

Illus. by W. England

If you choose to hold something other than the ice axe in your hand or use the hand in some other way, the ice axe vanishes until the hand is empty again.

Material Component: A shard of ice, glass, or crystal.

ICE CLAW

Evocation [Cold]
Level: Sorcerer/wizard 7
Components: V, S, F
Casting Time: 1 standard action
Range: Medium (100 ft. + 10 ft./level)
Effect: 10-ft. ice claw
Duration: 1 round/level (D)
Saving Throw: None
Spell Resistance: Yes

You finish this evocation and a great white claw appears before you, cold air wafting off its crystalline surface.

This spell creates a massive reptilian claw made of ice. The ice claw can make one grapple attack per round. Its attack bonus and grapple modifier are equal to your caster level + your Int modifier or Cha modifier (for wizards and sorcerers, respectively) + 7 for the claw's Strength (24). In any round when the claw is grappling a target, it deals 1d8 points of cold damage.

The claw can attack in the round it appears. Directing it to change targets is a standard action. It always attacks from your direction and does not get a flanking bonus or help a combatant get one. The claw has as many hit points as you do when undamaged and has AC 20 (+10 natural). It takes damage as a normal creature, but most magical effects that do not deal damage do not affect it. The claw cannot push through a *wall of force* or enter an *antimagic field*. It suffers the full effects of a *prismatic wall* or *prismatic sphere*. The claw has your saving throw bonuses. *Disintegrate* or a successful *dispel magic* destroys it. It has immunity to cold and vulnerability to fire.

Focus: A white leather glove and a piece of clear rock crystal.

ICE DAGGER

Evocation [Cold]
Level: Sorcerer/wizard 1
Components: V, S, M
Casting Time: 1 standard action
Range: Close (25 ft. + 5 ft./2 levels)
Effect: Dagger of ice
Duration: Instantaneous
Saving Throw: None
Spell Resistance: Yes

The melted ice cupped in your palm crystallizes into a daggerlike shard of ice that then

flies at your foe, exploding into a ball of icy fragments at its feet.

The ice dagger created by this spell launches itself at a target. Treat the attack as a thrown splash weapon (PH 158) that requires a ranged touch attack to hit. The ice dagger deals 1d4 points of cold damage to the target per caster level (maximum 5d4), and splash damage of 1 point of cold damage to adjacent creatures.

Material Component: A few drops of water made from melted ice.

ICE FLOWERS

Transmutation [Cold]
Level: Cleric 6, druid 5
Components: V, S
Casting Time: 1 standard action
Range: Long (400 ft. + 40 ft./level)
Area: 20-ft.-radius burst
Duration: Instantaneous
Saving Throw: Reflex half
Spell Resistance: No

A lance of ice and earth thrusts up where you point, flinging pebbles, rocks, and dirt into the sky. Stone rains down, covering the ground with debris.

This spell causes moisture in the ground at a point you designate to freeze into a mound of solid ice covered by a layer of soil, which bursts violently through the surface. This flings dangerous ice shards and small stones throughout the area, turning the surface of the ground in the spell's area into dense rubble (DMG 90). The shards and stones deal 1d6 points of damage per caster level (maximum 15d6). Half the damage is cold damage. The origin point of the spell must be on the ground. This spell has no effect in desert terrain or on solid stone.

ICE GAUNTLET

Evocation [Cold]
Level: Cleric 1
Components: V, DF
Casting Time: 1 standard action
Range: Personal
Target: You
Duration: 1 minute/level (D)

All warmth leaves your hand as at first a sheen of white frost covers it, then larger crystals of clear ice form around it. In seconds a large bristling ball of rock-hard ice spikes surrounds your fist, a cold mist enshrouding your forearm.

You can attack with your fist in all respects as if you were wearing a *+1 spiked gauntlet*. The *+1 spiked gauntlet* deals normal damage for your size and 1d4 points of cold damage. Damage reduction applies to the ice gauntlet's normal damage, but it does not affect the cold damage. If you fail a saving throw against a fire effect, the ice gauntlet melts and the spell ends.

An icelance spell pins a gnoll to a tree

ICE KNIFE

Conjuration (Creation) [Cold]
Level: Assassin 2, sorcerer/wizard 2
Components: S, M
Casting Time: 1 standard action
Range: Long (400 ft. + 40 ft./level)
Effect: One icy missile
Duration: Instantaneous
Saving Throw: Fortitude partial or Reflex half; see text
Spell Resistance: Yes

You shake your hand as if to free it from some substance you disdain. As you do, a magical shard of ice blasts from your hand and speeds to its target, the sound of cracking ice following in its wake.

You must succeed on a normal ranged attack to hit (with a +2 bonus on the attack roll for every two caster levels). If it hits, an ice knife deals 2d8 points of cold damage and 2 points of Dexterity damage (a successful Fortitude save negates the Dexterity damage). Creatures that have immunity to cold also take no Dexterity damage automatically.

A knife that misses creates a shower of ice crystals in a 10-foot-radius burst (see Missing with a Thrown Weapon, PH 158, to determine where the shard hits). The icy burst deals 1d8 points of cold damage to all creatures within the area (Reflex half).

Material Component: A drop of water or piece of ice.

ICELANCE

Conjuration (Creation)
Level: Druid 3, sorcerer/wizard 3
Components: V, S, F
Casting Time: 1 standard action
Range: Medium (100 ft. + 10 ft./level)
Effect: One lance of ice
Duration: Instantaneous
Saving Throw: Fortitude partial
Spell Resistance: Yes

You clutch the quartz in your hand, focusing the energy of the spell into a sharp spear. With a thought, you send it whistling through the air at your foe.

You must succeed on a normal ranged attack to strike a target with an *icelance*. You gain a +4 bonus on your attack roll. If you hit, the icelance deals 6d6 points of damage to the target. Half of this damage is piercing damage; the rest is cold damage. In addition, the target must make a Fortitude save or be stunned for 1d4 rounds. Regardless of the result of the attack, the icelance shatters upon its first use.

Focus: A 50-gp clear quartz gemstone. Alternatively, if you are in a cold region, you can substitute 10 pounds of ice or snow for the quartz.

Illus. by J. Nelson

ILLUSORY FEAST

Illusion (Pattern) [Mind-Affecting]
Level: Sorcerer/wizard 5
Components: V, S, M
Casting Time: 1 standard action
Range: Long (400 ft. + 40 ft./level)
Area: 40-ft.-radius spread
Duration: 1 round/level
Saving Throw: Will negates
Spell Resistance: Yes

Your stomach growls as an entire feast appears in the distance. You perceive the composition of the feast continuously shifting, its contents sometimes appealing to the point where you almost forget it is an illusion.

Tantalizing food and drink appears, causing creatures in the area to stop what they are doing and eat. A creature in the area that fails its save stops its current activities, drops held or carried items, and begins consuming the illusory food and drink. The food looks, feels, smells, tastes, and even sounds real to the affected creature, and it appears to be whatever kind of food the creature prefers. The creature is considered dazed. An attack on an affected creature frees it from the spell immediately. Sightless creatures are affected by this spell due to its effect on all the senses. Creatures that do not eat are unaffected by this spell.

Material Component: A piece of trail rations.

ILLUSORY PIT

Illusion (Glamer)
Level: Sorcerer/wizard 6
Components: V, S
Casting Time: 1 round
Range: Medium (100 ft. + 10 ft./level)
Area: 10-ft. cube/level
Duration: Concentration + 1 round/level
Saving Throw: Will disbelief
Spell Resistance: No

You shove downward with your hand, speaking the spell's arcane words as you do so. The ground disappears where you indicate, forming an impossibly deep pit.

You create the illusion of a pit, and each creature entering or within the area is forced to make a Will save or believe the floor on which it stands has become a bottomless chasm. Those that fail their saves fall prone and are unable to take any action except clawing desperately at the floor in the hopes of stopping their apparent fall. An attack on an affected creature frees it from the effect of the illusion but leaves it stunned for 1 round. Likewise, when the spell ends, creatures that believed they were falling are stunned for 1 round.

Flying creatures passing over an illusory pit are unaffected by the spell.

IMBUE FAMILIAR WITH SPELL ABILITY

Universal
Level: Sorcerer/wizard 6
Components: V, S
Casting Time: 1 standard action
Range: Touch
Target: Familiar touched
Duration: 1 hour/level
Saving Throw: Will negates (harmless)
Spell Resistance: Yes (harmless)

Upon completion of this spell, you feel as if you had just cast a number of spells in quick succession. Your familiar gives you a knowing nod.

This spell allows you to transfer a number of your spells and the ability to cast them into your familiar. Spontaneous spellcasters, such as sorcerers, can imbue a familiar with any spells they know how to cast, subject to the restrictions below. Arcanists who prepare spells, such as wizards, can imbue a familiar with any spell they have currently prepared. In either case, you can imbue one spell per three caster levels, with a maximum spell level of one-third your caster level, rounded down (maximum 5th level). Multiple castings of *imbue familiar with spell ability* have no effect on these limits.

The transferred spell's variable characteristics (range, duration, area, and so on) function according to your level. Once you cast *imbue familiar with spell ability* on your familiar, both the spell slot from which you cast the spell and the spell slots of the transferred spells remain unavailable for the preparation or casting of new spells until the familiar uses the transferred spells or *imbue familiar with spell ability* expires.

The spell can be dispelled; if this happens, the spells transferred are lost as if the familiar had cast them. In an *antimagic field*, the familiar loses the ability to cast the imbued spells, but regains it again if it leaves the field (as long as the spell's duration hasn't expired).

If any transferred spell requires a focus or material component, you must have it on your person when the spells are cast (components are consumed as normal without requiring you to bring them to hand). Any XP costs from a transferred spell are deducted from your total when the familiar casts the spell.

IMPERIOUS GLARE

Necromancy [Fear, Mind-Affecting]
Level: Sorcerer/wizard 6
Components: S
Casting Time: 1 standard action
Range: Close (25 ft. + 5 ft./2 levels)
Targets: One living creature/level, no two of which are more than 30 ft. apart
Duration: 1 round/level
Saving Throw: Will negates; see text
Spell Resistance: Yes

You regard your foes with a steely glare that would peel paint from a wagon. Motes of dark energy dance before your eyes and they, to a body, freeze in fear.

The targets must make successful Will saves or cower. The saving throw DC to resist this effect is either the normal save DC for the spell or the save DC for your natural frightful presence ability, whichever is higher. You cannot cast this spell if you do not have a frightful presence ability, either natural or magically bestowed (such as from the *aura of terror* spell, for example).

IMPLACABLE PURSUER

Divination
Level: Assassin 4, blackguard 4, ranger 4
Components: V, S
Casting Time: 1 minute
Range: Long (400 ft. + 40 ft./level); see text
Target: One creature
Duration: 1 hour/level (D)
Saving Throw: Will negates; see text
Spell Resistance: Yes

With this spell, you become an unerring tracker, instantly aware of your quarry's location whenever it's on the move.

The *implacable pursuer* spell gives you the direction and distance to the target creature whenever it finishes a turn more than 10 feet away from where it started. If you are a ranger, you apply your favored enemy bonus to the DC of the Will save.

Once you successfully target a creature with *implacable pursuer*, you know its location as long as the subject is moving, no matter where it goes on the same plane. Even if it leaves the plane, *implacable pursuer* tells you what plane the subject creature went to. The spell then provides no further information until you and the subject creature are on the same plane, in which case the spell resumes functioning normally.

IMPROVISATION

Transmutation
Level: Bard 1
Components: V, S, M
Casting Time: 1 standard action
Range: Personal
Target: You
Duration: 1 round/level (D)

With an elaborate flourish and call for luck, you toss the dice in your hand into the air. Immediately you feel as though fate favors you, filling you with confidence.

You gain access to a floating "pool" of luck, which manifests as bonus points you can use as desired to improve your odds of success at various tasks. This bonus pool consists of 2 points per caster level, which you can spend as you like to improve attack rolls, skill checks, and ability checks, although no single check can receive a bonus greater than one-half your caster level. You must declare any bonus point usage before the appropriate roll is made. Used points disappear from the pool, and any points remaining when the spell ends are wasted. These points count as luck bonuses for the purpose of stacking.

For example, a 14th-level bard pauses while chasing a pickpocket to cast *improvisation*. At any time during the next 14 rounds, he could use the points to provide himself a +7 luck bonus on a Spot check, a +7 luck bonus on a Climb check, and a +7 luck bonus on two of his attacks.

Material Component: A pair of dice.

INCITE

Enchantment (Compulsion) [Mind-Affecting]
Level: Bard 1, cleric 1, sorcerer/wizard 1
Components: V, S
Casting Time: 1 swift action
Range: Close (25 ft. + 5 ft./2 levels)
Target: Creatures in a 10-ft. burst
Duration: 1 minute/level
Saving Throw: Will negates
Spell Resistance: Yes

You cast this spell and your opponent is swallowed in a spiral of sparkling motes that urge your targets to act.

Affected creatures are not allowed to delay or to ready an action. If a subject is currently delaying, it acts as soon as the spell is cast. If the subject currently has an action readied, it loses that action.

INCORPOREAL ENHANCEMENT

Necromancy [Evil]
Level: Sorcerer/wizard 3
Components: V, S, M
Casting Time: 1 round
Range: Close (25 ft. + 5 ft./2 levels)
Target: One incorporeal undead/level
Duration: 24 hours
Saving Throw: None
Spell Resistance: No

Calling upon the dark power of the Plane of Negative Energy, you bolster the power of incorporeal undead.

The undead affected by this spell gain a +1 deflection bonus to Armor Class, +1d8 bonus hit points, a +1 enhancement bonus on attack rolls, and a +2 bonus to turn resistance. Each of these enhancements improves by the base amount for every five caster levels beyond 5th, so that a 20th-level caster grants undead +4 to AC, +4d8 bonus hit points, +4 on attack rolls, and +8 to turn resistance.

INCORPOREAL NOVA

Necromancy [Death]
Level: Cleric 5, sorcerer/wizard 6
Components: V, S
Casting Time: 1 standard action
Range: Medium (100 ft. + 10 ft./level)
Target: Incorporeal and gaseous creatures within a 50-ft.-radius burst
Duration: Instantaneous
Saving Throw: Will negates
Spell Resistance: Yes

A nova of dissolution dissipates the immaterial bodies of incorporeal and gaseous creatures, destroying them instantly.

The spell destroys 1d4 HD worth of creatures per caster level (maximum 20d4) in the area. Usually, creatures such as shadows, wraiths, spectres, ghosts, and similar creatures are destroyed, though vampires and living creatures in gaseous form are also affected, as are other incorporeal creatures. Creatures with the fewest HD are affected first; among creatures with equal HD, those that are closest to the point of origin of the burst are affected first. No creature with 9 or more HD is affected, and HD that are not sufficient to affect a creature are wasted.

INDOMITABILITY

Abjuration
Level: Sorcerer/wizard 5
Components: V, S
Casting Time: 1 standard action
Range: Touch
Target: Creature touched
Duration: 1 minute/level or until discharged
Saving Throw: None (harmless)
Spell Resistance: Yes (harmless)

The spell's energy makes you feel impervious to wounds, if only for a limited time.

The *indomitability* spell protects its recipient from the first incapacitating attack the creature suffers during the spell's duration. An incapacitating attack is one that would reduce the recipient to fewer than 1 hit point. The attack must be one that deals damage; the *indomitability* spell offers no protection from nondamaging effects or attacks that kill or destroy without dealing any damage, such as death effects. Regardless of how much damage the attack deals, the recipient of the *indomitability* spell takes only enough damage to be reduced to 1 hp. The remaining damage from the attack is ignored. Once the spell protects the subject in this manner, the spell is discharged.

INFERNAL THRENODY

Evocation [Evil, Sonic]
Level: Bard 3
Components: V, S
Casting Time: 1 round
Range: 50 ft.
Area: 50-ft.-radius emanation centered on you
Duration: 1 round/level (D)
Saving Throw: Will negates
Spell Resistance: Yes

The melody you create is a low but melodious dirge that blankets the area in a barely perceptible red aura. You feel invigorated with dark power.

You can strike up a pulsing, powerful rhythm that temporarily boosts by 2 the effective caster level of each evil-aligned divine spellcaster within range. This increase does not grant access to additional spells, but it does improve all spell effects that are dependent on caster level. Within the spell's area, each evil-aligned divine spellcaster gains a +4 profane bonus on Charisma checks to rebuke undead, and each good-aligned divine spellcaster takes a –4 profane penalty on Charisma checks to turn undead.

INFERNAL TRANSFORMATION

Transmutation [Evil]
Level: Cleric 7

This spell functions like *lesser infernal transformation,* except when you cast this spell, you assume the physical appearance and many of the qualities and abilities of a bone devil (MM 52). While under the effect of the spell, your creature type changes to outsider (baatezu, evil, lawful), and your size changes to Large. You have the space and reach of a bone devil (10 feet/10 feet). You gain a +4 profane bonus to Strength and Constitution and darkvision out to 60 feet. You gain damage reduction 5/good.

You also grow a tail like that of a scorpion. Whenever you take a full attack action, you can use the tail to make an additional attack each round at your highest attack bonus. A successful attack deals 3d4 points of damage + your Str modifier. This attack overcomes damage reduction as if it were an evil weapon. Creatures hit by the tail attack must make a Fortitude saving throw (DC 10 + 1/2 character level + Con modifier) or be subjected to poison (injury, initial damage 1d6 Str, secondary damage 2d6 Str). Your equipment grows to match your new size and form, allowing the tail attack to function even if you are wearing heavy armor or other restrictive clothing. You gain the ability to speak and understand Infernal.

Illus. by C. Frank

Indominability makes a deadly blow merely dangerous

INFERNAL TRANSFORMATION, LESSER

Transmutation [Evil]
Level: Cleric 4
Components: V, S, DF
Casting Time: 1 standard action
Range: Personal
Target: You
Duration: 1 round/level (D)

Your blood runs cold as a feeling of utter evil imbues you with unholy power. A cackle of sadistic glee escapes your changing mouth, and you feel your body grow in both size and power.

When you cast this spell, you assume the physical appearance and many of the qualities and abilities of a bearded devil (MM 52). While under the effect of the spell, your creature type changes to outsider (baatezu, evil, lawful), and your size changes to Medium. You have the space and reach of a bearded devil (5 feet/5 feet). You gain a +2 profane bonus to Strength and Constitution and darkvision out to 60 feet.

You grow a snaky beard. Whenever you take a full attack action, you can use the beard to make an additional attack each round at your highest attack bonus plus all appropriate modifiers. A successful attack deals 1d8 points of damage + your Str modifier. This attack overcomes damage reduction as if it were an evil weapon. Creatures hit by the beard attack must make a Fortitude saving throw (DC 10 + 1/2 character level + Con modifier) or be affected by the devil chills disease (DMG 292). You gain the ability to speak and understand Infernal.

INFERNAL WOUND

Transmutation [Evil]
Level: Cleric 2, sorcerer/wizard 2
Components: V, S
Casting Time: 1 standard action
Range: Touch
Target: Weapon touched
Duration: 1 round/level
Saving Throw: None
Spell Resistance: No

You wave your hands over the blade and it takes on a gray pallor. Its attacks will now leave a lingering, painful memory in their wake.

A creature injured by a weapon with *infernal wound* cast upon it loses 2 additional hit points each round for the duration of the spell (regardless of how many times it is struck during that time). The continuing hit point loss can be stopped by a Heal check (DC 10 + spell level + your relevant ability modifier), a *cure* spell, or a *heal* spell.

INFERNO

Transmutation [Fire]
Level: Druid 5
Components: V, S, M
Casting Time: 1 standard action
Range: Close (25 ft. + 5 ft./2 levels)
Target: One creature
Duration: 6 rounds; see text
Saving Throw: Fortitude negates and Reflex partial; see text
Spell Resistance: Yes

Singling out the target, you call upon elemental forces to surround it in fire.

The target of the *inferno* takes 6d6 points of fire damage unless it makes a Fortitude save. In each round thereafter, the fire deals 1d6 fewer points of damage (minimum 1d6) until the spell ends or the subject manages to extinguish the flames. Thus, the fire deals 5d6 points of damage in the second round, 4d6 points in the third round, and so forth. Flammable, nonmagical items carried by the target automatically fail their saves to resist this damage.

After the first round, the subject can attempt a DC 15 Reflex save as a full-round action to extinguish the flames before taking additional damage. Rolling on the ground (the subject becomes prone) allows the target a +2 bonus on this save. Leaping into a large body of water or magically extinguishing the flames automatically ends the effect.

Material Component: A gob of beeswax.

INFESTATION OF MAGGOTS

Necromancy
Level: Druid 3
Components: V, S, M
Casting Time: 1 standard action
Range: Touch
Target: Creature touched
Duration: 1 round/2 levels
Saving Throw: Fortitude negates
Spell Resistance: Yes

The infestation of maggots spell harms and horrifies its victims

You touch your foe with the dust of dead flies on your fingers, giving birth to hundreds of writhing maggots in his flesh.

With a successful melee touch attack, you infest a creature with maggotlike creatures. If the touched creature fails a Fortitude saving throw, the magical maggots deal 1d4 points of Constitution damage each round at the beginning of your turn. The subject makes a new Fortitude save each round to negate the damage in that round and end the effect.

The infestation can be removed with a *remove disease* or *heal* spell.

Material Component: A handful of dead, dried flies.

INHIBIT

Enchantment (Compulsion) [Mind-Affecting]
Level: Bard 1, cleric 1, sorcerer/wizard 1
Components: V, S
Casting Time: 1 standard action
Range: Medium (100 ft. + 10 ft./level)
Target: One creature
Duration: Instantaneous
Saving Throw: Will negates
Spell Resistance: Yes

You cast this spell and a spiral of dark motes surrounds your foe, slowing and distracting him from the task at hand.

You inhibit your foe from acting. The subject is forced to delay until the following round, acting immediately before you on your initiative count.

INKY CLOUD

Conjuration (Creation)
Level: Cleric 2, sorcerer/wizard 2
Components: V, S, M
Casting Time: 1 standard action
Range: 30 ft.
Area: 30-ft.-radius spread centered on you
Duration: 10 minutes/level
Saving Throw: None
Spell Resistance: No

Black bubbles of ink boil up from the vial in your hand and quickly spread to fill all the water around you with darkness, blocking your vision.

You create an inky cloud that billows out from your location. The cloud obscures all sight, including darkvision, beyond 5 feet. A creature within 5 feet has concealment. Creatures farther away have total concealment.

A moderate current disperses the cloud in 4 rounds; a strong current disperses the cloud in 1 round.

This spell functions only underwater.

Illus. by D. Martin

Material Component: A small vial containing the ink of a squid or octopus.

INSIDIOUS RHYTHM

Enchantment (Compulsion) [Mind-Affecting]
Level: Bard 1
Components: V, S
Casting Time: 1 immediate action
Range: Medium (100 ft. + 10 ft./level)
Target: One creature
Duration: 1 minute/level
Saving Throw: Will negates
Spell Resistance: Yes

You recite a foolhardy ditty, tapping your foot in time. With a wink and a grin you mark your target, who shortly thereafter follows suit.

The subject takes a –4 penalty on Intelligence-based skill checks and Concentration checks due to an endlessly recycling melody stuck in its mind. Whenever the subject attempts to cast, concentrate on, or direct a spell, it must succeed on a Concentration check (DC equal to *insidious rhythm's* save DC + spell's level) or fail at the attempt.

INSIGHTFUL FEINT

Divination
Level: Assassin 1, sorcerer/wizard 1
Components: V
Casting Time: 1 swift action
Range: Personal
Target: You
Duration: 1 round

With a chuckle you whisper the words that will make your ruse more effective.

You gain a +10 insight bonus on the next single Bluff check that you make to feint in combat (if it is made before the start of your next turn). You can make the feint as a move action, or once as a free action if you have the Improved Feint feat.

INSPIRATIONAL BOOST

Enchantment (Compulsion) [Mind-Affecting, Sonic]
Level: Bard 1
Components: V, S
Casting Time: 1 swift action
Range: Personal
Target: You
Duration: 1 round or special; see text

You concentrate on assisting your friends as you begin the short chant and simple hand-chopping motion necessary to cast the spell. As you finish, the spell's chant allows you to segue easily into bolstering your allies.

While this spell is in effect, the morale bonus granted by your inspire courage bardic music increases by 1.

The effect lasts until your inspire courage effect ends. If you don't begin to use your inspire courage ability before the beginning of your next turn, the spell's effect ends.

INSTANT LOCKSMITH

Divination
Level: Assassin 1, sorcerer/wizard 1
Components: V, S
Casting Time: 1 swift action
Range: Personal
Target: You
Duration: 1 round

You point at a mechanism, twist your hand, and make a clicking sound with your tongue. You now have a better idea of how the mechanism works.

You can make one Disable Device check or one Open Lock check in this round as a free action. You gain a +2 insight bonus on the check.

INSTANT REFUGE

Evocation
Level: Sorcerer/wizard 9
Components: V, S, M, XP
Casting Time: 10 minutes
Range: Personal
Target: You
Duration: Until discharged

You set invisible arcane triggers within your mind and body, allowing you to escape great peril in an instant.

This powerful variant of the *contingency* spell automatically transfers you and everything you carry or touch (except for other creatures or objects that weigh more than 50 pounds) to a locale you name.

When casting *instant refuge,* you must specify the locale and detail up to six specific conditions that trigger the spell. When any of these situations occurs, you are whisked away to the location. The location can be any place you have visited, even on another plane.

Material Component: A concoction made from demon skin and rare herbs worth 250 gp.

XP Cost: 100 XP.

INSTANT SEARCH

Divination
Level: Assassin 1, ranger 1, sorcerer/wizard 1
Components: V, S
Casting Time: 1 swift action
Range: Personal
Target: You
Duration: 1 round

By pointing at a small area nearby and whistling briefly, you release the power of the spell, granting you knowledge of the area you indicated.

You can make one Search check in this round as a free action. You gain a +2 insight bonus on the check.

INTERPLANAR MESSAGE

Evocation [Language-Dependent]
Level: Cleric 3
Components: V, S
Casting Time: 1 standard action
Range: See text
Target: One creature
Duration: 24 hours/level or until discharged
Saving Throw: Will negates (harmless)
Spell Resistance: Yes (harmless)

Your spell creates a bond between yourself and the creature you touch, a bond unbroken even by the distance between planes.

This spell allows you to send a limited message of twenty-five words or less to the targeted creature, who can be on another plane when the message is received.

Casting the spell takes a standard action, during which you touch the creature you intend to communicate with. That creature should be able to understand a language you know (otherwise, when the magic is activated, the creature knows that you sent the message, but has no idea what the message is). At any time afterward, you can send your interplanar message to that creature.

The message pops into the target's mind, awake or asleep, and the target is aware that the message has been delivered. If the message arrives when the target is asleep, it might appear as a vivid dream that the target remembers upon awakening.

This spell does not obligate nor force the creature you communicate with to act. The target cannot reply to tell you its plans or intentions. The message travels through the Astral Plane to reach its target, so the spell cannot reach planes separate from (not coterminous to or coexistent with) the Astral Plane.

You can have only one interplanar message active at any given time.

INTERPLANAR TELEPATHIC BOND

Divination
Level: Sorcerer/wizard 6
Components: V, S, M
Casting Time: 1 standard action
Range: Close (25 ft. + 5 ft./2 levels)
Targets: You plus one willing creature/3 levels, no two of which are more than 30 ft. apart
Duration: 10 minutes/level (D)
Saving Throw: None
Spell Resistance: No

You crush the eggshells as you cast this spell, indicating your comrades in the party. Now, regardless of where they might end up, you will be able to communicate with them.

This spell functions like *Rary's telepathic bond* (PH 268), except that the communication functions both on the same plane and across planes.

Material Component: Pieces of eggshell from two different kinds of creatures.

INVISIBILITY, SUPERIOR

Illusion (Glamer)
Level: Sorcerer/wizard 8
Components: V, S
Casting Time: 1 standard action
Range: Personal or touch
Target: You or a creature or object weighing no more than 100 lb./level
Duration: 1 minute/level (D)
Saving Throw: Will negates (harmless)
Spell Resistance: No

As you complete the spell, your senses dull somewhat. Upon releasing the spell's energy on your desired subject, your senses clear, although the spell's recipient can no longer be perceived.

This powerful glamer functions like *invisibility* (PH 245), except that it masks image, scent, and sound alike, concealing the subject from all senses except touch. As with *greater invisibility*, this spell doesn't end if the subject attacks. While invisible, the subject exudes no scent and is undetectable by scent, blindsense, tremorsense, and blindsight.

Superior invisibility renders the recipient immune to detection by *see invisibility, faerie fire, glitterdust, invisibility purge*, and *dust of appearance*, although creatures under the effect of the spell can be detected by *true seeing*. Certain mundane conditions (such as leaving footprints) can also render a subject detectable.

INVISIBILITY, SWIFT

Illusion (Glamer)
Level: Assassin 2, bard 1
Components: V
Casting Time: 1 swift action
Range: Personal
Target: You
Duration: 1 round

With a whispered syllable you complete the spell. You notice that others look past you as if you weren't there.

This spell functions like *invisibility* (PH 245), except as noted above.

IRON BONES

Level: Cleric 4, sorcerer/wizard 4

A brief flash engulfs your undead ally, and through its flesh you can see its skeleton. The skeleton glows a dusky red for a moment.

This spell functions like *stone bones* (page 208), except that the subject creature's skeleton changes to iron. The creature gains a +6 natural armor bonus to AC.

Arcane Focus: A miniature skull made out of iron or steel.

IRON SILENCE

Transmutation
Level: Assassin 2, bard 2, cleric 2
Components: V, S, DF
Casting Time: 1 standard action
Range: Touch
Target: One suit of armor touched/3 levels
Duration: 1 hour/level (D)
Saving Throw: Will negates (harmless, object)
Spell Resistance: Yes (harmless, object)

As you imitate a clanking noise you brush your hand over the armor you wish to silence. The armor glows softly orange for a moment before the glow fades. A closer look reveals what looks like orange grease in the joints of the armor.

While this spell is in effect, the armor check penalty from the affected suit or suits of armor does not apply on Hide and Move Silently checks. Only wearers proficient in the armor's use get this benefit when wearing the affected armor. The armor check penalty still applies to other skill checks as normal.

IRONGUARD

Abjuration
Level: Sorcerer/wizard 7
Components: V, S, F, M

This spell functions like *lesser ironguard*, except that the subject you touch is immune to magic metal as well.

Material Component: A tiny shield of wood, glass, or crystal.

Focus: A small nugget of adamantine worth 100 gp.

IRONGUARD, LESSER

Abjuration
Level: Sorcerer/wizard 5
Components: V, S, M
Casting Time: 1 standard action
Range: Touch
Target: Creature touched
Duration: 1 round/level
Saving Throw: Will negates (harmless)
Spell Resistance: Yes (harmless)

Illus. by L. Parrillo

With few words and a gesture, a necromancer gives his skeletal allies bones of iron

You watch as your target's skin lightens and takes on a translucent look.

The subject of *lesser ironguard* becomes immune to nonmagical metal. Metal items (including metal weapons) simply pass through you, and you can walk through metal barriers such as iron bars. Magic metal affects you normally, as do spells, spell-like abilities, and supernatural effects. Attacks delivered by metal items (such as poison on a dagger) affect you normally. If the spell expires while metal is inside you, the metal object is shunted out of your body (or you away from the metal, if it is an immovable object such as a set of iron bars). You and the object each take 1d6 points of damage as a result (ignoring the object's hardness for determining damage to it).

Because you pass through metal, you can ignore armor bonuses from nonmagic metal armor on opponents you attack with unarmed attacks.

Material Component: A tiny shield of wood, glass, or crystal.

IRONGUTS

Abjuration
Level: Bard 1, cleric 1, sorcerer/wizard 1
Components: V, S, M
Casting Time: 1 standard action
Range: Touch
Target: Creature touched
Duration: 10 minutes/level
Saving Throw: Will negates
Spell Resistance: Yes

You mutter the spell and uncork a bottle with a noxious concoction of scorpion venom, toad sweat, adder venom, and the strained brains of carrion crawlers. The poisonous liquid evaporates into a black cloud that surrounds your hand as you reach out to touch the target.

You enable a creature to better fight off the effect of poison. The subject is filled with antitoxin and gains a +5 alchemical bonus on Fortitude saves against all kinds of poisons, whether injury, contact, ingestion, or inhalation. After the spell ends, the subject is nauseated for 1 round.

Material Component: A vial containing the diluted poison of four different creatures.

IRONTHUNDER HORN

Transmutation [Sonic]
Level: Bard 1, sorcerer/wizard 2
Components: V, S
Casting Time: 1 standard action
Range: 30 ft.
Area: Cone-shaped burst
Duration: Instantaneous
Saving Throw: Reflex negates
Spell Resistance: Yes

The last words of your spell boom out with a thundering roar, knocking the foes in your path off their feet.

You create a deep resonant vibration that can shake creatures off their feet. Creatures in the area must succeed on a Reflex saving throw or fall prone.

JAGGED TOOTH

Transmutation
Level: Druid 3, ranger 2
Components: V, S

Casting Time: 1 standard action
Range: Close (25 ft. + 5 ft./2 levels)
Target: One natural slashing or piercing weapon of target creature
Duration: 10 minutes/level
Saving Throw: Will negates (harmless)
Spell Resistance: Yes (harmless)

You feel your own teeth sharpen momentarily as you complete this spell. As the magical energy surrounds your intended target, it flexes its muscles in appreciation of its weapon's deadlier capabilities.

This spell doubles the critical threat range of one natural weapon that deals either slashing or piercing damage. Multiple effects that increase a weapon's threat range don't stack.

JAWS OF THE WOLF

Transmutation
Level: Druid 4
Components: V, S, F
Casting Time: 1 standard action
Range: Close (25 ft. + 5 ft./2 levels)
Effect: One or more created worgs
Duration: 1 round/level (D)
Saving Throw: None
Spell Resistance: No

You cast small wooden statuettes on the ground and they immediately grow into adult worgs. The worgs growl at your foes, their jaws slathered with spittle.

You turn small wooden carvings into a number of worgs (MM 256) equal to one for every two caster levels. These worgs appear between you and your opponents. They act on their own but obey your mental commands. If the worgs move beyond the range of the spell, or at the end of the spell, the worgs become carvings again. Killing a worg destroys its focus item.

Focus: One carving of a worg for each that you create (25 gp each).

JOYFUL NOISE

Abjuration
Level: Bard 1
Components: S
Casting Time: 1 standard action
Range: 10 ft.
Area: 10-ft.-radius emanation centered on you
Duration: Concentration; see text
Saving Throw: None
Spell Resistance: No

You stomp your foot on the ground, creating a ripple of noise that unleashes suppressed sounds behind it.

You create sonic vibrations that negate any magical *silence* effect in the area. This zone of negation moves with you and lasts as long as you continue to concentrate.

The *silence* effect is not dispelled but simply held in abeyance; it remains in effect outside the area of the *joyful noise* effect.

JUNGLERAZER

Necromancy
Level: Druid 3, sorcerer/wizard 3
Components: V, S, M
Casting Time: 1 standard action
Range: 120 ft.
Area: 120-ft. line
Duration: Instantaneous
Saving Throw: Reflex half
Spell Resistance: Yes

Illus. by C. Dien

The junglerazer spell turns forest to ash and ruins plant creatures

Invisible destructive energy springs silently forth from you, instantly destroying all natural plant life in the area and leaving a path of ash in its wake.

Fey, vermin, plants and plant creatures, and animals caught in the area take 1d10 points of negative energy damage per caster level (maximum 10d10).

Material Component: A pinch of ash from a burnt plant.

JUNGLE'S RAPTURE

Transmutation
Level: Druid 5
Components: V, S
Casting Time: 1 standard action
Range: Close (25 ft. + 5 ft./2 levels)
Target: One living nonplant creature
Duration: Permanent (D)
Saving Throw: Will negates
Spell Resistance: Yes

Spitting, you curse the creature, knowing that in days it will be either dead or just another weed. As you watch, its body becomes more rigid, and the first whorls of wood grain can be seen on its skin.

The creature targeted by this spell immediately takes 1d6 points of Dexterity drain. This drain manifests as a hardening of the limbs and skin as the victim's flesh slowly turns to wood. Each day that passes, the victim takes an additional 1d6 points of Dexterity drain. Even if drained points are restored (through *restoration*, for example), the target creature still takes Dexterity drain each day until the spell is lifted. Once a victim of *jungle's rapture* is drained to 0 Dexterity, it immediately transforms into a normal plant of the same size as its original body. Aside from radiating an aura of transmutation magic, the plant is a normal plant with no Intelligence, Wisdom, or Charisma scores.

Jungle's rapture is a curse, and as such it cannot be dispelled. It can be removed with a *break enchantment, limited wish, miracle,* or *wish* spell. *Remove curse* works only if the caster level of that spell is equal to or higher than your caster level at the time you cast *jungle's rapture.*

The kelpstrand spell entangles and grapples its target

Illus. by J. Thomas

KELPSTRAND

Conjuration (Creation)
Level: Druid 2
Components: V, S, M
Casting Time: 1 standard action
Range: Close (25 ft. + 5 ft./2 levels)
Targets: One creature/3 levels, no two of which are more than 30 ft. apart
Duration: 1 round/level
Saving Throw: None
Spell Resistance: No

You stretch out your hand and long strands of wet kelp streak out to envelop your foes.

Make a ranged touch attack at each target. If you hit a creature, you immediately make an opposed grapple check against the creature as a free action without provoking attacks of opportunity. You add your caster level and your Wisdom bonus to the result of your grapple check rather than your Strength bonus and size bonus. If you succeed, the target becomes entangled in the thick strands of kelp and is grappled. Each round, the target can attempt to escape the kelpstrand by making a successful grapple or Escape Artist check against the kelpstrand's grapple check. You are not considered grappling yourself while using this spell. Once you shoot your strands of kelp, you need not take any action to maintain the effect.

A creature targeted with multiple kelpstrands has to make separate grapple or Escape Artist checks against each kelpstrand currently grappling it to escape. If you cast this spell while you are within 300 feet of the ocean shore, you gain a +4 bonus on any grapple checks made to determine the outcome of a kelpstrand grapple.

Material Component: A piece of dried seaweed.

KISS OF THE VAMPIRE

Necromancy
Level: Sorcerer/wizard 7
Components: V, S, M
Casting Time: 1 standard action
Range: Personal
Target: You
Duration: 1 round/level

Drawing upon the powers of unlife, you give yourself abilities similar to those of a vampire. You become gaunt and pale with feral, red eyes.

You gain damage reduction 10/magic, and you can use any one of the following abilities each round as a standard action.

- *enervation*, as a melee touch attack
- *vampiric touch*, as a melee touch attack
- *charm person*
- *gaseous form* (self only)

While you are using this spell, *inflict* spells heal you and *cure* spells hurt you. You are treated as if you were undead for the purpose of all spells and effects. A successful turn (or rebuke) attempt against an undead of your Hit Dice requires you to make a Will saving throw (DC 10 + turning character's Cha modifier) or be panicked (or cowering) for 10 rounds. A turn attempt that would destroy (or command) undead of your Hit Dice requires you to make a Will save (DC 15 + turning character's Cha modifier) or be stunned (or charmed as by *charm monster*) for 10 rounds.

Any charm effect you create with this spell ends when the spell ends, but all other effects remain until their normal duration expires.

Material Component: A black onyx worth at least 50 gp that has been carved with the image of a fang-mouthed face.

KNIGHT'S MOVE

Transmutation (Teleportation)
Level: Cleric 3, paladin 2
Components: V, S, DF
Casting Time: 1 swift action
Range: 5 ft./2 levels; see text
Target: You
Duration: Instantaneous

The ground before you appears overlaid with a chessboard pattern, with certain squares of the chessboard glowing softly red. Time stops for you as you move without walking to the indicated location.

You can teleport with a limited distance and a circumspect form of movement. You can instantly move up to 5 feet per two caster levels with this spell, but you must end this movement in a square that leaves you flanking an enemy.

KNOW GREATEST ENEMY

Divination
Level: Blackguard 1, paladin 1
Components: V, DF
Casting Time: 1 standard action
Range: 60 ft.
Area: Cone-shaped emanation
Duration: Concentration, up to 1 round/level
Saving Throw: None
Spell Resistance: Yes

Your eyes flash green, turning golden as your survey your opponents. To your eyes, the weakest of them are limned with a pale green nimbus, which intensifies with power. The most powerful is wrapped in a brilliant, shimmering green aura.

This spell evaluates the creatures in the area and determines the relative power level of each. Creatures are evaluated as follows.

CR	Strength
4 or lower	Weak
5–10	Moderate
11–15	Strong
16 or higher	Overwhelming

Among creatures within the same category, you know which is the most powerful, but not why. For example, among a group of ogres (CR 2), you would know one of them (an ogre with two levels of barbarian, CR 4) was the most powerful, but not know if it was because the ogre had class levels, a template (such as half-fiendish), or for another reason.

Any spell of 3rd level or higher that prevents scrying attempts on a creature (such as *nondetection*) or an area (such as *false vision*) thwarts this spell's ability to evaluate that creature or creatures within that area.

KNOW OPPONENT

Divination
Level: Bard 3, cleric 3
Components: S, DF
Casting Time: 1 standard action
Range: Close (25 ft. + 5 ft./2 levels)
Target: One creature
Duration: Instantaneous
Saving Throw: Will negates
Spell Resistance: Yes

You feel your eyes glow with magical energy as you complete the spell. You see luminous words appear in the air above your spell's target. The words describe the creature's strengths or weaknesses, as you desire.

You gauge the strengths and weaknesses of an opponent to gain combat advantages. Upon casting this spell, you learn a number of strengths or weaknesses of the target equal to one, plus one strength or weakness per two caster levels (maximum four). You can choose to learn strengths, weaknesses, or some combination thereof that you specify. If a creature has more strengths or weaknesses than you can learn with a single casting, you learn the most powerful ones first. Thus, if a monster can use *finger of death* at will and has resistance to sonic 5, you would learn about *finger of death* first.

Strengths can include attack forms and special abilities (including spell-like abilities or supernatural abilities). Weaknesses include vulnerability to an energy type.

For example, suppose a 7th-level cleric casts *know opponent* on a black-armored warrior, choosing to learn one strength and two weaknesses. The warrior fails his save, and the DM informs the cleric's player that the opponent has the ability to drain energy (a strength), is adversely affected by sunlight, and can be repelled by a holy symbol (both weaknesses). The cleric then concludes that he faces a vampire and breaks out the wooden stakes.

KNOW VULNERABILITIES

Divination
Level: Bard 2, cleric 3, sorcerer/wizard 4
Components: V, S
Casting Time: 1 standard action
Range: Close (25 ft. + 5 ft./2 levels)
Target: One creature
Duration: Instantaneous
Saving Throw: Will negates
Spell Resistance: Yes

Your eyes turn red, then take on a golden hue. As you look at the creature, you see small runes dancing around its head. Each rune identifies a particular vulnerability or resistance—red for resistances, green for vulnerabilities.

You learn any special qualities, vulnerabilities, and resistances the target creature has. Vulnerabilities include anything that causes the creature more than the normal amount of damage (such as a creature with the cold subtype having vulnerability to fire or a crystalline creature's susceptibility to the *shatter* spell). Resistances include any effects that reduce or negate damage the creature takes and immunities to particular attacks. The spell identifies resistances and vulnerabilities granted by spell effects.

For example, if cast upon a balor, you learn that it has damage reduction 15/cold iron and good; spell resistance 28; immunity to poison, fire, and electricity; resistance to acid 10 and cold 10; and that it does not have any particular vulnerabilities.

LAND WOMB

Abjuration
Level: Druid 4, ranger 4
Components: V, S
Casting Time: 1 standard action
Range: Touch
Target: You and one other creature/level
Duration: 10 minutes/level (D)
Saving Throw: Will negates
Spell Resistance: Yes

Others watch you speak the spell, and the earth opens up and swallows you whole. You remain safe and secure beneath the ground, untouched by events above.

You cannot enter a land womb through stone or rock, only through tillable soil. The land womb holds you secure 10 feet below the surface. Anyone in a land womb cannot be perceived by divination spells of 4th level or less.

You can bring one additional creature per caster level with you into the land womb. All creatures to be brought into the *land womb* must be touching each other (for instance, holding hands in a ring).

Land womb creates an underground space large enough to hold all target creatures. While space is tight, spellcasting by targets is still possible while in the confines of the spell's effect. You can no longer hear or see anything on the surface by nonmagical means.

You can end the spell at will, but those who are with you cannot. At the end of the spell's duration, all within the land womb return to the spot where they stood before the spell took effect.

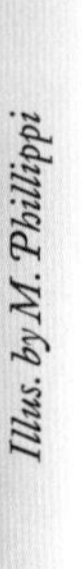

LANGUOR

Transmutation
Level: Druid 4
Components: V, S
Casting Time: 1 standard action
Range: Close (25 ft. + 5 ft./2 levels)
Effect: Ray
Duration: 1 round/level
Saving Throw: Will partial
Spell Resistance: Yes

With a low thrumming sound, a blue beam lances from your finger to strike your foe and weaken him.

You must succeed on a ranged touch attack with the ray to strike a target. This ray causes creatures it hits to become weak and slow for the spell's duration. A struck creature takes a penalty to Strength equal to 1d6+1 per two caster levels (maximum 1d6+10). In addition, a subject that fails a Will save is *slowed*.

The spell's *slow* effect counters and is countered by *haste*.

Lawful sword gives a paladin the upper hand over chaotic foes

LAST BREATH

Transmutation
Level: Druid 4
Components: V, S
Casting Time: 1 standard action
Range: Touch
Target: Dead creature touched
Duration: Instantaneous
Saving Throw: None
Spell Resistance: Yes (harmless)

Rushing to the body of your fallen ally, you call out magic words that will bring back life and breath to your friend.

Last breath restores life to a recently deceased creature, creating a new body for the returning spirit to inhabit. However, the spell must be cast within 1 round of the victim's death. This spell functions like *reincarnate* (PH 270), except that the reincarnated creature receives no level loss, no Constitution loss, and no loss of spells. The creature has –1 hit points (but is stable).

Material Component: Rare oils and unguents worth a total of at least 500 gp, spread over the remains.

LAUNCH BOLT

Transmutation
Level: Sorcerer/wizard 0
Components: V, S, M
Casting Time: 1 standard action
Range: Touch
Target: One crossbow bolt in your possession
Duration: Instantaneous
Saving Throw: None
Spell Resistance: No

The crossbow bolt in your hand glows a bright red, then flies off at your foe.

You cast this spell on a crossbow bolt, causing it to fly at a target of your choice as if you had fired it from a light crossbow, using a ranged attack roll. The bolt has a range increment of 80 feet. Any properties of the crossbow bolt (such as magical abilities, masterwork quality, and so on) or feats you possess (such as Point Blank Shot, Weapon Focus [light crossbow], and so on) apply. Drawing a bolt for this spell is a free action.

Material Component: The crossbow bolt to be fired (1 sp).

LAUNCH ITEM

Transmutation
Level: Sorcerer/wizard 0
Components: S
Casting Time: 1 standard action
Range: Touch
Target: One Fine item in your possession, weighing up to 10 lb.

Duration: Instantaneous
Saving Throw: None
Spell Resistance: No

You hold the item and windmill your arm in an underhanded toss. When it leaves your hand, it is bathed in an orange glow and flies farther than you could throw any item.

You cause a Fine item in your possession to fly at great speed to a target or location you specify, out to medium range (100 ft. + 10 ft./level).

This spell is normally used to launch dangerous items (flasks of acid, thunderstones, and so on) farther than you could normally throw them. You can use this spell to make an attack with a splash weapon. If you choose to do so, you must make an attack roll as normal, but you suffer no penalties for range.

LAWFUL SWORD

Evocation
Level: Paladin 4
Components: V, S **Casting Time:** 1 standard action
Range: Touch
Target: Weapon touched
Duration: 1 round/level
Saving Throw: None
Spell Resistance: No

Calling to mind thoughts of justice, you run your fingers along the weapon, imbuing it with power.

This spell functions like *holy sword* (PH 242), except as follows. The weapon functions as a +5 *axiomatic weapon* (+5 enhancement bonus on attack rolls and damage rolls, lawful-aligned, deals an extra 2d6 points of damage against chaotic opponents). It also emits a *magic circle against chaos* effect (as the spell).

LAY OF THE LAND

Divination
Level: Bard 4, druid 4, ranger 1
Components: V, S, F/DF
Casting Time: 3 rounds
Range: Personal
Target: You
Duration: Instantaneous

You cast this spell and are surrounded with a nimbus of green light. In your mind, a map unfolds of the surrounding area, showing the cities, hamlets, and known ruins as if penned by a cartographer. The light fades but the knowledge of the map remains.

You instantly gain an overview of the area around you. *Lay of the land* gives basic information relevant to major landmarks, such as rivers, lakes, and settlements (of at least hamlet size). It indicates the direction and distance to each from the current location. You have a good understanding of the terrain up to 50 miles from your current location.

Unlike *find the path,* this spell does not give information on traps, passwords, or impediments to a journey.

Arcane Focus: A small piece of lodestone.

LEGION'S (SPELL NAME)

Any spell whose name formerly began with *legion's* has been renamed to a *mass* spell, and is alphabetized in this chapter according to the second word of the spell name.

LESSER (SPELL NAME)

Any spell whose name begins with *lesser* is alphabetized in this chapter according to the second word of the spell name. Thus, the description of a *lesser* spell appears near the description of the spell on which it is based, unless that spell appears in the *Player's Handbook.*

LIFE BOLT

Necromancy
Level: Sorcerer/wizard 2
Components: V, S
Casting Time: 1 standard action
Range: Medium (100 ft. + 10 ft./level)
Effect: Up to five rays
Duration: Instantaneous
Saving Throw: None
Spell Resistance: Yes

Holding your palm outward, you intone the spell and empower it with a bit of your own life. A golden ray beams forth from your hand, striking an undead creature where its heart should have been.

You draw forth some of your own life force to create a beam of positive energy that harms undead. You must make a ranged touch attack to hit, and if the ray hits an undead creature, it deals 1d12 points of damage. Creating each beam deals you 1 point of nonlethal damage.

For every two caster levels beyond 1st, you can create an additional ray, up to a maximum of five rays at 9th level. If you shoot multiple rays, you can have them strike a single creature or several creatures. You must designate targets before you check for spell resistance or roll damage. All rays must be aimed at enemies that are all within 30 feet of each other.

LIFE WARD

Abjuration
Level: Cleric 4
Components: V, S, DF
Casting Time: 1 standard action
Range: Touch
Target: Creature touched
Duration: 1 minute/level
Saving Throw: Will negates
Spell Resistance: Yes

With a brush of your hand you surround the creature in crawling shadows, a cloak of negative energy that whirls and swims across the creature's body.

A creature warded by this spell gains protection from the effects of positive energy, including magical healing. The spell can be cast upon undead to offer additional protection against the turning abilities of clerics. The subject is immune to all positive energy effects, including conjuration (healing) spells, channeled positive energy such as from the turn undead ability, or other effects that derive their power from positive energy.

This spell offers protection from the blinding effect of the Positive Energy Plane, and warded creatures gain no temporary hit points while there.

LIFE'S GRACE

Abjuration
Level: Cleric 5
Components: V, S, DF
Casting Time: 1 standard action
Range: Touch
Target: Living creature touched
Duration: 1 minute/level
Saving Throw: Will negates (harmless)
Spell Resistance: Yes (harmless)

You say a brief prayer and touch your holy symbol to a creature. Symbols of warding and safety appear and flow out to cover the creature in a web of protective magic before fading from sight, absorbed into the creature's form.

The living creature touched becomes immune to all death spells, magical death effects, energy drain, and any negative energy effects. In addition, the subject is immune to undead special attacks that deal ability damage, ability drain, and magical disease (such as mummy rot), even if these attacks do not have a magical source. (For example, the spell prevents poison damage from the poisonous bite of an undead creature.) This spell does not prevent such attacks from undead originating from spells, magic items, or class abilities; only the special attacks from the undead's base nature are affected.

In addition, the subject's armor or clothing is considered ghost touch armor, and its armor bonus counts against incorporeal attacks. (A suit of clothing is considered armor that gives +0 AC for this purpose, though it can be enhanced with spells such as *magic vestment*.)

This spell doesn't remove negative levels that the subject has already gained, nor does it affect the saving throw necessary 24 hours after gaining a negative level.

LIGHT OF LUNIA

Evocation [Good, Light]
Level: Celestia 1, cleric 1, sorcerer/wizard 1
Components: V, S
Casting Time: 1 standard action
Range: Medium (100 ft. + 10 ft./level)
Target and Effect: You and up to two rays; see text
Duration: 10 minutes/level (D) or until discharged; see text
Saving Throw: None
Spell Resistance: Yes; see text

You invoke the powers of good and you begin to glow with the silver light of fabled Lunia, the first layer of the Seven Mounting Heavens of Celestia.

The silvery radiance created by this spell emanates from you in a 30-foot radius, and dim light extends for an additional 30 feet.

Beginning one turn after you cast this spell, you can choose to expend some or all of the *light of Lunia* as a ray of light. You must succeed on a ranged touch attack with the ray to strike a target. You can make a single ranged touch attack that deals 1d6 points of damage, or 2d6 points of damage against undead or evil outsiders, with a range of 30 feet. Spell resistance applies to this attack. This dims your silvery radiance to half (15-foot light, with dim light for an additional 15 feet). You can choose to fire one additional ray with the same characteristics either on the same round or on a subsequent round. Firing the second ray quenches your radiance and ends the spell.

LIGHT OF MERCURIA

Evocation [Good, Light]
Level: Cleric 2, sorcerer/wizard 2

This spell functions like *light of Lunia*, except that the radiance created is golden. Your light rays deal 2d6 points of damage, or 4d6 points of damage against undead and evil outsiders.

LIGHT OF VENYA

Evocation [Good, Light]
Level: Cleric 3, sorcerer/wizard 3

This spell functions like *light of Lunia*, except that a soft, pearly radiance is created. Your light rays deal 3d6 points of damage, or 6d6 points of damage against undead and evil outsiders. Alternatively, you can choose for the ray to heal 1d6 points of damage + your divine spellcaster level (maximum 1d6+10) to a living, non-evil creature.

LIGHTFOOT

Transmutation
Level: Assassin 1, ranger 1
Components: V
Casting Time: 1 swift action
Range: Personal
Target: You
Duration: 1 round

You mutter the words of this short spell and dive down the hallway, dancing between the armed guards and out the gate.

You provoke no attacks of opportunity for moving.

LIGHTNING RING

Evocation [Electricity]
Level: Sorcerer/wizard 8
Components: V, S, M
Casting Time: 1 round
Range: Personal
Effect: Ring of electricity
Duration: 1 round/2 levels
Saving Throw: See text
Spell Resistance: Yes

Your body quakes as a ring of crackling electricity explodes from your chest to whirl about you.

The ring of electricity moves with you and does not interfere with your spellcasting or attacks, or with others attacking you. As long as the *lightning ring* is in effect, you gain resistance to electricity 20. At the beginning of your turn each round, adjacent creatures take 10d6 points of electricity damage, or half that with a successful Reflex save.

In addition, each round as a free action at the beginning of your turn, you can direct two lightning bolts that deal 5d6 points of electricity damage each, exactly as the *lightning bolt* spell (caster level 5th), in any directions you choose. Each bolt can be aimed separately. A creature struck by one of these bolts can make a Reflex save for half damage. The DC for this save is calculated for an 8th-level spell, even though the bolts mimic a 3rd-level spell.

Material Components: A small glass ring and a bit of fur from any animal.

LIONHEART

Abjuration [Mind-Affecting]
Level: Paladin 1
Components: V, S, M
Casting Time: 1 standard action
Range: Touch
Target: Creature touched
Duration: 1 round/level
Saving Throw: Will negates (harmless)
Spell Resistance: Yes (harmless)

You touch your ally while intoning the spell. Where your finger touches, a warm glow appears, then fades.

The subject gains immunity to fear effects.

Material Component: A hair from a lion's mane.

LION'S CHARGE

Transmutation
Level: Druid 3, ranger 2
Components: V
Casting Time: 1 swift action
Range: Personal
Target: You
Duration: 1 round

You cast the spell and a nimbus of yellow energy in the form of a lion surrounds you.

This spell grants you the pounce special ability (MM 313), allowing you to make a full attack at the end of a charge.

LION'S ROAR

Evocation [Sonic]
Level: Cleric 8, Courage 8
Components: V, S, DF
Casting Time: 1 standard action
Range: 120 ft.
Area: 120-ft.-radius burst centered on you
Duration: Instantaneous or 1 minute/level
Saving Throw: Fortitude partial or Will negates (harmless); see text
Spell Resistance: Yes or Yes (harmless); see text

You open your mouth and emit a tremendous roar, a sound like a lion but as loud as a mountain falling.

All enemies within the spell's area take 1d8 points of sonic damage per two caster levels (maximum 10d8) and are stunned for 1 round. A successful Fortitude save halves the damage and negates the stunning effect.

In addition, all allies within the spell's area gain a +1 morale bonus on attack rolls and saves against fear effects, plus temporary hit points equal to 1d8 + caster level (to a maximum of 1d8+20 temporary hit points at caster level 20th).

LISTENING COIN

Divination (Scrying)
Level: Bard 3
Components: V, S, F
Casting Time: 1 standard action
Range: Touch
Effect: Magical sensor
Duration: 1 hour/level (D)
Saving Throw: None
Spell Resistance: No

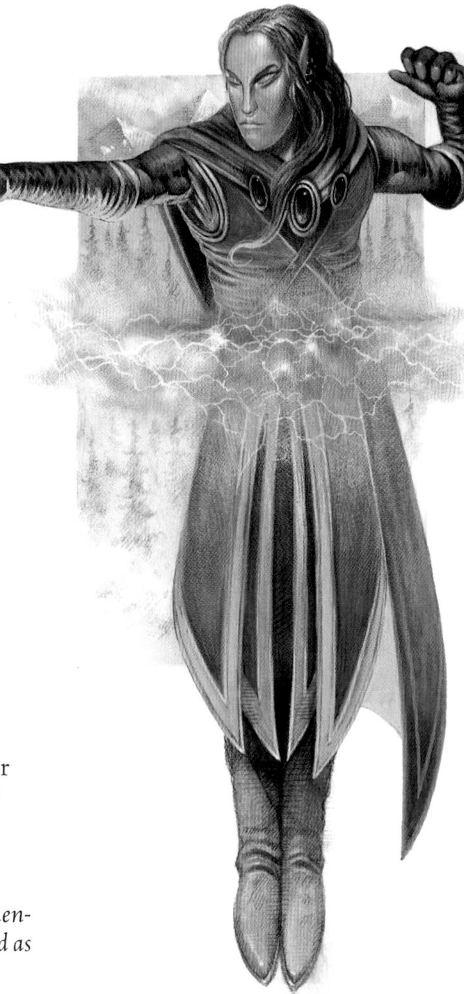

A wizard uses the lightning ring spell to shock her foes

Rubbing two coins together with your fingers, you whisper arcane words into them. Holding one to your ear surreptitiously, you hand over the other.

You turn two ordinary coins into magic listening devices—one a sensor and the other a receiver. After casting the spell, you simply give the sensor coin away, either surreptitiously or overtly. By holding the receiver coin up to your ear, you can hear whatever transpires near the sensor as if you were there (much like a *clairaudience* effect). If the sensor coin is in a pocket, pouch, or sack, the DC of the Listen check increases by 5.

The coins continue to function no matter how far apart they are, although they fall silent if they're on different planes.

Focus: The pair of coins.

LISTENING LORECALL

Divination
Level: Druid 2, ranger 2
Components: V, S, DF
Casting Time: 1 standard action
Range: Personal
Target: You
Duration: 10 minutes/level

You feel conscious of your ears as they warm noticeably. Sounds that seem as though they should be muffled become clear to you.

You gain a +4 insight bonus on Listen checks. In addition, if you have 5 or more ranks in Listen, you gain blindsense out to 30 feet. If you have 12 or more ranks in Listen, you gain blindsight out to 15 feet.

A *silence* spell or effect negates the blindsense or blindsight granted by a *listening lorecall* spell.

LIVELY STEP

Transmutation
Level: Bard 2, sorcerer/wizard 2
Components: V, S, F
Casting Time: 1 standard action
Range: 30 ft.
Area: 30-ft.-radius emanation centered on you
Duration: Up to 12 hours
Saving Throw: Will negates (harmless)
Spell Resistance: Yes (harmless)

Beating a small drum and singing a marching tune, you exhort your allies to struggle on.

Once you cast this spell, the speed of you and all allies within 30 feet of you increases by 10 feet.

You and other affected creatures can only benefit from this spell by refraining from taking any actions other than move actions. When one of the affected creatures takes any other kind of action, this spell ends.

Focus: A small drum.

Illus. by W. England

LIVING PRINTS

Divination
Level: Ranger 1
Components: V, S
Casting Time: 1 standard action
Range: Personal
Target: You
Duration: 1 hour/level

You eyes glow green and you can now see the trails laid down almost a month ago, as clearly as if your quarry had just passed through.

You perceive tracks as if they had just been made. You must notice the prints normally with a successful Search or Survival check, but this eliminates any penalties to your tracking due to the passage of time or any rainfall since the making of the trail. This spell has no effect on tracks more than thirty days old.

LIVING UNDEATH

Necromancy
Level: Cleric 2
Components: V, S, DF
Casting Time: 1 standard action
Range: Touch
Target: Creature touched
Duration: 1 minute/level
Saving Throw: Fortitude negates (harmless)
Spell Resistance: Yes (harmless)

You invoke the will of your gods and your skin sags and becomes sallow, your eyes hollow, and your flesh foul and rotted.

This spell imparts a physical transformation upon the subject, not unlike the process that produces a zombie. While the subject does not actually become undead, its vital processes are temporarily bypassed with no seeming ill effect. The subject is not subject to sneak attacks and critical hits for the duration of the spell, as if it were undead.

While the spell is in effect, the subject takes a –4 penalty to its Charisma score (to a minimum of 1).

LOVE'S LAMENT

Enchantment (Compulsion) [Mind-Affecting]
Level: Bard 3
Components: V
Casting Time: 1 standard action
Range: 60 ft.
Area: Cone-shaped burst
Duration: Instantaneous
Saving Throw: Will negates
Spell Resistance: Yes

Dirgelike music fills the area, reminding those in range of lost loves and life's disappointments.

Creatures within the area of this spell that fail their saves take 1d6 points of Wisdom damage and are nauseated for 1d4 rounds.

LOW-LIGHT VISION

Transmutation
Level: Assassin 1, druid 1, ranger 1, sorcerer/wizard 1
Components: V, M
Casting Time: 1 standard action
Range: Touch
Target: Creature touched
Duration: 1 hour/level
Saving Throw: Will negates (harmless)
Spell Resistance: Yes (harmless)

You pass your hand over the subject's eyes and murmur the arcane words. Its eyes grow larger, and when it opens them, the pupils are speckled with tiny silvers of starlight.

The subject creature gains low-light vision.

Arcane Material Component: A small candle.

LOYAL VASSAL

Abjuration [Lawful]
Level: Paladin 2
Components: V, S, DF
Casting Time: 1 standard action
Range: Touch
Targets: One willing creature touched/3 levels
Duration: 10 minutes/level; see text
Saving Throw: Will negates (harmless)
Spell Resistance: Yes (harmless)

Upon invoking the divine words, glowing silver runes encircle your allies' heads. The runes quickly fade, but the resolve they instilled remain.

You protect the subjects against mind-affecting spells and abilities, giving them a +3 sacred bonus on saving throws against such effects. The spell also helps prevent them from being magically compelled to harm you or anyone else affected by this spell. Any attempt to make a loyal vassal do so (whether the originating effect occurred before or after this spell was cast) counts as a suicidal order, triggering appropriate responses and possibly ending the controlling spell. If the subjects willingly attempt to harm you, the spell is broken for them immediately.

LUCENT LANCE

Transmutation [Light]
Level: Cleric 6, sorcerer/wizard 5
Components: V, S, F
Casting Time: 1 standard action
Range: Close (25 ft. + 5 ft./2 levels)
Effect: Ray
Duration: Instantaneous
Saving Throw: None
Spell Resistance: Yes; see text

The eternal energies of light and darkness you call upon to cast this spell cause the ambient light near you to coalesce around the crystal rod in your hand. The light erupts in a coruscating beam of radiance shaped like a needle-sharp lance.

You must succeed on a ranged touch attack with the ray to strike a target. A creature struck is blinded for 1 round, and dazzled for 1 round per caster level. A creature sensitive to bright light (such as a drow, duergar, or kuo-toa) takes penalties as if it had been exposed to full daylight for 1 round if struck by the beam, even if it resists the spell's other effects.

In addition to this dazzling effect, *lucent lance* deals damage based on the level of light available within your square. In bright light, it deals 1d6 points of damage per caster level (maximum 15d6). In shadowy illumination, it deals 1d4 points of damage per caster level (maximum 15d4). If no light is present in your square, the spell cannot be cast at all.

Focus: A clear glass or crystal rod.

LUMINOUS GAZE

Evocation [Light]
Level: Sorcerer/wizard 1
Components: V, S
Casting Time: 1 standard action
Range: Personal
Target: You
Duration: 1 round/level

At the corners of your vision you see a brightly glowing light. Wherever you look, that area fills with light as bright as a torch.

This spell causes your eyes to glow with an unearthly radiance. The glow from your eyes provides light as per the *light* spell. Each creature within a 20-foot radius of you is dazzled as long as they remain with range. Sightless creatures are unaffected.

MADDENING SCREAM

Enchantment (Compulsion) [Mind-Affecting]
Level: Madness 8
Components: V
Casting Time: 1 standard action
Range: Touch
Target: Living creature touched
Duration: 1d4+1 rounds
Saving Throw: None
Spell Resistance: Yes

With an incomprehensible word and the touch of a hand wrapped in black magic, you reduce your foe to a screaming lunatic.

This spell makes it impossible for the victim to do anything other than race about caterwauling. The creature must move its speed each turn, unless somehow prevented, and can take no other action. The spell gives the subject a –4 penalty to Armor Class, its Reflex saving throws fail except on a roll of 20, and the subject cannot use a shield.

MADDENING WHISPERS

Enchantment (Compulsion) [Mind-Affecting]
Level: Sorcerer/wizard 8
Components: V
Casting Time: 1 round
Range: Close (25 ft. + 5 ft./2 levels)
Targets: One creature/level
Duration: 1 round/level
Saving Throw: Will negates
Spell Resistance: Yes

As you mutter this spell, your words burrow into your foes' minds like hungry maggots, spawning dark and disturbing thoughts.

You can choose to inflict one of the following conditions upon any creatures that fail their saving throws.

Lucent lance bores a hole through a shadow

Hysteria: The subjects fall into fits of uncontrollable laughing or crying (equal chance for either). This hysteria affects subjects as though they were nauseated; they are unable to attack, cast spells, concentrate on spells, or do anything else requiring attention. The only action a subject can take is a single move action per turn.

Panic: The subjects become panicked. If cornered, a panicked creature cowers.

Violent Hallucinations: The subjects perceive any nearby creatures as dangerous enemies, attacking the nearest ones and fighting until the subjects are slain or until no more creatures are in sight.

Stupor: The subjects curl up on the floor and remain oblivious to events around them. Characters in a stupor are effectively stunned and prone.

MAELSTROM

Conjuration (Creation) [Water]
Level: Druid 8, Ocean 8
Components: V, S, DF
Casting Time: 1 round
Range: Long (400 ft. + 40 ft./level)
Effect: A whirlpool 120 ft. wide and 60 ft. deep
Duration: 1 round/level
Saving Throw: Reflex negates; see text
Spell Resistance: No

Whirling about your hand and pulling it down, your magic reaches out and does the same to the water but on a titanic scale, creating a vortex of sucking waves.

Maelstrom causes a deadly vortex to form in water. A body of water in which you form the *maelstrom* must be at least 120 feet wide and 60 feet deep, or the spell is wasted.

Waterborne creatures or objects within 50 feet of the vortex (below and on all sides) must make successful Reflex saves or be sucked in. Trained swimmers can attempt Swim checks instead if their skill modifier is higher than their Reflex save bonus. Waterborne vessels avoid being sucked in if their operators make Profession (sailor) checks against the same DC as the spell's saving throw. These creatures and objects take 3d8 points of damage upon being sucked in.

Once inside, creatures and objects take 3d8 points of bludgeoning damage each round at the beginning of your turn. They remain trapped for 2d4 rounds, after which time they are ejected to any square adjacent to the bottom of the vortex (your choice). Ejected subjects might be sucked back into the vortex, but they receive a new Reflex save. Subjects of Large or smaller size are ejected from the bottom of the

Illus. by J. Engle

Illus. by B. Hagan

An aquatic druid can wreak havoc with the maelstrom spell, all the while unseen by his foes

vortex. Larger subjects are ejected from the top.

MAGE ARMOR, GREATER

Conjuration (Creation) [Force]
Level: Sorcerer/wizard 3
Components: V, S

An invisible sheen of armor-shaped force surrounds you.

This spell functions like *mage armor* (PH 249), except that it requires no material component and its tangible field of force provides a +6 armor bonus to Armor Class.

MAGE ARMOR, MASS

Conjuration (Creation) [Force]
Level: Sorcerer/wizard 3
Range: Close (25 ft. + 5 ft./2 levels)
Targets: One creature/level, no two of which are more than 30 ft. apart

You feel arcane energy encompass you, granting you a sense of serenity. As you choose your targets for the spell, you see each one glow briefly with a silver aura.

This spell functions like *mage armor* (PH 249), except that it affects multiple creatures.

MAGE HAND, GREATER

Transmutation
Level: Sorcerer/wizard 1
Components: V, S
Casting Time: 1 standard action
Range: Medium (100 ft. + 10 ft./level)
Target: One object or creature weighing up to 40 lb.
Duration: Concentration
Saving Throw: Will negates
Spell Resistance: Yes

You cast the spell, and your hand is suffused with a ghostly white radiance. You point your finger at the target across the room, and it slowly rises in the air.

A *greater mage hand* spell can lift an object and move it at will from a distance. As a move action, you can propel the target up to 20 feet in any direction, although the spell ends if the distance between you and the subject ever exceeds the spell's range.

A creature can negate the effect against an object it possesses with a successful Will save or if you fail to overcome its spell resistance.

An object can be telekinetically manipulated as if with one hand. For example, a lever or rope can be pulled, a key can be turned, an object rotated, and so on, if the force required is within the weight limitation. The spell has an effective Strength of 10.

MAGIC FANG, SUPERIOR

Transmutation
Level: Druid 4, ranger 4
Components: V, S
Casting Time: 1 standard action
Range: Personal

Target: You
Duration: 1 round/level

You speak the old words of the incantation, and your hands glow with a yellow aura that flashes at the tips of your digits.

Superior magic fang gives every natural weapon you possess an enhancement bonus on attack rolls and damage rolls equal to +1 per four caster levels (maximum +5 at 20th level).

MAGIC MIASMA

Abjuration
Level: Sorcerer/wizard 9
Components: V, S, M
Casting Time: 1 standard action
Range: Medium (100 ft. + 10 ft./level)
Area: 30-ft.-radius emanation centered on a point in space
Duration: 1 round/level
Saving Throw: None; see text
Spell Resistance: No

A thick, sparkling cloud of billowing mist rolls into being from the point you indicate.

This potent spell conjures a cloud of mist that functions as a *solid fog* spell (PH 281). In addition, any spells cast within the fog have a –4 penalty to the spellcaster's caster level, and the save DC of any such spell is reduced by 2. Creatures within the fog, or that enter the fog, must succeed on a Will save or suffer the reduction in caster level and DC even after they leave the fog, for the duration of the spell.

Material Component: A small piece of quilted cloth, which must be soaked in water while the spell is cast.

MALEVOLENT MIASMA

Conjuration (Creation)
Level: Sorcerer/wizard 2
Components: V, S, F
Casting Time: 1 standard action
Range: Close (25 ft. + 5 ft./2 levels)
Area: 15-ft.-radius burst
Duration: Instantaneous
Saving Throw: Fortitude negates
Spell Resistance: No

You click the stones together in your hand and a gray fog, tinged with darker, malevolent streaks, springs up in the midst of your enemies.

The spell produces a toxic fog that deals 1d4 points of nonlethal damage per level (maximum 5d4). Creatures in the area that hold their breath are still subject to the effect. Creatures that are immune to poison are not affected by this spell.

Focus: Three polished gray stones.

MAKE MANIFEST

Transmutation
Level: Cleric 4, sorcerer/wizard 6
Components: V, S
Casting Time: 1 standard action
Range: Close (25 ft. + 5 ft./2 levels)
Target: One creature
Duration: 1 round/level
Saving Throw: Will negates
Spell Resistance: Yes

You cast a spell that reaches into another plane and pulls another creature to your realm.

You can cause one creature on a coexistent plane (DMG 150), along with its personal belongings, to suddenly appear on your plane of existence. An affected creature appears in the location analogous to the space it occupied on the coexistent plane. For example, the *make manifest* spell allows you to cause a target on the Ethereal Plane to appear on the Material Plane, and vice versa. This spell does not grant the ability to pinpoint the location of ethereal creatures.

For the duration of the spell, the target creature retains all its abilities except for those that allow it to enter other planes. For example, a ghost brought in from the Ethereal Plane would be unable to return to the Ethereal Plane but would remain incorporeal. At the end of the spell's duration, the target creature returns to whatever plane it was on before it was targeted by the spell, even if it has moved beyond the range of *make manifest*.

MAKE MANIFEST, MASS

Transmutation
Level: Cleric 6, sorcerer/wizard 8
Components: V, S, M
Area: 25-ft.-radius emanation centered on a point in space
Saving Throw: None

You toss a handful of copper dust into the air, and it clings to creatures invisible to you. Suddenly they're visible and in your presence.

This spell functions like *make manifest*, except that all creatures and unattended objects on coterminous and coexistent planes within the area of this spell are instantly brought onto your plane.

For the duration of the spell, the target creatures retain all their abilities except for those that allow them to enter other planes. At the end of *mass make manifest*'s duration, objects and creatures return to their plane of origin, even if they have left the spell's area.

Material Component: A handful of copper dust.

MANTLE OF CHAOS

Abjuration [Chaos]
Level: Cleric 3, Limbo 3
Components: V, S
Casting Time: 1 standard action
Range: Personal
Target: You
Duration: 10 minutes/level (D)
Saving Throw: None
Spell Resistance: Yes

You invoke the powers of chaos, and a flickering yellow field of anarchic energy surrounds you.

The power of this spell grants you spell resistance equal to 12 + your caster level against spells with the lawful descriptor.

MANTLE OF EVIL

Abjuration [Evil]
Level: Blackguard 3, cleric 3, Hades 3

You invoke the powers of evil, and a dark, wavering field of unholy energy wraps around you like a cloak.

This spell functions like *mantle of chaos*, except that *mantle of evil* grants spell resistance against spells with the good descriptor.

MANTLE OF GOOD

Abjuration [Good]
Level: Cleric 3, Elysium 3, paladin 3

You invoke the powers of good, and a shimmering white field of holy energy swaddles you.

This spell functions like *mantle of chaos*, except that *mantle of good* grants spell resistance against spells with the evil descriptor.

MANTLE OF THE ICY SOUL

Transmutation [Cold]
Level: Cleric 6, druid 5
Components: V, S, M
Casting Time: 1 standard action
Range: Touch
Target: Creature touched
Duration: 1 hour/level
Saving Throw: Will negates
Spell Resistance: Yes

As you touch the creature, a chill sweeps through you and down your arm. As the spell takes effect, the creature's body changes hue, becoming an icy blue.

The subject creature gains the cold subtype, granting it immunity to cold and vulnerability to fire (the creature takes half again as much damage from fire effects). A fire creature subjected to this spell does not gain the cold subtype, but it loses the fire subtype for the duration.

Material Component: A pinch of sapphire dust worth 10 gp.

MANTLE OF LAW

Abjuration [Law]
Level: Cleric 3, Mechanus 3, paladin 3

You invoke the powers of law, and a constant blue field of axiomatic energy surrounds you.

This spell functions like *mantle of chaos*, except that *mantle of law* grants spell resistance against spells with the chaotic descriptor.

MANYJAWS

Evocation [Force]
Level: Sorcerer/wizard 3
Components: V, S, M
Casting Time: 1 standard action
Range: Medium (100 ft. + 10 ft./level)
Effect: One pair of disembodied, flying jaws per caster level (maximum ten pairs)
Duration: Concentration, up to 3 rounds
Saving Throw: See text
Spell Resistance: Yes

You clamp your teeth together with the last gesture, and several disembodied jaws of blue force appear and float toward your foes, gnashing their teeth.

Manyjaws gives wizards a potent offense they can use while taking other actions

Illus. by R. Spears

When you cast this spell, you summon several pairs of mystical, disembodied jaws that fly about and attack your foes. These pairs of jaws can be commanded to attack separate targets, or multiple pairs can be sent to attack a single foe. The jaws originate at your location and fly out to attack their targets, moving at a fly speed of 40 feet with perfect maneuverability. You can redirect as many of the jaws as you desire as a standard action.

Each round on your action, each pair of jaws automatically hits its target and deals 1d6 points of damage, or half that amount with a successful Reflex save. A creature targeted by multiple pairs of jaws in a single round makes only one saving throw, with success halving the total damage.

Material Component: A pair of teeth.

MARK OF THE HUNTER

Divination
Level: Ranger 3
Components: V, S, M
Casting Time: 1 standard action
Range: Medium (100 ft. + 10 ft./level)
Target: One creature, which must be a favored enemy
Duration: 1 minute/level
Saving Throw: Will negates
Spell Resistance: Yes

By pointing your finger at one of your favored enemies, you mark it with a glowing rune that only you can see.

Your favored enemy bonuses against a foe with a *mark of the hunter* are 4 higher than they would otherwise be.

Furthermore, the rune limns your enemy, making the foe easier for you to attack. The subject of a *mark of the hunter* spell gains no bonus to Armor Class against your attacks from any cover less than total cover, nor does it gain a miss chance against your attacks from any concealment less than total concealment. Other effects that grant a miss chance (such as incorporeality) work normally.

Material Component: A bit of skin or bone from the relevant favored enemy type or subtype.

MARK OF THE OUTCAST

Necromancy
Level: Blackguard 1, cleric 2, druid 2
Components: V, S, DF
Casting Time: 1 standard action
Range: Close (25 ft. + 5 ft./2 levels)
Target: One creature
Duration: Permanent
Saving Throw: Will negates
Spell Resistance: Yes

You select your victim for punishment and invoke the ancient words of anathema. A dull purple splotch in the shape of a skull manifests itself on your victim's flesh, visible to all.

This spell creates an indelible mark on the subject's face (or other upper body part, if the subject doesn't have a head). The mark is visible to normal vision, low-light vision, and darkvision. The wearer of such a mark takes a –5 circumstance penalty on Bluff and Diplomacy checks and a –2 penalty to Armor Class.

The mark cannot be dispelled, but it can be removed with a *break enchantment, limited wish, miracle, remove curse,* or *wish* spell.

MARKED OBJECT

Divination
Level: Assassin 2, ranger 1, sorcerer/wizard 2
Components: V, S, F
Casting Time: 1 minute
Range: Personal
Target: You
Duration: 24 hours/level

By holding the small item to your nose and reciting the ancient words of power you unleash the spell. You immediately have a sense of the object's owner such that you believe you could find further indications of the creature's passage.

Upon casting this spell, you become attuned to the specific creature that owns the spell's focus item. (A creature is considered to own an item if it was the last creature to carry the item on its person for 24 hours or more. You do not count when considering what creature was last to carry an item.) This attunement grants you a +10 bonus on Search and Survival checks made to track the item's owner or find evidence of the owner's passage. This spell does not give you insight into who or what the creature you are attuned to is or where that creature ultimately might be. Also, the spell does not provide a trail that is not already there nor provide you with the benefit of the Track feat.

Arcane Focus: An object owned by the creature or a piece of the creature to be tracked, such as a tuft of hair or a fingernail.

MASS (SPELL NAME)

Any spell whose name begins with *mass* is alphabetized in this chapter according to the second word of the spell name. Thus, the description of a *mass* spell appears near the description of the spell on which it is based, unless that spell appears in the *Player's Handbook*.

MASTER AIR

Transmutation
Level: Druid 2
Components: V, S, F
Casting Time: 1 standard action
Range: Personal
Target: You
Duration: 1 round/level

You hold a feather aloft and intone the spell. Great translucent wings unfold from your back. You leap up and are airborne.

You sprout a pair of insubstantial feathery or batlike (your choice) wings.

You can fly at a speed of 90 feet with good maneuverability (60 feet if you're wearing medium or heavy armor). Using *master air* requires as much concentration as walking, so you can attack or cast spells normally. You can charge but not run, and you cannot carry aloft more weight than your maximum load (PH 161), plus any armor you wear.

Should the spell duration expire while you are still aloft, the magic fails slowly. You drop 60 feet per round for 1d6 rounds. If you reach the ground in that amount of time, you land safely. If not, you fall the rest of the distance, taking falling damage normally. Since dispelling a spell effectively ends it, you also fall in this way if the *master air* spell is dispelled.

Focus: A wing feather from any bird or the wing bone of any bat.

MASTER EARTH

Transmutation
Level: Druid 7
Components: V, S, F
Casting Time: 1 standard action
Range: Personal
Target: You
Duration: Instantaneous

The ground below your feet suddenly seems insubstantial, and you sink below the surface, moving through dirt and stone as easily as if you were flying through the air.

You travel straight through the earth itself to a destination you choose.

The movement is instantaneous and has no distance limitations (though the location must be on the same world). You need only think of where you want to go. If you don't think of an exact location, the earth carries you to the periphery of the general area you imagine.

The earth never leaves you stranded inside it. It always puts you back to the surface even if it cannot deliver you to your chosen destination. It takes you as far as it can. Underground, creature-built structures don't hinder you as long as you can move around them.

This spell functions only on the Material Plane.

Focus: The fossil of any animal.

MASTER'S TOUCH

Divination
Level: Bard 1, sorcerer/wizard 1
Components: V, F
Casting Time: 1 swift action
Range: Personal
Target: You
Duration: 1 minute/level (D)

Holding aloft an item you wish to use effectively, you address it directly with a command to obey your desire to wield it.

You gain proficiency with a single weapon or shield you hold in your hands when the spell is cast. The lack of a somatic component means the spell can be cast in the middle of a fight while you keep ready whatever items stand between you and danger.

Proficiency is granted for only a single, specific item, although multiple castings allow for multiple proficiencies. For example, if you hold a short sword and a rapier, with a buckler strapped to your off hand, you could cast the spell three times, once for each weapon and once for the shield.

This spell does not grant proficiency for a kind or category of item (such as short swords) but only for the one specific item held in your hand at the time the spell is cast (this short sword). Should you set that item down or otherwise lose your grip on it, the proficiency does not transfer to a different item of the same kind you might pick up. However, if you recover the original item before the spell's effect runs out, you are still proficient with that specific weapon or shield for the duration.

Focus: The item in whose use you wish to be proficient.

MAW OF CHAOS

Abjuration [Chaotic]
Level: Sorcerer/wizard 9
Components: V, S, M
Casting Time: 1 standard action
Range: Medium (100 ft. + 10 ft./level)
Area: 15-ft.-radius emanation centered on a point in space
Duration: 1 round/level
Saving Throw: Will partial
Spell Resistance: Yes

At the culmination of casting the spell you open your mouth wide as if to yawn. In imitation, the air cracks and splits, opening into a yawning area of roiling blue-green energy resembling a great mouth.

All creatures in the area take 1d6 points of damage per caster level in the round when you cast the spell and each round thereafter at the start of your turn. Those damaged must also make a Will saving throw or be dazed for 1 round.

Second, the chaotic energy makes it difficult to concentrate. Any activity that involves concentration (such as casting a spell or using a spell-like ability) requires a Concentration check (DC 25 + spell level) to succeed.

Creatures with the chaotic subtype are unaffected by this spell.

Material Component: A jawbone with teeth.

MAW OF STONE

Transmutation
Level: Cavern 7
Components: V, S, DF
Casting Time: 1 standard action
Range: Close (25 ft. + 5 ft./2 levels)
Effect: One cave mouth or natural tunnel up to 20 ft. in diameter
Duration: 10 minutes/level (D)
Saving Throw: Reflex partial; see text
Spell Resistance: No

The rock comes alive, opening into a huge maw of deadly stone.

You cause a single natural opening or natural chamber to become animated. The opening or chamber cannot move, but it can attack. You can order it to attack any creature, or a specific type of creature. You also can order it to attack under a specific circumstance, such as when creatures try to leave or when they touch something.

An animated opening can attack only creatures that try to move through it. An animated chamber can attack every creature inside. Only one *maw of stone* can be in effect on a particular opening or chamber at a time.

The animated opening has an attack bonus equal to your level +10. The *maw of stone* deals damage equal to 2d8 points + your caster level.

An animated opening can make one immediate attack against a creature passing through. If it succeeds, the target must make a Reflex save or it cannot pass through the maw.

The animated stone has an Armor Class of 15 and hardness 8. Dealing 60 points of damage to it ends the spell.

MECHANUS MIND

Enchantment (Compulsion) [Lawful, Mind-Affecting]
Level: Mechanus 2, sorcerer/wizard 2
Components: V, S
Casting Time: 1 standard action
Range: Touch
Target: Creature touched
Duration: 1 minute/level
Saving Throw: Fortitude negates (harmless)
Spell Resistance: Yes (harmless)

You speak the words of the spell and your mind feels clearer and more organized, as if it were mere drawers where everything was put in its proper place. Your face grows calmer and unexpressive, but your thoughts are more rational and ordered.

The subject gains a +4 resistance bonus on Will saving throws to resist mind-affecting spells and abilities.

While in the grip of *Mechanus mind*, the subject also becomes more analytical and less emotional. The subject gains a +2 competence bonus on Intelligence-based checks, but takes a –2 penalty on Charisma-based checks.

MEMORY ROT

Evocation
Level: Druid 5
Components: V, S
Casting Time: 1 standard action
Range: Close (25 ft. + 5 ft./2 levels)
Target: One living creature
Duration: Instantaneous
Saving Throw: Fortitude negates
Spell Resistance: Yes

You blow across your open palm at your opponent, and your breath coalesces into a cloud of glowing yellow spores that surround your foe's head, driving through its scalp into the brain beneath.

You create a cloud of spores that infests the brain of the subject creature, gradually destroying its mind. The spores deal 1d6 points of Intelligence damage immediately. The spores then gradually eat away at the subject's brain, dealing 1 point of Intelligence drain each round thereafter at the beginning of your turn. The subject can attempt a Fortitude save each round to combat the effect of the spores. A successful save ends the spores' advance and halts any further Intelligence drain.

MESMERIZING GLARE

Enchantment (Compulsion) [Mind-Affecting]
Level: Bard 2, sorcerer/wizard 3
Components: S
Casting Time: 1 standard action
Range: Close (25 ft. + 5 ft./2 levels)
Targets: One living creature/level, no two of which are more than 30 ft. apart
Duration: 1 round/level
Saving Throw: Will negates
Spell Resistance: Yes

You say nothing, but your eyes glow with a warm, friendly fire. Others stop to regard you, and once enraptured, they cannot look away.

Directing your gaze toward the target creatures, you cause them to stop and stare blankly at you. Creatures that fail their saving throws become *fascinated*.

METAL MELT

Transmutation [Fire]
Level: Sorcerer/wizard 4
Components: V, S, M

Casting Time: 1 standard action
Range: Close (25 ft. + 5 ft./2 levels)
Target: Nonmagical metal object weighing up to 5 lb./level
Duration: 1 round
Saving Throw: Will negates (object)
Spell Resistance: Yes (object)

You uncork the vial and pour out its contents, and the armor you designate begins to soften and flow.

You alter the physical properties of a metal object so that it runs like water. The melted metal does not change temperature but flows as a liquid for 1 round and then returns to its normal solid state, usually in a form resembling a puddle. An item in a creature's possession is allowed a Will save, using the creature's saving throw bonus unless its own is higher.

Material Component: A drop of mercury in a vial.

MIASMA

Evocation
Level: Druid 6
Components: V, S, DF
Casting Time: 1 standard action
Range: Close (25 ft. + 5 ft./2 levels)
Target: One living creature
Duration: 3 rounds/level
Saving Throw: Fortitude negates; see text
Spell Resistance: Yes

You hiss out a red mist that streaks toward your target despite prevailing winds and claws into his mouth and nose, choking him.

By filling the subject's mouth and throat with unbreathable gas, you prevent it from doing much more than coughing and spitting. An affected creature cannot speak, cast spells with verbal components, use breath weapons, or utter command words to activate magic items, but it can otherwise act normally.

The subject can hold its breath for 2 rounds per point of Constitution but must make a Constitution check (DC 10 +1 per previous success) each round thereafter to continue doing so. Failure on any such check (or voluntary resumption of breathing) causes the subject to fall unconscious (0 hp). On the next round, the subject drops to –1 hit points and is dying; on the third round, it suffocates (DMG 304).

Metal melt can cause a metal weapon to run like water

MIASMA OF ENTROPY

Necromancy
Level: Druid 4, sorcerer/wizard 5
Components: V, S
Casting Time: 1 standard action
Range: 30 ft.
Area or Target: Cone-shaped burst or one solid object; see text
Duration: Instantaneous
Saving Throw: Fortitude half or Will negates (object); see text
Spell Resistance: Yes (object)

A red mist rises from the ground as you intone this spell, billowing outward from you. Within it you see leaves curl up, scrolls rot from their spindles, and the leather armor of your foes drip from their vulnerable forms.

Miasma of entropy causes accelerated decay in all wood, leather, and other natural materials in the spell's area. It destroys nonmagical objects of wood, leather, paper, and other formerly living organic matter. All such objects within the area rot into slimy, pulpy masses. Objects weighing more than 1 pound per caster level are not affected, but all other objects of the appropriate composition are ruined.

Alternatively, you can target *miasma of entropy* against a single solid object of nonliving nonmagical organic matter that weighs up to 10 pounds per caster level.

MIND POISON

Necromancy
Level: Sorcerer/wizard 3
Components: V, S, M
Casting Time: 1 standard action
Range: Touch
Target: Living creature touched
Duration: Instantaneous; see text
Saving Throw: Fortitude negates; see text
Spell Resistance: Yes

You spit on your fingers and whip your hand in a snakelike motion, imbuing it with poisoning magic.

You infect the subject with a poison that saps willpower, dealing 1d10 points of Wisdom damage immediately and another 1d10 points of Wisdom damage 1 minute later. Each instance of damage can be negated by a Fortitude save (DC 10 + 1/2 your caster level + your Int or Cha modifier, for wizards or sorcerers, respectively).

Material Component: A piece of a toadstool.

Illus. by D. Martin

MINDLESS RAGE

Enchantment (Compulsion) [Mind-Affecting]
Level: Bard 2, sorcerer/wizard 2
Components: V, S, F
Casting Time: 1 standard action
Range: Medium (100 ft. + 10 ft./level)
Target: One creature
Duration: 1 round/level
Saving Throw: Will negates
Spell Resistance: Yes

By waving a scarlet cloth and shouting taunts at your intended subject, you gain its undivided attention.

You fill the subject with so great a rage that it can do nothing but focus on engaging you in personal physical combat. The target must be able to see you when you cast this spell. If the subject later loses line of sight to you, the spell immediately ends. (A subject can't voluntarily break line of sight with you, such as by closing its eyes, to end this spell prematurely.)

If the subject threatens you, it must make a full attack against you using a melee weapon or a natural weapon. If the subject doesn't threaten you at the start of its turn, it must move toward you (taking nothing but move actions) and end its movement as close to you as possible. If it gets close enough with a single move action to threaten you, it stops and makes a melee attack against you as normal.

While under the effect of a *mindless rage* spell, the subject can make use of all its normal melee combat skills, abilities, and feats—either offensive or defensive. However, the subject can't make ranged attacks, cast spells, or activate magic items that require a command word, a spell trigger, or spell completion to function. The subject can't make any attack against a creature other than you.

The subject of this spell, though overcome with rage, is by no means rendered idiotic or suicidal. For example, an affected creature will not charge off a cliff in an attempt to reach you.

An interesting side effect of *mindless rage* occurs when the spell affects any character or creature that has the rage ability (such as a barbarian). In these cases, the *mindless rage* spell automatically activates the creature's rage ability (and counts as one of the creature's uses of rage for that day).

Focus: A scarlet handkerchief or similar piece of cloth, waved in the target's direction while you vocalize the verbal component.

MINOR DISGUISE

Transmutation
Level: Bard 0
Components: V, S
Casting Time: 1 standard action
Range: Personal
Target: You
Duration: 1 hour

Your fingertips glow blue, and you add a few details to enhance your disguise.

You use magic to make minor, cosmetic changes in your appearance. The spell does not change the actual structure of either your features or body. It can add color to hair, paint wrinkles upon your face, give you a scar, or darken your teeth. This spell gives you a +2 competence bonus on the next Disguise check you make during its duration.

MISER'S ENVY

Enchantment (Compulsion) [Mind-Affecting]
Level: Bard 2, sorcerer/wizard 3
Components: V, S, M
Casting Time: 1 standard action
Range: Close (25 ft. + 5 ft./2 levels)
Target: One living creature
Duration: 1 round/level
Saving Throw: Will negates
Spell Resistance: Yes

Upon invoking the power of this spell, both the dwarf and the small idol across the room glow with a violet shade. The dwarf starts moving toward it, his eyes tinged violet with greed.

When you cast this spell, you designate a target creature and specify an object, both of which must be within the spell's range. If the target creature fails its saving throw, it becomes consumed by a powerful desire for the object. For the duration of the spell, the creature seeks to obtain the object (going so far as to attack anyone holding or wearing it).

Once the creature gains possession of the object, it protects the item greedily, attacking anyone who approaches within 30 feet or who otherwise appears to be trying to take the object away. If no one approaches within 30 feet or seems interested in trying to take the object, the subject can act normally.

Dragons, due to their greedy nature, take a –4 penalty on their saving throws against this spell.

Material Component: A copper piece.

MOMENT OF CLARITY

Abjuration
Level: Paladin 1
Components: V, S, DF
Casting Time: 1 standard action
Range: Touch
Target: Creature touched
Duration: Instantaneous
Saving Throw: None
Spell Resistance: No

You feel a dark, oppressive weight pressing against your mind. When you touch your target, the weight lifts. The creature you touched seems now to be battling with a similar oppression.

When you cast this spell and touch a creature that is under the influence of a mind-affecting spell or ability, that creature immediately receives another saving throw against the effect's original DC to break free of the effect. If the spell or ability did not originally permit a saving throw, this spell has no effect.

MONSTROUS THRALL

Enchantment (Compulsion) [Mind-Affecting]
Level: Domination 9
Components: V, S
Casting Time: 1 standard action
Range: Medium (100 ft. + 10 ft./level)
Target: One creature
Duration: 24 hours/level
Saving Throw: Will negates
Spell Resistance: Yes

Calling upon your reserves of personal power, you reach outward with your mind and gain control of the will of your foe.

This spell functions like *true domination* (page 224), except that the subject can be any creature and is permanently *dominated* if it fails its initial Will save.

A subject ordered to take an action against its nature receives a saving throw with a –4 penalty to resist taking that particular action. If the save succeeds, the subject still remains your thrall despite its minor mutiny. Once a subject makes a successful saving throw to resist a specific order, it makes all future saving throws to resist taking that specific action without a penalty.

MOON BLADE

Evocation
Level: Moon 3
Components: V, S, M/DF
Casting Time: 1 standard action
Range: 0 ft.
Effect: A swordlike beam
Duration: 1 minute/level (D)
Saving Throw: None
Spell Resistance: Yes

A 3-foot-long blazing beam of moonlight springs forth from your hand.

You call a swordlike beam of moonlight into your hand. Anyone who can cast *moon blade* can wield the beam with proficiency. However, if you are proficient with any type of sword, you can wield the beam as if it were any type of sword and thus gain the benefits of any special sword skill you might have, such as Weapon Focus.

Attacks with a *moon blade* are melee touch attacks. Its strike saps vitality or life force, causing no visible wounds but dealing 1d8 points of damage +1 point per two caster levels (to a maximum of +10) to any type of creature except undead. Undead are visibly wounded by a *moon blade*. Their substance boils away from its touch, and they take 2d8 points of damage +1 point per caster level (to a maximum of +20) per blow. The blade is immaterial, and your Strength modifier does not apply to the damage.

A successful *moon blade* strike temporarily scrambles magic. On the target's next turn after a hit from a *moon blade*, the creature must make a Concentration check to use any spell or spell-like ability. The DC is equal to 10 + damage dealt + spell level. (An opponent hit by a *moon blade* while casting a spell must make the usual Concentration check to avoid losing the spell in addition to the check on its next turn.)

Arcane Material Component: A small candy made with wintergreen oil.

MOON BOLT

Evocation
Level: Cleric 4, druid 4
Components: V, S
Casting Time: 1 standard action
Range: Long (400 ft. + 40 ft./level)
Target: One living or undead creature, or two living or undead creatures that are no more than 15 ft. apart; see text
Duration: Instantaneous
Saving Throw: Fortitude half (living target) or Will negates (undead target)
Spell Resistance: Yes

Picturing a full moon in your mind you call upon the cyclical energies of the celestial body. You create a bolt of shimmering moonlight that streaks from your outstretched hand.

A *moon bolt* strikes unerringly against any living or undead creature in range.

A living creature struck by a *moon bolt* takes 1d4 points of Strength damage per three caster levels (maximum 5d4). If the subject makes a successful Fortitude saving throw, the Strength damage is halved.

An undead creature struck by a *moon bolt* must make a Will save or fall helpless for 1d4 rounds, after which time it is no longer helpless and can stand upright, but it takes a –2 penalty on attack rolls and Will saving throws for the next minute.

MOON LUST

Illusion (Pattern) [Mind-Affecting]
Level: Cleric 1
Components: V, S, F
Casting Time: 1 standard action
Range: Medium (100 ft. + 10 ft./level)
Target: One living creature
Duration: 1 round/level
Saving Throw: Will partial
Spell Resistance: Yes

Forcefully presenting a silver ingot in your hand, you extol the virtues of the moon's beauty in a language both beautiful and dead. The words of your loving declaration call forth a silver-white glow around your target that swiftly fades.

This spell instills in the target an obsessive fascination with the moon. If the target fails its save, it fixates on the moon, staring at the moon or imagining it in its mind, and is considered *fascinated* for the duration of the spell.

If the saving throw is successful, the subject is instead dazzled for the duration of the spell.

Sightless creatures are not affected by this spell.

Focus: A silver ingot worth 5 gp.

MOON PATH

Evocation [Force]
Level: Moon 5
Components: V, S, M/DF
Casting Time: 1 standard action
Range: Medium (100 ft. + 10 ft./level)
Effect: A variable-width, glowing white stair or bridge of translucent force up to 15 ft./level long; see text
Duration: 1 minute/level (D)
Saving Throw: None; see text
Spell Resistance: No

As you cast this spell, pure, pale moonlight shapes itself into a stair or bridge, as you desire.

Moon path allows you to create a stair or bridge from one spot to another. The effect is a railless ribbon of glowing white translucent force like a glass strip. The strip can be from 3 to 20 feet wide as you decide. (You can vary the width over the ribbon's length if you want.) It sticks to its endpoints unshakably, even if these endpoints are in midair.

At the time of casting, you designate up to one creature per caster level to receive extra protection while standing on or moving along the *moon path*. Protected creatures gain the benefit of a *sanctuary* effect. This functions like the 1st-level spell *sanctuary* except that the save DC is 15 + your Wis modifier, and any subject of the spell who attacks breaks the *sanctuary* effect for all subjects. Protected creatures also stick to the top of the *moon path* as though they have received *spider climb* spells. A creature loses both benefits immediately when it leaves the path.

Unlike a *wall of force*, a *moon path* can be dispelled. It is otherwise similar to a *wall of force* in that it needs no supports and it is immune to damage of all kinds. A *disintegrate* spell blasts a hole in the path 10 feet square, leaving the rest of the path intact. (If the *moon path* is 10 feet wide or less, this merely creates a 10-foot gap.) A hit from a *rod of cancellation*, a *sphere of annihilation*, or *Mordenkainen's disjunction* destroys a *moon path*. Spells and breath weapons cannot pass through a *moon path*, although *dimension door, teleport,* and similar effects can bypass the barrier. It blocks ethereal creatures as well as material creatures. Gaze attacks cannot operate through a *moon path*.

A *moon path* must be straight, continuous, and unbroken when formed. If its surface would be interrupted by any object or creature, the spell fails. The bridge version of the spell must be created flat. The stair version cannot rise or descend any more sharply than 45 degrees.

Arcane Material Component: A white handkerchief.

MOONBEAM

Evocation [Light]
Level: Moon 2
Components: V, S, M/DF
Casting Time: 1 standard action
Range: 30 ft.
Area: Cone-shaped emanation
Duration: 1 minute/level (D)
Saving Throw: None or Will negates; see text
Spell Resistance: No

As you complete this spell, a swath of pale moonlight springs from your hand.

On your turn each round, you can change the direction the cone of light points.

Light from a *moonbeam* spell does not adversely affect creatures that are sensitive to light, but lycanthropes in humanoid form caught in the cone must make a Will save to avoid involuntarily assuming their animal forms. A lycanthrope in animal form can change out of it on the creature's next turn (spending a round in animal form). However, if it is still in the area of the spell, it must succeed on a Will save to do so. Once a lycanthrope successfully saves against *moonbeam*, it is not affected by any more of your *moonbeam* spells for 24 hours.

Moonbeam penetrates any darkness spell of equal or lower level, but does not counter or dispel it. Darkness spells of higher level block a *moonbeam*.

Arcane Material Component: A pinch of white powder.

MOONBOW

Evocation [Electricity]
Level: Sorcerer/wizard 5
Components: V, S, M
Casting Time: 1 standard action
Range: Medium (100 ft. + 10 ft./level)
Effect: 3 motes of electricity
Duration: Instantaneous or up to 3 rounds; see text
Saving Throw: None
Spell Resistance: Yes

Sparks flit among your fingers as you call electricity from the surrounding air.

This spell conjures three glowing motes of electricity. You direct any number of the motes to fly off and strike targets within the spell's range. Multiple motes can be fired at the same target, or each can be sent against a separate target. You must succeed on a ranged touch attack with a mote to strike a target. Any creature struck by a mote takes 1d6 points of electricity damage per two caster levels (maximum 10d6).

If you do not immediately fire all the motes created by the spell, you can choose to fire as many of the remaining ones as you wish as a standard action during the next round. If a round passes in which you do not fire one of your motes, the spell ends and all remaining motes vanish.

Material Component: A small piece of moonstone.

MOONFIRE

Evocation [Light]
Level: Moon 9
Components: V, S, DF
Casting Time: 1 standard action
Range: 60 ft.
Area: Cone-shaped burst and cone-shaped emanation; see text
Duration: Instantaneous and 1 round/level; see text
Saving Throw: Reflex half and Will negates; see text
Spell Resistance: Yes

A cone of fiery white moonlight springs from your hand.

Living creatures in the area of a *moonfire* spell feel an unnatural chill and take 1d8 points of damage per two caster levels (maximum 10d8). Undead and shapechangers take 1d8 points of damage per caster level (maximum 20d8). This application of the spell allows a Reflex save for half damage.

All magical auras within the cone glow with a faint blue light for 1 round per caster level. Disguised, shapechanged, or polymorphed creatures and objects in the spell's area at the time the spell is cast must make Will saves or immediately return to their normal forms. Even if the save succeeds, they remain covered in ghostly white outlines that show their true forms for 1 round per caster level.

The entire area covered by the cone glows silver-white for 1 round per caster level. This radiance is as bright as the light of a full moon and negates electricity damage for 1 round per caster level unless the item or creature generating the electricity effect makes a caster level check (1d20 + item's caster level or creature's caster level) against a DC equal to 10 + your caster level. If an electricity effect is generated outside the glowing cone, the cone blocks the electricity effect unless the creature generating the effect succeeds on a caster level check. If an electricity effect is generated inside the glowing cone, the cone negates the electricity effect unless the creature generating the effect succeeds on a caster level check.

MOUNTAIN STANCE

Transmutation
Level: Druid 2, sorcerer/wizard 2
Components: V, S
Casting Time: 1 standard action
Range: Touch
Target: One creature
Duration: 1 minute/level
Saving Throw: Will negates (harmless)
Spell Resistance: No

By calling upon the primordial powers of elemental earth, you complete the spell. A feeling of stubborn determination fills your soul until you touch the spell's intended recipient. You see then in that creature a hint of the same feeling of determination.

While this spell is in effect, the subject can root itself to the ground as a free action. The subject gains a bonus equal to your caster level against any attempts to grapple, lift, push, bull rush, overrun, throw, trip, or otherwise force the subject to move against its will through either physical or magical means.

Mountain stance makes holding your ground easy

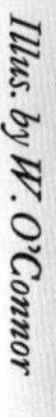

Illus. by W. O'Connor

If at any point such an effort succeeds and the subject is forced to move, the spell ends immediately. Any voluntary movement on the subject's part does not end the spell (although a creature cannot be rooted while it moves), and the subject can "reroot" itself elsewhere in the same manner as described above.

MURDEROUS MIST

Conjuration (Creation)
Level: Druid 4
Components: V, S
Casting Time: 1 standard action
Range: Close (25 ft. + 5 ft./2 levels)
Effect: Cloud spreads in a 30-ft. radius, 20 ft. high
Duration: 1 round/level
Saving Throw: Reflex partial; see text
Spell Resistance: No

Drawing the power of steaming volcanic vents into your body, you exhale, and a cloud of boiling steam roils away from you.

You create a cloud of scalding hot steam that moves in a straight line, away from you, at a speed of 10 feet per round. Anyone within the cloud takes 2d6 points of damage and is permanently blinded. If a creature within the area makes a successful Reflex saving throw, it takes only half damage and is not blinded.

Any creature within the cloud has concealment. Winds do not affect the cloud's direction or speed. However, a moderate wind (11+ mph) disperses the cloud in 4 rounds, and a strong wind (21+ mph) disperses it in 1 round.

NATURE'S AVATAR

Transmutation
Level: Druid 9
Components: V, S, DF
Casting Time: 1 swift action
Range: Touch
Target: Animal touched
Duration: 1 minute/level
Saving Throw: Will negates (harmless)
Spell Resistance: Yes (harmless)

With a touch, you gift your animal ally with nature's strength, resilience, and speed.

The affected animal gains a +10 morale bonus on attack rolls and damage rolls and 1d8 temporary hit points per caster level, plus the effect of a *haste* spell (PH 239).

NATURE'S BALANCE

Transmutation
Level: Druid 3
Components: V, S
Casting Time: 1 standard action
Range: Touch
Target: Creature touched
Duration: 10 minutes/level
Saving Throw: Fortitude negates (harmless)
Spell Resistance: Yes (harmless)

Touching your friend, you concentrate, imagining a light flowing from your body into his. As you do so, a blue glow flickers to life in the center of your chest, and it travels down your arm into his form, granting him a portion of your power.

You take a –4 penalty to your choice of Strength, Dexterity, or Constitution, and your subject gains an equivalent bonus to the same ability score. You get no saving throw to avoid the loss, but your subject can attempt a Fortitude save to avoid the gain, if desired.

NATURE'S FAVOR

Evocation
Level: Druid 2, ranger 2
Components: V, S, DF
Casting Time: 1 swift action
Range: Touch
Target: Animal touched
Duration: 1 minute
Saving Throw: Will negates (harmless)
Spell Resistance: Yes (harmless)

Rubbing the animal's side, you whisper the final bit of the spell's ritual. The animal glances at you before turning its attention to your foes, bristling as it does so.

You grant the subject animal a +1 luck bonus on attack rolls and damage rolls for every three caster levels you possess (maximum +5).

NATURE'S RAMPART

Transmutation
Level: Druid 3, ranger 3
Components: V, S, F
Casting Time: 10 minutes
Range: Medium (100 ft. + 10 ft./level)
Area: Structure up to 40 ft. square
Duration: Instantaneous
Saving Throw: None
Spell Resistance: No

With a final wave of your hand, the ground beneath your feet trembles and the landscape shifts into a new form.

You shape a natural setting into a formidable defensive position. Usually this spell is used to prepare an open outdoor area such as a hillside or a forest, but a large natural cavern could be shaped into a divine rampart. Artificial structures or features are not affected, although *nature's rampart* could be positioned to fill a gap between two buildings or barricade an unpaved road. The effect of the spell depends on the terrain:

Open Outdoor Site: A rampart or dike of earth 5 feet high and 5 feet thick at its base rises immediately behind a shallow ditch 5 feet wide and 5 feet deep along the perimeter of the site. Creatures behind the dike receive cover. Attackers approaching on foot must scramble down into the ditch and then climb 10 feet to reach the top of the dike (Climb DC 10).

Rough Outdoor Site or Cavern: Loose stones and boulders, dead wood, and patches of dense briars are arranged to form a defensible wall 5 feet high and 2 feet thick at the base around the perimeter of the site. Creatures behind the wall receive cover.

Marshy or Low-Lying Site: In areas such as marsh, bog, swamp, or tundra, *nature's rampart* cannot raise a wall, but instead creates a water-filled ditch 10 feet wide and 5 feet deep. Creatures forced to wade the ditch are reduced to 1/4 their normal speed (minimum 5 feet) and cannot charge or run.

Focus: A small quartz gem engraved with the image of an exquisite tiny castle, worth at least 100 gp.

NATUREWATCH

Necromancy
Level: Druid 0, ranger 1
Components: S
Casting Time: 1 standard action
Range: 30 ft.
Area: Cone-shaped emanation
Duration: 10 minutes/level
Saving Throw: None
Spell Resistance: No

Reaching out with your heart, you seek knowledge of the health of plants and animals in the area.

This spell is similar to *deathwatch* (PH 217), but it functions only on animals and plants. In addition, it also allows you to determine a variety of other mundane information about the animals and plants (whether or not the plants are dehydrated, the animals are malnourished, and so forth).

NAUSEATING BREATH

Conjuration (Creation)
Level: Cleric 3, sorcerer/wizard 3
Components: V, S, M
Casting Time: 1 standard action
Range: 30 ft.
Area: Cone-shaped burst
Duration: Instantaneous
Saving Throw: Fortitude negates
Spell Resistance: No

You windmill your arm to complete the spell and nearly gag before exhaling a great gout of putrid-smelling green gas.

You breathe out a cone of nauseating vapors. Any creature in the area must succeed on a Fortitude save or be nauseated for 1d6 rounds.

Material Component: A piece of fish at least one day old.

NEGATIVE ENERGY AURA

Necromancy
Level: Cleric 4
Components: V, S
Casting Time: 1 standard action
Range: Personal
Area: 10-ft.-radius emanation centered on you
Duration: 1 round/level

You speak the ancient words of this spell and an aura of black, crackling negative energy surrounds you.

Each round on your turn, every living creature within 10 feet of you loses 1 hit point per three caster levels (maximum 5). Undead creatures instead gain 2 hit points per round (though they can't exceed their full normal hit point total from this effect). Characters with immunity to negative energy effects are not affected by this aura. The aura does not affect you.

NERVESKITTER

Transmutation
Level: Sorcerer/wizard 1
Components: V, S
Casting Time: 1 immediate action
Range: Close (25 ft. + 5 ft./2 levels)
Target: One creature
Duration: 1 round
Saving Throw: None (harmless)
Spell Resistance: Yes

You suffuse your ally with a brief, blue glow. He jerks away from you, as if he can anticipate your next action.

You cast this spell when you and your party roll for initiative. Unlike other immediate actions, you can cast this spell while flat-footed. You enhance the subject's reactions in combat, granting it a +5 bonus on its initiative check for the current encounter. If the subject does not make an initiative check within 1 round, this spell has no effect.

NET OF SHADOWS

Illusion (Shadow) [Darkness]
Level: Sorcerer/wizard 1
Components: V, S
Casting Time: 1 standard action
Range: Close (25 ft. + 5 ft./2 levels)
Targets: One creature/level, no two of which are more than 25 ft. apart
Duration: 1d6 rounds
Saving Throw: Will negates
Spell Resistance: Yes

You cast the spell, and the surrounding shadows shift at your command, flying toward your targets and wrapping themselves around them.

This spell gives the subjects concealment, but the shifting magic shadows also inhibit the subjects' ability to ascertain their surroundings. The subjects can see only 5 feet through the shadows that coat them, and foes within that range have concealment from the subjects. Darkvision does not penetrate a *net of shadows.*

NIGHTMARE LULLABY

Enchantment (Compulsion) [Mind-Affecting, Sonic]
Level: Bard 2
Components: V, S
Casting Time: 1 standard action
Range: Medium (100 ft. + 10 ft./level)
Target: One creature
Duration: 1 round/level
Saving Throw: Will negates
Spell Resistance: Yes

Your music calms your foe, sending it to sleep while it remains upright. As you perform, it starts to twitch and moan, as if tormented by unseen fears.

This spell can put a target into a surreal, sleepwalking state. The target must make a Will saving throw or become *confused,* thinking it has entered a nightmare.

NIGHT'S CARESS

Necromancy [Evil]
Level: Sorcerer/wizard 5
Components: V, S
Casting Time: 1 standard action
Range: Touch
Target: Creature touched
Duration: Instantaneous
Saving Throw: Fortitude partial; see text
Spell Resistance: Yes

A touch from your hand, which sheds darkness like the blackest night, disrupts the life force of a living creature.

Your touch deals 1d6 points of damage per caster level (maximum 15d6) and 1d6+2 points of Constitution damage. (A successful Fortitude saving throw negates the Constitution damage.)

Illus. by R. Horsley

The nauseating breath spell can effectively incapacitate foes

The spell has a special effect on an undead creature. An undead touched by you takes no damage or Constitution loss, but it must make a successful Will saving throw or flee as if panicked for 1d4 rounds +1 round per caster level.

NIGHTSHIELD

Abjuration
Level: Cleric 1, sorcerer/wizard 1
Components: V, S
Casting Time: 1 standard action
Range: Personal
Target: You
Duration: 1 minute/level (D)

With a whisper-quiet whoosh, a field of shadowy energy cloaks your body.

This spell provides a +1 resistance bonus on saving throws; this resistance bonus increases to +2 at caster level 6th and +3 at caster level 9th. In addition, the spell negates *magic missile* attacks directed at you.

NIGHTSTALKER'S TRANSFORMATION

Transmutation
Level: Sorcerer/wizard 5
Components: V, S, M
Casting Time: 1 standard action
Range: Personal
Target: You
Duration: 1 round/level (D)

Moving the potion you hold in a circle before you, you finish speaking the words of the spell before quaffing the potion in one gulp. A moment later you feel discomfort as your connection to the arcane energies of the world around you slips away. In its place, you find your mind and body filled with abilities you lacked before.

You gain a +4 enhancement bonus to Dexterity, a +3 luck bonus to Armor Class, a +5 luck bonus on Reflex saving throws, a +5 competence bonus on Spot, Listen, Hide, and Move Silently checks, and proficiency with all simple weapons plus the hand crossbow, rapier, sap, shortbow, and short sword. You also gain the Weapon Finesse feat and the evasion ability (PH 50). You deal an extra 3d6 points of damage whenever you attack an opponent that you flank or an opponent denied its Dexterity bonus to Armor Class. This extra damage works like the rogue's sneak attack ability.

You lose your spellcasting ability for the duration of the spell, including your ability to use spell trigger or spell completion magic items, just as if the spells were no longer on your class list.

Material Component: A *potion of cat's grace,* which you drink (and whose effect is subsumed by this spell's effect).

NIMBUS OF LIGHT

Evocation [Light]
Level: Cleric 1, Purification 1
Components: V, S, DF
Casting Time: 1 standard action
Range: Personal
Target: You
Duration: 1 minute/level or until discharged (D)

A glittering corona of sunlight surrounds your body at a few inches distance—until you release it as a focused blast of divine energy.

The nimbus of light around you glows like a lantern, providing bright illumination in a 30-foot radius (and shadowy illumination for an additional 30 feet) from you.

As a move action, you can coalesce the energy from a *nimbus of light* around your outstretched arm, and then as a standard action fling it toward a foe within 30 feet. You must succeed on a ranged touch attack with the energy to strike a target. A *nimbus of light* deals 1d8 points of damage +1 point per round that has elapsed since you cast the spell (maximum 1d8 + caster level). Attacking with a *nimbus of light* ends the spell, whether your ranged touch attack is successful or not.

NIXIE'S GRACE

Transmutation [Water]
Level: Bard 6
Components: V, S, F
Casting Time: 1 standard action
Range: Personal
Target: You
Duration: 10 minutes/level
Saving Throw: None
Spell Resistance: No

You feel a longing for cool waters, and a forceful confidence manifests within you. Your movements and thoughts become filled with grace.

This potent spell infuses you with powerful fey magic, granting you many of the traits and abilities of a nixie (MM 235). Upon casting this spell, you gain a swim speed of 30 feet. You can breathe underwater, and you gain low-light vision and damage reduction 5/cold iron. You also gain a +6 enhancement bonus to Dexterity, a +2 enhancement bonus to Wisdom, and a +8 enhancement bonus to Charisma.

Focus: A lock of nixie's hair, freely given to you by a nixie.

OBEDIENT AVALANCHE

Conjuration (Creation) [Cold]
Level: Cold 9, sorcerer/wizard 9
Components: V, S
Casting Time: 1 standard action
Range: Medium (100 ft. + 10 ft./level)
Effect: 20-ft.-radius avalanche of snow centered on a point in space; see text
Duration: Instantaneous
Saving Throw: Reflex half or Reflex negates; see text
Spell Resistance: No

You summon an avalanche of snow out of a rift in midair, burying your foes and sending them to a frosty death.

An *obedient avalanche* spell affects creatures differently, depending on where they are in relation to the avalanche.

Within 20 feet of the Center Point: Creatures take 1d8 points of damage per two caster levels (maximum 10d8) and an additional 1d6 points of cold damage per two caster levels. A successful Reflex save halves the damage. Creatures who fail their saves are also buried (DMG 90). All squares within 20 feet of the center point are covered in heavy snow (DMG 94), which persists as long as ordinary snow would. A buried creature can free itself with a DC 20 Strength check as a full-round action, and can be dug free by others (a single creature working alone requires 1 minute to free a trapped creature). A trapped creature is unable to move, and cannot cast spells with somatic components, and any material components must be in hand.

Between 20 feet and 40 feet of the Center Point: Creatures take half as much damage from the impact of the avalanche as the creatures nearer the center point took (Reflex negates). Creatures who fail their saves must also resist the force of the snow moving past them as if they were being bull rushed. The snow has a +13 attack bonus (+5 for effective Strength of 20 and +8 for effectively being Huge) on the bull rush check, and it pushes characters away from the center point of the spell. All squares in the 20-foot to 40-foot ring are covered in snow (DMG 94), which persists as long as ordinary snow would.

Terrain and Structures: The avalanche uproots small trees and other vegetation automatically, and it leaves a trail of light rubble (DMG 91) even after the snow melts. Structures struck by an obedient avalanche take 1d6×10 points of damage.

An *obedient avalanche* extinguishes all flames it touches, whether they are normal or magical.

OMEN OF PERIL

Divination
Level: Cleric 1, druid 1, Liberation 1, ranger 1
Components: V, F
Casting Time: 1 round
Range: Personal
Target: You
Duration: Instantaneous

A brief supplication gives you a vision that hints at how dangerous the immediate future is likely to be.

Based on an assessment of your immediate surroundings and chosen path of travel, you receive one of three visions that reflect the next hour's journey: safety, peril, or great danger.

The base chance for receiving an accurate reply is 70% +1% per caster level, to a maximum of 90%; the DM makes the roll secretly.

If the *omen of peril* is successful, you get one of three visions, which lasts just a second or two.

- *Safety:* You aren't in any immediate danger. If you continue on your present course (or remain where you are if you have been stationary for some time before casting the spell), you will face no significant monsters, traps, or other challenges for the next hour or so.
- *Peril:* You will face challenges typical of an adventure: challenging but not overwhelming monsters, dangerous traps, and other hazards for the next hour or so.
- *Great Danger:* Your very life is at grave risk. You will likely face powerful NPCs or deadly traps in the next hour.

If the roll fails, you get one of the two incorrect results, determined randomly by the DM, and you don't necessarily know that you failed because the DM rolls secretly.

Choosing which vision is "correct" takes some educated guesswork on the part of the DM, who should assess the characters' likely courses of action and what dangers they're likely to face.

The exact form that an *omen of peril* takes depends on whether you worship a specific deity, venerate nature as a druid, or simply uphold abstract principles. A druid might see a white dove for safety, a dark cloud obscuring the sun for peril, and a forest fire for great danger. A cleric of Fharlanghn might get a vision of a straight road for safety, a crossroads for peril, and a washed-out bridge for great danger.

Unlike the more powerful *augury* spell (PH 202), an *omen of peril* doesn't respond to a specific question. It indicates only the level of danger likely for the next hour, not what form the danger will take.

Focus: A set of marked sticks, bones, or similar tokens worth at least 25 gp.

ONE WITH THE LAND

Transmutation
Level: Druid 2, ranger 2
Components: V, S
Casting Time: 1 standard action
Range: Personal
Target: You
Duration: 1 hour/level

You cast the spell and are bathed in a golden-green light from above. As it fades, you feel in touch with your natural surroundings.

You forge a strong link with nature that gives you greater insight into your environment. You gain a +2 competence bonus on Handle Animal, Hide, Move Silently, Search, Survival, and wild empathy checks.

ONE MIND

Divination
Level: Paladin 2

This spell functions like *lesser one mind*, except as noted here, and in addition it allows you and your special mount to predict each other's movements, giving you a significant edge in combat. You and your mount both gain a +2 bonus on attack rolls as long as you are mounted.

ONE MIND, GREATER

Divination
Level: Paladin 3

This spell functions like *one mind*, except as noted here, and in addition you and your mount gain a +2 bonus on melee damage rolls as long as you are mounted.

ONE MIND, LESSER

Divination
Level: Paladin 1
Components: V, S, DF
Casting Time: 1 standard action
Range: Personal
Target: You
Duration: 1 hour/level

Your mount begins to move in a predictable, complementary manner to yourself. It positions itself to maximize its effectiveness as a combat partner, and you feel that your actions instinctively do the same for it.

You temporarily strengthen the mental bond with your special mount when you cast this spell. When you are mounted on your special mount, the link with your mount sharpens your senses, giving you a +4 insight bonus on Spot and Listen checks and the scent ability (MM 314) for the duration of the spell. If your mount ever moves more than 10 feet from you, the spell ends.

OOZE PUPPET

Transmutation
Level: Sorcerer/wizard 6
Components: V, S
Casting Time: 1 standard action
Range: Medium (100 ft. + 10 ft./level)
Target: One ooze
Duration: 24 hours/level
Saving Throw: Fortitude negates
Spell Resistance: Yes

With a few chanted words and a mystic pass of your arm, your magic reaches out to invisibly surround the ooze, placing it under your control.

You telekinetically take control of the targeted ooze, manipulating it and forcing it to move and attack as you see fit. You can force the ooze to perform as you desire, within the limits of its abilities. Controlling the ooze's actions for an entire round is a move action for you. When the ooze is not directed to move, attack, or undertake any actions by you, telekinetic force holds it immobile. Once control is established, you must have line of sight to the ooze to manipulate it, but distance is not otherwise a factor, unless you and the ooze are on different planes (at which point the spell ends).

If a controlled ooze splits, such as a black pudding (MM 201) struck by a slashing weapon, you retain control of only one of the resultant oozes (choose randomly).

The ooze puppet spell telekinetically controls an ooze creature

Illus. by C. Dien

OPALESCENT GLARE

Necromancy [Death, Good]
Level: Arborea 4, Cleric 6, sorcerer/wizard 6
Components: V, S, DF
Casting Time: 1 standard action
Range: Personal
Target: You
Duration: Instantaneous
Saving Throw: Will partial; see text
Spell Resistance: Yes

You invoke the spell and your eyes begin to glow with a rippling pearly radiance, like those of a noble ghaele eladrin.

Inspired by the deadly gaze of the noble ghaele eladrin, you gain a gaze attack usable against creatures within 60 feet. If an evil creature with 5 or fewer Hit Dice meets your gaze (DMG 294), it dies unless it succeeds on a Will save. Even if the save succeeds, the creature is affected as though by a *fear* spell (PH 229) for 2d10 rounds.

Non-evil creatures and evil creatures with more than 5 Hit Dice are not slain by the gaze, and they suffer the *fear* effect only if they fail the Will save.

ORB OF ACID

Conjuration (Creation) [Acid]
Level: Sorcerer/wizard 4
Components: V, S
Casting Time: 1 standard action
Range: Close (25 ft. + 5 ft./2 levels)
Effect: One orb of acid
Duration: Instantaneous
Saving Throw: Fortitude partial; see text
Spell Resistance: No

An orb of acid about 3 inches across shoots from your palm at its target, dealing 1d6 points of acid damage per caster level (maximum 15d6). You must succeed on a ranged touch attack to hit your target.

A creature struck by the orb takes damage and becomes sickened by the acid's noxious fumes for 1 round. A successful Fortitude save negates the sickened effect but does not reduce the damage.

ORB OF ACID, LESSER

Conjuration (Creation) [Acid]
Level: Sorcerer/wizard 1
Components: V, S

Casting Time: 1 standard action
Range: Close (25 ft. + 5 ft./2 levels)
Effect: One orb of acid
Duration: Instantaneous
Saving Throw: None
Spell Resistance: No

Your quick, precise movements culminate in your open palm facing your target. An orb of dark green acid flies from your hand.

An orb of acid about 2 inches across shoots from your palm at its target, dealing 1d8 points of acid damage. You must succeed on a ranged touch attack to hit your target.

For every two caster levels beyond 1st, your orb deals an additional 1d8 points of damage: 2d8 at 3rd level, 3d8 at 5th level, 4d8 at 7th level, and the maximum of 5d8 at 9th level or higher.

ORB OF COLD

Conjuration (Creation) [Cold]
Level: Sorcerer/wizard 4
Effect: One orb of cold

This spell functions like *orb of acid*, except that it deals cold damage. In addition, a creature struck by an *orb of cold* must make a Fortitude save or be blinded for 1 round instead of being sickened.

ORB OF COLD, LESSER

Conjuration (Creation) [Cold]
Level: Sorcerer/wizard 1
Effect: One orb of cold

Your hand takes on a blue tint and your fingers turn numb and unresponsive as you complete the spell. From your chilled palm flies an orb composed of blue ice.

This spell functions like *lesser orb of acid*, except that it deals cold damage.

ORB OF ELECTRICITY

Conjuration (Creation) [Electricity]
Level: Sorcerer/wizard 4
Effect: One orb of electricity

This spell functions like *orb of acid*, except that it deals electricity damage. In addition, a creature wearing metal armor struck by an *orb of electricity* must make a Fortitude save or be entangled for 1 round instead of being sickened.

ORB OF ELECTRICITY, LESSER

Conjuration (Creation) [Electricity]
Level: Sorcerer/wizard 1
Effect: One orb of electricity

The air crackles around your outstretched hand and the smell of ozone assaults your nostrils as a ball of electrical energy, its surface crackling with bolts of lightning, streaks from your open palm.

This spell functions like *lesser orb of acid*, except that it deals electricity damage.

ORB OF FIRE

Conjuration (Creation) [Fire]
Level: Sorcerer/wizard 4
Effect: One orb of fire

This spell functions like *orb of acid*, except that it deals fire damage. In addition, a creature struck by an *orb of fire* must make a Fortitude save or be dazed for 1 round instead of being sickened.

ORB OF FIRE, LESSER

Conjuration (Creation) [Fire]
Level: Sorcerer/wizard 1
Effect: One orb of fire

Your hand heats to an uncomfortable temperature just moments before you release the spell's energy in the form of an orb of white flames speeding from your outward-facing palm.

This spell functions like *lesser orb of acid*, except that it deals fire damage.

ORB OF FORCE

Conjuration (Creation) [Force]
Level: Sorcerer/wizard 4
Components: V, S
Casting Time: 1 standard action
Range: Medium (100 ft. + 10 ft./level)
Effect: One orb of force
Duration: Instantaneous
Saving Throw: None
Spell Resistance: No

As you gather the energies of the spell, you feel against your palm a spherical weight that seems almost bonded to your skin. The sphere grows, until with a final precise movement, you release the translucent blue orb, sending it hurtling toward your intended target.

You create a globe of force 3 inches across, which streaks from your palm toward your target. You must succeed on a ranged touch attack to hit the target. The orb deals 1d6 points of damage per caster level (maximum 10d6).

ORB OF SOUND

Conjuration (Creation) [Sonic]
Level: Sorcerer/wizard 4
Effect: One orb of sonic energy

Symbols recognizable as musical notation—the visual representation of sound—appear in midair within the curve of your palm accompanied by the fractious sounds they represent. The notes begin to whirl and stretch, forming into a spherical whirlwind of cacophonic chaos, as you make ready to release the spell. At last, you send the sphere of noise toward your chosen target.

This spell functions like *orb of acid*, except that it deals 1d4 points of sonic damage per level (maximum 15d4). In addition, a creature struck by an *orb of sound* must make a Fortitude save or be deafened for 1 round instead of being sickened.

ORB OF SOUND, LESSER

Conjuration (Creation) [Sonic]
Level: Sorcerer/wizard 1
Effect: One orb of sonic energy

This spell functions like *lesser orb of acid*, except that it deals 1d6 points of sonic damage, plus an additional 1d6 points of damage per two caster levels beyond 1st: 2d6 at 3rd level, 3d6 at 5th level, 4d6 at 7th level, and the maximum of 5d6 at 9th level or higher.

OTYUGH SWARM

Conjuration (Creation)
Level: Pestilence 9
Components: V, S
Casting Time: 1 standard action
Range: Medium (100 ft. + 10 ft./level)
Effect: Three or more otyughs, no two of which are more than 30 ft. apart
Duration: Seven days or seven months (D)
Saving Throw: None
Spell Resistance: No

Illus. by J. Engle

You smell an otyugh swarm before you see it

Focusing your will on a disgusting pile of refuse, you cause toothed and tentacled horrors to rise up and stalk about at your command.

Otyugh swarm creates otyughs from a large collection of refuse and filth, such as a sewer or cesspool. You can choose to create 3d4 ordinary otyughs (MM 204) or 1d3+1 Huge otyughs with 15 HD (MM 292). The otyughs willingly aid you in combat or battle, perform a specific mission, or serve as bodyguards. They remain with you for seven days unless you dismiss them. If the otyughs are created only for guard duty, the duration of the spell is seven months. In this case, the otyughs must be ordered to guard only a specific site or location. Otyughs summoned to guard duty cannot move outside the spell's range.

You must create the otyughs in an area containing at least 6,000 pounds of sewage, refuse, or offal. After you cast the spell, otyughs not summoned for guard duty can leave the area of offal at your command.

OWL'S INSIGHT

Transmutation
Level: Druid 5
Components: V, S
Casting Time: 1 standard action
Range: Touch
Target: Creature touched
Duration: 1 hour
Saving Throw: Fortitude negates (harmless)
Spell Resistance: Yes (harmless)

As you cast this spell, your face is overlaid with the image of a snow owl. The image fades as you bestow your ally with comprehension.

The subject gains an insight bonus to Wisdom equal to 1/2 your caster level.

PANACEA

Conjuration (Healing)
Level: Cleric 4, druid 5
Components: V, S
Casting Time: 1 standard action
Range: Touch
Target: Creature touched
Duration: Instantaneous
Saving Throw: Will half (harmless); see text
Spell Resistance: Yes (harmless)

You kneel next to your afflicted comrade and speak the soft words of this spell. At your touch a golden radiance infuses your companion.

This spell channels positive energy into a creature to wipe away its afflictions. It immediately ends any of the following conditions affecting the subject: blinded, *confused*, dazed, dazzled, deafened, diseased, exhausted, fatigued, frightened, nauseated, panicked, paralyzed, shaken, sickened, and stunned. It negates sleep effects and the effect of the *feeblemind* spell, and ends any additional effects from poison, as the *neutralize poison* spell. It also cures 1d8 points of damage + 1 point per caster level (maximum +20).

Panacea does not remove ability damage, negative levels, or drained levels.

Used against an undead creature, *panacea* deals damage instead of curing the creature (which takes half damage if it makes a Will saving throw), but it has no other effect.

PAVILION OF GRANDEUR

Conjuration (Creation)
Level: Creation 9
Components: V, S, DF
Casting Time: 10 minutes
Range: Close (25 ft. + 5 ft./2 levels)
Effect: Extradimensional pavilion, up to five 10-ft. cubes/level (S), plus feast for 12 creatures/level
Duration: 24 hours/level (D) plus 12 hours; see text
Saving Throw: None
Spell Resistance: No

Thinking sweet thoughts of home and hearth, you conjure an invisible bastion of comfort and security.

You conjure up a grand pavilion-sized tent that has a single entrance on the plane from which the spell was cast. The entry point looks like a faint shimmering in the air that is 10 feet wide by 15 feet high. Only those you designate can enter the pavilion, and the entrance is shut and made invisible behind you when you enter. You can open it again from your own side at will. Once observers have passed beyond the entrance, they are in a spacious tent decorated in the colors of your faith. The lighting can vary between darkness and daylight, and the temperature between 40 and 90 degrees Fahrenheit, at your discretion when casting the spell.

The pavilion is sumptuously furnished, including a full meal for a dozen creatures per caster level. Anyone who spends 1 hour dining here gains benefits identical to those of a *heroes' feast* spell (PH 240). While in the pavilion, creatures heal naturally at double the normal rate (not including fast healing or regeneration).

PERINARCH

Transmutation
Level: Druid 4, Limbo 4, sorcerer/wizard 4
Components: V, S, DF
Casting Time: 1 standard action
Range: Close (25 ft. + 5 ft./2 levels)
Duration: 1 round/level; see text
Saving Throw: None (object) and Reflex negates; see text
Spell Resistance: No

Limbo impinges on all sides—colors, sounds, and elements. You speak the words and feel the power of the plane buckle within your mind, then relax as you impress order upon the chaos.

This spell grants temporary control over the terrain of Limbo. Normally, unless controlled, the Ever-Changing Chaos of Limbo (DMG 158) is just what the plane's name implies: a roiling soup of energy and elements. Natives learn to control it or to inhabit areas that have enjoyed some measure of control for a long period, but visitors to areas of "raw" limbo must make a DC 16 Wisdom check to gain control over the dangerous roil.

The *perinarch* spell gives you automatic control of a radius of raw Limbo (an area not already stabilized or within some other creature's control) in close range. Control allows you to reshape the raw limbo as you desire, adding

Illus. by B. Hagan

A pavilion of grandeur spell provides adventurers with a spectacular resting place between battles

or subtracting one of the four basic elements once per round as a standard action. A favorite among travelers from the Material Plane is a chunk of earth surrounded by a small atmosphere of air.

The effect of this spell overlaps with the control already (potentially) established with a Wisdom check. Your allies can give their control over to you concurrently with the spell being cast, if they so choose. Control cannot be wrested away from you while the spell is in effect (which is one of the best reasons to cast this spell, even if you have a high Wisdom). If you move more than 100 feet away from the area that you controlled, the order you imposed fades away.

You are unable to achieve any works of complexity within an area you control, but you can mix two or three elements in a crude fashion; a few examples are provided below. You can attempt to seize control of a new area that already contains foes; however, foes can make a Reflex save to get out of the area.

Thick Barrier: You can "thicken" empty air with dust and rock, creating a zone around yourself and your allies that outside creatures must hack or force a way through. Their speed drops to 5 feet, or 10 feet for Large or larger creatures.

Fiery Barrier: You can create a thick field of flame that deals 3d10 points of fire damage to any creature attempting to pass through it. The field also deals 3d10 points of fire damage for each round a creature lingers within it.

Complete Barrier: You can create a complete barrier of solid stone up to 1 foot thick encircling yourself and your allies, preventing access by any other than the most accomplished tunnelers. On the other hand, you can attempt to trap foes within their own bubble of solid stone.

PERINARCH, PLANAR

Transmutation
Level: Druid 9, Limbo 9, sorcerer/wizard 9

The god's domain was made entirely of water, but your spell creates a bubble of air and a place to stand.

This spell functions like *perinarch*, except that you can cast this spell on any highly morphic or divinely morphic plane (DMG 148).

Although only in the mind of the spell's target, phantasmal assailants inflict very real harm to the weak-willed

Illus. by R. Spears

PERSISTENT BLADE

Evocation [Force]
Level: Sorcerer/wizard 1
Components: V, S, F
Casting Time: 1 standard action
Range: Close (25 ft. + 5 ft./2 levels)
Effect: One dagger made of force
Duration: 1 round/level
Saving Throw: None
Spell Resistance: Yes

You hold a dagger in your hand and concentrate on it, evoking the power of the spell. A duplicate of the dagger, made of translucent force, appears besides it and flies off at your command.

You bring into being a tiny blade of force. The blade flies at a speed of 40 feet (perfect) and attacks any target within its range, as you desire, starting in the round when you cast the spell. The blade attacks on your turn once each round, striking with an attack bonus equal to your base attack bonus + 1/2 your Cha modifier or Int modifier (for sorcerers and wizards, respectively) and deals 1d4 points of damage, with a critical threat range of 19–20. If an ally also attacks the creature, the blade moves on your turn to flank the target. As a force effect, it can strike ethereal and incorporeal creatures. The blade cannot be attacked.

Each round after the first, you can use a standard action to switch the blade to a new target; otherwise, it continues to attack the same target.

If an attacked creature has spell resistance, the resistance is checked the first time the *persistent blade* strikes. If the blade is successfully resisted, the spell is dispelled. If not, the blade has its normal full effect on that creature for the duration of the spell.

Focus: A silvered dagger.

PHANTASMAL ASSAILANTS

Illusion (Phantasm) [Fear, Mind-Affecting]
Level: Sorcerer/wizard 2
Components: V, S
Casting Time: 1 standard action
Range: Close (25 ft. + 5 ft./2 levels)
Target: One living creature
Duration: Instantaneous
Saving Throw: Will disbelief (if interacted with), then Fortitude half; see text
Spell Resistance: Yes

You point at your intended target. Instantly, shadowy shapes form at your flank and rush toward the creature you indicate, surrounding it. Others nearby do not notice the images that plague your target.

You create phantasmal images of nightmare creatures in the target's mind, visible only as shadowy shapes to you and unseen by all others. If the target succeeds on an initial Will save, it recognizes that the images are not real, and the spell fails. If not, the phantasms strike the target, dealing 8 points of Wisdom damage and 8 points of Dexterity damage (4 points each on a successful Fortitude save). If the subject of a *phantasmal assailant* succeeds in disbelieving and is wearing a *helm of telepathy*, the spell can be turned back upon you with the same effect.

PHANTASMAL DECOY

Illusion (Phantasm) [Mind-Affecting]
Level: Ranger 3
Components: V, S
Casting Time: 1 standard action
Range: Medium (100 ft. + 10 ft./level)
Target: One living creature
Duration: 1 round/level
Saving Throw: Will negates, and Will disbelief (if interacted with)
Spell Resistance: Yes

Reaching into your foe's mind, you weave an illusion of his most hated foe.

You create a phantasmal image of the subject's most hated enemy by sifting through the subconscious mind of the subject. Only you and the spell's subject can see the phantasmal creature, and the phantasm seems blurry and indistinct to you. If the target fails its Will saving throw, you designate a space that the phantasm appears to occupy. The subject must attack the phantasm, or move to be adjacent to it. A creature that attacks the phantasm is allowed an additional saving throw to disbelieve the illusion. If moving up to the phantasm would cause the subject to cross dangerous terrain (such as a pool of lava), it does not move to be adjacent to the phantasm. It merely moves as close as it can and takes no further actions unless the phantasm moves to a space it can reach.

As a move action, you can move a *phantasmal decoy* up to 60 feet in any direction. Because it's not real, a *phantasmal decoy* isn't affected by terrain that slows movement (although you can slow its progress voluntarily if you like to help maintain the facade of realism).

PHANTASMAL DISORIENTATION

Illusion (Phantasm) [Mind-Affecting]
Level: Druid 6
Components: V, S
Casting Time: 1 standard action
Range: Medium (100 ft. + 10 ft./level)
Target: One living creature
Duration: 1 minute/level (D)
Saving Throw: Will negates; see text
Spell Resistance: Yes

You create ever-shifting phantasmal terrain and landmarks that confuse the subject when it tries to move. The very ground shifts and twists beneath the subject's feet, and the landscape moves of its own accord. The subject finds it nearly impossible to walk in a straight line.

The target of a *phantasmal disorientation* spell must make a Will save after this spell is cast to discern true landmarks from phantasmal ones. If the save succeeds, the creature moves and acts normally. If the save fails, it instead moves in a direction 90 degrees to either side (equal chance of going left or right), and cannot target any creature with ranged attacks or ranged spells. Because of the disorientation, the subject doesn't realize it's headed in the wrong direction until it meaningfully interacts with its environment (by making an attack or manipulating an object such as a door, for example). For the duration of the spell, an affected creature must succeed on a Will save each round to move normally.

A *phantasmal disorientation* spell affects only the direction of movement and attacks made at range. Creatures subject to it can still make melee attacks, cast personal or touch spells, or otherwise act normally.

PHANTASMAL THIEF

Conjuration (Creation)
Level: Greed 8, sorcerer/wizard 5
Components: V, S, M
Casting Time: 1 standard action
Range: Close (25 ft. + 5 ft./2 levels)
Effect: One invisible, mindless, shapeless thief
Duration: 1 round/level
Saving Throw: None
Spell Resistance: No

As you invoke this spell, the spool begins to spin, the thread vanishing as it unravels. There is a wrinkle of force that flashes briefly; then it evaporates, leaving only the promise of power behind.

An invisible force, not unlike the product of an *unseen servant* spell (PH 297), comes into being where you wish. On your turn, this force steals objects from others as you inaudibly direct it (a free action). A *phantasmal thief* can steal an object from a creature or can pick up an unattended object, as long as the object weighs no more than 1 pound per caster level. It cannot break into locked chests. A *phantasmal thief* has a Hide modifier (useful against those who can see invisible creatures) and a Move Silently modifier both equal to your caster level.

If a *phantasmal thief* goes undetected, it can steal any object a creature possesses but is not holding or wearing. Even objects in a *bag of holding* can be stolen. It can steal objects, bring objects to you, or put them back where they came from. It can take no other actions. A *phantasmal thief* needs 1 round to steal an object and another round to bring it to you.

A *phantasmal thief* can hold only one object at a time, and the object becomes invisible in its grasp.

A thief cannot take an item if it is detected by the creature it's trying to steal from (with a Listen or Spot check). However, the thief can repeat the attempt in the next round. It cannot be harmed in any way, although it can be dispelled.

A *phantasmal thief* can steal an object from a creature's hand by making a successful disarm attempt. It does so with a bonus on the disarm check equal to your caster level. If a *phantasmal thief* is used in this way, it disappears after it brings the stolen object to you.

Material Component: A spool of green thread.

PHANTOM BEAR

Conjuration (Summoning)
Level: Druid 9
Components: V, S, DF
Casting Time: 1 round
Range: Medium (100 ft. + 10 ft./level)
Effect: One summoned phantom bear
Duration: Concentration, up to 1 round/level
Saving Throw: None
Spell Resistance: No

The ghostly image of a great bear appears before you. It rises silently on its hind legs and violently falls onto its forepaws, still making no sound. Then it opens its mouth, releasing a tremendous roar.

This spell functions like *phantom wolf* (page 157), except that you conjure an incorporeal bear with a fearsome roar.

Phantom Bear **CR 14**

N Huge magical beast (incorporeal)
Init +9; **Senses** darkvision 60 ft.; Listen +20, Spot +20

AC 25, touch 25, flat-footed 16; Dodge, Mobility
hp 147 (14 HD)
Fort +13, **Ref** +17, **Will** +7

Speed fly 60 ft. (good)
Melee 2 claws +23 incorporeal touch (2d6 plus 3d6 cold) and bite +22 incorporeal touch (2d8 plus 3d6 cold)
Space 15 ft.; **Reach** 15 ft.
Base Atk +14; **Grp** —
Atk Options Combat Reflexes
Special Actions fearsome roar

Abilities Str —, Dex 29, Con 20, Int 11, Wis 17, Cha 28
SQ incorporeal traits
Feats Combat Reflexes, Dodge, Mobility, Multiattack, Weapon Focus (bite)
Skills Listen +20, Spot +20

Fearsome Roar (Su) 120-ft. radius, once every 1d4 rounds, Will DC 26 negates. Creatures within 30 feet become panicked, others within the area become frightened for 3d6 rounds if they fail their saves.

PHANTOM FOE

Illusion (Phantasm) [Mind-Affecting]
Level: Assassin 2, sorcerer/wizard 2
Components: V, S, F
Casting Time: 1 standard action
Range: Touch
Target: Creature touched
Duration: 1 round/level
Saving Throw: Will disbelief
Spell Resistance: No

By waving around a tiny pewter figurine and picturing in your mind the figurine attacking the target creature, you complete the spell. You feel a phantasmal force leap from the figurine toward your target.

If the target creature fails its saving throw, this spell creates in the subject's mind an illusory double of whichever creature currently threatens it that it deems most dangerous. The form of this *phantom foe* changes as appropriate whenever the target perceives a different threatening creature more dangerous than the last. This illusory double provides two effects.

First, the subject believes it is being flanked by the *phantom foe* and the real creature the foe duplicates. Thus, the duplicated creature is always considered to be flanking the subject in melee. A creature that can't be flanked is immune to this aspect of the spell.

Second, the subject of the spell is unable to determine that the *phantom foe* is not a real threat, and whenever the subject attempts to attack the creature duplicated by the *phantom foe*, that creature benefits from a 50% miss chance against attacks from the subject of the spell. Because this miss chance comes from the subject's inability to tell the *phantom foe* from the original, it is rolled separately from any miss chance that applies due to displacement or concealment.

Creatures other than the subject cannot see the *phantom foe*, although they can attempt to guess its location by how the target acts. If the subject is not threatened by any creature at the start of its turn, the spell ends.

Focus: A tiny pewter figure of a warrior that is worth 10 gp.

Illus. by E. Polak

The phantom stag spell provides a druid with a powerful mount to ride into battle

PHANTOM STAG

Conjuration (Creation)
Level: Druid 5
Components: V, S
Casting Time: 1 standard action
Range: 0 ft.
Effect: One quasi-real, staglike creature
Duration: 1 hour/level (D)
Saving Throw: None; see text
Spell Resistance: No

Putting your fingers to your lips to whistle, you blow a deer's call, and a great ghostly stag appears before you.

You conjure a Large, corporeal staglike creature that bears you or a person you designate into combat or overland at great speed. A *phantom stag* has a black body and head with sharp, silvery antlers, and smoke-colored, insubstantial hooves that make no sound. It has no saddle, bridle, or bit, but it is exceptionally alert to the nudges and balance changes of its rider.

The *phantom stag* has an AC of 20 (–1 size, +6 natural armor, +5 Dex) and 40 hit points +5 hit points per caster level. It attacks with its antlers at a +10 bonus, dealing 1d8+9 points of damage (doubled on a successful charge). It can also trample Medium or smaller foes, who must succeed on a Reflex save (18 + 1/2 your caster level) or take 1d6+9 points of damage as the stag moves through their space.

A *phantom stag* has a speed of 20 feet per caster level, to a maximum of 300 feet. It can bear its rider's weight plus up to 10 pounds per caster level in other gear. It ignores terrain elements such as undergrowth, rubble, or mud that would slow its movement.

Phantom stags gain certain powers according to caster level. A mount's abilities include those associated with any lower caster levels.

12th Level: The *phantom stag* can use *air walk* at will (as the spell, PH 196, no action required to activate this ability) for up to 1 round at a time, after which it falls to the ground. The *phantom stag* gains a +2 deflection bonus to AC.

14th Level: The *phantom stag* can fly at its speed (average maneuverability). The *phantom stag* gains a +4 deflection bonus to AC.

16th Level: The *phantom stag's* antlers have the ghost touch (DMG 224) and wounding (DMG 226) weapon special abilities. The *phantom stag* gains a +6 deflection bonus to AC.

18th Level: The *phantom stag* can use *etherealness* on behalf of its rider (as the spell, PH 228, caster level 18th). The *phantom stag* gains a +8 deflection bonus to AC.

PHANTOM THREAT

Illusion (Phantasm) [Mind-Affecting]
Level: Bard 1
Components: V, S
Casting Time: 1 standard action
Range: Close (25 ft. + 5 ft./2 levels)
Target: One creature
Duration: 1 round/level
Saving Throw: Will negates
Spell Resistance: Yes

Reaching out to your foe's mind, you cause him to feel as though a threat looms close behind no matter which way he turns.

You create the sensation in the subject's mind that it is threatened by more foes than it actually faces. Though the subject doesn't actually perceive any additional enemies (and thus doesn't waste any attacks on the phantasm), a creature affected by this spell is considered flanked, even if not threatened by other creatures. No amount of convincing by others can help the subject of this spell avoid its effect—only a successful saving throw against the spell when initially cast can help the target. A creature that can't be flanked is immune to this spell.

PHANTOM WOLF

Conjuration (Summoning)
Level: Druid 8
Components: V, S, DF
Casting Time: 1 round
Range: Medium (100 ft. + 10 ft./level)
Effect: One summoned phantom wolf
Duration: Concentration, up to 1 round/level
Saving Throw: None
Spell Resistance: No

Cupping a hand to your mouth, you howl like a wolf, and in a moment, mist coalesces into a wolflike form with terrible jaws.

PHANTOM WOLF — CR 12
N Large magical beast (incorporeal)
Init +9; **Senses** darkvision 60 ft.; Listen +20, Spot +20
Aura frightful presence

AC 25, touch 25, flat-footed 16; Dodge, Mobility
hp 113 (12 HD)
Fort +12, **Ref** +17, **Will** +7

Speed fly 60 ft. (good)
Melee bite +22 incorporeal touch (2d6 plus 3d6 cold)
Space 15 ft.; **Reach** 15 ft.
Base Atk +14; **Grp** —
Atk Options Combat Reflexes

Abilities Str —, Dex 29, Con 18, Int 11, Wis 17, Cha 26
SQ incorporeal traits
Feats Alertness, Combat Reflexes, Dodge, Mobility, Weapon Focus (bite)
Skills Listen +20, Spot +20

Frightful Presence (Su) 30-ft. radius, Will DC 24 negates. Creatures with less than 12 HD become frightened for 3d6 rounds if they fail their saves. An opponent that succeeds on the save is immune to that same phantom wolf's frightful presence for 24 hours.

You conjure forth an incorporeal white wolf with abnormally large, frosty jaws. This *phantom wolf* follows your mental commands, acting on your behalf as long as it remains within range and you continue to concentrate on it.

A *phantom wolf* appears where you designate and acts as you direct on your turn. You don't need to maintain line of effect once the spell is cast, but the spell ends if the *phantom wolf* is ever outside the spell's range.

PLAGUE OF RATS

Conjuration (Summoning)
Level: Pestilence 5
Components: V, S, DF
Casting Time: 1 round
Range: Medium (100 ft. + 10 ft./level)
Effect: One swarm of rats/2 levels, each of which is adjacent to at least one other swarm
Duration: 1 round/level
Saving Throw: None
Spell Resistance: No

Black balls of fur litter the ground, rolling about as they rapidly expand, growing tails, feet, and snarling, diseased mouths.

You summon a number of rat swarms (MM 239)—one per two caster levels—to a maximum of six swarms at 12th level. The swarms must be summoned so that each one is adjacent to at least one other swarm (that is, the swarms must fill one contiguous area). You can summon the rat swarms so that they share the spaces of other creatures. Each swarm attacks any creatures occupying its space. If no living creatures are within its space, a swarm attacks or pursues the nearest creature as best it can. You have no control over its target or direction of travel.

PLAGUE OF UNDEAD

Necromancy [Evil]
Level: Cleric 9, sorcerer/wizard 9
Components: V, S, M
Casting Time: 1 standard action
Range: Close (25 ft. + 5 ft./2 levels)
Targets: One or more corpses within range
Duration: Instantaneous
Saving Throw: None
Spell Resistance: No

Unleashing a cold rush of necromantic energy, you cause a host of undead to rise from the bodies of the fallen.

This spell turns the bones or bodies of dead creatures into undead skeletons (MM 225) or zombies (MM 265) with maximum hit points for their Hit Dice. If you can control them, these undead follow your spoken commands. The undead remain animated until destroyed (a destroyed skeleton or zombie can't be animated again).

Regardless of the specific numbers or kinds of undead created with this spell, you can't create more HD of undead with this spell than four times your caster level with a single casting of *plague of undead*.

The undead you create remain under your control indefinitely. No matter how many times you use this spell or *animate dead* (PH 198), however, you can control only 4 HD worth of undead creatures per caster level. The limit imposed by this spell and the *animate dead* spell are the same, meaning that creatures you animate with either spell count against this limit. If you exceed this number, all the newly created creatures fall under your control and any excess undead from previous castings of this spell or *animate dead* become uncontrolled. Any time you must release part of the undead that you control because of this spell or *animate dead*, you choose which undead are released until the total HD of undead you control is equal to four times your caster level.

The bones and bodies required for this spell follow the same restrictions as *animate dead*.

Material Component: A black sapphire worth 100 gp or several black sapphires with a total value of 100 gp.

Cleric who follow gods of pestilence can summon a plague of rats

Illus. by W. England

PLANAR BUBBLE

Abjuration
Level: Cleric 7, sorcerer/wizard 7
Components: V, S, M/DF
Casting Time: 1 standard action
Range: Touch
Area: 10-ft.-radius emanation from touched creature
Duration: 10 minutes/level
Saving Throw: Will negates (harmless)
Spell Resistance: No; see text

You cast the spell and sprinkle silver dust around you. Where it lands the dust sparkles and evaporates, and the elemental region around you calms and becomes more hospitable.

This spell creates an area around the subject creature that emulates its native planar environment. Thus, a character hailing from the Material Plane would have normal gravity, temperature, magic, and so on. This spell cast on a native of the Plane of Shadow (DMG 152) would make the area around the creature mimic its home plane's normal gravity, a mild neutral alignment, enhanced shadow spells, and impeded light or fire spells.

Arcane Material Component: A sprinkling of silver dust.

PLANAR EXCHANGE

Conjuration (Calling) [see text for *lesser planar exchange*]
Level: Cleric 6

This spell functions like *lesser planar exchange*, except as noted here. You trade places with an avoral guardinal (MM 141), bone devil (MM 52), or babau demon (MM 40). The called creature has full access to all its abilities, with one exception: A demon or devil you conjure can't summon other creatures. If the creature is slain, you take 3d6 points of damage and the spell ends.

PLANAR EXCHANGE, GREATER

Conjuration (Calling) [see text for *lesser planar exchange*]
Level: Cleric 8

This spell functions like *lesser planar exchange*, except as noted here. You trade places with a leonal guardinal (MM 142), barbed devil (MM 51), or hezrou demon (MM 44). The called creature has full access to all its abilities, with one exception: A demon or devil you conjure can't summon other creatures. If the creature is slain, you take 4d6 points of damage and the spell ends.

PLANAR EXCHANGE, LESSER

Conjuration (Calling)
Level: Cleric 4
Components: V, S, DF
Casting Time: 1 round
Range: 0 ft.
Effect: One called creature
Duration: 1 round/level (D)
Saving Throw: None
Spell Resistance: No

You cross your arms and close your eyes, intoning the ancient spell. There is a bright flash, and another creature stands in your place.

When you cast this spell, you call a celestial brown bear (MM 269), celestial griffon (MM 139), fiendish dire ape (MM 62), or fiendish tiger (MM 281), at your option, to your precise location. At the same instant, you are transported to that creature's home plane, where you exist in stasis for the duration of the spell. To a casual observer, it appears that you have transformed into the called creature (though an onlooker who makes a DC 25 Spot check notices the slight gap in time between your disappearance and the creature's appearance). If the called creature would not fit in the place you occupied when you cast the spell, the spell fails. If the called creature is slain, you take 2d6 points of damage, the spell ends, and you are returned to your origin plane in the space last occupied by the called creature.

A celestial creature (MM 31) called by this spell gains damage reduction 5/magic; resistance to acid 5, cold 5, and electricity 5; spell resistance equal to its HD +5; and a smite evil attack that provides a bonus equal to its HD on one damage roll.

A fiendish creature (MM 107) called by this spell gains damage reduction 5/magic; resistance to acid 5 and fire 5; spell resistance equal to its HD +5; and a smite good attack that provides a bonus equal to its HD on one damage roll.

You have full control over the creature's actions and can perceive the environment around the called creature as if you were seeing through its eyes, hearing through its ears, and so on.

While in stasis, you can't take any actions other than to control the called creature or to dismiss the spell, nor can anything on the creature's home plane affect you in any way. You also can't perceive anything around your body's location. When you dismiss the spell, or when the creature is slain, you appear in the creature's location, and it is returned to its home plane.

When you use a calling spell that calls a chaotic, evil, good, or lawful creature, it is a spell of that type.

PLANAR TOLERANCE

Level: Cleric 4, druid 4, Elysium 2, ranger 4, sorcerer/wizard 5
Duration: 1 hour/level

You have barely time to bark out a few elder words of power, but then the pressure subsides, and you know you are safe long enough to complete your mission.

This spell functions like *avoid planar effects* (page 19), except as noted above.

PLANE SHIFT, GREATER

Conjuration (Teleportation)
Level: Cleric 7, sorcerer/wizard 8

You and the others link hands, and you concentrate on the forked copper rod. You rap the fork against your thigh and speak the words of the spell. You know where you're going, and as the landscape around you fades, a new plane takes shape around you.

This spell functions like *plane shift* (PH 262), except that if you have visited the desired location, the spell takes you to the precise location (rather than 5 to 500 miles distant).

PLANT BODY

Transmutation
Level: Druid 5
Components: V, S, DF
Casting Time: 1 standard action
Range: Personal
Target: You
Duration: 10 minutes/level

Radiating out from your hands, moss and ivy covers your flesh until you resemble a shambling mound.

You imbue yourself with powerful transformative magic, gaining some of the characteristics of the plant type. Any spell or effect that would affect plant creatures also affects you, for the duration of *plant body*.

When subject to this spell, you are immune to extra damage from critical hits, mind-affecting spells and abilities, poison, sleep, paralysis, stunning, and polymorphing.

Your ability scores, skills, and feats are unaffected (although your new form might make it difficult or impossible for you to use certain skills or feats).

POISON THORNS

Transmutation
Level: Druid 5

Black, glistening thorns emerge from your skin, causing you no damage but endangering those who attack you in melee.

Illus. by L. Parrillo

Poison thorns protect a druid from a naga's coils

This spell functions like *thornskin* (page 219), except as noted above, and a scratch from the thorns is sufficient to deliver a dose of poison to your attacker. Any creature grappling you is exposed to the poison each round at the start of your turn. The poison from the thorns deals 1d4 points of Strength damage immediately and another 1d4 points of Strength damage 1 minute later. Each instance of damage can be negated by a successful Fortitude save (DC 10 + 1/2 your caster level + your Wis modifier).

Material Component: A dried black rose.

POISON VINES

Conjuration (Creation)
Level: Druid 4
Saving Throw: Fortitude negates; see text
Spell Resistance: Yes

In an instant you cause glistening green vines to spring up at your command.

This spell functions like *vine mine* (page 230), except that the vines you create are poisonous (contact, 1d6 Dex/2d6 Dex). A successful Fortitude save is required only upon the first entry into the spell's area (and again 1 minute later); creatures don't have to save each time they enter (or each round they remain within). You are immune to the poison of the vines you create, and you can select a number of other targets equal to your caster level to share this immunity.

PORTAL ALARM

Abjuration
Level: Bard 2, sorcerer/wizard 2
Components: V, S, M
Casting Time: 1 standard action
Range: Close (25 ft. + 5 ft./2 levels)
Target: One interplanar gate or portal
Duration: 2 hours/level (D)
Saving Throw: None
Spell Resistance: No

You cast a tiny bell at the portal, and it rings as you finish the last gesture of the spell. With the completion of the spell, the bell vanishes in midair, but it continues to ring for a few moments more.

Portal alarm sounds a mental or audible alarm each time a creature of Tiny or larger size passes through the magic gate or portal the spell is cast upon. You decide at the time of casting whether the *portal alarm* will be mental or audible.

Mental Alarm: A mental alarm alerts you (and only you) as long as you remain within 1 mile of the warded area and on the same plane. You notice a mental tremor that would awaken you from a normal sleep but does not otherwise disturb concentration (it would not interfere with spellcasting). A *silence* spell has no effect on a mental alarm.

Audible Alarm: An audible *portal alarm* produces the sound of a hand bell, buzzer, or other similar repeating sound that can be heard clearly up to 60 feet away, and it pierces closed doors and extends onto other planes. The ringing can be heard faintly up to 180 feet away and lasts for 1 round. Creatures within the area of a *silence* spell cannot hear the ringing, and if the portal itself is within the area of a *silence* spell, no alarm is sounded.

Ethereal and astral creatures trigger a *portal alarm* if they pass through the portal.

You can set a *portal alarm* with a password, determined at the time of the casting, and this password can be discerned with the *analyze portal* spell (page 10). Those speaking the password before passing through the portal do not set off the alarm.

Material Component: A tiny bell.

PORTAL ALARM, IMPROVED

Abjuration
Level: Bard 4, sorcerer/wizard 4
Components: V, S, F
Duration: 8 hours/level (D)

This spell functions like *portal alarm*, with the following additions.

- You can designate the alarm set off by an *improved portal alarm* to be mental, audible, or both.
- If a mental alarm is chosen, you receive a mental picture of all creatures that have passed through the portal and which direction they passed through. The mental image provides information as if you were

standing 10 feet away from the portal.
- You can enable another creature to receive the mental alarm instead of yourself. You must touch the creature, which receives a Will saving throw to negate the effect, if applicable.

Focus: A small leather pouch containing three brass bells.

PORTAL BEACON

Transmutation
Level: Cleric 1, sorcerer/wizard 1
Components: V, S
Casting Time: 1 standard action
Range: Close (25 ft. + 5 ft./2 levels)
Target: One interplanar gate or portal
Duration: 1 hour/level
Saving Throw: None
Spell Resistance: No

Mentally marking the appearance and location of the portal, you implant that knowledge into others, allowing them to be drawn to the portal like a lodestone to metal.

You alter a magic gate or portal so it sends out a mental beacon for up to six creatures, including yourself if you choose. These individuals must be known to you but need not be present at the time of casting. Once you cast *portal beacon*, these creatures know the direction and distance to the targeted portal for the spell's duration.

Moving to a plane other than the two connected by the portal ends the spell for that creature but leaves it intact for others. You can have any number of *portal beacons* tuned to you without impairing other abilities or actions.

POSITIVE ENERGY AURA

Conjuration (Healing)
Level: Cleric 4
Components: V, S
Casting Time: 1 standard action
Range: Personal
Area: 10-ft.-radius emanation centered on you
Duration: 1 round/level
Saving Throw: None
Spell Resistance: No

You speak the eldritch phrases of power and an aura of white, shining, positive energy surrounds you.

Each round on your turn, every living creature within 10 feet of you gains 1 hit point per three caster levels (maximum 5). Creatures can't exceed their full normal hit point totals as a result of this effect. Undead creatures take 2 points of damage per round. Characters with immunity to positive energy effects are not affected by this aura. A *positive energy aura* does not affect you.

PRIMAL FORM

Transmutation
Level: Druid 3, sorcerer/wizard 3
Components: V, S, DF
Casting Time: 1 standard action
Range: Personal
Target: You
Duration: 1 minute/level (D)

By calling on the ancient and timeless magical energies of the elements, you complete the spell. Immediately your form begins to change, taking on aspects of the element you envisioned while casting the spell.

When you cast this spell, choose an element (air, earth, fire, or water). You assume the physical appearance and many of the qualities and abilities of a Medium elemental of the chosen element (MM 96–100). *Primal form* also grants you the elemental subtype of the chosen element.

You gain a +4 bonus on saving throws against mind-affecting spells and abilities. There is a 25% chance that critical hits and sneak attacks scored on you are negated, as if you were wearing armor with the light fortification special ability (DMG 219). You cannot cast spells, and you lose any spell-like, supernatural, and extraordinary abilities of your own form. You gain additional abilities depending on the element you chose when you cast the spell:

Air: Fly speed 20 feet (perfect).
Earth: Damage reduction 5/—.
Fire: 1d4 fire damage, resistance to fire 10, burn (MM 98).
Water: Swim 90 feet, drench (MM 101).

Your equipment melds into your new form and becomes nonfunctional.

PRISMATIC EYE

Evocation
Level: Sorcerer/wizard 7
Components: V, S, F
Casting Time: 1 standard action
Range: Medium (100 ft. + 10 ft./level)
Effect: Magical eye
Duration: 1 round/level
Saving Throw: See text
Spell Resistance: Yes

With a popping sound, a moist, apple-sized eye with a rainbow-hued iris appears and sends a beam of colored light at the foe you designate.

The prismatic eye spell becomes more dangerous with multiple castings

Illus. by C. Frank

You create a visible orb that can produce ray effects duplicating the beams of a *prismatic spray* spell (PH 264). You can move the eye up to your speed as a move action, but it cannot go beyond the spell's range.

Starting in the round the eye appears, you can command it to fire a ray (50-foot range) as a free action once per round. You must succeed on a ranged touch attack with a ray to strike a target, but each ray uses a +6 bonus on attack rolls instead of your ranged attack bonus.

A target struck by a ray suffers the effect of one beam of a *prismatic spray* spell (roll 1d8 to determine the effect, rerolling any result of 8), except that the save DC (if applicable) is 19. After a particular color of ray has been used, it is no longer available to the eye, and die rolls that indicate the same color are rerolled. Once all seven rays have been fired, the eye remains until the spell's duration expires. You can still move it, but it can fire no more rays.

The eye is a Fine object with AC 18 (+8 size) and 9 hit points. It uses your save bonuses for saving throws.

Focus: A polished, rainbow-hued abalone shell.

PRISMATIC RAY

Evocation
Level: Sorcerer/wizard 5
Components: V, S
Casting Time: 1 standard action
Range: Medium (100 ft. + 10 ft./level)
Effect: Ray
Duration: Instantaneous
Saving Throw: See text
Spell Resistance: Yes

You feel within you, as the spell nears completion, various energies locked in a battle within your body. As nausea threatens to overcome you, you croak out the final syllables of arcane power and point your hand. A single beam of brilliantly colored light then shoots from your outstretched hand.

You must succeed on a ranged touch attack with the ray to strike a target. On a successful attack, a creature with 6 Hit Dice or fewer is blinded for 2d4 rounds by the *prismatic ray* in addition to suffering a randomly determined effect:

1d8	Color of Beam	Effect
1	Red	20 points fire damage (Reflex half)
2	Orange	40 points acid damage (Reflex half)
3	Yellow	80 points electricity damage (Reflex half)
4	Green	Poison (Kills; Fortitude partial, take 1d6 Con damage instead)
5	Blue	Turned to stone (Fortitude negates)
6	Indigo	Insane, as *insanity* spell (Will negates)
7	Violet	Sent to another plane (Will negates)
8	—	Two effects; roll twice more, ignoring any "8" results

PROBE THOUGHTS

Divination [Mind-Affecting]
Level: Mind 6, sorcerer/wizard 6
Components: V, S
Casting Time: 1 minute
Range: Close (25 ft. + 5 ft./2 levels)
Target: One living creature
Duration: Concentration, up to 1 round/level
Saving Throw: Will negates; see text
Spell Resistance: Yes

Reaching out with your thoughts, you break through your target's mental defenses and reap answers to your desires.

All of the subject's memories and knowledge are accessible to you, ranging from memories deep below the surface to those still easily called to mind. You can learn the answer to one question per round, to the best of the subject's knowledge. You pose the questions telepathically, and the answers to those questions are imparted directly to your mind. You and the subject do not need to speak the same language, though less intelligent creatures might yield up only appropriate visual images in answer to your questions. The subject is not aware that its mind is being probed, unless you wish to make it aware.

If the subject moves beyond the range of the spell, the effect ends.

PROGRAMMED AMNESIA

Enchantment (Compulsion) [Mind-Affecting]
Level: Sorcerer/wizard 9
Components: V, S, M
Casting Time: 10 minutes
Range: Close (25 ft. + 5 ft./2 levels)
Target: One living creature
Duration: Permanent
Saving Throw: Will negates
Spell Resistance: Yes

As you finish the complicated procedure necessary to cast the spell, your target's mind opens up to you like a book. You see the target's memories like stories and know that you can rewrite them as a master bard rewrites the inferior works of his apprentices.

You can selectively destroy, alter, or implant memories in the subject creature as you see fit. Casting the spell gives you access to all of the subject's thoughts and memories, allowing you to implement as many of the following specific effects as you like.

Memory Erasure: Memories possessed by the subject can be erased, including knowledge of specific events, people, or places. You can erase up to one full week of memories from the subject's mind.

Memory Implant: You can create false memories in the subject's mind as you see fit. You can implant memories of being friends with a hated enemy, events that didn't really take place, or betrayals by people the subject regards as friends.

Negative Levels: You can bestow a number of negative levels equal to 1/2 the subject's character level (rounding down, minimum 1st level) or less. This effect represents erasure of class knowledge and training. These negative levels never become permanent level loss, but they cannot be removed by spells such as *restoration,* instead returning at a rate of one level per day.

Persona Rebuilding: By erasing the subject's previous personality and implanting a false set of memories, you can build a new persona for the creature, altering its alignment, beliefs, values, and personality traits. (Some class abilities might be affected by alignment changes.)

Programmed Trigger: You can program the subject to delay the onset of any of the above effects until a specific event takes place, such as the receipt of a coded message, capture by enemies, or arrival at some destination. Similarly, you could specify some or all of the alterations you create in a subject to be removed by a specific event.

The nature of *programmed amnesia* is such that a subject given new memories (whether willing or not) might be given cause to suspect that those memories are false, based on how complete your programming is. For example, a paladin subject to a persona rebuilding effect that changes her alignment to neutral loses her paladin abilities. Unless you impart a specific believable memory of why she changed alignment, the character will perceive this unexplained gap in her memory and might take steps (such as seeking a magical cure for her "amnesia") that could negate the spell's effect (see below).

Generally, your subject must be either willing to undergo the spell or restrained in some way so that it cannot leave or interfere with the casting. *Programmed amnesia* cannot be dispelled, and so is normally permanent unless you care to specify events that will end the effect. Its effect can also be removed by a *greater restoration*, *miracle*, or *wish* spell.

Material Component: A set of small crystal lenses set in gold loops worth 500 gp.

PROTECTION FROM NEGATIVE ENERGY

Abjuration
Level: Cleric 2
Components: V, S
Casting Time: 1 standard action
Range: Touch
Target: Creature touched
Duration: 10 minutes/level
Saving Throw: Will negates (harmless)
Spell Resistance: Yes (harmless)

Swaddling your ally in a protective field drawn by your hand like a blanket, you guard him against negative energy attacks.

The warded creature gains partial protection against negative energy effects. For as long as the spell lasts, it subtracts 10 from the hit point damage dealt by any negative energy effect (such as an *inflict* spell) that adversely affects it.

Negative energy effects that don't deal hit point damage to the subject, such as an *energy drain* spell, affect the subject normally.

PROTECTION FROM POSITIVE ENERGY

Abjuration
Level: Cleric 2
Components: V, S
Casting Time: 1 standard action
Range: Touch
Target: Creature touched
Duration: 10 minutes/level
Saving Throw: Will negates
Spell Resistance: Yes

A black seed of magic floats above your finger, and you implant it in the creature before you, guarding it against positive energy.

The warded creature gains partial protection against positive energy effects. For as long as the spell lasts, it subtracts 10 from the hit point damage dealt by any positive energy effect (such as a *cure* spell) that adversely affects it.

Positive energy effects that don't deal hit point damage to the subject, such as turning attempts, affect the subject normally.

PROTÉGÉ

Transmutation
Level: Bard 4
Components: V, S
Casting Time: 1 round
Range: Touch
Target: One creature with Intelligence 3 or higher
Duration: 1 minute/level (D)
Saving Throw: Will negates (harmless)
Spell Resistance: Yes (harmless)

You admonish your chosen subject even as you offer a supportive slap on the back. With that simple action, you complete the spell and see in your target a realization of its new abilities.

You briefly grant some bard abilities to a creature of your choice. The subject of the spell can then function as a bard of one-half your current bard level with respect to bardic music and bardic knowledge. However, *protégé* imparts no spellcasting ability and does not grant access to spells not normally available to the subject. For Perform checks and bardic music prerequisites, the creature uses its own ranks in Perform or one-half of your ranks (modified by its own Charisma modifier), whichever is better.

PUPPETEER

Enchantment (Compulsion) [Mind-Affecting]
Level: Bard 3
Components: V, S
Casting Time: 1 standard action
Range: Medium (100 ft. + 10 ft./level)
Target: One creature
Duration: 1 round/level (D)
Saving Throw: Will negates
Spell Resistance: Yes

In casting this spell, you see what others do not—strings of silver energy running from your hands and feet to your target's wrists and ankles. You wave, and she waves back, in an awkward, resisting fashion. You start walking toward the edge of the cliff. . . .

You force the subject to mimic your actions. The subject matches your motions exactly, though it takes a –4 penalty to Dexterity and Strength. Its movements look awkward, and its actions aren't as effective as if it were actually doing them itself. You can try to make the subject commit a suicidal act, but it receives another Will save to break the spell. If that save is successful, the subject collapses, helpless and in a comatose state, for 1d4 rounds.

Anyone observing the subject of this spell can determine that the subject's actions are being controlled by making a DC 15 Sense Motive check (or DC 10 if the controlling bard is also visible).

This spell doesn't grant the subject extraordinary, supernatural, spell-like abilities, or spellcasting abilities, even if you have and use such abilities during the spell's duration.

QUICK MARCH

Transmutation
Level: Cleric 2, paladin 2
Components: V, S, DF
Casting Time: 1 swift action
Range: Medium (100 ft. + 10 ft./level)
Targets: Allies in a 20-ft.-radius burst
Duration: 1 round
Saving Throw: Will negates (harmless)
Spell Resistance: Yes (harmless)

When you cast this spell, your feet and those of your allies glow with a yellow nimbus of light.

Quick march increases your allies' base land speed by 30 feet. (This adjustment is considered an enhancement bonus.) There is no effect on other modes of movement, such as burrow, climb, fly, or swim. As with any effect that increases a creature's speed, this spell affects maximum jumping distance.

QUICK POTION

Transmutation
Level: Sorcerer/wizard 2
Components: V, S
Casting Time: 1 minute
Range: Touch
Target: Flask of water touched
Duration: 1 hour/level
Saving Throw: Will negates (object)
Spell Resistance: Yes (object)

You mutter the last of the spell's words and wave your fingers over the flask. Coppery sparks drop from your fingertips and suffuse the water with a deep rusty shade. As the sparks dissolve fully, you begin casting your next spell.

You transform the water in a flask so that it is capable of storing a spell in the manner of a potion. On your next turn, you or another spellcaster can cast a spell into the water, transforming the water into a potion of the appropriate type. Only spells suitable for making potions can be used in this way.

QUILL BLAST

Conjuration (Creation)
Level: Druid 5
Components: V, S, M
Casting Time: 1 standard action
Range: 20 ft.
Area: 20-ft.-radius spread centered on you
Duration: Instantaneous
Saving Throw: Reflex half; see text
Spell Resistance: Yes

Needle-sharp quills emerge from your skin as you begin casting this spell, then fly outward in every direction when you complete the spell.

Creatures within the spread of a *quill blast* are hit by one or more quills, depending on their size: Tiny or smaller, 4 quills; Small, 6 quills; Medium, 8 quills; Large, 10 quills; and Huge or larger, 12 quills.

Small or larger creatures that make their saves are struck by half as many quills; Tiny or smaller creatures that make their saves avoid the quills completely.

Each quill deals 1d6 points of damage and lodges itself into the creature it hits. Lodged quills impose a noncumulative –1 penalty on attack rolls, saves, and checks. All quills can be removed safely as a standard action with a DC 20 Heal check. Otherwise, removing the quills deals an extra 1d6 points of damage.

Material Component: A porcupine quill.

QUILLFIRE

Transmutation
Level: Druid 3
Components: V, S
Casting Time: 1 standard action
Range: Personal
Target: You
Duration: 1 round/level

You evoke the power of nature, and the back of your hand bristles with a spikelike growth of quills.

Your hand sprouts poisonous quills that you can use in melee or as a ranged attack.

The quills deal 1d8 points of damage. They can be thrown (range increment 10 feet). The quills are poisonous (injury DC equal DC of *quillfire*, 1d6 Str/1d6 Str).

RADIANT ASSAULT

Evocation [Light]
Level: Cleric 7, sorcerer/wizard 7
Components: V, S, F
Casting Time: 1 standard action
Range: Long (400 ft. + 40 ft./level)
Area: 20-ft.- radius burst
Duration: Instantaneous
Saving Throw: Will partial
Spell Resistance: Yes

With outstretched hand, you gesture toward the area where the spell will come into effect. An instant later a blast of multicolored light fills that area.

This spell releases energy in the form of a multitude of rainbow-colored beams that erupt in every direction within the area designated by you. This kaleidoscopic burst of energy deals 1d6 points of damage per caster level (maximum 15d6), and all creatures within the burst are dazed for 1d6 rounds. Those that succeed on a Will save take only half normal damage and are dazzled for 1d6 rounds instead.

Sightless creatures are unaffected by this spell.

Focus: An eye from any outsider that has 4 or more Hit Dice.

RAGING FLAME

Transmutation [Fire]
Level: Druid 1, sorcerer/wizard 1
Components: V, S
Casting Time: 1 standard action
Range: Medium (100 ft. + 10 ft./level)
Area: 30-ft.-radius spread
Duration: 1 minute
Saving Throw: None
Spell Resistance: No

Hot, burning passion fills your soul as you complete the spell. You release the passionate energy into the chosen area, causing fires there to flare with their own elemental desire to burn.

This spell inflames existing fire, giving it a passion to burn. All normal fires within the affected area flare up, burning twice as hot and twice as bright. The illumination radii of all nonmagical fires double (so a torch casts bright illumination in a 40-foot radius), and all nonmagical fires deal double damage (so a creature that catches on fire takes 2d6 points of fire damage per round). Fire that leaves the area remains affected by the spell.

Fire affected by this spell burns out twice as quickly, so a torch that is the subject of a *raging flame* spell burns out in 30 minutes instead of the normal hour.

Magical fire in the area, such as from a *produce flame* or *fireball* spell, burns hotter, dealing +1 point of fire damage per die.

Raging flame counters or dispels the effect of *slow burn* (page 192).

RAINBOW BEAM

Evocation [Light]
Level: Sorcerer/wizard 2
Components: V, S, F
Casting Time: 1 standard action
Range: Close (25 ft. + 5 ft./2 levels)
Effect: Ray
Duration: Instantaneous
Saving Throw: None
Spell Resistance: Yes

You fire a ray of swirling, multihued light drawn from radiant energies. The light's hues wind together but remain independent.

You must succeed on a ranged touch attack with the ray to strike a target. If you hit, the subject is dazzled for 1 minute. The spell also deals 1d12 points of damage per three caster levels (maximum 5d12). A *rainbow beam* deals a random type of damage as determined by the following table. If two types of energy are indicated, *rainbow beam* deals half its damage from each type of energy indicated. Creatures apply energy resistance separately to each type of damage.

1d8	Color	Damage Type
1	red	fire
2	orange	acid
3	yellow	electricity
4	green	poison
5	blue	cold
6	indigo	sonic
7	violet	force
8	multihued	roll twice (ignore further results of 8)

Focus: A small clear gem or crystal prism worth at least 10 gp.

RAINBOW BLAST

Evocation [Light]
Level: Sorcerer/wizard 3
Components: V, S, M
Casting Time: 1 standard action
Range: 120 ft.
Area: 120-ft. line
Duration: Instantaneous
Saving Throw: Reflex half
Spell Resistance: Yes

From your splayed fingers shoots a beam of mixed energy and multihued lights. The beam burns and freezes, sizzles and screams.

This spell is a wide-spectrum blast of radiant energy composed of all five energy types. *Rainbow blast* deals 1d6 points of damage from each of the five energy types (acid, cold, electricity, fire, and sonic), for a total of 5d6 points of damage. Creatures apply resistance to energy separately for each type of damage.

As you gain in levels, the damage die increases in size. At 7th level the spell deals 5d8 points of damage, at 9th level it deals 5d10 points of damage, and at 11th level it deals 5d12 points of damage—one die for each of the five energy types.

Focus: A small clear gem or crystal prism worth at least 50 gp.

RAISE FROM THE DEEP

Transmutation [Water]
Level: Sorcerer/wizard 4
Components: V
Casting Time: 1 minute
Range: Long (400 ft. + 40 ft./level); see text
Target: One creature or object
Duration: 1 hour/level
Saving Throw: Fortitude negates (object)
Spell Resistance: Yes (object)

Water roils and foams as the shipwreck rises to the surface. Floating now effortlessly, it bobs up and down, never sinking more than an inch.

A rainbow blast spell strikes foes with every type of energy

Illus. by M. Phillippi

The subject of this spell gains magical buoyancy and floats on the surface of the water for the duration of the spell, despite its weight or normal buoyancy. It cannot swim below the surface of the water. Creatures that must breathe water can still do so. If the subject is underwater at the time this spell is cast, it rises toward the surface at a speed of 150 feet. The magic of the spell prevents the subject from taking damage from the speed of the ascent.

This spell is particularly effective at raising sunken ships from the deep. If you know the exact details of the shipwreck (its appearance, its name, the date of its creation, its history, and the circumstances of its sinking), the vertical distance between you and the subject is not a factor. When cast to raise a shipwreck, the spell brings up all surviving fragments of the ship, along with any loose objects that are in contact with the ship or enclosed inside it. The ship and its fragments remain on the surface of the ocean until the spell's duration ends, at which point the ship sinks again if it has not been repaired. (Multiple consecutive castings of the spell might be needed to keep the ship afloat long enough to be fully repaired.)

RAM'S MIGHT

Transmutation
Level: Druid 1, ranger 1
Components: V, S
Casting Time: 1 standard action
Range: Personal
Target: You
Duration: 1 minute/level

You complete the casting, and your hands tingle. Ridged, hornlike ripples appear over your knuckles, nails, and the backs of your hands.

You gain a +2 enhancement bonus to Strength, and your unarmed attacks deal lethal instead of nonlethal damage. You are considered armed. The spell has no other effect; you can cast spells and manipulate objects normally.

RAPID BURROWING

Transmutation
Level: Druid 1, ranger 1
Components: V, S, DF
Casting Time: 1 standard action
Range: Touch
Target: Creature touched
Duration: 10 minutes/level
Saving Throw: Fortitude negates (harmless)
Spell Resistance: Yes (harmless)

Splaying your fingers like a mole's forepaws completes the spell. With your touch, the target's digging appendages increase in size and sharpness.

This spell increases the touched creature's burrow speed by 20 feet. It has no effect on other modes of movement, nor does it grant the subject a burrow speed or the ability to burrow through stone if the creature cannot already do so.

RAY OF CLUMSINESS

Transmutation
Level: Sorcerer/wizard 1
Components: V, S
Casting Time: 1 standard action
Range: Close (25 ft. + 5 ft./2 levels)
Effect: Ray
Duration: 1 minute/level
Saving Throw: None
Spell Resistance: Yes

A crackling ray leaps from your outstretched hand. The green ray seems almost sluggish in reaching its target, though it takes only an eyeblink to do so.

You must succeed on a ranged touch attack with the ray to strike a target. The energy of the ray stiffens the subject's muscles and joints, making it more difficult for the subject to move. The subject takes a penalty to Dexterity equal to 1d6+1 per two caster levels (maximum penalty 1d6+5, minimum Dexterity 1).

RAY OF DEANIMATION

Abjuration
Level: Sorcerer/wizard 4
Components: V, S
Casting Time: 1 standard action
Range: Close (25 ft. + 5 ft./2 levels)
Effect: Ray
Target: One construct
Duration: Instantaneous
Saving Throw: None
Spell Resistance: No

A copper-red ray bursts from your outstretched hand. The sound of grinding gears and breaking metal accompanies the ray's flight.

This ray interferes with magical animation, degenerating the magic bound within constructs and effectively causing damage. You must succeed on a ranged touch attack with the ray to strike a target. The ray deals 1d6 points of damage per caster level to the subject (maximum 15d6).

RAY DEFLECTION

Abjuration
Level: Bard 4, sorcerer/wizard 4
Components: V, S, F
Casting Time: 1 standard action
Range: Personal
Target: You
Duration: 1 minute/level
Saving Throw: None
Spell Resistance: No

As the spell is cast, a brief shimmering field appears around you. Small motes of silver float within the field.

For the duration of the spell, you are protected against ranged touch attacks, including ray spells and ray attacks made by creatures. Any ray attack directed at you is automatically reflected harmlessly away.

Focus: A glass prism.

RAY OF DIZZINESS

Enchantment (Compulsion) [Mind-Affecting]
Level: Bard 3, sorcerer/wizard 3
Components: V, S, F
Casting Time: 1 standard action
Range: Medium (100 ft. + 10 ft./level)
Effect: Ray
Duration: 1 round/level
Saving Throw: None
Spell Resistance: Yes

You release a drab violet ray from your palm. The ray shoots toward your target in a spiraling corkscrew.

You strike out at your enemy with a ray that causes intense feelings of vertigo. You must succeed on a ranged touch attack with the ray to strike a target. A struck subject experiences strong feelings of vertigo and can take only a move action or a standard action each round (but not both, and it cannot take a full-round action).

Focus: A small top.

RAY OF ENTROPY

Necromancy
Level: Sorcerer/wizard 6
Components: V, S
Casting Time: 1 standard action
Range: Close (25 ft. + 5 ft./2 levels)
Effect: Ray
Duration: 1 minute/level
Saving Throw: None
Spell Resistance: Yes

You release a crackling black ray. The smell of decay fills the air.

When you cast this spell, you unleash a ray of negative energy that consumes the life energy of the subject. You must succeed on a ranged touch attack with the ray to strike a target. If your attack is successful against a living creature, the ray makes the subject weaker, slower, and less healthy. The subject takes a –4 penalty to Strength, Constitution, and Dexterity for the duration of the spell.

RAY OF FLAME

Evocation [Fire]
Level: Sorcerer/wizard 1
Components: V, S, F
Casting Time: 1 standard action
Range: Close (25 ft. + 5 ft./2 levels)
Effect: Ray
Duration: Instantaneous
Saving Throw: See text
Spell Resistance: Yes

A burning ray shoots out at the target from your upturned palm. The sound of a crackling fire follows the ray's path.

You must succeed on a ranged touch attack with the ray to strike a target. If your attack is successful, the ray deals 1d6 points of fire damage per two caster levels (maximum 5d6). The target must also make a Reflex save or catch fire, taking 1d6 points of fire damage each round until the flames are put out (requiring a DC 15 Reflex save; see Catching on Fire, DMG 303).

Focus: A small, polished glass lens.

RAY OF ICE

Evocation [Cold]
Level: Sorcerer/wizard 2
Components: V, S, M
Casting Time: 1 standard action
Range: Close (25 ft. + 5 ft./2 levels)
Effect: Ray
Duration: Instantaneous
Saving Throw: See text
Spell Resistance: Yes

Beware the wizard who masters rays

A cyan ray beams from your fingertips. You shudder with cold as the ray leaves your hand.

You launch a ray of numbing cold at your enemy. You must succeed on a ranged touch attack with the ray to strike a target. If successful, the ray deals 1d6 points of cold damage per two caster levels (maximum 5d6). The target must also make a Reflex save or be frozen to the ground with its feet encased in ice. A frozen creature cannot move, receives no Dexterity bonus to AC, and incurs a –2 penalty on attack rolls.

A frozen creature can free itself with a DC 18 Strength check or by dealing 15 points of damage to the ice.

Material Component: Ice or a vial of melted mountain snow.

RAY OF LIGHT

Evocation [Light]
Level: Bard 6, sorcerer/wizard 6
Components: V, S
Casting Time: 1 standard action
Range: Close (25 ft. + 5 ft./2 levels)
Effect: Ray
Duration: Instantaneous
Saving Throw: None
Spell Resistance: Yes

Your palm emits a ray of light. The ray gives off a soft, continuous glow.

You direct a short ray at the eyes of a target. You must succeed on a ranged touch attack with the ray to strike a target. With a successful ranged touch attack, the subject is blinded for 1d4 rounds.

RAY OF SICKNESS

Necromancy
Level: Sorcerer/wizard 2
Components: V, S
Casting Time: 1 standard action
Range: Close (25 ft. + 5 ft./2 levels)
Effect: Ray
Duration: 1 round/level
Saving Throw: None
Spell Resistance: Yes

Holding your outstretched hand palm down, you fire a sickly green ray. Your hand feels cold and clammy for a few seconds after the ray flies forth.

You must succeed on a ranged touch attack with the ray to strike a target. If your ranged touch attack hits, the subject becomes sickened.

RAY OF STUPIDITY

Enchantment (Compulsion) [Mind-Affecting]
Level: Sorcerer/wizard 2
Components: V, S, M
Casting Time: 1 standard action
Range: Close (25 ft. + 5 ft./2 levels)
Effect: Ray
Duration: Instantaneous
Saving Throw: None
Spell Resistance: Yes

A bright yellow beam bursts from your extended fingertips. The beam emits an

Illus. by S. Belledin

"uh" sound, like someone trying to think of a word.

This ray clouds the mind of your enemy, damaging its intellect. You must succeed on a ranged touch attack with the ray to strike a target. A subject struck by the ray takes 1d4+1 points of Intelligence damage. If the target is a wizard, she might temporarily lose the ability to cast some or all of her spells if her Intelligence drops too low.

Material Component: A miniature cone-shaped hat.

RAY OF WEAKNESS

Necromancy
Level: Sorcerer/wizard 2
Components: V, S
Casting Time: 1 standard action
Range: Close (25 ft. + 5 ft./2 levels)
Effect: Ray
Duration: 1 minute/level
Saving Throw: None
Spell Resistance: Yes

A dark ray flies forth from your hand. The air fills with the smell of blood.

You must succeed on a ranged touch attack with the ray to strike a target. The target of this ray feels weaker and takes a –2 penalty on attack rolls. Its speed is reduced by 10 feet.

RAZORFANGS

Transmutation
Level: Sorcerer/wizard 2
Components: V
Casting Time: 1 standard action
Range: Personal
Target: You
Duration: 1 round/level

You speak the words of this spell and your claws shine with lustrous yellow radiance, growing more slender and sharper as you watch.

Choose one of your natural weapons that deals slashing or piercing damage (such as a bite or a single claw). That natural weapon's threat range doubles (in most cases, becoming 19–20). The effect of this spell does not stack with any other effects that increase a weapon's threat range.

REALITY MAELSTROM

Evocation
Level: Sorcerer/wizard 9
Components: V, S, M
Casting Time: 1 standard action
Range: Medium (100 ft. + 10 ft./level)
Area: 20-ft.-radius emanation centered on a point in space, and 40-ft.-radius emanation centered on the same point; see text
Duration: 1 round
Saving Throw: Will negates, Reflex negates; see text
Spell Resistance: Yes

A lightning strike and a tearing sound as loud as thunder fills the area as a hole in space opens. Wind rushes into the void, and objects nearby lift into the air as everything is drawn inexorably toward the rip in reality.

You tear a temporary hole in reality itself that sucks all loose material and living creatures into it, sending them to a random plane (see sidebar). Everything sucked into the *reality maelstrom* goes to the same plane.

Reality maelstrom has a primary area and a secondary area. The primary area is the hole itself: a sphere with a 20-foot radius centered on the spell's point of origin. Within that area, all unattended objects weighing 100 pounds or less are sucked into the maelstrom, as are all individuals who fail a Will saving throw.

Reality maelstrom creates a hole in the cosmology of the planes

Illus. by C. Dien

The rip also creates a windstorm of air that affects objects and creatures in the secondary area of the spell. The secondary area is all the space farther than 20 feet from the spell's point of origin but not farther than 40 feet away. All unattended objects within the secondary area that weigh 50 pounds or less are drawn into the primary area of the maelstrom. Individuals within the secondary area must make a Reflex saving throw. Those who fail are sucked into the primary area and must then make a Will saving throw to avoid being drawn into the maelstrom.

Individuals who succeed on either saving throw can move and attack as normal.

A *reality maelstrom* is a one-way portal, so nothing ever emerges from the hole the spell makes.

Material Component: A golden hoop no less than 1 inch across.

REAVING DISPEL

Abjuration
Level: Sorcerer/wizard 9
Saving Throw: See text
Spell Resistance: No

Bringing to your lips some of the most elemental words of arcane power, you feel stirring within you the spirits of ancient mages as you prepare to absorb the spell energies you have targeted. Your body shakes uncontrollably, as if eagerly anticipating the power behind those spells.

This spell functions like *dispel magic* (PH 223), except that your caster level for your dispel check is a maximum of +20 instead of +10, and (as with *greater dispel magic*) you have a chance to dispel any effect that *remove curse* can remove, even if *dispel magic* can't dispel that effect. When casting a targeted dispel or counterspell, you can choose to reave each spell you successfully dispel, stealing its power and effect for yourself. When making a targeted dispel, make a Spellcraft check (DC 25 + spell level) to identify the target spell or each ongoing spell currently in effect on the target creature or object.

Each spell you dispel with a targeted dispel can be reaved if you so desire, and the spell's effects are redirected to you, continuing as if cast on you by the original caster with no interruption to or extension of duration. Once you reave the spell, you identify it if you haven't done so already (see below). If the subject was the caster and the spell is dismissible, you can dismiss it as if you had cast it yourself. Likewise, if the subject was the caster and the spell requires concentration, you must concentrate to maintain the spell's effect as if you had cast it yourself.

You can still attempt to reave a spell you didn't identify with your Spellcraft check, but doing so can be risky if you don't know the specifics of the spell's effect. For example, if you fail to identity an ongoing spell effect on an enemy character and choose to reave anyway, you might find yourself under the influence of the *dominate person* effect that character was suffering from. Any spell resistance you might have has no effect against harmful spells you might inadvertently reave, but you get the same chance to save against those spell effects as the original target.

If you choose to reave a spell you have successfully counterspelled with *reaving dispel*, you seize control of the spell after the enemy caster completes it, and you can redirect the spell to whatever targets or area you wish (including the original caster, if appropriate). Again, you must make a Spellcraft check (DC 25 + spell level) to identify the spell you intend to reave, but you are free to choose to redirect a spell whose effect, range, and area you don't know. If the redirected spell's correct casting conditions aren't met (because you guess at an improper target or range, for example), the spell fails.

RANDOM PLANAR DESTINATIONS

Spells such as *prismatic spray, reality maelstrom,* and *scramble portal,* and items such as an *amulet of the planes* and a *staff of power* can send an individual to a random plane. The list of available planes varies according to the cosmology you've chosen. An example using the D&D cosmology is presented in the next column.

Transitive Planes such as the Ethereal Plane, the Astral Plane, and the Plane of Shadow should not be considered for such random destinations.

The layer and exact location on the particular plane is up to the DM. Transportation to a random plane does not guarantee survival there, and individuals who risk such effects should be aware of the dangers.

If an individual is someplace other than the Material Plane when randomly switching planes, simply replace the plane of origin's entry on the table with the Material Plane. Thus, a *staff of power* broken on the Elemental Plane of Fire sends the wielder to the Material Plane if a 91 is rolled.

Random Planar Destinations

d%	Plane
01–05	Heroic Domains of Ysgard
06–10	Ever-Changing Chaos of Limbo
11–15	Windswept Depths of Pandemonium
16–20	Infinite Layers of the Abyss
21–25	Tarterian Depths of Carceri
26–30	Gray Waste of Hades
31–35	Bleak Eternity of Gehenna
36–40	Nine Hells of Baator
41–45	Infernal Battlefield of Acheron
46–50	Clockwork Nirvana of Mechanus
51–55	Peaceable Kingdoms of Arcadia
56–60	Seven Mounting Heavens of Celestia
61–65	Twin Paradises of Bytopia
66–70	Blessed Fields of Elysium
71–75	Wilderness of the Beastlands
76–80	Olympian Glades of Arborea
81–89	Concordant Domain of the Outlands
90–91	Elemental Plane of Fire
92–93	Elemental Plane of Earth
94–95	Elemental Plane of Air
96–97	Elemental Plane of Water
98	Positive Energy Plane
99	Negative Energy Plane
100	Demiplane of DM's choice

Reaving dispel can be used to cast an area dispel with the increased maximum caster level, but any magical effects so dispelled cannot be reaved.

REBUKE

Enchantment (Compulsion) [Fear, Mind-Affecting]
Level: Sorcerer/wizard 2, Hades 2
Components: V, S, F
Casting Time: 1 standard action
Range: Close (25 ft. + 5 ft./2 levels)
Target: One living creature
Duration: 1 round/level
Saving Throw: Will negates
Spell Resistance: Yes

You rap the switch in your hand and then sharply against your thigh, finishing the final gesture that will bring discomfort to your foe.

When the spell is cast, the subject is dazed for 1 round and shaken for the duration of the spell. Furthermore, a spellcaster targeted by *rebuke* must make a successful Concentration check (DC equal to the save DC for this spell + the level of the spell being cast) to cast spells while under its effect.

Focus: A stick at least 1 foot long.

REBUKE, FINAL

Enchantment (Compulsion) [Fear, Mind-Affecting]
Level: Sorcerer/wizard 7
Saving Throw: Will partial

You jab the stick into your side and twist it, causing yourself some discomfort but creating a killing pain in the target.

This spell functions like *rebuke*, except that the target dies instantly if it fails its saving throw. A creature that survives this effect is dazed for 1 round.

REBUKE, GREATER

Enchantment (Compulsion) [Fear, Mind-Affecting]
Level: Sorcerer/wizard 4

This spell functions like *rebuke*, except that the subject is cowering for 1d4 rounds instead of being dazed for 1 round.

REBUKING BREATH

Necromancy
Level: Sorcerer/wizard 4
Components: S
Casting Time: 1 swift action
Range: Personal
Target: Your breath weapon
Duration: 1 round

Your expel your breath weapon, and it is filled with dancing white sparks that swarm around your foes and freeze them with fear.

For this spell to function, you must have a breath weapon, either as a supernatural ability or as the result of casting a spell such as *dragon breath* (page 73). When you successfully cast this spell, you imbue your breath weapon with negative energy that rebukes undead in its area. Undead within the area of your breath weapon that fail their saving throws against it cower as if in awe for 1 round.

RECIPROCAL GYRE

Abjuration
Level: Sorcerer/wizard 5
Components: V, S, M
Casting Time: 1 standard action
Range: Medium (100 ft. + 10 ft./level)
Target: One creature or object
Duration: Instantaneous
Saving Throw: Will half, then Fortitude negates; see text
Spell Resistance: No

You finger the tiny loop of wire in your hands as you complete the spell. You manipulate the magical aura of the target, creating a damaging feedback reaction, and the target explodes with white sparks.

The subject takes 1d12 points of damage per functioning spell or spell-like ability currently affecting it (maximum 25d12). In addition, any creature so affected that fails its Will save must then succeed on a Fortitude save or be dazed for 1d6 rounds.

Only spells specifically targeted on the creature in question can be used to create the backlash of a *reciprocal gyre*, so spells that affect an area can't be used to deal reciprocal damage to creatures within their area. Likewise, persistent or continuous effects from magic items can't be used to deal reciprocal damage, but targeted spell effects can be.

Material Component: A tiny closed loop of copper wire.

RECITATION

Conjuration (Creation)
Level: Cleric 4, Purification 3
Components: V, S, DF
Casting Time: 1 standard action
Range: 60 ft.
Area: All allies within a 60-ft.-radius burst centered on you
Duration: 1 round/level
Saving Throw: None
Spell Resistance: Yes

By reciting a sacred passage or declaration, you invoke your deity's blessing upon yourself and your allies.

The spell affects all allies within the spell's area at the moment you cast it. Your allies gain a +2 luck bonus to AC, on attack rolls, and on saving throws, or a +3 luck bonus if they worship the same deity as you.

Divine Focus: In addition to your holy symbol, this spell requires a sacred text as a divine focus.

RED TIDE

Evocation [Water]
Level: Druid 8
Components: V, S, DF
Casting Time: 1 standard action
Range: Medium (100 ft. + 10 ft./level)
Area: 30-ft.-radius burst
Duration: Instantaneous
Saving Throw: Fortitude partial; see text
Spell Resistance: Yes

As you complete the spell, a surging, frothing wave of thick, red seawater washes over everything in the area.

All creatures in the area of a *red tide* spell are immediately knocked prone and must make a Fortitude saving throw.

A creature that makes its Fortitude save against a *red tide* is sickened for 1 minute. A creature that fails this saving throw is nauseated for 1 minute, and it takes 2d6 points of Strength damage. After 1 minute, the nausea ends but the creature must make a second Fortitude saving throw or take an additional 2d6 points of Strength damage. Creatures that are immune to poison are immune to these effects of a *red tide*.

Creatures with the fire subtype take 1d6 points of damage per caster level (maximum 20d6), or half with a successful Reflex save.

The tainted water evoked by this spell vanishes almost immediately, and any objects or creatures in the area do not emerge wet.

REDUCE PERSON, GREATER

Transmutation
Level: Sorcerer/wizard 5
Duration: 10 minutes/level

The creature shrinks rapidly before your eyes.

This spell functions like *reduce person* (PH 269), except as noted above.

REFLECTIVE DISGUISE

Illusion (Glamer)
Level: Bard 2, sorcerer/wizard 2
Components: V, S
Casting Time: 1 standard action
Range: Personal
Target: You
Duration: 10 minutes/level

You invoke the spell and, to your eyes, you are covered with a glittering net of sparks and spangles. To the eyes of the drow in the underground marketplace, you look like just another dark elf.

A *reflective disguise* spell causes any intelligent creature viewing you to perceive you as the same species and gender as itself, provided that its size category is no more than one step different from your own. The spell changes perceptions of clothing, race, and gender. *Reflective disguise* does not give you any knowledge of the abilities or mannerisms of the reflected form, nor does it alter the perceived tactile (touch), audible (sound), or olfactory (smell) properties of you or your equipment.

A creature that interacts with the glamer, beyond simply viewing it, gets a Will save to recognize it as an illusion. For example, a creature that touched you and realized that the tactile sensation did not match the visual one would be entitled to such a save. A creature with the scent ability automatically gets a Will save if you are within its scent range.

Red tide bowls over, nauseates, and weakens foes

REFLECTIVE DISGUISE, MASS

Illusion (Glamer)
Level: Bard 5, sorcerer/wizard 6
Range: Close (25 ft. + 5 ft./2 levels)
Targets: One creature/2 levels, no two of which are more than 30 ft. apart
Duration: 12 hours (D)
Saving Throw: Will negates
Spell Resistance: Yes

You cast the spell, and your allies all suddenly appear to be members of the same orc tribe you plan to infiltrate.

This spell functions like *reflective disguise*, except you can change the appearance of other creatures as well. Affected creatures resume their normal appearances if slain.

An unwilling target can negate the spell's effect on itself by making a successful Will save or with spell resistance.

REFUSAL

Abjuration
Level: Sorcerer/wizard 5
Components: V, S, M
Casting Time: 1 standard action
Range: Medium (100 ft. + 10 ft./level)
Effect and Area: Invisible ward that occupies two 10-ft. squares/level (S)
Duration: 1 hour/level
Saving Throw: Will negates; see text
Spell Resistance: Yes

A metallic stretching sound, as if a thin sheet of metal were bowed then released, echoes forth from your outstretched hand. You can see for just an instant a glowing grid that defines the protected area of your spell.

You create a special ward that prevents unauthorized spellcasters or creatures with spell-like abilities from entering an area. Any creature that has spells prepared, spell slots available for casting without preparation, or innate spell-like abilities must succeed on a Will save or be halted by an invisible barrier that prevents passage. The DC of the Will save increases by a number equal to the spell level of the highest-level spell the creature has prepared or is capable of casting (so that a 10th-level sorcerer who hasn't yet depleted his 5th-level spell slots for the day adds 5 to the save DC). You can choose to designate a password or special condition (such as character race, alignment, possession of a token, or any other observable or detectable characteristic) by which spellcasting characters and creatures can enter the *refusal*-warded area.

Creatures that have no spellcasting capability or spell-like abilities (including spellcasters who have used up their spell slots and creatures with spell trigger or spell completion magic items) can pass through the barrier with no difficulty. Spellcasters and creatures that have spell-like abilities and that are already within the area you protect when you create the ward are not compelled to leave or restricted in their movement within it (and spells and spell-like abilities can pass through the barrier in either direction with no difficulty). However, if such creatures

Illus. by J. Nelson

leave the area, they must succeed on saving throws as described above to return.

Creatures attempting to use any teleportation spell or effect to enter the warded area make the normal saving throw. They are shunted harmlessly to the nearest safe space outside the warded area if they fail.

Material Component: A pinch of dust from a wizard's tomb.

REGAL PROCESSION

Conjuration (Summoning)
Level: Paladin 3, sorcerer/wizard 3
Effect: One mount/level

You toss a bit of horsehair into the air, and as it drifts toward the ground, an array of finely adorned mounts appears.

This spell functions like *mount* (PH 256), except you can summon several mounts. Each comes with a bit and bridle, riding saddle, saddle blanket, ribbons, adornments, and a banner. You select the colors of the horses and the livery, either or both of which can include a heraldic or personal symbol.

REJECTION

Abjuration
Level: Cleric 6
Components: V, S
Casting Time: 1 standard action
Range: 60 ft.
Area: Cone-shaped burst
Duration: Instantaneous
Saving Throw: Fortitude negates
Spell Resistance: Yes

With a stern word of disallowance, you cast the spell. A barely perceptible hum sounds in the direction you indicate.

A creature in the area must succeed on a Fortitude saving throw or be pushed away from you to a distance of 5 feet per caster level. If the creature is pushed into a wall or similarly solid surface, it takes 1d6 points of damage for every 10 feet it was moved.

Movement forced by this spell can take the creature beyond the spell's range.

REJUVENATION COCOON

Conjuration (Healing)
Level: Druid 5
Components: V, S, M
Casting Time: 1 standard action
Range: Touch
Target: Willing creature touched
Duration: 2 rounds
Saving Throw: Will negates (harmless)
Spell Resistance: Yes (harmless)

Feasting on a rejuvenative corpse gives undead the power to heal wounds

Illus. by R. Spears

You pass your hand over the body of your friend, drawing a cocoon of glowing yellow-green energy about him.

When you cast the spell, the *rejuvenation cocoon* forms around the subject. One round after the cocoon forms, it heals the subject of 10 points of damage per caster level (maximum 150 hit points) and purges the subject of poison and disease. At the end of the second round, the *rejuvenation cocoon* dissipates and the subject emerges, able to move and act freely.

The cocoon is made of force, but it is somewhat flexible and responds to pressure from the inside of the cocoon. The subject can't move from the space it is in while cocooned, however.

The cocoon has hardness 10 and 10 hit points per caster level. If it is destroyed, the spell ends.

Material Component: A cocoon of a butterfly.

REJUVENATIVE CORPSE

Necromancy [Evil]
Level: Cleric 3
Components: V, S, DF
Casting Time: 1 minute
Range: Touch
Target: One humanoid that died within the past week
Duration: 24 hours or until discharged; see text
Saving Throw: Will negates (object)
Spell Resistance: Yes (object)

Hunger gnaws at your innards as you complete the spell. Your hands glow with black crackling energy, which discharges into the corpse you touch. For a moment, the corpse glows with a similar blackness before fading.

You charge a dead body with negative energy, giving it the ability to heal an undead creature that dines upon its flesh. The corpse remains charged with this energy for up to 24 hours. If an undead creature eats a full meal of the corpse's flesh within this time (a humanlike undead creature, such as a ghoul, generally taking 10 minutes), the undead gains fast healing 1 upon completing its feast, which lasts for the next 5 minutes. This effect does not stack with any fast healing the undead has from other sources. This spell does not allow the undead to regrow or attach lost body parts. Eating the flesh discharges the spell from the corpse.

You can cast this spell multiple times on a corpse, allowing more than one undead to benefit from eating it, though a single undead gorging itself on multiple "meals" does not gain any extra benefit while the first meal is in effect (the fast healing does not stack). A typical Medium corpse is usually enough for ten such meals, a Small corpse five, Tiny two, and Diminutive one.

A living creature that eats a charged corpse must succeed on a Fortitude saving throw or immediately contract filth fever (DMG 292; no incubation time). Creatures that are neither alive nor undead and eat the charged corpse are unaffected.

REMOVE SCENT

Transmutation
Level: Bard 1, druid 1, ranger 1, sorcerer/wizard 1
Components: V, S, M
Casting Time: 1 standard action
Range: Touch
Target: Creature touched
Duration: 10 minutes/level
Saving Throw: Will negates
Spell Resistance: Yes

With a touch of a wax-covered finger to the subject, you inhale deeply and smell nothing.

This spells hides the scent of the creature or object touched for the duration of the spell. The scent ability (MM 314) cannot detect a creature under the effect of a *remove scent* spell. It also negates the harmful effects of the noxious stench exuded by certain creatures, such as ghasts, for the duration of the spell.

Material Component: A pinch of unscented candle wax.

RENEWAL PACT

Conjuration (Healing)
Level: Cleric 7, Pact 7
Components: V, S, M, DF
Casting Time: 10 minutes
Range: Touch
Target: Willing living creature touched
Duration: Permanent until triggered
Saving Throw: Will negates (harmless)
Spell Resistance: Yes (harmless)

Calling upon your deity to aid your ally, you bind a protective spell to your friend, leaving a tattoolike mark of your deity's holy symbol on his skin.

This spell remains dormant until the subject is subjected to one or more of the following adverse conditions: ability damage, blinded, *confused*, dazed, dazzled, deafened, diseased, exhausted, fatigued, feebleminded, insanity, nauseated, sickened, stunned, or poisoned. One round after the subject is affected by a condition that triggers the *renewal pact*, the subject receives a *panacea* spell (page 152) at a caster level equal to that of the caster of the *renewal pact*.

A creature can be subject to only one *renewal pact* at a time. Casting *renewal pact* on a subject who already has an untriggered *renewal pact* voids the earlier pact.

Material Component: A topaz worth at least 500 gp.

REPAIR CRITICAL DAMAGE

Transmutation
Level: Sorcerer/wizard 4

The smell of grease and the distant echo of clanking gears greet your senses as you complete this spell. Upon touching the intended construct, the grease smell and gear sounds disappear. Major dents and scratches disappear from the construct, as do cuts, tears, and abrasions.

This spell functions like *repair light damage*, except that you repair 4d8 points of damage +1 point per caster level (maximum +20).

REPAIR LIGHT DAMAGE

Transmutation
Level: Sorcerer/wizard 1
Components: V, S
Casting Time: 1 standard action
Range: Touch
Target: Construct touched
Duration: Instantaneous
Saving Throw: None
Spell Resistance: No

As a sculptor massaging a rough spot of clay into something less abrasive, your touch smooths over the dents and dings of the construct you touch.

When laying your hand upon a construct that has at least 1 hit point remaining, you transmute its structure to repair the damage it has taken. The spell repairs 1d8 points of damage +1 point per caster level (maximum +5).

REPAIR MINOR DAMAGE

Transmutation
Level: Sorcerer/wizard 0

As if with the eye of an expert craftsman, your touch draws out a minor dent in the construct's surface.

This spell functions like *repair light damage*, except that you repair 1 point of damage to a construct.

REPAIR MODERATE DAMAGE

Transmutation
Level: Sorcerer/wizard 2

Your touch eliminates the wear and tear from the construct's body.

This spell functions like *repair light damage*, except that you repair 2d8 points of damage +1 point per caster level (maximum +10) to a construct.

REPAIR SERIOUS DAMAGE

Transmutation
Level: Sorcerer/wizard 3

With a touch, you mold the battered construct's form to be more like it was on its day of creation.

This spell functions like *repair light damage*, except that you repair 3d8 points of damage +1 point per caster level (maximum +15) to a construct.

REPLICATE CASTING

Transmutation [see text]
Level: Sorcerer/wizard 9
Components: V, S
Casting Time: 1 round; see text
Range: See text
Effect: One spell or spell-like ability
Duration: See text
Saving Throw: See text
Spell Resistance: See text

The enemy mage raises her hands, and a cone of swirling, multicolored winds appears at her fingertips. Then she laughs and says, "Can you do that?"

You smile and reply, "I can now."

You duplicate the effect of any one spell or spell-like ability you have seen within the last round. This spell can duplicate only spells and spell-like abilities of 8th level or lower. This duplication functions like the ability of a *wish* spell to duplicate another spell, except that it is not limited by type of spell (divine or arcane) or by what school the effect is from. If the casting time of the spell you observed is greater than 1 round, the casting time of this spell is increased to the same.

A duplicated spell or spell-like ability functions as if you had the appropriate spell prepared and were casting it yourself. If the spell or ability has an XP cost, you must pay that XP cost. If the spell has a costly material component, you must provide that component or pay an additional XP cost equal to the gold piece value of that component divided by 5.

RESIST ENERGY, MASS

Abjuration
Level: Cleric 3, druid 3, sorcerer/wizard 4
Range: Close (25 ft. + 5 ft./2 levels)
Targets: One creature/level, no two of which are more than 30 ft. apart

You call upon the protective energies of magical power, surrounding your subjects in temporarily visible fields of energy. Although the fields fade from view, you can still just barely sense their existence.

This spell functions like *resist energy* (PH 272), except that it affects all targeted creatures.

RESIST PLANAR ALIGNMENT

Abjuration
Level: Cleric 1, druid 1, Hades 2, Limbo 2, paladin 1, ranger 1, sorcerer/wizard 1
Components: V, S, DF
Casting Time: 1 standard action
Range: Touch
Target: Creature touched
Duration: 10 minutes/level
Saving Throw: Fortitude negates (harmless)
Spell Resistance: Yes (harmless)

You can tell that your target feels the oppression of the plane around you, the rank evil of the place. A few spoken phrases, backed by magical power, and that oppression seems to lift.

This abjuration grants a creature limited protection from a plane's alignment traits (DMG 149). When the subject visits a plane with an alignment trait, this spell grants it immunity to penalties on its Charisma-based checks that mildly aligned planes impose on visitors of opposed alignments. The Charisma-, Wisdom-, and Intelligence-based check penalties associated with strongly aligned planes are halved while the spell's duration lasts.

RESISTANCE, GREATER

Abjuration
Level: Bard 4, cleric 4, druid 4, sorcerer/wizard 4
Duration: 24 hours

Just as you touch the spell's subject, a feeling of peace and watchful guardianship fills your being.

This spell functions like *resistance* (PH 272), except as noted here. You grant the subject a +3 resistance bonus on saves.

RESISTANCE, SUPERIOR

Abjuration
Level: Bard 6, cleric 6, druid 6, sorcerer/wizard 6
Duration: 24 hours

As you finish casting the spell, you feel imbued with the feeling that something greater than yourself is protecting you. When you touch your intended subject and release the spell, the feeling disappears.

This spell functions like *resistance* (PH 272), except as noted here. You grant the subject a +6 resistance bonus on saves.

RESONATING BOLT

Evocation [Sonic]
Level: Bard 4, sorcerer/wizard 3
Components: V, S
Casting Time: 1 standard action
Range: 60 ft.
Area: 60-ft. line
Duration: Instantaneous
Saving Throw: Reflex half
Spell Resistance: Yes

Your quick movements and rapid utterances release the spell's energy, culminating in a final cry that unleashes a tremendous bolt of sonic energy from your open hand.

The bolt of sonic energy deals 1d4 points of sonic damage per caster level (maximum 10d4) to each creature within its area. In addition, a *resonating bolt* deals full damage to objects and can easily shatter or break interposing barriers. If the bolt destroys a barrier, it can continue beyond the barrier if its range permits; otherwise, it stops.

RESTORATION, MASS

Conjuration (Healing)
Level: Cleric 7
Casting Time: 1 round
Range: Close (25 ft. + 5 ft./2 levels)
Targets: One creature/level, no two of which are more than 30 ft. apart

Hurling diamond dust into the air, you call out to your deity, and a sparkling aura briefly surrounds those you wish to heal.

This spell functions like *restoration* (PH 272), except as noted above.

RESURGENCE

Abjuration
Level: Blackguard 1, cleric 1, paladin 1
Components: V, S, DF
Casting Time: 1 standard action
Range: Touch
Target: Creature touched
Duration: Instantaneous
Saving Throw: Will negates (harmless)
Spell Resistance: Yes (harmless)

By laying hands on your ally and saying a brief prayer, you convince a higher power to grant him a second chance.

The subject of a *resurgence* spell can make a second attempt to save against an ongoing spell, spell-like ability, or supernatural ability, such as *dominate person*. If the subject of *resurgence* is affected by more than one ongoing magical effect, the subject chooses one of them to retry the save against. If the subject succeeds on the saving throw on the second attempt, the effect ends immediately. *Resurgence* never restores hit points or ability score damage, but it does eliminate any conditions such as shaken, fatigued, or nauseated that were caused by a spell, spell-like ability, or supernatural ability.

If a spell, spell-like ability, or supernatural ability doesn't allow a save (such as *power word stun*), then *resurgence* won't help the subject recover.

RESURGENCE, MASS

Abjuration
Level: Blackguard 3, cleric 3, paladin 3
Range: Close (25 ft. + 5 ft./2 levels)
Targets: One creature/level, no two of which are more than 30 ft. apart

Throwing out your hand and calling upon your deity for favor, you give your allies a chance to free themselves of the baleful magic.

This spell functions like *resurgence*, except as noted here. The spell grants a second save attempt against a single spell or ability chosen by you. For instance, if three of your allies have been *mind blasted* by mind flayers and two others have been turned into toads by *baleful polymorph* spells, you must choose to affect either the *mind blast* (granting three new save attempts) or the *baleful polymorphs* (granting two new save attempts).

REVEILLE

Necromancy [Language-Dependent]
Level: Bard 2
Components: V, S
Casting Time: 1 round
Range: Touch
Target: One recently dead creature
Duration: 5 rounds
Saving Throw: None
Spell Resistance: No

You touch the body and intone a lament, calling out to the living memory of the creature. Tendrils of mystical energy sparkle around the creature's lips, and it begins to speak.

You cause a creature that has been dead for up to three days to reveal information about events that led up to its death. The corpse speaks tersely in its native language, using no more than a dozen words or so in a round. In the first round, it describes the last thing it saw. In the second, it describes its dying wish. In the third, it describes the attack that killed it. In the fourth, it tells who killed it. In the fifth, it tells why it believes it was killed.

REVENANCE

Conjuration (Healing)
Level: Bard 6, blackguard 4, cleric 4, paladin 4
Components: V, S, DF
Casting Time: 1 standard action
Range: Touch
Target: Dead ally touched
Duration: 1 minute/level
Saving Throw: None; see text
Spell Resistance: Yes (harmless)

You rush to your fallen companion amid the chaos of the battle and cry out the words that will bring her back for one last fight.

This spell brings a dead ally temporarily back to life. The subject can have been dead for up to 1 round per level. Your target functions as if a *raise dead* spell (PH 268) had been cast upon her, except that she does not lose a level and has half of her full normal hit points. She is alive (not undead) for the duration of the spell and can be healed normally, but dies as soon as the spell ends. While under the effect of this spell, the subject is not affected by spells that raise the dead.

The subject gains a +1 morale bonus on attack rolls, damage rolls, saves, and checks against the creature that killed her.

REVERSE ARROWS

Abjuration
Level: Sorcerer/wizard 3
Components: V, S, F
Casting Time: 1 standard action
Range: Personal
Target: You
Duration: 10 minutes/level or until discharged

As you clasp the shell in one hand and the ball of sap in the other, a silver radiance flecked with blue lines surrounds you. You pocket the items, but the radiance remains.

This spell functions like *protection from arrows* (PH 266), except as noted here. If any projectile fired from a ranged weapon that strikes you has all its damage negated by your damage reduction (10/magic), the projectile is turned back upon the creature that fired it. The attacker's attack roll is used to determine if the reversed projectile strikes the attacker, but the damage is rerolled. If the attacker is also protected by a *reverse arrows* spell, it is possible for the projectile to bounce between both individuals until one of the spells is discharged from accumulated damage.

Once this spell has prevented a total of 10 points of damage per caster level (maximum 100 points), it is discharged.

Focus: A piece of shell from a tortoise and a ball of tree sap.

REVIVE OUTSIDER

Conjuration (Healing)
Level: Cleric 6
Components: V, S, M, DF
Casting Time: 1 minute
Range: Touch
Target: Dead outsider touched
Duration: Instantaneous
Saving Throw: None; see text
Spell Resistance: Yes (harmless)

Sprinkling the components of its home plane over the body of the outsider, you chant and pass around the corpse three times. With the final words of the spell, the outsider's eyes open, alive once more.

You restore life to a dead outsider, as with the *raise dead* spell (PH 268). You can restore to life any creature of the outsider type of up to your level in Hit Dice, and the creature can have been dead for any length of time.

Material Components: A bit of soil, water, or other unworked, natural material from the outsider's native plane, and a diamond worth at least 5,000 gp.

REVIVE UNDEAD

Necromancy [Evil]
Level: Deathbound 5, sorcerer/wizard 6
Components: V, S, M
Casting Time: 1 minute
Range: Touch
Target: Destroyed undead creature touched
Duration: Instantaneous
Saving Throw: None
Spell Resistance: No

Even fallen angels can be brought to life and light again with the revive outsider spell

Illus. by W. O'Connor

Touching the corpse of the creature, you whisper to its departed spirit, calling it back—but not to life.

Your restore animation to an undead creature destroyed by hit point loss (even a zombie or skeleton, which can't normally be reanimated once destroyed). You can revive a destroyed undead creature that has been inactive for up to one day per caster level. In addition, the subject's animating spirit must be free and willing to return. If the subject's animating spirit is not willing to return, the spell does not work; therefore, subjects that want to revive receive no saving throw.

Revive undead restores hit points to the subject up to a total of 1 hit point per Hit Die. The body of the undead to be revived must be whole. Otherwise, missing parts are still missing when the creature is reanimated. None of the dead creature's equipment or possessions are affected in any way by this spell.

An undead that has been destroyed by a turning effect can't be revived by this spell.

The subject of the spell loses one level or Hit Die (if it doesn't have a character class level, it loses a HD) when it is revived. This level loss cannot be repaired by any spell. If the subject is 1st level, it loses 2 points of Charisma instead. An undead that was destroyed with spells prepared has a 50% chance of losing any given spell upon being revived, in addition to losing spells for losing a level. A spellcasting undead creature that doesn't prepare spells (such as a sorcerer) has a 50% chance of losing any given unused spell slot as if it had been used to cast a spell, in addition to losing spell slots for losing a level.

Material Component: A black pearl worth at least 5,000 gp.

REVIVIFY

Conjuration (Healing)
Level: Cleric 5
Components: V, S, M
Casting Time: 1 standard action
Range: Touch
Target: Dead creature touched
Duration: Instantaneous
Saving Throw: None; see text
Spell Resistance: Yes (harmless)

The diamonds vaporize from your hand as you cast this spell, and the vapors they give off wrap around your fallen companion, dragging her soul back into her mortal form.

Revivify miraculously restores life to a recently deceased creature. However, the spell must be cast within 1 round of the victim's death. Before the soul of the deceased has completely left the body, this spell halts its journey while repairing somewhat the damage to the body. This spell functions like *raise dead* (PH 268), except that the raised creature receives no level loss, no Constitution loss, and no loss of spells. The creature has –1 hit points (but is stable).

Material Component: Diamonds worth at least 1,000 gp.

RHINO'S RUSH

Transmutation
Level: Paladin 1, ranger 1, Wrath 1
Components: V, S
Casting Time: 1 swift action
Range: Personal
Target: You
Duration: 1 round

A violent fury consumes you. You seek nothing more than to charge at your enemies and bash in their heads.

This spell allows you to propel yourself in a single deadly charge. The first charge attack you make before the end of the round deals double damage on a successful hit.

RIGHTEOUS AURA

Abjuration [Good, Light]
Level: Paladin 4
Components: V, S, DF
Casting Time: 1 standard action
Range: Personal
Target: You
Duration: 1 hour/level

You invoke the powers of good and law, and in response to your pleas, you glow with the golden radiance of the sun.

You are bathed in an unearthly glow for the duration of the spell, as if a *daylight* spell (PH 216) had been cast on you. You get a +4 sacred bonus to Charisma.

If you die, your body is converted into an explosive blast of energy in a 20-foot-radius burst centered where you fell, dealing 2d6 points of damage per caster level (maximum 20d6) to all evil creatures in the burst's area. Good creatures in the area are healed by the same amount, and undead take double this damage. Spell resistance cannot prevent this damage, but a successful Reflex save reduces it to half. Your body is disintegrated, so you cannot be raised with a *raise dead* spell. Spells that do not require an intact body, such as *true resurrection*, can be used to bring you back to life as normal.

RIGHTEOUS FURY

Transmutation
Level: Paladin 3
Components: V, S, DF
Casting Time: 1 standard action
Range: Personal
Target: You
Duration: 1 minute/level

You pull a holy aura about you that glows a golden red.

Summoning the power of your deity, you charge yourself with positive energy. This gives you 5 temporary hit points per caster level (maximum 50) and a +4 sacred bonus to Strength. These temporary hit points last for up to 1 hour.

RIGHTEOUS WRATH OF THE FAITHFUL

Enchantment (Compulsion) [Mind-Affecting]
Level: Cleric 5, Purification 7
Components: V, S, DF
Casting Time: 1 standard action
Range: 30 ft.
Targets: Allies within a 30-ft.-radius burst centered on you
Duration: 1 round/level
Saving Throw: None
Spell Resistance: Yes

When you cast this spell, you fire your allies and companions with a divine madness or fury, greatly enhancing their combat ability.

Allies gain one additional melee attack each round, at their highest attack bonus, when making a full attack. (This additional attack is not cumulative with other effects that grant extra attacks, such as a *haste* spell.) They also gain a +3 morale bonus on melee attack rolls and damage rolls. (This bonus on melee attack rolls does stack with the bonus provided by *haste*.)

RING OF BLADES

Conjuration (Creation)
Level: Cleric 3
Components: V, S, M
Casting Time: 1 standard action
Range: Personal
Target: You
Duration: 1 minute/level

As you twirl the small dagger in your hand, it slowly fades from existence and is replaced by dozens of larger blades swirling about you in a horizontal ring.

This spell conjures a horizontal ring of swirling metal blades around you. The ring extends 5 feet from you, into all squares adjacent to your space, and it moves with you as you move. Each round, at the beginning of your turn, and also when you cast the spell, the blades deal 1d6 points of damage +1 point per caster level (maximum +10) to all creatures in the affected area.

Spell resistance does not apply to the damage dealt, but a creature's damage reduction does apply. The blades are treated as magic, silvered, and slashing for the purpose of overcoming damage reduction.

Material Component: A small dagger.

RUBY RAY OF REVERSAL

Abjuration
Level: Sorcerer/wizard 6
Components: V, S, F
Casting Time: 1 standard action
Range: Medium (100 ft. + 10 ft./level)
Target: One natural or magical hazard; see text
Duration: Instantaneous
Saving Throw: None
Spell Resistance: No

From your fingertips springs a thin line of bright red light to negate the hazard before you.

Each version of this spell can target one of the hazards described below and "correct" it in the manner described. Unless specifically stated otherwise, this spell affects magical and mundane hazards of the indicated type equally. For example, a *ruby ray of reversal* can eliminate the webs of a monstrous spider or the effect of a *web* spell.

- Any trap targeted by the ray is sprung. This version of the spell can have adverse effects on creatures standing within a trap's area. You must be aware of a trap to cast *ruby ray of reversal* on it.
- The spell unties knots and causes chains, manacles, and similar restraining devices to fall away. *Entangle* and similar magical effects are dispelled. Doors (or chests, drawers, cabinets, and so on) that are locked, barred, or under the effect of an *arcane lock* spell are opened.
- A 5-foot-diameter hole is created in a *wall of force*, *forcecage*, or similar spell or effect. This function of the spell does not destroy the targeted effect, but creatures trapped by it might be able to wriggle free.
- A creature that has been polymorphed, turned to stone, or otherwise transformed from its natural state is returned to its natural form.
- A *magic jar* spell is dispelled if a *ruby ray of reversal* targets the crystal holding the caster's soul.

- Webs, slime, grease, and other substances that would hamper movement are destroyed in a 20-foot-radius spread.

Focus: A ruby worth at least 500 gp.

RUIN DELVER'S FORTUNE

Transmutation
Level: Bard 4, sorcerer/wizard 4
Components: V
Casting Time: 1 immediate action
Range: Personal
Target: You
Duration: 1d4 rounds

In desperate need, you cry out a word imbued with power, granting you a bit of extra luck when you need it most.

When the spell is cast, choose from one of the following effects.

- Gain a luck bonus on Fortitude saving throws equal to your Charisma modifier, and immunity to poison.
- Gain a luck bonus on Reflex saving throws equal to your Charisma modifier, and the evasion ability.
- Gain a luck bonus on Will saving throws equal to your Charisma modifier, and immunity to fear effects.
- Gain temporary hit points equal to 4d8 + your Cha modifier. These hit points vanish at the end of the spell's duration.

You can cast this spell multiple times. Each time you do, choose a different benefit.

RUSHING WATERS

Conjuration (Creation) [Water]
Level: Druid 4
Components: V, S, DF
Casting Time: 1 standard action
Range: Medium (100 ft. + 10 ft./level)
Area: 15-ft.-radius spread
Duration: Instantaneous
Saving Throw: None; see text
Spell Resistance: No

You invoke the powers of nature, and a great fountain rises up before you, sending waves in all directions.

Cold water gushes in a great wave outward from the point you choose, violently spreading to the limits of the area. This wave makes a bull rush attempt against each creature in the affected area without provoking attacks of opportunity. The wave has a +15 bonus on the opposed Strength check. If the wave wins the opposed Strength check, the defender is moved 5 feet directly away from the spell's point of origin, plus an additional 5 feet for every 5 points by which the wave's check result exceeds that of the defender. Any creature moved 5 or more feet by *rushing waters* must succeed on a Reflex save or fall prone.

The wave also drenches anything in its area and extinguishes any normal fire as large as a bonfire.

The rust ray spell can destroy a weapon in the blink of an eye

Illus. by C. Frank

RUST RAY

Transmutation
Level: Sorcerer/wizard 3
Components: V, S, M
Casting Time: 1 standard action
Range: Close (25 ft. + 5 ft./2 levels)
Effect: Ray
Target: One nonmagical ferrous object or one ferrous creature
Duration: Instantaneous
Saving Throw: None or Fortitude negates (object); see text
Spell Resistance: No

You unleash a russet ray at a metallic object. The air around you smells of hot metal.

This russet ray corrodes metal that it touches. You must succeed on a ranged touch attack with the ray to strike a target. It can effectively destroy any nonmagical iron or iron alloy object. Such objects struck by a *rust ray* take 2d6 points of damage +1 per two caster levels (maximum +10), ignoring hardness. You can also target a weapon being wielded or metal armor being worn. Metal armor affected by this ray takes normal damage from the spell and loses 1d4 points of Armor Class through corrosion. If an item is reduced to 0 hit points, it is destroyed. Ferrous creatures struck by the ray take the same damage as objects.

Magic items can negate the effect with a successful Fortitude saving throw.

Material Component: Rust particles or a piece of a rust monster.

SACRED HAVEN

Abjuration [Good]
Level: Paladin 4
Components: V, S, DF
Casting Time: 1 standard action
Range: 30 ft.
Targets: You and allies in a 30-ft.-radius burst centered on you
Duration: 1 minute/level
Saving Throw: Will negates (harmless)
Spell Resistance: Yes (harmless)

A rosy glow passes from your hand and briefly spreads around you.

You and affected allies gain a +2 sacred bonus to Armor Class. In addition, while protected by this spell, an affected creature retains its Dexterity bonus to Armor Class when flat-footed or when struck by an invisible attacker.

For the duration of the spell, you gain awareness of the health of all affected creatures, as with the *status* spell (PH 284), and you need not be able to touch the affected creatures to heal them with your lay on hands ability. Use of the lay on hands ability still requires a standard action, but it can be done at any range, as long as you and your target are on the same plane.

SAFE CLEARING

Abjuration
Level: Ranger 3
Components: V, S
Casting Time: 10 minutes
Range: 30 ft.
Area: 30-ft.-radius emanation centered on you
Duration: 1 hour/level
Saving Throw: Will negates; see text
Spell Resistance: Yes

You press your hand against the ground and intone the ancient words. A green radiance spreads from your hand, forming a ring of translucent jade flames. "We're safe," you tell your allies, "for the moment."

You make an area safe from attacks. This spell's benefit functions much like that of the *sanctuary* spell (PH 274). The area of a *safe clearing* spell is immobile. Any creature attempting to strike or otherwise directly attack anyone within the *safe clearing*, or any creature attempting to enter the area, must make a Will save. Success means the creature can act normally and is not affected by this casting of the spell. Failure means it can't attack anyone in the area or even enter the area for the duration of the spell. Those not attempting to attack creatures in the warded area remain unaffected. This spell does not prevent creatures in the warded area from being attacked or affected by area spells.

A creature within the area that makes an attack is no longer protected by the spell, and can be targeted normally.

SAFETY

Abjuration
Level: Cleric 3
Components: V, S
Casting Time: 1 standard action
Range: Touch
Target: Creature touched
Duration: 10 minutes/level
Saving Throw: None or Will negates (harmless)
Spell Resistance: No or Yes (harmless)

After an intonation and clasping of the subject creature, you grant it knowledge of where safety lies.

The recipient of this spell can find the shortest, most direct direction to a place of safety, with safety being defined as a location where the individual is not taking immediate damage from the environment, and immediate damage is not imminent. It does not provide the means for the subject to move in that direction.

A *safety* spell points out the shortest distance out of a poisonous cloud, or the direction one should dig to reach the surface if entombed in earth. It does not function against the *maze* spell, because that spell deals no physical damage. Nor does the spell provide knowledge of or protection against the creatures that inhabit those safe places.

In the D&D cosmology (DMG 150), *safety* has the following effects when cast on specific planes.

Plane of Shadow: Shortest route out of darklands.

Elemental Plane of Air: Nearest windproof shelter, shortest route out of smoke bank.

Elemental Plane of Earth: Nearest air pocket or open cavern.

Elemental Plane of Fire: Shortest route out of magma pools or other unusually hot places.

Elemental Plane of Water: Nearest pocket of breathable air; shortest route out of hot spot, ice pocket, or red tide.

Negative Energy Plane: Nearest doldrum area with the minor negative-dominant trait.

Positive Energy Plane: Nearest edge zone with the minor positive-dominant trait.

Limbo: Nearest area of stabilized limbo.

Pandemonium: Nearest shelter from a windstorm.

Carceri: Shortest route out of a Minethys sandstorm.

Gehenna: Nearest flat ledge, nearest shelter from Mungoth's acidic snow.

Nine Hells: Nearest shelter from fireballs on Avernus, rockslides on Malbolge, or cold on Cania.

Acheron: Nearest shelter from Ocanthus bladestorms.

On planes you create yourself, *safety* might provide other information.

This spell is mostly used in hostile environments, such as one of the Inner Planes, to locate the nearest pocket of habitable space.

If *safety* is cast and then followed by a *plane shift* spell (PH 262), the *plane shift* sends the subject of *safety* to a place of relative safety on that plane. It is transported to a pocket of air on the Elemental Plane of Water, for example, or a cool spot on the Elemental Plane of Fire.

SALTRAY

Evocation
Level: Druid 2
Components: V, S
Casting Time: 1 standard action
Range: Close (25 ft. + 5 ft./2 levels)
Effect: Ray
Duration: Instantaneous
Saving Throw: Fortitude partial
Spell Resistance: Yes

A thin shaft of whirling salt crystals lances out from your crooked finger to strike and shred your foe.

You must succeed on a ranged touch attack with the ray to strike a target. A creature struck by a *saltray* takes 1d6 points of damage per two caster levels (maximum 5d6) and must make a Fortitude save or be stunned for 1 round.

SANCTUARY, MASS

Abjuration
Level: Balance 5, cleric 5
Range: Close (25 ft. + 5 ft./2 levels)
Targets: One creature/level, no two of which are more than 30 ft. apart

You cast this spell and you are infused with a clear, silvery aura. You touch each of your companions in turn, and they are infused with the aura as well.

This spell functions like *sanctuary* (PH 274), except that it affects multiple creatures.

SANDBLAST

Evocation
Level: Druid 1
Components: V, S, DF
Casting Time: 1 standard action
Range: 10 ft.
Area: 10-ft.-radius burst centered on you
Duration: Instantaneous
Saving Throw: Reflex half
Spell Resistance: Yes

Whipping your hand in a wide arc, you spray sand from your fingers in a powerful blast.

Creatures in the area take 1d6 points of nonlethal damage. Any creature that fails its Reflex save is also stunned for 1 round. You are not harmed by the spell.

SARCOPHAGUS OF STONE

Conjuration (Creation) [Earth]
Level: Cleric 6
Components: V, S, M, DF
Casting Time: 1 standard action
Range: Close (25 ft. + 5 ft./2 levels)
Target: 1 Medium or smaller creature
Duration: Instantaneous
Saving Throw: Reflex negates
Spell Resistance: No

The earth quakes as stone erupts from the ground and takes the form of a sarcophagus.

This spell creates an airtight stone coffin around the target. The stone is 1 inch thick, has hardness 8, and requires 15 points of damage to break through. Decreasing its size does not change the thickness of the walls; the coffin is always just large enough to hold the subject. This coffin is sealed upon formation and impervious to air and gas. A creature trapped within it has 1 hour worth of air, and after that time must hold its breath or begin to suffocate (DMG 304). A creature that has no need to breathe (such as a construct, elemental, or undead) needs not fear suffocation, but it remains trapped until it breaks free or is freed.

A creature within the coffin can attack the stone with a natural weapon or light melee weapon. A creature can attempt a DC 26 Strength check to break free of the stone, and allies can also help to break the trapped creature free.

Material Component: A fragment of a sarcophagus.

Encasing a foe in a sarcophagus of stone proves an effective—albeit grisly—tactic

Illus. by R. Spears

SCALE WEAKENING

Transmutation
Level: Sorcerer/wizard 2
Components: V, S, M
Casting Time: 1 standard action
Range: Close (25 ft. + 5 ft./2 levels)
Effect: Ray
Duration: 1 minute/level (D)
Saving Throw: None
Spell Resistance: Yes

As you cast this spell, the snakeskin vaporizes. A dull gray ray projects from your hand. Where the ray strikes, your foe's skin seems brittle and more frail.

You must succeed on a ranged touch attack with the ray to strike a target. The subject's natural armor bonus is reduced by 1 point per three caster levels (maximum reduction 5 points at 15th level). This spell can't reduce a creature's natural armor bonus to less than 0, nor does it have any effect on an enhancement bonus to natural armor (such as that granted by the *barkskin* spell).

Material Component: A shed snakeskin.

SCATTERSPRAY

Transmutation
Level: Sorcerer/wizard 1
Components: V, S
Casting Time: 1 standard action
Range: Close (25 ft. + 5 ft./2 levels)
Targets: Six or more Diminutive or Fine objects, all within 1 ft. of each other, whose total weight does not exceed 25 lb.
Duration: Instantaneous
Saving Throw: See text
Spell Resistance: No

With a single word and gesture, you send small, unattended objects flying about the room.

You can point to a collection of little, unsecured items and cause them to fly off in all directions simultaneously. The spray of items creates a burst with a 10-foot radius. If the items are fairly hard or sharp (such as stones, sling bullets, or coins), creatures in the burst take 1d8 points of damage. A successful Reflex save negates this damage. Eggs, fruit, and other soft objects can be used, but the damage is then nonlethal damage.

SCENT

Transmutation
Level: Druid 2, ranger 1
Components: V, S, M
Casting Time: 1 standard action
Range: Touch
Target: Creature touched
Duration: 10 minutes/level
Saving Throw: None
Spell Resistance: Yes (harmless)

At your touch, the creature inhales deeply, experiencing a new world of sensory input.

You give the creature touched the scent ability (MM 314).

Material Component: A sprinkle of mustard and pepper.

SCINTILLATING SCALES

Abjuration
Level: Sorcerer/wizard 2
Components: V
Casting Time: 1 standard action
Range: Personal
Target: You
Duration: 1 minute/level

You invoke the words of this spell, and your skin glistens and shimmers with a silvery protective aura that makes you shine.

This spell transforms your natural armor bonus to Armor Class into a deflection bonus to your Armor Class. While your overall Armor Class might not change, the deflection bonus applies to melee touch attacks and ranged touch attacks, including incorporeal touch attacks. If you have no natural armor bonus, this spell has no effect.

SCINTILLATING SPHERE

Evocation [Electricity]
Level: Sorcerer/wizard 3
Components: V, S, M
Casting Time: 1 standard action
Range: Long (400 ft. + 40 ft./level)
Area: 20-ft.-radius burst
Duration: Instantaneous
Saving Throw: Reflex half
Spell Resistance: Yes

You pinch the marble between your fingers and intone the spell. It flies from your fingers, trailing a smell of ozone, and grows into a ball of multicolored sparks that detonate in a burst of spherical lightning.

A *scintillating sphere* is a massive electrical discharge that deals 1d6 points of electricity damage per caster level (maximum 10d6) to every creature and unattended object within the area.

Material Component: A glass marble.

SCORCH

Evocation [Fire]
Level: Sorcerer/wizard 2
Components: V, S, F
Casting Time: 1 standard action
Range: 30 ft.
Area: 30-ft. line
Duration: Instantaneous
Saving Throw: Reflex half
Spell Resistance: Yes

A jet of roaring flame bursts from your outstretched hand, scorching any creature in its path.

Scorch deals 1d8 points of damage per two caster levels, to a maximum of 5d8 points of damage, to each target it hits.

Focus: A red dragon's scale.

SCOURGE

Necromancy
Level: Pestilence 7
Components: V, S, F, DF
Casting Time: 1 standard action
Range: Long (400 ft. + 40 ft./level)
Targets: One living creature/level, no two of which are more than 50 ft. apart
Duration: Instantaneous
Saving Throw: Fortitude negates
Spell Resistance: Yes

Picking out those you wish revenge upon, you cause their bodies to erupt in painful and debilitating blackened boils, magenta blotches, violet lesions, seeping abscesses, and malignant cysts.

The target creatures are infected with a vile disease unless they succeed on a Fortitude save. Once it has infected a creature, the disease immediately deals 1d6 points of Strength and Dexterity damage, and it deals the same damage each subsequent day. A creature is allowed an additional saving throw each day to avoid that day's damage. As with mummy rot (DMG 292), successful saves do not allow the creature to recover. The symptoms persist until the creature finds some magical means to remove the disease.

The disease can be removed by first casting *break enchantment* or *remove curse* on the subject (requiring a DC 20 caster level check for either spell), after which a *remove disease, heal,* or similar spell will cure the victim.

Focus: A black whip or riding crop, which is cracked in the direction of the intended victims during the casting of the spell.

SCRAMBLE PORTAL

Transmutation [Chaotic]
Level: Sorcerer/wizard 4
Components: V, S, M
Casting Time: 1 standard action
Range: Close (25 ft. + 5 ft./2 levels)
Target: One interplanar *gate* or portal
Duration: 1 round/level
Saving Throw: None (for portal)
Spell Resistance: No

You raise your hand and send a roiling ball of crackling, multicolored energy at the portal, knowing its chaotic power will give portal users a surprise.

You randomize the destination of one interplanar *gate* or portal for the duration of the spell. Anyone who passes through the portal from either side is sent to a random plane instead of the portal's normal destination.

Material Component: A cracked mirror.

SEAL PORTAL

Abjuration
Level: Sorcerer/wizard 6
Components: V, S, M
Casting Time: 1 standard action
Range: Close (25 ft. + 5 ft./2 levels)
Target: One interplanar *gate* or portal
Duration: Permanent (D)
Saving Throw: None
Spell Resistance: No

You cast a silver bar in the direction of the portal and it vanishes, becoming a semi-translucent net of silver magic that briefly encases the portal before disappearing.

You can permanently seal an interplanar *gate* or portal. The spell prevents any use of the portal, although *seal portal* can be dispelled by a *dispel magic* spell. A *knock* spell does not function on a sealed portal, but a *chime of opening* dispels *seal portal* if *seal portal* was cast by a spellcaster of lower than 15th level.

Once a portal is opened, *seal portal* does not remain in effect and must be cast again.

Material Component: A silver bar worth 50 gp.

SECOND WIND

Transmutation
Level: Paladin 1
Components: V, S, DF
Casting Time: 1 standard action
Range: Touch
Target: Creature touched
Duration: Instantaneous and 1 hour/level; see text
Saving Throw: Will negates (harmless)
Spell Resistance: Yes (harmless)

You feel slightly winded but energized, as if having just run a long distance but knowing you could run farther. When touching the spell's intended recipient, your breathing returns to normal but you note the spell's subject heaves a deep, refreshing breath.

This spell removes fatigue from a subject and provides a +4 bonus on Constitution checks for the duration of the spell. If the subject creature is exhausted when you cast this spell, its condition is improved to fatigued.

SEEK ETERNAL REST

Conjuration (Healing)
Level: Paladin 3
Components: V, DF
Casting Time: 1 standard action
Range: Personal
Target: You
Duration: 1 hour/level

You invoke the greater powers and are infused with a great, golden glow.

You improve your ability to turn undead. For the purpose of turning or destroying undead, you are treated as a cleric of your paladin level.

SENSE HERETIC

Divination
Level: Paladin 1
Components: V, S, DF
Casting Time: 1 standard action
Range: Touch
Target: Object touched
Duration: 10 minutes/level (D)
Saving Throw: None
Spell Resistance: No

Holding the target item aloft, you quietly chant the last few words to cast the spell. The item immediately flares a soft blue color, which fades almost immediately.

This spell is usually cast on a weapon or a holy symbol. If an evil creature that has the ability to cast divine spells comes within 100 feet of the item, the item begins to glow with a faint blue radiance. You cannot tell where, or in which direction, the detected creature is, only that such a creature is within range. The spell can penetrate barriers, but 1 foot of stone, 1 inch of common metal, a thin sheet of lead, or 3 feet of wood or dirt blocks it.

SENSORY DEPRIVATION

Illusion (Phantasm) [Mind-Affecting]
Level: Sorcerer/wizard 4
Components: V, S, M
Casting Time: 1 standard action
Range: Medium (100 ft. + 10 ft./level)
Target: One creature
Duration: 1 round/level
Saving Throw: Will disbelief
Spell Resistance: Yes

Your vision blurs, and sounds seem muffled as you cast the spell. Upon completing it, you release the spell's energy, freeing your senses from that which dampened them. The target of your spell glows for an instant with a black aura.

Rather than creating an illusion of something, this spell creates an illusion of absolute nothingness. The spell effect surrounds the subject in a dark, clinging shadow that only it perceives, which blocks all auditory, olfactory, taste, and visual sensations. In addition, it blocks finely tuned senses of touch such as those that provide a creature with tremorsense. A subject that fails its save is blinded and deafened, and it gains no benefit from blindsense, blindsight, scent, or tremorsense.

The subject retains any telepathic or empathic links it might possess with other creatures while affected by the spell.

Material Component: Black silk cloth tied like a blindfold.

SERENE VISAGE

Illusion (Glamer)
Level: Bard 1, sorcerer/wizard 1
Components: V, S
Casting Time: 1 standard action
Range: Personal
Target: You
Duration: 1 minute/level

By casting this spell, you imbue yourself with an ephemeral quality that induces others to trust what you say.

Simple illusions aid your attempts to be persuasive. You gain an insight bonus equal to one-half your caster level (maximum +10) on Bluff checks.

SERVANT HORDE

Conjuration (Creation)
Level: Sorcerer/wizard 3
Components: V, S, M
Casting Time: 1 standard action
Range: Close (25 ft. + 5 ft./2 levels)
Effect: Invisible, mindless, shapeless servants
Duration: 1 hour/level
Saving Throw: None
Spell Resistance: No

As you complete this spell, you sense a number of invisible entities form around you.

This spell creates a number of *unseen servants* (PH 297) equal to 2d6 +1 per level (maximum +15).

Material Component: A small stick to which many lengths of knotted thread are attached.

SHADOW BINDING

Illusion (Shadow)
Level: Sorcerer/wizard 3
Components: V, S, M
Casting Time: 1 standard action
Range: Close (25 ft. + 5 ft./2 levels)
Area: 10-ft.-radius burst
Duration: 1 round/level
Saving Throw: Will negates
Spell Resistance: Yes

As the links of chain in your hand dissipate to feed the arcane energies of your spell, a multitude of ribbonlike shadows instantaneously explodes outward from an indicated point nearby.

Creatures in the area that fail a Will save are entangled and unable to move. Breaking free of a *shadow binding* requires a DC 20 Strength check or a DC 20 Escape Artist check, taken as a full-round action.

Material Component: A few links of iron chain.

Shadow binding only entraps the weak-willed

competence bonus on Escape Artist, Hide, and Move Silently checks. Your shadowy form also provides you with concealment. This shadowy concealment is not negated by a *see invisibility* spell, but a *true seeing* spell counteracts the effect. Standing within the radius of a *daylight* spell or in bright natural sunlight temporarily suppresses the concealment effect.

In addition, if you have 5 ranks in Escape Artist, you can attempt to slip through a solid object or barrier up to 5 feet thick with a DC 20 Escape Artist check, though doing this ends the spell as soon as the attempt is completed (regardless of success). If you have 10 ranks in Escape Artist, you can attempt to pass through an object or barrier up to 10 feet thick. If you have 15 ranks in Escape Artist, you can attempt to pass through a barrier composed of magical force (or similar magical obstacles).

Material Component: A small piece of black cloth taken from a funeral shroud.

SHADOW CACHE

Illusion (Shadow)
Level: Bard 3, sorcerer/wizard 3
Components: V, S
Casting Time: 1 standard action
Range: Touch
Area: 1-ft.-diameter circle
Duration: 1 minute/level (D)
Saving Throw: No
Spell Resistance: No

With a flourish, you open an invisible portal. Plunging your arm inside, you see your hand vanish as though it were invisible.

You can temporarily stash small items on the Plane of Shadow (DMG 152) or permanently dispose of them there. This spell opens a small portal to the Plane of Shadow that is invisible on the Material Plane and appears as a small disk on the Plane of Shadow.

You can reach into the Plane of Shadow through the portal created by *shadow cache*, but only small, nonliving objects can pass entirely through the hole. The cache can hold up to 30 cubic feet of material, or 250 pounds.

You can recover objects placed in the portal throughout the duration of the spell, or by casting another *shadow cache* later. A *shadow cache* remains stationary at the point where you create it. Items placed in a *shadow cache* can possibly be picked up by natives of the Plane of Shadow, and in any event are slowly moved by the morphic trait of the plane. For every 24 hours that passes, there is a 10% chance each day that objects placed on the Plane of Shadow with *shadow cache* are gone (either moved or taken).

The spell cannot be cast on the Plane of Shadow itself, but only on planes coexistent with the Plane of Shadow.

SHADOW FORM

Illusion (Shadow)
Level: Assassin 4, sorcerer/wizard 5
Components: V, S, M
Casting Time: 1 standard action
Range: Personal
Target: You
Duration: 1 minute/level (D)

Shadows rise from the ground to envelop you. The shadows easily move with you, guiding your steps and how to hold your body.

While this spell is in effect, you gain a number of benefits. The shadows wrapping your form grant you a +4

SHADOW HAND

Illusion (Shadow)
Level: Sorcerer/wizard 5
Components: V, S
Casting Time: 1 standard action
Range: Close (25 ft. + 5 ft./2 levels)
Effect: Medium shadowy hand
Duration: 1 round/level (D)
Saving Throw: None
Spell Resistance: Yes

You intone the spell, and an enormous hand made out of thick gray fog floats in the air before you.

You create a floating Medium hand made of shadow material. A *shadow hand* is an opaque gray color, 5 feet long, and 5 feet wide with its fingers outstretched. It can grant total concealment against a single opponent you designate, carry materials as *Tenser's floating disk* (PH 294), or point or gesture as a normal hand does.

The hand has an AC of 18 (+6 natural, +2 deflection) and has half as many hit points as your full normal total. It can be damaged just as *Bigby's interposing hand* (PH 204) can be, and it makes all saving throws as if it were you.

Changing the hand's task or target is a standard action, and it can move anywhere in range. If not given any

Illus. by L. Parrillo

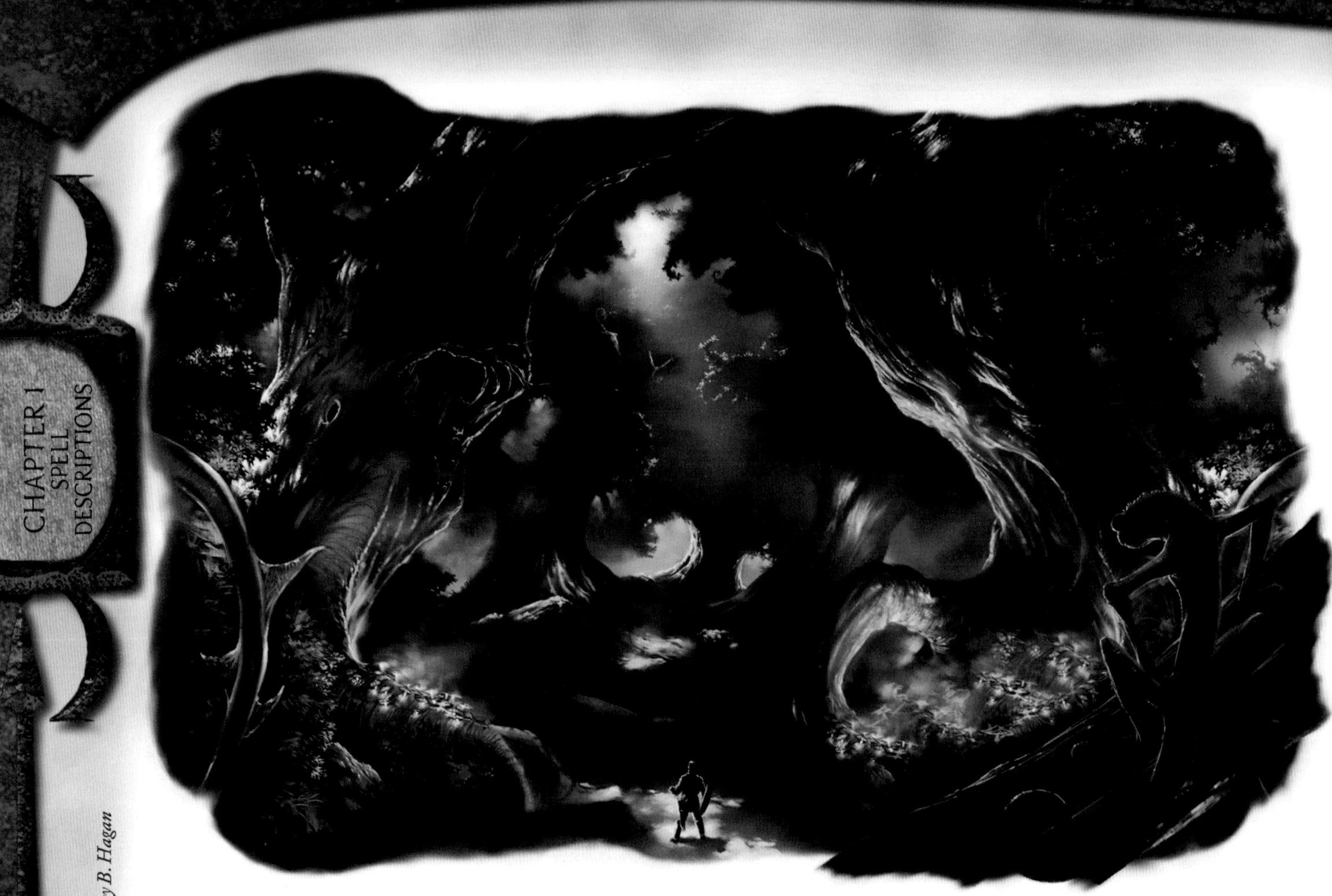

The shadow landscape spell brings a bit of the Plane of Shadow to the Material Plane

Illus. by B. Hagan

commands, the hand follows you at your speed, maintaining the same distance from you. The spell ends if the hand moves out of the spell's range.

If carrying items and commanded to do something else, the hand drops whatever it is holding to complete its task (you can order the hand to rid itself of items gently as a standard action). Unlike *Tenser's floating disk*, it does not have to follow you at a fixed distance—you direct where the hand goes.

SHADOW LANDSCAPE

Illusion (Shadow)
Level: Druid 9
Components: V, S, DF
Casting Time: 1 hour
Range: Long (400 ft. + 40 ft./level)
Area: One-mile-radius spread centered on a point in space
Duration: 24 hours/level (D)
Saving Throw: Reflex partial; see text
Spell Resistance: Yes

By infusing the nearby landscape with power stolen from the Plane of Shadow, you make the surrounding terrain a more savage, dangerous place.

The spell's exact effects vary with the terrain upon which it is cast.

Desert: The spell transforms a desert into a place where no one goes willingly. The average temperature increases by 30 degrees, or decreases by 30 degrees if the desert is actually a tundra (see Cold Dangers and Heat Dangers, DMG 302–303). Sandstorms (or snowstorms if in a tundra) blow through a *shadow landscape* desert on an hourly basis.

Forest: Forests augmented with a *shadow landscape* spell become frightening places where a canopy of rotting leaves blocks the sun and all the trees are strangely twisted. Spaces with light undergrowth have heavy undergrowth instead, and spaces covered with heavy undergrowth grasp at passersby as if an *entangle* spell (PH 227) had been cast on them (save DC equal to the *shadow landscape*'s DC).

Hill: Even gentle hills become more treacherous under the effect of a *shadow landscape* spell. Light undergrowth becomes heavy undergrowth in hill terrain, and slopes seem steeper than their elevation would indicate. It takes 2 squares of movement to move uphill on a gradual slope, and 4 squares to move uphill on a steep slope. Cliffs have frequent overhangs and are made of crumbling rock, requiring a DC 25 Climb check to ascend or descend.

Marsh: Marshes seem swampier and more forbidding. Half the undergrowth spaces in the marsh become quicksand (DMG 88).

Mountain: The mountains become places of jagged peaks, slippery slopes, and howling winds. Cliffs and chasms require a DC 25 Climb check to scale. Creatures who fail Climb checks or make loud noises have a 10% chance of starting an avalanche (DMG 90). Altitude effects are one category worse: areas lower than 5,000 feet are treated as the 5,000- to 15,000-foot category, and anything above 5,000 feet is treated as being above 15,000 feet.

Plain: Only natural grasslands change as a result of *shadow landscape*, but they become wide-open spaces with stands of thick bushes where thunderstorms and tornados are frequent. Half the spaces with undergrowth (light or heavy) grasp at passersby as if an *entangle* spell (PH 227) had been cast on them (save DC equal to the *shadow landscape*'s DC).

Underground: Ordinary dungeons aren't affected by *shadow landscape*, but naturally occurring caverns are. Natural stone floors take 4 squares of movement per space to enter. Stalagmites cover 10% of the available floor space.

In addition to terrain-specific effects, a *shadow landscape* spell worsens the weather within the spell's area. When rolling random weather (DMG 94), roll twice and take the higher result. In plains terrain, roll three times and take the highest result. This effect does not apply underground.

You don't suffer the terrain-specific effects (entangling terrain, hindrances to movement, altitude effects, higher Climb DCs, and so on) of a *shadow landscape* you created. When you cast *shadow landscape*, you can designate one creature per four caster levels as a designated traveler. Creatures so designated don't suffer the terrain-specific effects of the spell, but they're still subject to the bad weather.

You can also designate one or more animals, plants, or magical beasts native to the spell's area as shadow guardians of the landscape. You can designate 1 HD of creatures per caster level, split up however you like. For example, a 20th-level druid could designate two treants (7 HD each) and a dire wolf (6 HD) as shadow guardians. As long as the designated guardians remain within the spell's area, they have a friendly attitude toward you and the travelers you have designated, and they also gain the following special qualities: resistance to cold 10, darkvision out to 60 feet, damage reduction 5/magic, evasion, and low-light vision. If the creature already has one or more of these special qualities, use the better value.

SHADOW PHASE

Transmutation
Level: Assassin 4, sorcerer/wizard 3
Components: V, S
Casting Time: 1 standard action
Range: Touch
Target: Creature touched
Duration: 1 round/level (D)
Saving Throw: Fortitude negates (harmless)
Spell Resistance: Yes (harmless)

Your hand becomes slightly translucent as you complete the arcane gestures of the spell. As you touch the intended recipient, your hand appears solid again, while the subject's flesh takes on a dark, wispy, insubstantial appearance.

The spell temporarily transposes some of the subject's tissue with shadow-stuff, making the subject partially incorporeal. This partially incorporeal state does not allow the subject to pass through walls or other solid objects.

Nonmagical physical attacks directed against the spell's subject suffer a 50% miss chance. Magical attacks, such as supernatural and spell-like abilities, spells, and magic weapons, suffer a 20% miss chance.

SHADOW MASK

Illusion (Shadow)
Level: Sorcerer/wizard 2
Components: V, S, M
Casting Time: 1 standard action
Range: Personal
Target: You
Duration: 10 minutes/level (D)

You draw raw energy from the Plane of Shadow to obscure your face.

You cause a mask of shadows to form around your face. It does not impede your vision, cannot be physically removed, completely hides your features, and protects you against certain attacks. You receive a +4 bonus on saving throws against light or darkness spells and any spells that rely on bright light for damaging effects, such as the *flare* spell or the fireworks effect of *pyrotechnics*. You also gain a 50% chance each round to avoid having to make a saving throw against gaze attacks, just as if you averted your eyes. If you avert your eyes while using *shadow mask*, you get to check twice to see if you avoid having to make the saving throw.

When the spell's duration ends, the *shadow mask* fades over the course of 1d4 rounds (rather than immediately), giving you time to keep your face hidden by other means. A successful *dispel magic* cast against a *shadow mask* effectively ends the spell and causes the same slow fading.

Material Component: A mask of black cloth.

SHADOW RADIANCE

Illusion (Shadow)
Level: Sorcerer/wizard 2
Components: V, S, M
Casting Time: 1 standard action
Range: Medium (100 ft. + 10 ft./level)
Area: 20-ft.-radius burst centered on a point in space
Duration: 1 round/level
Saving Throw: Will disbelief (if interacted with)
Spell Resistance: Yes

Whispering the final syllable of the complicated formula, you cast the spell. Instantly, a blast of bright light fills the targeted area. From your vantage point, the spell's light glows like a torch, although you note some creatures turn away from it as if it were a blinding radiance.

This spell creates an intensifying illusion of bright light that affects all creatures within the area (except those that are sightless or blinded). Viewers that fail their saving throws see a burst of bright light on the first round and become blinded for 1 round. On subsequent rounds for the rest of the spell's duration, the affected creatures continue to perceive a bright light. If they take penalties in bright illumination, they take them for the duration of their exposure to this light. Additionally, they are dazzled while in the area of the spell. Those who escape the area of a *shadow radiance* spell completely recover within 1 round. Those who make their saves and those outside the initial burst see only the equivalent of torchlight emanating from the center of the area.

Material Component: A flame at least the size of a torch.

SHADOW SPRAY

Illusion (Shadow)
Level: Sorcerer/wizard 2
Components: V, S, M
Casting Time: 1 standard action
Range: Medium (100 ft. + 10 ft./level)
Area: 5-ft.-radius burst
Duration: Instantaneous
Saving Throw: Fortitude negates
Spell Resistance: Yes

As you finish casting this spell, ribbonlike shadows burst outward from the midst of your foes.

You cause a multitude of ribbonlike shadows to instantaneously explode outward from the point of origin. Creatures in the area take 4 points of Strength damage and are dazed for 1 round.

Material Component: A handful of black ribbons.

SHADOW WELL

Illusion (Shadow)
Level: Sorcerer/wizard 4
Components: V, S
Casting Time: 1 standard action
Range: Close (25 ft. + 5 ft./2 levels)
Target: One creature
Duration: 1 round/level
Saving Throw: Will negates; see text
Spell Resistance: Yes

You spit out the words of the spell, and the shadow of your foe darkens, becoming a solid black pit. Your opponent pinwheels its arms as it topples backward into the darkness.

You cause the target's shadow to become a temporary gateway to a pocket realm within the Plane of Shadow. The target must make a Will save or be pulled into the gateway. Inside the pocket realm, the creature sees a deserted, gloomy duplicate of the real world, while shadowy phantasms stalk and taunt it without causing actual harm. Each round, the creature can attempt another Will save to return from the *shadow well*. Otherwise, the subject returns to the real world when the spell's duration expires.

Being trapped in a *shadow well* can be terrifying; upon returning to the real world, the subject must succeed on another Will save or be frightened for 1d4 rounds.

Upon leaving the pocket realm, the subject reappears in the spot it had been in when the *shadow well* spell was cast. If this spot is filled with a solid object, the subject appears in the nearest adjacent empty space.

Spells and abilities that move a creature within a plane, such as *teleport* and *dimension door*, do not help a creature escape a *shadow well* spell, although a *plane shift* spell allows it to flee to another plane as normal. The target might still become frightened upon leaving.

SHADOWBLAST

Evocation [Light]
Level: Cleric 4, druid 4
Components: V, S, M
Casting Time: 1 standard action
Range: Long (400 ft. + 40 ft./level)
Area: 20-ft.-radius spread
Duration: Instantaneous
Saving Throw: Fortitude negates
Spell Resistance: Yes

Light flashes bright and white for an instant in the area of this spell, dispersing portals to the Plane of Shadow and stunning the unnatural creatures that fear the light.

Natives of the Plane of Shadow caught in a *shadowblast* are stunned for 1d6 rounds if they fail a Fortitude saving throw. Shadow natives that are also undead or vulnerable to light take an additional 2d10 points of damage if they fail a second Fortitude save. Creatures that fail either Fortitude save cannot use spell-like or supernatural abilities to open any portal to the Plane of Shadow for 3d6 minutes.

Shadowblast closes all portals, *gates*, and other openings to the Plane of Shadow in its area. Creatures on the other side of a portal are unaffected by *shadowblast*.

Material Component: A handful of grave dirt, squeezed tightly and flung.

SHADOWFADE

Illusion (Shadow)
Level: Sorcerer/wizard 5
Components: V, S
Casting Time: 1 standard action
Range: Close (25 ft. + 5 ft./2 levels)
Effect: One 10-ft. portal to the Plane of Shadow
Duration: 1 minute/level
Saving Throw: Will negates
Spell Resistance: Yes

Summoning to mind a dark reflection of the world around you, you inscribe a doorway into the air with your hand, opening a portal to the Plane of Shadow.

You open a 10-foot-diameter portal onto the Plane of Shadow, allowing you and creatures you designate within range to pass into that area. This does not grant you the ability to open another such portal automatically, so the spell is often used as a temporary hiding place or a method of gaining access to the Plane of Shadow.

The portal remains for the duration of the spell, and other creatures can pass through it in either direction if they make a Will save. The portal is invisible from the Material Plane and looks like a white hole on the Plane of Shadow.

You must be in a region of heavy shadows to cast *shadowfade*. The spell can be cast only on a plane coexistent with the Plane of Shadow (DMG 152), and it cannot be cast on the Plane of Shadow itself.

SHADOWY GRAPPLER

Illusion (Shadow)
Level: Sorcerer/wizard 6
Components: V, S, M
Range: Medium (100 ft. + 10 ft./level)
Target: One creature
Duration: 1 round/level (D)
Saving Throw: Will partial; see text
Spell Resistance: Yes

You feel a spectral force form near you, as if some intangible shadow being stood nearby. Upon choosing the target of your spell, you sense the shadowy force depart from your side, moving as fast as thought toward the creature you designated as your target. You see the target creature move as if attacked by an unseen foe.

Upon casting this spell, you create a shadowy force that automatically grabs the target (PH 156). The shadowy force immediately attempts to establish a hold on the target with a grapple check bonus equal to the DC of this spell. If the target succeeds on its saving throw, the grapple check bonus of the *shadowy grappler* is cut in half. For example, a sorcerer with a 16 Charisma who casts this spell creates a *shadowy grappler* with a grapple check bonus of +19 if the target fails its save and +9 if the target makes its save.

Every round on your turn, the *shadowy grappler* makes a grapple check against the target. Once it has a hold, the shadowy force attempts to pin the target on the following round. If the grappler establishes a pin, it uses the option to prevent the target from speaking. The grappler always attempts to maintain a grapple or work toward a pin.

A *shadowy grappler* occupies the same square as the target and moves with the target for as long as the spell lasts. Other creatures cannot join the grapple, either to assist the target or the grappler.

Material Component: A dried squid tentacle.

SHARD STORM

Evocation [Force]
Level: Sorcerer/wizard 5
Components: V, S, M
Casting Time: 1 standard action
Range: Medium (100 ft. + 10 ft./level)
Effect: One or more 20-ft.-radius bursts of piercing force
Duration: 1 round/level
Saving Throw: Reflex half
Spell Resistance: Yes

Tossing the shard from your grasp, you complete the spell. An instant later, translucent shards of arcane energy blast the area you designated. In addition to deadly shards, the area fills with the chiming sound of shattering glass.

Immediately upon completion of this spell, and once per round thereafter, you can cause minuscule shards of magical force to explode out in a 20-foot-radius burst from the point of origin. The storm deals 3d6 points of force damage to all creatures within the radius. A successful Reflex save halves the damage.

Each round at the beginning of your turn, creatures in the area take an additional 3d6 points of force damage. You can use a free action to suppress the storm for that round.

Material Component: A small shard of clear glass or crystal.

Shard storm harms corporeal and incorporeal foes alike

SHARE HUSK

Divination
Level: Druid 2
Components: V, S, M
Casting Time: 1 standard action
Range: Touch
Target: Animal touched
Duration: 1 minute/level
Saving Throw: Will negates (harmless)
Spell Resistance: Yes

As the bit of dried food vanishes from your hand, you gain a wolf's-eye view of the world—and a wolf's-nose view as well.

You sense through an animal's senses, seeing through its eyes and hearing through its ears. While doing so, you use either your Listen or Spot modifiers or the animal's, whichever is better. This spell gives you no special ability to understand what you sense.

You can switch your perceptions between the animal's and your own on your turn as a free action. You and the animal must be on the same plane for the spell to function.

Material Component: An edible treat that would appeal to the animal (vegetable or meat).

SHARPTOOTH

Transmutation
Level: Sorcerer/wizard 4
Components: V, S
Casting Time: 1 standard action
Range: Personal
Target: You
Duration: 1 round/level

You cast this spell, and your jaws glow with yellow, eldritch power, your muscles grow more powerful, and your teeth become sharper.

Choose one of your natural weapons (or your unarmed strike if you have no natural weapons). For the duration of the spell, that method of attack deals damage as though you were one size category larger than your actual size. This spell does not stack with itself.

SHATTERFLOOR

Evocation [Sonic]
Level: Sorcerer/wizard 3
Components: V, S, F
Casting Time: 1 standard action
Range: Medium (100 ft. + 10 ft./level)
Area: 15-ft.-radius spread
Duration: Instantaneous
Saving Throw: Reflex half
Spell Resistance: Yes

Illus. by R. Horsley

You strike the bell with the hammer and evoke a loud thrumming vibration. It quickly builds to a painful crescendo, then fades. In its wake it leaves a circle of crushed stone and rubble.

Creatures and objects in the area take 1d4 points of sonic damage per caster level (maximum 10d4), and can make a saving throw to take half damage. If the floor of the area is made of stone, wood, ice, or material with hardness less than those, the floor is pulverized, resulting in an area of difficult terrain composed of soft dust, wood fragments, or loose crushed ice, as appropriate.

Focus: A miniature hammer and bell worth at least 10 gp.

SHELTERED VITALITY

Abjuration
Level: Cleric 4, druid 4
Components: V, S, DF
Casting Time: 1 standard action
Range: Touch
Target: Living creature touched
Duration: 1 minute/level
Saving Throw: Fortitude negates (harmless)
Spell Resistance: Yes (harmless)

Pressing your hand to the creature's chest, you utter a low chant, and a warm glow passes from your hand into the subject.

The subject gains immunity to fatigue, exhaustion, and ability damage or ability drain (regardless of the source).

SHIELD OF FAITH, MASS

Abjuration
Level: Cleric 4
Range: Close (25 ft. + 5 ft./2 levels)
Targets: One creature/level, no two of which are more than 30 ft. apart

You hold your arms aloft and implore the power you venerate. Your comrades are bathed in a silver light, and over their hearts appears the symbol of your god, showing the deity's protection.

This spell functions like *shield of faith* (PH 278), except that it affects multiple allies at a distance.

Illus. by D. Martin

The shieldbearer spell can prove better than the shield spell

SHIELD OF WARDING

Abjuration [Good]
Level: Cleric 3, paladin 2
Components: V, S
Casting Time: 1 standard action
Range: Touch
Target: One shield or buckler touched
Duration: 1 minute/level
Saving Throw: Will negates (object, harmless)
Spell Resistance: No

You press your palm against the shield and speak the words of power. A silver radiance, in the shape of your holy symbol spreads over the shield.

The touched shield or buckler grants its wielder a +1 sacred bonus to Armor Class and on Reflex saves, +1 per five caster levels (maximum +5 at 20th level). The bonus applies only when the shield is worn or carried normally (but not, for instance, if it is slung over the shoulder).

SHIELDBEARER

Transmutation
Level: Sorcerer/wizard 1
Components: V, S
Casting Time: 1 standard action
Range: Touch
Target: Shield touched
Duration: 1 round/level
Saving Throw: None
Spell Resistance: No

A feeling of protectiveness and guardianship fills you as you complete the spell. Touching the target shield, you point to the creature it is meant to protect and watch as the shield rises in the air and floats gently toward the indicated creature.

A *shieldbearer* spell allows you to enchant one shield so that it hovers near and attempts to protect one creature of your choice. The spell's recipient is chosen at the time of casting and cannot be changed. The enchanted shield remains within 1 foot of the creature for the duration of the spell. The shield's subject is then granted a shield bonus to AC as if it was wearing the shield. The spell permits the enchanted shield's subject to use a two-handed weapon or a weapon in each hand and still benefit from the shield's effect.

Shield bonuses from multiple sources, including multiple castings of this spell, do not stack.

SHIFTING PATHS

Illusion (Glamer)
Level: Druid 7, sorcerer/wizard 8
Components: V, S
Casting Time: 10 minutes
Range: Medium (100 ft. + 10 ft./level)
Area: 1-mile radius + 1 mile/level

Duration: 1 hour/level
Saving Throw: Will disbelief (if interacted with)
Spell Resistance: Yes

As if a massive cloth were sweeping it away, the path before you becomes hidden in shadows and false underbrush. At the same moment, a new path appears from the point you designate, wandering off in a different direction.

This spell simultaneously hides a path or road specified by you, while simultaneously creating an illusory path. The illusory path starts at a point chosen by you within the range of the spell. It continues in the direction you indicate, to the limit of the spell's area, where it ends abruptly. The illusory path avoids obstacles and provides no bridges, stairs, ladders, ramps, or other methods of traversing such obstacles. There is no way to force the illusory path to lead over a cliff or across a river more than 4 feet deep.

Those who fail their Will saves struggle along the illusory path. If vegetation or rough terrain slows their progress, they believe the path is sloping enough to justify the reduced speed. Those who succeed on their Will saves see both paths, but the illusory path is shadowy and obviously unreal.

SHOCK AND AWE

Enchantment [Mind-Affecting]
Level: Assassin 1, bard 1, sorcerer/wizard 1
Components: V, S
Casting Time: 1 swift action
Range: Close (25 ft. + 5 ft./2 levels)
Targets: One creature/level, no two of which are more than 30 ft. apart.
Duration: 1 round
Saving Throw: None
Spell Resistance: Yes

Upon completing this spell, you feel a nagging compulsion to divert your attention from your enemies. Shaking off the feeling, you note with satisfaction that your targeted enemies seem even more distracted than you.

This spell distracts its targets, preventing them from reacting with the deftness they might otherwise possess. Only effective when cast in the surprise round of combat and against flat-footed creatures, this spell causes those it affects to take a –10 penalty on their next initiative check. Targets that cannot be caught flat-footed (such as a rogue with uncanny dodge) cannot be affected by this spell.

SHROUD OF FLAME

Evocation [Fire]
Level: Sorcerer/wizard 5
Components: V, S, M
Casting Time: 1 standard action
Range: Medium (100 ft. + 10 ft./level)
Target: One creature
Duration: 1 round/level
Saving Throw: None
Spell Resistance: Yes

You snap your fingers, and a small explosion of black smoke results. Nearby, one of your foes bursts into flames.

This spell causes a creature to take 2d6 points of fire damage in each round of the spell's duration. The *shroud of flame* around the creature sheds bright illumination out to 40 feet and negates any concealment the creature might have.

Immersing the subject creature in a nonflammable liquid ends the spell.

Material Component: A pinch of saltpeter, a small piece of phosphorus, and a scrap of lace cloth or a spiderweb.

SHROUD OF UNDEATH

Necromancy
Level: Cleric 2, sorcerer/wizard 2
Components: V, S, M
Casting Time: 1 standard action
Range: Personal
Target: You
Duration: 10 minutes/level (D)

You are bathed with a dappled white light. Where it strikes your body, your flesh grows momentarily pale and ancient, then returns to normal.

You shroud yourself with invisible negative energy so that nonintelligent undead creatures perceive you as a fellow undead, ignoring you. Your appearance does not change, and while intelligent undead do not immediately recognize you as alive, they are likely to question whether you are actually undead. If used in conjunction with a disguise or illusion to appear undead, this spell gives you a +5 bonus on your Disguise check.

When you are affected by this spell, *inflict* spells heal you and *cure* spells hurt you. You are treated as if you were undead for the purpose of all spells and effects that specifically affect undead creatures. A successful turning or rebuking attempt against you (treating you as an undead of your Hit Dice) ends this spell but does not otherwise affect you.

If you attack an undead creature while this spell is in effect, the spell immediately ends.

Material Component: Dust or bone fragments from any destroyed undead creature.

SIGN

Enchantment (Compulsion) [Mind-Affecting]
Level: Cleric 1
Components: V, S, M
Casting Time: 1 standard action
Range: Personal
Target: You
Duration: 10 minutes/level or until discharged

The tea leaves burst into flames between your fingers, and for a brief moment you see the future in the billowing smoke.

You get a +4 bonus on your next initiative check.

Material Component: A small piece of dried goat intestine or some tea leaves.

SIGN OF SEALING

Abjuration
Level: Sorcerer/wizard 3
Components: V, S, M
Casting Time: 1 round
Range: Close (25 ft. + 5 ft./2 levels)
Target: One door, chest, or other opening up to 30 sq. ft./level
Duration: Permanent
Saving Throw: Reflex half; see text
Spell Resistance: No

While pointing at the target, you trace the lines of a complicated sigil that visually appears where it is to seal. The sigil glows with latent magical energy.

You seal a door, chest, or similar closure with a prominent magical sigil that bars entry and prevents opening. A door or object protected by this spell can be opened only by breaking (add 10 to the normal break DC) or by the use of *knock* or *dispel magic*. If the door or object is forced open by any means (magical or physical), the *sign of sealing* deals 1d4 points of damage per caster level (maximum 10d4) in a 30-foot radius (Reflex half).

A *knock* spell doesn't negate or automatically bypass a *sign of sealing*, but will suppress the sign for 10 minutes on a successful caster level check (DC 11 + the caster level of the sign's creator). A *sign of sealing* is a magic trap that can be disarmed with a DC 28 Disable Device check. You can pass your own sign safely, and it remains set behind you.

Material Component: A crushed emerald worth 100 gp.

SIGN OF SEALING, GREATER

Abjuration
Level: Sorcerer/wizard 6
Casting Time: 10 minutes
Target: One door, chest, or other opening or open space up to 30 sq. ft./level

This spell functions like *sign of sealing*, except that it can also be used to seal an open space (such as a corridor or an archway), creating a magical barrier of force that repels any creature attempting to pass. In addition, doors and objects protected by a *greater sign of sealing* are strengthened, increasing their hardness by 10 and granting them an extra 5 hit points per caster level. Any object protected by a *greater sign of sealing* is treated as a magic item for the purpose of making saving throws and gains a +4 resistance bonus on saving throws. If its seal is broken, a *greater sign of sealing* deals 1d6 points of damage per caster level (maximum 20d6) in a 40-foot radius (Reflex half).

A *greater sign of sealing* cannot be passed with a *knock* spell, but it can be dispelled (DC 15 + the caster level of the sign's creator). It can be disarmed with a DC 31 Disable Device check.

Material Component: A crushed emerald worth at least 500 gp.

SILENT PORTAL

Illusion (Glamer)
Level: Assassin 1, sorcerer/wizard 0
Components: S
Casting Time: 1 standard action
Range: Close (25 ft. + 5 ft./2 levels)
Target: One portal

The sink spell defeats even the best swimmer

Illus. by B. Hagan

Duration: 1 minute/level (D)
Saving Throw: Will negates (object)
Spell Resistance: Yes (object)

The door squeaks slightly as you force it. You pause and wave your finger in a pattern along the opening and it silences.

This simple cantrip negates the sound of opening and closing a single portal (door, window, gate, drawer, chest lid, or the like). Even the squeakiest door opens without a sound when under the effect of this spell. *Silent portal* covers only the normal means of opening and closing the targeted portal. Breaking a window or kicking in a door still makes noise, but opening a door that is loosely hanging by its hinges does not (since this is the normal way a door would be opened). Portals composed of magical energy are not affected by this spell.

In the case of magic or even intelligent portals, spell resistance and a Will save (DC 10 + caster's ability modifier + other modifiers as appropriate) apply.

SILVERBEARD

Transmutation
Level: Paladin 1
Components: V, DF
Casting Time: 1 standard action
Range: Personal
Target: You
Duration: 1 minute/level

You evoke the greater powers of good, and your beard stiffens, turning metallic and reaching halfway down your chest, giving you greater protection.

Your beard grows and turns to pure and magically hardened silver, providing you with a +2 sacred bonus to AC. If you do not have a beard, you grow one for the duration of this spell (even if you are a creature that cannot normally grow a beard, such as an elf or a female human). You get a +2 circumstance bonus on Diplomacy checks against dwarves.

SINK

Transmutation
Level: Cleric 3, druid 3
Components: V, S, DF
Casting Time: 1 standard action
Range: Close (25 ft. + 5 ft./2 levels)
Targets: One creature/3 levels, no two of which are more than 30 ft. apart
Duration: 1 round
Saving Throw: Will negates
Spell Resistance: Yes

Casting this spell makes the water around the spell's targets roil. Each target begins struggling against the water, as if trying hard merely to stay afloat.

When this spell is cast, it causes the targets, which must be currently in water or another liquid, to sink. Each subject descends 100 feet down into the liquid (or to the bottom, if the liquid is not deep enough). Affected creatures can then swim up normally. Once on the bottom, a creature must still make a Swim check to move, or else it can move along the bottom at one-quarter its land speed.

SIRINE'S GRACE

Evocation
Level: Bard 4, druid 5
Components: V, S, M
Casting Time: 1 standard action
Range: Personal
Target: You
Duration: 1 round/level

Upon completion of this spell, you are infused with unearthly grace and confidence.

For the duration of this spell, you gain a +4 enhancement bonus to Charisma and Dexterity, a deflection bonus to AC equal to your Charisma modifier, and a +8 bonus on Perform checks. You also gain a swim speed of 60 feet and the ability to breathe water. You can move and attack normally while underwater, even with slashing or bludgeoning weapons.

Material Component: A shard of mirror.

SKELETAL GUARD

Necromancy [Evil]
Level: Sorcerer/wizard 8
Components: V, S, M
Casting Time: 1 standard action
Range: Touch
Target: One or more fingerbones
Duration: Instantaneous
Saving Throw: None
Spell Resistance: No

Shaking the fingerbones in your hand like dice, you coat them in shadowy energy. As you cast them to the ground to complete the spell, animate skeletons spring up where you threw the bones.

You create a number of loyal skeletons from fingerbones. Treat all skeletons as human warrior skeletons (MM 226), except that each one has turn resistance equal to your caster level – 1. You can create one skeleton per caster level. These skeletons count toward the number of Hit Dice of undead you can have in your control (4 HD per caster level, as with *animate dead*).

Material Component: One finger bone from a humanoid and one onyx gem worth 50 gp per skeleton to be created.

SKULL WATCH

Necromancy
Level: Cleric 3, sorcerer/wizard 3
Components: V, S, F
Casting Time: 1 standard action
Range: Touch
Target: One humanoid skull
Duration: Permanent
Saving Throw: See text
Spell Resistance: No

You lift the skull into the air and it floats gently out of your grasp, its eye sockets locked on a distant point.

The skull affected by a *skull watch* spell floats gently 5 feet off the ground, facing a direction you choose. It monitors an area 20 feet wide by 90 feet long, though walls and other opaque barriers can curtail this area. If any Tiny or larger living creature enters the area guarded by the skull, it emits a piercing shriek that can be heard up to a quarter mile away. Every creature within 60 feet of the skull when it shrieks must make a Fortitude save or be deafened for 1d6 rounds. Whether or not you can hear this audible alarm, you instantly become aware that the effect has been triggered, provided you are on the same plane as it is. The alarm resets 1d4 rounds later.

When you cast the spell, you can specify creatures that will not trigger the alarm. The skull can be moved from its original position by anyone who can get to it without entering its monitored area. The skull has AC 12, hardness 1, and 1 hit point per caster level. You are not magically made aware of the skull's destruction if it has not been triggered.

Focus: The humanoid skull upon which the spell is cast.

SLAPPING HAND

Evocation [Force]
Level: Sorcerer/wizard 2
Components: V, S, F
Casting Time: 1 standard action
Range: Medium (100 ft. + 10 ft./level)
Effect: One Tiny hand
Duration: Instantaneous
Saving Throw: None; see text
Spell Resistance: Yes

You complete the spell and blow into the leather glove. Immediately a blue-white, translucent hand appears next to the enemy and smacks it across the side of the head—not enough to hurt it, but hard enough to give others nearby a chance to attack.

This spell distracts the subject, causing it to immediately provoke attacks of opportunity from creatures threatening its space. The spell allows no saving throw, but a slapped creature can negate the effect with a DC 20 Concentration check.

Focus: A leather glove.

SLASHING DARKNESS

Evocation
Level: Cleric 3
Components: V, S
Casting Time: 1 standard action
Range: Medium (100 ft. + 10 ft./level)
Effect: Ray
Duration: Instantaneous
Saving Throw: None
Spell Resistance: Yes

You complete this spell and a hissing, hurtling ribbon of pure darkness flies from your hand.

You must succeed on a ranged touch attack with the ray to strike a target. A creature struck by this ray of negative energy takes 1d8 points of damage per two caster levels (maximum 5d8). An undead creature instead heals 1d8 points of damage per two caster levels (maximum 5d8).

SLIDE

Transmutation
Level: Sorcerer/wizard 1
Components: V
Casting Time: 1 standard action
Range: Close (25 ft. + 5 ft./2 levels)
Target: One creature
Duration: Instantaneous
Saving Throw: Will negates
Spell Resistance: Yes

When you speak the word that activates the spell, the soles of your ally's feet glow yellow

Illus. by E. Polak

Green slime from a slime wave spell devours everything but stone

as he is lifted slightly off the ground. He slips five feet across the ground, into position to flank his opponent.

You slide the subject creature along the ground a distance of 5 feet in any direction. (If the creature is flying or otherwise not on the ground, it moves parallel to the ground.) You can't slide the subject into a space that is occupied by an ally, an enemy, or a solid object; if you attempt to do so, the spell automatically ends. You cannot slide the subject up or down, but you can slide it over the edge of a cliff or other drop-off if you desire.

This movement does not provoke attacks of opportunity.

SLIDE, GREATER

Transmutation
Level: Sorcerer/wizard 2
Range: Medium (100 ft. + 10 ft./level)

This spell functions like *slide*, except as described above, and you can slide the subject creature 20 feet in a straight line. This movement likewise does not provoke attacks of opportunity.

SLIME WAVE

Conjuration (Summoning)
Level: Cleric 7, druid 7
Components: V, S, M
Casting Time: 1 standard action
Range: Close (25 ft. + 5 ft./2 levels)
Area: 15-ft.-radius spread
Duration: 1 round/level
Saving Throw: Reflex negates
Spell Resistance: No

You finish the spell, and a horrendous wave of green slime explodes outward from the spot where you point.

You create a wave of green slime (DMG 76) that begins at the point of origin you choose and violently spreads to the limit of the area. The wave splashes and splatters as it passes; some slime clings to any wall or ceiling the wave touches. Green slime devours flesh and organic materials on contact, and even dissolves metal. Each creature in the area is covered with one patch of green slime. Unlike normal green slime, the slime created by this spell gradually evaporates, disappearing by the end of the duration.

Material Component: A few drops of stagnant pond water.

SLOW BURN

Transmutation [Fire]
Level: Druid 1, sorcerer/wizard 1
Components: V, S, M/DF
Casting Time: 1 standard action
Range: Medium (100 ft. + 10 ft./level)
Area: 30-ft.-radius spread
Duration: 1 minute
Saving Throw: None
Spell Resistance: No

The desire to live into old age grips you as you near completion of this spell. The feeling passes as you designate the area of the spell, where the flames there flicker for a moment as if a gust of wind had hit them.

This spell lends fuel to existing fires within the spell's area, allowing them to burn off the intangible power of passion as much as from physical substance. Because these fires consume less of the physical fuel that sustain them, they burn for twice as long without losing any of their intensity, but their illumination radius is halved.

In addition, an affected fire is much harder to extinguish. It takes twice as long to put out a fire that is under the effect of this spell, and if a roll is required (such as the Reflex save required to extinguish flames if a creature is on fire), two successful rolls over 2 rounds are required to successfully put out the fire. If one such roll fails, the creature must begin trying to extinguish the flames again as if it had never succeeded on the first roll.

Magical fire used against a target in this spell's area, such as from a *produce flame* or *fireball* spell, does not burn as effectively, and fire damage from such sources is reduced by 1 point per die.

Slow burn counters or dispels the effect of *raging flame* (page 164).

Arcane Material Component: An oil-filled hourglass.

SMELL OF FEAR

Transmutation
Level: Ranger 1
Components: V, S
Casting Time: 1 standard action
Range: Touch
Target: Creature touched
Duration: 1 minute/level
Saving Throw: Will negates
Spell Resistance: Yes

Your hand glows red briefly upon casting this spell, and after you slap your foe on the back, you try to hide a grin.

You bestow on your target an aroma that attracts predatory animals. They prefer to attack the subject over other targets, and animals attacking the subject creature gain a +1 bonus per three caster levels (maximum +3) on attack rolls and damage rolls.

SNAKE'S SWIFTNESS

Transmutation
Level: Druid 1, sorcerer/wizard 2
Components: V, S, M/DF
Casting Time: 1 standard action
Range: Close (25 ft. + 5 ft./2 levels)
Target: One allied creature
Duration: Instantaneous
Saving Throw: Will negates (harmless)
Spell Resistance: Yes (harmless)

You toss the scales into the air, and they vanish in a sparkling mist as you indicate your target. Without hesitating, that creature draws and fires an arrow into the fray.

The subject can immediately make one melee or ranged attack. Taking this action doesn't affect the subject's normal place in the initiative order. This is a single attack and follows the standard rules for attacking.

This spell does not allow the subject to make more than one additional attack in a round. If the subject has already made an additional attack, due to a prior casting of this spell, from the *haste* spell, or from any other source, this spell fails.

Arcane Material Component: A few scales from a snake.

SNAKE'S SWIFTNESS, MASS

Transmutation
Level: Druid 2, sorcerer/wizard 3
Range: Medium (100 ft. + 10 ft./level)
Targets: Allied creatures in a 20-ft.-radius burst

You hold the snake scales high overhead, and they evaporate in a flash of light. That radiance carries to every ally in your command—and as one, they unleash a volley of attacks.

This spell functions like *snake's swiftness*, except that it affects multiple allies out to medium range.

SNAKEBITE

Transmutation
Level: Druid 3, ranger 4
Components: V, S
Casting Time: 1 standard action
Range: Personal
Target: You
Duration: 1 round/level (D)

You cast the spell, and one of your arms turns into a venomous bright-green snake with a fanged, biting mouth that drips poison.

This spell transforms one of your arms into a poisonous serpent. As an attack action, you can strike an opponent with your snake arm by making a successful melee attack. The bite from the venomous serpent deals damage equal to 1d3 points + your Str modifier, and it carries a toxic venom that deals 2 points of Constitution damage as initial and secondary damage. Each instance of ability damage can be negated by a Fortitude save (DC equal to this spell's DC).

You can't hold a weapon with your transformed hand, but your other hand can be used to wield weapons or cast spells with somatic components. Attacking with the transformed hand and a weapon incurs the standard two-weapon fighting penalties (PH 160).

You can be under the effect of only one *snakebite* spell at any given time.

SNIPER'S EYE

Transmutation
Level: Assassin 4
Components: V, S, F
Casting Time: 1 standard action
Range: Personal
Target: You
Duration: 1 round/level (D)

Holding the glass lens before you, you take a series of slow, deep breaths. Whispered words of arcane power seep past your lips with each exhalation. As you complete the spell you feel infused with deadly ability.

When you cast *sniper's eye*, you gain the following benefits.

- +10 competence bonus on Spot checks.
- Darkvision out to 60 feet.
- The ability to make a ranged sneak attack at a range of up to 60 feet, rather than 30 feet.
- The ability to make a death attack with a ranged weapon rather than just with a melee weapon. The target must be within 60 feet.

This spell doesn't grant you the ability to make a sneak attack or death attack if you don't already have that ability.

Sniper's eye attunes you completely to the vantage point you had when you cast the spell. You understand the nuances of the breeze and every angle and shadow—from that spot. If you move even 5 feet from the place where you cast the spell, you lose the benefits of *sniper's eye* until you return to that spot.

Focus: A magnifying glass lens.

SNIPER'S SHOT

Divination
Level: Assassin 1, ranger 1, sorcerer/wizard 1
Components: V, S
Casting Time: 1 swift action
Range: Personal
Target: You
Duration: 1 round

While muttering a short chant you focus your awareness, looking only at the areas of your foe that seem most vital to its survival.

Your ranged attacks made before the start of your next turn can be sneak attacks regardless of the distance between you and your target. You must still fulfill the other conditions for making a sneak attack against the target.

This spell doesn't grant you the ability to make a sneak attack if you don't already have that ability.

SNOWBALL SWARM

Evocation [Cold]
Level: Sorcerer/wizard 2
Components: V, S, M
Casting Time: 1 standard action
Range: Medium (100 ft. + 10 ft./level)
Area: 10-ft.-radius burst
Duration: Instantaneous
Saving Throw: Reflex half
Spell Resistance: Yes

As you cast this spell, those around you sense an unnatural chill. This vanishes, though, as you release a burst of frost-filled power in the midst of your foes.

A flurry of magic snowballs erupts from a point you select. The swarm of snowballs deals 2d6 points of cold damage to creatures and objects within the burst. For every two caster levels beyond 3rd, the snowballs deal an extra 1d6 points of damage, to a maximum of 5d6 at 9th level or higher.

Material Component: A piece of ice or a small white rock chip.

SNOWSHOES

Transmutation
Level: Cleric 1, druid 1, ranger 1
Components: V, S
Casting Time: 1 standard action
Range: Touch
Target: Creature touched
Duration: 1 hour/level (D)
Saving Throw: Will negates (harmless)
Spell Resistance: Yes (harmless)

A chill grips you as you complete the spell and touch your intended subject. The feet of the spell's subject glow with an ice-blue radiance that fades but lingers. The creature rises slightly out of the snow, as if it weighed much less.

The affected creature can walk lightly over ice and snow without having its speed reduced. The affected creature gains a 10-foot enhancement bonus to speed and is not required to make a Balance check or Reflex save to walk on ice and snow without slipping and falling, to avoid cracking ice it walks over, or to avoid falling through cracked ice. In addition, the affected creature does not leave a more readily discernible trail through ice and snow than it does on solid ground, denying trackers potential bonuses to follow the affected creature's path. (See Weather, DMG 93–95, and Cold Dangers, DMG 302, for more details on the effects of weather and ice.)

SNOWSHOES, MASS

Transmutation
Level: Cleric 3, druid 3, ranger 3
Range: Close (25 ft. + 5 ft./2 levels)
Target: One creature/level, no two of which are more than 30 ft. apart

The feet of all the designated creatures glow with an ice-blue aura. Each subject in turn rises slightly to the top of the snow, as if it were held aloft by the cold blue sheen.

This spell functions like *snowshoes*, except as noted above.

SOLIPSISM

Illusion (Phantasm) [Mind-Affecting]
Level: Sorcerer/wizard 7
Components: V
Casting Time: 1 standard action
Range: Medium (100 ft. + 10 ft./level)

The snowshoes spell gives a druid the upper hand when fighting foes in the snow

Illus. by J. Engle

Target: One creature
Duration: 1 round/level (D)
Saving Throw: Will negates
Spell Resistance: Yes

Pangs of loneliness grip your heart as you complete the spell. Upon choosing your target, the feeling subsides even as a ghostly pale yellow mist swirls around your target for a moment.

You manipulate the senses of one creature so that it perceives itself to be the only real creature in all of existence and everything around it to be merely an illusion.

If the target fails its save, it is convinced of the unreality of every situation it might encounter. It takes no actions, not even purely mental actions, and instead watches the world around it with bemusement. The subject becomes effectively helpless and takes no steps to defend itself from any threat, since it considers any hostile action merely another illusion.

SONGBIRD

Transmutation
Level: Bard 0
Components: V, S
Casting Time: 1 round
Range: Personal
Target: You
Duration: Performance +1 hour or until discharged; see text

You intone this simple spell and your control over your voice improves, your unruly hair straightens, and your flesh radiates a healthy glow. You're ready for showtime.

You acquire an even greater charisma when you perform. Anyone who hears or views your performance becomes favorably inclined toward you. This spell grants you a +1 competence bonus on your next Charisma-based check involving any one person who saw the performance. This effect lasts for the duration of your performance and up to 1 hour immediately following. You must begin the performance within 1 hour of casting the spell for it to have any effect.

SONIC BLAST

Evocation [Sonic]
Level: Sorcerer/wizard 1
Components: V, S
Casting Time: 1 standard action
Range: Close (25 ft. + 5 ft./2 levels)
Target: One creature
Duration: Instantaneous
Saving Throw: Will partial
Spell Resistance: Yes

The words of your spell twist upon each other and grow stronger. Then, like a cluster of bees, they streak toward your target and detonate in a screaming bellow around him.

You blast the target with loud and high-pitched sounds. The subject takes 1d4 points of sonic damage per two caster levels (maximum 5d4) and must make a Will save or be deafened for 1d4 rounds. This spell has no effect if cast into the area of a *silence* spell.

SONIC RUMBLE

Evocation [Sonic]
Level: Sorcerer/wizard 5
Components: V, S, F
Casting Time: 1 standard action
Range: 30 ft.
Area: Cone-shaped burst
Duration: Concentration, up to 1 round/level
Saving Throw: Reflex half
Spell Resistance: Yes

Your final words of the spell become a deep, rumbling hum, as loud as the din of a battlefield, and they blast outward from you in a cone.

You create a cone of powerful sound. If used to attack, the cone deals 1d6 points of sonic damage per two levels (maximum 10d6) each round a creature is within the area; a successful Reflex save reduces this damage by half. Targets within the area of a *silence* spell are immune.

Focus: A hollow cone of brass and gold worth 50 gp.

SONIC SNAP

Evocation [Sonic]
Level: Sorcerer/wizard 0
Components: V, S
Casting Time: 1 standard action
Range: Close (25 ft. + 5 ft./2 levels)
Target: One creature or object
Duration: Instantaneous
Saving Throw: Will partial
Spell Resistance: Yes

You bark the last word of the spell, and that word takes life, streaking toward your target and exploding in a shout.

You create a brief but loud noise adjacent to the target. The subject takes 1 point of sonic damage and must succeed on a Will saving throw or be deafened for 1 round. This spell has no effect if cast into the area of a *silence* spell.

SONIC WEAPON

Transmutation [Sonic]
Level: Bard 2, sorcerer/wizard 2
Components: V
Casting Time: 1 standard action
Range: Touch
Target: Weapon touched
Duration: 1 minute/level (D)

Holding the weapon to your mouth, you whisper the spell's arcane words, shrouding the weapon in visible sound like a thin sheen of water.

While the spell is in effect, the affected weapon deals an extra 1d6 points of sonic damage with each successful attack. The sonic energy does not harm the weapon's wielder. Bows, crossbows, and slings that are affected by this spell bestow the sonic energy upon their ammunition.

SONIC WHIP

Evocation [Sonic, Mind-Affecting]
Level: Bard 2
Components: V, S, M
Casting Time: 1 standard action
Range: 0 ft.
Effect: A whip of force
Duration: 1 round/level
Saving Throw: Will negates; see text
Spell Resistance: No

As you make a cracking sound and hold out your hand, the small silk whip within your grasp dissipates and a life-sized whip of hissing blue force appears in your grasp. With expert precision, you manage to make the invisible whip in your hand crack.

This spell creates a whip of sonic energy that you wield as if you had proficiency with it. Simply cracking a *sonic whip* as a free action keeps normal animals (but not dire animals, magical beasts, or vermin) at bay unless they succeed on a Will save. Affected animals stay at least 30 feet away from you for the duration of the spell, as space permits. On a successful ranged attack with the whip, any normal animal you strike must succeed on a Will save or become frightened.

Against other creature types, you can use a *sonic whip* in combat as if it were a normal whip.

Material Component: A miniature silk whip.

SONOROUS HUM

Evocation [Sonic]
Level: Bard 2, cleric 3, sorcerer/wizard 3
Components: V, S
Casting Time: 1 standard action
Range: Personal
Target: You
Duration: 1 minute/level (D)

You finish casting this spell, and the area around you is abuzz with a low, droning hum that improves your concentration.

After you cast this spell, the next spell you cast within the duration that requires concentration to maintain is maintained for you until the *sonorous hum* spell expires. This effect allows you to cast other spells, even another spell that also requires concentration. If the spell maintained by the *sonorous hum* has a shorter duration than that of this spell, the maintained spell expires as it normally would, and you gain no further benefits from this casting of *sonorous hum*. The sound created by the spell is as loud as a person in armor walking at a slow pace trying not to make noise (normally a DC 5 Listen check to detect). You can end the spell as a free action.

For example, you could cast this spell, then cast *detect thoughts*, and this spell maintains the concentration on *detect thoughts* while you cast *discern lies* and maintain concentration on that spell yourself. You control all aspects of both spells, so you could change the orientation of the *detect thoughts* effect and select a different target for your *discern lies* spell in the same round.

A sound lance is visible as waves in the air

Illus. by C. Dien

If you take damage, you must still make a Concentration check to maintain the spell.

SOUND LANCE

Evocation [Sonic]
Level: Cleric 4, sorcerer/wizard 3
Components: V, S
Casting Time: 1 standard action
Range: Medium (100 ft. + 10 ft./level)
Target: One creature or object
Duration: Instantaneous
Saving Throw: Fortitude half
Spell Resistance: Yes

You unleash a shrill, piercing cry at your target, which takes the barely visible form of a translucent lance hurtling through the air.

This spell causes a projectile of intense sonic energy to leap from you to a target within range. The sound deals 1d8 points of sonic damage per caster level (maximum 10d8). A *sound lance* cannot penetrate the area of a *silence* spell.

SPARK OF LIFE

Necromancy
Level: Cleric 3, druid 4
Components: V, S
Casting Time: 1 standard action
Range: Touch
Target: Undead creature touched
Duration: 1 round/level

Saving Throw: Will negates
Spell Resistance: Yes

A touch from your hand outlines an undead creature in a faint yellow glow, making it vulnerable to many of the dangers that can harm living creatures.

For the duration of the spell, the undead creature is subject to extra damage from critical hits (and thus sneak attacks), nonlethal damage, ability drain, energy drain, fatigue, exhaustion, and damage to its physical ability scores (though it still lacks a Constitution score and thus can't take Constitution damage) as if it were alive.

It loses its immunity to effects that require a Fortitude save, as well as its invulnerability to poison, sleep effects, paralysis, stunning, disease, and death effects. However, an undead affected by this spell gains a bonus on its Fortitude saves equal to its Charisma bonus (if any). (The bonus doesn't apply to Fortitude saves against effects that also affect objects.) It must breathe, eat, and sleep just like a normal living creature (though the last two aren't likely to come into play thanks to the spell's short duration).

While it is under the effect of this spell, both negative energy (such as *inflict* spells) and positive energy (such as *cure* spells) heal damage to the undead creature, rather than damaging it.

An undead creature affected by this spell retains all of its other traits.

SPAWN SCREEN

Necromancy
Level: Cleric 2, sorcerer/wizard 2
Components: V, S, DF
Casting Time: 1 standard action
Range: Touch
Targets: One creature/level
Duration: 1 hour/level
Saving Throw: Will negates (harmless)
Spell Resistance: Yes (harmless)

Hoping that your friend will not have need of the spell, you ensure that his death in the coming battle won't result in an even greater abomination.

The subject does not rise as an undead spawn should it perish from an undead's attack that normally would turn it into a spawn, such as from the bite of a ghoul (MM 118). This spell doesn't prevent the subject from perishing or provide anything other than insurance that the subject's body and spirit cannot be hijacked by an acquisitive undead creature.

The protection applies if the duration is still in effect when the subject first dies; the spell need not linger in its effect during the period immediately prior to a spawn's rise. This spell cannot be cast on the body of a creature that has already been killed by a spawn-creating undead.

SPEAK TO ALLIES

Transmutation [Language-Dependent]
Level: Bard 2, sorcerer/wizard 2
Targets: Any number of allied creatures, no two of which are more than 30 ft. apart

As you rub the small piece of copper wire, it begins to buzz with the latent magical energy of the spell. When you finally release the spell's energy, you hear the words you wish to share with your allies in your mind—and moments later you hear their unspoken replies.

This spell functions like *message* (PH 253), except as noted above and that you and the recipients don't have to mouth the words or whisper, which means that those skilled in reading lips have no opportunity to learn the messages.

SPECTRAL TOUCH

Necromancy
Level: Sorcerer/wizard 6
Components: V, S
Casting Time: 1 standard action
Range: Touch
Targets: One creature/level
Duration: 1 round/level (D); see text
Saving Throw: Fortitude negates
Spell Resistance: Yes

A touch from your hand, which crackles with black energy, weakens the life force of living creatures.

Each melee touch attack you successfully make during the spell's duration channels negative energy that bestows one negative level on the target and grants you 5 temporary hit points. This spell cannot give you more temporary hit points than your normal starting hit points (your hit point total cannot exceed two times your normal starting hit points). Both the negative level and the temporary hit points last for up to 1 hour. You can use this attack once per round for a number of rounds equal to your caster level. Any charges of the spell not used by the time the duration expires are lost.

An undead creature you touch instead gains 5 temporary hit points and you lose a like amount (no save). Temporary hit points gained in this way last for up to 1 hour.

SPECTRAL WEAPON

Illusion (Shadow)
Level: Assassin 3, bard 4, sorcerer/wizard 3
Components: V, S
Casting Time: 1 swift action
Range: 0 ft.
Effect: One shadowy blade
Duration: 1 round/level (D)
Saving Throw: See text
Spell Resistance: Yes

You summon forth semisolid shadowstuff and force it to coalesce into a shape only you can wield. The shadow-formed weapon looks real at first glance, though it appears darkened as if perpetually in shadows. Wisps of shadow tendrils constantly follow the weapon as you move it about.

Using material from the Plane of Shadow, you can fashion a quasi-real melee weapon of any type with which you are proficient. This *spectral weapon* appears in your hand and behaves as a normal weapon of its type, with two exceptions. First, you resolve attacks with your *spectral weapon* as melee touch attacks instead of melee attacks. Second, any foe you hit is entitled to a Will save to recognize the weapon's shadowy, semi-insubstantial nature. If the save is successful, that opponent takes only half damage from the weapon on that attack and all subsequent attacks, and is only 50% likely to suffer any special effects of your attacks (such as a death attack delivered with the weapon).

You can maintain only one *spectral weapon* at a time, and only you can wield it. The weapon dissipates when you let go of it or when the spell's duration expires, whichever comes first.

SPEECHLINK

Divination
Level: Bard 3
Components: V, S
Casting Time: 1 standard action
Range: Touch
Targets: You and one creature touched
Duration: 10 minutes/level (D)
Saving Throw: None
Spell Resistance: No

Tapping your finger to the side of your head and to your intended subject, you whisper words of greeting to complete the spell. You then hear your subject's voice as if it were speaking directly into your ear.

You and a willing subject can communicate verbally no matter how much distance you put between yourselves on the same plane. Either participant can end the spell at any time. *Speechlink* allows you and your allies each to hear the other's vocalizations, whatever their volume. It does not transfer other sounds from either participant's location. This spell works on any creatures, including animals, but does not convey any special language comprehension ability.

SPELL ENGINE

Abjuration [Force]
Level: Wizard 8
Components: V, S, M, XP
Casting Time: 10 minutes
Range: Close (25 ft. + 5 ft./2 levels)
Effect: 5-ft.-radius magical wheel
Duration: See text
Saving Throw: None
Spell Resistance: Yes; see text

You speak a word of abjuration and thrust aloft the bone disk and silver wheel, held together by a single tear. The disk and wheel begin to spin, then vanish, but you feel the power of the mystic engine created nearby.

Upon casting this spell, you can swap out any or all of your prepared spells for other spells from your spellbook. Each prepared spell must be swapped for a spell of the same level. Empty spell slots from a spell cast earlier in the day (including the casting of this spell) cannot be refreshed.

Preparing spells within the light provided by a spell engine takes only half as long as normal.

Material Components: A disk of polished bone, one of your tears, and a silver wheel worth 500 gp.

XP Cost: 250 XP.

SPELL ENHANCER

Transmutation
Level: Sorcerer/wizard 4
Components: V
Casting Time: 1 swift action
Range: Personal
Target: You
Duration: 1 round

You utter an ancient word tied to the fundamental principles of magic and immediately begin casting another spell.

This spell enhances the next spell you cast, making it more difficult for targets to resist. The next spell you cast this round is cast at +2 caster level, and its save DC increases by 1.

SPELL FLOWER

Transmutation
Level: Cleric 1, sorcerer/wizard 1
Components: V, S
Casting Time: 1 standard action
Range: Personal
Target: You
Duration: 1 round/level

Joining mysterious phrases with the simple motion of flexing your fingers, you imbue your hands with receptive magical energy that crackles and glows a soft orange.

You are able to hold the charge for one touch spell per arm of your body as long as you don't use a charged limb to cast another spell or touch anything with it. Each touch spell you cast resides in a different forelimb. For the duration of this spell, any touch spells you cast are discharged only if you cast another spell with that forelimb or touch something with that forelimb.

For example, a human sorcerer casts this spell, then casts *chill touch* and holds the charge in his left hand, then casts *shocking grasp* and holds the charge in his right hand. Because of the *spell flower,* he can hold the charge on both of these spells at the same time. If he casts another spell with a somatic component (which requires the use of one of his hands), he immediately loses one of his held touch spells (his choice), but if the spell he casts is also a touch spell, he can immediately hold the charge in the available hand. If he chooses to attack with a touch spell, it works normally. Since he has multiple limbs that are considered armed, he can make an off-hand attack with the other touch spell in the same round, with the normal penalties for fighting with two weapons (PH 160).

A spectral weapon appears fearsome at first glance

Illus. by D. Martin

A marilith spellcaster could do the same as the sorcerer in the previous example, except that she could hold the charge on up to six touch spells. She could also use any of her spell-like or supernatural abilities, since those do not interfere with holding a charge.

If the *spell flower* effect ends, the most recent touch spell cast remains as a held charge and all other held spells dissipate.

SPELL IMMUNITY, LESSER

Abjuration
Level: Cleric 2
Components: V, S
Casting Time: 1 standard action
Range: Touch
Target: Creature touched
Duration: 10 minutes/level
Saving Throw: Will negates (harmless)
Spell Resistance: Yes (harmless)

Silvery motes of light begin to snow down as you complete the spell, shifting to its recipient upon your successful touch. The motes coalesce into a nimbus that contracts and holds to the subject as a silvery sheen.

This spell protects one creature from a single 1st- or 2nd-level spell. The creature effectively has unbeatable spell resistance regarding the chosen spell. *Lesser spell immunity* can't protect a creature from a spell to which spell resistance doesn't apply. This spell works against other spells, spell-like effects, and innate spell-like abilities. It does not protect against supernatural or extraordinary abilities, such as breath weapons or gaze attacks. Only a particular spell can be protected against, not a school of spells or a group of spells with similar effects; thus, a creature given immunity to *inflict light wounds* is still susceptible to *inflict moderate wounds*.

A creature can have only one *lesser spell immunity* or *spell immunity* (PH 282) in effect at a time.

SPELL MATRIX

Transmutation
Level: Sorcerer/wizard 7
Effect: Matrix that holds two of your spells

This spell functions like *lesser spell matrix*, except that you can store up to two spells of up to 3rd level, and you take 2d6 points of damage instead of 1d6 upon casting. The matrix closes after 2 rounds and no more spells can be added, even if it is not full.

In addition, you can decide to link the two spells stored in the matrix into a spell sequence if both are 2nd level or lower. You can then discharge the two linked spells as a single swift action, just as if you were casting the lone spell from a *spell matrix*.

Focus: A sapphire with a minimum value of 1,000 gp.

SPELL MATRIX, GREATER

Transmutation
Level: Sorcerer/wizard 9
Effect: Matrix that holds three of your spells

This spell functions like *lesser spell matrix*, except that you can store up to three spells of up to 3rd level, and you take 3d6 points of damage instead of 1d6 upon casting. The matrix closes after 3 rounds and no more spells can be added, even if it is not full.

In addition, you can designate one spell or one spell sequence held in the matrix to come into effect under a condition you dictate when casting *greater spell matrix*. The spell (or sequence of spells) to be activated by the triggering condition must be of a type that affects your own person, such as *levitate* or *feather fall*. The conditions required to bring the desired spell or spells into effect must be clear, although they can be general. In all cases, *greater spell matrix* immediately brings into effect the designated spell or sequence of spells, which is cast instantaneously when the designated circumstances occur. You cannot choose to have the spell or spells not activate when the triggering event occurs.

Focus: A diamond with a minimum value of 1,500 gp.

SPELL MATRIX, LESSER

Transmutation
Level: Sorcerer/wizard 5
Components: V, S, F
Casting Time: 1 standard action
Range: Personal
Effect: Matrix that holds one of your spells
Duration: 10 minutes/level (D)

Concentrating as you intone the arcane words, you envision your mind as a maze of paths and doors. You get a chill as the spell completes and some of the doors open.

You prepare a magical matrix that allows you to store one of your spells and use it later as a swift action.

In the round after you cast *lesser spell matrix*, you can cast one spell of up to 3rd level to be stored in it. The matrix closes after 1 round, whether or not you have stored a spell in it. Only a spell that can be altered by the Quicken Spell feat can be placed in the matrix, and any spell stored there is treated as a prepared spell. Casting *lesser spell matrix* deals 1d6 points of damage to you, and this damage cannot be healed by any means while the matrix exists.

While the matrix is active, you can cast the spell stored in it as a swift action. Once it is cast from the matrix, the spell is gone.

A *dispel magic* spell that successfully dispels the matrix also dispels the spell held inside it. If you are affected by an *antimagic field*, the duration of the matrix is interrupted, but the spell does not activate. The matrix becomes active again when you emerge from the *antimagic field*. If you die while the spell is still held in the matrix, both the spell and the matrix dissipate harmlessly.

Focus: A piece of amber with a minimum value of 500 gp.

SPELL RESISTANCE, MASS

Abjuration
Level: Cleric 7
Range: Close (25 ft. + 5 ft./2 levels)
Targets: One creature/level, no two of which are more than 30 ft. apart
Duration: 1 round/level

Wrapping your allies in protective magic, you give them the ability to shrug off spells.

This spell functions like *spell resistance* (PH 282), except as noted here.

SPELL VULNERABILITY

Transmutation
Level: Cleric 4, sorcerer/wizard 3
Components: V, S
Casting Time: 1 round
Range: Close (25 ft. + 5 ft./2 levels)
Target: One creature
Duration: 1 minute/level
Saving Throw: Fortitude negates
Spell Resistance: No

A violet spray springs from your fingertips and wraps around your opponent. It fades into a dull purple glow, which attracts spell energies as opposed to shrugging them off.

This spell reduces the subject's spell resistance by 1 per caster level (maximum reduction 15). This reduction can't lower a subject's spell resistance below 0.

SPHERE OF ULTIMATE DESTRUCTION

Conjuration (Creation)
Level: Sorcerer/wizard 9
Components: V, S, M
Casting Time: 1 standard action
Range: Medium (100 ft. + 10 ft./level)
Effect: 2-ft.-radius sphere
Duration: 1 round/level (D)
Saving Throw: Fortitude partial; see text
Spell Resistance: Yes

As you successfully complete the intricate gestures and tongue-tying syllables of this spell, you conjure a featureless black sphere of nothingness. Matter that touches the sphere disappears, causing a slight breeze to form that blows endlessly in the direction of the all-consuming blackness.

You create a terrible sphere that destroys anything it touches. The sphere flies up to 30 feet per round. The sphere stops moving when it enters a space containing a creature, automatically striking it. You must actively direct it to a new target as a move action.

When struck by the sphere, a subject takes 2d6 points of damage per caster level (maximum 40d6). Any creature reduced to 0 or fewer hit points by this spell is disintegrated, leaving behind only a trace of fine dust (though its equipment is unaffected). When used against an object, the sphere disintegrates as much as one 10-foot cube of nonliving matter. A creature or object that makes a successful Fortitude save is partially affected, taking only 5d6 points of damage. If this damage reduces the creature or object to 0 or fewer hit points, it is disintegrated.

The effects of the sphere count as a *disintegrate* spell for the purpose of destroying a *wall of force* or any other spell or effect specifically affected by *disintegrate*. If the sphere moves beyond the spell's range, it winks out.

Material Component: A pinch of dust from a disintegrated creature.

SPIDER CURSE

Transmutation [Mind-Affecting]
Level: Spider 6
Components: V, S, DF
Casting Time: 1 minute
Range: Medium (100 ft. + 10 ft./level)
Target: One Medium or smaller humanoid
Duration: 24 hours/level
Saving Throw: Will negates
Spell Resistance: Yes

You pour the power of the spell into the body of another. That creature, now but a vessel of your will, takes the shape of a centaurlike spider creature called a drider.

You turn a humanoid into a creature resembling a drider (MM 89) that obeys your mental commands.

The transmuted subject gains a spider's body with a humanoid head, arms, and torso, just like a drider.

The subject has a drider's speed, natural armor, bite attack, and poison (but see below). The subject gains a +4 bonus to Strength, Dexterity, and Constitution. The subject becomes size Large, with a space of 10 feet and a reach of 5 feet. The subject gains a –1 penalty to AC and on attack rolls due to size.

The subject retains its Intelligence, Wisdom, and Charisma scores, level and class,

A sphere of ultimate destruction destroys everything it touches

Illus. by M. Phillippi

hit points (despite any change in Constitution), alignment, base attack bonus, and base saves. (New Strength, Dexterity, and Constitution scores might affect final Armor Class, attack, and save bonuses.) The subject's equipment remains and continues to function as long as it fits a drider's body shape. Otherwise it is subsumed into the new form and ceases to function for the duration of the spell. Retained items include anything worn on the upper body (head, neck, shoulders, hands, arms, and waist). Nonfunctioning items include anything worn on the legs, feet, or the whole body (armor, robes, vestments, and boots).

The subject's bite delivers a poison with a Fortitude save DC of 16 + your Wisdom bonus. Initial and secondary damage is 1d6 points of Strength damage.

Your control over the subject is like that provided by a *dominate person* spell (PH 224). (You telepathically control the creature as long as it remains within range.)

SPIDER PLAGUE

Conjuration (Summoning) [see text]
Level: Cleric 6
Components: V, S
Casting Time: 1 round
Range: Close (25 ft. + 5 ft./2 levels)
Effect: Five summoned spiders
Duration: 1 round/level
Saving Throw: None
Spell Resistance: No

Your eyes rolling wildly in their sockets, you cackle the last few words to call upon your deity's power. A number of massive spiders spring up from the earth in the location you indicate.

This spell summons five celestial or fiendish Large monstrous spiders (MM 289). They appear where you designate and act immediately, on your turn. They attack your opponents to the best of their ability. If you can communicate with the spiders, you can direct them not to attack, to attack particular enemies, or to perform other actions.

A celestial spider summoned by this spell has damage reduction 5/magic; resistance to acid 5, cold 5, and electricity 5; spell resistance 9; and a smite evil attack that provides a +4 bonus on one damage roll.

A fiendish creature (MM 107) summoned by this spell has damage reduction 5/magic; resistance to acid 5 and fire 5; spell resistance 9; and a smite good attack that provides a +4 bonus on one damage roll.

When you use a summoning spell to summon an evil or good creature, it is a spell of that type.

SPIDER POISON

Necromancy
Level: Assassin 3, sorcerer/wizard 3
Components: V, S, M
Casting Time: 1 standard action
Range: Touch
Target: Living creature touched
Duration: Instantaneous; see text
Saving Throw: Fortitude negates
Spell Resistance: Yes

You hold the husk of the spider in your hand and speak the words of the spell. The husk vanishes, but leaves in your palm the brief glowing image of a spider.

You poison a subject by making a successful melee touch attack. The poison deals 1d6 points of Strength damage immediately and another 1d6 points of Strength damage 1 minute later. Each instance of damage can be negated by a Fortitude save (DC 10 + 1/2 your caster level + your relevant spellcasting ability modifier (Intelligence for wizards and assassins, Charisma for sorcerers).

Material Component: A poisonous spider, alive or dead.

SPIDER SHAPES

Transmutation
Level: Spider 9
Components: V, S, DF
Casting Time: 1 standard action
Range: Close (25 ft. + 5 ft./2 levels)
Targets: One willing creature/level, all within 30 ft. of each other
Duration: 1 hour/level (D)
Saving Throw: None; see text
Spell Resistance: Yes (harmless)

You channel the power of the spell into the willing masses before you, granting them the blessed forms of spiders.

This spell functions like *polymorph* (PH 283), except that you polymorph up to one willing creature per level into a monstrous spider (MM 288) of any size from Tiny to Huge as you decide. Unlike with *polymorph*, this spell allows the subjects to gain a spider's poisonous bite. All the creatures you transmute must become spiders of the same size.

Subjects remain in the spider form until the spell expires or you dismiss the spell for all subjects. In addition, an individual subject can choose to resume its normal form as a full-round action. Doing so ends the spell for that creature only.

SPIDERFORM

Transmutation
Level: Drow 5
Components: V, S, DF
Casting Time: 1 standard action
Range: Personal
Target: You
Duration: 1 hour/level (D)

You invest the power of the spell into yourself, twisting and bending your own form into that of a spider.

You can polymorph into a drider (MM 89) or a Tiny, Small, Medium, or Large monstrous spider (MM 288). You regain lost hit points as if you rested for a day on the initial transformation. The spell lasts until you decide to resume your normal shape.

You acquire the physical and natural abilities of the creature you polymorph into, including natural size, Strength, Dexterity, and Constitution, armor, attack routines, and movement capabilities.

You also acquire the poisonous bite and web-spinning ability of whichever spider form you choose.

You retain your Intelligence, Wisdom, and Charisma scores, level and class, hit points (despite any change in Constitution), alignment, base attack bonus, and base saves. (New Strength, Dexterity, and Constitution scores might affect final attack and save bonuses.) You can cast spells and use magic items if you choose drider form, but no other spider form is capable of spellcasting or manipulating devices.

If you choose drider form, your equipment remains and continues to function as long as it fits a drider's body shape. Retained items include anything worn on the upper body (head, neck, shoulders, hands, arms, and waist). Otherwise your equipment is subsumed into the new form and ceases to function for the duration of the spell.

SPIDERSKIN

Transmutation
Level: Druid 3, sorcerer/wizard 3
Components: V, S, M/DF
Casting Time: 1 standard action
Range: Touch
Target: Creature touched
Duration: 10 minutes/level
Saving Throw: Will negates (harmless)
Spell Resistance: Yes (harmless)

You cast this spell upon yourself, and your flesh glows yellow. The glow quickly subsides, but you feel your flesh thicken, its surface growing harder and more like a carapace.

The spell grants the recipient a +1 enhancement bonus to its existing natural armor bonus, a +1 racial bonus on saves against poison, and a +1 racial bonus on Hide checks for every three caster levels you have. This means that the bonuses to natural armor, saves, and Hide checks improve to +2 at caster level 6th, +3 at caster level 9th, +4 at 12th, and +5 at 15th.

The enhancement bonus provided by *spiderskin* stacks with the subject's natural armor bonus, but not with other enhancement bonuses to natural armor. A creature without natural armor has an effective natural armor bonus of +0, much as a character wearing only normal clothing has an armor bonus of +0.

Arcane Material Component: The leg of a spider.

SPIKES

Transmutation
Level: Cleric 3, druid 3

With the sound of twisting wood, the weapon you touch grows sharp spikes like rose thorns.

This spell functions like *brambles* (page 38), except that the affected weapon gains a +2 enhancement bonus on its attack rolls, and its threat range is doubled. This effect does not stack with other effects that increase a weapon's threat range, such as the Improved Critical feat.

SPIRIT WORM

Necromancy
Level: Sorcerer/wizard 1
Components: V, S, M
Casting Time: 1 standard action
Range: Touch
Target: Living creature touched
Duration: 1 round/level, up to 5 rounds; see text
Saving Throw: Fortitude negates; see text
Spell Resistance: Yes

You press the bit of blackened bone against your foe and intone the spell. The bone vanishes, leaving a mottled bruise where it touched.

You create a lingering decay in the spirit and body of the target. If the target fails its saving throw, it takes 1 point of Constitution damage each round while the spell lasts (maximum 5 points). The victim can attempt a Fortitude saving throw each round, and success negates the Constitution damage for that round and ends the spell.

Material Component: A piece of fire-blackened ivory or bone carved in the shape of a segmented worm.

SPIRITJAWS

Evocation [Force]
Level: Druid 3
Components: V, S, M
Casting Time: 1 standard action
Range: Medium (100 + 10 ft./level)
Effect: Jaws of force
Duration: 1 round/level (D)
Saving Throw: None
Spell Resistance: Yes

You call upon the power of the dinosaurs to complete the spell. A set of ghostly dinosaur jaws comes into being and attacks the creature you designate.

This spell creates a set of powerful jaws of force. The jaws attempt to grapple the designated opponent, starting with one attack in the round the spell is cast and continuing each round thereafter. The jaws use your base attack bonus (possibly allowing them multiple attacks per round in subsequent rounds) + your Wis modifier as their attack bonus. If an initial attack hits, the jaws deal 2d6 points of damage and attempt to start a grapple as a free action. The jaws' bonus on grapple checks is equal to their attack bonus + 4.

Once the opponent is grappled, the jaws deal 2d6 points of damage with each subsequent grapple check. The target is considered to be grappling and cannot move; it no longer threatens squares and loses its Dexterity bonus to AC against opponents not grappling it.

The jaws always strike from your direction. They do not get a bonus for flanking or help a combatant get one. Your feats do not affect the jaws. If the jaws move beyond the range of the spell, they vanish. As a magical force effect, the jaws cannot be damaged, but *disintegrate* or a *sphere of annihilation* destroys the effect.

The grappled target can cast a spell only if it has no somatic component, the material components are in hand, and a Concentration check (DC 20 + spell level) is made. A creature grappled by the jaws can attempt to escape by succeeding on a grapple check against the jaws or by making a successful Escape Artist check as a standard action opposed by the jaws' grapple check.

As a free action, you can direct the jaws to pin a grappled opponent instead of dealing damage with a grapple check. If the jaws win the opposed grapple check, the opponent is pinned. A pinned opponent is immobile and must break the pin before it can escape the grapple. Creatures other than those grappling the pinned target gain a +4 bonus on attack rolls to hit it. If the jaws have multiple attacks, you can use them to damage a pinned target or to make more grapple attempts against it.

Each round after the first, you can use a move action to direct the jaws to a new target. If you do not, the jaws continue to attack the previous round's target. On any round that the jaws switch targets, they get one attack. Subsequent rounds of attacking that target allow the jaws to make multiple attacks if your base attack bonus would allow it.

If you become unable to command the jaws, they vanish.

Material Component: A piece of bone from a dinosaur's jaw.

SPIRITUAL CHARIOT

Conjuration (Creation) [Force]
Level: Blackguard 3, paladin 2
Components: V, S, DF
Casting Time: 1 standard action

Range: Close (25 ft. + 5 ft./2 levels)
Target: One special mount
Duration: 1 hour/level
Saving Throw: None
Spell Resistance: No

You cast this spell, and a large and ornate chariot made of transparent, faintly glowing azure energy forms behind your mount.

You conjure a chariot of force. When it appears, your special mount is harnessed to it. It can hold one Medium creature or two Small creatures plus the driver (usually the paladin).

Although the chariot seems large and sturdy, it and its occupants have no weight for the purpose of the mount's load, so the mount can travel at full speed. If the chariot is ever unhitched from the special mount, it disappears. The chariot's driver gains a +4 sacred bonus on Handle Animal checks. The chariot is made of magical force and has immunity to most types of damage. It interacts with other spells as a *wall of force* (PH 298) does. Those in the chariot have cover based on their size and the position of their attackers. In most situations, Medium creatures inside the chariot gain cover.

SPIRITWALL

Necromancy [Fear, Mind-Affecting]
Level: Sorcerer/wizard 5
Components: V, S, M
Casting Time: 1 standard action
Range: Medium (100 ft. + 10 ft./level)
Effect: Swirling wall whose area is up to one 10-ft. square/level, or a sphere or hemisphere with a radius of up to 1 ft./level
Duration: 1 minute/level (D)
Saving Throw: None; see text
Spell Resistance: No

With a deep groan, as if you were being subjected to eternal pain, you unleash the spell. A mass of green-white forms resembling tortured spirits forms nearby. The mass continues the low groaning you uttered while casting the spell.

One side of the wall, selected by you, emits a low groaning that causes creatures within 60 feet of that side to make a Will save or become frightened and flee for 1d4 rounds. Any living creature that touches the wall takes 1d10 points of damage as its life force is disrupted. A living creature passing through the wall takes 1d10 points of damage and must make a Fortitude save or gain one negative level.

The barrier is semimaterial and opaque, providing cover and total concealment against physical attacks, and it blocks line of effect for magical effects (spells, spell-like abilities, and supernatural abilities).

Material Component: A clear cut gemstone.

SPLINTERBOLT

Conjuration (Creation)
Level: Druid 2
Components: V, S, M
Casting Time: 1 standard action
Range: Close (25 ft. + 5 ft./2 levels)
Effect: One or more streams of splinters
Duration: Instantaneous
Saving Throw: None
Spell Resistance: No

A spiritwall can only effectively bar the living

Illus. by L. Parrillo

You extend your hand toward your foe, flicking a single sliver of wood into the air, and a splinter larger than a titan's javelin whistles through the air.

You must make a ranged attack to hit the target. If you hit, the *splinterbolt* deals 4d6 points of piercing damage. A *splinterbolt* threatens a critical hit on a roll of 18–20.

You can fire one additional *splinterbolt* for every four levels beyond 3rd (to a maximum of three at 11th level). You can fire these *splinterbolts* at the same or different targets, but all *splinterbolts* must be aimed at targets within 30 feet of each other and fired simultaneously.

A creature's damage reduction, if any, applies to the damage from this spell. The damage from *splinterbolt* is treated as magic and piercing for the purpose of overcoming damage reduction.

Material Component: A splinter of wood.

SPONTANEOUS SEARCH

Divination
Level: Sorcerer/wizard 1
Components: V, S, M
Casting Time: 1 round
Range: Touch
Target: Creature touched
Duration: 1 round
Saving Throw: Will negates (harmless)
Spell Resistance: Yes (harmless)

With a leisurely wave and a declaration of boredom, you complete the spell. You instantly become aware of the location and types of objects in the spell's area, as if you had made a quick search.

The subject of this spell knows the contents of a 20-foot-radius burst, as if it had taken 10 on a Search check for each object and space in the burst radius, including noting the location of traps (though only a rogue can locate those traps with a DC greater than 20).

Material Component: A silk glove.

STABILIZE

Conjuration (Healing)
Level: Paladin 2, cleric 2
Components: V, S, DF
Casting Time: 1 swift action
Area: 50-ft.-radius burst centered on you
Duration: Instantaneous
Saving Throw: Will negates (harmless); see text
Spell Resistance: Yes (harmless)

Filled with compassion and concern, you draw upon your deity's power. A burst of golden energy springs forth, spreading from you. Those still alive around you seem less bloody and in less pain.

This spell, designed to work on the battlefield, allows you to stabilize the dying all around you. A burst of positive energy spreads out from you, healing 1 point of damage to all living creatures in the affected area, whether allied or not. This spell deals 1 point of damage to undead creatures, which are allowed a Will saving throw to negate the effect.

STALKING BRAND

Transmutation
Level: Ranger 1
Components: S
Casting Time: 1 standard action
Range: Close (25 ft. + 5 ft./2 levels)
Target: One creature
Duration: 24 hours/level
Saving Throw: None
Spell Resistance: Yes

With a wave of your hand, you cause a tiny mark to appear upon the target's forehead. "I will know you in any form or visage," you say.

This spell marks your target with a tiny symbol visible only to you and to *detect magic*. The brand appears as you envision it, approximately 1 inch in diameter. You can see the brand even if the subject uses magical means to change or hide its appearance. Spells such as *disguise self*, *polymorph*, and *invisibility* do not hide the brand. To your eyes, the mark glows a light green.

STALWART PACT

Evocation
Level: Cleric 5, Pact 5
Components: V, S, M, DF
Casting Time: 10 minutes
Range: Touch
Target: Willing living creature touched
Duration: Permanent until triggered, then 1 round/level
Saving Throw: Will negates (harmless)
Spell Resistance: Yes (harmless)

You touch your ally and empower him with a spell that will later take effect in dire need.

Once this spell is cast, it remains dormant until the subject is reduced to half or less of its full normal hit points. Once the subject has taken enough damage to reduce it to half or lower hit points, it immediately gains 5 temporary hit points per two caster levels (maximum 35 hit points at 14th level), damage reduction 5/magic, and a +2 luck bonus on saving throws. The hit points, damage reduction, and saving throw bonus disappear when the spell ends.

Material Component: Incense worth 250 gp.

STANDING WAVE

Transmutation
Level: Druid 3
Components: V, S, DF
Casting Time: 1 standard action
Range: Close (25 ft. + 5 ft./2 levels)
Effect: Waves under a creature or object within range
Duration: 10 minutes/level (D)
Saving Throw: Reflex negates
Spell Resistance: Yes

Roaring a binding phrase, you take command of the water, causing a wave to rise and propelling it in the direction you desire.

You command the waters to lift a creature or object and propel it forward. An object so lifted can contain creatures or other objects. The maximum size of the creature or object the wave can lift depends on your caster level.

Caster Level	Size of Creature or Object
5th	Medium
7th	Large
9th	Huge
11th	Gargantuan
13th	Colossal

Standing wave moves the lifted creature or object in a straight line at a

Illus. by F. Vohwinkel

The standing wave spell is useful for moving foes—and for simply moving

speed of 60 feet over water. The spell dissipates when the wave contacts land, lowering its burden harmlessly to shore. If you are riding in or standing on the object, the object continues to move until you are no longer in or on the object or the spell is dismissed; otherwise, the object is moved to the extent of the spell's range when you cast the spell.

STARVATION

Transmutation
Level: Druid 4
Components: V, S, M
Casting Time: 1 standard action
Range: Close (25 ft. + 5 ft./2 levels)
Target: One living creature
Duration: Instantaneous
Saving Throw: Fortitude partial
Spell Resistance: Yes

Your stomach growls as you near completion of the spell. As you declare the target of the spell, your hunger disappears, but you note with satisfaction that your target seems wracked with pain.

You inflict wracking hunger pangs on the target creature. It must make a Fortitude save or take 1d6 points of nonlethal damage per caster level (maximum 10d6) and become fatigued. A creature that makes a successful save takes half damage and is not fatigued by the spell.

A fatigued creature becomes exhausted when doing anything that causes the creature to become fatigued (such as dangerous environmental temperatures or ending a barbarian rage). A fatigued creature that fails its saving throw against *starvation* takes nonlethal damage as normal and becomes exhausted.

Material Component: A piece of spoiled food.

STEELDANCE

Transmutation
Level: Sorcerer/wizard 3
Components: V, S, F
Casting Time: 1 standard action
Range: Medium (100 ft. + 10 ft./level)
Targets: Two daggers
Duration: 1 round/level
Saving Throw: None
Spell Resistance: No

You place the two daggers in your outstretched palm and cast the spell. They rise from your hands, glowing with a dim blue radiance.

The two daggers hover about you, attacking foes that come near. On your turn, each blade can make an attack at an adjacent opponent, with an attack bonus equal to your caster level + your relevant ability modifier. The damage they deal is equal to the normal weapon damage (1d4 for daggers) + your ability modifier (Intelligence for wizards and Charisma for sorcerers). The weapons are treated as magic for the purpose of overcoming damage reduction.

Your blades can be attacked with sunder or disarm attempts as if you were wielding them, and they use the above attack bonus to resolve such situations. Disarming a weapon under the effect of *steeldance* ends the spell for that weapon.

Focus: Two bladed weapons, such as daggers or longswords.

STICK

Transmutation
Level: Bard 0, sorcerer/wizard 0
Components: V, S, M
Casting Time: 1 standard action
Range: Touch
Target: Nonmagical, unattended object weighing up to 5 lb.
Duration: Instantaneous
Saving Throw: Will negates (object)
Spell Resistance: Yes (object)

Lacking someone to hold the item where you need it, you mutter and wave your hand in a simple gesture before sticking the item in place.

Stick affixes one object weighing up to 5 pounds to another object. The two items can be separated with even a small amount of force, such as a wind stronger than 10 mph, a *mage hand* or *unseen servant* spell, or a move action by any corporeal creature (which provokes attacks of opportunity).

Material Component: A bit of dried glue.

STICKY FINGERS

Transmutation
Level: Assassin 1, bard 1
Components: S
Casting Time: 1 standard action
Range: Personal
Target: You
Duration: 1 round

Your fingers exude a slightly viscous secretion and become more nimble. When touched together, your fingertips stick slightly.

This spell grants you a +10 bonus on Sleight of Hand checks.

STICKY SADDLE

Transmutation
Level: Paladin 1
Components: V, S, DF
Casting Time: 1 immediate action
Range: Personal
Target: You
Duration: 1 minute/level (D)

A colorless glow surrounds you and your mount for an instant. When the glow fades, you feel more attentive to the movements of your mount even while an unseen force holds you fast to it.

This spell "glues" you to your mount. It becomes impossible for you to fall or be thrown off your mount. Prying you from the saddle requires a DC 20 Strength check, and you gain a +10 bonus on Ride checks related to staying in the saddle. The spell must be cast after you are seated on your mount. If you are not seated on your mount when the spell is cast, the spell fails. If the spell is cast while you are riding bareback, you are "stuck" to the mount's back. Otherwise, you are merely stuck to the saddle, but the saddle is attached to the mount normally. If you are knocked unconscious while this spell is in effect, you automatically remain in the saddle. The spell can be dismissed as an immediate action, and it does not impede the rider from making a soft fall if the mount is dropped in battle.

STING RAY

Enchantment (Compulsion) [Mind-Affecting]
Level: Bard 2, sorcerer/wizard 2
Components: V, S, M
Casting Time: 1 standard action
Range: Close (25 ft. + 5 ft./2 levels)
Effect: Ray
Duration: 1 round/level

Saving Throw: Will partial
Spell Resistance: Yes

From your outstretched hand leaps forth a ray of glittering energy apparently composed of countless minuscule writhing insects. The hum of minute chitinous bodies scrambling over one another fills the air.

You must succeed on a ranged touch attack with the ray to strike a target. When this ray successfully strikes, it creates a sensation of many tiny insects biting and crawling on the victim's body. The target can attempt a Will save each round to shake off the effect. Until the spell is shrugged off, the victim is hampered by the unsettling feeling of all the stinging and biting, and is able to perform only a single move or standard action each round. The victim also takes a –2 penalty to AC.

In addition, if the victim attempts to cast a spell, it must succeed on a Concentration check with a DC equal to the *sting ray's* DC + the level of the spell the subject is attempting to cast. For example, if a 6th-level sorcerer with a Charisma score of 16 casts *sting ray* on a wizard casting a *fireball*, the Concentration check DC is 19 (16 [*sting ray* DC] + 3 [*fireball* spell level]).

A successful Will save negates the effect restricting the subject's action to one move or one standard action each round, nor does the subject need to make a Concentration check each time it wishes to cast a spell. However, the subject still takes the penalty to AC for the duration of the spell with a successful save.

Material Component: Four dried stinging insects (bees, wasps, and so on).

STOLEN BREATH

Necromancy [Air]
Level: Sorcerer/wizard 2
Components: V, S, F
Casting Time: 1 standard action
Range: Medium (100 ft. + 10 ft./level)
Target: One living creature that breathes air
Duration: Instantaneous; see text
Saving Throw: None
Spell Resistance: Yes

With a clenched fist, you make a tugging motion toward your target. A transparent, barely perceptible hand appears to plunge into your target's mouth.

With this spell, you steal all the air from the subject's lungs, causing it to suffer a momentary respiratory crisis. It can take shallow breaths and act normally but is considered sickened for 1 minute. At any time during this minute, the subject can take a full-round action to get its wind back, ending the condition.

Focus: A stoppered glass vial.

STONE BODY

Transmutation
Level: Cleric 6, sorcerer/wizard 6
Components: V, S, M
Casting Time: 1 standard action
Range: Personal
Target: You
Duration: 1 minute/level (D)

As the echoes of your spellcasting die, your flesh begins to stiffen and turn gray, gaining the rough texture and consistency of stone.

This spell transforms your body into living stone, which grants you several powerful resistances and abilities.

You gain damage reduction 10/adamantine. You are immune to blindness,

Illus. by J. Engle

Sticky saddle gives a caster the ability to stay in the saddle, no matter how her mount moves

extra damage from critical hits, ability score damage, deafness, disease, drowning, poison, stunning, and all spells or attacks that affect your physiology or respiration, because you have no physiology or respiration while this spell is in effect. You gain a +4 enhancement bonus to Strength, but you take a –4 penalty to Dexterity (minimum Dexterity 1). Your speed is reduced to one-half normal, and your weight increases by a factor of three.

If you are targeted with *transmute rock to mud*, you are *slowed* for 2d6 rounds with no saving throw. A *transmute mud to rock* heals you of all your lost hit points. A *stone to flesh* spell cast on you automatically ends this spell.

Arcane Material Component: A small piece of stone that was once part of a stone golem, a greater earth elemental, or a castle's outer wall.

STONE BONES

Transmutation
Level: Cleric 2, sorcerer/wizard 2
Components: V, S, F
Casting Time: 1 standard action
Range: Touch
Target: Corporeal undead creature touched
Duration: 10 minutes/level
Saving Throw: Will negates (harmless)
Spell Resistance: Yes (harmless)

A brief flash engulfs your ally, and through his flesh you can see his skeleton. The skeleton glows a foggy gray for a moment, thickening with eldritch power, then all is as it was before.

You cause the skeleton of the target corporeal undead to become thicker and as strong as stone. This gives the subject a +3 enhancement bonus to its existing natural armor.

Arcane Focus: A miniature skull carved of granite.

Illus. by J. Thomas

Stone shatter sends a heartrendingly pure note to the center of any stone

STONE SHAPE, GREATER

Transmutation [Earth]
Level: Cleric 5, druid 5, sorcerer/wizard 7
Target: Stone or stone objects touched, up to 10 cu. ft. + 10 cu. ft./level

You mutter the ancient words, and your hands glow yellow where they touch the stone. Where you touch, the stone seems as soft as clay.

This spell functions like *stone shape* (PH 284), except that it affects a much larger quantity of stone.

STONE SHATTER

Evocation [Sonic]
Level: Bard 4
Components: V, S
Casting Time: 1 standard action
Range: Close (25 ft. + 5 ft./level)
Target: One stone object or creature
Duration: Instantaneous
Saving Throw: None or Fortitude half; see text
Spell Resistance: No

You call up energies from deep within you and utter a perfect note. The stone rocks as it is struck, and cracks appear in its form.

You aim a single note of perfect pitch toward an unattended stone object weighing no more than 2 pounds per caster level, or toward a stone creature, causing it to shatter. A stone object is destroyed, whereas a stone creature (of any weight) takes 1d6 points of damage per caster level (maximum 15d6), with a Fortitude save for half damage.

STONE SPHERE

Evocation [Earth]
Level: Sorcerer/wizard 4
Components: V, S, M
Casting Time: 1 standard action
Range: Medium (100 ft. + 10 ft./level)
Effect: One 5-ft.-diameter stone sphere
Duration: 1 round/level
Saving Throw: Reflex negates; see text
Spell Resistance: Yes

You toss the marble in the air, and it vanishes as you speak the words of the spell. A larger version of the marble, five feet across, appears in the hallway and bears down on your foe.

You create a smoothly polished, 5-foot-diameter sphere of stone that moves under your control at a speed of 30 feet. A *stone sphere* has AC 5, hardness 8, and 500 hit points.

In the round when you cast the spell, the *stone sphere* appears at the spot you designate within the spell's range, and you can direct its movement as a free action. In subsequent rounds, you must actively direct the *stone sphere* in order to move it; otherwise, it remains motionless. Directing the movement of a *stone sphere* in any round after its initial appearance requires a move action.

If you move a *stone sphere* into a square occupied by an enemy, it stops moving and deals 1d6 points of damage per two caster levels (maximum 5d6) to every creature in that square. A successful Reflex save negates the damage.

Material Component: A smooth sphere of marble 1 inch in diameter.

STONE SPIDERS

Transmutation
Level: Spider 7
Components: V, S, DF
Casting Time: 1 round
Range: Close (25 ft. + 5 ft./2 levels)
Targets: Three pebbles, no two of which are more than 30 ft. apart
Duration: 1 round/level (D)
Saving Throw: None
Spell Resistance: No

You imbue three small stones with magical power, causing them to twist and grow into large stone spiders.

This spell transforms three pebbles into stone constructs that resemble monstrous spiders. The constructs can be any size from Tiny to Huge as you decide, but all the constructs you create must be the same size. The constructs have the same statistics as monstrous spiders (MM 288) of the appropriate size, except as noted here.

- Their natural armor bonus increases by 6.
- They have damage reduction 10/magic.
- Their poison has a Fortitude save DC of 10 + 1/2 your caster level + your Wis modifier. Initial and secondary damage is 1d3 points of Strength damage.

If the constructs can hear your commands, you can direct them not to attack, to attack particular enemies, or to perform other actions. Otherwise, they simply attack your enemies to the best of their ability.

STONEHOLD

Conjuration (Creation) [Earth]
Level: Druid 6
Components: V, S
Casting Time: 1 standard action
Range: Medium (100 ft. + 10 ft./level)
Area: One 10-ft. square/level
Duration: 24 hours/level
Saving Throw: See text
Spell Resistance: Yes (object)

When the energy of this spell bursts forth, the ground erupts with multiple human-sized arms made of solid rock. As you finish casting, they retreat beneath the stone surface, a trap set for future trespassers.

This spell conjures thick stony arms that spring forth from any rock or stone formation whenever anyone passes near it. Each 10-foot square in the spell's area contains one stone arm.

Any creature that enters the area of the spell is immobilized by the arms unless it succeeds on a Reflex save. Such a creature is rooted in place and unable to move. It can take actions normally; it just can't move from the space it currently occupies. Held creatures take 1d6+5 points of damage each round, at the beginning of your turn. Creatures that succeed on the Reflex save can move through the area normally. Creatures that start their turn in the affected area must attempt another Reflex save or be affected by the spell.

A held creature can attempt a DC 20 Strength check or a DC 25 Escape Artist check to break free, and can also break free by dealing enough damage to destroy the arm. An arm has AC 15, hardness 8, and 15 hit points.

Before they attack, the arms remain beneath the surface of the stone. They can be discovered (but not disarmed) as a magic trap can be.

STONY GRASP

Transmutation [Earth]
Level: Sorcerer/wizard 3
Effect: Animated stone arm
Duration: 1 round/level

By thrusting your arm downward, you complete the casting of the spell. Nearby, a roughly formed arm about the size of a human erupts from the ground and grasps at the air.

This spell functions like *earthen grasp* (page 76), except as noted here. The stony arm can appear from any natural surface, including unworked rock, earth, mud, grass, or sand. The stone arm has AC 18, hardness 8, and 4 hit points per caster level.

Material Component: A miniature hand sculpted from stone.

STORM OF ELEMENTAL FURY

Conjuration (Summoning)
Level: Druid 7
Components: V, S
Casting Time: 1 round
Range: Long (400 ft. + 40 ft./level)
Effect: 40-ft.-radius storm cloud, 200 ft. above the ground
Duration: 4 rounds
Saving Throw: See text
Spell Resistance: Yes

With a thunderous boom, a black storm cloud appears over your enemies, striking them with a terrifying combination of effects from the Elemental Planes.

Each round, the storm generates one of the following effects, starting with the first effect, then progressing to the second, until it has run its 4-round course.

1st Round: A *storm of elemental fury* buffets the area immediately beneath it with a whirling windstorm (DMG 94–95). Ranged attacks within the area of the storm are impossible, and Small or smaller creatures must succeed on a Fortitude save or be blown away. Medium creatures must make their Fortitude save or be knocked prone, and Large or larger creatures must succeed on a Fortitude save to move that round. Flying creatures that fail their saves are instead blown in a random direction, traveling 1d6×5 feet if Large or larger, 1d6×10 feet if Medium, and 2d6×10 feet if Small or smaller. Spells cast within the area are disrupted unless the caster succeeds on a Concentration check against a DC equal to the *storm of elemental fury*'s save DC + the level of the spell the caster is trying to cast.

2nd Round: Chunks of rock fall from the sky, dealing 5d6 points of damage (no save) to all creatures in the storm.

3rd Round: A deluge of rain extinguishes unprotected flames and perhaps protected ones as well (50% chance). The torrential downpour reduces visibility to 5 feet and cuts movement in half.

4th Round: Flame pelts the area beneath the storm cloud, dealing 1d6 points of fire damage per caster level (maximum 15d6) (Reflex half).

STORM TOWER

Abjuration [Air]
Level: Druid 7
Components: V, S
Casting Time: 1 round
Range: Long (400 ft. + 40 ft./level)
Area: Cylinder (20-ft. radius, 100 ft. high)
Duration: 1 round/level (D)
Saving Throw: Fortitude negates; see text
Spell Resistance: Yes

You form an enormous tower of dark, swirling storm clouds and howling wind.

Storm tower gives a druid respite from foes

Illus. by W. O'Connor

A *storm tower* absorbs any electricity damage dealt to those within it. *Magic missiles* cannot be cast into, out of, or within a *storm tower*. The *storm tower* is composed of windstorm-strength winds (DMG 95), making ranged attacks impossible within it, though it has no effect on the movement of creatures within it. However, only Gargantuan or Colossal creatures can pass through the outer edge of the *storm tower*; all creatures of smaller size must succeed on a Fortitude saving throw to enter; otherwise, they are checked at the edge.

Anyone within a *storm tower* has concealment relative to those outside the tower. The howling winds of a *storm tower* also apply a –10 penalty on Listen checks made within 50 feet of it (including all those made inside the tower).

STORMRAGE

Transmutation [Electricity]
Level: Cleric 8, druid 8
Components: V, S, DF
Casting Time: 1 standard action
Range: Personal
Target: You
Duration: 1 minute/level (D)

You harness the powers of wind and storm to move, protect yourself, and attack.

You can fly at a speed of 40 feet, and you gain immunity to thrown weapons and projectile ranged attacks. You are unaffected by natural or magical wind, easily able to hold your position and not subject to other effects of extreme wind.

Finally, you can discharge a bolt of electricity from your eyes once per round. You enemies' spell resistance applies to these lightning attacks. Doing this is a standard action that does not provoke attacks of opportunity, has a range of 100 feet, and requires a ranged touch attack. You gain a +3 bonus on the attack roll if the opponent is wearing metal armor, made out of metal, or carrying a lot of metal. If you hit, the bolt deals 1d6 points of electricity damage per two caster levels (maximum 10d6), with no saving throw allowed.

STRATEGIC CHARGE

Abjuration
Level: Blackguard 1, paladin 1
Components: V, DF
Casting Time: 1 swift action
Range: Personal
Target: You
Duration: 1 round/level

A red nimbus surrounds you as you move smoothly across the crowded battlefield.

You gain the benefit of the Mobility feat (PH 98), even if you not meet the prerequisites. You do not have to be charging to gain this benefit.

STRENGTH OF STONE

Transmutation
Level: Paladin 2
Components: V, S, DF
Casting Time: 1 swift action
Range: Personal
Target: You
Duration: 1 round

You call upon the fortitude of the powers of good, and your flesh turns an ivory-gray hue as you draw power up through the earth itself.

The spell grants you a +8 enhancement bonus to Strength. The spell ends instantly if you lose contact with the ground. This means you cannot jump, tumble, charge, run, or move more than your speed in a round (because these acts cause both of your feet to leave the ground) without breaking the spell. A natural stone wall or ceiling counts as the ground for the purpose of this spell (so you could climb a cavern wall and not lose the spell).

STUN RAY

Conjuration (Creation) [Electricity]
Level: Sorcerer/wizard 7
Components: V, S, M
Casting Time: 1 standard action
Range: Close (25 ft. + 5 ft./2 levels)
Effect: Ray
Duration: 1d4+1 rounds; see text
Saving Throw: Fortitude partial; see text
Spell Resistance: Yes

A quick jolt of electricity darts from your raised hand. The slight smell of ozone lingers afterward.

You blast an enemy with a scintillating ray of electricity. You must succeed on a ranged touch attack with the ray to strike a target. The target is stunned for 1d4+1 rounds by the ray of electricity. If the subject makes a successful Fortitude save, it is stunned for only 1 round. Creatures that have immunity to electricity are not affected by this spell.

Material Component: A coiled copper wire.

STUNNING BREATH

Transmutation
Level: Sorcerer/wizard 5
Components: S
Casting Time: 1 swift action
Range: Personal
Target: Your breath weapon
Duration: Instantaneous

You breathe out, and your breath weapon is mixed with heavy, blue spheres of magical energy. Those that survive your onslaught are left standing but stunned.

For this spell to function, you must have a breath weapon that deals hit point damage, either as a supernatural ability or as the result of casting a spell such as *dragon breath* (page 73). When you successfully cast this spell, you imbue your breath weapon with concussive force that can stun those caught in its area. Creatures that take damage from the breath weapon must make successful Fortitude saves (DC equal to your breath weapon save DC) or be stunned for 1 round.

STUNNING BREATH, GREATER

Transmutation
Level: Sorcerer/wizard 8

This spell functions like *stunning breath*, except that creatures that fail their Fortitude saves are stunned for 2d4 rounds.

SUBMERGE SHIP

Evocation [Water]
Level: Sorcerer/wizard 7
Components: V, S, F
Casting Time: 10 minutes
Range: Touch
Target: Ship touched
Duration: 1 hour/level
Saving Throw: None
Spell Resistance: No

Holding forth a miniature rudder, you touch the target ship. Immediately you feel connected to it, knowing the intricate details of its construction. You sense an invisible aura surrounding the ship and permeating its every space. Although it seems to be riding lower in the water than its weight would suggest, you instinctively know that you can control its every movement.

You grant the ship touched a swim speed of 60 feet and the ability to move beneath the surface of the water. You can control the ship's speed and direction as a free action. All interior spaces of the ship remain dry even if a doorway or porthole is open while the ship is underwater. Any creature aboard the ship when the spell is cast can move about the ship with ease (including climbing and jumping) as if it were afloat on a calm sea. Such creatures can breathe water for the duration of the spell as long as they remain within 10 feet of the ship. External forces, such as a storm or an angry dragon, can still jostle the ship and cause it to shake and possibly knock passengers and objects from it, but nothing falls from the ship as a result of your direction of its movement.

You can transfer control of the ship to another individual by giving that individual the miniature rudder you used as a focus to cast the spell. If the focus is ever lost or becomes unattended, the spell's duration expires.

Once the spell ends (either because the duration expired, the focus was lost or became unattended, or the magic was successfully dispelled), the magic lingers for 1 additional round per caster level. During this time, the ship ascends toward the water's surface at a rate of 60 feet per round. If the ship is still underwater when this additional time runs out, it immediately sinks, and its passengers risk drowning.

Focus: A miniature wooden rudder inlaid with silver, worth 2,500 gp.

SUBVERT PLANAR ESSENCE

Transmutation
Level: Cleric 5, sorcerer/wizard 6
Components: V, S, M/DF
Casting Time: 1 standard action
Range: Medium (100 ft. + 10 ft./level)
Area: 20-ft.-radius emanation centered on a point in space
Duration: 1 round/level
Saving Throw: Fortitude negates
Spell Resistance: Yes

Taking command of the forces that connect your plane to others, you reach out with your will and deaden an area to the influence of the Outer Planes on its natives.

The submerge ship spell allows everyone to travel beneath the waves

Outsiders within the emanation of a *subvert planar essence* spell find their connection disrupted with the planar forces that created them. Outsiders that fail their saves have their damage reduction and spell resistance each reduced by 10.

For example, a barbed devil subject to *subvert planar essence* would have no damage reduction and spell resistance 13, while a pit fiend would have damage reduction 5/good and silver, and spell resistance 22.

An outsider attempts a Fortitude save and checks spell resistance when it first enter the spell's area. If it makes the save or the spell fails to overcome its spell resistance, that creature is thereafter unaffected by this casting of *subvert planar essence* and can enter and exit the spell area without making further saves. Outsiders that fail their saves and have their spell resistance overcome by the spell are affected as long as they remain within the spell's area, and they are automatically affected if they leave and reenter the area.

Arcane Material Component: A tuning fork made from cold iron.

SUDDEN STALAGMITE

Conjuration (Creation) [Earth]
Level: Druid 4
Components: V, S
Casting Time: 1 standard action
Range: Medium (100 ft. + 10 ft./level)
Target: One creature
Duration: Instantaneous
Saving Throw: Reflex half
Spell Resistance: No

You point your finger upward and utter a curt shout. Immediately, a razor-sharp stalagmite bursts from the ground to impale your foe.

This spell creates a stalagmite about 1 foot wide at its base and up to 10 feet tall. If it encounters a ceiling before it reaches full size, it stops growing. The stalagmite grows from the ground under the target creature and shoots upward. An airborne creature within 10 feet of the ground gains a +4 bonus on its saving throw, and airborne creatures more than 10 feet above the ground cannot be harmed by this spell.

The stalagmite deals 1d6 points of piercing damage per caster level (maximum 10d6). In addition, a target that fails to make a saving throw against this spell and takes damage from it is impaled on the stalagmite and cannot move from its current location until it makes a DC 15 Escape Artist check. The stalagmite can be removed in other ways as well, such as with a *stone shape* spell. The victim can break free with a DC 25 Strength check, although doing this deals it 3d6 points of slashing damage.

A creature's damage reduction, if any, applies to the damage from this spell. The damage from *sudden stalagmite* is treated as piercing for the purpose of overcoming damage reduction.

SUMMON BABAU DEMON

Conjuration (Summoning) [Chaotic, Evil]
Level: Cleric 6
Components: V, S, DF
Casting Time: 1 round
Range: Close (25 ft. + 5 ft./2 levels)
Effect: One summoned babau demon
Duration: Concentration, up to 1 round/level + 1 round
Saving Throw: None
Spell Resistance: No

A puff of smoke erupts from the ground, smelling of brimstone and burning corpses. From the smoke strides the leathery form of a babau demon.

This spell summons a babau demon (MM 40) from the Infinite Layers of the Abyss. It appears where you designate and acts immediately, on your turn. It understands your speech (regardless of your language), and it follows your commands to the best of its ability. You must concentrate to maintain the spell's effect, but commanding the creature is a free action.

A summoned creature cannot summon or otherwise conjure another creature, nor can it use any teleportation or planar travel abilities.

SUMMON BEARDED DEVIL

Conjuration (Summoning) [Evil, Lawful]
Level: Cleric 5
Components: V, S, DF
Casting Time: 1 round
Range: Close (25 ft. + 5 ft./2 levels)
Effect: One summoned bearded devil
Duration: Concentration, up to 1 round/level + 1 round
Saving Throw: None
Spell Resistance: No

A fire flares from the ground, then subsides immediately. In the place of the first is the hunchbacked form of a barbazu, brandishing a saw-toothed glaive.

This spell summons a bearded devil (MM 52) from the Nine Hells of Baator. It appears where you designate and acts immediately, on your turn. It understands your speech (regardless of your language), and it follows your commands to the best of its ability. You must concentrate to maintain the spell's effect, but commanding the creature is a free action.

A summoned creature cannot summon or otherwise conjure another creature, nor can it use any teleportation or planar travel abilities.

SUMMON BRALANI ELADRIN

Conjuration (Summoning) [Chaotic, Good]
Level: Cleric 5
Components: V, S, DF
Casting Time: 1 round
Range: Close (25 ft. + 5 ft./2 levels)
Effect: One summoned bralani eladrin
Duration: Concentration, up to 1 round/level + 1 round
Saving Throw: None
Spell Resistance: No

A glowing blue seal appears on the ground and then subsides immediately. When it has vanished entirely, a bralani eladrin appears.

This spell summons a bralani eladrin (MM 93) from the Olympian Glades of Arborea. It appears where you designate and acts immediately, on your turn. It understands your speech (regardless of your language), and it follows your commands to the best of its ability. You must concentrate to maintain the spell's effect, but commanding the creature is a free action.

Illus. by J. Thomas

SUMMON ELEMENTAL MONOLITH

Conjuration (Summoning) [see text]
Level: Cleric 9, druid 9, sorcerer/wizard 9
Components: V, S, M
Casting Time: 1 round
Range: Medium (100 ft. + 10 ft./level)
Effect: One summoned elemental monolith
Duration: Concentration, up to 1 round/level
Saving Throw: None
Spell Resistance: No

You call into being a gigantic, roughly humanoid creature composed entirely of elemental matter. The creature immediately attacks a nearby enemy.

You conjure a tremendously powerful creature known as an elemental monolith (*Complete Arcane* 156). It appears at the spot you designate and acts immediately on your turn, attacking your opponents to the best of its ability. You must concentrate to maintain the spell's effect, but commanding the creature is a free action.

If you speak the elemental monolith's language and are close enough to communicate with it, you can direct it not to attack, to attack particular enemies, or to perform other actions. A monolith can't be summoned into an environment hostile to it in any way (for example, you couldn't summon a fire monolith underwater or an earth monolith high in midair).

When you use a summoning spell to summon an air, earth, fire, or water creature, it becomes a spell of that type.

Material Component: A gem worth 100 gp—aquamarine for air, tourmaline for earth, garnet for fire, or pearl for water.

SUMMON ELEMENTITE SWARM

Conjuration (Summoning) [see text]
Level: Druid 4
Components: V, S
Casting Time: 1 round
Range: Close (25 ft. + 5 ft./2 levels)
Effect: One summoned elementite swarm
Duration: Concentration, up to 1 round/level + 1 round
Saving Throw: None
Spell Resistance: No

You summon what looks like a host of small pebbles, which immediately descend upon your foes.

This spell summons an elementite swarm (*Planar Handbook* 114)—air, earth, fire, or water, at your option—from the appropriate Elemental Plane. It appears where you designate and acts immediately, on your turn. It understands your speech (regardless of your language), and it follows your commands to the best of its ability. You must concentrate to maintain the spell's effect, but commanding the creature is a free action.

When you use a summoning spell to summon an air, earth, fire, or water creature, it is a spell of that type.

SUMMON ELYSIAN THRUSH

Conjuration (Summoning) [Good]
Level: Bard 2, cleric 2
Components: V, S, DF
Casting Time: 10 minutes
Range: Close (25 ft. + 5 ft./2 levels)
Effect: One summoned Elysian thrush
Duration: 8 hours
Saving Throw: None
Spell Resistance: No

You evoke the powers of Elysium and of song, and the bird responds. It is about two feet long, with a resplendent orange breast and multicolored feathers. It settles upon a branch and begins to sweetly warble.

This spell summons an Elysian thrush (*Planar Handbook* 118), a birdlike creature native to the Blessed Fields of Elysium. The creature has no significant combat utility, but its song accelerates the natural healing rate of living creatures. Those within 30 feet who listen to the thrush's song while resting recover at twice the normal natural healing rate.

SUMMON GREATER ELEMENTAL

Conjuration (Summoning) [see text]
Level: Druid 6
Components: V, S, DF
Casting Time: 1 round
Range: Close (25 ft. + 5 ft./2 levels)
Effect: One summoned elemental
Duration: Concentration, up to 1 round/level + 1 round
Saving Throw: None
Spell Resistance: No

You call upon the powers of nature, and they respond to your command. A huge wave wells up before you, dark eyes within it regarding you from beneath the water. You point at the boat in the bay, and say, "Sink it."

This spell summons a greater elemental (MM 96–100)—air, earth, fire, or water, at your option—from the appropriate Elemental Plane. The greater elemental appears where you designate and acts immediately, on your turn. It understands your speech (regardless of your language), and it follows your commands to the best of its ability. You must concentrate to maintain the spell's effect, but commanding the creature is a free action.

When you use a summoning spell to summon an air, earth, fire, or water creature, it is a spell of that type.

SUMMON HOUND ARCHON

Conjuration (Summoning) [Good, Lawful]
Level: Cleric 4
Components: V, S, DF
Casting Time: 1 round
Range: Close (25 ft. + 5 ft./2 levels)
Effect: One summoned hound archon
Duration: Concentration, up to 1 round/level + 1 round
Saving Throw: None
Spell Resistance: No

You invoke the powers of good and law, and a brilliant beam stabs from the heavens above. Out of that beam strides a red-fleshed, dog-headed humanoid with a greatsword.

This spell summons a hound archon (MM 16) from the Seven Mounting Heavens of Celestia. It appears where you designate and acts immediately, on your turn. It understands your speech (regardless of your language), and it follows your commands to the best of its ability. You must concentrate to maintain the spell's effect, but commanding the creature is a free action.

A summoned creature cannot summon or otherwise conjure another creature, nor can it use any teleportation or planar travel abilities.

SUMMON UNDEAD I

Conjuration (Summoning) [Evil]
Level: Blackguard 1, cleric 1, sorcerer/wizard 1
Components: V, S, F/DF
Casting Time: 1 round
Range: Close (25 ft. + 5 ft./2 levels)
Effect: One summoned creature
Duration: 1 round/level
Saving Throw: None
Spell Resistance: No

The undead you summon appear in a burst of smoke and fog. The vapor swiftly dissipates, but you can't shake the impression of screaming faces in the cloud's tendrils.

This spell functions like *summon monster* I (PH 285), except that you summon an undead creature.

Summon undead I conjures one of the creatures from the 1st-level list in the accompanying sidebar. You choose which creature to summon, and you can change that choice each time you cast the spell. Summoned undead do not count toward the total Hit Dice of undead that you can control with *animate dead* or the other command undead abilities. No undead creature you summon can have more Hit Dice than your caster level +1.

Focus: A tiny bag, a small (not lit) candle, and a carved bone from any humanoid.

SUMMON UNDEAD II

Conjuration (Summoning) [Evil]
Level: Blackguard 2, cleric 2, sorcerer/wizard 2
Effect: One or more summoned creatures, no two of which are more than 30 ft. apart

Summon undead puts control of undead minions in the hands of even apprentice wizards

This spell functions like *summon undead* I, except that you can summon one undead from the 2nd-level list or two undead of the same kind from the 1st-level list.

SUMMON UNDEAD III

Conjuration (Summoning) [Evil]
Level: Blackguard 3, cleric 3, sorcerer/wizard 3
Effect: One or more summoned creatures, no two of which are more than 30 ft. apart

This spell functions like *summon undead* I, except that you can summon one undead from the 3rd-level list, two undead of the same kind from the 2nd-level list, or four undead of the same kind from the 1st-level list.

SUMMON UNDEAD IV

Conjuration (Summoning) [Evil]
Level: Blackguard 4, cleric 4, sorcerer/wizard 4
Effect: One or more summoned creatures, no two of which are more than 30 ft. apart

This spell functions like *summon undead* I, except that you can summon one undead from the 4th-level list, two undead of the same kind from the 3rd-level list, or four undead of the same kind from a lower-level list.

SUMMON UNDEAD V

Conjuration (Summoning) [Evil]
Level: Cleric 5, sorcerer/wizard 5
Effect: One or more summoned creatures, no two of which are more than 30 ft. apart

This spell functions like *summon undead* I, except that you can summon one undead from the 5th-level list, two undead of the same kind from the 4th-level list, or four undead of the same kind from a lower-level list.

SUMMON UNDEAD LISTS

1st Level: Human warrior skeleton (*MM* 226), kobold zombie (*MM* 266)
2nd Level: Owlbear skeleton (*MM* 226), bugbear zombie (*MM* 267).
3rd Level: Ghoul (*MM* 118), troll skeleton (*MM* 227), ogre zombie (*MM* 267).
4th Level: Allip (*MM* 10), ghast (*MM* 119), wyvern zombie (*MM* 267).
5th Level: Mummy (*MM* 190), shadow (*MM* 221), vampire spawn (*MM* 253), wight (*MM* 255).

SUPERIOR (SPELL NAME)

Any spell whose name begins with *superior* is alphabetized in this chapter according to the second word of the spell name. Thus, the description of a

Illus. by R. Spears

superior spell appears near the description of the spell on which it is based, unless that spell appears in the *Player's Handbook*.

SUPPRESS BREATH WEAPON

Enchantment (Compulsion) [Mind-Affecting]
Level: Bard 3, sorcerer/wizard 3
Components: V
Casting Time: 1 standard action
Range: Close (25 ft. + 5 ft./2 levels)
Target: One creature that has a breath weapon
Duration: 1 minute/level
Saving Throw: Will negates
Spell Resistance: No

You shout out the words of this spell and the creature's throat constricts, a blue ring of runes visible around its neck.

The subject of this spell cannot use its breath weapon for the duration of the spell.

SUPPRESS GLYPH

Abjuration
Level: Cleric 3
Components: V, S
Casting Time: 1 standard action
Range: 100 ft.
Area: 100-ft.-radius burst centered on you.
Duration: 1 minute/level
Saving Throw: Will negates (object)
Spell Resistance: Yes (object)

You cast the spell, and a dancing crown of ruby runes orbits your head briefly.

You gain an enhanced awareness of magical writing within range. Magical writing such as a *glyph of warding, explosive runes, sepia snake sigil*, or *symbol* is covered by a blue nimbus of light (which sheds light equal to a candle). This effect reveals the location of the writing without triggering it. For every source of magical writing, you can make a dispel check (1d20 + your caster level, maximum +10) against a DC equal to 11 + the writing's caster level. If you are successful, the magical writing is suppressed for 1 minute per caster level. You and other creatures could then read a book warded by *explosive runes*, or open a drawer guarded by a *glyph of warding*, or pass through a doorway protected by a *symbol* without effect.

This spell covers and negates any active or triggered magical writing (such as a quickly scribed *symbol of fear* or a triggered *symbol of death*), although creatures that have already succumbed to the effect of the writing are unaffected. Once this spell ends, all magical writing in the area can be triggered normally, and active or triggered writings resume their function if they have any duration left.

SUREFOOT

Abjuration
Level: Ranger 1
Components: V, S
Casting Time: 1 standard action
Range: Personal
Target: You
Duration: 10 minutes/level

You speak a few words and motion toward your feet, which begin to glow with a green hue.

Your steps are sure and true, even on the narrowest ledges. You gain a +10 competence bonus on Balance, Climb, Jump, and Tumble checks. In addition, you do not lose your Dexterity bonus to AC when balancing or climbing.

SUREFOOTED STRIDE

Transmutation
Level: Bard 2, druid 1, ranger 1, sorcerer/wizard 2
Components: V, S
Casting Time: 1 standard action
Range: Personal
Target: You
Duration: 1 minute/level
Saving Throw: None
Spell Resistance: No

You become as surefooted as any mountain goat, and the power of your magic makes walking in treacherous terrain child's play.

You can move through difficult terrain (PH 163) at full speed for the duration of this spell, and you can even run, charge, and tumble through such terrain as though it were clear terrain. You also gain a +2 competence bonus on Climb checks.

SUREFOOTED STRIDE, MASS

Transmutation
Level: Bard 5, druid 4, ranger 4, sorcerer/wizard 5
Range: Close (25 ft. + 5 ft./2 levels)
Target: One creature/level, no two of which are more than 30 ft. apart

This spell functions like *surefooted stride*, except as noted here.

SUSPENDED SILENCE

Illusion (Glamer)
Level: Sorcerer/wizard 3
Components: V, S, M
Casting Time: 1 standard action
Range: Touch
Target: One object
Duration: 24 hours or until discharged, then 6 rounds; see text
Saving Throw: None (object)
Spell Resistance: No (object)

You sprinkle the object with a handful of gem dust, and the last words of your spell fade like they are being dragged into a hole. Then the normal sounds of the world reestablish themselves, but the spell within is set to be unleashed later.

When you touch the object and give the command word you designate, the object becomes the subject of a *silence* spell. The effect of the *silence* spell moves with the object and lasts for 6 rounds.

Material Component: A feather and a handful of gem dust worth 50 gp.

SWAMP LUNG

Conjuration (Creation)
Level: Druid 7
Components: V, S, DF
Casting Time: 1 standard action
Range: Medium (100 ft. + 10 ft./level)
Target: One living creature with a respiratory system
Duration: Instantaneous
Saving Throw: Fortitude negates
Spell Resistance: No

You take a deep breath and feel the power of the spell surround you. Choosing your target, you unleash the spell's energy. A sea-green halo forms around your target's head. Moments later, the targeted creature begins coughing up water.

This spell causes stagnant swamp water to flood the target's lungs. If the target is unable to breathe water, it must cough it out. If it makes the save, then this expulsion is done with little effort. If it fails the save, the creature falls prone in a coughing fit for 1d6 rounds and is helpless during that time. Furthermore, on a failed save, the subject contracts filth fever (DMG 292).

Creatures able to breathe water must make the Fortitude save in order to avoid the disease, but are otherwise unaffected.

SWAMP STRIDE

Conjuration (Teleportation)
Level: Druid 5, ranger 4
Components: V, S, DF
Casting Time: 1 standard action
Range: Personal
Target: You
Duration: 1 hour/level or until expended; see text

Instinctively, you know the depth of the nearest pool of water, as well as other pools nearby of a similar depth. In your mind's eye you see the pools connected to one another magically, as if each were a doorway with a tunnel linking it to all the others.

This spell functions like *tree stride* (PH 296), but it is used for diving into pools of water rather than trees. Each pool must be at least 1 foot deep, and the exit pool of water must be similar in depth to the entry pool (within 1 foot). Unlike with *tree stride*, each jump has a maximum range of 500 feet. All other effects and limitations are the same.

SWIFT (SPELL NAME)

Any spell whose name begins with *swift* is alphabetized in this chapter according to the second word of the spell name. Thus, the description of a *swift* spell appears near the description of the spell on which it is based, unless that spell appears in the *Player's Handbook*.

SWIM

Transmutation [Water]
Level: Druid 2, sorcerer/wizard 2
Components: V, S, M
Casting Time: 1 round
Range: Medium (100 ft. + 10 ft./level)
Target: One creature
Duration: 10 minutes/level (D)
Saving Throw: None
Spell Resistance: Yes (harmless)

Making the sound of crashing waves with your throat completes the spell. With a wave of your hand, your subject seems more streamlined, with a hint of webbed appendages.

This spell gives the recipient a swim speed of 30 feet (although not the ability to breathe water or hold one's breath beyond normal limits). As long as the creature isn't carrying more than a light load, it can swim without making Swim checks. It also gains a +8 bonus on any Swim checks to perform special actions or avoid hazards, though it still takes the normal penalty for weight carried (–1 per 5 pounds). The recipient can choose to take 10 on Swim checks, even if rushed or threatened, and can use the run action while swimming if it swims in a straight line.

If the creature is carrying more than a light load, it must make Swim checks to move (taking the normal penalty for weight carried), but all other benefits of the spell still apply.

Material Component: A goldfish scale.

SWIM, MASS

Transmutation [Water]
Level: Druid 4
Targets: One creature/level, no two of which are more than 30 ft. apart

Choosing carefully the recipients of your spell, you cause a blue-green glow to emanate from each one. Moments later, the emanation fades, leaving the chosen creatures looking more lithe but with more robust limbs.

The spell functions like *swim*, except that it affects multiple creatures.

SWORD OF DARKNESS

Necromancy [Evil]
Level: Sorcerer/wizard 7
Components: V, S, M
Effect: Black blade of negative energy

You shatter the sword in your hand against a stone, bringing into being a similar weapon made entirely of black energy. As soon as it forms, the black blade attacks.

This spell functions like *sword of deception* (see below), except that you cause a black blade of pure negative energy to appear and attack opponents at a distance, as directed by you. Instead of dealing damage, a *sword of darkness* bestows one negative level on each successful hit against a living creature, threatens a critical hit on a roll of 19–20, and bestows two negative levels on a critical hit. Negative levels usually have a chance of permanently draining the subject's levels, but the negative levels from *sword of darkness* don't last long enough to do so. However, if the subject gains at least as many negative levels as it has Hit Dice, it dies.

If the sword strikes an undead creature, it grants that creature 5 temporary hit points per two caster levels (maximum 25 temporary hit points) that last for up to 1 hour.

Material Component: A bastard sword or longsword, which is shattered against a stone while casting the spell.

SWORD OF DECEPTION

Evocation [Force]
Level: Sorcerer/wizard 4
Components: V, S, F
Casting Time: 1 standard action
Range: Medium (100 ft. + 10 ft./level)
Effect: Pale green blade of force
Duration: 1 round/level (D)
Saving Throw: None
Spell Resistance: Yes

Swinging a miniature replica of a sword as if it were real, you bring into being a full-sized representation of your replica made entirely of pale green force. The blade immediately attacks your enemy.

You cause a blade of pale green force to appear and strike the opponent you designate, starting with one attack in the round when the spell is cast and continuing each round thereafter. Though it makes regular melee attacks, the sword strikes as a spell, not a weapon (and so can strike incorporeal creatures). A *sword of deception* always strikes from your direction, and so it can't be used to flank with your attacks, but it could flank with your allies.

The blade attacks with a base attack bonus equal to your caster level, dealing 1d8 points of damage per hit and threatening a critical hit on a roll of 19–20. In addition, each successful hit provides a

–2 penalty on the target's next saving throw roll (–4 on a successful critical hit). This penalty is cumulative (to a maximum of –5 on a single creature) and lasts until the creature is forced to make a saving throw in a dangerous situation or receives the benefit of a *remove curse* spell.

Each round, a *sword of deception* continues to attack the previous round's target unless you use a standard action to switch it to a new target within range. In any round when the weapon switches targets, it gets one attack as a standard action (as it does in the round when the spell is cast). The weapon can make multiple attack rolls against a single target with a full attack action if its base attack bonus permits. A *sword of deception* cannot be attacked or damaged (though it can be dispelled as any other spell).

If an attacked creature has spell resistance, make a caster level check the first time the sword attacks. If the check is successful, the sword can attack that creature with normal effect for the duration of the spell. If not, the *sword of deception* is dispelled. If the target goes beyond the spell range or out of your sight, the *sword of deception* returns to you and hovers.

Focus: A miniature replica of a sword and a set of loaded dice.

SYMBOL OF SPELL LOSS

Abjuration
Level: Cleric 5, sorcerer/wizard 5
Components: V, S
Casting Time: 10 minutes
Range: 0 ft.; see text
Effect: One symbol
Duration: See text
Saving Throw: Will negates
Spell Resistance: No

You trace the symbol and feel a pull as it tugs against the magical energy in your mind.

This spell functions like *symbol of death* (PH 289), except that when it is triggered, the symbol begins to attack the minds of spellcasters within 60 feet. Each must attempt a Will saving throw every round they are within range, at the beginning of their turn. Failure means that the highest-level spell prepared by the spellcaster (or highest-level spell slot, if the character casts spells spontaneously) is lost for the day. The symbol remains active for 10 minutes per level or until it has erased fifty levels of spells. The symbol attacks creatures with spell-like abilities as if they had spells, consuming a daily use of the highest-level ability the creature possesses, or suppressing an ability usable at will for 1 round.

SYMPHONIC NIGHTMARE

Enchantment (Compulsion) [Mind-Affecting]
Level: Bard 6, cleric 7, sorcerer/wizard 7
Components: V, S, F
Casting Time: 1 standard action
Range: Touch; see text
Target: Living creature touched; see text
Duration: 24 hours/level (D)
Saving Throw: Will negates
Spell Resistance: Yes

A dark and ominous aura forms around you as you complete the spell. Distant chords of a harsh and terrible symphony—as if multiple orchestras played different pieces simultaneously—echo continuously in the air as you reach for your victim.

A creature targeted by this spell loses the ability to dream during sleep or rest. Rather, in place of dreams, the subject's slumbering mind is filled with the sounds of a discordant orchestra. After the victim's first attempt to sleep, it incurs a –2 penalty on Wisdom-based skill checks. This penalty persists as long as the *symphonic nightmare* maintains its hold. This spell affects all creatures that sleep or enter sleeplike trances, although creatures without the need to sleep are effectively immune.

In addition, the creature's sleep is now haunted. It can no longer gain complete rest from sleeping or resting. The subject does not regain hit points or heal ability damage naturally, nor is it able to prepare spells if doing so requires a full night's rest.

The creature is, however, now immune to the *dream* and *nightmare* spells, as well as to other effects that cause nightmares (such as the night hag's dream haunting ability).

You can lift the effect of this curse at will, but it is otherwise difficult to remove a *symphonic nightmare* before its duration expires. A *remove curse* cast at a higher caster level than the *symphonic nightmare* spell removes it, as does a successful *break enchantment*. Otherwise, a *wish* or *miracle* is required to lift the curse.

This spell can also be cast on a creature you are scrying, or on a creature distant from you if you hold something the creature carried within the past 24 hours.

Focus: A small statue of an opened skull, within which is arranged a miniature orchestra. The quality of this component must be extraordinary, and it carries a value of 1,000 gp.

SYNOSTODWEOMER

Transmutation
Level: Sorcerer/wizard 7
Components: V, S
Casting Time: 1 swift action
Range: Personal
Target: One of your spells
Duration: 1 round

You cast this spell, and you picture a forge in your mind. You think of the forge as you cast your next spell, but that spell does not manifest. Instead, your hands glow with a golden curative radiance.

You channel the spell energy from a spell you know into healing magic. After you cast this spell, the next spell you cast in the same round is converted to positive energy. When you cast the second spell, you touch yourself or another creature, curing 1d8 points of damage for every spell level of the spell you cast. If the spell you cast was prepared with a metamagic feat, you use the level of the spell slot the spell occupied.

TACTICAL PRECISION

Divination [Mind-Affecting]
Level: Bard 2
Components: V, S, M
Casting Time: 1 standard action
Range: Close (25 ft. + 5 ft./2 levels)
Targets: One creature/level, no two of which are more than 30 ft. apart
Duration: 1 round/level
Saving Throw: Will negates (harmless)
Spell Resistance: Yes (harmless)

You hold aloft a toy soldier and shake it at your allies, calling them to arms as you do so. The toy soldier dissipates, but you feel a connection to your allies as though you could hear each one whispering her intended actions before she performed them.

When you cast this spell, you grant your allies greater insight into one another's actions, allowing them to better coordinate their attacks. If two affected allies flank the same creature, each gains a +2 insight bonus on melee attack rolls and deals an extra 1d6 points of damage against the flanked creature. Creatures not subject to extra damage from sneak attacks are immune to this extra damage.

Material Component: A toy soldier.

TARGETING RAY

Divination
Level: Bard 1, sorcerer/wizard 1
Components: V, S, F
Casting Time: 1 standard action
Range: Medium (100 ft. + 10 ft./level)
Effect: Ray
Duration: 1 round/level
Saving Throw: None
Spell Resistance: No

From your clenched fist you produce a luminous ray. The ray pulsates between the target creature and you.

The ray acts as a rangefinder for you and any allies. You must succeed on a ranged touch attack with the ray to strike a target. It provides a +1 insight bonus per three caster levels on ranged attacks directed at the subject for the duration of the spell. Your allies need not see you, but they must be able to see the ray. You can otherwise act normally for the duration of the spell. Allies who can see the target of the ray receive the bonus even if you lose line of sight to the target.

Focus: A small metal or stone tube.

TELEPATHIC AURA

Divination
Level: Paladin 4
Components: S, DF
Casting Time: 1 standard action
Range: 100 ft.
Area: 100-ft.-radius emanation centered on you
Duration: 10 minutes/level (D)
Saving Throw: None
Spell Resistance: No

You make a silent gesture with your holy symbol and think about your fellowship with your companions. In a moment, they all look up as if someone called their names.

You can mentally communicate with all allies within range, though this is one-way communication. (You can send thoughts, but you cannot receive thoughts in response.) Anything you choose to send is received by all creatures you perceive as allies within the emanation (you cannot send thoughts only to certain allies), and they all understand you regardless of language. Allies with Intelligence scores lower than 3 understand basic commands but not complex information ("Attack" is understood, but "Ignore the foot soldiers and attack the spellcasters" gets the same reaction as "Attack").

TELEPATHIC BOND, LESSER

Divination [Mind-Affecting]
Level: Mind 3, sorcerer/wizard 3
Components: V, S
Casting Time: 1 standard action
Range: 30 ft.
Targets: You and one willing creature within 30 ft.
Duration: 10 minutes/level
Saving Throw: None
Spell Resistance: No

As you send your thoughts outward, your mind brushes against the consciousness of your friend and it welcomes you, forming a bond that no distance can break.

You forge a telepathic bond with another creature with an Intelligence score of 6 or higher. You can communicate telepathically through the bond regardless of language. No special power or influence is established as a result of the bond. Once the bond is formed, it works over any distance (although not from one plane to another).

THORNSKIN

Transmutation
Level: Druid 3
Components: V, S, M
Casting Time: 1 standard action
Range: Personal
Target: You
Duration: 1 round/level (D)

You push a thorn against your skin to complete the spell. Instead of piercing your skin, the thorn melds into it. An instant later, hundreds of similar thorns sprout all over your body.

Your skin sprouts thorns when this spell is cast, increasing the damage you deal with an unarmed strike and making you difficult to grab. As well as dealing lethal damage with your unarmed strikes (if you don't already do so), you deal an extra 1d6 points of piercing damage (so that a human under the effect of *thornskin* would deal 1d3 points of bludgeoning damage + 1d6 points of piercing damage with an unarmed strike). In addition, any creature that hits you with a natural weapon or unarmed strike (including all successful grapple checks) takes 5 points of piercing damage.

A creature's damage reduction, if any, applies to the damage from this spell. The damage from *thornskin* is treated as piercing for the purpose of overcoming damage reduction.

Material Component: A thorn.

THUNDERHEAD

Evocation [Electricity]
Level: Druid 1, sorcerer/wizard 1
Components: V, S, M
Casting Time: 1 standard action
Range: Close (25 ft. + 5 ft./2 levels)
Target: One creature
Duration: 1 round/level
Saving Throw: Reflex negates; see text
Spell Resistance: Yes

Black mist forms near the ground and sweeps upward to join a small cloud forming above the creature you designate as your target. Miniature peals of thunder erupt from the cloud.

Thunderhead creates a small thundercloud over the subject's head. The cloud moves with the subject, following it unerringly even if he becomes invisible or leaves the region. In every round of the spell's duration, a miniature bolt of lightning leaps from the thundercloud to strike the subject. Each bolt deals 1 point of electricity damage that is negated by a successful Reflex save.

Material Component: A small piece of copper wire.

THUNDERLANCE

Evocation [Force]
Level: Sorcerer/wizard 4
Components: V, S, M
Casting Time: 1 standard action
Range: 0 ft.
Effect: A spearlike beam
Duration: 1 round/level (D)
Saving Throw: None
Spell Resistance: No

A faint gray shimmering force in the general shape of a staff or spear springs from your hand.

When you cast this spell, you create a deadly lance of force. You can freely make a *thunderlance* retract or grow to any length from 1 foot to 20 feet, but it always remains a straight lance of force. This effect gives you a natural reach of 20 feet. You can use a *thunderlance* to make powerful melee attacks.

You can wield a *thunderlance* in one or two hands, dealing a base 3d6 points of damage (crit 20/×3). Instead of using your Strength modifier, you use the higher of your Intelligence modifier or Charisma modifier as a bonus on attack rolls and damage rolls.

If you successfully strike a target protected by any force effect of 3rd level or lower, such as a *shield* or *mage armor* spell, the *thunderlance* might dispel the force effect in addition to damaging the target. Make a dispel check against the level of the caster who created the effect. If you succeed, the effect is dispelled. The *thunderlance* remains whether you succeed or fail on this check.

Material Component: A small metal spear.

The thunderhead spell seems a nuisance, but it can be deadly

Illus. by D. Martin

THUNDEROUS ROAR

Evocation [Sonic]
Level: Druid 3
Components: V, S, DF
Casting Time: 1 standard action
Range: Long (400 ft. + 40 ft./level)
Area: 20-ft.-radius burst
Duration: Instantaneous
Saving Throw: Fortitude partial; see text
Spell Resistance: Yes

Calling upon the lost voices of dead creatures, you cause the targeted area to become filled with the enraged roaring of a thousand dinosaurs. The ground beneath the area shakes with the sound.

The resulting blast of sound from the casting of *thunderous roar* can be heard for miles, but the spell affects only those in its area. All creatures in the affected area take 1d6 points of sonic damage per two caster levels (maximum 5d6). A successful Fortitude saving throw halves the damage. Additionally, any creature that takes damage from this spell must make a Reflex saving throw or be knocked prone from the force of the roar. Crystalline creatures take 1d6 points of sonic damage per caster level (maximum 10d6).

TIDAL SURGE

Evocation [Water]
Level: Druid 6
Components: V, S
Casting Time: 1 standard action
Range: Medium (100 ft. + 10 ft./level)
Targets: One creature or all creatures in a 20-ft.-radius burst
Duration: Instantaneous
Saving Throw: Reflex half
Spell Resistance: Yes

An explosion of water rushes out from the point you designate, bowling over your enemies.

When you cast this spell, you create a huge wave of water that slams into one or more targets within range. If no large, natural source of water (a river, lake, or ocean) exists within the spell's range, you can affect only one target. If such a source of water exists within the range of the spell, the spell creates a burst centered on a location you designate. In either case, the water deals 1d6 points of damage per caster level (maximum 15d6) to the target or to creatures within the burst.

In addition, all affected creatures are subjected to a bull rush attack, forcing them to make opposed Strength checks against the wave of water. The water has a +5 bonus on the opposed Strength check, or a +10 bonus if the spell is cast near a source of water. You designate the direction the wave pushes when you cast the spell; creatures that lose the opposed Strength check are pushed back 5 feet, plus an additional 5 feet for every 5 points by which the wave beats their Strength checks, in the chosen direction. It is possible for a wave arising from a body of water to push characters into the water.

The wave puts out torches, campfires, exposed lanterns, and other open flames if they are carried by the target or located within the area and they are Large or smaller. If the wave hits a magical fire, those flames are targeted by a *dispel magic* effect as if you had cast the spell.

TIGER'S TOOTH

Transmutation
Level: Druid 2
Components: V
Casting Time: 1 swift action
Duration: 1 round

You speak quickly, and your animal companion glows briefly, the glow focusing around its natural weapons.

This spell functions like *magic fang* (PH 250), except as noted above.

TORTOISE SHELL

Transmutation
Level: Druid 6
Components: V, S, DF
Casting Time: 1 standard action
Range: Touch
Target: Living creature touched
Duration: 10 minutes/level
Saving Throw: None
Spell Resistance: Yes (harmless)

In the blink of an eye, the creature you touched grows the armor plating of a tortoise across its torso and a tough, leathery skin elsewhere.

Tortoise shell grants a +6 enhancement bonus to the subject's existing natural armor bonus. This enhancement bonus increases by 1 for every three caster levels beyond 11th, to a maximum of +9 at 20th level.

The enhancement bonus provided by *tortoise shell* stacks with the target's natural armor bonus, but not with other enhancement bonuses to natural armor. A creature without natural armor has an effective natural armor of +0, much as a character wearing only normal clothing has an armor bonus of +0.

Tortoise shell slows a creature's movement as if it were wearing heavy armor. An elf subject to *tortoise shell*, for example, would have a speed of 20 feet and could run only 60 feet per round. The spell affects only a creature's speed; *tortoise shell* doesn't carry an armor check penalty or an arcane spell failure chance.

TOUCH OF MADNESS

Enchantment [Mind-Affecting]
Level: Madness 2
Components: V, S
Casting Time: 1 standard action
Range: Touch
Target: Creature touched
Duration: 1 round/level
Saving Throw: Will negates
Spell Resistance: Yes

Your hand glows with roiling purple light as you reach out to deliver lunacy with your touch.

You can cause one living creature to become dazed by making a successful touch attack. If the target creature does not make a successful Will save, its mind is clouded and it takes no actions for 1 round per caster level.

TOWERING OAK

Illusion (Glamer)
Level: Ranger 1
Components: V, S
Casting Time: 1 swift action
Range: Personal
Target: You
Duration: 1 round/level

You evoke the power of the forests, giving yourself the ability to speak for them. You loom over others like a mighty tree dwarfs lesser plants.

You draw on the oak's strength to improve your ability to intimidate your enemies. You gain a +10 competence bonus on Intimidate checks and a +2 enhancement bonus to Strength.

TRAIN ANIMAL

Enchantment (Charm) [Mind-Affecting]
Level: Druid 2, ranger 2
Components: V, S, DF
Casting Time: 10 minutes
Range: Touch
Target: Animal touched
Duration: 1 hour/level
Saving Throw: Will negates (harmless)
Spell Resistance: Yes (harmless)

At last, you near the end of the spell's complicated procedure. As the final act of the ritual, you call out the tricks you wish to teach the animal you are touching. Your hand tingles for a moment as the spell takes effect.

While this spell is in effect, the affected animal gains a number of additional tricks equal to half your caster level (maximum five).

This spell does not modify an animal's attitude toward you, nor does it guarantee that an animal will cooperate when instructed to perform the newly learned tricks.

TRANSCRIBE SYMBOL

Abjuration
Level: Sorcerer/wizard 6
Components: V, S, F
Casting Time: 1 standard action
Range: Touch
Target: Magic symbol touched
Duration: 10 minutes or until discharged
Saving Throw: None
Spell Resistance: No

Mimicking the marks of the sigil on the slate you hold, you render yourself immune to detection by the magic symbol.

You place a protective spell upon your hand that allows you to touch an untriggered magic sigil (such as a *glyph of warding* or a *symbol of death*) without setting it off. The touched sigil is removed from its location and held as magical potential on your hand, as though it were a touch spell.

To pick up a sigil in this manner, you must make a successful caster level check (DC 20 + the target glyph's spell level). Failure indicates that you have triggered the glyph or symbol. If you successfully transfer the sigil to your hand, you can use a standard action to place it on a surface (not a creature) of the sort on which it can normally be scribed. The transferred sigil works normally thereafter and retains all its original triggering conditions, although its current location might make its triggers difficult or impossible to achieve.

You can maintain the magic sigil on your hand as long as you concentrate. If your concentration lapses or the spell duration expires while the sigil is thus stored as potential, it immediately triggers upon you (and only you), even if you normally would not meet its trigger conditions. The effect has the same saving throw and spell resistance as the original spell did. The only safe way to rid yourself of the stored sigil is to place it upon a suitable surface.

Focus: A piece of slate that has been scoured bare and smooth on one side.

TRANSFIX

Enchantment (Compulsion) [Mind-Affecting]
Level: Sorcerer/wizard 7
Components: V, S, M
Casting Time: 1 round
Range: Medium (100 ft. + 10 ft./level)
Area: 10-ft.-radius emanation centered on a point in space
Duration: 1 hour/level
Saving Throw: Will negates; see text
Spell Resistance: Yes

With a declaration, you finish your casting. Immediately, beings in the affected area cease moving, standing as still as statues.

This spell causes any Medium or smaller humanoids within the area of the spell to become paralyzed. When casting the spell, you must specify a condition that will end it ("Wait here until the dragon arrives"), even if that condition can never feasibly be met ("Stay here until the sun shines at night"). Subjects in the area that fail their saves immediately become aware of the condition, but they cannot communicate it due to their paralyzed state (although someone could use a spell such as *detect thoughts* to ascertain the condition). For every hour the creatures are transfixed before the condition is met, they are allowed another saving throw to break free of the spell's effect.

As long as the spell operates, any Medium or smaller humanoid that enters its area must make a successful saving throw or become transfixed with the same exit conditions (they too become aware of the exit conditions on becoming transfixed). Likewise, any creatures removed from the area are freed from the spell's effect.

An affected creature that is attacked gains a new saving throw to break free of the enchantment.

Material Component: A drop of pine resin.

Transcribe symbol allows a wizard to pick up and move a protective glyph

Illus. by F. Vohwinkel

TRANSLOCATION TRICK

Conjuration [Teleportation]
Level: Sorcerer/wizard 4
Components: V
Casting Time: 1 standard action
Range: Medium (100 ft. + 10 ft./level)
Targets: You and one creature
Duration: 10 minutes/level
Saving Throw: Will negates; see text
Spell Resistance: Yes

You utter the words, and in an instant you and your target are switched—you take its position and form, and it appears where you had stood moments before, looking to others as you appear.

You and the other target switch locations, as if simultaneously using *dimension door* spells (PH 221) and exchange appearances, as if using *disguise self* spells (PH 222) to appear as each other. Your target can negate this spell with a successful saving throw.

If you or your target exceed the capacity of the *dimension door* spell or if you and your target have bodies that are so different that the *disguise self* spell could not disguise you as your target, this spell fails.

Magic that penetrates disguises (such as *true seeing*) reveals the identities of you and your target. Otherwise, you are considered to be disguised as your target and vice versa for the duration of the spell. You get a +10 bonus on Disguise checks to impersonate the target.

When the spell ends, you and your target revert to your true appearances in your current locations. You do not switch places again.

TRANSMUTE ROCK TO LAVA

Transmutation [Earth, Fire]
Level: Druid 9, sorcerer/wizard 9
Components: V, S
Casting Time: 1 standard action
Range: Medium (100 ft. + 10 ft./level)
Area: One 10-ft. cube
Duration: Instantaneous
Saving Throw: Reflex half; see text
Spell Resistance: No

As you release the spell's energy, the targeted area of stone instantly turns to molten lava, and the uncomfortable burning in your chest immediately ceases.

You transform natural, uncut, or unworked rock of any sort into an equal volume of red-hot molten lava. All creatures in the spell's area that make successful Reflex saves take 6d6 points of fire damage, provided they can physically escape the area on their next turn. Creatures that fail their saves, or those unable to escape the area, take 20d6 points of fire damage in each round they remain in the area.

Creatures in the lava have their speed reduced to 5 feet and take a –2 penalty on attack rolls and to Armor Class. Even after leaving the area of the spell, creatures that were exposed to the lava take half damage (either 3d6 or 10d6) for 1 additional round.

If *transmute rock to lava* is cast upon the ceiling of a cavern or tunnel, the lava falls to the floor and spreads out in a 15-foot-radius pool at a depth of approximately 1-1/2 feet. The rain of lava deals 2d6 points of fire damage to anyone caught directly beneath (Reflex half). In addition, creatures take 10d6 points of fire damage each round when they are caught in the area of the pool.

Although constructions of worked stone can't be targeted with this spell, casting it on unworked stone below or adjacent to such structures deals 10d6 points of fire damage per round to any part of the structure in contact with the lava. Wooden structures in contact with lava instantly burst into flame.

The lava cools naturally from its surface toward its center, and it no longer deals fire damage after 2d6 hours as it slowly reverts to stone. Though a 15-foot-radius pool can take as long as two days to completely cool, the core of a 10-foot cube of lava might remain molten for a month or more.

Magical or enchanted stone is not affected by the spell.

TRAVELER'S MOUNT

Transmutation
Level: Blackguard 1, druid 1, paladin 1, ranger 1
Components: V, S
Casting Time: 1 standard action
Range: Touch
Target: Animal or magical beast touched
Duration: 1 hour/level
Saving Throw: Will negates
Spell Resistance: Yes

With words of encouragement, you make the creature better able to handle the rigors of overland travel, at the expense of its ability to fight.

The touched animal or magical beast gets a 20-foot enhancement bonus to its speed, and it can hustle without taking damage or becoming fatigued as long as the spell is in effect. While bearing a rider, the mount no longer attacks in combat. The steed willingly bears its rider into battle; it just can't use its own natural weapons for the duration of the spell.

The treasure scent spell allows a spellcaster to sniff out riches

TREASURE SCENT

Divination
Level: Bard 3, druid 3, sorcerer/wizard 4
Components: V, S
Casting Time: 1 standard action
Range: Personal
Target: You
Duration: 1 hour/level

A multihued glow of metallic colors surrounds you. The swirling glow manifests as a thin mist that forces itself up into your nose. Suppressing a sneeze, you note with excitement the unmistakable scent of treasure.

You can detect copper, silver, gold, platinum, and gems within 30 feet, as well as differentiate between the five kinds of valuables.

When you detect one of these types of valuables, the exact location of the source is not revealed—only its presence and direction. Whenever you come within 5 feet of the treasure, you can pinpoint its exact location. The spell can penetrate barriers, but 1 foot of stone, 1 inch of common metal, a thin sheet of lead, or 3 feet of wood or dirt blocks it.

TREMOR

Evocation [Earth]
Level: Cleric 3, druid 3
Components: V, S, DF
Casting Time: 1 standard action
Range: Medium (100 ft. + 10 ft./level)
Area: 40-ft.-radius spread
Duration: 1 round/3 levels
Saving Throw: See text
Spell Resistance: No

When you cast this spell, a small, localized tremor shakes the ground in the area. Detritus and loose debris rattle with the small quake, and creatures caught in the area stumble and fall.

This minor quake is not strong enough to damage structures. The effect lasts for 1 round per three caster levels, during which time any spellcaster on the ground in the area must succeed on a Concentration check (DC 15 + spell level) or lose any spell she is casting. A

Illus. by W. England

creature attempting to use a skill that would provoke attacks of opportunity (such as Disable Device, Heal, Open Lock, and Use Rope, among others) must succeed on a DC 15 Concentration check, or the action automatically fails and is wasted. Each creature in the area must make a Reflex save each round or be knocked prone.

TREMORSENSE

Transmutation
Level: Ranger 2, sorcerer/wizard 3
Components: V, S, F/DF
Casting Time: 1 standard action
Range: Personal
Target: You
Duration: 10 minutes/level (D)

You cast this spell and know where each of your opponents stands. Their presence is marked in your mind like ripples radiating along the surface of a pond.

You can automatically pinpoint the location of any object or creature within 30 feet that is in contact with the ground.

Arcane Focus: A fleck of skin from a creature that has tremorsense.

TRIADSPELL

Transmutation
Level: Cleric 5
Components: V, S
Casting Time: 1 standard action
Range: Personal
Target: You
Duration: Instantaneous

You complete the casting, and deep within your mind, you feel one of your prepared spells subdividing into three parts, each as powerful as its original.

You alter one of your prepared spells so that you can cast it three times before it is expended. The prepared spell must be of 3rd level or lower, and once the *triadspell* is cast, you can cast the altered spell two additional times (a total of three times) before it is expended. The altered spell functions normally and requires components or XP for each use as if you were casting three separate spells. If you later choose to prepare a different spell in that spell slot, any extra castings provided by the *triadspell* are lost. You cannot cast *triadspell* more than once upon a single prepared spell.

TRUE CREATION

Conjuration (Creation)
Level: Creation 8
Components: V, S, M, XP
Casting Time: 10 minutes
Range: 0 ft.
Effect: Unattended, nonmagical object of nonliving matter, up to 1 cu. ft./level
Duration: Instantaneous
Saving Throw: None
Spell Resistance: No

With one last invocation to your deity, you end the spell and bring into being the object you desire.

You create a nonmagical, unattended object of any sort of matter. Items created are permanent and cannot be negated by dispelling magic or negating powers. For all intents and purposes, these items are completely real. The volume of the item created cannot exceed 1 cubic foot per caster level. You must succeed on an appropriate skill check to make a complex item, such as a Craft (bowmaking) check to make straight arrow shafts or a Craft (gemcutting) check to make a cut and polished gem.

Unlike the items brought into being by the lower-level spells *minor creation* and *major creation*, objects created by the casting of *true creation* can be used as material components.

Material Component: A small piece of matter of the same type of item you plan to create—a sliver of wood to create arrow shafts, a tiny piece of the appropriate stone to create a polished gem, and so forth.

XP Cost: Half the item's gold piece value in XP, or 50 XP, whichever is more.

TRUE DOMINATION

Enchantment (Compulsion) [Mind-Affecting]
Level: Domination 8
Components: V, S
Casting Time: 1 standard action
Range: Medium (100 ft. + 10 ft./level)
Target: One humanoid
Duration: 24 hours/level
Saving Throw: Will negates; see text
Spell Resistance: Yes

Reaching out with your thoughts, you grasp the mind of your foe and take command of its actions.

You can control the actions of any humanoid. You establish a telepathic link with the subject's mind. If a common language is shared, you can generally force the subject to perform as you desire, within the limits of its abilities. If no common language is shared, you can communicate only basic commands, such as "Come here," "Go there," "Fight," and "Stand still." You know what the subject is experiencing, but you do not receive direct sensory input from it.

Subjects have a chance of resisting this control by making a Will save to avoid the effect when the spell is cast. Those affected by the spell and then forced to take actions against their nature receive a new saving throw with a –4 penalty. Obviously self-destructive orders might be carried out, unless the subject can make a saving throw with the –4 penalty. Once control is established, the range at which it can be exercised is unlimited, as long as you and the subject are on the same plane. You need not see the subject to control it.

Protection from evil or a similar spell can prevent you from exercising control or using the telepathic link while the subject is so warded, but it does not prevent the establishment of domination or dispel it.

TSUNAMI

Conjuration (Creation) [Water]
Level: Druid 9
Components: V, S, M
Casting Time: 1 round
Range: Long (400 ft. + 40 ft./level)
Effect: 20-ft./level-wide, 10-ft.-long, 40-ft.-high wave of water; see text
Duration: Concentration, up to 1 round/level (D)
Saving Throw: Fortitude partial (object)
Spell Resistance: No

The eldest, most powerful forces of elemental water heed your summons and obey your request. These forces of pure elemental power gather together a wall of water that moves inexorably in the direction of your choice, crushing all that it encounters.

This spell creates a towering tsunami and sends it forth in a powerful wave to smash all in its path. The *tsunami* starts at any point you select within range of the spell and then moves at a speed of 60 feet in any direction chosen by you. Once the direction is set, the *tsunami* cannot change course. The *tsunami* deals 1d6 points of bludgeoning damage per caster level (maximum 20d6) to all in its path. Anything struck can make a Fortitude saving throw for half damage. Gargantuan or larger creatures that fail the save are knocked prone. Huge or smaller creatures that fail the save are picked up and carried with the wave. Each round a victim is carried by the *tsunami,* it takes the bludgeoning damage again and can make an additional Fortitude save for half damage. Creatures being carried by a *tsunami* cannot move in any other way. They can otherwise act normally, but must make a Concentration check (DC 20 + spell level) to cast a spell. Creatures caught in a *tsunami* take a –4 penalty to Dexterity and a –2 penalty on attack rolls. They can escape the wave by making successful DC 20 Swim checks, as long as they end their movement outside the effect of the *tsunami.*

Any creature that comes in contact with a *tsunami* as a result of movement during its turn is considered to have been struck by the *tsunami*'s movement. A creature can attempt to extract another creature caught by a *tsunami,* providing the rescuer resists being swept up or knocked down by the *tsunami* and can reach the victim Extracting a victim in this manner requires a DC 20 Strength check.

A *tsunami*'s progress can be halted by anything that would normally block line of effect along its path, assuming the *tsunami* does not destroy the intervening object or creature. If only a portion of the *tsunami* is blocked, the rest of it continues on.

Although this spell can be cast on dry land, it is most effective when cast on the open sea. In this case, saving throws to avoid full damage are made with a –4 penalty, and the width of the *tsunami* increases to 40 feet per caster level. A *tsunami* that begins on water but then travels onto land immediately shrinks to its land size and speed. A *tsunami* does not vanish if it moves beyond the spell's initial range.

Material Component: A crown of coral set with pearls (total value of at least 5,000 gp).

TUNNEL SWALLOW

Conjuration (Creation) [Earth]
Level: Sorcerer/wizard 6
Components: V, S, M
Casting Time: 1 standard action
Range: Medium (100 ft. + 10 ft./level)
Target: Tunnel section up to 20 ft. in diameter and up to 50 ft. long
Duration: Instantaneous
Saving Throw: Reflex partial; see text
Spell Resistance: No

You unleash the power of this spell, and the walls of the tunnel begin to roil and shift on all sides, clenching in rapid succession as they fling your opponents down the hallway.

You cause a section of tunnel to flex with peristaltic convulsions, crushing its contents and moving them along its length in the direction you designate. Each creature and object in the affected tunnel section is crushed for 1d6 points of damage per level (maximum 15d6) and is moved from its former position to a point just outside the affected tunnel section. A creature that makes a successful Reflex saving throw takes only half damage and is moved halfway from its former position in the tunnel toward the designated end of the tunnel section. When the spell duration expires, the tunnel returns to its former shape and size, with no harm done to its structure.

Tunnel swallow affects both worked and natural tunnels, as well as corridors in surface buildings, but does not harm the structure.

Movement caused by this spell does not provoke attacks of -opportunity.

Material Component: A lump of chewed vegetable or meat.

UNBINDING

Abjuration
Level: Liberation 9, sorcerer/wizard 9
Components: V, S, M, DF
Casting Time: 1 round
Range: 180 ft.
Area: 180-ft.-radius burst centered on you
Duration: Instantaneous
Saving Throw: None
Spell Resistance: No

A burst of white energy erupts from your body to destroy spells that contain, constrain, or seal.

The tsunami spell can wash the natural world clean of unbalancing force

Illus. by J. Engle

An *unbinding* spell negates *charm* and *hold* spells of all types; *arcane locks* and similar closures; and spells that create physical or magical barriers, such as *wall of fire, wall of force, guards and wards, temporal stasis,* and *slow* spells, among others. The effect of a *statue* spell is also ended, and a *magic jar* is shattered—forever destroyed—and the life force within snuffed out. In addition, any spell that holds magical effects, including other spells (*magic mouth, imbue with spell* ability, and so on), immediately releases them at a range of 0 feet.

Protective spells such as *protection from evil, shield, globe of invulnerability,* and similar spells are not affected by an *unbinding.* Petrified creatures are neither revealed nor restored. Individuals bound to service are not freed (including creatures such as familiars, invisible stalkers, genies, and elementals). An *antimagic field* is not affected, nor does the effect of *unbinding* penetrate one. A *magic circle against evil* (or another alignment) that currently holds a creature imprisoned is dispelled.

Curses and *geas/quest* spells are negated only if you are of a level equal to or greater than that of the original caster.

All these effects occur without regard to the caster's wishes. Spell effects on the person of the caster, or effects or items being carried or worn by the caster, remain undisturbed, but any others within the area are affected, including those of allies. The opening of locks or other closures triggers any alarms or traps attached to them. Any released creature might or might not be friendly to the caster.

Material Components: A lodestone and a pinch of saltpeter.

UNDEAD BANE WEAPON

Transmutation
Level: Cleric 4, paladin 3
Components: V, S, DF
Casting Time: 1 standard action
Range: Touch
Target: Weapon touched or fifty projectiles (all of which must be in contact with each other at the time of casting)
Duration: 1 hour/level
Saving Throw: Will negates (harmless, object)
Spell Resistance: Yes (harmless, object)

Your hand glows with a dull light, and when you touch the weapon, the light shifts to it, so that it sheds a serene gray radiance as bright as a candle.

You give a weapon the undead bane special ability in addition to any other properties it has. Against undead, your weapon's enhancement bonus is 2 higher than normal, and it deals an extra 2d6 points of damage against undead. The spell has no effect if cast upon a weapon that already has the undead bane special ability.

Alternatively, you can affect up to fifty arrows, bolts, or bullets. The projectiles must be of the same kind, and they have to be together, such as in the same quiver. Projectiles, but not thrown weapons, lose their transmutation after one attack.

The weapon is treated as good-aligned for the purpose of overcoming damage reduction.

UNDEAD LIEUTENANT

Necromancy
Level: Sorcerer/wizard 3
Components: V, S
Casting Time: 1 standard action
Range: Close (25 ft. + 5 ft./2 levels)
Target: One undead creature; see text
Duration: 24 hours
Saving Throw: Will negates (harmless)
Spell Resistance: Yes (harmless)

You cast your spell on the foul creature, and for a brief moment your own face appears atop its ruined body.

You empower the subject undead with the authority of command over undead in your control. The targeted undead must have Intelligence 5 or higher. Undead under your control obey the target undead as if it were you. You can give orders to the undead normally, superseding the orders of the subject of this spell. The number of undead you can control is increased by an amount equal to your caster level as long as the *undead lieutenant* is active. If the target undead creature is destroyed, the spell ends.

You can have only one *undead lieutenant* at any time.

UNDEAD TORCH

Necromancy
Level: Sorcerer/wizard 3
Components: V, S, M
Casting Time: 1 standard action
Range: Close (25 ft. + 5 ft./2 levels)
Targets: One corporeal undead/level, no two of which are more than 30 ft. apart
Duration: 1 round/level
Saving Throw: Will negates (harmless)
Spell Resistance: Yes (harmless)

You make a dark incantation and smash the firefly between your thumb and forefinger. The undead bursts into blue flames that do not burn.

The subject creature deals an extra 2d6 points of damage on melee attacks against living creatures. If an attacked creature has spell resistance, the resistance is checked the first time the undead subject attacks it. If your caster level check fails, the creature is unaffected by that casting of the *undead torch.*

If the undead creature is destroyed, the *undead torch* continues to burn at the location of its destruction until the duration ends, and living creatures that pass through that area take 2d6 points of damage. If the undead creature assumes a nonphysical state (such as a vampire assuming gaseous form), the spell disperses harmlessly.

Material Component: A living or dead firefly or glowworm.

UNDEATH'S ETERNAL FOE

Abjuration [Good]
Level: Cleric 9
Components: V, S, DF
Casting Time: 1 standard action
Range: Close (25 ft. + 5 ft./2 levels)
Targets: One creature/5 levels
Duration: 1 round/level
Saving Throw: None (harmless)
Spell Resistance: Yes (harmless)

You invoke the power of good and indicate each of your party members in turn. A crystal blue aura springs up around each of them, fortifying them against the assaults of undead.

You grant one or more creatures special abilities that allow them to effectively destroy undead.

All subjects receive a *death ward* effect (PH 217). The subjects also have immunity to the special attacks and abilities of undead that deal ability damage, ability drain, fear effects, disease, paralysis, or poison. Targets can make melee and ranged attacks against ethereal or incorporeal undead as if they were using *ghost touch* weapons. They also gain a +4 sacred bonus to AC against attacks by undead.

UNDERMASTER

Transmutation [Earth]
Level: Druid 9, sorcerer/wizard 9
Components: V, M
Casting Time: 1 standard action
Range: Personal
Target: You
Duration: 5 rounds

You invoke the mighty powers of the earth and it rises about you, limning you from below with brilliant green radiance. The power surges within your hands as you are invested with its might, and you bend that might to your own will.

You take up the mantle of the earth, gaining power over it as long as you stand upon or beneath its surface. While energized with the awesome power of this spell, you can choose a spell from those listed below once per round and use it as a spell-like ability. Using a spell in this way requires a standard action, even if the spell would normally have a longer casting time (such as *move earth*).

The spells granted by *undermaster* are *earth lock, earthquake, excavate, flesh to stone, meld into stone, move earth, reverse gravity, soften earth and stone, statue, stone shape, stone tell, stone to flesh, transmute mud to rock, transmute rock to mud, tunnel swallow, wall of stone*, and *xorn movement*.

Material Component: A deep blue spinel worth 500 gp.

UNDERSONG

Transmutation
Level: Bard 1
Components: V
Casting Time: 1 standard action
Range: Personal
Target: You
Duration: 10 minutes/level

When you cast this spell, a familiar and soothing song wells up in your mind.

This spell brings to your mind a song that helps you retain your concentration. The song does not distract you from any task at hand—on the contrary, by humming along to the tune, you can focus your mind with ease. As long as this spell is in effect, you can make a Perform check in place of a Concentration check.

The undead torch spell lends an undead greater power to harm the living

UNHOLY STORM

Conjuration (Creation) [Evil, Water]
Level: Blackguard 3, cleric 3
Components: V, S, M, DF
Casting Time: 1 standard action
Area: Cylinder (20-ft. radius, 20 ft. high)
Duration: 1 round/level (D)
Saving Throw: None
Spell Resistance: No

You call upon the forces of evil, and a heavy rain begins to fall in the area you indicate, its raindrops foul and steaming.

A driving rain falls around you. It falls in a fixed area once created. The storm reduces hearing and visibility, resulting in a –4 penalty on Listen, Spot, and Search checks. It also applies a –4 penalty on ranged attacks made into, out of, or through the storm. Finally, it automatically extinguishes any unprotected flames and has a 50% chance to extinguish protected flames (such as those of lanterns).

The rain damages good creatures, dealing 2d6 points of damage per round (good outsiders take double damage).

Material Component: A flask of unholy water (25 gp).

UNLUCK

Divination
Level: Bard 3, sorcerer/wizard 3
Components: V, S, M
Casting Time: 1 standard action
Range: Close (25 ft. + 5 ft./2 levels)
Target: One creature
Duration: 1 round/level
Saving Throw: Will negates
Spell Resistance: Yes

Spewing a curse of bad luck, you fling a piece of broken mirror at your target. The mirror shard dissipates harmlessly as soon as it leaves your hand, and the sound of rolling dice is perceptible for an instant.

When you cast this spell, you negatively influence the randomness of fortune for the target. Whenever the affected creature undertakes an action involving random chance (specifically, whenever any die roll is made for the

Illus. by L. Parrillo

creature, including attack rolls, damage rolls, and saving throws), two separate rolls are made and the worse result applied.

A creature carrying a *stone of good luck* is immune to the effect of *unluck*.

Material Component: A piece of a broken mirror.

UNYIELDING ROOTS

Transmutation
Level: Druid 8
Components: V, S, DF
Casting Time: 1 standard action
Range: Touch
Target: Willing creature touched
Duration: 1 round/level (D)
Saving Throw: Fortitude negates (harmless)
Spell Resistance: Yes (harmless)

The creature you touch grows thick tree roots that anchor it to the ground and provide it with life-sustaining healing.

The creature you touch must be standing on or otherwise touching the ground for this spell to have an effect on it. For the duration of the spell, the touched creature can't move from its current space, nor can it be moved from its space by bull rushes, overruns, magic such as *Bigby's forceful hand*, or any effect short of a massive earthquake. Such attempts simply fail. If an overrun attempt is made against a creature with *unyielding roots*, the rooted creature must block rather than avoid the overrun. The rooted creature automatically wins the Strength check to stop the overrun and can make a Strength check (opposed by the overrunning creature's Strength or Dexterity check) to knock the overrunning creature prone.

The roots draw life energy from the ground that feed the touched creature, healing up to 30 points of damage per round, neutralizing poisons automatically, and wiping away negative levels (as the *restoration* spell). The touched creature gets a +4 bonus on Fortitude and Will saves as long as the roots remain, but a –4 penalty on Reflex saves.

UPDRAFT

Conjuration (Creation) [Air]
Level: Cleric 1, druid 1
Components: V, S, M
Casting Time: 1 swift action
Range: Personal
Target: You
Duration: Instantaneous

A druid can use the updraft spell to rise high above a battle

Illus. by W. O'Connor

Detritus and loose debris on the ground beneath you begins to spin about, caught in a small vortex. The vortex quickly coalesces into a column of dirty gray-brown air thick enough to hold you aloft.

Updraft conjures forth rushing air that propels you upward. You gain 10 feet per level of altitude, and then gently float back down to the ground. At any point during your descent, you can move up to 5 feet laterally.

Material Component: A miniature propeller or windmill.

VALIANT FURY

Transmutation
Level: Courage 5
Components: V, S, DF
Casting Time: 1 standard action
Range: Close (25 ft. + 5 ft./2 levels)
Target: One living creature
Duration: 1 round/level
Saving Throw: Will negates (harmless)
Spell Resistance: Yes (harmless)

Pointing your holy symbol at your ally as you chant, you imbue him with fighting spirit.

The affected creature gains a +4 morale bonus to Strength and Constitution, and a +2 morale bonus on Will saves.

In addition, when making a full attack, the affected creature can make one additional attack with any weapon it is holding. The attack is made using the creature's full base attack bonus, plus any modifiers appropriate to the situation. This effect is not cumulative with similar effects, such as that provided by the *haste* spell.

VEIL OF SHADOW

Evocation [Darkness]
Level: Assassin 2, blackguard 2, cleric 2, sorcerer/wizard 2
Components: V, S
Casting Time: 1 standard action
Range: Personal
Target: You
Duration: 1 minute/level

You speak the words of this spell, and tendrils of purple darkness rise from the ground, surrounding you and concealing you from your foes.

Swirling wisps of darkness obscure your form, granting you concealment. The 20% miss chance is in effect even if the attacker has darkvision.

This spell effect is dispelled in daylight or in the area of a light spell of 3rd level or higher.

See invisibility does not counter a *veil of shadow's* concealment effect, but a *true seeing* spell does.

VEIL OF UNDEATH

Necromancy [Evil]
Level: Cleric 8, sorcerer/wizard 8
Components: V, S, M
Casting Time: 1 standard action
Range: Personal
Target: You
Duration: 10 minutes/level

Upon completion of the spell, you exhale your last breath and accept a brief embrace from death.

You gain many of the traits common to undead creatures. While the spell lasts, you have immunity to mind-affecting spells and abilities, poison, sleep, paralysis, stunning, disease, death, extra damage from critical hits, nonlethal damage, death from massive damage, ability drain, energy drain, fatigue, exhaustion, damage to physical ability scores, and any effect requiring a Fortitude save unless it is harmless or affects objects. You need not breathe, eat, or sleep.

Like an undead creature, you are damaged by *cure* spells and healed by *inflict* spells.

You don't actually gain the undead type from casting this spell.

Material Component: A finger from a zombie.

VIGOR

Conjuration (Healing)
Level: Cleric 3, druid 3
Duration: 10 rounds + 1 round/level (max 25 rounds)

This spell functions like *lesser vigor,* except as noted here and that it grants fast healing 2.

VIGOR, GREATER

Conjuration (Healing)
Level: Cleric 5, druid 5
Duration: 10 rounds + 1 round/level (max 35 rounds)

This spell functions like *lesser vigor,* except as noted here and that it grants fast healing 4.

VIGOR, LESSER

Conjuration (Healing)
Level: Cleric 1, druid 1
Components: V, S
Casting Time: 1 standard action
Range: Touch
Target: Living creature touched
Duration: 10 rounds + 1 round/level (max 15 rounds)
Saving Throw: Will negates (harmless)
Spell Resistance: Yes (harmless)

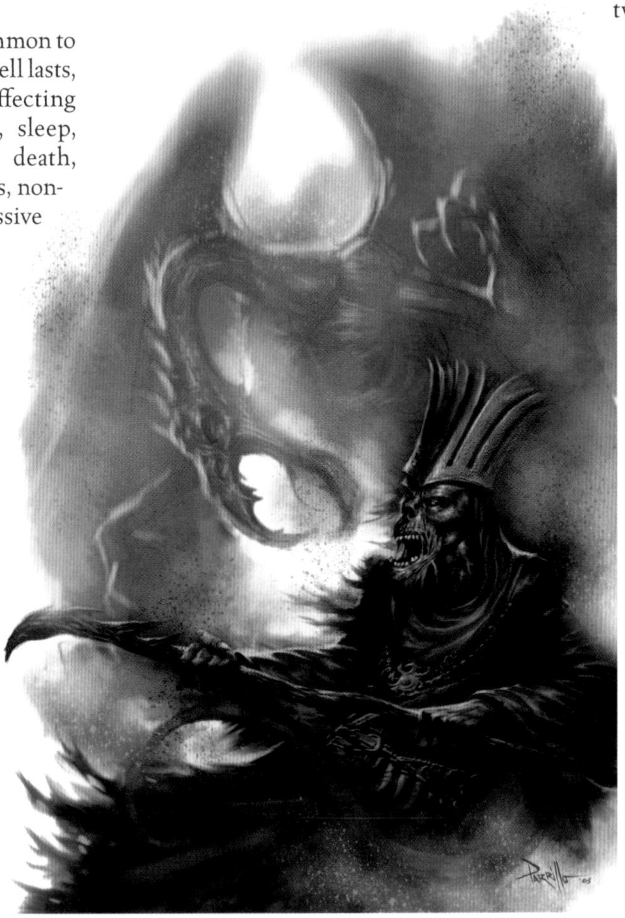

The vile death spell grants an undead creature some of the power of a fiend

The sounds of battle ring in your ears as you lay hands on your fallen comrade. You can spare neither time nor magic to do more right now, but the blood flow slows to a trickle and her breathing becomes less labored, even as you are called to the aid of another.

The subject gains fast healing 1, enabling it to heal 1 hit point per round until the spell ends and automatically becoming stabilized if it begins dying from hit point loss during that time. *Lesser vigor* does not restore hit points lost from starvation, thirst, or suffocation, nor does it allow a creature to regrow or attach lost body parts.

The effects of multiple *vigor* spells do not stack; only the highest-level effect applies.

VIGOR, MASS LESSER

Conjuration (Healing)
Level: Cleric 3, druid 3
Range: 20 ft.
Target: One creature/2 levels, no two of which are more than 30 ft. apart
Duration: 10 rounds + 1 round/level (max 25 rounds)

This spell functions like *lesser vigor,* except that it affects multiple creatures.

VIGOROUS CIRCLE

Conjuration (Healing)
Level: Cleric 6, druid 6
Duration: 10 rounds + 1 round/level (max 40 rounds)

This spell functions like *mass lesser vigor,* except as noted here and that it grants fast healing 3.

VILE DEATH

Conjuration (Calling) [Evil]
Level: Cleric 9, sorcerer/wizard 9
Components: V, S, M, XP
Casting Time: 1 hour
Range: Touch
Target: One corporeal undead creature
Duration: Permanent (D)
Saving Throw: None
Spell Resistance: Yes

The ground tears at your feet, and you can hear the distant screams of people in pain. An unwholesome red light emanates from the tear and coalesces into the translucent form of a fiend. It sneers at you as the earth closes, then it turns to look at the undead host you chose as the spell's subject. Both the undead and the fiend shudder as they meld together and the red glow dissipates.

Illus. by L. Parrillo

You summon the spirit of a fiend from the depths of the Nine Hells or the Abyss and bind it into the body of a corporeal undead creature—a bodak, a devourer, a ghast, a ghoul, a mohrg, a mummy, a nightshade, a skeleton, a vampire, a vampire spawn, a wight, or a zombie.

Binding the fiend applies the fiendish template (MM 108) to the undead creature. The resulting creature is independent of you, and can act on its own. Its initial attitude toward you is indifferent.

Material Component: A bit of brimstone and a bloodstone worth at least 500 gp.

XP Cost: 100 XP.

VINE MINE

Conjuration (Creation)
Level: Druid 3
Components: V, S, M
Casting Time: 1 standard action
Range: Medium (100 ft. + 10 ft./level)
Area: 10-ft.-radius/level spread
Duration: 10 minutes/level
Saving Throw: See text
Spell Resistance: Yes

You hold the crown of ivy leaves aloft, invoking the powers of nature, and an explosion of plant growth fills the area—plants over which you have control.

You create and direct the rapid growth of vines. When you cast the spell, choose one of the following effects.

- Climbing aid (treat as knotted ropes)
- Bind helpless targets (Escape Artist DC 25 to escape)
- Hamper movement (as heavy undergrowth)
- Camouflage (add +4 competence bonus on Hide checks)

As a standard action, you can redirect the vines' growth (thus changing the effect).

Material Component: A crown of ivy leaves.

VINE STRIKE

Divination
Level: Druid 1, ranger 1
Components: V, DF
Casting Time: 1 swift action
Range: Personal
Target: You
Duration: 1 round

As you intone the sounds of the spell, your sight temporarily dims under a green gloom. An eyeblink later, the dimness disappears, and you feel a new connection with the natural order, as if it were directing where to land your blow.

While this spell is in effect, you have a special connection to the forces of nature that allows you to deliver sneak attacks on plant creatures as if they were not immune to sneak attacks. To attack a plant creature in this manner, you must still meet the other requirements for making a sneak attack.

This spell applies only to sneak attack damage. It gives you no ability to affect plant creatures with critical hits, nor does it confer any special ability to overcome the damage reduction or other defenses of plant creatures.

VIPERGOUT

Conjuration (Summoning) [see text]
Level: Sorcerer/wizard 3
Components: V, S, M
Casting Time: 1 standard action
Range: Close (25 ft. + 5 ft./2 levels)
Effect: 1d4+3 summoned creatures
Duration: 1 round/level
Saving Throw: None
Spell Resistance: Yes

A churning in your stomach overtakes you as you complete the spell. Something slithers up your throat, and you vomit serpents.

This spell summons 1d4+1 celestial or fiendish Medium vipers (MM 280), which leap forth from your mouth to attack your enemies.

A celestial viper summoned by this spell has resistance to acid 5, cold 5, and electricity 5; spell resistance 7; and a smite evil attack that provides a +2 bonus on one damage roll.

A fiendish viper summoned by this spell has resistance to acid 5 and fire 5; spell resistance 7; and a smite good attack that provides a +2 bonus on one damage roll.

Starting in the round you complete the spell, you can spit three vipers as a standard action or one viper as a move action. (Thus, if you move and then cast this spell, you cannot spit any vipers until your next turn, but if you cast this spell without moving, you can spit forth one viper as your move action in that round.) Spat vipers land at your feet in an adjacent square of your choice and act on the same round, on your turn, just as creatures summoned by a *summon monster* spell do.

The snakes are not actually present in your mouth, and they do not interfere with your breathing. However, until you have brought forth all the snakes summoned by the spell, you cannot speak, cast spells with verbal components, or activate items that require speech. When the spell's duration expires, all the vipers disappear, and any not yet brought forth are lost.

When you use a summoning spell to summon a good creature or an evil creature, it is a spell of that type.

Material Component: A snakeskin.

VISAGE OF THE DEITY

Transmutation [Evil or Good]
Level: Cleric 6, Mysticism 6

This spell functions like *lesser visage of the deity*, except that you take on many qualities of a celestial or fiendish creature, as follows.

- You take on a shining, metallic appearance (for good clerics) or a more fearsome appearance (for evil clerics).
- You gain the ability to smite evil (for good clerics) or good (for evil clerics) once a day. Add your Charisma modifier to your attack roll and your character level to your damage roll against a foe of the appropriate alignment.
- You gain darkvision out to 60 feet.
- You gain resistance to acid 20, cold 20, and electricity 20 (for good clerics) or resistance to cold 20 and fire 20 (for evil clerics).
- You gain damage reduction 10/magic.
- You gain spell resistance 20.

Your creature type does not change (you do not become an outsider).

VISAGE OF THE DEITY, GREATER

Transmutation [Evil or Good]
Level: Cleric 9, Competition 9, Mysticism 9, Purification 9

This spell functions like *lesser visage of the deity,* except that you take on many qualities of a half-celestial or half-fiendish creature.

Your creature type changes to outsider for the duration of the spell. Unlike other outsiders, you can be brought back from the dead if you are killed in this form.

Good clerics undergo the following transformations.

- You grow feathered wings that allow you to fly at twice your normal speed (good maneuverability).
- You gain +1 natural armor.
- You gain low-light vision.
- You gain resistance to acid 10, cold 10, and electricity 10.
- You gain immunity to disease.
- You gain a +4 racial bonus on saving throws against poison.
- You gain damage reduction 10/magic.
- You gain spell resistance 25.
- You gain the following bonuses to your ability scores: +4 Str, +2 Dex, +4 Con, +2 Int, +4 Wis, +4 Cha.

Evil clerics undergo the following transformations.

- You grow batlike wings that allow you to fly at your normal speed (average maneuverability).
- You gain +1 natural armor.
- You gain bite and claw attacks. If you are size Medium or larger, your bite deals 1d6 points of damage and each claw attack deals 1d4 points of damage. If you are Small, your bite deals 1d4 points of damage and each claw attack deals 1d3 points of damage.
- You gain darkvision out to 60 feet.
- You gain immunity to poison.
- You gain resistance to acid 10, cold 10, electricity 10, and fire 10.
- You gain damage reduction 10/magic.
- You gain spell resistance 25.
- You gain the following bonuses to your ability scores: +4 Str, +4 Dex, +2 Con, +4 Int, +2 Cha.

VISAGE OF THE DEITY, LESSER

Transmutation [Evil or Good]
Level: Blackguard 4, cleric 3, Mysticism 3, paladin 4
Components: V, S, DF
Casting Time: 1 standard action
Range: Personal
Target: You
Duration: 1 round/level

As you end your prayer, you can feel the hand of your deity upon you. Your appearance reflects her divine power, and her touch grants you resistance from some of the damage of this world.

You gain a +4 enhancement bonus to Charisma. You also gain resistance to acid 10, cold 10, and electricity 10 if you are good, or resistance to cold 10 and fire 10 if you are evil.

VISCID GLOB

Conjuration
Level: Sorcerer/wizard 5
Components: V, S, M
Casting Time: 1 standard action
Range: Medium (100 ft. + 10 ft./level)
Target: One creature
Duration: 1 hour/level
Saving Throw: Reflex negates
Spell Resistance: Yes

You speak the words of this spell and toss the small ball of silk in the air. It turns into a 5-foot-wide glob of dripping, green-gray goo, and the sticky mass rockets toward your target.

When you attack with a *viscid glob,* you make a ranged touch attack against the target. If you miss, the glob might strike a nearby square or creature (see Missing with a Thrown Weapon, PH 158). Once you have established the direction of the miss, roll 1d4 to determine the number of squares away from the target square that the glob lands.

A Medium or smaller creature struck by the glob must make a successful Reflex save or be instantly stuck in place. A stuck creature can speak but is otherwise limited to purely mental actions (such as casting spells with no somatic or material components) and attempts to free itself by means of a Strength check or Escape Artist check (against a DC equal to this spell's DC) made as a full-round action. A Large or larger creature stuck in the goo can't move from the spot where it is glued, but it can otherwise act normally.

The glob dissipates when the spell duration expires. Until then, it remains sticky, and any creature touching it (for example, a creature attempting to pull out an ally) must make a successful Reflex save or become stuck itself. A creature stuck by such secondary contact is not trapped as thoroughly as a creature targeted by the glob, however, so the DC of the Strength check or Escape Artist check required to get free is reduced by 5.

Material Component: A tiny ball of spider silk.

VISION OF GLORY

Divination
Level: Cleric 1, paladin 1
Components: V, S, DF
Casting Time: 1 standard action
Range: Touch
Target: Creature touched
Duration: 1 minute or until discharged
Saving Throw: None
Spell Resistance: Yes

You touch your ally, and her eyes mist over momentarily. You know she is seeing an image of her deity, imploring her to battle in his name.

You give the subject creature a brief vision of a divine entity that is giving it support and inspiring it to continue. The creature gets a morale bonus equal to your Charisma modifier on a single saving throw. It must choose to use the bonus before making the roll to which it applies. Using the bonus discharges the spell.

VITRIOLIC SPHERE

Conjuration (Creation) [Acid]
Level: Sorcerer/wizard 5
Components: V, S, M
Casting Time: 1 standard action
Range: Long (400 ft. + 40 ft./level)
Area: 10-ft.-radius burst
Duration: Instantaneous; see text
Saving Throw: Reflex partial; see text
Spell Resistance: No

Although a safe zone exists at the center of a vortex of teeth, some creatures are too large to take advantage of it

Illus. by W. Reynolds

At the successful casting of the spell, you conjure a sizzling emerald sphere. The sphere immediately shatters, drenching all in the area with a potent acid.

Affected creatures take 6d6 points of acid damage. Creatures that succeed on their Reflex saving throws take half of this damage. Creatures that fail their Reflex saves take full damage, and also take 6d6 points of acid damage in each of the following 2 rounds.

Material Component: A tiny glass vial filled with aqua regia.

VOICE OF THE DRAGON

Transmutation
Level: Bard 4, Dragon 4, sorcerer/wizard 4
Components: V, S
Casting Time: 1 standard action
Range: Personal
Target: You
Duration: 10 minutes/level (D)

As you speak the words of the spell and inscribe the motions in the air, your voice deepens, taking on a resonance that makes the listener think of authority, power, and great age.

You gain a +10 enhancement bonus on Bluff, Diplomacy, and Intimidate checks. You also gain the ability to speak and understand (but not read) Draconic.

At any time before the spell's duration expires, you can use a standard action to target a creature with a *suggestion* effect, which functions identically to the spell of that name (PH 285), including range, duration, and other effects. Doing this causes the *voice of the dragon* spell to end, though the *suggestion* itself lasts for the normal duration thereafter.

Special: Sorcerers cast this spell at +1 caster level.

VORTEX OF TEETH

Evocation [Force]
Level: Druid 4, sorcerer/wizard 4
Components: V, S, M
Casting Time: 1 standard action
Range: Medium (100 ft. + 10 ft./level)
Area: Hollow cylinder (40-ft. radius, 20 ft. high, with a 5-ft.-radius safe zone at the center)
Duration: 1 round/level (D)
Saving Throw: None
Spell Resistance: Yes

A huge school of transparent piranhas swims rapidly through the air in the area you indicate. These magic fish are made of force and tear into the bodies of creatures as though ravenous.

Creatures in the area take 3d8 points of damage per round at the beginning of your turn. Because this spell is a force effect, it harms incorporeal creatures.

Material Component: A fish tooth.

VULNERABILITY

Transmutation
Level: Assassin 4, cleric 5, sorcerer/wizard 5
Components: V, S
Casting Time: 1 standard action
Range: Touch
Target: Creature touched
Duration: 1 round/level
Saving Throw: Will negates
Spell Resistance: Yes

You invoke the power of this spell and a purple mist swirls around your opponent, weakening its mystic protections.

This spell lowers the subject's damage reduction by 5 (to a minimum of 5). For instance, if you successfully cast *vulnerability* on a dragon with damage reduction 10/magic, its damage reduction becomes 5/magic.

For every four caster levels beyond 9th, the subject's damage reduction lowers by an additional 5: a reduction of 10 at caster level 15th and a reduction of 15 at caster level 19th.

WAIL OF DOOM

Necromancy [Fear, Mind-Affecting, Sonic]
Level: Bard 5
Components: V
Casting Time: 1 standard action
Range: 30 ft.
Area: Cone-shaped burst
Duration: Instantaneous + 1 round/level or 1 round; see text
Saving Throw: Will partial; see text
Spell Resistance: Yes

You unleash a terrible cry of malice and anger. The very air darkens with black energy as your cry echoes away from you.

Anyone caught in the area of this spell suffers excruciating pain and becomes demoralized. Each creature takes 1d4 points of damage per caster level (maximum 15d4) and becomes panicked for 1 round per caster level. A successful Will save halves the damage, reduces the panicked effect to shaken, and reduces the duration of the shaken effect to 1 round.

WALL OF CHAOS

Abjuration [Chaotic]
Level: Cleric 4, sorcerer/wizard 4

You invoke the abjuration, and a wall of multicolored energy springs up, becoming translucent and vanishing in a flash.

This spell functions like *wall of good* (see below), except that lawful creatures are blocked.

WALL OF DISPEL MAGIC

Abjuration
Level: Cleric 5, sorcerer/wizard 5
Components: V, S, DF
Casting Time: 1 standard action
Range: Close (25 ft. + 5 ft./2 levels)
Effect: A straight wall whose area is up to one 10-ft. square/level
Duration: 1 minute/level
Saving Throw: None
Spell Resistance: No

You cast the spell and a translucent wall springs up, a shimmering field of faded colors that swirls and merges with itself like the surface of a soap bubble.

This spell creates a transparent, permeable barrier. Anyone passing through it becomes the target of a *dispel magic* effect (PH 223) at your caster level. A summoned creature targeted in this way can be dispelled by the effect.

A *wall of dispel magic* cannot be seen or felt by ordinary means, or even with a *see invisibility* spell. *Detect magic* indicates the presence of the effect, and *true seeing* reveals its presence.

WALL OF EVIL

Abjuration [Evil]
Level: Cleric 4, sorcerer/wizard 4

You invoke the abjuration and a wall of red and black energy springs up, only to fade away to invisibility.

This spell functions like *wall of good* (see below), except that good creatures are blocked.

WALL OF GEARS

Conjuration (Creation)
Level: Mechanus 6, sorcerer/wizard 6
Components: V, S, M
Casting Time: 1 standard action
Range: Medium (100 ft. + 10 ft./level)
Effect: A straight wall of moving gears whose area is up to one 10-ft. square/level; see text
Duration: 1 minute/level
Saving Throw: See text
Spell Resistance: No

You pop the gear into your mouth and make a humming, buzzing incantation. The sound takes on a life of its own, and springing from the ground is a huge wall made of machinery, all spinning, clattering and moving about, endangering all who are close to it.

This spell creates a 6-inch-thick wall of moving iron cogs, wheels, gears, pistons, and assorted mechanical parts. Each 5-foot square of the wall's surface has hardness 10 and 90 hit points.

Both sides of the wall have hundreds of moving parts that flail out, dealing 1d6 points of damage per two caster levels (maximum 15d6) to all creatures within 10 feet. A successful Reflex save halves this damage.

Material Component: A small gear.

WALL OF GLOOM

Illusion (Shadow) [Darkness, Fear, Mind-Affecting]
Level: Sorcerer/wizard 2
Components: V, S, M
Casting Time: 1 standard action
Range: Medium (100 ft. + 10 ft./level)
Effect: A straight wall whose area is up to one 10-ft. square/level
Duration: Concentration + 1 round/level
Saving Throw: None
Spell Resistance: No

Rubbing the fleece between your fingers, you hold up your hand and shout an arcane word. In an instant, a wall of dark shadow appears in the indicated location. Dark whispers, barely perceptible, constantly issue forth from the far side of the wall, causing a cold chill to run up your spine.

You create a barrier of ominous shadow that obscures vision and blocks line of sight, including darkvision. The wall is insubstantial, so creatures can move through it without penalty.

Wall of gloom counters or dispels any light spell of equal or lower level.

Material Component: A bit of fleece from a black sheep.

WALL OF GOOD

Abjuration [Good]
Level: Cleric 4, sorcerer/wizard 4
Components: V, S, M/DF
Casting Time: 1 standard action
Range: Close (25 ft. + 5 ft./2 levels)
Effect: A straight wall whose area is up to one 10-ft. square/level or a sphere or hemisphere with a radius of up to 5 ft./2 levels
Duration: 10 minutes/level
Saving Throw: See text
Spell Resistance: Yes

You invoke the abjuration, and a cascade of brilliant white energy springs up in a wall that becomes invisible almost instantly.

You create an immobile barrier that inhibits evil creatures. An evil summoned creature cannot pass through the wall in either direction, and any other evil creature must succeed

Illus. by D. Martin

A wall of gears strikes those who try to break though it

on a Will save each time it attempts to move through the wall. If the saving throw is failed, the creature's movement is stopped, and it can take no other action that round.

A *wall of good* must be continuous and unbroken when formed. If it is cast so that an object or creature breaks its surface, the spell fails.

Arcane Material Component: Powdered silver worth 25 gp.

WALL OF GREATER DISPEL MAGIC

Abjuration
Level: Cleric 8, sorcerer/wizard 8

You cast the spell and a translucent wall springs up, its shimmering field pulsing with strong, malignant shades that spin and twist into each other.

This spell functions like *wall of dispel magic* (see above), except that the effect is that of *greater dispel magic* (PH 223).

WALL OF LAW

Abjuration [Lawful]
Level: Cleric 4, sorcerer/wizard 4

You invoke the abjuration, and a wall of translucent silver energy springs up before fading away to nothingness.

This spell functions like *wall of good* (see above), except that chaotic creatures are blocked.

WALL OF LIGHT

Evocation [Light]
Level: Cleric 3, sorcerer/wizard 3
Components: V, S, M
Casting Time: 1 standard action
Range: Close (25 ft. + 5 ft./2 levels)
Effect: A straight wall whose area is up to one 10-ft. square/level or a sphere or hemisphere with a radius of up to 5 ft./2 levels
Duration: 1 minute/level (D)
Saving Throw: None
Spell Resistance: Yes; see text

A blinding flash accompanies the completion of this spell as a wall of pure light springs into being.

This spell causes a wall of dazzling yellow-white light to come into being at any point within range. The wall is opaque to all other creatures, though you can see through it without difficulty. A *wall of light* has no physical substance and does not otherwise hinder attacks, movement, or spells passing through it, although it blocks line of sight for other creatures.

A creature that passes through a *wall of light* becomes dazzled for the duration of the spell. Spell resistance applies when passing through the wall. Sightless creatures and those already dazzled are not affected by passing through a *wall of light*.

A *wall of light* sheds light equivalent to a *daylight* spell. *Wall of light* counters or dispels any darkness spell of equal or lower level.

Material Component: A pinch of powdered sunstone.

WALL OF LIMBS

Evocation
Level: Sorcerer/wizard 5
Components: V, S
Casting Time: 1 round
Range: Medium (100 ft. + 10 ft./level)
Effect: A wall of whirling limbs up to 20 ft. long/level, or a ring of whirling limbs with a radius of up to 5 ft./2 levels, either form 20 ft. high
Duration: 1 round/level (D)

Saving Throw: Reflex negates; see text
Spell Resistance: Yes

By flexing your arm and speaking the repetitive words of power, you unleash the spell. In the distance, the ground is covered in a writhing mass. As you watch, over the course of a few seconds, the writhing mass rises up and forms a wall of thousands of wriggling arms resembling your own.

An immobile, vertical curtain of whirling limbs springs into existence. The limbs resemble your own forelimbs.

A creature attempting to move through the wall takes 5d6 points of damage and must succeed on a DC 18 Strength check or become stuck within the wall and unable to move (a charging creature gains a +2 bonus on the Strength check). The creature takes 5d6 points of damage each round at the beginning of your turn until freed. A creature can free itself with a DC 18 Strength check, or by dealing 30 points of damage to a 5-foot section of wall.

A creature that starts its turn next to a *wall of limbs* must succeed on a DC 18 Strength check or be grabbed by the flailing arms and become stuck, as above.

If you evoke the wall so that it appears where creatures are, each creature takes damage as if passing through the wall. Each such creature can avoid the wall (ending up on the side of its choice) and thus take no damage by making a successful Reflex save.

A *wall of limbs* provides cover against attacks made through it.

WALL OF SAND

Conjuration (Creation) [Earth]
Level: Cleric 4, druid 5, sorcerer/wizard 4
Components: V, S, M/DF
Range: Medium (100 ft. + 10 ft./level)
Effect: A straight wall whose area is up to one 10-ft. square/level (S)
Duration: Concentration + 1 round/level
Saving Throw: None
Spell Resistance: No

With a rush of hot air, a swirling wall of blowing sand leaps into being.

This spell conjures up a 10-foot-thick, viscous, opaque wall of swirling sand. The spell must be cast so that it rests on a solid surface. Once cast, the wall is immobile. The sand is sufficiently thick to block ranged attacks, providing normal cover appropriate for its size, but creatures can attempt to force their way through it. Moving through a *wall of sand* is difficult, requiring a full-round action and a Strength check. A creature moves 5 feet through a *wall of sand* for every 5 points by which its Strength check result exceeds 10.

Creatures within a *wall of sand* are considered blinded and deafened, and they are unable to speak or breathe. Thus, they might begin to suffocate (DMG 304) if they remain within the wall too long. Spells with verbal components cannot be cast within the wall, and any other spell requires a successful Concentration check (DC 20 + spell level).

Creatures with reach can attempt to attack through the wall, but targets have total concealment and total cover, and the attacker must have a general idea where the target is located.

Any open, unprotected flame thrust into a *wall of sand* is instantly extinguished.

Arcane Material Component: A handful of sand.

WALL OF SMOKE

Conjuration (Creation)
Level: Druid 1, sorcerer/wizard 1
Components: V, S
Casting Time: 1 standard action
Range: Close (25 ft. + 5 ft./2 levels)
Effect: A straight wall whose area is up to one 10-ft. square/level (S)
Duration: 1 round/level
Saving Throw: Fortitude partial; see text
Spell Resistance: No

You wave your hand in a circular motion, and black smoke swirls into existence as a dark wall.

This spell creates a thin wall of black smoke. The wall is stationary once created. The wall blocks sight to a limited degree. Creatures on opposite sides of the wall that cannot see over it gain concealment from each other. A creature can pass through a *wall of smoke*, but it must make a Fortitude save to avoid being nauseated for 1 round.

A moderate wind (11+ mph), such as from a *gust of wind* spell, destroys the wall in 1 round.

This spell does not function underwater.

WALL OF WATER

Conjuration (Creation) [Water]
Level: Druid 4, sorcerer/wizard 4
Components: V, S, M
Casting Time: 1 standard action
Range: Medium (100 ft. + 10 ft./level)
Effect: A straight wall whose area is up to one 10-ft. square/level (S)
Duration: 10 minutes/level
Saving Throw: Reflex negates; see text
Spell Resistance: No

A wall springs up in the area you designate. Composed of a sheet of water rising vertically, the transparent wall does not prevent you from seeing beyond it. The water of the wall is calm as a lake on a windless day.

This spell creates a 10-foot-thick wall of fresh water or seawater (as selected by you). The water forms around objects and creatures in its area, plunging these creatures and objects underwater. A creature in the area where the water is created can make a Reflex save to move to a random side of the wall before it forms completely. This movement must occur on the creature's next turn, or it immediately suffers the full effect of being in the wall.

Creatures can move through a *wall of water* by making Swim checks, or can walk along the floor at half speed; the water itself is considered to be calm water. Any open flames in the area when the water forms are immediately extinguished. Creatures with the fire subtype take 2d6 points of damage +1 point per caster level each round they remain partially or wholly in the wall.

Although the wall is transparent, it provides cover to any targets inside against attacks launched from outside the wall. It cannot be destroyed by physical damage, nor can it be drained off to a different location. Water brought out of the wall in a container instantly evaporates as the wall itself forms more water to replace what was removed.

Material Component: A sponge.

WAR CRY

Enchantment (Compulsion) [Mind-Affecting, Sonic]
Level: Bard 2
Components: V, S
Casting Time: 1 swift action
Range: Personal
Target: You
Duration: 1 round

You jab your weapon into the air as if in triumph, letting out a cry of victory before you have even made your attack. Foes around you seem surprised by your display even as the feeling grows within you that you cannot fail.

You gain a +4 morale bonus on attack rolls and damage rolls made as part of a charge.

If you deal damage with a charge attack, your foe must succeed on a Will save or become panicked for 1 round (spell resistance applies to this effect).

WARNING SHOUT

Transmutation [Sonic]
Level: Paladin 1
Components: V
Casting Time: 1 immediate action
Range: 30 ft.
Targets: All allies within 30 feet
Duration: Instantaneous
Saving Throw: None
Spell Resistance: No

You shout a few words imbued with power by your faith, and your next words ring out clear and far despite other noise or intervening barriers.

All allies within range are no longer considered flat-footed, even if they have not yet acted in the current combat.

Anyone sleeping naturally (as opposed to magically induced sleep, such as from a *sleep* spell) within the area is woken by a *warning shout*.

WATERSPOUT

Conjuration (Creation) [Water]
Level: Druid 7, Ocean 7
Components: V, S, DF
Casting Time: 1 round
Range: Long (400 ft. + 40 ft./level)
Effect: Cylinder (5-ft. radius, 80 ft. high)
Duration: 1 round/level
Saving Throw: Reflex negates
Spell Resistance: No

Water whirls into the air, swirling upward with a thunderous noise like a tornado of fluid.

Waterspout causes water to rise up into a whirling, cylindrical column. You can direct the movement of the waterspout as a move action.

With a war cry spell, a roar of triumph brings victory closer

Illus. by C. Frank

A *waterspout* moves at a speed of 30 feet. You can concentrate on controlling the *waterspout's* every movement or specify a simple program, such as move straight ahead, zigzag, circle, or the like. Directing a *waterspout's* movement or changing its programmed movement is a move action for you. A *waterspout* always moves during your turn in the initiative order. If the *waterspout* exceeds the spell's range, it collapses and the spell ends.

A *waterspout* batters creatures and objects it touches, and it often sucks them up. Any creature or object that comes in contact with it must succeed on a Reflex save or take 3d8 points of damage. Medium or smaller creatures that fail their saves are sucked into the spout and held suspended in its powerful currents, taking 2d6 points of damage each round (no save). Trapped creatures remain inside for 1d3 rounds before the *waterspout* ejects them out the top of the spout, and they fall back to the surface (taking 8d6 points of falling damage) 1d8×5 feet from the base of the *waterspout*.

Waterborne creatures or objects within 10 feet of the spout (below and on all sides) also must make successful Reflex saves or be sucked into the spout if they are Medium or smaller. Anything sucked into the spout takes 3d8 points of damage and is then trapped for 1d3 rounds as described above.

Only the smallest of watercraft, such as canoes, kayaks, or coracles, can be sucked into the spout. The occupant of any such craft can make a Profession (sailor) check instead of a Reflex save if it so chooses to avoid being sucked up.

WAVE OF GRIEF

Enchantment [Evil, Mind-Affecting]
Level: Bard 2, blackguard 2, cleric 2
Components: V, S, M
Casting Time: 1 standard action
Range: 30 ft.
Area: Cone-shaped burst
Duration: 1 round/level
Saving Throw: Will negates
Spell Resistance: Yes

Emitting a mournful wail, you send out a pulse of magic imbued with sorrow and sadness.

All within the cone when the spell is cast take a –3 penalty on attack rolls, saving throws, ability checks, and skill checks.

Material Component: Three tears.

WEAPON OF ENERGY

Transmutation [see text]
Level: Cleric 3, sorcerer/wizard 3
Components: V, S
Casting Time: 1 standard action
Range: Touch
Target: One weapon
Duration: 1 round/level

Saving Throw: Fortitude negates (object, harmless)
Spell Resistance: Yes (harmless, object)

Your hand glows slightly. With a touch, you transfer the glow from your hand onto the intended weapon.

You cause a weapon to gain the ability to deal energy damage in addition to its other abilities, similar to how a flaming burst weapon deals extra fire damage on a hit or a critical hit. The weapon can deal acid, cold, electricity, or fire damage, chosen by you at the time of casting. The weapon deals an extra 1d6 points of damage of that energy type on a successful hit. On a critical hit, the weapon deals an additional 1d10 points of energy damage. If the weapon's critical multiplier is ×3, add 2d10 points of energy damage instead, and if the multiplier is ×4, add 3d10 points of energy damage.

This spell can be cast on a weapon that already deals energy damage, and if the weapon already creates the same type of damage as the spell, the effects stack. For example, if cast on a *+1 flaming longsword* to give it additional fire damage, the weapon now deals an extra 2d6 points of fire damage per hit.

This spell has a descriptor that is the same as the energy created by the target weapon. For example, *weapon of energy* is a fire spell when used to give a weapon bonus fire damage.

WEAPON OF IMPACT

Transmutation
Level: Bard 3, cleric 3, sorcerer/wizard 3
Components: V, S
Casting Time: 1 standard action
Range: Touch
Target: One bludgeoning weapon or fifty bludgeoning projectiles, all of which must be in contact with one another at the time of casting
Duration: 10 minutes/level
Saving Throw: Fortitude negates (harmless, object)
Spell Resistance: Yes (harmless, object)

You pass your hands over the weapon, and its head glows with a blue-gold radiance.

This spell makes a bludgeoning weapon have greater impact, improving its ability to deal telling blows. This transmutation doubles the threat range of the weapon. If the spell is cast on sling bullets or other bludgeoning projectiles, the *weapon of impact* effect on a particular projectile ends after one use, whether or not the missile strikes its intended target.

Multiple effects that increase a weapon's threat range, such as the Improved Critical feat, don't stack.

WEAPON OF THE DEITY

Transmutation
Level: Blackguard 3, cleric 3, paladin 3
Components: V, DF
Casting Time: 1 standard action
Range: Touch
Target: Weapon touched
Duration: 1 round/level
Saving Throw: Fortitude negates (harmless, object)
Spell Resistance: Yes (harmless, object)

Wielding the weapon your deity favors, you call upon that divine force to imbue it with power.

You must be holding your deity's favored weapon to cast this spell. You can use the weapon as if you had proficiency with it even if you normally do not. The weapon gains a +1 enhancement bonus on attack rolls and damage rolls and an additional special ability (see the list below). A double weapon gains this enhancement bonus and special ability for only one of its two ends, as chosen by you.

When you reach caster level 9th, the enhancement bonus of the weapon increases to +2. At 12th level, the bonus rises to +3, at 15th level it is +4, and at 18th level it becomes +5.

The list below includes deities from the core pantheon as well as other deities described in D&D supplements, along with the five alignment components. If a cleric worshiping a different deity casts this spell, the DM should assign an appropriate weapon special ability of the same power level as those given here.

Deities
Bahamut: *+1 frost heavy pick*
Boccob: *+1 spell storing quarterstaff*
Corellon Larethian: *+1 keen longsword*
Ehlonna: *+1 frost longsword*
Erythnul: *+1 mighty cleaving morningstar*
Fharlanghn: *+1 defending quarterstaff*
Garl Glittergold: *+1 throwing battleaxe*
Gruumsh: *+1 returning shortspear*
Heironeous: *+1 shock longsword*
Hextor: *+1 mighty cleaving heavy flail*
Kord: *+1 mighty cleaving greatsword*
Kurtulmak: *+1 shock shortspear*
Lolth: *+1 keen whip*
Moradin: *+1 throwing warhammer*
Nerull: *+1 keen scythe*
Obad-Hai: *+1 defending quarterstaff*
Olidammara: *+1 keen rapier*
Pelor: *+1 flaming heavy mace*
St. Cuthbert: *+1 mighty cleaving heavy mace*
Vecna: *+1 frost dagger*
Wee Jas: *dagger of venom*
Tiamat: *+1 flaming heavy pick*
Yondalla: *+1 defending short sword*

Alignments
Good: *+1 frost warhammer*
Evil: *+1 mighty cleaving light flail*
Neutral: *+1 defending heavy mace*
Law: *+1 flaming longsword*
Chaos: *+1 shock battleaxe*

WEAPON SHIFT

Transmutation
Level: Bard 2, sorcerer/wizard 1
Components: V, S, M
Casting Time: 1 standard action
Range: Touch
Target: One melee weapon of up to 15 lb.
Duration: 1 minute/level
Saving Throw: Fortitude negates (object)
Spell Resistance: Yes (object)

Waving the folded sheet of parchment before you, you firmly grasp the target weapon. A barely perceptible rust-brown glow engulfs it, then grows into a shining radiance of molten-metal red. As the radiance subsides, you note with satisfaction that the weapon now has the desired shape.

A *weapon shift* spell allows you to temporarily transform any one melee weapon into a different melee weapon. Thus, a greatclub could be transformed into a greatsword, a light pick into a morning star, or a dagger into a battleaxe.

Improvised weapons and double weapons cannot be targeted or be the result of this spell. Magic weapons transformed retain all their special abilities as long as the new form could legally have those abilities, and weapons made from special materials retain their special materials.

Material Component: A piece of parchment folded into the shape of the weapon type desired.

WEATHER EYE

Divination
Level: Druid 3
Components: V, S, M, F
Casting Time: 1 hour
Range: 1 mile + 1 mile/level
Area: 1-mile radius + 1-mile/level centered on you
Duration: Instantaneous
Saving Throw: None
Spell Resistance: No

Using your connection to the divine forces and nature, you gaze into your scrying device and summon images to mind of what the future holds for the weather.

You can accurately predict the natural weather up to one week into the future. If unnatural forces currently affect the weather, then *weather eye* reveals the spells or abilities in effect, though not the source of those abilities.

Material Component: Incense.

Focus: A scrying device of some kind (bowl, mirror, crystal ball, and so forth).

WEIGHED IN THE BALANCE

Necromancy
Level: Balance 9
Components: V
Casting Time: 1 standard action
Range: 30 ft.
Area: Creatures in a 30-ft.-radius spread centered on you
Duration: Instantaneous
Saving Throw: Will negates
Spell Resistance: Yes

You speak the words of power, and a warm orange fire radiates from you, aiding those that believe in the true balance, and harming all others.

This spell harms or heals creatures within its area based on their alignments and life status. The effect does the most harm to those creatures most extreme in alignment and most out of balance with the natural world.

For living creatures that have an alignment with no neutral component (LG, CG, LE, or CE), this spell acts as an *inflict critical wounds* spell (PH 244).

For living creatures that have an alignment with a neutral component and one other (NG, LN, CN, or NE), this spell acts as an *inflict moderate wounds* spell (PH 244).

For living creatures that have a neutral alignment (N) and all undead creatures, this spell acts as a *heal* spell (PH 239), dealing damage to undead but acting as a beneficial spell to neutral creatures.

WHIRLING BLADE

Transmutation
Level: Bard 2, sorcerer/wizard 2
Components: V, S, F
Casting Time: 1 standard action
Range: 60 ft.
Effect: 60-ft. line
Duration: Instantaneous
Saving Throw: None
Spell Resistance: No

With weapon in hand, you finish the last of the arcane gestures and words that activate the power of the spell. As you cast the spell, you hurl a single slashing weapon at your foes. The blade, carried along both by your might and your magical prowess, slashes at your foes while whirling forward.

You hurl a weapon held at the time of casting, and it magically attacks all enemies along a line to the extent of the spell's range. You make a normal melee attack, just as if you were attacking with the weapon in melee, against each foe in the weapon's path, but you can choose to substitute your Intelligence modifier or your Charisma modifier (as appropriate for your spellcasting class) for your Strength modifier on the weapon's attack rolls and damage rolls. Even if your base attack bonus would normally give you multiple attacks, a whirling blade gets only one attack (at your best attack bonus) against each target. The weapon deals damage just as if you had swung it in melee, including any bonuses you might have from ability scores or feats.

No matter how many targets your weapon hits or misses, it instantly and unerringly returns to your hand after attempting the last of its attacks.

Focus: A slashing melee weapon that you hurl.

Illus. by J. Engle

A whirling blade makes attacks against many foes

WHIRLWIND, GREATER

Evocation [Air]
Level: Druid 9, Windstorm 9
Components: V, S
Casting Time: 1 standard action
Range: Medium (100 ft. + 10 ft./level)
Effect: 20-ft.-radius tornado, up to 5 ft./level high, centered on a point in space
Duration: 1 round/level
Saving Throw: Fortitude partial
Spell Resistance: Yes

Wind whips into a frenzy and becomes a tornado that wreaks destruction as you direct, flinging your foes into the air and destroying nearby structures.

This spell is a more potent version of *whirlwind* (PH 301). A *greater whirlwind* affects creatures differently, depending on their size and where they are in relation to the twister.

Near the Tornado: Large or smaller creatures who start their turn within 60 feet of the center of a *greater whirlwind* must succeed on a Fortitude save or be dragged 1d4×10 feet toward the center of the twister, taking 1d4 points of nonlethal damage per 10 feet dragged.

Huge creatures within 40 feet of the twister must succeed on a Fortitude save or be knocked prone. Gargantuan and Colossal creatures within 40 feet of the twister must succeed on a Fortitude save before moving away from the twister.

Flying creatures of Huge size or smaller that fail their Fortitude saves are sucked to the center of the twister, taking 2d6 points of damage from the battering and buffeting. Gargantuan flying creatures must succeed on a Fortitude save or be pulled 1d6×10 feet toward the center of the twister. Colossal flyers must likewise make Fortitude saves or be pulled 1d6×5 feet toward the twister's center.

Any Huge or smaller creature that comes in contact with the spell effect must succeed on a Reflex save or take 3d6 points of damage. A Large or smaller creature that fails its first save must succeed on a second one or be picked up bodily by the cyclone and held suspended in its powerful winds. Any creature picked up is ejected 3 rounds later.

Inside the Tornado: Creatures that start their turn inside the tornado take 6d6 points of damage for each round they remain inside at the beginning of your turn. Creatures inside the tornado can't do much; attacks, spellcasting, and movement are impossible within a *greater whirlwind*. When the *greater whirlwind* ejects a creature, it reappears 4d6×5 feet away from the twister's center in a random direction, and 4d6×5 feet off the ground (immediately falling if it can't fly).

Terrain and Structures: The tornado uproots trees and other vegetation automatically, and it leaves a trail of dense rubble (DMG 90) wherever it goes. Structures within a greater whirlwind take 2d6×10 points of damage per round. In a round or two, that amount of damage is sufficient to destroy any building made of materials less sturdy than reinforced masonry.

No ranged attacks can pass through the twister. A *greater whirlwind* extinguishes all flames it touches. Listen checks are impossible within a *greater whirlwind.*

A *greater whirlwind* remains stationary unless you direct it elsewhere as a move action. It moves up to 60 feet per round.

WILD RUNNER

Transmutation
Level: Druid 4, ranger 4
Components: V, S, DF
Casting Time: 1 standard action
Range: Personal
Target: You
Duration: 10 minutes/level (D)

A vibrant green glow surrounds you, and you feel your body begin to change shape. You grow several inches in height and become aware of a bending and lengthening of your spine. Glancing back, you see a second pair of hoofed legs and a swishing tail.

When you cast this spell, you assume the physical appearance and many of the qualities and abilities of a centaur (MM 32). While under the effect of the spell, your creature type changes to monstrous humanoid, and your size changes to Large. You have the space and reach of a centaur (10 feet/5 feet). You gain the Strength, Dexterity, and Constitution of an average centaur (Str 18, Dex 14, Con 15), but you retain your own mental ability scores. Your base land speed becomes 50 feet. You gain darkvision out to 60 feet. You can still use any extraordinary, spell-like, and supernatural abilities possessed by your normal form. You gain all the advantages of a quadruped form (greater carrying capacity, +4 bonus to resist trip attacks, and so on); this includes the ability to fight effectively while carrying a rider. You can still use your equipment and cast spells normally.

WIND AT BACK

Evocation
Level: Druid 4
Components: V, S
Casting Time: 1 standard action
Range: Medium (100 ft. + 10 ft./level)
Targets: One creature/level, no two of which are more than 30 ft. apart
Duration: 12 hours
Saving Throw: Fortitude negates (harmless)
Spell Resistance: Yes (harmless)

You intone the words that will give you and your allies speed and stamina for the long journey ahead. Your companions are bathed in a soft green radiance as the spell is cast.

This spell doubles the overland speed (PH 164) of all subjects, assuming they are all traveling together in the same direction, including pack animals and mounts. This spell does not affect nonliving material. The spell does not affect tactical speed.

WIND TUNNEL

Evocation
Level: Druid 5
Components: V, S
Casting Time: 1 standard action
Range: Close (25 ft. + 5 ft./2 levels)
Targets: One creature/level
Duration: 1 round/level
Saving Throw: Fortitude negates (harmless)
Spell Resistance: Yes (harmless)

You evoke the powers of the sky, and the wind picks up around you. It blows from your back, now, and wraps itself around your allies' missiles, sending them to their targets more surely.

You call on the wind to assist your allies' accuracy. A *wind tunnel* improves the accuracy of your allies' ranged weapons, granting each subject a +5 competence bonus on ranged attacks. Further, it doubles the range increment of these weapons.

WINGBIND

Evocation [Force]
Level: Sorcerer/wizard 4
Components: V, S
Casting Time: 1 standard action
Range: Medium (100 ft. + 10 ft./level)
Target: One creature
Duration: 1 round/level (D)
Saving Throw: Reflex negates
Spell Resistance: Yes

The flying creature lets out a surprised howl and then plummets to the ground, its wings flat against its body and struggling against a green glowing net.

A web of force surrounds the target, entangling it like a net. This spell functions like *earthbind* (page 76), except that an ensnared creature immediately falls to the ground, taking falling damage.

An entangled creature can escape with a successful Escape Artist check against a DC equal to the save DC of the spell. Like a *wall of force* (PH 298), this web of force is impervious to most attacks: It is immune to damage of all kinds, cannot be burst with a Strength check, and is unaffected by most spells, including *dispel magic*. Also like a *wall of force*, the web is immediately destroyed by *disintegrate*, a *rod of cancellation*, a *sphere of annihilation*, or *Mordenkainen's disjunction*.

WINGED MOUNT

Transmutation
Level: Blackguard 4, paladin 4
Component: V, S, DF
Casting Time: 1 standard action
Range: Touch
Target: Your touched special mount
Duration: 10 minutes/level
Saving Throw: Fortitude negates (harmless)
Spell Resistance: Yes (harmless)

You touch your special mount and it sprouts giant, feathery white wings.

This spell grants your special mount a fly speed of 60 feet (good). The mount is slowed as normal because of weight carried, barding worn, and environmental factors.

WINGS OF AIR

Transmutation
Level: Druid 2, sorcerer/wizard 2
Components: V
Casting Time: 1 standard action
Range: Touch
Target: Winged creature touched
Duration: 1 minute/level
Saving Throw: None (harmless)
Spell Resistance: No (harmless)

You place your hand on the creature's shoulders, and a warm yellow radiance infuses it, spreading out to the tips of its wings.

The creature you touch becomes more agile in the air, able to make quicker turns, and more maneuverable when flying. The subject must be capable of flight using wings. The creature's maneuverability improves by one grade—from clumsy to poor, poor to average, average to good, or good to perfect.

A single creature cannot benefit from multiple applications of this spell at one time.

WINGS OF AIR, GREATER

Transmutation
Level: Druid 4, sorcerer/wizard 4

This spell functions like *wings of air*, except that the creature's maneuverability improves by two grades—from clumsy to average, poor to good, or average to perfect.

The wind tunnel spell guides ranged attacks to their targets

Illus. by W. O'Connor

WINGS OF THE SEA

Transmutation
Level: Cleric 1, druid 1, ranger 1, sorcerer/wizard 1
Components: S, M
Casting Time: 1 standard action
Range: Touch
Target: Creature touched
Duration: 1 minute/level
Saving Throw: Fortitude negates (harmless)
Spell Resistance: Yes (harmless)

The webbing between your fingers grows to reach your fingertips as you complete the spell.

In the instant you touch the spell's intended subject, however, the webbing between your fingers returns to normal even as the subject's means of watery movement grow.

This spell increases the touched creature's swim speed by 30 feet. It has no effect on other modes of movement, nor does it give the subject a swim speed if it does not already have one.

Material Component: A drop of water.

WINTER CHILL

Transmutation [Cold]
Level: Druid 1
Components: V, S
Casting Time: 1 standard action
Range: Close (25 ft. + 5 ft./2 levels)
Target: One creature
Duration: Instantaneous
Saving Throw: Fortitude negates
Spell Resistance: Yes

You make a sound like whistling wind and inscribe a snowflake shape in the air, willing a chill to overcome your foe.

The target creature must succeed on a Fortitude save or take 1d6 points of cold damage and become fatigued. A creature with immunity to cold is not affected by this spell.

WINTER'S EMBRACE

Evocation [Cold]
Level: Druid 2
Components: V, S
Casting Time: 1 standard action
Range: Close (25 ft. + 5 ft./2 levels)
Target: One creature
Duration: 1 round/level
Saving Throw: Fortitude negates
Spell Resistance: Yes

You clutch at the air as though grabbing a nearby creature, and then you blow on your fist. As you do so, ice and snow appear around your foe.

A target that fails its save takes 1d8 points of cold damage per round at the beginning of your turn. Each round, the subject can make a new Fortitude saving throw to avoid taking damage that round. The second time a subject takes damage from a single casting of *winter's embrace*, it becomes fatigued. The fourth time it takes damage from the same spell, it becomes exhausted.

WITHER LIMB

Necromancy [Evil]
Level: Deathbound 4
Components: V, S
Casting Time: 1 standard action
Range: Close (25 ft. + 5 ft./2 levels)
Target: Limbs of one humanoid
Duration: Permanent
Saving Throw: Fortitude negates
Spell Resistance: Yes

Uttering a rumbling phrase, you point at your foe and watch with delight as its limbs wither and twist, becoming useless.

You choose to wither either the arms or the legs of a humanoid. Withered legs force a subject to fall prone while at the same time reducing the subject's land speed to 5 feet. Withered arms make it impossible for the subject to use objects or cast spells with somatic components.

A withered limb can be restored to normal by a successful *dispel magic* from a spellcaster of a level higher than the level of the *wither limb* caster.

Wood rot destroys wooden items and harms plant creatures

WITHERING PALM

Necromancy
Level: Cleric 7
Components: V, S
Casting Time: 1 standard action
Range: Touch
Target: Living creature touched
Duration: Instantaneous
Saving Throw: Fortitude negates
Spell Resistance: Yes

A black shroud of magical energy surrounds your hands. Beneath the shroud your hands look withered and aged, like uncared-for ancient leather on the verge of crumbling to dust.

Your successful melee touch attack deals 1 point of Strength damage and 1 point of Constitution damage per two caster levels to the target (maximum of 10 points each). If you score a critical hit, the subject takes ability drain instead, but the effect is not doubled.

WOOD ROT

Transmutation
Level: Druid 4
Components: V, S, M
Casting Time: 1 standard action
Range: Touch
Target: One nonmagical wooden object or a volume of wood; or one plant creature
Duration: Instantaneous or 1 round/level; see text
Saving Throw: None
Spell Resistance: No

By crushing a live termite between your teeth and reciting the necessary words of power, you finish casting the spell.

When you cast this spell, an insidious rot immediately taints any wooden object or plant creature you touch. Any unattended nonmagical wooden item smaller than 6 feet in diameter, or a 3-foot-radius volume of a larger wooden object (such as a wooden door), is instantly destroyed by *wood rot*.

Illus. by C. Dien

In combat, you can use the spell to attempt to sunder any wooden or wooden-hafted weapon; the weapon or its wooden portion is destroyed on a successful melee touch attack. Attempting to sunder a weapon generally provokes attacks of opportunity, and *wood rot* has no effect on wooden or wooden-hafted weapons that strike you, even if you hold the charge.

Against wooden shields or armor, you also make a melee touch attack. Such targets too large to be destroyed outright take a –1d6 penalty to their armor or shield bonus on a successful hit and are rendered unusable if the penalty exceeds the bonus. Any attack against a wooden object discharges the spell, and wooden magic items are immune to the effect of *wood rot*.

Against plant creatures, *wood rot* deals 3d6 points of damage +1 point per caster level (maximum +15) on a successful attack. Against plant creatures, the spell lasts for 1 round per level, and you can make one melee touch attack per round. Once it is used to make an attack against a plant creature, *wood rot* cannot be used to attack or destroy wooden items.

Material Component: A live termite.

WOOD WOSE

Conjuration (Creation)
Level: Druid 1
Components: V, S, DF
Casting Time: 1 standard action
Range: Close (25 ft. + 5 ft./2 levels)
Effect: One nature servant
Duration: 1 hour/level
Saving Throw: None
Spell Resistance: No

Whistling up nature's power and waving a branch of holly, you create a helper for the task at hand.

A *wood wose* is a translucent green nature spirit that you can command to perform simple natural tasks. It can build a campfire, gather herbs, feed an animal companion, catch a fish, or perform any other simple task that doesn't involve knowledge of technology. It cannot, for example, open a latched chest, since it doesn't know how a latch works.

A *wood wose* can perform only one activity at a time, but it repeats the same activity if told to do so. Thus, if you commanded it to gather leaves, it would continue to do so while you turned your attention elsewhere, as long as you remained within range.

A *wood wose* has an effective Strength of 2, so it can lift 20 pounds or drag 100 pounds. It can trigger traps, but the 20 pounds of force it can exert is not enough to activate most pressure plates. It has a land speed of 15 feet and a fly speed of 15 feet (perfect).

A *wood wose* cannot attack in any way; it is never allowed an attack roll or a saving throw. It cannot be killed, but it dissipates if it takes 6 points of damage from area attacks. If you attempt to send the wose beyond the spell's range (measured from your current position), it ceases to exist.

WORD OF BALANCE

Evocation [Sonic]
Level: Balance 7, druid 7
Components: V
Casting Time: 1 standard action
Range: 30 ft.
Targets: Creatures in a 30-ft.-radius spread centered on you
Duration: Instantaneous
Saving Throw: None or Will negates; see text
Spell Resistance: Yes

You utter the elder words of balance. Those who stray too far from the path of evenhandedness pay the price for their sins as the words judge them.

Any lawful good, chaotic good, lawful evil, or chaotic evil creature that hears a *word of balance* suffers ill effects according to its Hit Dice, as given below, with no saving throw. These effects are cumulative.

HD	Effect
Equal to caster level	Nauseated
Up to caster level –1	Weakened, nauseated
Up to caster level –5	Paralyzed, weakened, nauseated
Up to caster level –10	Killed

Nauseated: The creature is limited to a single move action for 1 round but can defend itself normally.

Weakened: The creature's Strength decreases by 2d6 points for 2d4 rounds.

Paralyzed: The creature is paralyzed and helpless for 1d10 minutes.

Killed: The creature dies if living or is destroyed if undead.

If you are on your home plane when you cast this spell, every lawful good, chaotic good, lawful evil, and chaotic evil elemental and outsider within the area is instantly banished back to its home plane unless it makes a successful Will saving throw at a –4 penalty. Creatures so banished cannot return for at least 24 hours. The banishment effect occurs whether or not the creatures actually hear the *word of balance*, though those that do also suffer the appropriate effects (see above).

Creatures whose HD exceed your caster level are unaffected by *word of balance*.

WORD OF BINDING

Conjuration (Creation)
Level: Paladin 3
Components: V, DF
Casting Time: 1 standard action
Range: Close (25 ft. + 5 ft./level)
Target: One Medium or smaller humanoid or monstrous humanoid
Duration: 1 round/level (D)
Saving Throw: Reflex negates
Spell Resistance: Yes

When you cast this spell and call to the target, shining steel manacles appear around its wrists and ankles.

You create masterwork steel manacles that attempt to bind your target. A successful Reflex save allows the target to dodge the forming manacles; otherwise it is bound at its wrists and ankles.

The imprisoned creature can slip free with a DC 35 Escape Artist check or a DC 28 Strength check. The manacles have hardness 10 and hit points equal to 10 + 1 per caster level. The manacles automatically scale to fit any Medium or smaller humanoid creature. While imprisoned by the manacles, the subject cannot take any actions requiring the use of its hands and can move only 5 feet per round. The manacles come complete with an average quality lock (Open Lock DC 25).

WOUNDING WHISPERS

Abjuration [Sonic]
Level: Bard 3
Components: V, S
Casting Time: 1 standard action
Range: Personal
Target: You
Duration: 1 round/level (D)

The words of this spell produce hissing, sibilant echoes that spin around you, invoking doom upon those who dare to harm you.

Any creature striking you with its body or a handheld weapon takes 1d6 points of sonic damage +1 point per caster level. If a creature has spell resistance, it applies to this damage. Weapons with reach, such as longspears, do not endanger their users in this way.

You cannot use this spell to deal damage to another target (for instance, with an unarmed attack or by forcing the whispers against a target). Only if another creature touches you does the effect deal damage.

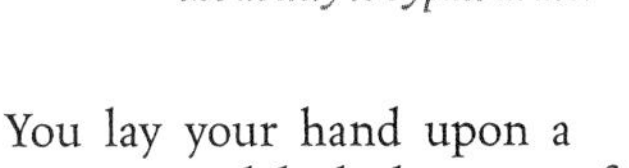

The wraithstrike spell gives a spellcaster the ability to bypass armor

Illus. by W. O'Connor

WRACK

Necromancy [Evil]
Level: Cleric 4, sorcerer/wizard 5
Components: V, S
Casting Time: 1 standard action
Range: Close (25 ft. + 5 ft./2 levels)
Target: One humanoid
Duration: 1 round/level + 3d10 minutes; see text
Saving Throw: Fortitude negates
Spell Resistance: Yes

With the final word of the spell, your chosen foe is wracked with such pain that it doubles over and collapses. Its face and hands blister and drip fluid, and its eyes cloud with blood, rendering it blind.

This spell causes your target to experience excruciating pain. For the duration of the spell, the subject falls prone and is blinded and helpless. Even when the spell ends, the subject is still shaken for 3d10 minutes.

WRACKING TOUCH

Necromancy
Level: Druid 2, sorcerer/wizard 2
Components: V, S
Casting Time: 1 standard action
Range: Touch
Target: Creature touched
Duration: Instantaneous
Saving Throw: Fortitude half
Spell Resistance: Yes

You cry out with malice and clench your fist, completing the spell. The spell's terrible energy causes your fist to shake involuntarily, sending spasms up your arm.

You lay your hand upon a creature and deal 1d6 points of damage +1 point per caster level (maximum +10). In addition, if you have the sneak attack ability, you also deal sneak attack damage to the affected creature unless the creature is immune to extra damage from critical hits. The creature still takes the spell damage even if it does not take the sneak attack damage. Unlike a normal use of sneak attack, your target need not be flanked or denied its Dexterity bonus to take sneak attack damage from this spell.

WRAITHSTRIKE

Transmutation
Level: Assassin 3, sorcerer/wizard 2
Components: V, S
Casting Time: 1 swift action
Range: Personal
Target: You
Duration: 1 round

By presenting your weapon with an overly dramatic flourish and calling out with a sickly-sounding moan, you complete the spell. As you do so, your weapon becomes translucent almost to the point that you cannot see it, though it still weighs as heavily in your hand.

While this spell is in effect, your melee attacks are resolved as melee touch attacks rather than normal melee attacks.

WRATHFUL CASTIGATION

Enchantment (Compulsion) [Mind-Affecting]
Level: Sorcerer/wizard 8
Components: V, S, F
Casting Time: 1 standard action
Range: Close (25 ft. + 5 ft./2 levels)
Target: One living creature
Duration: 1 round/level (D)
Saving Throw: See text
Spell Resistance: Yes

You brandish the whip, and your target begins to shake uncontrollably, then collapses on the ground, its spasms eventually fading as it dies.

This spell causes wracking pain and violent convulsions, ending in death. The target creature must make a Will save or writhe in pain, helpless, before it dies 1 round later at the start of your turn. A creature that makes the Will save must also succeed on a second Will save or be dazed and take a –4 penalty on saving throws for the duration of the spell.

Focus: A whip.

XORN MOVEMENT

Transmutation **Level:** Sorcerer/wizard 5
Components: V, S, F
Casting Time: 1 standard action
Range: Touch
Target: Creature touched
Duration: 1 round/level; see text
Saving Throw: Will negates (harmless)
Spell Resistance: Yes (harmless)

You concentrate on the piece of the xorn's hide. As you intone the spell it begins to glow yellow, and then the glow spreads over your entire form. You complete the spell and slip effortlessly between the gaps in the earth itself, leaving nothing disturbed in your wake.

The subject of this spell can move through natural earth and stone (but not worked stone, brick, or metal) as a xorn does, leaving behind no tunnel or sign of passage. Furthermore, the subject can breathe normally while entombed in earth and natural rock. A *move earth* spell cast on an area the subject occupies flings it back 30 feet and stuns it for 1 round. A successful Fortitude save negates the stunning effect.

Xorn movement lasts a minimum of 1 round/level. If the subject has not emerged into a large enough open space to contain its body comfortably when the spell expires, it is shunted off to the nearest such open space, taking 1d6 points of damage per 5 feet so traveled.

Focus: A scale from a xorn's hide.

ZEAL

Abjuration
Level: Competition 2, blackguard 2, paladin 2
Components: V, S
Casting Time: 1 swift action
Range: Personal
Target: You
Duration: 1 round/level

You invoke a divine shield to protect you as you close with a chosen opponent.

Choose a foe as you cast this spell. You gain a +4 deflection bonus to AC against all attacks of opportunity from opponents other than the chosen foe. Also, you can move through enemies as if they were allies for the duration of this spell, as long as you finish your movement closer to your chosen foe than when you began it.

ZEALOT PACT

Evocation
Level: Cleric 6, Competition 6, Pact 6
Components: V, S, DF, XP
Casting Time: 10 minutes
Range: Touch
Target: Willing living creature touched
Duration: Permanent until triggered; then 1 round/level
Saving Throw: Will negates (harmless)
Spell Resistance: Yes (harmless)

By binding the subject to your deity, you give it the ability to crush the deity's enemies.

Once this spell is cast, the *zealot pact* remains dormant until the subject successfully hits a foe whose alignment is exactly opposite that of your deity. The subject's subsequent melee attacks gain a +4 bonus and deal double damage. Once the spell is active, the subject must attack foes of opposite alignment every round if able to do so, or the spell effect ends. The subject knows which creatures within 60 feet are of opposite alignment.

If you create a *zealot pact* with a neutral deity (such as Obad-Hai), choose one alignment from among the following that triggers the *zealot pact:* lawful good, lawful evil, chaotic evil, or chaotic good.

A creature can be subject to only one *zealot pact* at a time. Casting *zealot pact* on a subject that already has an untriggered *zealot pact* voids the earlier pact.

XP Cost: 500 XP.

ZONE OF RESPITE

Abjuration
Level: Cleric 5, sorcerer/wizard 5
Components: V, S, M
Casting Time: 2 rounds
Range: 20 ft.
Area: 20-ft.-radius emanation centered on you
Duration: 1 minute/level
Saving Throw: None
Spell Resistance: Yes

Smearing blood between your fingers, you inscribe a ward in the air and cast the power of that ward over a wide area.

You create a region that is temporarily protected against interplanar intrusion. This includes spells and abilities that use other planes, including *dimension door, teleport, plane shift,* and travel through such planes as the Astral Plane, the Ethereal Plane, and the Plane of Shadow.

Summoning and calling spells do not function within a *zone of respite,* but summoned and called creatures outside a *zone of respite* can be sent inside it.

Gate spells and other portals cannot be created within a *zone of respite,* but existing portals are unaffected by the spell. Creatures on coterminous or coexistent planes (DMG 150) must retreat to the edge of the *zone of respite* and cannot enter the corresponding area on the coterminous or coexistent plane.

Material Component: A small amount of blood from a gorgon.

ZONE OF REVELATION

Divination
Level: Cleric 5
Components: V, S, M/DF
Casting Time: 1 standard action
Range: Close (25 ft. + 5 ft./2 levels)
Area: 5-ft.-radius/level emanation centered on a point in space
Duration: 1 minute/level
Saving Throw: None
Spell Resistance: Yes

After making a dramatic gesture and uttering a few words of power, you close your eyes and open them again, revealing all that is hidden.

All creatures and objects within a *zone of revelation* are made visible. This includes invisible creatures, as well as those on coexistent planes such as the Ethereal Plane and the Plane of Shadow (DMG 150). Natives of these planes do not lose any abilities but are simply made visible.

Zone of revelation suppresses but does not dispel *invisibility, etherealness,* or other spells. Once a formerly invisible object or creature leaves the area, it becomes invisible again. Ethereal creatures in the spell's area become nonethereal until they move beyond the spell's range.

Arcane Material Component: A handful of dust from the grave clothes of an undead creature.

Illus. by D. Martin

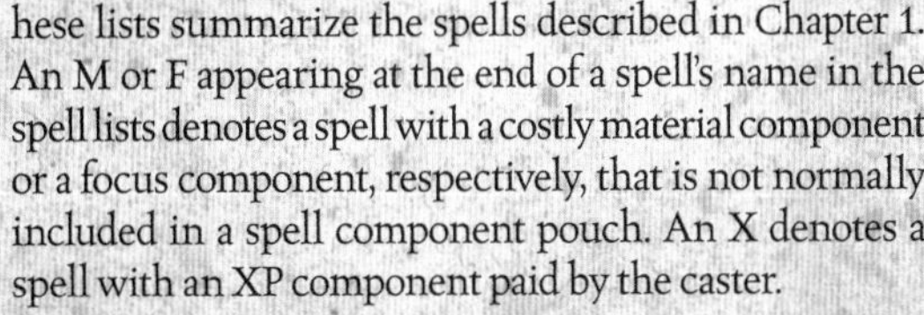

These lists summarize the spells described in Chapter 1. An M or F appearing at the end of a spell's name in the spell lists denotes a spell with a costly material component or a focus component, respectively, that is not normally included in a spell component pouch. An X denotes a spell with an XP component paid by the caster.

ASSASSIN SPELLS

1ST-LEVEL ASSASSIN SPELLS

Critical Strike: For 1 round you gain +1d6 damage, doubled threat range, and +4 on attack rolls to confirm critical threats.
Dead End: Removes spoor of one creature/level.
Distract Assailant: One creature is flat-footed for 1 round.
Ebon Eyes: Subject can see through magical darkness.
Insightful Feint: Gain +10 on your next Bluff check to feint in combat.
Instant Locksmith: Make Disable Device or Open Lock check at +2 as free action.
Instant Search: Make Search check at +2 as free action.
Lightfoot: Your move does not provoke attacks of opportunity for 1 round.
Low-Light Vision: See twice as far as a human in poor illumination.
Shock and Awe: Flat-footed creatures get –10 on initiative.

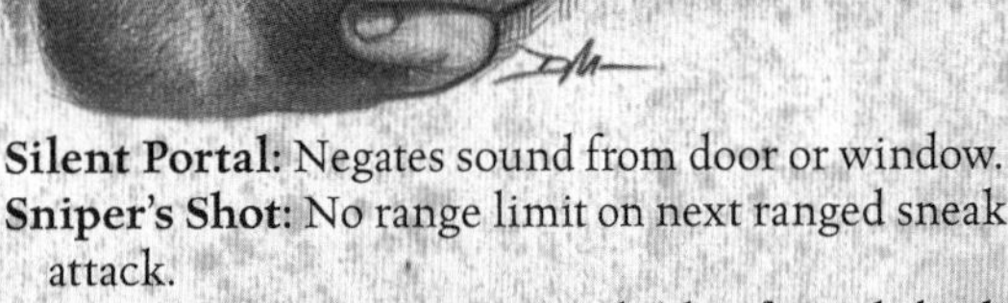

Silent Portal: Negates sound from door or window.
Sniper's Shot: No range limit on next ranged sneak attack.
Sticky Fingers: You get +10 on Sleight of Hand checks.

2ND-LEVEL ASSASSIN SPELLS

Absorb Weapon: Hide a weapon, gain a Bluff check with a +4 bonus on feint attempts when you draw it.
Blade of Pain and Fear: Creates blade of gnashing teeth.
Fell the Greatest Foe: Deal extra damage to creatures larger than you.
Fire Shuriken: Magical shuriken deal 3d6 fire damage.
Ice Knife: Magical shard of ice deals 2d8 cold damage plus 2 Dex damage, or deals 1d8 cold damage in 10-ft.-radius burst.
Invisibility, Swift: You are invisible for 1 round or until you attack.
Iron Silence: Armor touched has no armor check penalty on Hide and Move Silently for 1 hour/level.
Marked Object: You gain bonus to track a specific being.
Phantom Foe[M]**:** Subject is always flanked by one creature.
Veil of Shadow: Darkness grants you concealment.

3RD-LEVEL ASSASSIN SPELLS

Amorphous Form: Subject becomes puddlelike and can slip through cracks quickly.
Fangs of the Vampire King: Grow vampire fangs.
Find the Gap: Your attacks ignore armor and natural armor.
Spectral Weapon: Use quasi-real weapon to make touch attacks.
Spider Poison: Touch deals 1d6 Str damage, repeats in 1 minute.
Wraithstrike: Your melee attacks strike as touch attacks for 1 round.

4TH-LEVEL ASSASSIN SPELLS

Cursed Blade: Wounds dealt by weapon can't be healed without *remove curse*.
Heart Ripper: Kills living creature with up to your caster level in HD.
Hide from Dragons: Dragons can't perceive one subject/2 levels.
Implacable Pursuer: You know where prey is, as long as it's moving.
Shadow Form: Gain +4 on Hide, Move Silently, and Escape Artist checks, and concealment; you can move through obstacles if you have ranks in Escape Artist.
Shadow Phase: Subject becomes partially incorporeal.
Sniper's Eye: Gain +10 Spot, darkvision, 60-ft. range for sneak attacks, and death attacks with ranged weapons.
Vulnerability: Reduces an opponent's damage reduction.

An assassin casts absorb weapon in order to retain a secret advantage

Illus. by M. Cotie

BARD SPELLS

0-LEVEL BARD SPELLS (CANTRIPS)

Ghostharp: Object records, plays a song at your command.
Minor Disguise: Makes slight changes to your appearance.
Songbird: Perform and gain +1 on your next Cha check.
Stick: Glues an object weighing 5 pounds or less to another object.

1ST-LEVEL BARD SPELLS

Accelerated Movement: Balance, Climb, or Move Silently at normal speed with no penalty on skill check.
Amplify: Lowers Listen DC by 20.
Appraising Touch: Gain +10 bonus on Appraise checks.
Beastland Ferocity: Subject fights without penalty while disabled or dying.
Cheat: Caster rerolls when determining the success of a game of chance.
Crabwalk: Touched creature gains bonus while charging.
Critical Strike: For 1 round you gain +1d6 damage, doubled threat range, and +4 on attack rolls to confirm critical threats.
Dead End: Removes spoor of one creature/level.
Distort Speech: Subject's speech is 50% unintelligible, so it might miscast spells.
Distract: Subjects take –4 on Concentration, Listen, Search, and Spot.
Expeditious Retreat, Swift: Your speed increases by 30 ft. for 1 round.
Focusing Chant: Gain +1 on attack rolls, skill checks, and ability checks.
Guiding Light: +2 on ranged attacks against creatures in illuminated area.
Healthful Rest: Subjects heal at twice the normal rate.
Herald's Call: Creatures of 5 HD or less within 20 ft. *slowed* for 1 round.
Improvisation: You gain a pool of luck bonus points equal to twice your caster level and can spend them to improve attack rolls, skill checks, and ability checks.
Incite: Subjects can't ready actions or delay.
Inhibit: Subject delays until next round.
Insidious Rhythm: Subject has –4 penalty on Intelligence-based skill checks and Concentration checks, and must make Concentration check to cast spells.
Inspirational Boost: The bonuses granted by your inspire courage ability increase by 1.
Invisibility, Swift: You are invisible for 1 round or until you attack.
Ironguts: Subject gains +5 bonus on saving throws against poison.
Ironthunder Horn: Intense vibrations trip those in area.
Joyful Noise: You negate *silence* in a 10-ft.-radius emanation for as long as you concentrate.
Master's Touch: You gain proficiency in a weapon or shield touched for 1 minute/level.
Phantom Threat: Subject thinks it's flanked.
Remove Scent: Hides touched creature's scent.
Serene Visage: Gain insight bonus on Bluff checks equal to half your level.
Shock and Awe: Flat-footed creatures get –10 on initiative.

Sticky Fingers: You get +10 on Sleight of Hand checks.
Targeting Ray: You and allies are +1 to hit/3 levels against subject.
Undersong: Make Perform checks instead of Concentration checks.

2ND-LEVEL BARD SPELLS

Alarm, Greater[F]**:** As *alarm*, and it works on coexistent planes.
Battle Hymn: Allies can reroll one Will save/round.
Bladeweave: Your melee attack dazes your opponent.
Bonefiddle[F]**:** Spectral fiddle bow deals 3d6 damage/round.
Circle Dance: Indicates direction to known individual.
Cloak Pool: Hide a color pool on the Astral Plane from view.
Cloud of Bewilderment: Generates a nauseating 10-ft-cube.
Curse of Impending Blades: Subject takes –2 penalty to AC.
Dark Way: Creates temporary unbreakable bridge supporting up to 200 lb./level.
Delusions of Grandeur: Subject thinks it is better than it is.
Discolor Pool: Change the color of a color pool on the Astral Plane.
Disquietude: Subject avoids physical contact with others.
Dissonant Chant: Concentration checks more difficult within area of spell.
Distracting Ray: Ray forces spellcaster to make Concentration check.
Entice Gift: Subject gives caster what it's holding.
Fly, Swift: Gain fly speed of 60 ft. for 1 round.
Grace: Silvery light grants +2 Dexterity, +10 feet to land speed, melee attacks treated as good; take –20 to Hide checks.
Harmonic Chorus: Give another caster +2 to caster level and +2 on save DCs as long as you concentrate.
Heartfire: Subjects outlined by fire, take 1d4 damage/round.
Iron Silence: Armor touched has no armor check penalty on Hide and Move Silently for 1 hour/level.
Know Vulnerabilities: Determine subject's vulnerabilities and resistances.
Lively Step: You and allies gain +10 increase to speed.
Mesmerizing Glare: Your gaze fascinates creatures.
Mindless Rage: Subject compelled to attack you physically for 1 round/level.
Miser's Envy: Subject jealously covets a nearby object.
Nightmare Lullaby: Subject is *confused*.
Portal Alarm: You are alerted when a creature passes through a warded portal.
Reflective Disguise: Viewers see you as their own species and gender.
Reveille: Dead creature speaks a short sentence about what caused its death.
Sonic Weapon: Weapon touched deals +1d6 sonic damage with each hit.
Sonic Whip: Whip of magical force keeps animals at bay and can frighten animals as ranged touch attack.
Sonorous Hum: Removes need to concentrate to maintain next spell cast.
Speak to Allies: Subjects can converse at distance without moving lips.
Sting Ray: Subject of ray can take only standard or move action, has –2 AC, and must make Concentration checks to cast spells.
Summon Elysian Thrush: Summon an Elysian thrush, which accelerates natural healing.
Surefooted Stride: You can move over rubble as easily as you can over open ground.
Tactical Precision: Allies gain additional +2 bonus on attack rolls and +1d6 additional damage against flanked foes.
War Cry: Gain +4 on attack rolls and damage rolls if you charge. Any opponent you damage must save or become panicked for 1 round.
Wave of Grief: Cone imposes –3 penalty on attacks, checks, and saves.
Weapon Shift: Touched weapon changes form.
Whirling Blade: Hurled slashing weapon magically attacks all foes in 60-ft. line.

3RD-LEVEL BARD SPELLS

Allegro: You and your allies gain +30 ft. speed for 1 minute/level.
Analyze Portal: Find a nearby portal and discover its properties.
Creaking Cacophony: Sound distracts and makes foes vulnerable to sonic damage.
Curse of Impending Blades, Mass: Enemies take –2 penalty to AC.
Dirge of Discord: All within 20 ft. take –4 on attack rolls and Dexterity, and reduce speed by 50%.
Dissonant Chord: Deal 1d8/2 levels sonic damage in 10-ft. burst.
Dolorous Blow: Weapon's threat range is doubled and threats are automatically confirmed.
G'elsewhere Chant: Teleport subject to random safe place within 100 ft.
Haunting Tune: 1 subject/level becomes shaken.
Hymn of Praise: Add +2 to caster level of all good divine casters within range.
Infernal Threnody: Add +2 to caster level to all evil divine casters within range.
Know Opponent: Learn strengths and weaknesses of foe.
Listening Coin: You can eavesdrop through a magic coin.
Love's Lament: Cone deals 1d6 Wisdom damage and causes nausea.
Puppeteer: Subject mimics your actions.
Ray of Dizziness: Subject can take only move or standard actions.
Shadow Cache: You open a small portal to the Plane of Shadow through which you can put an item for later retrieval.
Speechlink: You and one other creature can talk, no matter how far apart.
Suppress Breath Weapon: Subject can't use breath weapon.
Treasure Scent: You detect valuable metals and gems.
Unluck: Subject remakes all rolls, uses worse result for 1 round/level.

Weapon of Impact: As *keen edge*, but aids bludgeoning weapons.

Wounding Whispers: Sonic aura damages foes that strike you.

4TH-LEVEL BARD SPELLS

Cacophonic Shield: Shield 10 ft. from you blocks sounds, deals 1d6 sonic damage +1/level, and deafens creatures passing through.

Celebration: Intoxicate subjects.

Ethereal Mount: You conjure swift mounts on the Ethereal Plane.

Fugue[F]**:** Your Perform check creates variety of effects.

Lay of the Land: You gain an overview of the geography around you.

Ray Deflection: Ray attacks are reflected away.

Portal Alarm, Improved: Warded portal alerts you or a creature designated by you to creatures passing through it.

Protégé: Subject can use bardic music and bardic knowledge as bard of half your level.

Resistance, Greater: Subject gains +3 on saving throws.

Resonating Bolt: Sonic energy deals 1d4 damage/level (max 10d4).

Ruin Delver's Fortune: Cast on another creature's turn and choose one of several benefits.

Sirine's Grace: You gain bonuses to Charisma and Dexterity, AC, and Perform checks, and can breathe water.

Spectral Weapon: Use quasi-real weapon to make touch attacks.

Stone Shatter: Shatter a stone object or creature.

Voice of the Dragon: +10 on Bluff, Diplomacy, and Intimidate checks; can use one *suggestion*.

Travel through the Ethereal Plane is faster on the back of an ethereal mount

Illus. by F. Vohwinkel

5TH-LEVEL BARD SPELLS

Blink, Greater: Controlled blinking between the Material and Ethereal Planes grants defenses for 1 round/level.

Body Harmonic[F]**:** Piercing tone deals 1d10 damage to one ability/round.

Bolts of Bedevilment: One ray/round, dazes 1d3 rounds.

Cacophonic Burst: Noise deals 1d6/level sonic damage to all within area.

Dragonsight: Gain low-light vision, darkvision, and blindsense.

Hidden Lodge: Creates sturdy cottage camouflaged to blend into natural surroundings.

Hide from Dragons: Dragons can't perceive one subject/2 levels.

Reflective Disguise, Mass: Viewers see subjects as their own species and gender.

Surefooted Stride, Mass: As *surefooted stride* but multiple subjects.

Wail of Doom: Deal 1d4 damage/level in 30-ft. cone, plus subjects panicked or shaken.

6TH-LEVEL BARD SPELLS

Dirge: Enemies take 2 points of Str and Dex damage/round.

Hindsight[M]**:** You see into the past.

Nixie's Grace: You gain a swim speed, water breathing, low-light vision, damage reduction 5/cold iron, and enhancements to Dexterity and Wisdom.

Ray of Light: Ray blinds subject.

Revenance: Restores dead creature to life for 1 minute/level.

Resistance, Superior: Subject gains +6 on saving throws.

Symphonic Nightmare[M]**:** Discordant noise haunts subject's sleep.

BLACKGUARD SPELLS

1ST-LEVEL BLACKGUARD SPELLS

Blessed Aim: +2 bonus for allies' ranged attacks.

Divine Sacrifice: You sacrifice hit points to deal extra damage.

Golden Barding: Your mount gets force armor.

Faith Healing: Cures 8 hp +1/level (max +5) to worshiper of your deity.

Know Greatest Enemy: Determines relative power level of creatures within the area.

Mark of the Outcast: Subject takes –5 penalty on Bluff and Diplomacy checks and –2 penalty to AC.

Resurgence: You grant subject a second chance at a saving throw.

Strategic Charge: Gain the benefits of the Mobility feat.

Summon Undead I: Summons undead to fight for you.

Traveler's Mount: Creature moves faster but can't attack.

2ND-LEVEL BLACKGUARD SPELLS

Blade of Pain and Fear: Creates blade of gnashing teeth.

Curse of Ill Fortune: Subject takes –3 penalty on attacks, checks, and saves.

Demonhide: Evil creature gains DR 10/cold iron or good.

Hand of Divinity: Gives +2 sacred or profane bonus on saves to worshiper of your deity.

Summon Undead II: Summons undead to fight for you.

Veil of Shadow: Darkness grants you concealment.
Wave of Grief: Cone imposes –3 penalty on attacks, checks, and saves.
Zeal: You move through foes to attack the enemy you want.

3RD-LEVEL BLACKGUARD SPELL

Fangs of the Vampire King: Grow vampire fangs.
Mantle of Evil: You gain SR 12 + caster level against spells with the good descriptor.
Resurgence, Mass: As *resurgence,* but multiple subjects.
Spiritual Chariot: Creates ghostly chariot behind your mount.
Summon Undead III: Summons undead to fight for you.
Unholy Storm[M]**:** Evil-aligned rain falls in 20-ft. radius.
Weapon of the Deity: Your weapon gains enhancement bonus and special ability.

4TH-LEVEL BLACKGUARD SPELLS

Implacable Pursuer: You know where prey is, as long as it's moving.
Revenance: Restores dead creature to life for 1 minute/level.
Summon Undead IV: Summons undead to fight for you.
Visage of the Deity, Lesser: You gain +4 Cha and resistance 10 to certain energy types.
Winged Mount: Your mount grows wings and flies at speed of 60 ft.

CLERIC SPELLS

0-LEVEL CLERIC SPELL (ORISON)

Amanuensis: Copy nonmagical text.

1ST-LEVEL CLERIC SPELLS

Anarchic Water[M]**:** Makes chaotic-aligned anarchic water.
Axiomatic Water[M]**:** Makes lawful-aligned axiomatic water.
Blessed Aim: +2 bonus for allies' ranged attacks.
Blood Wind: Subject uses natural weapon at range.
Cold Fire: Fire becomes blue and white, emits cold.
Conviction: Subject gains +2 or higher save bonus.
Delay Disease: Ravages of disease staved off for a day.
Dispel Ward: As *dispel magic,* but affects only wards.
Ebon Eyes: Subject can see through magical darkness.
Faith Healing: Cures 8 hp +1/level (max +5) to worshiper of your deity.
Foundation of Stone: +2 AC, +4 bonus to resist bull rush and trip attacks.
Grave Strike: You can sneak attack undead for 1 round.
Guiding Light: +2 on ranged attacks against creatures in illuminated area.
Healthful Rest: Subjects heal at twice the normal rate.
Ice Gauntlet: A spiked gauntlet of ice forms around your fist.
Incite: Subjects can't ready actions or delay.
Inhibit: Subject delays until next round.
Ironguts: Subject gains +5 bonus on saving throws against poison.
Light of Lunia: You radiate silvery light, which you can expend as 2 bolts that deal 1d6 damage.
Moon Lust: Subject obsesses about moon, is *fascinated* or dazzled.
Nightshield: You gain resistance bonus on saves, and spell absorbs *magic missile* damage.
Nimbus of Light: Light illuminates you until released as an attack.
Omen of Peril[F]**:** You know how dangerous the future will be.
Portal Beacon: You grant others knowledge of a magic portal's location.
Resist Planar Alignment: Subject can resist penalties for being of an opposed alignment on an aligned Outer Plane.
Resurgence: You grant subject a second chance at a saving throw.
Sign: You gain +4 bonus on next initiative check.
Snowshoes: Subject walks easily on ice and snow.
Spell Flower: Hold the charge on one touch spell per forelimb.
Summon Undead I: Summons undead to fight for you.
Updraft: Column of wind lifts you aloft.
Vigor, Lesser: Creature heals 1 hp/round (max 15 rounds).
Vision of Glory: Subject gains morale bonus equal to your Cha modifier to one saving throw.
Wings of the Sea: +30 ft. to subject's swim speed.

2ND-LEVEL CLERIC SPELLS

Aura Against Flame: Ignores 10 fire damage/round and extinguishes fires.
Avoid Planar Effects: Provides temporary protection against overtly damaging planar traits.
Balor Nimbus: Your flaming body damages foes in grapple.
Body Blades: You gain spikes, harm grapplers.
Brambles: Wooden weapon grows spikes that deal +1 damage/level (max +10).
Close Wounds: Cure 1d4 damage +1/level, even on another's turn.
Curse of Ill Fortune: Subject takes –3 penalty on attacks, checks, and saves.
Dark Way: Creates temporary unbreakable bridge supporting up to 200 lb./level.
Deific Vengeance: Deity's punishment deals 1d6 damage/2 levels (max 5d6).
Divine Insight: You gain insight bonus of 5 + caster level on one single skill check.
Divine Interdiction: Turn/rebuke attempts fail within the area.
Divine Protection: Allies gain +1 to AC, saves.
Energized Shield, Lesser: Shield provides user resistance 5, shield bash deals +1d6 damage.
Extend Tentacles: +5 ft. to reach of tentacle attack.
Frost Breath: Icy breath deals 1d4 damage/2 levels.
Fuse Arms: Multiple arms/tentacles become one pair of stronger limbs.
Ghost Touch Armor: Armor works normally against incorporeal attacks.
Hand of Divinity: Gives +2 sacred or profane bonus to worshiper of your deity.

Healing Lorecall: If you have 5 or more ranks in Heal, you can remove harmful conditions with conjuration (healing) spells.
Infernal Wound: Weapon deals persistent, bleeding wounds.
Inky Cloud: Obscures sight underwater beyond 5 ft.
Iron Silence: Armor touched has no armor check penalty on Hide and Move Silently checks for 1 hour/level.
Light of Mercuria: You radiate golden light, which you can expend as 2 bolts that deal 1d6 damage, 2d6 against undead and evil outsiders.
Living Undeath: Subject becomes immune to extra damage from critical hits and sneak attacks.
Mark of the Outcast: Subject takes –5 penalty on Bluff and Diplomacy checks and –2 penalty to AC.
Protection from Negative Energy: Ignore 10 points of negative energy damage per attack.
Protection from Positive Energy: Ignore 10 points of positive energy damage per attack.
Quick March: Allies' speed increases by 30 ft. for 1 round.
Shroud of Undeath: Negative energy shroud makes undead perceive you as undead.
Spawn Screen: Subject resists being transformed into an undead spawn if slain.
Spell Immunity, Lesser: As *spell immunity*, but only 1st- and 2nd-level spells.
Stabilize: Cures 1 point of damage to all creatures in area.
Stone Bones: Corporeal undead gains +3 natural armor bonus.
Summon Elysian Thrush: Summon an Elysian thrush, which accelerates natural healing.
Summon Undead II: Summons undead to fight for you.
Veil of Shadow: Darkness grants you concealment.
Wave of Grief: Cone imposes –3 penalty on attacks, checks, and saves.

3RD-LEVEL CLERIC SPELLS

Aid, Mass: Allies gain +1 on attack rolls, +1 against fear, 1d8 temporary hp +1/level (max +15).
Air Breathing: Subjects can breathe air freely.
Align Weapon, Mass: Allies' weapons become good, evil, lawful, or chaotic.
Anarchic Storm[M]**:** Chaotic-aligned rain falls in 20-ft. radius.
Antidragon Aura[M]**:** Allies gain bonus to AC and saves against dragons.
Attune Form: Grant creature temporary protection against overtly damaging planar traits.
Awaken Sin: Subject faces its sins, takes 1d6 nonlethal damage/level (10d6 max).
Axiomatic Storm[M]**:** Lawful-aligned rain falls in 20-ft. radius.
Blade of Pain and Fear: Creates blade of gnashing teeth.
Blindsight: Subject gains blindsight 30 ft. for 1 minute/ level.
Chain of Eyes: See through other creatures' eyes.
Checkmate's Light: Your weapon becomes a +1 axiomatic weapon and bolsters the morale of allies.
Circle Dance: Indicates direction to known individual.
Cloak of Bravery: You and your allies gain a bonus on saves against fear.
Clutch of Orcus: Deals 1d12 damage/round and paralyzes foe.
Conviction, Mass: Allies gain +2 or higher save bonus.
Corona of Cold: Aura of cold protects you, damages others.
Darkfire: Dark flames deal 1d6 damage/2 levels, touch or thrown.
Demon Dirge: Demons are stunned and take 3d6 damage/round for 1d4 rounds.
Devil Blight: Damage and stun baatezu; damage other lawful and evil creatures.
Downdraft: Flying creatures knocked down.
Energized Shield: Shield provides user resistance 10, shield bash deals +2d6 damage.
Energy Vortex: Burst of energy centered on you damages nearby creatures.
Favorable Sacrifice[M]**:** Subject gains better protection the more gems you sacrifice.
Fell the Greatest Foe: Deal extra damage to creatures larger than you.
Flame of Faith: Gives weapon the flaming burst special ability.
Ghost Touch Weapon: Weapon works normally against incorporeal creatures.
Girallon's Blessing: Subject gains one additional pair of arms.
Grace: Silvery light grants +2 Dexterity, +10 feet to land speed, melee attacks treated as good; take –20 to Hide checks.
Hamatula Barbs: Subjects grow barbs, which damage foes that attack subject in melee.
Holy Storm[M]**:** Good-aligned rain falls in 20-ft. radius.
Ice Axe: You create a battleaxe made of ice.
Interplanar Message: You send a short mental message that can reach a subject regardless of planar boundaries.
Knight's Move: You instantly move to flank a subject.
Know Opponent: Learn strengths and weaknesses of foe.
Know Vulnerabilities: Determine subject's vulnerabilities and resistances.
Light of Venya: You radiate pearly light, which you can expend as 2 bolts that deal 2d6 damage, 4d6 against undead and evil outsiders.
Mantle of Chaos/Evil/Good/Law: You gain SR 12 + caster level against spells with opposite alignment descriptor.
Nauseating Breath: Exhale a cone of nauseating gas.
Rejuvenative Corpse: Negative energy fills corpse, feeding undead healed.
Resist Energy, Mass: Creatures ignore damage from specified energy type.
Resurgence, Mass: As *resurgence*, but multiple subjects.
Ring of Blades: Blades surround you, damaging other creatures (1d6 damage +1/level).
Safety: Touched creature knows shortest route to safety.
Shield of Warding: Shield grants +1 bonus on AC and Reflex saves/5 levels (max +5).
Sink: Subject sinks in water, must make Swim checks.
Skull Watch: Skull shrieks when creature enters warded area.
Slashing Darkness: Ray deals 1d8/2 levels damage or heals undead the same amount.

Snowshoes, Mass: As *snowshoes*, affects one creature/level.
Sonorous Hum: Removes need to concentrate to maintain next spell cast.
Spark of Life: Undead creature loses most immunities.
Spikes: As *brambles*, but weapon gains +2 bonus and doubled threat range.
Summon Undead III: Summons undead to fight for you.
Suppress Glyph: You notice but do not trigger magical writing traps.
Tremor: Subjects knocked prone.
Unholy Storm[M]**:** Evil-aligned rain falls in 20-ft. radius.
Vigor: As *lesser vigor*, but 2 hp/round (max 25 rounds).
Vigor, Mass Lesser: As *lesser vigor*, but multiple subjects (max 25 rounds).
Visage of the Deity, Lesser: You gain +4 Cha and resistance 10 to certain energy types.
Wall of Light: Creates wall of light, can dazzle creatures.
Weapon of Energy: Weapon deals extra energy damage.
Weapon of Impact: As *keen edge*, but aids bludgeoning weapons.
Weapon of the Deity: Your weapon gains enhancement bonus and special ability.

4TH-LEVEL CLERIC SPELLS

Assay Spell Resistance: +10 bonus on caster level checks to defeat one creature's spell resistance.
Astral Hospice[M]**:** While on the Astral Plane, open a portal to a demiplane so natural healing can occur.
Blindsight, Greater: Subject gains blindsight 60 ft. for 1 minute/level.
Castigate: Verbal rebuke damages those whose alignment differs from yours.
Consumptive Field: Draw life from all creatures in 30-ft. radius with –1 or fewer hit points.
Contingent Energy Resistance: Energy damage triggers a *resist energy* spell.
Delay Death: Losing hit points doesn't kill subject.
Glowing Orb[F]**:** Creates permanent magical light; you control brightness.
Hand of the Faithful: Immobile zone of warding stuns those worshiping different deities from yours.
Holy Transformation, Lesser: You change into protectar, gain abilities.
Hypothermia: Causes 1d6 cold damage/level, fatigue.
Infernal Transformation, Lesser: You change into bearded devil, gain abilities.
Iron Bones: Corporeal undead gains +6 natural armor bonus.
Life Ward: Grants immunity to healing spells and positive energy effects.
Make Manifest: You cause a creature on a coexistent plane to appear on your plane.
Moon Bolt: 1d4 Strength damage/3 levels; undead made helpless.
Negative Energy Aura: 10-ft. radius surrounding you deals 1 hp/3 levels for 1 round/level.
Panacea: Removes most afflictions.
Planar Exchange, Lesser: Trade places with one of four lesser planar creatures (your choice).
Planar Tolerance: Provides long-term protection against overtly damaging planar traits.
Positive Energy Aura: 10-ft. radius surrounding you heals 1 hp/3 levels for 1 round/level.
Recitation: Your allies get bonus on AC, attacks and saves.
Resistance, Greater: Subject gains +3 on saving throws.
Revenance: Restores dead creature to life for 1 minute/level.
Shadowblast: Blast of light stuns and damages natives to the Plane of Shadow.
Sheltered Vitality: Subject gains immunity to fatigue, exhaustion, ability damage, and ability drain.
Shield of Faith, Mass: Allies gain +3 or higher AC bonus.
Sound Lance: Sonic energy deals 1d8/level damage.
Spell Vulnerability: Reduce creature's spell resistance by 1/caster level (max reduction 15).
Summon Hound Archon: Summon a hound archon to follow your commands.
Summon Undead IV: Summons undead to fight for you.

Illus. by C. Frank

Devil blight is the perfect spell for dealing with baatezu

Undead Bane Weapon: Weapon gains undead bane property and is considered good-aligned.
Wall of Chaos/Evil/Good/Law: Wall blocks creatures of opposite alignment.
Wall of Sand: Swirling sand blocks ranged attacks, slows movement through.
Wrack: Renders creature helpless with pain.

5TH-LEVEL CLERIC SPELLS

Aura of Evasion[M]: All within 10 ft. gain evasion against breath weapons.
Blistering Radiance: Light dazzles creatures, deals 2d6 fire damage in 50-ft.-radius spread.
Call Zelekhut[X]: A zelekhut performs one duty for you.
Contagion, Mass: As *contagion*, but 20-ft. radius.
Crawling Darkness: Shroud of tentacles conceals and protects you.
Curse of Ill Fortune, Mass: Enemies take –2 penalty on attack rolls and saves.
Death Throes: Your body explodes when you die.
Divine Agility: Subject gains +10 to Dexterity for 1 round/level.
Doomtide: Black mist obscures sight, dazes those inside.
Dragon Breath: You choose a dragon type and mimic its breath weapon.
Earth Reaver: Eruption deals 7d6 damage to all in area.
Incorporeal Nova: Destroy incorporeal undead.
Life's Grace: Grants immunity to many undead attacks and protection against incorporeal attacks.
Revivify[M]: Restore recently dead to life with no level loss.
Righteous Wrath of the Faithful: Your allies gain extra attack, +3 on attack rolls and damage rolls.
Sanctuary, Mass: One creature/level can't be attacked, and can't attack.
Stalwart Pact[M]: You gain combat bonuses automatically when reduced to half hit points or lower.
Stone Shape, Greater: Sculpts 10 cu. ft. + 10 cu. ft./level of stone into any shape.
Subvert Planar Essence: Reduces subject's damage reduction and spell resistance.
Summon Bearded Devil: Summon a bearded devil to follow your commands.
Summon Bralani Eladrin: Summon a bralani eladrin to follow your commands.
Summon Undead V: Summons undead to fight for you.
Symbol of Spell Loss: Triggered rune absorbs spells yet to be cast.
Triadspell: Cast a prepared spell three times.
Vigor, Greater: As *lesser vigor*, but 4 hp/round.
Vulnerability: Reduces an opponent's damage reduction.
Wall of Dispel Magic: Creatures passing through a transparent wall become subjects of targeted *dispel magic*.
Zone of Respite: Prevents teleportation and similar effects from functioning in the area.
Zone of Revelation: Makes invisible and ethereal creatures visible.

Clerics prepare for the day by praying for spells

Illus. by M. Cotie

6TH-LEVEL CLERIC SPELLS

Barghest's Feast[M]: Destroy corpse, potentially preventing its return to life.
Bolt of Glory: Positive energy ray deals extra damage to evil outsiders and undead.
Cold Snap: You lower temperature in area.
Cometfall: Comet falls atop foes, damaging them and knocking them prone.
Energy Immunity: Subject and equipment gain immunity to damage of specified energy type.
Ghost Trap: Incorporeal creatures turn corporeal.
Hide the Path[F]: Area warded against divinations.
Ice Flowers: Ice and earth deal 1d6 damage/level.
Lucent Lance: Ambient light forms lance, deals various damage.
Make Manifest, Mass: As *make manifest* but affecting all creatures in the area.
Mantle of the Icy Soul[M]: Touched creature gains the cold subtype.
Opalescent Glare: Kill creatures with a look, or make them very afraid.
Planar Exchange: Trade places with one of three planar creatures (your choice).
Rejection: Creatures within cone are blasted away from you.
Revive Outsider[M]: You restore life to a dead outsider.
Sarcophagus of Stone: Sarcophagus entombs subject.
Spider Plague: Summons Large monstrous spiders to fight for you.
Stone Body: Your body becomes living stone.
Summon Babau Demon: Summon a babau demon to follow your commands.
Resistance, Superior: Subject gains +6 on saving throws.
Vigorous Circle: As *mass lesser vigor* except 3 hp/round (max 40 rounds).

Visage of the Deity: As *lesser visage of the deity*, but you become celestial or fiendish.
Zealot Pact[X]: You automatically gain combat bonuses when you attack someone of opposite alignment.

7TH-LEVEL CLERIC SPELLS

Bestow Curse, Greater: As *bestow curse*, but more severe penalties.
Blood to Water: 2d6 Constitution damage to subjects.
Brain Spider: Eavesdrop on thoughts of up to eight other creatures.
Brilliant Blade: Weapon or projectiles shed light, ignore armor.
Call Kolyarut[X]: A kolyarut performs one duty for you.
Consumptive Field, Greater: Draw life from all creatures in 30-ft. radius with 9 or fewer hit points.
Death Dragon: You gain +4 natural armor, +4 deflection, and natural attacks.
Energy Ebb: Give subject one negative level/round for 1 round/level.
Evil Glare: Paralyze creatures with your glare.
Fortunate Fate: Subject immediately receives a *heal* if it would be killed by damage.
Holy Star: Mote of energy protects you, attacks foes.
Holy Transformation: You change into hound archon, gain abilities.
Infernal Transformation: You change into bone devil, gain abilities.
Planar Bubble: Create bubble around creature that emulates its native planar environment.
Plane Shift, Greater: *Plane shift* accurately to your desired destination.
Radiant Assault: 1d6 damage/level, victims dazed or dazzled.
Renewal Pact[M]: Creature is automatically healed if adverse condition affects it.
Restoration, Mass[M]: As *restoration*, but multiple subjects.
Slime Wave: Creates a 15-ft. spread of green slime.
Spell Resistance, Mass: As *spell resistance*, but multiple subjects.
Symphonic Nightmare[M]: Discordant noise haunts subject's sleep.
Withering Palm: Touch attack deals 1 point Str damage plus 1 point Con damage/2 levels.

8TH-LEVEL CLERIC SPELLS

Bodak's Glare[F]: You slay a creature, which turns into a bodak 24 hours later.
Brilliant Aura: Allies' weapons become brilliant energy, ignoring armor.
Death Pact[M]: Deity brings subject back from the dead automatically.
Death Ward, Mass: As *death ward*, but more subjects.
Fierce Pride of the Beastlands: Summon celestial lions and celestial dire lions to follow your commands.
General of Undeath: Increases your maximum HD of controlled undead by your level.
Heat Drain: Subjects take 1d6 cold damage/level, you gain equal amount hp.
Lion's Roar: Deals 1d8 points of damage/2 levels to enemies; allies get +1 on attacks and saves against fear, plus temporary hp.
Planar Exchange, Greater: Trade places with one of three greater planar creatures (your choice).
Stormrage: You can fly and fire lightning from your eyes.
Veil of Undeath: You gain undead traits.
Wall of Greater Dispel Magic: Creatures passing through a transparent wall become subjects of targeted *greater dispel magic*.

9TH-LEVEL CLERIC SPELLS

Abyssal Army: Summons demons to fight for you.
Awaken Construct[X]: Construct gains humanlike sentience.
Call Marut[X]: A marut performs one duty for you.
Heavenly Host: Summons archons to fight for you.
Hellish Horde: Summons devils to fight for you.
Hunters of Hades[M]: Summons a pair of pack fiends or a retriever to follow your commands.
Plague of Undead[M]: Animates horde of undead.
Summon Elemental Monolith[M]: Calls powerful elemental creature to fight for you.
Undeath's Eternal Foe: Subjects receive negative energy protection and immunity to most undead special attacks.
Vile Death[MX]: Undead creature gains fiendish template.
Visage of the Deity, Greater: As *lesser visage of the deity*, but you become half-celestial or half-fiendish.

DRUID SPELLS

0-LEVEL DRUID SPELLS (ORISONS)

Dawn: Sleeping/unconscious creatures in area awaken.
Naturewatch: As *deathwatch*, but on animals and plants.

1ST-LEVEL DRUID SPELLS

Animate Fire: Turn campfire into Small elemental.
Animate Water: Turn quantity of water into Small elemental.
Animate Wood: Turn Small or smaller wooden item into animated object.
Aspect of the Wolf: You change into a wolf and gain some of its abilities.
Aura Against Flame: Ignores 10 fire damage/round and extinguishes fires.
Babau Slime: Secrete a body-covering acid that damages attacking foes.
Beast Claws: Your hands become slashing natural weapons.
Beastland Ferocity: Subject fights without penalty while disabled or dying.
Beget Bogun[MX]: You create a Tiny nature servant.
Branch to Branch: You gain +10 competence bonus on Climb checks in trees and can brachiate through forest.
Breath of the Jungle: Fog makes poison and diseases harder to resist.
Buoyant Lifting: Underwater creatures rise to surface.
Camouflage: Grants +10 bonus on Hide checks.

Claws of the Bear: Your hands become weapons that deal 1d8 damage.
Climb Walls: Touched creature gains increased climbing ability.
Cloudburst: Hampers vision and ranged attacks, puts out normal fires.
Cold Fire: Fire becomes blue and white, emits cold.
Crabwalk: Touched creature gains bonus while charging.
Deep Breath: Your lungs are filled with air.
Delay Disease: Ravages of disease staved off for a day.
Enrage Animal: Animal rages like barbarian, not fatigued.
Foundation of Stone: +2 AC, +4 bonus to resist bull rush and trip attacks.
Hawkeye: Increase range increments by 50%, +5 on Spot checks.
Healthful Rest: Subjects heal at twice the normal rate.
Horrible Taste: Touched creature or object nauseates biting or swallowing foes.
Low-Light Vision: See twice as far as a human in poor illumination.
Omen of Peril[F]**:** You know how dangerous the future will be.
Raging Flame: Fires burn twice as hot, half as long.
Ram's Might: Gain +2 to Strength and your unarmed attacks deal normal damage.
Rapid Burrowing: +20 ft. to subject's burrow speed.
Remove Scent: Hides touched creature's scent.
Resist Planar Alignment: Subject can resist penalties for being of an opposed alignment on an aligned Outer Plane.
Sandblast: You fire hot sand that deals 1d6 nonlethal damage, stuns enemies.
Slow Burn: Fires burn twice as long.
Snake's Swiftness: Subject immediately makes one attack.
Snowshoes: Subject walks easily on ice and snow.
Surefooted Stride: You can move over rubble as easily as you can over open ground.
Thunderhead: Small lightning bolts deal 1 damage/round.
Traveler's Mount: Creature moves faster but can't attack.
Updraft: Column of wind lifts you aloft.
Vigor, Lesser: Creature heals 1 hp/round (max 15 rounds).
Vine Strike: You can sneak attack plant creatures for 1 round.
Wall of Smoke: Wall of black smoke obscures vision and nauseates those who pass through.
Wings of the Sea: +30 ft. to subject's swim speed.
Winter Chill: Creature takes 1d6 cold damage and is fatigued.
Wood Wose: Nature spirit does simple tasks for you.

2ND-LEVEL DRUID SPELLS

Align Fang: Natural weapon becomes good, evil, lawful, or chaotic.
Avoid Planar Effects: Provides temporary protection against overtly damaging planar traits.
Balancing Lorecall: You gain a +4 bonus on Balance checks and can balance on difficult surfaces if you have 5 or more ranks in Balance.
Binding Winds: Air prevents subject from moving, hinders ranged attacks.
Bite of the Wererat: You gain the Dexterity and attacks of a wererat.
Blinding Spittle: Ranged touch attack blinds subject.
Blood Frenzy: Grants extra use of rage.
Body of the Sun: Your body emanates fire, dealing 1d4 fire damage/2 levels.
Brambles: Wooden weapon grows spikes that deal +1 damage/level (max +10).
Briar Web: Area slows creatures and thorns deal 1 point of damage/5 ft. moved.
Burrow: Subject can burrow with a speed of 30 feet.
Camouflage, Mass: As *camouflage*, but multiple subjects.
Cloud Wings: +30 ft. to subject's fly speed.
Countermoon: Forces lycanthrope to its natural form.
Creeping Cold[F]**:** Creature feels chill that increases with each round.
Daggerspell Stance: You gain +2 insight bonus on attack rolls and damage rolls if you make a full attack, SR 5 + caster level if you fight defensively, and DR 5/magic if you use the total defense action.
Decomposition: Wounds deal 3 extra points of damage each round.
Earthbind: Subject creature can't fly.
Earthen Grace: Subject takes only nonlethal damage from stone and earth.
Earthfast: Doubles the hit points of stone structure or rock formation and increases hardness to 10.
Easy Trail: You make a temporary trail through any kind of undergrowth.
Embrace the Wild: You gain an animal's senses for 10 minutes/level.
Fins to Feet: Transforms tails and fins into legs and feet.
Frost Breath: Icy breath deals 1d4 damage/2 levels.
Healing Lorecall: If you have 5 or more ranks in Heal, you can remove harmful conditions with conjuration (healing) spells.
Healing Sting: Touch deals 1d12 damage +1/level; caster gains damage as hp.
Heartfire: Subjects outlined by fire, take 1d4 damage/round.
Kelpstrand: Strands of kelp grapple foes.
Listening Lorecall: You gain +4 on Listen checks, plus blindsense or blindsight if you have 5 or more ranks in Listen.
Mark of the Outcast: Subject takes –5 penalty on Bluff and Diplomacy checks and –2 penalty to AC.
Master Air: You sprout insubstantial wings and can fly.
Mountain Stance: Subject becomes hard to move.
Nature's Favor: Animal touched gains luck bonus on attack rolls and damage rolls of +1/3 levels.
One with the Land: Link with nature gives a +2 bonus on nature-related skill checks.
Saltray: Ray deals 1d6 damage/2 levels and stuns.
Scent: Grants the scent special ability.
Share Husk: See and hear through the senses of a touched animal.
Snake's Swiftness, Mass: Allies each immediately make one attack.

Splinterbolt: 4d6 piercing damage to subjects hit by ranged attack.
Swim: Subject gains swim speed, +8 bonus on Swim checks.
Tiger's Tooth: One natural weapon of subject gets +1/4 levels on attack rolls and damage rolls (max +5) for 1 round.
Train Animal: Affected animal gains additional tricks equal to 1/2 caster level for 1 hour/level.
Wings of Air: Subject's flight maneuverability improves by one step.
Winter's Embrace: Creature takes 1d8 cold damage/round and might become exhausted.
Wracking Touch: Deal 1d6 damage +1/level; you also deal sneak attack damage if you have any.

3RD-LEVEL DRUID SPELLS

Air Breathing: Subjects can breathe air freely.
Align Fang, Mass: Allies' natural weapons become good, evil, lawful, or chaotic.
Attune Form: Grant creature temporary protection against overtly damaging planar traits.
Bite of the Werewolf: You gain the Strength and attacks of a werewolf.
Blindsight: Subject gains blindsight 30 ft. for 1 minute/level.
Bottle of Smoke[F]: Uncorking bottle creates fast horse made of smoke.
Capricious Zephyr: Gale-force winds push creatures.
Charge of the Triceratops: Subject grows horns and skull plate, gains gore attack.
Circle Dance: Indicates direction to known individual.
Corona of Cold: Aura of cold protects you, damages others.
Creaking Cacophony: Sound distracts and makes foes vulnerable to sonic damage.
Crumble: You erode building or other structure.
Dehydrate: Deals Con damage to subject.
Downdraft: Flying creatures knocked down.
Energy Vortex: Burst of energy centered on you damages nearby creatures.
Entangling Staff: Quarterstaff can grapple and constrict foes.
Fire Wings: Your arms become wings that enable flight, deal 2d6 fire damage.
Fly, Swift: Gain fly speed of 60 ft. for 1 round.
Forestfold: Gain +10 competence bonus on Hide and Move Silently checks in one type of terrain.
Giant's Wrath: Pebbles you throw become boulders.
Girallon's Blessing: Subject gains one additional pair of arms.
Heatstroke: Subject creature takes nonlethal damage and becomes fatigued.
Hypothermia: Causes 1d6 cold damage/level, fatigue.
Icelance[F]: Changes ice into lance, which attacks subject for 6d6 damage and stuns for 1d4 rounds.
Infestation of Maggots: Touch attack deals 1d4 Con damage/round.
Jagged Tooth: Doubles the critical threat range of natural weapons.
Junglerazer: Fey, vermin, plants, and animals take 1d10 damage/level.
Lion's Charge: You can make a full attack on a charge for 1 round.
Nature's Balance: You transfer 4 ability score points to the subject for 10 minutes/level.
Nature's Rampart[F]: You mold the terrain to provide fortifications.
Primal Form: You change into elemental, gain some abilities.
Quillfire: Your hand sprouts poisonous quills useful for melee or ranged attacks.
Resist Energy, Mass: Creatures ignore damage from specified energy type.
Sink: Subject sinks in water, must make Swim checks.
Snakebite: Your arm turns into poisonous snake you can use to attack.
Snowshoes, Mass: As *snowshoes*, affects one creature/level.
Spiderskin: Subject gains increasing bonus to natural armor bonus, saves against poison, and Hide checks.
Spikes: As *brambles*, but weapon gains +2 bonus and doubled threat range.
Spirit Jaws: Ghostly jaws grapple creature, deal 2d6 damage.
Standing Wave: Magically propels boat or swimming creature.
Thornskin: Your unarmed attacks deal +1d6 damage; natural and unarmed attacks against you take 5 damage.
Thunderous Roar: Roar deals 1d6 damage/2 levels, deafens.
Treasure Scent: You detect valuable metals and gems.
Tremor: Subjects knocked prone.
Vigor: As *lesser vigor*, but 2 hp/round (max 25 rounds).
Vigor, Mass Lesser: As *lesser vigor*, but multiple subjects (max 25 rounds).
Vine Mine: Vines grow rapidly, giving various effects.
Weather Eye: You accurate predict weather up to one week ahead.

4TH-LEVEL DRUID SPELLS

Arc of Lightning: Line of electricity arcs between two creatures (1d6/level damage).
Bite of the Wereboar: You gain the Strength and attacks of a wereboar.
Blindsight, Greater: Subject gains blindsight 60 ft. for 1 minute/level.
Burrow, Mass: As *burrow*, but affects 1/level subjects.
Chain of Eyes: See through other creatures' eyes.
Contagious Touch: You infect one creature/round with chosen disease.
Contingent Energy Resistance: Energy damage triggers a *resist energy* spell.
Creeping Cold, Greater[F]: As *creeping cold*, but longer duration and more damage.
Enhance Wild Shape: Your wild shape ability gains a bonus.
Essence of the Raptor: Base speed becomes 60 feet, gain skill bonuses and scent.
Eye of the Hurricane: Storm pushes creatures, calm at center.

Jaws of the Wolf[F]: One carving/2 levels turns into a worg.
Land Womb: You and one creature/level hide within the earth.
Languor: Ray slows subject and diminishes its Strength.
Last Breath[M]: Reincarnate recently deceased creature with no level loss.
Lay of the Land: You gain an overview of the geography around you.
Magic Fang, Superior: Your natural weapons gain +1 enhancement bonus/4 levels.
Miasma of Entropy: Rot all natural materials in 30-ft. cone-shaped burst.
Moon Bolt: 1d4 Strength damage/3 levels; undead made helpless.
Murderous Mist: Steam deals 2d6 damage, blinds creatures.
Perinarch: Gain greater control over Limbo's morphic essence.
Planar Tolerance: Provides long-term protection against overtly damaging planar traits.
Poison Vines: Vines grow and poison creatures stuck within them.
Resistance, Greater: Subject gains +3 on saving throws.
Rushing Waters: Wave makes bull rush attack.
Shadowblast: Blast of light stuns and damages natives to the Plane of Shadow.
Sheltered Vitality: Subject gains immunity to fatigue, exhaustion, ability damage, and ability drain.
Spark of Life: Undead creature loses most immunities.
Starvation: Hunger pangs deal 1d6 damage/level, cause fatigue.
Sudden Stalagmite: Impaling stalagmite damages and holds foes.
Summon Elementite Swarm: Summon an elementite swarm to follow your commands.
Surefooted Stride, Mass: As *surefooted stride* but multiple subjects.
Swim, Mass: As *swim*, but one creature/level.
Vortex of Teeth: 3d8 points of damage due to force per round to all creatures in the area.
Wall of Water: Creates shapeable transparent wall of water.
Wild Runner: Change into centaur, gain some abilities.
Wind at Back: Doubles overland speed of subjects for 12 hours.
Wings of Air, Greater: Subject's flight maneuverability improves by two steps.
Wood Rot: Destroy wooden items or deal 3d6 damage + 1/level (max +15) to plant creatures.

5TH-LEVEL DRUID SPELLS

Anticold Sphere: Sphere hedges out cold creatures and protects you from cold.
Bite of the Weretiger: You gain the Strength and attacks of a weretiger.
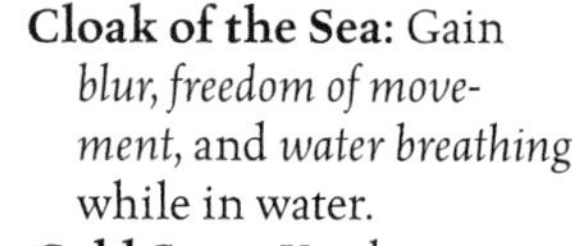
Cloak of the Sea: Gain *blur, freedom of movement*, and *water breathing* while in water.
Cold Snap: You lower temperature in area.
Contagion, Mass: As *contagion*, but 20-ft. radius.
Dance of the Unicorn: Purifying mist washes the air clean of smoke, dust, and poisons.
Dire Hunger: Subject grows fangs, attacks creatures near it.
Echo Skull: See, hear, and speak through a prepared animal skull for 1 hour/level.
Fireward: As *quench*, but also suppresses magical fire effects in affected area.
Freeze: Ray immobilizes subject and deals 6d6 cold damage/round.
Heal Animal Companion: As *heal* on your animal companion.
Ice Flowers: Ice and earth deal 1d6 damage/level.
Inferno: Creature bursts into flames and takes fire damage per round.
Jungle's Rapture: Curse causes 1d6 Dexterity drain.
Mantle of the Icy Soul[M]: Touched creature gains the cold subtype.
Memory Rot: Spores deal 1d6 Int damage to subject, plus 1 Int drain/round.
Owl's Insight: Subject gains Wis bonus equal to half your level for 1 hour.
Panacea: Removes most afflictions.
Phantom Stag: Magic stag appears for 1 hour/level.
Plant Body: Subject's type changes to plant.
Poison Thorns: You grow thorns that poison your attackers.
Quill Blast: You fling quills in spread, dealing damage and imposing penalties.
Rejuvenation Cocoon: Energy cocoon shields creature, then heals it.

Most druids use a sprig of mistletoe or holly for their focus, but others choose a different symbol for their devotion to nature

Illus. by W. England

Sirine's Grace: You gain bonuses to Charisma and Dexterity, AC, and Perform checks, and can breathe water.
Stone Shape, Greater: Sculpts 10 cu. ft. + 10 cu. ft./level of stone into any shape.
Swamp Stride: As *tree stride*, but with bodies of water.
Vigor, Greater: As *lesser vigor*, but 4 hp/round.
Wall of Sand: Swirling sand blocks ranged attacks, slows movement through.
Wind Tunnel: Ranged weapons gain +5 bonus and double range increment.

6TH-LEVEL DRUID SPELLS

Anger of the Noonday Sun: Blinds creatures within 20 ft., damages undead.
Animate Snow: You animate snow to attack foes.
Aspect of the Earth Hunter: Change into bulette and gain some of its abilities.
Bite of the Werebear: You gain the Strength and attacks of a werebear.
Blood Sirocco: Wind bowls over foes and draws away their blood.
Cometfall: Comet falls atop foes, damaging them and knocking them prone.
Dinosaur Stampede: Spectral dinosaurs deal 1d12 damage +1/level.
Drown: Subject immediately begins to drown.
Energy Immunity: Subject and equipment gain immunity to damage of specified energy type.
Enveloping Cocoon: Entraps subject creature and denies save for attached spell.
Extract Water Elemental: Pulls water from victim, forms water elemental.
Fires of Purity: Subject bursts into magical flame, becoming a dangerous weapon.
Hide the Path[F]: Area warded against divinations.
Hungry Gizzard: Gizzard engulfs victim, grapples and deals damage.
Miasma: Gas fills creature's mouth, suffocating it.
Phantasmal Disorientation: Fools creature's sense of direction, making movement difficult.
Stonehold: Stony arm trap grapples and damages creatures.
Summon Greater Elemental: Summon a greater elemental to follow your commands.
Resistance, Superior: Subject gains +6 on saving throws.
Tidal Surge: Wave of water deals 1d6/level damage and bull rushes.
Tortoise Shell: Creature gains +6 natural armor, +1/3 levels above 11th.
Vigorous Circle: As *mass lesser vigor*, but 3 hp/round (max 40 rounds).

7TH-LEVEL DRUID SPELLS

Aura of Vitality: Subjects gain +4 to Str, Dex, and Con.
Brilliant Blade: Weapon or projectiles shed light, ignore armor.
Cloudwalkers: Subjects can fly outdoors at speed of 60 ft.
Master Earth: Travel through the earth to any location.
Shifting Paths: Illusion hides path, creates false new path.
Slime Wave: Creates a 15-ft. spread of green slime.
Storm of Elemental Fury: Magic cloud creates windstorm, then hail of stones, then rainstorm, then flame.
Storm Tower: Swirling clouds absorb electricity and *magic missiles* and prevent ranged attacks.
Swamp Lung: Water in lungs makes subject helpless, diseased.
Waterspout: Waterspout you control picks up and damages foes.
Word of Balance: Kills, paralyzes, weakens, or nauseates nonneutral creatures.

8TH-LEVEL DRUID SPELLS

Awaken, Mass[X]: As *awaken*, but multiple creatures.
Bombardment: Falling rocks deal 1d8 damage/level and bury subjects.
Brilliant Aura: Allies' weapons become brilliant energy, ignoring armor.
Cocoon[X]: Preserves a corpse and reincarnates with no loss of level.
Deadfall: Falling wood causes damage and knocks foes prone.
Maelstrom: Water vortex traps and damages creatures and objects.
Phantom Wolf: Incorporeal wolf fights for you.
Red Tide: Nauseating water knocks foes prone and deals Strength damage.
Stormrage: You can fly and fire lightning from your eyes.
Unyielding Roots: Creature grows roots that keep it stationary and heal it every round.

9TH-LEVEL DRUID SPELLS

Cast in Stone: Petrifying gaze attack.
Death Ward, Mass: As *death ward*, but more subjects.
Drown, Mass: As *drown*, but affects multiple subjects.
Nature's Avatar: Animal gains +10 on attack rolls and damage rolls, *haste*, and 1d8 hp/level.
Perinarch, Planar: Gain control over a small area of any divinely morphic plane.
Phantom Bear: Incorporeal bear fights for you.
Shadow Landscape: Makes natural terrain more dangerous, creates guardians that you command.
Summon Elemental Monolith[M]: Calls powerful elemental creature to fight for you.
Transmute Rock to Lava: Transforms one 10-ft. cube with subsequent fire damage and effects.
Tsunami: Massive wave deals 1d6 damage/level.
Undermaster[M]: You gain earth-related spell-like abilities.
Whirlwind, Greater: As *whirlwind*, but larger and more destructive.

PALADIN SPELLS

1ST-LEVEL PALADIN SPELLS

Axiomatic Water[M]: Makes lawful-aligned axiomatic water.
Bless Weapon, Swift: Weapon strikes true against evil foes for 1 round.
Blessed Aim: +2 bonus for allies' ranged attacks.

Clear Mind: +4 on saves against mind-affecting spells and abilities.
Deafening Clang: Weapon deals sonic damage, deafens.
Divine Sacrifice: You sacrifice hit points to deal extra damage.
Energized Shield, Lesser: Shield provides user resistance 5, shield bash deals +1d6 damage.
Faith Healing: Cures 8 hp +1/level (max +5) to worshiper of your deity.
Find Temple: You know direction of your deity's nearest temple.
Golden Barding: Your mount gets force armor.
Grave Strike: You can sneak attack undead for 1 round.
Holy Spurs: Special mount's speed increases by 40 ft. for 1 round.
Know Greatest Enemy: Determines relative power level of creatures within the area.
Lionheart: Subject gains immunity to fear.
Moment of Clarity: Subject gains second save against mind-affecting spell or ability.
One Mind, Lesser: You gain +4 on Spot and Listen checks while mounted.
Resist Planar Alignment: Subject can resist penalties for being of an opposed alignment on an aligned Outer Plane.
Resurgence: You grant subject a second chance at a saving throw.
Rhino's Rush: Next charge deals double damage.
Second Wind: Dispel fatigue, grant bonus on Constitution checks.
Sense Heretic: Glow reveals when evil creature is near.
Silverbeard: You grow a hard silver beard that gives +2 bonus to armor.
Sticky Saddle: You become stuck to special mount, gain +10 Ride checks.
Strategic Charge: You gain the benefits of the Mobility feat.
Traveler's Mount: Creature moves faster but can't attack.
Vision of Glory: Subject gains morale bonus equal to your Cha modifier to one saving throw.
Warning Shout: Allies are no longer flat-footed.

2ND-LEVEL PALADIN SPELLS

Angelskin: Lawful good creature gains DR 5/evil.
Aura of Glory: Remove any fear effect from allies.
Awaken Sin: Subject faces its sins, takes 1d6/level nonlethal damage (10d6 max).
Checkmate's Light: Your weapon becomes a +1 axiomatic weapon and bolsters the morale of allies.
Cloak of Bravery: You and your allies gain a bonus on saves against fear.
Divine Insight: You gain insight bonus of 5 + caster level on one single skill check.
Divine Protection: Allies gain +1 to AC, saves.
Energized Shield: Shield provides user resistance 10, shield bash deals +2d6 damage.
Fell the Greatest Foe: Deal extra damage to creatures larger than you.
Flame of Faith: Gives weapon the flaming burst special ability.

Illus. by F. Vohwinkel

Spiritual chariot allows a mount to run unencumbered by the rider

Hand of Divinity: Gives +2 sacred or profane saving throw bonus to worshiper of your deity.
Holy Mount: Special mount gains celestial template.
Knight's Move: You instantly move to flank a subject.
Loyal Vassal: Ally gains +3 against mind-affecting spells and abilities and cannot be compelled to harm you.
One Mind: As *lesser one mind*, but also gain +2 to attack while mounted.
Quick March: Allies' speed increases by 30 ft. for 1 round.
Shield of Warding: Shield grants +1 bonus on AC and Reflex saves/5 levels (max +5).
Spiritual Chariot: Creates ghostly chariot behind your mount.
Stabilize: Cures 1 point of damage to all creatures in area.
Strength of Stone: +8 Str bonus that ends if you lose contact with the ground.
Zeal: You move through foes to attack the enemy you want.

3RD-LEVEL PALADIN SPELLS

Axiomatic Storm[M]: Lawful-aligned rain falls in 20-ft. radius.
Blessing of Bahamut: You gain damage reduction 10/magic.
Diamondsteel[M]: Metal armor provides damage reduction.
Find the Gap: Your attacks ignore armor and natural armor.
Hand of the Faithful: Immobile zone of warding stuns those worshiping different deities from yours.
Holy Storm[M]: Good-aligned rain falls in 20-ft. radius.
Mantle of Good/Law: You gain SR 12 + caster level against spells with opposite alignment descriptor.
One Mind, Greater: As *one mind*, but also gain +2 to damage while mounted.
Regal Procession: As *mount*, but you summon several mounts.
Resurgence, Mass: As *resurgence*, but multiple subjects.
Righteous Fury: Gain temporary hp, +4 to Strength.
Seek Eternal Rest: Turn undead as cleric of your level.
Undead Bane Weapon: Weapon gains undead bane property and is considered good-aligned.
Weapon of the Deity: Your weapon gains enhancement bonus and special ability.
Word of Binding: Magical manacles restrain foe.

4TH-LEVEL PALADIN SPELLS

Castigate: Verbal rebuke damages those whose alignment differs from yours.
Draconic Might: Gain +5 to Str, Con, Cha; +4 natural armor; immunity to magic sleep effects and paralysis.
Favor of The Martyr: Subject gains immunity to nonlethal damage, charm and compulsion effects, and other adverse conditions.
Lawful Sword: Weapon becomes +5 axiomatic weapon and emits magic circle against chaos.
Revenance: Restores dead creature to life for 1 minute/level.
Righteous Aura: You detonate on death, healing good creatures and damaging others (2d6/level damage).
Sacred Haven: Creatures gain +2 AC, retain Dex bonus, and you can lay on hands at range.
Telepathic Aura: One-way mental communication to allies within 100 feet.
Visage of the Deity, Lesser: You gain +4 Cha and resistance 10 to certain energy types.
Winged Mount: Your mount grows wings and flies at speed of 60 ft.

A ranger's spells can make potent weapons

RANGER SPELLS

1ST-LEVEL RANGER SPELLS

Accelerated Movement: Balance, Climb, or Move Silently at normal speed with no penalty on skill check.
Arrow Mind: You threaten nearby squares with your bow and fire without provoking attacks of opportunity.
Aspect of the Wolf: You change into a wolf and gain some of its abilities.
Blades of Fire: Your melee weapons deal +1d8 fire damage for 1 round.
Bloodhound: You gain an immediate retry if you fail a Survival check while tracking.
Branch to Branch: You gain +10 competence bonus on Climb checks in trees and can brachiate through forest.
Camouflage: Grants +10 bonus on Hide checks.
Claws of the Bear: Your hands become weapons that deal 1d8 damage.
Climb Walls: Touched creature gains increased climbing ability.
Crabwalk: Touched creature gains bonus while charging.
Dawn: Sleeping/unconscious creatures in area awaken.
Deep Breath: Your lungs are filled with air.
Detect Favored Enemy: You know if favored enemies are within 60 ft.
Easy Trail: You make a temporary trail through any kind of undergrowth.
Embrace the Wild: You gain an animal's senses for 10 minutes/level.
Enrage Animal: Animal rages like barbarian, not fatigued.
Guided Shot: You ignore distance, cover, concealment penalties with your ranged attacks for 1 round.

Illus. by R. Spears

Hawkeye: Increase range increments by 50%, +5 on Spot checks.
Healing Lorecall: If you have 5 or more ranks in Heal, you can remove harmful conditions with conjuration (healing) spells.
Horrible Taste: Touched creature or object nauseates biting or swallowing foes.
Hunter's Mercy: Your next hit with a bow is automatically a critical hit.
Instant Search: Make Search check at +2 as free action.
Lay of the Land: You gain an overview of the geography around you.
Lightfoot: Your move does not provoke attacks of opportunity for 1 round.
Living Prints: You perceive tracks as if they had just been made.
Low-Light Vision: See twice as far as a human in poor illumination.
Marked Object: You gain bonus to track a specific being.
Naturewatch: As *deathwatch*, but on animals and plants.
Omen of Peril[F]: You know how dangerous the future will be.
Ram's Might: Gain +2 to Strength and your unarmed attacks deal normal damage.
Rapid Burrowing: +20 ft. to subject's burrow speed.
Remove Scent: Hides touched creature's scent.
Resist Planar Alignment: Subject can resist penalties for being of an opposed alignment on an aligned Outer Plane.
Rhino's Rush: Next charge deals double damage.
Scent: Grants the scent special ability.
Smell of Fear: Subject's aroma attracts animal attacks.
Sniper's Shot: No range limit on next ranged sneak attack.
Snowshoes: Subject walks easily on ice and snow.
Stalking Brand: Subject marked with symbol you can see despite disguises.
Surefoot: +10 bonus on Balance, Climb, Jump, and Tumble checks.
Surefooted Stride: You can move over rubble as easily as you can over open ground.
Towering Oak: +10 bonus on Intimidate checks.
Traveler's Mount: Creature moves faster but can't attack.
Vine Strike: You can sneak attack plant creatures for 1 round.
Wings of the Sea: +30 ft. to subject's swim speed.

2ND-LEVEL RANGER SPELLS

Align Fang: Natural weapon becomes good, evil, lawful, or chaotic.
Balancing Lorecall: You gain a +4 bonus on Balance checks and can balance on difficult surfaces if you have 5 or more ranks in Balance.
Briar Web: Area slows creatures and thorns deal 1 point of damage/5 ft. moved.
Burrow: Subject can burrow with a speed of 30 feet.
Camouflage, Mass: As *camouflage*, but multiple subjects.
Curse of Impending Blades: Subject takes –2 penalty to AC.
Easy Climb: You make a vertical surface easy to climb (DC 10).
Exacting Shot: Your ranged weapon automatically confirms critical hits against favored enemies.
Fell the Greatest Foe: Deal extra damage to creatures larger than you.
Haste, Swift: Move faster, +1 on attacks, AC, Reflex saves.
Jagged Tooth: Doubles the critical threat range of natural weapons.
Lion's Charge: You can make a full attack on a charge for 1 round.
Listening Lorecall: You gain +4 on Listen checks, plus blindsense or blindsight if you have 5 or more ranks in Listen.
Nature's Favor: Animal touched gains luck bonus on attack rolls and damage rolls of +1/3 levels.
One with the Land: Link with nature gives a +2 bonus on nature-related skill checks.
Train Animal: Affected animal gains additional tricks equal to 1/2 caster level for 1 hour/level.
Tremorsense: Grants tremorsense to a range of 30 feet.

3RD-LEVEL RANGER SPELLS

Align Fang, Mass: Allies' natural weapons become good, evil, lawful, or chaotic.
Arrow Storm: You make one ranged attack against each foe within one range increment.
Blade Storm: You make melee attacks against every foe you threaten.
Blade Thirst: Slashing weapon glows and gains +3 bonus.
Bottle of Smoke[F]: Uncorking bottle creates fast horse made of smoke.
Burrow, Mass: As *burrow*, but affects 1/level subjects.
Charge of the Triceratops: Subject grows horns and skull plate, gains gore attack.
Curse of Impending Blades, Mass: Enemies take –2 penalty to AC.
Decoy Image: Figment mimics you and allies.
Find the Gap: Your attacks ignore armor and natural armor.
Forestfold: You gain +10 competence bonus on Hide and Move Silently checks in one type of terrain.
Heal Animal Companion: As *heal* on your animal companion.
Mark of the Hunter: Rune on creature makes it easier to attack.
Nature's Rampart[F]: You mold the terrain to provide fortifications.
Phantasmal Decoy: Creates illusory enemy for foe to chase.
Safe Clearing: As *sanctuary*, but protects an area and lasts 1 hour/level.
Snowshoes, Mass: As *snowshoes*, affects one creature/level.

4TH-LEVEL RANGER SPELLS

Aspect of the Earth Hunter: Change into bulette and gain some of its abilities.
Deeper Darkvision: Subject can see 90 ft. in magical darkness.
Foebane: Your weapon becomes +5 and deals +2d6 damage against a favored enemy.

Implacable Pursuer: You know where prey is, as long as it's moving.
Land Womb: You and one creature/level hide within the earth.
Magic Fang, Superior: Your natural weapons gain +1 enhancement bonus/4 levels.
Planar Tolerance: Provides long-term protection against overtly damaging planar traits.
Snakebite: Your arm turns into poisonous snake you can use to attack.
Surefooted Stride, Mass: As *surefooted stride* but multiple subjects.
Swamp Stride: As *tree stride*, but with bodies of water.
Wild Runner: Change into centaur, gain some abilities.

SORCERER/ WIZARD SPELLS

0-LEVEL SORCERER/WIZARD SPELLS (CANTRIPS)

Conj **Caltrops:** Creates caltrops in 5-ft.-by-5-ft. square, + 5-ft. square/2 levels beyond 1st (max 5).
Evoc **Electric Jolt:** Ranged touch attack deals 1d3 electricity damage.
Sonic Snap: Subject takes 1 point of sonic damage and is deafened 1 round.
Illus **Silent Portal:** Negates sound from door or window.
Trans **Amanuensis:** Copy nonmagical text.
Launch Bolt: Launches a crossbow bolt up to 80 ft.
Launch Item: Hurls Fine item up to Medium range.
Repair Minor Damage: Repairs 1 point of damage to any construct.
Stick: Glues an object weighing 5 pounds or less to another object.

1ST-LEVEL SORCERER/WIZARD SPELLS

Abjur **Dispel Ward:** As *dispel magic*, but affects only wards.
Ectoplasmic Armor: Gain armor bonus against incorporeal touch attacks.
Ironguts: Subject gains +5 bonus on saving throws against poison.
Nightshield: You gain resistance bonus on saves, and spell absorbs *magic missile* damage.
Resist Planar Alignment: Subject can resist penalties for being of an opposed alignment on an aligned Outer Plane.
Conj **Benign Transposition:** Two willing subjects switch places.
Blades of Fire: Your melee weapons deal +1d8 fire damage for 1 round.
Buzzing Bee: Bee gives subject –10 penalty on Move Silently and hinders Concentration checks.
Corrosive Grasp: 1 touch/level deals 1d8 acid damage.
Deep Breath: Your lungs are filled with air.
Hail of Stone[M]**:** Stones deal 1d4 points of damage/level to creatures in the area (max 5d4).
Orb of Acid, Lesser: Ranged touch attack deals 1d8 acid damage + 1d8/2 levels beyond 1st (max 5d8).
Orb of Cold, Lesser: Ranged touch attack deals 1d8 cold damage + 1d8/2 levels beyond 1st (max 5d8).
Orb of Electricity, Lesser: Ranged touch attack deals 1d8 electricity damage + 1d8/2 levels beyond 1st (max 5d8).
Orb of Fire, Lesser: Ranged touch attack deals 1d8 fire damage + 1d8/2 levels beyond 1st (max 5d8).
Orb of Sound, Lesser: Ranged touch attack deals 1d6 sonic damage + 1d6/2 levels beyond 1st (max 5d6).
Summon Undead I: Summons undead to fight for you.
Wall of Smoke: Wall of black smoke obscures vision and nauseates those who pass through.
Div **Appraising Touch:** Gain +10 bonus on Appraise checks.
Arrow Mind: You threaten nearby squares with your bow and fire without provoking attacks of opportunity.
Critical Strike: For 1 round you gain +1d6 damage, doubled threat range, and +4 on attack rolls to confirm critical threats.
Golem Strike: You can sneak attack constructs for 1 round.
Guided Shot: You ignore distance, cover, concealment penalties with your ranged attacks for 1 round.
Insightful Feint: Gain +10 on your next Bluff check to feint in combat.
Instant Locksmith: Make Disable Device or Open Lock check at +2 as free action.
Instant Search: Make Search check at +2 as free action.
Master's Touch: You gain proficiency in a weapon or shield touched for 1 minute/level.
Sniper's Shot: No range limit on next ranged sneak attack.
Spontaneous Search: Instantly Search area as if having taken 10.
Targeting Ray: You and allies are +1 to hit/3 levels against subject.
Ench **Distract:** Subjects take –4 on Concentration, Listen, Search, and Spot.
Distract Assailant: One creature is flat-footed for 1 round.
Incite: Subjects can't ready actions or delay.
Inhibit: Subject delays until next round.
Shock and Awe: Flat-footed creatures get –10 on initiative.
Evoc **Blood Wind:** Subject uses natural weapons at range.

Guiding Light: +2 on ranged attacks against creatures in illuminated area.
Ice Dagger: Grenadelike weapon deals subject 1d4/level cold damage, plus area damage.
Light of Lunia: You radiate silvery light, which you can expend as 2 bolts that deal 1d6 damage.
Luminous Gaze: Your eyes emit light, dazzle creatures.
Persistent Blade: Blade of force attacks subject, automatically flanks.
Ray of Flame: Ray deals 1d6/2 levels fire damage, ignites subject.
Sonic Blast: Subject takes 1d4/2 levels sonic damage plus deafness.
Thunderhead: Small lightning bolts deal 1 damage/round.

Illus **Dead End**: Removes spoor of one creature/level.
Net of Shadows: Ordinary shadows provide concealment to all in the area.
Serene Visage: Gain insight bonus on Bluff checks equal to half your level.

Necro **Backbiter**: Weapon strikes wielder.
Spirit Worm: Subject takes 1 point Con damage every round for 1 round/level.

Trans **Accelerated Movement**: Balance, Climb, or Move Silently at normal speed with no penalty on skill check.
Babau Slime: Secrete a body-covering acid that damages attacking foes.
Breath Flare: Your breath weapon dazzles subjects.
Cheat: Caster rerolls when determining the success of a game of chance.
Cutting Hand: Your hand gains a +2 enhancement bonus and deals 1d6 damage.
Ebon Eyes: Subject can see through magical darkness.
Expeditious Retreat, Swift: Your speed increases by 30 ft. for 1 round.
Fist of Stone: Gain +6 Str and natural slam attack.
Horrible Taste: Touched creature or object nauseates biting or swallowing foes.
Low-Light Vision: See twice as far as a human in poor illumination.
Mage Hand, Greater: As *mage hand*, but medium range and up to 40 lb.
Nerveskitter: Subject gains +5 bonus on initiative checks.
Portal Beacon: You grant others knowledge of a magic portal's location.
Raging Flame: Fires burn twice as hot, half as long.
Ray of Clumsiness: Victim takes 1d6 Dexterity penalty +1/2 levels.
Remove Scent: Hides touched creature's scent.
Repair Light Damage: Repairs 1d8 damage +1/level (max +5) to any construct.
Scatterspray: Group of small objects flies apart in a burst.
Shieldbearer: Shield floats near subject to offer protection.
Slide: Move subject 5 feet.
Slow Burn: Fires burn twice as long.
Spell Flower: Hold the charge on one touch spell per forelimb.
Weapon Shift: Touched weapon changes form.
Wings of the Sea: +30 ft. to subject's swim speed.

Univ **Familiar Pocket**: Garment or container becomes extradimensional safe haven for your familiar.

2ND-LEVEL SORCERER/WIZARD SPELLS

Abjur **Aiming at the Target**: +10 bonus on Concentration checks for previously cast spell.
Alarm, Greater[F]: As *alarm*, and it works on coexistent planes.
Daggerspell Stance: You gain +2 insight bonus on attack rolls and damage rolls if you make a full attack, SR 5 + caster level if you fight defensively, and DR 5/magic if you use the total defense action.
Dissonant Chant: Concentration checks more difficult within area of spell.
Distracting Ray: Ray forces spellcaster to make Concentration check.
Earth Lock[M]: Constricts tunnel, preventing access.
Ectoplasmic Feedback: Incorporeal attackers take 1d6 damage + 1/level.
Portal Alarm: You are alerted when a creature passes through a warded portal.
Scintillating Scales: Your natural armor bonus turns into a deflection bonus.

Conj **Baleful Transposition**: Two subjects switch places.
Cloud of Bewilderment: Generates a nauseating 10-ft. cube.
Create Magic Tattoo[M]: Subject receives a magic tattoo with various effects.
Ice Knife: Magical shard of ice deals 2d8 cold damage plus 2 Dex damage, or deals 1d8 cold damage in 10-ft.-radius burst.
Inky Cloud: Obscures sight underwater beyond 5 ft.
Malevolent Miasma: Cloud of fog deals 1d4 nonlethal damage/level.
Summon Undead II: Summons undead to fight for you.

Div **Balancing Lorecall**: You gain a +4 bonus on Balance checks and can balance on difficult surfaces if you have 5 or more ranks in Balance.
Chain of Eyes: See through other creatures' eyes.
Discern Shapechanger[M]: Penetrates disguises and identifies shapechanging creatures.
Marked Object: You gain bonus to track a specific being.

Ench **Entice Gift**: Subject gives caster what it's holding.
Mechanus Mind: Reformat subject's mind to be coldly calculating.
Mindless Rage: Subject compelled to attack you physically for 1 round/level.

Ray of Stupidity: Victim takes 1d4+1 Intelligence damage.
Rebuke: Subject is dazed 1 round, then shaken.
Sting Ray: Subject of ray can take only standard or move action, has –2 AC, and must make Concentration checks to cast spells.

Evoc
Battering Ram: Deals 1d6 damage plus bull rush.
Blast of Force: Attack deals 1d6 damage/2 levels (max 5d6).
Burning Sword: Weapon gains flaming burst special ability.
Combust: Subject takes 1d8/level fire damage and might catch fire.
Electric Loop: Deals 1d6/2 levels electricity damage plus stunning to a single creature.
Ethereal Chamber: You entrap an ethereal subject in a chamber of force.
Fireburst: Creatures within 10 feet take 1d8/level fire damage.
Flame Dagger: Beam of fire deals 1d4 damage +1/level.
Force Ladder[F]**:** Creates an immobile ladder of force.
Frost Breath: Icy breath deals 1d4 damage/2 levels.
Light of Mercuria: You radiate golden light, which you can expend as 2 bolts that deal 1d6 damage, 2d6 against undead and evil outsiders.
Rainbow Beam[F]**:** Ray dazzles and deals 1d12 damage/3 levels of random type.
Ray of Ice: Ray deals 1d6 cold damage/2 levels.
Scorch: Jet of flame deals 1d8/2 levels (max 5d8).
Slapping Hand: Hand makes creature provoke attacks of opportunity.
Snowball Swarm: Snowballs deal 2d6 points of cold damage in 10-ft. burst.
Veil of Shadow: Darkness grants you concealment.

Illus
Bladeweave: Your melee attack dazes your opponent.
Cloak Pool: Hide a color pool on the Astral Plane from view.
Dark Way: Creates temporary unbreakable bridge supporting up to 200 lb./level.
Delusions of Grandeur: Subject thinks it is better than it is.
Discolor Pool: Change the color of a color pool on the Astral Plane.
Disguise Undead: Change appearance of one corporeal undead.
Phantasmal Assailants: Nightmare creatures strike subject for 8 Wis damage, 8 Dex damage.
Phantom Foe[M]**:** Subject is always flanked by one creature.
Reflective Disguise: Viewers see you as their own species and gender.
Shadow Mask: Grants +4 on saves against light spells, protection from gaze attacks.
Shadow Radiance: Area filled with intense light that grows brighter.
Shadow Spray: Deals 4 points of Str damage and dazes.
Wall of Gloom: Shadow barrier obscures vision.

Necro
Bonefiddle[F]**:** Spectral fiddle bow deals 3d6 damage/round.
Curse of Impending Blades: Subject takes –2 penalty to AC.
Death Armor[F]**:** Black aura damages creatures attacking you.
Desiccating Bubble: Globe of air damages by evaporating moisture from subject.
Ghoul Glyph: Glyph wards area, paralyzes victims.
Life Bolt: 1 ray/2 levels draws 1 hp from you to deal 1d12 damage to undead.
Ray of Sickness: Subject becomes sickened.
Ray of Weakness: Subject takes –2 on attacks, –10 ft. speed.
Shroud of Undeath: Negative energy shroud makes undead perceive you as undead.
Spawn Screen: Subject resists being transformed into an undead spawn if slain.
Stolen Breath: Subject has wind knocked out of it.
Wracking Touch: Deal 1d6 damage +1/level; you also deal sneak attack damage if you have any.

Trans
Augment Familiar: Your familiar becomes more powerful.
Balor Nimbus: Your flaming body damages foes in grapple.
Belker Claws: Touch attack deals 2d12 damage and lingers +1 round/3 levels.
Body of the Sun: Your body emanates fire, dealing 1d4 fire damage/2 levels.
Bristle: Armor spikes attack with wearer.
Earthbind: Subject creature can't fly.
Earthen Grasp: Arm made of earth and soil grapples foes.
Extend Tentacles: +5 ft. to reach of tentacle attack.
Fearsome Grapple: You grow tentacles that help you grapple.

Few wooden doors can withstand a battering ram spell

Illus. by J. Nelson

Fins to Feet: Transforms tails and fins into legs and feet.
Fly, Swift: Gain fly speed of 60 ft. for 1 round.
Fuse Arms: Multiple arms/tentacles become one pair of stronger limbs.
Ghost Touch Armor: Armor works normally against incorporeal attacks.
Heroics: Fighter gains one fighter bonus feat.
Hurl: Thrown weapon returns to thrower.
Infernal Wound: Weapon deals persistent, bleeding wounds.
Ironthunder Horn: Intense vibrations trip those in area.
Lively Step: You and allies gain +10 increase to speed.
Mountain Stance: Subject becomes hard to move.
Quick Potion: Creates a potion that must be used within 1 hour/level.
Razorfangs: Your bite or claw attack threatens a critical hit on a 19 or 20.
Repair Moderate Damage: Repairs 2d8 damage +1/level (max +10) to any construct.
Scale Weakening: Subject's natural armor weakens.
Slide, Greater: Move subject 20 feet.
Snake's Swiftness: Subject immediately makes one attack.
Sonic Weapon: Weapon touched deals +1d6 sonic damage with each hit.
Speak to Allies: Subjects can converse at distance without moving lips.
Stone Bones: Corporeal undead gains +3 natural armor bonus.
Surefooted Stride: You can move over rubble as easily as you can over open ground.
Swim: Subject gains swim speed, +8 bonus on Swim checks.
Whirling Blade: Hurled slashing weapon magically attacks all foes in 60-ft. line.
Wings of Air: Subject's flight maneuverability improves by one step.
Wraithstrike: Your melee attacks strike as touch attacks for 1 round.

3RD-LEVEL SORCERER/WIZARD SPELL

Abjur **Anticipate Teleportation[F]:** Predict and delay the arrival of creatures teleporting into range by 1 round.
Antidragon Aura[M]: Allies gain bonus to AC and saves against dragons.
Avoid Planar Effects: Provides temporary protection against overtly damaging planar traits.
Earthen Grace: Subject takes only nonlethal damage from stone and earth.
Eradicate Earth: Deals 1d8 points of damage/level to earth creatures (max 10d8).
Reverse Arrows: As *protection from arrows*, but negated arrows turn back upon their source.
Sign of Sealing[M]: Magical sigil protects door or chest, deals 1d4/level damage (max 10d4) if opened.

Conj **Acid Breath:** Cone of acid deals 1d6 damage/level (max 10d6).
Bands of Steel: Metallic bands immobilize or entangle subject for 1 round/level.
Contagious Fog: 20-ft.-radius cloud of fog inflicts disease.
Corpse Candle: Ghostly hand and candle sheds light, affects incorporeal creatures.
Icelance[F]: Changes ice into lance, which attacks subject for 6d6 damage and stuns for 1d4 rounds.
Mage Armor, Greater: Gives subject +6 armor bonus.
Mage Armor, Mass: As *mage armor*, but one creature/level.
Nauseating Breath: Exhale a cone of nauseating gas.
Regal Procession: As *mount*, but you summon several mounts.
Servant Horde: Create 2d6 unseen servants +1/level (max +15).
Summon Undead III: Summons undead to fight for you.
Vipergout: You spit forth celestial or fiendish vipers that attack your foes.

Div **Analyze Portal:** Find a nearby portal and discover its properties.
Circle Dance: Indicates direction to known individual.
Telepathic Bond, Lesser: Link with subject within 30 ft. for 10 minutes/level.
Unluck: Subject remakes all rolls, uses worse result for 1 round/level.

Ench **Mesmerizing Glare:** Your gaze fascinates creatures.
Miser's Envy: Subject jealously covets nearby object.
Ray of Dizziness: Subject can take only move or standard actions.
Suppress Breath Weapon: Subject can't use its breath weapon.

Evoc **Blacklight:** Create an area of total darkness.
Blade of Pain and Fear: Creates blade of gnashing teeth.
Capricious Zephyr: Gale-force winds push creatures.
Chain Missile: Multiple missiles deal 1d4+1 damage each, then strike secondary targets.
Flashburst: Flash of light dazzles and blinds creatures in area.
Glowing Orb[F]: Creates permanent magical light; you control brightness.
Great Thunderclap: Loud noise causes stunning, deafness, and knocks prone in a large area.
Hailstones: Frigid globes deal 5d6 cold damage.
Light of Venya: You radiate pearly light, which you can expend as 2 bolts that deal 2d6 damage, 4d6 against undead and evil outsiders.

Manyjaws: One set of jaws/level attacks enemies for 1d6 damage.
Rainbow Blast[F]**:** Line deals 1d6 damage of each energy type.
Resonating Bolt: Sonic energy deals 1d4 damage/level (max 10d4).
Scintillating Sphere: 20-ft.-radius burst deals 1d6 electricity/level.
Shatterfloor: Deals 1d4 sonic/level plus damages floor surface.
Sonorous Hum: Removes need to concentrate to maintain next spell cast.
Sound Lance: Sonic energy deals 1d8/level damage.
Wall of Light: Creates wall of light, can dazzle creatures.

Illus **Claws of Darkness:** Claws deal 1d8 cold damage and have reach.
Cone of Dimness: Subjects believe they are engulfed in magical darkness.
Shadow Binding: Ribbonlike shadows entangle creatures in 10-ft.-radius burst.
Shadow Cache: You open a small portal to the Plane of Shadow through which you can put an item for later retrieval.
Spectral Weapon: Use quasi-real weapon to make touch attacks.
Suspended Silence[M]**:** Object becomes programmed to create an area of silence at your command.

Necro **Curse of Impending Blades, Mass:** Enemies take –2 penalty to AC.
Disrupt Undead, Greater: As *disrupt undead*, but 1d8 damage/level.
Healing Touch: Heal subject 1d6/2 levels, but take damage equal to half.
Incorporeal Enhancement: Grant bonuses to incorporeal undead.
Junglerazer: Fey, vermin, plants, and animals take 1d10 damage/level.
Mind Poison: Your poisonous touch deals Wis damage.
Skull Watch: Skull shrieks when creature enters warded area.
Spider Poison: Touch deals 1d6 Str damage, repeats in 1 minute.
Undead Lieutenant: Chosen undead can give orders to undead in your control.
Undead Torch: Undead creature gains blue aura that gives +2d6 damage against living creatures.

Trans **Air Breathing:** Subjects can breathe air freely.
Amorphous Form: Subject becomes puddlelike and can slip through cracks quickly.
Bite of the Wererat: You gain the Dexterity and attacks of a wererat.
Deeper Darkvision: Subject can see 90 ft. in magical darkness.
Demon Dirge: Demons are stunned and take 3d6 damage/round for 1d4 rounds.
Devil Blight: Damage and stun baatezu; damage other lawful and evil creatures.
Diamondsteel[M]**:** Metal armor provides damage reduction.
Dolorous Blow: Weapon's threat range is doubled and threats are automatically confirmed.
Dragonskin: You gain a bonus to natural armor plus energy resistance 10.
False Gravity: Travel on a solid surface as if that surface had its own gravity.
Giant's Wrath: Pebbles you throw become boulders.
Girallon's Blessing: Subject gains one additional pair of arms.
Hamatula Barbs: Subjects grow barbs, which damage foes that attack subject in melee.
Primal Form: You change into elemental, gain some abilities.
Repair Serious Damage: Repairs 3d8 damage +1/level (max +15) to any construct.
Rust Ray: Metal objects take 2d6 damage +1/2 levels.
Shadow Phase: Subject becomes partially incorporeal.
Snake's Swiftness, Mass: Allies each immediately make one attack.
Spell Vulnerability: Reduce creature's spell resistance by 1/caster level (max reduction 15).
Spiderskin: Subject gains increasing bonus to natural armor, saves against poison, and Hide checks.
Steeldance: Blades hover around you and attack foes.
Stony Grasp: Arm made of soil and rock grapples foes.
Tremorsense: Grants tremorsense to a range of 30 feet.
Weapon of Energy: Weapon deals extra energy damage.
Weapon of Impact: As *keen edge*, but aids bludgeoning weapons.

Univ **Enhance Familiar:** Your familiar receives +2 bonus on saves, combat rolls, and AC for 1 hour/level.
Fortify Familiar: Your familiar gains 2d8 temporary hp, +2 to armor, 25% chance to avoid extra sneak attack and critical hit damage.

4TH-LEVEL SORCERER/WIZARD SPELLS

Abjur **Dispelling Screen:** Targeted *dispel magic* on any creatures and unattended items, +10 max on caster level check.
Forceward: Creates a sphere of force that protects against force effects and keeps out incorporeal creatures.
Portal Alarm, Improved: Warded portal alerts you or a creature designated by you to creatures passing through it.
Ray Deflection: Ray attacks are reflected away.
Ray of Deanimation: Ray deals 1d6 damage/level to constructs.

Resistance, Greater: Subject gains +3 on saving throws.

Resist Energy, Mass: Creatures ignore damage from specified energy type.

Wall of Chaos/Evil/Good/Law[M]: Wall blocks creatures of opposite alignment.

Conj **Blast of Flame:** 60-ft. cone of fire (1d6/level damage).

Bloodstar[F]: Hovering construct does Con damage each time foe is damaged.

Ethereal Mount: You conjure swift mounts on the Ethereal Plane.

Orb of Acid: Ranged touch, 1d6/level acid damage and subject might be sickened.

Orb of Cold: Ranged touch, 1d6/level cold damage and subject might be blinded.

Orb of Electricity: Ranged touch, 1d6/level electricity damage and subject might be entangled.

Orb of Fire: Ranged touch, 1d6/level fire damage and subject might be dazed.

Orb of Force: Globe of force deals 1d6/level damage (max 10d6).

Orb of Sound: Ranged touch, 1d4/level sonic damage and subject might be deafened.

Summon Undead IV: Summons undead to fight for you.

Translocation Trick: You and subject switch places and appear as each other.

Wall of Sand: Swirling sand blocks ranged attacks, slows movement through.

Wall of Water: Creates shapeable transparent wall of water.

Div **Assay Spell Resistance:** +10 bonus on caster level checks to defeat one creature's spell resistance.

Know Vulnerabilities: Determine subject's vulnerabilities and resistances.

Treasure Scent: You detect valuable metals and gems.

Ench **Battle Hymn:** Allies can reroll one Will save/round.

Rebuke, Greater: Subject cowers for 1d4 rounds.

Evoc **Blistering Radiance:** Light dazzles creatures, deals 2d6 fire damage in 50-ft.-radius spread.

Defenestrating Sphere[F]: Cloudy gray sphere knocks enemies prone, hurls them upward for subsequent falling damage.

Dragon Breath: You choose a dragon type and mimic its breath weapon.

Energy Spheres: Five colored spheres attack with or negate acid, cold, electricity, fire, and sonic energy.

Explosive Cascade: Bouncing flame ball deals 1d6/level fire damage.

Floating Disk, Greater: As *floating disk*, but you can ride it.

Force Chest: 2-ft-cube chest made of force.

Force Claw: Claw of force guards an area, making opportunity attacks.

Force Missiles: Unerring missiles of force strike for 2d6 damage and explode in a burst.

Forcewave: Bull rushes all creatures within 10 ft.

Stone Sphere: 3-ft.-diameter stone sphere rolls over your enemies.

Sword of Deception: Blade of energy attacks independently, deals 1d4 damage, penalizes subsequent save.

Thunderlance: Lance of force deals 3d6 damage and might dispel force effects.

Vortex of Teeth: 3d8 points of damage due to force per round to all creatures in the area.

Wingbind: A net of force entangles the subject, causing it to fall from the sky.

Illus **Sensory Deprivation:** All of subject's senses are blocked.

Shadow Well: Subject enters gloomy pocket plane and emerges frightened.

Necro **Burning Blood:** Subject takes 1d8 acid damage plus 1d8 fire damage/round.

Rebuking Breath: Your breath weapon rebukes undead.

Trans **Attune Form:** Grant creature temporary protection against overtly damaging planar traits.

Backlash: Subject takes damage if it uses spells against another creature.

Bite of the Werewolf: You gain the Strength and attacks of a werewolf.

Blinding Breath: Your breath weapon blinds subjects.

Wingbind swiftly brings low-flying foes to ground

Illus. by J. Nelson

Corporeal Instability: Transform a creature into an amorphous mass.
Darkvision, Mass: As *darkvision*, but affects one/level subjects.
Displacer Form: You change into displacer beast, gain some abilities.
Entangling Staff: Quarterstaff can grapple and constrict foes.
Fire Stride: Teleport from one fire to another.
Flame Whips: Your forelimbs deal 6d6 fire damage.
Flight of the Dragon: You grow dragon wings.
Iron Bones: Corporeal undead gains +6 natural armor bonus.
Metal Melt: Melts metal object without heat.
Perinarch: Gain greater control over Limbo's morphic essence.
Raise from the Deep: Creature or sunken ship made buoyant.
Repair Critical Damage: Repairs 4d8 damage +1/level (max +20) to any construct.
Ruin Delver's Fortune: Cast on another creature's turn and choose one of several benefits.
Scramble Portal: You randomize the destination of a magic portal.
Sharptooth: One of your natural weapons deals damage as if you were one size larger.
Spell Enhancer: Lets you cast another spell in the same round at +2 caster level.
Voice of the Dragon: +10 on Bluff, Diplomacy, and Intimidate checks; can use one *suggestion*.
Wings of Air, Greater: Subject's flight maneuverability improves by two steps.

5TH-LEVEL SORCERER/WIZARD SPELLS

Abjur **Anticold Sphere:** Sphere hedges out cold creatures and protects you from cold.
Contingent Energy Resistance: Energy damage triggers a *resist energy* spell.
Dispelling Breath: Your breath weapon acts as a targeted *dispel magic* to all creatures in its area.
Duelward: +4 on Spellcraft checks, counterspell as an immediate action.
Ironguard, Lesser: Subject becomes immune to nonmagical metal.
Indomitability: Subject can't be reduced below 1 hp.
Planar Tolerance: Provides long-term protection against overtly damaging planar traits.
Reciprocal Gyre: Creature or object takes 1d12 damage/level of spell affecting it (max 25d12).
Refusal: Spellcasters and creatures with spell-like abilities are prevented from entering an area.
Symbol of Spell Loss: Triggered rune absorbs spells yet to be cast.
Wall of Dispel Magic: Creatures passing through a transparent wall becomes subjects of targeted *dispel magic*.
Zone of Respite: Prevents teleportation and similar effects from functioning in the area.

Conj **Acid Sheath**[F]**:** Sheath of acid damages those who attack you, enhances acid spells.
Arc of Lightning: Line of electricity arcs between two creatures (1d6/level damage).
Call Zelekhut[X]**:** A zelekhut performs one duty for you.
Dimension Door, Greater: Short-range, multiple-use *dimension door.*
Dragon Ally, Lesser[X]**:** Exchange services with a 9 HD dragon.
Hidden Lodge: Creates sturdy cottage camouflaged to blend into natural surroundings.
Phantasmal Thief: Creates an unseen force that steals from others.
Summon Undead V: Summons undead to fight for you.
Viscid Glob: Ranged touch attack hurls 5-ft.-diameter glob of glue at subject.
Vitriolic Sphere: Potent acid deals 6d6 acid damage plus possible damage in following 2 rounds.

Evoc **Ball Lightning:** Energy ball deals 1d6/level electricity damage.
Cacophonic Burst: Noise deals 1d6/level sonic damage to all within area.
Cacophonic Shield: Shield 10 ft. from you blocks sounds, deals 1d6 sonic damage +1/level, and deafens creatures passing through.
Cyclonic Blast: Deals 1d6 damage/level, knocks down creatures.
Fire Shield, Mass: Creatures attacking allies take damage; allies are protected from fire or cold.
Firebrand[M]**:** One 5-ft. burst/level deals 1d6 fire/level plus burning for 1 round.
Fireburst, Greater: Subjects within 15 ft. take 1d10/level fire damage.
Moonbow: Three motes of electricity each deal 1d6/2 levels electricity damage to subjects.
Prismatic Ray: Ray of light blinds subject, deals random effect.
Shard Storm: Blast deals 3d6 damage to creatures in area.
Shroud of Flame: Subject bursts into flames, taking 2d6 fire damage/round.
Sonic Rumble[F]**:** Cone of sound deals damage.
Wall of Limbs: Whirling limbs deal 5d6 damage and grab creatures passing through.

Illus **Illusory Feast:** Subjects become dazed by illusory food.
Shadow Form: Gain +4 on Hide, Move Silently, and Escape Artist checks, and concealment; you can move through obstacles if you have ranks in Escape Artist.
Shadow Hand: Medium hand blocks opponents or carries items.
Shadowfade: Opens a portal to the Plane of Shadow.

Necro **Death Throes:** Your body explodes when you die.
Graymantle: Inhibits creature's ability to heal and regenerate for 1 round/level.

Miasma of Entropy: Rot all natural materials in 30-ft. cone-shaped burst.
Night's Caress: Touched foe takes 1d6 points of damage/level plus 1d6+2 Con damage.
Spiritwall: Wall of spirit-forms causes panic, deals 1d10 damage if touched, can bestow negative levels if passed through.
Wrack: Renders creature helpless with pain.

Trans **Bite of the Wereboar**: You gain the Strength and attacks of a wereboar.
Blink, Greater: Controlled blinking between the Material and Ethereal Planes grants defenses for 1 round/level.
Breath Weapon Substitution: Your breath weapon deals a different kind of damage than normal.
Draconic Might: Gain +5 to Str, Con, Cha; +4 natural armor; immunity to magic sleep and paralysis effects.
Draconic Polymorph: As *polymorph*, but improved.
Dragonsight: Gain low-light vision, darkvision, and blindsense.
Earth Reaver: Eruption deals 7d6 damage to all in area.
Enlarge Person, Greater: Subject remains enlarged for 1 hour/level.
Ethereal Breath: Your breath weapon manifests on the Ethereal Plane.
Fiendform: Assume form and abilities of fiendish creature, demon, or devil.
Fly, Mass: One creature/level flies at speed of 60 ft.
Gutsnake: 10-ft. tentacle grows from your stomach and attacks your enemies.
Lucent Lance: Ambient light forms lance, deals various damage.
Nightstalker's Transformation[M]: Gain +4 Dex, +3 luck bonus to AC, +5 luck bonus on Ref saves, +3d6 sneak attack, and evasion.
Reduce Person, Greater: Subject remains reduced for 10 minutes/level.
Spell Matrix, Lesser[F]: Magical matrix stores a 3rd-level or lower spell to be cast later as quickened spell.
Stunning Breath: Your breath weapon also stuns creatures for 1 round.
Surefooted Stride, Mass: As *surefooted stride* but multiple subjects.
Vulnerability: Reduces an opponent's damage reduction.
Xorn Movement: Touched creature swims through earth like a xorn.

6TH-LEVEL SORCERER/WIZARD SPELLS

Abjur **Anticipate Teleportation, Greater**[F]: Predict and delay the arrival of creatures teleporting into range by 3 rounds.
Aura of Evasion[M]: All within 10 ft. gain evasion against breath weapons.
Ruby Ray of Reversal[F]: Ray negates magical or mundane hazards.
Seal Portal[M]: Seal an interplanar portal or *gate*.
Sign of Sealing, Greater[M]: Magical sigil protects door, chest, or open space, deals 1d6/level damage (max 20d6) if opened.

Conj **Resistance, Superior**: Subject gains +6 on saving throws.
Transcribe Symbol: Safely moves an untriggered magical symbol to another location.
Tunnel Swallow: Tunnel's peristaltic convulsions deal 1d6 points of damage/level (max 15d6).
Wall of Gears: Creates wall of moving gears that deals 1d6 damage/2 levels to creatures within 10 ft.

Div **Probe Thoughts**: Read subject's memories, one question/round.
Interplanar Telepathic Bond: Link lets allies communicate across planes.

Conj **Acid Storm**[M]: Deals 1d6/level acid damage (max 15d6) in a 20-ft. radius.
Fire Spiders: Swarm of Fine fire elementals deals fire damage in an area.
Freezing Fog: Fog slows creatures, obscures vision, hinders movement.
Gemjump[F]: Teleport to the location of a specially prepared gem.

Evoc **Fires of Purity**: Subject bursts into magical flame, becoming a dangerous weapon.
Howling Chain[F]: Chain of force trips and attacks opponents.
Ray of Light: Ray blinds subject.

Illus **Dream Casting**: Alter subject's dreams to produce desired effect.
Illusory Pit: Creatures in area are knocked prone while believing they're falling.
Reflective Disguise, Mass: Viewers see subjects as their own species and gender.
Shadowy Grappler: Illusory force grapples subject.

Necro **Aura of Terror**: You gain an aura of fear, or your frightful presence becomes more effective.
Contagion, Mass: As *contagion*, but 20-ft. radius.
Fleshshiver: Subject is stunned for 1 round, takes 1d6/level damage, and is nauseated for 1d4+2 rounds.
Ghoul Gauntlet: Convert victim to a ghoul under your control.
Imperious Glare: You cause subjects to cower in fear.
Incorporeal Nova: Destroy incorporeal undead.
Opalescent Glare: Kill creatures with a look, or make them very afraid.
Ray of Entropy: Subject takes –4 Strength, Dexterity, and Constitution.
Revive Undead[M]: Restores undeath to undead that was destroyed up to 1 day/level ago.
Spectral Touch: Your touch bestows one negative level/round.

Trans **Bite of the Weretiger**: You gain the Strength and attacks of a weretiger.

Brilliant Blade: Weapon or projectiles shed light, ignore armor.
Cloak of the Sea: Gain *blur, freedom of movement,* and *water breathing* while in water.
Extract Water Elemental: Pulls water from victim, forms water elemental.
HardeningM: Increases object's hardness by 1 point/2 levels.
Make Manifest: You cause a creature on a coexistent plane to appear on your plane.
Ooze Puppet: You telekinetically control an ooze.
Stone Body: Your body becomes living stone.
Subvert Planar Essence: Reduces subject's damage reduction and spell resistance.

Univ **Imbue Familiar with Spell Ability:** You transfer spells and casting ability into your familiar.

7TH-LEVEL SORCERER/WIZARD SPELL

Abjur **Antimagic Ray**M: Subject loses all magical powers.
Dispelling Screen, Greater: Targeted *dispel magic* on any creatures and unattended items, +20 max on caster level check.
Energy Immunity: Subject and equipment gain immunity to damage of specified energy type.
Ghost Trap: Incorporeal creatures turn corporeal.
Hide from Dragons: Dragons can't perceive one subject/2 levels.
IronguardF: Subject becomes immune to all metal.
Planar Bubble: Create bubble around creature that emulates its native planar environment.

Conj **Call Kolyarut**X: A kolyarut performs one duty for you.
Dragon AllyX: As *lesser dragon ally,* but up to 15 HD.
Stun Ray: Subject stunned 1d4+1 rounds.

Ench **Hiss of Sleep:** You induce comatose slumber in subjects.
Rebuke, Final: As *rebuke,* except the subject must save or die.
Symphonic NightmareM: Discordant noise haunts subject's sleep.
Transfix: Humanoids freeze in place until condition you specify is met.

Evoc **Emerald Flame Fist:** Touch attack deals 3d6 + fire damage 1/level (max +20); subject can be engulfed by flame for additional damage.
Ice Claw: Claw of ice grapples and deals cold damage.
Prismatic Eye: Orb produces individual prismatic rays as touch attacks.
Radiant Assault: 1d6 damage/level, victims dazed or dazzled.
Submerge Ship: You control ship mentally while it travels underwater.

Illus **Solipsism:** Subject believes it alone exists.

Necro **Arrow of Bone**M: Missile or thrown weapon gains +4 bonus, subject takes 3d6 damage +1/level (max +20) or is slain.
Avasculate: Reduce foe to half hp and stun.
Awaken UndeadX: Grant sentience to otherwise mindless undead.
Barghest's FeastM: Destroy corpse, potentially preventing its return to life.
Energy Ebb: Give subject one negative level/round for 1 round/level.
Evil Glare: Paralyze creatures with your glare.
Kiss of the VampireM: You gain vampirelike supernatural abilities, but are vulnerable to attacks that harm undead.
Sword of Darkness: Blade of negative energy bestows one or more negative levels.

Trans **Animate Breath:** Your breath weapon becomes an elemental.
Bite of the Werebear: You gain the Strength and attacks of a werebear.
Body of War: You change into warforged titan, gain some abilities.
Brilliant Aura: Allies' weapons become brilliant energy, ignoring armor.
Elemental Body: You take on the qualities of a type of elemental.

Wizards study spells from many sources in preparation for a journey

Illus. by W. England

Energy Transformation Field[MX]: Area absorbs magic energy to power a predetermined spell.
Glass Strike: Turns subject into glass.
Spell Matrix[F]: Stores up to two spells of 3rd level or lower to be released later.
Stone Shape, Greater: Sculpts 10 cu. ft. + 10 cu. ft./level of stone into any shape.
Synostodweomer: Channel a spell into positive energy to cure 1d8/spell level.

8TH-LEVEL SORCERER/WIZARD SPELLS

Abjur **Spell Engine**[MX]: *Wizard only.* Swap out prepared spells for other spells in your spellbook.
Wall of Greater Dispel Magic: Creatures passing through a transparent wall become subjects of targeted *greater dispel magic*.
Conj **Fierce Pride of the Beastlands**: Summon celestial lions and celestial dire lions to follow your commands.
Plane Shift, Greater: *Plane shift* accurately to your desired destination.
Ench **Maddening Whispers**: You induce confusion and madness in subjects.
Wrathful Castigation: Subject dies or is dazed and –4 on saves for 1 round/level.
Evoc **Field of Icy Razors**[F]: Creatures in area take normal and cold damage, might be slowed.
Lightning Ring: Ring of lightning gives you resistance to electricity 20, damages adjacent creatures, and emits two lightning bolts per round.
Illus **Shifting Paths**: Illusion hides path, creates false new path.
Invisibility, Superior: Subject is invisible to sight, hearing, and scent for 1 minute/level, and can attack.
Necro **Avascular Mass**: Reduce foe to half hp and stun, entangle in 20-ft. radius from victim.
Bestow Curse, Greater: As *bestow curse*, but more severe penalties.
Blackfire: Subject is engulfed in black flame, takes 1d4 Con damage and becomes nauseated; flames and effects can spread to adjacent living creatures.
Heart of Stone[FX]: Exchange your heart with stone heart to gain damage reduction, resistance to energy for 1 year.
Skeletal Guard[M]: Create one skeleton/level with turn resistance.
Veil of Undeath: You gain undead traits.
Trans **Excavate**: Creates a permanent passage in earth and walls.
Flensing: Pain and trauma deal 2d6 damage, 1d6 Con damage, 1d6 Cha damage for up to 4 rounds.
Ghostform: You assume incorporeal form and gain some incorporeal traits and bonuses.
Make Manifest, Mass: As *make manifest* but affecting all creatures in the area.
Stunning Breath, Greater: Your breath weapon also stuns creatures for 2d4 rounds.

9TH-LEVEL SORCERER/WIZARD SPELLS

Abjur **Absorption**: You absorb spell energy to power spells of your own.
Effulgent Epuration: Creates one sphere/level to negate hostile magic.
Magic Miasma: *Solid fog* reduces caster level by –4.
Maw of Chaos: Chaotic energy dazes, deals damage, impedes concentration.
Reaving Dispel: On a targeted *dispel*, steal spell power and effects for yourself.
Unbinding: Frees everyone in range from spells that constrain or bind.
Conj **Abyssal Army**: Summons demons to fight for you.
Black Blade of Disaster: Floating magic weapon disintegrates subjects.
Call Marut[X]: A marut performs one duty for you.
Dragon Ally, Greater[X]: As *lesser dragon ally*, but up to 21 HD.
Heavenly Host: Summons archons to fight for you.
Hellish Horde: Summons devils to fight for you.
Obedient Avalanche: Snowy avalanche crushes and buries your foes.
Sphere of Ultimate Destruction: Featureless black sphere does 2d6/level damage, disintegrates.
Summon Elemental Monolith[M]: Calls powerful elemental creature to fight for you.
Vile Death[MX]: Undead creature gains fiendish template.
Div **Eye of Power**: As *arcane eye*, but you can cast spells of 3rd level or lower through it.
Hindsight[M]: You see into the past.
Ench **Programmed Amnesia**[M]: Destroy, alter, or replace memories in subject creature.
Evoc **Instant Refuge**[MX]: Transport to a safe location of your choice.
Reality Maelstrom: Hole in reality sends creatures and objects to another plane.
Necro **Enervating Breath**: Your breath weapon also bestows 2d4 negative levels.
Plague of Undead[M]: Animates horde of undead.
Trans **Awaken Construct**[X]: Construct gains humanlike sentience.
Breath Weapon Admixture: Add a second kind of energy to your breath weapon.
Perinarch, Planar: Gain control over a small area of any divinely morphic plane.
Replicate Casting: Duplicate observed spell or spell-like ability.
Spell Matrix, Greater[F]: Stores up to three spells of 3rd level or lower to be released later.
Transmute Rock to Lava: Transforms one 10-ft. cube with subsequent fire damage and effects.
Undermaster[M]: You gain earth-related spell-like abilities.

Appendix: Domain Spells

The following domains supplement those described in Chapter 11 of the *Player's Handbook*. In the lists that follow, a dagger (†) following a spell name signifies a spell described in this book.

BALANCE DOMAIN

Granted Power: Once per day, as a free action, you can add your Wisdom modifier to your Armor Class. This bonus lasts for 1 round per cleric level.

Balance Domain Spells

1 **Make Whole:** Repairs an object.
2 **Calm Emotions:** Calms creatures, negating emotion effects.
3 **Clarity of Mind†:** +4 bonus on saves against mind-affecting spells and abilities, allows reroll of concealment miss chance.
4 **Dismissal:** Forces a creature to return to native plane.
5 **Sanctuary, Mass†:** One creature/level can't be attacked, and can't attack.
6 **Banishment:** Banishes 2 HD/level of extraplanar creatures.
7 **Word of Balance†:** Kills, paralyzes, weakens, or nauseates nonneutral creatures.
8 **Protection from Spells[MF]:** Confers +8 resistance bonus.
9 **Weighed in the Balance†:** Harms or heals creatures within 30 feet of you.

CAVERN DOMAIN

Granted Power: You gain the stonecunning ability (PH 15). If you already have stonecunning, your racial bonus on checks to notice unusual stonework increases to +4.

Cavern Domain Spells

1 **Detect Secret Doors:** Reveals hidden doors within 60 ft.
2 **Darkness:** 20-ft. radius of supernatural shadow.
3 **Meld into Stone:** You and your gear merge with stone.
4 **Leomund's Secure Shelter:** Creates sturdy cottage.
5 **Passwall:** Creates passage through wood or stone wall.
6 **Find the Path:** Shows most direct way to a location.
7 **Maw of Stone†:** Animates cavern opening or chamber.
8 **Earthquake:** Intense tremor shakes 5-ft./level radius.
9 **Imprisonment:** Entombs subject beneath the earth.

CELERITY DOMAIN

Granted Power: Your land speed is faster than the norm for your race by 10 feet. This benefit is lost if you are wearing medium or heavy armor or carrying a medium or heavy load.

Celerity Domain Spells

1 **Expeditious Retreat:** Your speed increases by 30 ft.
2 **Cat's Grace:** Subject gains +4 to Dex for 1 minute/level.
3 **Blur:** Attacks miss subject 20% of the time.
4 **Haste:** One creature/level moves faster, +1 on attack rolls, AC, and Reflex saves.
5 **Tree Stride:** Step from one tree to another far away.
6 **Wind Walk:** You and your allies turn vaporous and travel fast.
7 **Cat's Grace, Mass:** As *cat's grace*, one subject/level.
8 **Blink, Greater†:** Controlled blinking between the Material and Ethereal Planes grants defenses for 1 round/level.
9 **Time Stop:** You act freely for 1d4+1 rounds.

CHARM DOMAIN

Granted Power: You can boost your Charisma by 4 points once per day. Activating this power is a free action. The Charisma increase lasts 1 minute.

Charm Domain Spells

1 **Charm Person:** Makes one person your friend.
2 **Calm Emotions:** Calms creatures, negating emotion effects.
3 **Suggestion:** Compels subject to follow stated course of action.
4 **Good Hope:** Subjects gain +2 on attack rolls, damage rolls, saves, and checks.
5 **Charm Monster:** Makes monster believe it is your ally.
6 **Geas/Quest:** As *lesser geas*, plus it affects any creature.
7 **Insanity:** Subject suffers continuous *confusion*.
8 **Demand:** As *sending*, plus you can send *suggestion*.
9 **Dominate Monster:** As *dominate person*, but any creature.

COLD DOMAIN

Granted Power (Su): You can turn or destroy fire creatures as a good cleric turns undead. You can also rebuke or command cold creatures as an evil cleric rebukes undead. Use these abilities a number of times per day equal to 3 + your Cha modifier.

Cold Domain Spells

1 **Chill Touch:** One touch/level deals 1d6 damage and possibly 1 Str damage.
2 **Chill Metal:** Cold metal damages those who touch it.
3 **Sleet Storm:** Hampers vision and movement.
4 **Ice Storm:** Hail deals 5d6 damage in cylinder 40 ft. across.
5 **Wall of Ice:** Ice plane creates wall with 15 hp +1/level, or hemisphere can trap creatures inside.
6 **Cone of Cold:** 1d6/level cold damage.
7 **Control Weather:** Changes weather in local area.
8 **Polar Ray:** Ranged touch attack deals 1d6/level cold damage.
9 **Obedient Avalanche†:** Snowy avalanche crushes and buries your foes.

COMMUNITY DOMAIN

Granted Power: Use *calm emotions* as a spell-like ability once per day. Gain a +2 bonus on Diplomacy checks.

Community Domain Spells

1 **Bless:** Allies gain +1 on attack rolls and saves against fear.
2 **Status:** Monitors condition, position of allies.
3 **Prayer:** Allies +1 on most rolls, enemies –1 penalty.
4 **Tongues:** Speak any language.
5 **Rary's Telepathic Bond:** Link lets allies communicate.
6 **Heroes' Feast:** Food for one creature/level cures and grants combat bonuses.

7 **Refuge**[M]: Alters item to transport its possessor to you.
8 **Mordenkainen's Magnificent Mansion**[F]: Door leads to extradimensional mansion.
9 **Heal, Mass:** As *heal*, but with several subjects.

COMPETITION DOMAIN

Granted Power (Ex): You gain a +1 bonus on opposed checks you make.

Competition Domain Spells

1 **Remove Fear:** Suppresses fear or gives +4 on saves against fear for one subject + one per 4 levels.
2 **Zeal†:** You move through foes to attack the enemy you want.
3 **Prayer:** Allies +1 bonus on most rolls, enemies –1 penalty.
4 **Divine Power:** You gain attack bonus, +6 to Str, and 1 hp/level.
5 **Righteous Might:** Your size increases, and you gain combat bonuses.
6 **Zealot Pact†**[X]: You automatically gain combat bonuses when you attack someone of opposite alignment.
7 **Regenerate:** Subject's severed limbs grow back, cures 4d8 damage +1/level (max +35).
8 **Moment of Prescience:** You gain insight bonus on single attack roll, check, or save.
9 **Visage of the Deity, Greater†:** As *lesser visage of the deity*, but you become half-celestial or half-fiendish.

COURAGE DOMAIN

Granted Power (Su): You radiate an aura of courage that grants all allies within 10 feet (including yourself) a +4 morale bonus on saving throws against fear effects. This ability functions only while you are conscious.

Courage Domain Spells

1 **Remove Fear:** Suppresses fear or gives +4 on saves against fear for one subject + one per 4 levels.
2 **Aid:** +1 on attack rolls and saves against fear, 1d8 temporary hp +1/level (max +10).
3 **Cloak of Bravery:** You and your allies gain a bonus on saves against fear.
4 **Heroism:** Gives +2 bonus on attack rolls, saves, skill checks.
5 **Valiant Fury†:** +4 Str, Con; +2 Will saves, extra attack.
6 **Heroes' Feast:** Food for one creature/level cures and grants combat bonuses.
7 **Heroism, Greater:** Gives +4 bonus on attack rolls, saves, skill checks; immunity to fear; temporary hp.
8 **Lion's Roar†:** Deals 1d8 points of damage/2 levels to enemies; allies get +1 on attacks and saves against fear, temporary hp.
9 **Cloak of Bravery, Greater†:** You and your allies become immune to fear and get +2 bonus on attacks.

CRAFT DOMAIN

Granted Power: You cast conjuration (creation) spells at +1 caster level and gain Skill Focus as a bonus feat for one Craft skill of your choice.

Craft Domain Spells

1 **Animate Rope:** Makes a rope move at your command.
2 **Wood Shape:** Rearranges wooden objects to suit you.
3 **Stone Shape:** Sculpts stone into any shape.
4 **Minor Creation:** Creates one cloth or wood object.
5 **Wall of Stone:** Creates a stone wall that can be shaped.
6 **Fantastic Machine†:** Creates a machine to perform a single simple task.
7 **Major Creation:** As *minor creation*, plus stone and metal.
8 **Forcecage**[M]: Cube or cage of force imprisons all inside.
9 **Fantastic Machine, Greater†** Creates a machine to perform multiple tasks.

CREATION DOMAIN

Granted Power: You cast conjuration (creation) spells at +1 caster level.

Creation Domain Spells

1 **Create Water:** Creates 2 gallons/level of pure water.
2 **Minor Image:** As *silent image*, plus some sound.
3 **Create Food and Water:** Feeds three humans (or one horse)/level.
4 **Minor Creation:** Creates one cloth or wood object.
5 **Major Creation:** As *minor creation*, plus stone and metal.
6 **Heroes' Feast:** Food for one creature/level cures and grants combat bonuses.
7 **Permanent Image**[M]: Includes sight, sound, and smell.
8 **True Creation†**[X]: As *major creation*, but permanent.
9 **Pavilion of Grandeur†:** A feast and a great pavilion are created.

DARKNESS DOMAIN

Granted Power: You gain Blind-Fight as a bonus feat.

Darkness Domain Spells

1 **Obscuring Mist:** Fog surrounds you.
2 **Blindness/Deafness:** Makes subject blinded or deafened.
3 **Blacklight†** Create an area of total darkness.
4 **Armor of Darkness†:** Shroud grants deflection bonus, darkvision, and other effects.
5 **Darkbolt†:** Multiple bolts deal 2d8 damage and daze creatures.
6 **Prying Eyes:** 1d4 +1/level floating eyes scout for you.
7 **Nightmare:** Sends vision dealing 1d10 damage, fatigue.
8 **Power Word Blind:** Blinds creature with 200 hp or less.
9 **Power Word Kill:** Kills one creature with 100 hp or less.

DEATHBOUND DOMAIN

Granted Power: Your limit for creating undead animated with spells increases to three times your caster level instead of the normal two times caster level.

Deathbound Domain Spells

1 **Chill of the Grave†:** Ray causes cold damage.
2 **Blade of Pain and Fear†:** Creates blade of gnashing teeth.
3 **Fangs of the Vampire King†:** Grow vampire fangs.
4 **Wither Limb†:** Cause enemy's limbs to wither.
5 **Revive Undead†**[M]: Restores undeath to undead that was destroyed up to 1 day/level ago.
6 **Awaken Undead†**[X]: Grant sentience to otherwise mindless undead.

7 **Avasculate†:** Reduce foe to half hp and stun.
8 **Avascular Mass†:** Reduce foe to half hp and stun, entangle in 20-ft. radius from victim.
9 **Wail of the Banshee:** Kills one creature/level.

DOMINATION DOMAIN

Granted Power: You gain Spell Focus (enchantment) as a bonus feat.

Domination Domain Spells

1 **Command:** One subject obeys selected command for 1 round.
2 **Enthrall:** Captivates all within 100 ft. + 10 ft./level.
3 **Suggestion:** Compels subject to follow stated course of action.
4 **Dominate Person:** Controls humanoid telepathically.
5 **Command, Greater:** As *command*, but affects one subject/level.
6 **Geas/Quest:** As *lesser geas*, plus it affects any creature.
7 **Suggestion, Mass:** As *suggestion*, plus one subject/level.
8 **True Domination†:** As *dominate person*, but save at –4.
9 **Monstrous Thrall†:** As *true domination*, but permanent and affects any creature.

DRAGON DOMAIN

Granted Power: Add Bluff and Intimidate to your list of cleric class skills.

Dragon Domain Spells

1 **Magic Fang:** One natural weapon of subject creature gets +1 on attack rolls and damage rolls.
2 **Resist Energy:** Ignores 10 (or more) points of damage/attack from specified energy type.
3 **Magic Fang, Greater:** One natural weapon of subject creature gets +1/4 levels on attack rolls and damage rolls (max +5).
4 **Voice of the Dragon†:** +10 on Bluff, Diplomacy, and Intimidate checks; can use one *suggestion*.
5 **True Seeing**[M]: Lets you see all things as they really are.
6 **Stoneskin**[M]: Ignore 10 points of damage per attack.
7 **Dragon Ally†**[X]: As *lesser dragon ally*, but up to 15 HD.
8 **Suggestion, Mass:** As *suggestion*, plus one subject/level.
9 **Dominate Monster:** As *dominate person*, but any creature.

DREAM DOMAIN

Granted Power: You are immune to fear effects.

Dream Domain Spells

1 **Sleep:** Puts 4 HD of creatures into magical slumber.
2 **Augury**[MF]: Learns whether an action will be good or bad.
3 **Deep Slumber:** Puts 10 HD of creatures to sleep.
4 **Phantasmal Killer:** Fearsome illusion kills subject or deals 3d6 damage.
5 **Nightmare:** Sends vision dealing 1d10 damage, fatigue.
6 **Dream Sight†:** Your spirit can hear and see at a distance for 1 minute/level.
7 **Scrying, Greater**[F]: As *scrying*, but faster and longer.
8 **Power Word Stun:** Stuns creature with 150 hp or less.
9 **Weird:** As *phantasmal killer*, but affects all within 30 ft.

DROW DOMAIN

Granted Power: You gain Lightning Reflexes as a bonus feat.

Drow Domain Spells

1 **Cloak of Dark Power†:** Cloak protects subject from effects of sunlight.
2 **Clairaudience/Clairvoyance:** See or hear at a distance for 1 minute/level.
3 **Suggestion:** Compels subject to follow stated course of action.
4 **Discern Lies:** Reveals deliberate falsehoods.
5 **Spiderform†:** Polymorph into drider or Large spider.
6 **Dispelling Screen, Greater†:** Targeted *dispel magic* on any creatures and unattended items, +20 max on caster level check.
7 **Word of Chaos:** Nonchaotic subject is killed, *confused*, stunned, or deafened.
8 **Planar Ally, Greater:** As *lesser planar ally*, but up to 24 HD.
9 **Gate**[X]: Connects two planes for travel or summoning.

DWARF DOMAIN

Granted Power: You gain Great Fortitude as a bonus feat.

Dwarf Domain Spells

1 **Magic Weapon:** Weapon gains +1 bonus.
2 **Bear's Endurance:** Subject gains +4 to Con for 1 minute/level.
3 **Glyph of Warding**[M]: Inscription harms those who pass it.
4 **Magic Weapon, Greater:** +1 bonus/4 levels (max +5).
5 **Fabricate:** Transforms raw material into finished items.
6 **Stone Tell:** Talk to natural or worked stone.
7 **Dictum:** Kills, paralyzes, slows, or deafens nonlawful subjects.
8 **Protection from Spells**[MF]: Confers +8 resistance bonus.
9 **Elemental Swarm:** Summons multiple elementals.*
*Earth spell only.

ELF DOMAIN

Granted Power: You gain the Point Blank Shot feat.

Elf Domain Spells

1 **True Strike:** +20 on your next attack roll.
2 **Cat's Grace:** Subject gains +4 to Dex for 1 minute/level.
3 **Snare:** Creates a magic booby trap.
4 **Tree Stride:** Step from one tree to another far away.
5 **Commune with Nature:** Learn about terrain for 1 mile/level.
6 **Find the Path:** Shows most direct way to a location.
7 **Liveoak:** Oak becomes treant guardian.
8 **Sunburst:** Blinds all within 80 ft., deals 6d6 damage.
9 **Antipathy:** Object or location affected by spell repels certain creatures.

ENVY DOMAIN

Granted Powers: Add Bluff to your list of cleric class skills. In addition, you cast spells that damage or drain ability scores or bestow negative levels at +1 caster level.

ENVY DOMAIN SPELLS

1 **Disguise Self:** Changes your appearance.
2 **Ray of Enfeeblement:** Ray deals 1d6+1/2 levels Str penalty.
3 **Touch of Idiocy:** Subject takes 1d6-point penalty to Int, Wis, and Cha.
4 **Vampiric Touch:** Touch deals 1d6/2 levels damage; caster gains damage as hp.
5 **Crushing Despair:** Subjects take –2 on attack rolls, damage rolls, saves, and checks.
6 **Magic Jar**[F]**:** Enables possession of another creature.
7 **Limited Wish**[X]**:** Alters reality—within spell limits.
8 **Simulacrum**[MX]**:** Creates partially real double of a creature.
9 **Wish**[X]**:** As *limited wish*, but with fewer limits.

FAMILY DOMAIN

Granted Power (Su): Once per day as a free action, you can protect a number of creatures equal to your Charisma modifier (minimum one creature) with a +4 dodge bonus to AC. This ability lasts 1 round per level. An affected creature loses this protection if it moves more than 10 feet from you. You can affect yourself with this ability.

Family Domain Spells

1 **Bless:** Allies gain +1 on attack rolls and saves against fear.
2 **Shield Other**[F]**:** You take half of subject's damage.
3 **Helping Hand:** Ghostly hand leads subject to you.
4 **Imbue with Spell Ability:** Transfer spells to subject.
5 **Rary's Telepathic Bond:** Link lets allies communicate.
6 **Heroes' Feast:** Food for one creature/level cures and grants combat bonuses.
7 **Refuge**[M]**:** Alters item to transport its possessor to you.
8 **Protection from Spells**[MF]**:** Confers +8 resistance bonus.
9 **Prismatic Sphere:** As *prismatic wall*, but surrounds on all sides.

FATE DOMAIN

Granted Power (Ex): You gain the uncanny dodge ability. If you have another class that gives you uncanny dodge, your cleric levels add to that class's level for determining when you gain the improved uncanny dodge class feature (PH 26).

Fate Domain Spells

1 **True Strike:** +20 on your next attack roll.
2 **Augury**[MF]**:** Learns whether an action will be good or bad.
3 **Bestow Curse:** –6 to an ability score; –4 on attack rolls, saves, and checks; or 50% chance of losing each action.
4 **Status:** Monitors condition, position of allies.
5 **Mark of Justice:** Designates action that will trigger curse on subject.
6 **Geas/Quest:** As *lesser geas*, plus it affects any creature.
7 **Vision**[MX]**:** As *legend lore*, but quicker and strenuous.
8 **Mind Blank:** Subject is immune to mental/emotional magic and scrying.
9 **Foresight:** "Sixth sense" warns of impending danger.

FORCE DOMAIN

Granted Power (Su): By manipulating cosmic forces of inertia, once per day you can reroll any damage roll (for a weapon, a spell, or an ability) and take the better of the two rolls.

Force Domain Spells

1 **Mage Armor:** Gives subject +4 armor bonus.
2 **Magic Missile:** 1d4+1 damage; +1 missile/2 levels above 1st (max 5).
3 **Blast of Force†:** Attack deals 1d6 damage/2 levels (max 5d6).
4 **Otiluke's Resilient Sphere:** Force globe protects but traps one subject.
5 **Wall of Force:** Wall is immune to damage.
6 **Repulsion:** Creatures can't approach you.
7 **Forcecage**[M]**:** Cube or cage of force imprisons all inside.
8 **Otiluke's Telekinetic Sphere:** As *Otiluke's resilient sphere*, but you move sphere telekinetically.
9 **Bigby's Crushing Hand:** Large hand provides cover, pushes, or crushes your foes.

GLORY DOMAIN

Granted Power: Turn undead with a +2 bonus on the turning check and +1d6 on the turning damage roll.

Glory Domain Spells

1 **Disrupt Undead:** Deals 1d6 damage to one undead.
2 **Bless Weapon:** Weapon strikes true against evil foes.
3 **Searing Light:** Ray deals 1d8/2 levels damage, more against undead.
4 **Holy Smite:** Damages and blinds evil creatures.
5 **Holy Sword:** Weapon becomes +5, deals +2d6 damage against evil.
6 **Bolt of Glory†:** Positive energy ray deals extra damage to evil outsiders and undead.
7 **Sunbeam:** Beam blinds and deals 4d6 damage.
8 **Crown of Glory†**[M]**:** You gain +4 Charisma and inspire your allies.
9 **Gate**[X]**:** Connects two planes for travel or summoning.

GLUTTONY DOMAIN

Granted Power: For a total time per day of 1 round per cleric level you possess, you can increase your size as if you were affected by the *enlarge person* spell. Activating the power or ending it is a free action.

Gluttony Domain Spells

1 **Goodberry:** 2d4 berries each cure 1 hp (max 8 hit points/24 hours)
2 **Death Knell:** Kills dying creature; you gain 1d8 temporary hp, +2 to Str, and +1 caster level.
3 **Create Food and Water:** Feeds three humans (or one horse)/level.
4 **Vampiric Touch:** Touch deals 1d6/2 levels damage; caster gains damage as hp.
5 **Baleful Polymorph:** Transforms subject into harmless animal.
6 **Heroes' Feast:** Food for one creature/level cures and grants combat bonuses.
7 **Stone to Flesh:** Restores petrified creatures.
8 **Bite of the King†:** Swallow enemies whole.
9 **Trap the Soul**[MF]**:** Imprisons subject within gem.

GNOME DOMAIN

Granted Power: You cast illusion spells at +1 caster level.

Gnome Domain Spells

1 **Silent Image:** Creates minor illusion of your design.
2 **Gembomb**†[M]: Gem becomes a bomb that deals 1d8 force damage/2 levels.
3 **Minor Image:** As *silent image*, plus some sound.
4 **Minor Creation:** Creates one cloth or wood object.
5 **Hallucinatory Terrain:** Makes one type of terrain appear like another (field into forest, or the like).
6 **Fantastic Machine:** Creates a machine to perform a single simple task.
7 **Screen:** Illusion hides area from vision, scrying.
8 **Otto's Irresistible Dance:** Forces subject to dance.
9 **Summon Nature's Ally IX***: Summons creature to fight.
*Earth elementals or animals only.

GREED DOMAIN

Granted Power: You gain a +2 competence bonus on Appraise, Open Lock, and Sleight of Hand checks.

Greed Domain Spells

1 **Cheat**†: Caster rerolls when determining the success of a game of chance.
2 **Entice Gift**† Subject gives caster what it's holding.
3 **Knock:** Opens locked or magically sealed door.
4 **Fire Trap**[M]: Opened object deals 1d4 damage +1/level.
5 **Fabricate:** Transforms raw material into finished items.
6 **Guards and Wards:** Array of magical effects protects area.
7 **Teleport Object:** As *teleport*, but affects a touched object.
8 **Phantasmal Thief**†: Creates an unseen force that steals from others.
9 **Sympathy**[F]: Object or location attracts certain creatures.

HALFLING DOMAIN

Granted Power: Once per day for 10 minutes, you add your Charisma modifier to your Climb, Jump, Move Silently, and Hide checks. Activating this ability is a free action.

Halfling Domain Spells

1 **Magic Stone:** Three stones gain +1 on attack rolls, deal 1d6+1 damage.
2 **Cat's Grace:** Subject gains +4 to Dex for 1 minute/level.
3 **Magic Vestment:** Armor or shield gains +1 enhancement/4 levels.
4 **Freedom of Movement:** Subject moves normally despite impediments.
5 **Mordenkainen's Faithful Hound:** Phantom dog can attack, guard.
6 **Move Earth:** Dig trenches and build walls.
7 **Shadow Walk:** Step into shadow to travel rapidly.
8 **Word of Recall:** Teleports you back to designated place.
9 **Foresight:** "Sixth sense" warns of impending danger.

HATRED DOMAIN

Granted Power (Su): Once per day as a free action, choose one opponent. Against that foe you gain a +2 profane bonus on attack rolls, saving throws, and Armor Class for 1 minute.

Hatred Domain Spells

1 **Doom:** One subject takes –2 on attack rolls, damage rolls, saves, and checks.
2 **Scare:** Panics creatures of less than 6 HD.
3 **Bestow Curse:** –6 to an ability score; –4 on attack rolls, saves, and checks; or 50% chance of losing each action.
4 **Rage:** Gives +2 to Str and Con, +1 on Will saves, –2 to AC.
5 **Righteous Might:** Your size increases and you gain combat bonuses.
6 **Forbiddance**[M]: Blocks planar travel, damages creatures of different alignment.
7 **Blasphemy:** Kills, paralyzes, weakens, or dazes non-evil subject.
8 **Antipathy:** Object or location affected by spell repels certain creatures.
9 **Wail of the Banshee:** Kills one creature/level.

HUNGER DOMAIN

Granted Power: You gain a bite attack. If you are Small, your bite attack deals 1d4 points of damage; Medium, 1d6; or Large, 1d8. You are proficient with your bite, and considered armed. If you already have a natural bite attack, use the higher of the two damage values. This is considered a secondary natural attack.

Hunger Domain Spells

1 **Ghoul Light**†: Light provides turn resistance.
2 **Ghoul Glyph**†: Glyph wards area, paralyzes victims.
3 **Ghoul Gesture**†: Ray paralyzes subject.
4 **Enervation:** Subject gains 1d4 negative levels.
5 **Ghoul Gauntlet**†: Convert victim to a ghoul under your control.
6 **Eyes of the King**† Summon fiendish dire bats.
7 **Field of Ghouls**†: Transform dying creatures into ghouls.
8 **Bite of the King**†: Swallow enemies whole.
9 **Energy Drain:** Subject gains 2d4 negative levels.

ILLUSION DOMAIN

Granted Power: You cast all illusion spells at +1 caster level.

Illusion Domain Spells

1 **Silent Image:** Creates minor illusion of your design.
2 **Minor Image:** As *silent image*, plus some sound.
3 **Displacement:** Attacks miss subject 50%.
4 **Phantasmal Killer:** Fearsome illusion kills subject or deals 3d6 damage.
5 **Persistent Image:** As *major image*, but no concentration required.
6 **Mislead:** Turns you invisible and creates illusory double.
7 **Project Image:** Illusory double can talk and cast spells.
8 **Screen:** Illusion hides area from vision, scrying.
9 **Weird:** As *phantasmal killer*, but affects all within 30 ft.

INQUISITION DOMAIN

Granted Power: Gain a +4 bonus on dispel checks.

Inquisition Domain Spells

1 **Detect Chaos:** Reveals chaotic creatures, spells, or objects.
2 **Zone of Truth:** Subjects within range cannot lie.
3 **Detect Thoughts:** Allows "listening" to surface thoughts.
4 **Discern Lies:** Reveals deliberate falsehoods.

5 **True Seeing**[M]: Lets you see all things as they really are.
6 **Geas/Quest**: As *lesser geas*, plus it affects any creature.
7 **Dictum**: Kills, paralyzes, slows, or deafens nonlawful subjects.
8 **Shield of Law**[F]: +4 AC, +4 resistance, and SR 25 against chaotic spells.
9 **Imprisonment**: Entombs subject beneath the earth.

LIBERATION DOMAIN

Granted Power (Su): If you are affected by a charm, compulsion, or fear effect and fail your saving throw, you can attempt the save again 1 round later at the same DC. You get only this one extra chance to succeed on your saving throw.

Liberation Domain Spells

1 **Omen of Peril**†[F]: You know how dangerous the future will be.
2 **Undetectable Alignment**: Conceals alignment for 24 hours.
3 **Rage:** Subjects gain +2 to Str and Con, +1 on Will saves, –2 to AC.
4 **Freedom of Movement**: Subject moves normally despite impediments.
5 **Break Enchantment**: Frees subjects from enchantments, alterations, curses, and petrification.
6 **Dispel Magic, Greater:** As *dispel magic*, but up to +20 on check.
7 **Refuge**[M]: Alters item to transport its possessor to you.
8 **Mind Blank**: Subject is immune to mental/emotional magic and scrying.
9 **Unbinding**†: Frees everyone in range from spells that constrain or bind.

LUST DOMAIN

Granted Power (Su): Once per day as a free action, you gain an enhancement bonus to Charisma equal to your cleric level. The power lasts for 1 round.

Lust Domain Spells

1 **Charm Person**: Makes one person your friend.
2 **Invisibility**: Subject is invisible for 1 minute/level or until it attacks.
3 **Clairaudience/Clairvoyance**: See or hear at a distance for 1 minute/level.
4 **Planar Ally, Lesser**[X]: Exchange services with a 6 HD extraplanar creature.
5 **Scrying**[F]: Spies on subject from a distance.
6 **Symbol of Persuasion**[M]: Triggered rune charms nearby creatures.
7 **Refuge**[M]: Alters item to transport its possessor to you.
8 **Sympathy**[F]: Object or location attracts certain creatures.
9 **Trap the Soul**[MF]: Imprisons subject within gem.

MADNESS DOMAIN

Granted Power: You subtract 1 from all Wisdom-based skill checks and all Will saves. However, once per day, you can see and act with the clarity of true madness: Add one-half your level to a single Wisdom-based skill check or Will save. You must choose to use this benefit before the check or save is rolled.

Madness Domain Spells

1 **Confusion, Lesser:** One creature acts randomly for 1 round.
2 **Touch of Madness**†: Dazes one creature for 1 round/level.
3 **Rage:** Subjects gain +2 to Str and Con, +1 on Will saves, –2 to AC.
4 **Confusion**: Makes subject behave oddly for 1 round/level.
5 **Bolts of Bedevilment**†: One ray/round, dazes 1d3 rounds.
6 **Phantasmal Killer**: Fearsome illusion kills subject or deals 3d6 damage.
7 **Insanity**: Subject suffers continuous *confusion*.
8 **Maddening Scream**†: Subject has –4 AC, no shield, Reflex save on 20 only.
9 **Weird**: As *phantasmal killer*, but affects all within 30 ft.

MENTALISM DOMAIN

Granted Power (Sp): Once per day as a standard action, you can generate a mental ward, granting a creature you touch a resistance bonus on its next Will saving throw equal to your level +2. The mental ward is an abjuration effect with a duration of 1 hour.

Mentalism Domain Spells

1 **Confusion, Lesser:** One creature acts randomly for 1 round.
2 **Detect Thoughts**: Allows "listening" to surface thoughts.
3 **Clairaudience/Clairvoyance**: See or hear at a distance for 1 minute/level.
4 **Modify Memory**: Changes 5 minutes of subject's memories.
5 **Mind Fog**: Subjects in fog get –10 to Wisdom and Will checks.
6 **Rary's Telepathic Bond**: Link lets allies communicate.
7 **Antipathy**: Object or location affected by spell repels certain creatures.
8 **Mind Blank**: Subject is immune to mental/emotional magic and scrying.
9 **Astral Projection**[M]: Projects you and companions onto the Astral Plane.

METAL DOMAIN

Granted Power: You gain Martial Weapon Proficiency and Weapon Focus as bonus feats for either the light hammer or the warhammer (your choice).

Metal Domain Spells

1 **Magic Weapon**: Weapon gains +1 bonus.
2 **Heat Metal**: Make metal so hot it damages those who touch it.
3 **Keen Edge**: Doubles normal weapon's threat range.
4 **Rusting Grasp**: Your touch corrodes iron and alloys.
5 **Wall of Iron**[M]: 30 hp/4 levels; can topple onto foes.
6 **Blade Barrier**: Wall of blades deals 1d6/level damage.
7 **Transmute Metal to Wood**: Metal within 40 ft. becomes wood.
8 **Iron Body**: Your body becomes living iron.
9 **Repel Metal or Stone**: Pushes away metal and stone.

MIND DOMAIN

Granted Power: You gain a +2 bonus on Bluff, Diplomacy, and Sense Motive checks.

Mind Domain Spells

1 **Comprehend Languages:** You understand all spoken and written languages.
2 **Detect Thoughts:** Allows "listening" to surface thoughts.
3 **Telepathic Bond, Lesser:** Link with subject within 30 ft. for 10 minutes/level.
4 **Discern Lies:** Reveals deliberate falsehoods.
5 **Rary's Telepathic Bond:** Link lets allies communicate.
6 **Probe Thoughts†:** Read subject's memories, one question/round.
7 **Brain Spider†:** Eavesdrop on thoughts of up to eight other creatures.
8 **Mind Blank:** Subject is immune to mental/emotional magic and scrying.
9 **Weird:** As *phantasmal killer*, but affects all within 30 ft.

MOON DOMAIN

Granted Power: Turn or destroy lycanthropes as a good cleric turns or destroys undead. You can use this ability a number of times per day equal to 3 + your Cha modifier.

Moon Domain Spells

1 **Faerie Fire:** Outlines subject with light, canceling *blur*, concealment, and the like.
2 **Moonbeam†:** Forces lycanthropes to regain human shape.
3 **Moon Blade†:** Creates sword that does 2d8 damage +1/two level, scrambles magic.
4 **Fear:** Subjects within cone flee for 1 round/level.
5 **Moon Path†:** Creates invisible stair or bridge.
6 **Permanent Image**[M]: Includes sight, sound, and smell.
7 **Insanity:** Subject suffers continuous *confusion*.
8 **Animal Shapes:** One ally/level polymorphs into chosen animal.
9 **Moonfire†:** Cone of light damages creatures, reveals hidden things, negates electricity damage.

MYSTICISM DOMAIN

Granted Power (Su): Once per day, you can use a free action to channel your deity's power to grant yourself a luck bonus on your saving throws equal to your Charisma modifier (minimum +1). The effect lasts for 1 round per cleric level.

Mysticism Domain Spells

1 **Divine Favor:** You gain +1/3 levels on attack rolls and damage rolls.
2 **Spiritual Weapon:** Magic weapon attacks on its own.
3 **Visage of the Deity, Lesser†:** You gain +4 Cha and resistance 10 to certain energy types.
4 **Weapon of the Deity†:** Your weapon gains enhancement bonus and special ability.
5 **Righteous Might:** Your size increases and you gain combat bonuses.
6 **Visage of the Deity†:** As *lesser visage of the deity*, but you become celestial or fiendish.
7 **Blasphemy/Holy Word***: Kills, paralyzes, weakens, or dazes non-evil/non-good subjects.
8 **Holy Aura/Unholy Aura**[F*]: +4 AC, +4 resistance, and SR 25 against evil/good spells.
9 **Visage of the Deity, Greater†:** As *lesser visage of the deity*, but you become half-celestial or half-fiendish.
* Choose good or evil version based on your alignment.

NOBILITY DOMAIN

Granted Power (Sp): Once per day as a standard action, you can inspire allies, giving them a +2 morale bonus on saving throws, attack rolls and damage rolls, ability checks, and skill checks. Allies must be able to hear you speak for 1 round. This effect lasts for a number of rounds equal to your Charisma bonus (minimum 1 round).

Nobility Domain Spells

1 **Divine Favor:** You gain +1/3 levels on attack rolls and damage rolls.
2 **Enthrall:** Captivates all within 100 ft. + 10 ft./level.
3 **Magic Vestment:** Armor or shield gains +1 enhancement/4 levels.
4 **Discern Lies:** Reveals deliberate falsehoods.
5 **Command, Greater:** As *command*, but affects one subject/level.
6 **Geas/Quest:** As *lesser geas*, plus it affects any creature.
7 **Repulsion:** Creatures can't approach you.
8 **Demand:** As *sending*, plus you can send *suggestion*.
9 **Storm of Vengeance:** Storm rains acid, lightning, and hail.

OCEAN DOMAIN

Granted Power (Su): You have the supernatural ability to breathe water as if under the effect of a *water breathing* spell, for up to 1 minute per level. This effect occurs automatically as soon as it applies, lasts until it runs out or is no longer needed, and can operate multiple times per day (up to the total daily time limit).

Ocean Domain Spells

1 **Endure Elements:** Exist comfortably in hot or cold environments.
2 **Sound Burst:** Deals 1d8 sonic damage to subjects, might also stun them.
3 **Water Breathing:** Subjects can breathe underwater.
4 **Freedom of Movement:** Subject moves normally despite impediments.
5 **Wall of Ice:** Ice plane creates wall with 15 hp +1/level, or hemisphere can trap creatures inside.
6 **Otiluke's Freezing Sphere:** Freezes water or deals cold damage.
7 **Waterspout†:** Waterspout you control picks up and damages foes.
8 **Maelstrom†:** Water vortex traps and damages creatures and objects.
9 **Elemental Swarm:** Summons multiple elementals.*
*Cast as a water spell only.

ORACLE DOMAIN

Granted Power: You cast all divination spells at +2 caster level.

Oracle Domain Spells

1 **Identify**[M]: Determines properties of magic item.
2 **Augury**[MF]: Learns whether an action will be good or bad.
3 **Divination**[M]: Provides useful advice for specific proposed action.
4 **Scrying**[F]: Spies on subject from a distance.
5 **Commune**[X]: Deity answers one yes-or-no question/level.

6 **Legend Lore**MF: Lets you learn tales about a person, place, or thing.
7 **Scrying, Greater**F: As *scrying*, but faster and longer.
8 **Discern Location:** Reveals exact location of creature or object.
9 **Foresight:** "Sixth sense" warns of impending danger.

ORC DOMAIN

Granted Power (Su): You gain the smite power, the ability to make a single melee attack with a bonus on the damage roll equal to your cleric level (if you hit). You must declare the smite before making the attack. It is usable once per day. If used against a dwarf or an elf, you get a +4 bonus on the smite attack roll.

Orc Domain Spells

1 **Cause Fear:** One creature of 5 HD or fewer flees for 1d4 rounds.
2 **Produce Flame:** 1d6 damage +1/level, touch or thrown.
3 **Prayer:** Allies +1 on most rolls, enemies –1 penalty.
4 **Divine Power:** You gain attack bonus, +6 to Str, and 1 hp/level.
5 **Prying Eyes:** 1d4 +1/level floating eyes scout for you.
6 **Eyebite:** Subject becomes panicked, sickened, and comatose.
7 **Blasphemy:** Kills, paralyzes, weakens, or dazes non-evil subject.
8 **Cloak of Chaos**F: +4 to AC, +4 resistance, and SR 25 against lawful spells.
9 **Power Word Kill:** Kills one creature with 100 hp or less.

PACT DOMAIN

Granted Power: Add Appraise, Intimidate, and Sense Motive to your list of cleric class skills.

Pact Domain Spells

1 **Command:** One subject obeys selected command for 1 round.
2 **Shield Other**F: You take half of subject's damage.
3 **Speak With Dead:** Corpse answers one question/2 levels.
4 **Divination**M: Provides useful advice for specific proposed action.
5 **Stalwart Pact**†M: You gain combat bonuses automatically when reduced to half hit points or lower.
6 **Zealot Pact**†X: You automatically gain combat bonuses when you attack someone of opposite alignment.
7 **Renewal Pact**†M: Creature is automatically healed if adverse condition affects it.
8 **Death Pact**†M: Deity brings subject back from the dead automatically.
9 **Gate**X: Connects two planes for travel or summoning.

PESTILENCE DOMAIN

Granted Power: You gain immunity to the effects of all diseases, though you can still carry infectious diseases.

Pestilence Domain Spells

1 **Doom:** One subject takes –2 on attacks, damage, saves, and checks.
2 **Summon Swarm:** Summons swarm of bats, rats, or spiders.
3 **Contagion:** Infects subject with chosen disease.
4 **Poison:** Touch deals 1d10 Con damage, repeats in 1 minute.
5 **Plague of Rats**† Summons horde of rats.
6 **Curse of Lycanthropy**†: Kills subject and summons wererats.
7 **Scourge**†: Inflicts a disease that must be magically cured, one subject/level.
8 **Horrid Wilting:** Deals 1d6/level damage within 30 ft.
9 **Otyugh Swarm**†: Creates 3d4 otyughs or 1d3+1 Huge otyughs.

PLANNING DOMAIN

Granted Power: You gain Extend Spell as a bonus feat.

Planning Domain Spells

1 **Deathwatch:** Reveals how near death subjects within 30 ft. are.
2 **Augury**MF: Learns whether an action will be good or bad.
3 **Clairaudience/Clairvoyance:** Hear or see at a distance for 1 minute/level.
4 **Status:** Monitors condition, position of allies.
5 **Detect Scrying:** Alerts you of magical eavesdropping.
6 **Heroes' Feast:** Food for one creature/level cures and grants combat bonuses.
7 **Scrying, Greater**F: As *scrying*, but faster and longer.
8 **Discern Location:** Reveals exact location of creature or object.
9 **Time Stop:** You act freely for 1d4+1 rounds.

PORTAL DOMAIN

Granted Power: You can detect an active or inactive portal as if it were a normal secret door (Search DC 20).

Portal Domain Spells

1 **Summon Monster I:** Calls extraplanar creature to fight for you.
2 **Analyze Portal:** Find a nearby portal and discover its properties.
3 **Dimensional Anchor:** Bars extradimensional movement.
4 **Dimension Door:** Teleports you a short distance.
5 **Teleport:** Instantly transports you as far as 100 miles/level.
6 **Banishment:** Banishes 2 HD/level of extraplanar creatures.
7 **Etherealness:** Travel to Ethereal Plane with companions.
8 **Maze:** Traps subject in extradimensional maze.
9 **Gate**X: Connects two planes for travel or summoning.

PRIDE DOMAIN

Granted Power: Whenever you roll a 1 on a saving throw, you can immediately reroll the save. You must keep the result of the second roll, even if it is another 1.

Pride Domain Spells

1 **Hypnotism:** Fascinates 2d4 HD of creatures.
2 **Eagle's Splendor:** Subject gains +4 Cha for 1 minute/level.
3 **Heroism:** Gives +2 bonus on attack rolls, saves, skill checks.
4 **Divine Power:** You gain attack bonus, +6 to Str, and 1 hp/level.
5 **Reduce Person, Mass:** Reduces several creatures.

6 **Forbiddance**^{M}: Blocks planar travel, damages creatures of different alignment.
7 **Heroism, Greater**: Gives +4 bonus on attack rolls, saves, skill checks; immunity to fear; temporary hp.
8 **Spell Immunity, Greater:** As *spell immunity,* but up to 8th-level spells.
9 **Charm Monster, Mass:** As *charm monster,* but all within 30 ft.

PURIFICATION DOMAIN

Granted Power: You cast all abjuration spells at +1 caster level.

Purification Domain Spells

1 **Nimbus of Light†**: Sunlight illuminates you until released as an attack.
2 **Deific Vengeance†**: Deity's punishment deals 1d6 damage/2 levels (max 5d6).
3 **Recitation†** Your allies get bonus on AC, attacks and saves.
4 **Castigate†**: Verbal rebuke damages those whose alignment differs from yours.
5 **Dance of the Unicorn†**: Purifying mist washes the air clean of smoke, dust, and poisons.
6 **Fires of Purity†**: Subject bursts into magical flame, becoming a dangerous weapon.
7 **Righteous Wrath of the Faithful†**: Your allies gain extra attack, +3 on attack rolls and damage rolls.
8 **Sunburst†**: Blinds all within 80 ft., deals 6d6 damage.
9 **Visage of the Deity, Greater†**: As *lesser visage of the deity,* but you become half-celestial or half-fiendish.

RENEWAL DOMAIN

Granted Power (Su): If you fall below 0 hit points, you regain a number of hit points equal to 1d8 + your Charisma modifier. This ability functions once per day. If an attack brings you to –10 hit points or lower, you die before this power takes effect.

Renewal Domain Spells

1 **Charm Person**: Makes one person your friend.
2 **Restoration, Lesser**: Dispels magical ability penalty or repairs 1d4 ability damage.
3 **Remove Disease**: Cures all diseases affecting subject.
4 **Reincarnate**: Brings dead subject back to life in random body.
5 **Atonement**^{FX}: Removes burden of misdeeds from subject.
6 **Heroes' Feast**: Food for one creature/level cures and grants combat bonuses.
7 **Restoration, Greater**^{X}: As *restoration,* plus restores all levels and ability scores.
8 **Polymorph Any Object**: Changes any subject into anything else.
9 **Freedom**: Releases creature from *imprisonment.*

RETRIBUTION DOMAIN

Granted Power (Su): Once per day, if you have been harmed by someone in combat, you can make a strike of vengeance with a melee or ranged weapon against that foe on your next action. If this strike hits, you deal maximum damage.

Retribution Domain Spells

1 **Shield of Faith**: Aura grants +2 or higher deflection bonus.
2 **Bear's Endurance**: Subject gains +4 to Con for 1 minute/level.
3 **Speak with Dead**: Corpse answers one question/2 levels.
4 **Fire Shield**: Creatures attacking you take fire damage; you're protected from heat or cold.
5 **Mark of Justice**: Designates action that will trigger curse on subject.
6 **Banishment**: Banishes 2 HD/level of extraplanar creatures.
7 **Spell Turning**: Reflect 1d4+6 spell levels back at caster.
8 **Discern Location**: Reveals exact location of creature or object.
9 **Storm of Vengeance**: Storm rains acid, lightning, and hail.

RUNE DOMAIN

Granted Power: You gain Scribe Scroll as a bonus feat.

Rune Domain Spells

1 **Erase**: Mundane or magical writing vanishes.
2 **Secret Page**: Changes one page to hide its real content.
3 **Glyph of Warding**^{M}: Inscription harms those who pass it.
4 **Explosive Runes**: Deals 6d6 damage when read.
5 **Planar Binding, Lesser**: Traps extraplanar creature of 6 HD or less until it performs a task.
6 **Glyph of Warding, Greater**: As *glyph of warding,* but up to 10d8 damage or 6th-level spell.
7 **Drawmij's Instant Summons**^{M}: Prepared object appears in your hand.
8 **Symbol of Death**^{M}: Triggered rune slays nearby creatures.
9 **Teleportation Circle**^{M}: Circle teleports any creature inside to designated spot.

SCALYKIND DOMAIN

Granted Power: Rebuke or command animals (reptilian creatures and snakes only) as an evil cleric rebukes or commands undead. You can use this ability a number of times per day equal to 3 + your Cha modifier.

Scalykind Domain Spells

1 **Magic Fang**: One natural weapon of subject creature gets +1 on attack rolls and damage rolls.
2 **Animal Trance***: Fascinates 2d6 animals.
3 **Magic Fang, Greater**: One natural attack of subject creature gets +1/4 levels on attack rolls and damage rolls (max +5).
4 **Poison**: Touch deals 1d10 Con damage, repeats in 1 minute.
5 **Animal Growth***: One animal/2 levels doubles in size.
6 **Eyebite**: Subject becomes panicked, sickened, and comatose.
7 **Vipergout**: You spit forth celestial or fiendish vipers that attack your foes.
8 **Animal Shapes***: One ally/level polymorphs into chosen animal.
9 **Shapechange**^{F}: Transforms you into any creature, and change forms once per round.

*Affects only ophidian and reptilian creatures.

APPENDIX

SLIME DOMAIN

Granted Power: Rebuke or command oozes as an evil cleric rebukes or commands undead. You can use this ability a number of times per day equal to 3 + your Cha modifier.

Slime Domain Spells

1 **Grease:** Makes 10-ft. square or one object slippery.
2 **Melf's Acid Arrow:** Ranged touch attack; 2d4 damage for 1 round + 1 round/3 levels.
3 **Poison:** Touch deals 1d10 Con damage, repeats in 1 minute.
4 **Rusting Grasp:** Your touch corrodes iron and alloys.
5 **Evard's Black Tentacles:** Tentacles grapple all within 15-ft. spread.
6 **Transmute Rock to Mud:** Transforms two 10-ft. cubes per level.
7 **Destruction**[F]: Kills subject and destroys remains.
8 **Power Word Blind:** Blinds creature with 200 hp or less.
9 **Implosion:** Kills one creature/round.

SLOTH DOMAIN

Granted Powers: You are closest to your god while lazing and relaxing. You take no penalty to Armor Class against melee attacks while prone.

Sloth Domain Spells

1 **Touch of Fatigue:** Touch attack fatigues subject.
2 **Unseen Servant:** Invisible force obeys your commands.
3 **Deep Slumber:** Puts 10 HD of creatures to sleep.
4 **Slow:** One subject/level takes only one action/round, –2 to AC, –2 on attack rolls.
5 **Symbol of Sleep**[M]: Triggered rune puts nearby creatures into catatonic slumber.
6 **Waves of Fatigue:** Several subjects become fatigued.
7 **Shadow Walk:** Step into shadow to travel rapidly.
8 **Waves of Exhaustion:** Several subjects become exhausted.
9 **Astral Projection**[M]: Projects you and companions onto the Astral Plane.

SPELL DOMAIN

Granted Power: You gain a +2 bonus on Concentration checks and Spellcraft checks.

Spell Domain Spells

1 **Mage Armor:** Gives subject +4 armor bonus.
2 **Silence:** Negates sound in 15-ft. radius.
3 **Anyspell†:** Prepare any arcane spell up to 2nd level.
4 **Rary's Mnemonic Enhancer**[F]: Wizard only. Prepares extra spells or retains one just cast.
5 **Break Enchantment:** Frees subjects from enchantments, alternations, curses, and petrification.
6 **Anyspell, Greater†:** Prepare any arcane spell up to 5th level.
7 **Limited Wish**[X]: Alters reality—within spell limits.
8 **Antimagic Field:** Negates magic within 10 ft.
9 **Mordenkainen's Disjunction:** Dispels magic, disenchants magic items.

SPIDER DOMAIN

Granted Power: Rebuke or command spiders as an evil cleric rebukes or commands undead. You can use this ability a number of times per day equal to 3 + your Cha modifier.

Spider Domain Spells

1 **Spider Climb:** Grants ability to walk on walls and ceilings.
2 **Summon Swarm:** Summons swarm of bats, rats, or spiders.
3 **Phantom Steed***: Magic mount appears for 1 hour/level.
4 **Giant Vermin:** Turns centipedes, scorpions, or spiders into giant vermin.
5 **Insect Plague:** Locust swarms attack creatures.
6 **Spider Curse†:** Turn humanoid subject into a drider.
7 **Stone Spiders†:** Transform pebbles into monstrous spider constructs.
8 **Creeping Doom:** Swarms of centipedes attack at your command.
9 **Spider Shapes†:** Polymorph one creature/level into monstrous spider.

*Has a vermin shape.

STORM DOMAIN

Granted Power: You gain resistance to electricity 5.

Storm Domain Spells

1 **Entropic Shield:** Ranged attacks against you have 20% miss chance.
2 **Gust of Wind:** Blows away or knocks down smaller creatures.
3 **Call Lightning:** Calls down lightning bolts (3d6 per bolt) from sky.
4 **Sleet Storm:** Hampers vision and movement.
5 **Ice Storm:** Hail deals 5d6 damage in cylinder 40 ft. across.
6 **Summon Monster VI***: Calls extraplanar creature to fight for you.
7 **Control Weather:** Changes weather in local area.
8 **Whirlwind:** Cyclone deals damage and can pick up creatures.
9 **Storm of Vengeance:** Storm rains acid, lightning, and hail.

SUFFERING DOMAIN

Granted Power (Sp): You can use a pain touch once per day. Make a melee touch attack against a living creature, which bestows on that creature a –2 penalty to Strength and Dexterity for 1 minute on a successful attack. This ability does not affect creatures that have immunity to extra damage from critical hits.

Suffering Domain Spells

1 **Bane:** Enemies take –1 on attack rolls and saves against fear.
2 **Bear's Endurance:** Subject gains +4 to Con for 1 minute/level.
3 **Bestow Curse:** –6 to an ability score; –4 on attack rolls, saves, and checks; or 50% chance of losing each action.
4 **Enervation:** Subject gains 1d4 negative levels.
5 **Feeblemind:** Subject's Int and Cha drop to 1.
6 **Harm:** Deals 10 points/level damage to subject.
7 **Eyebite:** Subject becomes panicked, sickened, and comatose.

8 **Symbol of Pain**^{M}: Triggered rune wracks nearby creatures with pain.
9 **Horrid Wilting:** Deals 1d6/level damage within 30 ft.

SUMMONER DOMAIN

Granted Power: You cast all conjuration (summoning) and conjuration (calling) spells at +2 caster level.

Summoner Domain Spells

1 **Summon Monster I:** Calls extraplanar creature to fight for you.
2 **Summon Monster II:** Calls extraplanar creature to fight for you.
3 **Summon Monster III:** Calls extraplanar creature to fight for you.
4 **Planar Ally, Lesser**^{X}: Exchange services with a 6 HD extraplanar creature.
5 **Summon Monster V:** Calls extraplanar creature to fight for you.
6 **Planar Ally:** As *lesser planar ally*, but up to 16 HD.
7 **Summon Monster VII:** Calls extraplanar creature to fight for you.
8 **Planar Ally, Greater:** As *lesser planar ally*, but up to 24 HD.
9 **Gate**^{X}: Connects two planes for travel or summoning.

TIME DOMAIN

Granted Power: You gain Improved Initiative as a bonus feat.

Time Domain Spells

1 **True Strike:** +20 on your next attack roll.
2 **Gentle Repose:** Preserves one corpse.
3 **Haste:** One creature/level moves faster, +1 on attack rolls, AC, and Reflex saves.
4 **Freedom of Movement:** Subject moves normally despite impediments.
5 **Permanency**^{X}: Makes certain spells permanent.
6 **Contingency**^{F}: Sets trigger condition for another spell.
7 **Legend Lore**^{MF}: Lets you learn tales about a person, place, or thing.
8 **Foresight:** "Sixth sense" warns of impending danger.
9 **Time Stop:** You act freely for 1d4+1 rounds.

TRADE DOMAIN

Granted Power (Sp): Once per day as a free action, you can use *detect thoughts*, affecting one subject and lasting a number of minutes equal to your Charisma bonus (minimum 1 minute).

Trade Domain Spells

1 **Message:** Whispered conversation at a distance.
2 **Gembomb†**^{M}: Gem becomes a bomb that deals 1d8 force damage/2 levels.
3 **Eagle's Splendor:** Subject gains +4 to Charisma for 1 minute/level.
4 **Sending:** Delivers short message anywhere, instantly.
5 **Fabricate:** Transforms raw material into finished items.
6 **True Seeing**^{M}: Lets you see all things as they really are.
7 **Mordenkainen's Magnificent Mansion**^{F}: Door leads to extradimensional mansion.
8 **Mind Blank:** Subject is immune to mental/emotional magic and scrying.
9 **Discern Location:** Reveals exact location of creature or object.

TYRANNY DOMAIN

Granted Power: Add +1 to the save DC of any enchantment (compulsion) spell you cast.

Tyranny Domain Spells

1 **Command:** One subject obeys selected command for 1 round.
2 **Enthrall:** Captivates all within 100 ft. + 10 ft./level.
3 **Discern Lies:** Reveals deliberate falsehoods.
4 **Fear:** Subjects within cone flee for 1 round/level.
5 **Command, Greater:** As *command*, but affects one subject/level.
6 **Geas/Quest:** As *lesser geas*, plus it affects any creature.
7 **Bigby's Grasping Hand:** Hand provides cover, pushes, or grapples.
8 **Charm Monster, Mass:** As *charm monster*, but all within 30 ft.
9 **Dominate Monster:** As *dominate person*, but any creature.

UNDEATH DOMAIN

Granted Power: You gain Extra Turning as a bonus feat.

Undeath Domain Spells

1 **Detect Undead:** Reveals undead within 60 ft.
2 **Desecrate**^{M}: Fills area with negative energy, making undead stronger.
3 **Animate Dead**^{M}: Creates undead skeletons and zombies.
4 **Death Ward:** Grants immunity to death spells and negative energy effects.
5 **Circle of Death**^{M}: Kills 1d4/level HD of creatures.
6 **Create Undead**^{M}: Creates ghouls, ghasts, mummies, or mohrgs.
7 **Control Undead:** Undead don't attack you while under your command.
8 **Create Greater Undead**^{M}: Create shadows, wraiths, specters, or devourers.
9 **Energy Drain:** Subject gains 2d4 negative levels.

WEALTH DOMAIN

Granted Power: Add Appraise to your list of cleric class skills. You gain Skill Focus (Appraise) as a bonus feat.

Wealth Domain Spells

1 **Alarm:** Wards an area for 2 hours/level.
2 **Obscure Object:** Masks object against scrying.
3 **Glyph of Warding**^{M}: Inscription harms those who pass it.
4 **Detect Scrying:** Alerts you of magical eavesdropping.
5 **Leomund's Secret Chest**^{F}: Hides expensive chest on Ethereal Plane; you retrieve it at will.
6 **Forbiddance**^{M}: Blocks planar travel, damages creatures of different alignment.
7 **Sequester:** Subject is invisible to sight and scrying; renders creature comatose.
8 **Discern Location:** Reveals exact location of creature or object.
9 **Antipathy:** Object or location affected by spell repels certain creatures.

WINDSTORM DOMAIN

Granted Power: Inclement weather has less of an effect on you. Rain and snow don't penalize your Spot and Search checks. You can move through snow-covered and icy terrain at your normal movement. Wind effects, whether natural or magical, affect you as if you were one size category larger.

Windstorm Domain Spells

1 **Obscuring Mist:** Fog surrounds you.
2 **Binding Winds:** Air prevents subject from moving, hinders ranged attacks.
3 **Call Lightning:** Calls down lightning bolts (3d6 per bolt) from sky.
4 **Ice Storm:** Hail deals 5d6 damage in cylinder 40 ft. across.
5 **Arc of Lightning†:** Line of electricity arcs between two creatures (1d6/level damage).
6 **Cloudwalkers†:** Subjects can fly outdoors at speed of 60 ft.
7 **Control Weather:** Changes weather in local area.
8 **Whirlwind:** Cyclone deals damage and can pick up creatures.
9 **Whirlwind, Greater†:** As *whirlwind*, but larger and more destructive.

WRATH DOMAIN

Granted Power: Once per day, you can subtract a number of points from your Wisdom score equal to or less than your cleric level. For every 2 points you subtract from your Wisdom score, add 1 point to your Strength score. You suffer all the effects of reduced Wisdom, including access to spells and bonus spells, reduction of Will saves, and penalties on Wisdom-based skills. This trade between ability scores lasts for 1 round per cleric level and cannot be ended prematurely.

Wrath Domain Spells

1 **Rhino's Rush†:** Next charge deals double damage.
2 **Bull's Strength:** Subject gains +4 Str for 1 minute/level.
3 **Rage:** Subjects gain +2 to Str and Con, +1 on Will saves, –2 to AC.
4 **Shout:** Deafens all within cone and deals 5d6 sonic damage.
5 **Righteous Might:** Your size increases, and you gain combat bonuses.
6 **Song of Discord:** Forces subjects to attack each other.
7 **Tenser's Transformation[M]:** You gain combat bonuses.
8 **Shout, Greater:** Devastating yell deals 10d6 sonic damage; stuns creatures, damages objects.
9 **Storm of Vengeance:** Storm rains acid, lightning, and hail.

PLANAR DOMAINS

A planar domain counts as both of a cleric's domain choices. The granted powers of a planar domain are more potent than those of other domains, and each level offers two spells from which a cleric can choose when preparing spells. Each day, a cleric with access to a planar domain chooses one of the two spells available to prepare in his domain spell slot for each spell level. Unlike other domains, planar domains each have an alignment requirement that must be met by a cleric who wants to access the domain.

A cleric need not select a specific deity to have access to a planar domain. A cleric who devotes himself to a specific alignment (LG, NG, CG, LN, CN, LE, NE, or CE) rather than a deity can select a planar domain in place of his two normal domain choices. If the DM wishes, he can make domains specific to other planes, using these as representative guides.

ABYSS DOMAIN

Requirement: Must be chaotic evil.

Granted Power (Su): Once per day as a free action, you can channel the furious power of the demons. This power grants you a +4 bonus to Strength but also gives you a –2 penalty to Armor Class. The effect lasts for 5 rounds and cannot be ended prematurely. Add Intimidate to your list of cleric class skills.

Abyss Domain Spells

1 **Align Weapon:** Weapon becomes evil or chaotic.
Cause Fear: One creature of 5 HD or fewer flees for 1d4 rounds.
2 **Bull's Strength:** Subject gains +4 to Strength for 1 minute/level.
Death Knell: Kills dying creature; you gain 1d8 temporary hp, +2 to Strength, and +1 caster level.
3 **Babau Slime†:** Secrete a body-covering acid that damages foes' weapons.
Summon Monster III: Calls extraplanar creature to fight for you.*
4 **Balor Nimbus†:** Subject's flaming body damages foes in grapple.
Poison: Touch deals 1d10 Con damage, repeats in 1 minute.
5 **Slay Living:** Touch attack kills subject.
Summon Monster V: Calls extraplanar creature to fight for you.*
6 **Bull's Strength, Mass:** As *bull's strength*, affects one subject/level.
Harm: Deals 10 points/level damage to subject.
7 **Destruction[F]:** Kills subject and destroys remains.
Summon Monster VII: Calls extraplanar creature to fight for you.*
8 **Finger of Death:** Kills one subject.
Bodak's Glare†: You slay a creature, which turns into a bodak 24 hours later.
9 **Implosion:** Kills one creature/round.
Summon Monster IX: Calls extraplanar creature to fight for you.*

* Chaotic evil creatures only.

ARBOREA DOMAIN

Requirement: Must be chaotic good.

Granted Power (Su): Once per day as a free action, you can channel the glory of the eladrin to grant yourself a morale bonus on weapon damage rolls and saves against charm and fear effects. This bonus is equal to your Charisma bonus (if any) and lasts for 1 minute. Add Survival to your list of cleric class skills.

Arborea Domain Spells

1 **Endure Elements:** Exist comfortably in hot or cold environments.
Longstrider: Your speed increases by 10 ft.
2 **Aid:** +1 on attack rolls and saves against fear, 1d8 temporary hp +1/level (max +10).

Eagle's Splendor: Subject gains +4 to Charisma for 1 minute/level.
3 **Heroism**: Gives +2 on attack rolls, saves, skill checks.
Summon Monster III: Calls extraplanar creature to fight for you.*
4 **Neutralize Poison**: Immunizes subject against poison, detoxifies venom in or on subject.
Opalescent Glare†: Kill creatures with a look, or make them very afraid.
5 **Break Enchantment**: Frees subjects from enchantments, alternations, curses, and petrification.
Summon Monster V: Calls extraplanar creature to fight for you.*
6 **Heroes' Feast**: Food for one creature/level cures and grants combat bonuses.
Eagle's Splendor, Mass: As *eagle's splendor*, affects one subject/level.
7 **Spell Turning**: Reflect 1d4+6 spell levels back at caster.
Summon Monster VII: Calls extraplanar creature to fight for you.*
8 **Heroism, Greater**: Gives +4 bonus on attack rolls, saves, skill checks; immunity to fear; temporary hp.
Mind Blank: Subject is immune to mental/emotional magic and scrying.
9 **Freedom**: Releases creature from *imprisonment*.
Summon Monster IX: Calls extraplanar creature to fight for you*
* Chaotic good creatures only.

BAATOR DOMAIN

Requirement: Must be lawful evil.

Granted Power (Su): You gain the ability to see perfectly in darkness of any kind, even that created by a *deeper darkness* spell. Add Bluff to your list of cleric class skills.

Baator Domain Spells

1 **Bane**: Enemies take –1 on attack rolls and saves against fear.
Disguise Self: Changes your appearance.
2 **Darkness**: 20-ft. radius of supernatural shadow.
Fox's Cunning: Subject gains +4 to Intelligence for 1 minute/level.
3 **Detect Thoughts**: Allows "listening" to surface thoughts.
Summon Monster III: Calls extraplanar creature to fight for you.*
4 **Deeper Darkness**: Object sheds supernatural shadow in 60-ft. radius.
Suggestion: Compels subject to follow stated course of action.
5 **Spell Resistance**: Subject gains SR 12 + level.
Summon Monster V: Calls extraplanar creature to fight for you.*
6 **Dominate Person**: Controls humanoid telepathically.
Fox's Cunning, Mass: As *fox's cunning*, but affects one subject/level.
7 **Repulsion**: Creatures can't approach you.
Summon Monster VII: Calls extraplanar creature to fight for you.*
8 **Demand**: As *sending*, plus you can send *suggestion*.
Spell Turning: Reflect 1d4+6 spell levels back at caster.
9 **Imprisonment**: Entombs subject beneath the earth.
Summon Monster IX: Calls extraplanar creature to fight for you.*
* Lawful evil creatures only.

CELESTIA DOMAIN

Requirement: Must be lawful good.

Granted Power (Su): Once per day as a free action, you can generate an aura of menace similar to that of the archons. The aura lasts for 1 minute. Any hostile enemy within a 20-foot radius of you must succeed on a Will save (DC 10 + 1/2 your cleric level + your Cha modifier) to resist its effects. Those who fail take a –2 penalty on attack rolls, Armor Class, and saves for 24 hours or until they successfully hit you. A creature that has resisted or broken the effect cannot be affected again by your aura for 24 hours. Add Sense Motive to your list of cleric class skills.

Celestia Domain Spells

1 **Light of Lunia†**: You radiate silvery light, which you can expend as two bolts that deal 1d6 damage.
Shield of Faith: Aura grants +2 or higher deflection bonus.
2 **Bear's Endurance**: Subject gains +4 to Con for 1 minute/level.
Shield Other[F]: You take half of subject's damage.
3 **Magic Vestment**: Armor or shield gains +1 enhancement/4 levels.
Summon Monster III: Calls extraplanar creature to fight for you.*
4 **Divine Power**: You gain attack bonus, +6 to Strength, and 1 hp/level.
Magic Weapon, Greater: +1 bonus/4 levels (max +5).
5 **Righteous Might**: Your size increases, and you gain combat bonuses.
Summon Monster V: Calls extraplanar creature to fight for you.*
6 **Blade Barrier**: Wall of blades deals 1d6/level damage.
Bear's Endurance, Mass: As *bear's endurance*, affects one subject/level.
7 **Regenerate**: Subject's severed limbs grow back, cures 4d8 damage +1/level (max +35).
Summon Monster VII: Calls extraplanar creature to fight for you.*
8 **Power Word Stun**: Stuns creatures with 150 or fewer hp.
Shield of Law[F]: +4 to AC, +4 resistance, and SR 25 against chaotic spells.
9 **Foresight**: "Sixth sense" warns of impending danger.
Summon Monster IX: Calls extraplanar creature to fight for you.*
* Lawful good creatures only.

ELYSIUM DOMAIN

Requirement: Must be neutral good.

Granted Power (Su): You gain the ability to smite evil with a single melee attack once per day. You add your Charisma bonus (if any) to your attack roll and deal an extra 1 point of damage per class level. This smite attack is treated as good-aligned for the purpose of overcoming damage reduction. At 5th level and every five levels thereafter, you can use this smite attack one additional time per day.

Elysium Domain Spells

1 **Charm Person:** Makes one person your friend.
Protection from Evil: +2 to AC and saves, counter mind control, hedge out elementals and outsiders.
2 **Enthrall:** Captivates all within 100 ft. + 10 ft./level.
Planar Tolerance†: Provides long-term protection against overtly damaging planar traits.
3 **Magic Circle against Evil:** As *protection* spell, but 10-ft. radius and 10 minutes/level.
Mantle of Good†: You gain SR 12 + caster level against spells with the evil descriptor.
4 **Charm Monster:** Makes monster believe it is your ally.
Holy Smite: Damages and blinds evil creatures.
5 **Dispel Evil:** +4 bonus against attacks.
Cure Light Wounds, Mass: Cures 1d8 damage +1/level for many creatures.
6 **Find the Path:** Shows most direct way to a location.
Mind Fog: Subjects in fog get –10 to Wisdom and Will checks.
7 **Control Weather:** Changes weather in local area.
Holy Word: Kills, paralyzes, blinds, or deafens non-good subjects.
8 **Holy Aura**[F]**:** +4 to AC, +4 resistance and SR 25 against evil spells.
Sunburst: Blinds all within 80 ft., deals 6d6 damage.
9 **Heal, Mass:** As *heal*, but with several subjects.
Moment of Prescience: You gain insight bonus on single attack roll, check, or save.

HADES DOMAIN

Requirement: Must be neutral evil.

Granted Power (Su): You gain the ability to smite good with a single melee attack once per day. You add your Charisma bonus (if any) to your attack roll and deal an extra 1 point of damage per class level. This smite attack is treated as evil-aligned for the purpose of overcoming damage reduction. At 5th level and every five levels thereafter, you can use this smite attack one additional time per day.

Hades Domain Spells

1 **Doom:** One subject takes –2 on attacks, damage, saves, and checks.
Protection from Good: +2 to AC and saves, counter mind control, hedge out elementals and outsiders.
2 **Resist Planar Alignment†:** Subject can resist penalties for being of an opposed alignment on an aligned Outer Plane.
Rebuke†: Subject is dazed 1 round, then shaken.
3 **Magic Circle against Good:** As *protection* spell, but 10-ft. radius and 10 minutes/level.
Mantle of Evil†: You gain SR 12 + caster level against spells with the good descriptor.
4 **Contagion:** Infects subject with chosen disease.
Unholy Blight: Damages and sickens good creatures.
5 **Crushing Despair:** Subjects take –2 on attack rolls, damage rolls, saves, and checks.
Dispel Good: +4 bonus against attacks by good creatures.
6 **Mind Fog:** Subjects in fog get –10 to Wisdom and Will checks.
Waves of Fatigue: Several subjects become fatigued.
7 **Blasphemy:** Kills, paralyzes, weakens, or dazes non-evil subject.
Plane Shift[F]**:** As many as eight subjects travel to another plane.
8 **Unholy Aura**[F]**:** +4 to AC, +4 resistance, and SR 25 against good spells.
Waves of Exhaustion: Several subjects become exhausted.
9 **Energy Drain:** Subject gains 2d4 negative levels.
Gate[X]**:** Connects two planes for travel or summoning.

LIMBO DOMAIN

Requirement: Must be chaotic neutral.

Granted Power (Su): You gain the ability to smite law with a single melee attack once per day. You add your Charisma bonus (if any) to your attack roll and deal an extra 1 point of damage per class level. This smite attack is treated as chaotic-aligned for the purpose of overcoming damage reduction. At 5th level and every five levels thereafter, you can use this smite attack one additional time per day.

Limbo Domain Spells

1 **Confusion, Lesser:** One creature acts randomly for 1 round.
Protection from Law: +2 to AC and saves, counter mind control, hedge out elementals and outsiders.
2 **Entropic Shield:** Ranged attacks against you have 20% miss chance.
Resist Planar Alignment†: Subject can resist penalties for being of an opposed alignment on an aligned Outer Plane.
3 **Magic Circle against Law:** As *protection* spell, but 10-ft. radius and 10 minutes/level.
Mantle of Chaos†: You gain SR 12 + caster level against spells with the lawful descriptor.
4 **Chaos Hammer:** Damages and slows lawful creatures.
Perinarch†: Gain greater control over Limbo's morphic essence.
5 **Baleful Polymorph:** Transforms subject into harmless animal.
Dispel Law: +4 bonus against attacks by lawful creatures.
6 **Animate Objects:** Objects attack your foes.
Insanity: Subject suffers continuous *confusion*.
7 **Song of Discord:** Forces subjects to attack each other.
Word of Chaos: Nonchaotic subject is killed, *confused*, stunned, or deafened.
8 **Cloak of Chaos**[F]**:** +4 to AC, +4 resistance, and SR 25 against lawful spells.
Otto's Irresistible Dance: Forces subject to dance.
9 **Perinarch, Planar†:** Gain control over a small area of any divinely morphic plane.
Shapechange[F]**:** Transforms you into any creature, and change forms once per round.

MECHANUS DOMAIN

Requirement: Must be lawful neutral.

Granted Power (Su): You gain the ability to smite chaos with a single melee attack once per day. You add your Charisma bonus (if any) to your attack roll and deal an extra 1 point of damage per class level. This smite attack is treated as lawful-aligned for the purpose of overcoming damage reduction. At 5th level and every five levels thereafter, you can use this smite attack one additional time per day.

Mechanus Domain Spells

1 **Command:** One subject obeys selected command for 1 round.
Protection from Chaos: +2 to AC and saves, counter mind control, hedge out elementals and outsiders.
2 **Calm Emotions:** Calms creatures, negating emotion effects.
Mechanus Mind†: Reformat subject's mind to be coldly calculating.
3 **Magic Circle against Chaos:** As *protection* spell, but 10-ft. radius and 10 minutes/level.
Mantle of Law†: You gain SR 12 + caster level against spells with the chaotic descriptor.
4 **Discern Lies:** Reveals deliberate falsehoods.
Order's Wrath: Damages and dazes chaotic creatures.
5 **Dispel Chaos:** +4 bonus against attacks by chaotic creatures.
Mark of Justice: Designates action that will trigger curse on subject.
6 **Hold Monster:** As *hold person*, but any creature.
Wall of Gears†: Creates wall of moving gears that deals 1d6 damage/2 levels to creatures within 10 ft.
7 **Dictum:** Kills, paralyzes, slows, or deafens nonlawful subjects.
Hold Person, Mass: As *hold person*, but all within 30 ft.
8 **Iron Body:** Your body becomes living iron.
Shield of Law[F]**:** +4 to AC, +4 resistance, and SR 25 against chaotic spells.
9 **Call Marut†:** A marut performs one duty for you.
Mordenkainen's Disjunction: Dispels magic, disenchants magic items.

SOURCES

Spell Compendium is a collection of material that previously appeared in a number of different products and other sources. Following is a list of those sources and their authors.

D&D Supplements
Complete Adventurer by Jesse Decker
Complete Arcane by Richard Baker
Complete Divine by David Noonan
Complete Warrior by Andy Collins, David Noonan, and Ed Stark
Draconomicon by Andy Collins, Skip Williams, and James Wyatt
Libris Mortis by Andy Collins and Bruce R. Cordell
Magic of Faerûn by Sean K Reynolds, Duane Maxwell, and Angel Leigh McCoy
Manual of the Planes by Andy Collins, Bruce R. Cordell, and David Noonan
Miniatures Handbook by Michael Donais, Skaff Elias, Rob Heinsoo, and Jonathan Tweet
Planar Handbook by Bruce R. Cordell and Gwendolyn F. M. Kestrel
Player's Guide to Faerûn by Richard Baker, Travis Stout, and James Wyatt
Savage Species by David Eckelberry, Rich Redman, and Jennifer Clarke Wilkes
Underdark by Bruce R. Cordell, Gwendolyn F. M. Kestrel, and Jeff Quick

Articles published on www.wizards.com/dnd
"Barb of the Mind" by Sean K Reynolds
"The Codicil of White" by Sean K Reynolds
"Earthmother's Weapons" by Sean K Reynolds
"Foundations of Stone" by James Jacobs
"Lesser Testament of Vraer" by Sean K Reynolds
"The Lost Coast" by James Jacobs
"Magic of Delight and Despair I" by Gwendolyn F. M. Kestrel
"Master Tactician" by Sean K Reynolds
"Obsul Ssussun" by Sean K Reynolds
"Sand and Sun" by James Jacobs
"Snow and Ice" by James Jacobs
"Spellbook Archive" by Ramon Arjona, Richard Baker, Andy Collins, Robert Holzmeier, and James Wyatt
"Spells of the Deep Underdark" by James Jacobs
"Spells of the Ruins" by James Jacobs
"Tar'Ael Veluuthra" by Sean K Reynolds
"Toxic Paradise" by James Jacobs

Articles published in *Dragon Magazine*
"Rays of Light" by Stephen Schubert, *Annual* #5
"Alister's Augmentations" by Owen K.C. Stephens, #275
"Abuse Your Illusions" by Rich Redman, #291
"Rune-Skulls of the Abbor-Alz" by James Jacobs, #292
"Blessings of War" by Amber E. Scott, #299
"A Clutch of Cantrips" by Kieran Turley and S. Deniz Bucak, #302
"Prayers of the Frostmaiden: The Spells of Auril" by Thomas M. Costa, #312
"Elder Serpents of Set" by Thomas M. Costa, #313
"Brotherhood of the Burning Heart" by Clifford Horowitz, #314
"Dust to Dust" by Ari Marmell, #314
"Guardians of the Deepest Seas" by James Jacobs, #314
"Masters of the Four Winds" by David Noonan, #314
"The Bloody Swords" by Sean K Reynolds, #315
"Sin Eaters of Eilistraee" by James Jacobs, #315
"Holy Strategists of the Red Knight" by Travis Stout, #317
"Children of Ka" by Ken Marable, #318
"Under Command: Forms of Legend" by Jesse Decker, #320
"Patterns of Shadow and Light" by Jason Nelson, #322
"Force Spells" by C. Wesley Clough, #323
"Seven Deadly Domains" by Hal Maclean, #323
"The Hidden Book" by Rich Burlew, #324
"Myths of the Shadow" by Rahul Kanakia, #325
"Tvash-Prull's Symphony" by James Jacobs, #328